Dictionaries of LSP Collocations

STUDIES IN LINGUISTICS, ANGLOPHONE LITERATURES AND CULTURES

Edited by Robert Kiełtyka and Agnieszka Uberman

VOLUME 35

PETER LANG

Anna Zagórska

Dictionaries of LSP Collocations

The Process of Compilation Based on Polish, English and Italian Banking Law

PETER LANG

Bibliographic Information published by the Deutsche Nationalbibliothek
The Deutsche Nationalbibliothek lists this publication in the Deutsche Nationalbibliografie; detailed bibliographic data is available online at http://dnb.d-nb.de.

Library of Congress Cataloging-in-Publication Data
A CIP catalog record for this book has been applied for at the Library of Congress.

This publication was financially supported by the University of Warsaw.

Cover illustration: Courtesy of Benjamin Ben Chaim

ISSN 2364-7558
ISBN 978-3-631-87152-2 (Print)
E-ISBN 978-3-631-89632-7 (E-PDF)
E-ISBN 978-3-631-89635-8 (EPUB)
DOI 10.3726/b20533

Peter Lang – Berlin · Bern · Bruxelles · New York · Oxford · Warszawa · Wien

This publication has been peer reviewed.

www.peterlang.com

I would like to thank Professor Elżbieta Jamrozik from the University of Warsaw for her extensive engagement, inspiring advice, and tremendous support on which I could always count.

Table of contents

Introduction

Despite the unquestionable importance of collocational knowledge for linguistic competence, collocations are still not given sufficient attention in LSP research, translation, and instruction. Besides, dictionaries of LSP collocations are very sparse and have been subject to limited amount of research, particularly as far as the process of their compilation is concerned. The gap in lexicographic research and practice is very serious and should be plugged by assiduous measures taken by academics. Without dictionaries of LSP collocations, it is unlikely that collocations will ever be devoted the necessary attention by LSP users. The neglect of collocations is in turn clearly undesirable, since without their knowledge it is impossible to fully master and correctly use a foreign language in any specialised field. Besides, the lack of dictionaries of LSP collocations clearly implies that collocations are problematic to lexicographers.

The present work aims at the creation of a model of multilingual dictionary of LSP collocations. The dictionary model is intended to contribute to the efficient interlingual communication in specialised domains, which will be the decisive factor in all the organisational and structural decisions. It is assumed that the model should be universal, i.e. usable in various specialised domains and with any combination of languages (cf. Parowenko 2007: 6). It is intended as an aid for those who aspire to compile dictionaries of LSP collocations.

The above-mentioned dictionary model is created on the example of Polish, English, and Italian banking law. Thus, the most significant part of this work comprises a collocational dictionary of Polish, English, Italian and banking law. Hopefully, the dictionary will prove to be a useful resource for translators, interpreters and LSP learners and teachers. Besides, it is recommended to lawyers and bank employees who use in their professional communication at least two of the above-mentioned languages.

The work is divided into two parts, the first of which consists of three chapters and is supposed to constitute a theoretical background. In the first of the chapters, attention is devoted to the notion of collocation, which is defined for the purposes of specialised lexicography. As for the second chapter, it describes the Polish, English and Italian language of law, most of all in terms of their lexical features. Furthermore, the third chapter is devoted to the process of dictionary creation. As the work aims at the creation of a dictionary model, the above-mentioned process is described as comprehensively as possible, with particular focus on LSP dictionaries and collocational dictionaries. Besides, special attention is given to dictionary structures as well as corpus linguistic tools which are employed in lexicographic work.

The second part of the work comprises a collocational dictionary of English, Italian and Polish banking law. Created with the aid of AntConc 3.4.3 concordance programme, it consists of three partially autonomous parts, containing Polish, English, and Italian collocations respectively. The entries in each of the dictionary parts contain cross-references to entries in the two other parts of the dictionary (cf. Hartmann 2001: 59, 65–66). The dictionary compilation process as well as the dictionary structure are presented in detail in Chapter 5. Besides, Chapter 4 contains a description of the employed corpus, consisting of Polish, English, and Italian normative acts which regulate the activity and organisation of banks.

The conclusions consist, among others, of a review of problems encountered in the dictionary compilation process as well as some suggestions for other LSP collocational dictionary authors. Besides, they contain a description of Polish, English and Italian language of banking law, most of all in terms of their lexical and collocational features. Hopefully, the work will lead to the creation of a useful resource for law and banking professionals as well as constitute a guide for those who aspire to create multilingual dictionaries of LSP collocations.

1. Collocations

The present chapter is devoted to the notion of collocation, which breeds considerable controversy among linguistic researchers. Inter alia, it explores various attempts to define the notion as well as various typologies of collocations. It also focuses on the role of collocation as an aspect of language knowledge. Besides, the chapter is concluded with an attempt to define the discussed notion. The proposed definition of collocation is not universal but intended for application in the process of creation of an LSP collocational dictionary.

1.1. The notion of collocation

Although collocations have been examined by a significant number of researchers, the term itself remains a subject of controversy. Linguistic literature provides various definitions of collocations. Besides, there are numerous terms which are related to the notion of collocation, and which are often equally controversial in terms of their meanings. To give an example, apart from the term collocation, English researchers mention *fixed expressions, multi-word items, phraseological units, lexical phrases, idioms, prefabricated phrases, prefabs*, etc. (Nuccorini 2003: 367, Nesselhauf 2005: 1). Polish researchers refer to *związki łączliwe, idiomy, skupienia nierozerwalne, połączenia frazeologiczne, połączenia konwencjonalne, analityzmy, frazemy, utarte zwroty*, etc. (Geller and Dąbrówka 2007: XI, Śliwiński 2008: 314–315, Białek 2009: 8, 2011: 8). In France, linguistic research is devoted to *locutions, expressions figées, expressions idiomatiques, phraséologismes* or *phrasèmes*. In Italy, it concerns *locuzioni, combinazioni di parole, unità fraseologiche* and *espressioni idiomatiche* (Nuccorini 2003: 367, Sułkowska 2013). The above-mentioned terms are employed alongside the term *collocation,* which was transferred to languages other than English, e.g. *kolokacja* (Polish), *collocazione* (Italian), and *collocation* (French). It should be mentioned, however, that the term under discussion was disseminated by British researchers, such as J. R. Firth and J. Sinclair.

The various terms relating to the notion of collocation often partially overlap, though they are not fully synonymous (Białek 2009: 8). In majority, they do not have definitions which would be universally acknowledged (Nuccorini 2003: 367). Nuccorini (2003: 368) notices that the variety of terms entails "different syntactic and semantic categorisations" as well as 'the inclusion or exclusion of various types of "phrases"'. Besides, it reflects 'the scientific, lexicological, and academic status of phraseology whose domain is not marked by clearcut boundaries and whose inner subdivisions merge along a continuum rather than forming separate, discrete classes' (Nuccorini 2003: 368). Accordingly, various phraseological and collocational dictionaries differ in their content and in the approaches to its description. Their authors adopt diverse theoretical principles in the course of selecting, classifying, and presenting the expressions included in dictionary entries (Nuccorini 2003: 368, cf. Gledhill 2000: 7–18, Nesselhauf 2005: 12–13).

As will be shown in subsection 1.1.2., the notion of collocation is highly problematic in terms of its definition. What is more, collocations have been devoted scarce amount of research, though they constitute a particularly significant aspect of language knowledge (see section 1.2.). One of the reasons is that the group of items which are termed as collocations is extremely heterogeneous. Moreover, collocations as a linguistic phenomenon are on the borderline between grammar and lexis, thus they constitute a particularly problematic subject of linguistic research. Their investigation requires various forms of linguistic analysis, which relate to semantic, lexical, syntactic, pragmatic and even phonological description. Nevertheless, the description and analysis of collocations is typically limited to only one level and frequently constitutes a part of wider linguistic research principally devoted to other arguments (Bartsch 2004: 27, Handl 2008: 48). For the sake of example, Firth (1957) considers collocations as one of the modes of meaning. Bartsch (2004) analyses them in terms of their structural and functional properties. Białek (2009) devotes attention to collocations as translation units. Rudnicka (2010) investigates their value assuming that they are a kind of lexicographic example of word usage. Finally, collocational research by Caldas-Coulthard and Moon (2010) relates to critical discourse analysis, whereas Scinetti (2014) compares the use of collocations by first and second language speakers of Italian.

1.1.1. Historical background

The term *collocation* is usually attributed to J. R. Firth, who uses it while discussing various modes of meaning. The researcher assumes that collocations convey some part of word meaning. To give an example, while considering the expression 'dark night' Firth (1957: 196) notes that 'one of the meanings of *night* is its collocability with *dark* and of *dark*, of course, collocation with *night*' (cf. Bursill-Hall 1966: 46–48, Lyons 1966: 295–296, Moon 1997: 41–42, Léon 2007). The researcher recommends the study of collocations as a form of research in the domain of descriptive linguistics. Besides, he notices that collocations can be divided into those 'general or usual' and those 'technical or personal', the latter being more restricted than the former (Firth 1957: 195).

Though Firth is commonly believed to be the father of collocational research, it should be mentioned that according to Barnbrook et al. (2013: 9) the term *collocation* in its linguistic understanding was present in texts already at the beginning of the XVIIIth century. Besides, it is used in *A Grammar of English Words*, which was first published already in 1938, to refer to 'a succession of two or more words that may best be learnt as if it were a single word' (Palmer 1947: x, cf. Nation 2001: 317, Bartsch 2004: 30–33). Its author, Palmer (1947: xi) distinguishes collocations from phrases, postulating that the former resemble single words in terms of their meanings and functions, whereas the latter 'are more in the nature of conversational formulas, sayings, proverbs etc.'. Finally, according to Akasu (2011: 45–46), the first collocational dictionary was published already in 1939 by Katsumata, with the title *Kenkyusha's Dictionary of English Collocations.*

In any case, it seems that the truly deep interest in collocations was sparked by the works by Firth, in particular *Papers in linguistics 1934–1957.* One of the subsequent breakthrough publications is probably *In memory of J. R. Firth (1966)*, where the notion of collocation is devoted attention by Halliday, Lyons and Sinclair. Inter alia, Lyons (1966: 295–296) rejects the Firthian view that collocations constitute a part of word meaning, though he admits that it is possible to convey the meaning of a word by presenting a well-chosen group of its collocates. Sinclair (1966) devotes attention to the methods of describing lexical items in terms of their collocational patterns. Additionally, he recommends investigating collocations with the aid of statistical tests (Sinclair 1966: 418, 428). Finally, Halliday (1966: 151) proposes some methods of describing collocations and notices that the collocating items are sometimes placed in different sentences, though 'there are limits of relevance to be set to a collocational span of this kind' (cf. Sinclair 1966: 413–414). Besides, the researcher notices that collocability is sometimes independent of parts of speech. For instance, apart from a *strong argument*, one may refer to *the strength of argument* or may *argue strongly* (Halliday 1966: 151, cf. Palmer 1976: 101).

In general, as Herbst (1996: 380–383) points out, collocational research can be conducted based on two distinct approaches, i.e. statistically oriented approach and significance oriented approach. In the former approach, collocations are perceived as co-occurrences of items within a given span of words. Special attention is devoted to co-occurrences whose frequency is greater than could be expected on the basis of chance. Contrastingly, in the latter approach, the significance of a given collocation is related to its semantic unpredictability (cf. Nesselhauf 2005: 11–12). Herbst (1996: 388) presents two main types of word combinations the approach is devoted to. Firstly, these are combinations in which one of the elements has a very restricted set of collocates. To give an example, the noun *flock* collocates with *sheep*. As the collocation constitutes a part of its meaning, the noun in question does not collocate with *cows*, for which the appropriate collocate is *herd*. As for the second type of combinations, one of their elements collocates with a limited set of items, which is, however, not motivated by its meaning. For the sake of example, the verb *to commit* collocates with *murder* and *crime*, but not with *burglary* or *theft* (Herbst 1996: 389–389, cf. Palmer 1976: 96–97).

The two approaches under discussion above relate to different understandings of the term *collocation*. The variety of opinions on what should be perceived as collocation is reflected in numerous definitions of the term, which will be devoted attention in the following subsection.

1.1.2. Defining and explaining the notion of collocation

The notion of collocation is defined and understood in a number of ways. Some example definitions of the term are quoted below:

> The term **collocation** will be used to refer to sequences of lexical items which habitually co-occur, but which are nonetheless fully transparent in the sense that each lexical constituent is also a semantic constituent. These are of course easy to distinguish from idioms; nonetheless, they do have a kind of semantic cohesion – the constituent elements are, to varying degrees, mutually selective. (Cruse 1986: 40)

> Collocations (…) are fixed, recurrent combinations of words in which each word basically retains its meaning. (Benson 1989: 85)

> Collocation is a term used to describe a group of words which occur repeatedly in a language. (Carter 1994: 47)

> A collocation is a predictable combination of words: *get lost, make up for lost time, speak your mind*. Some combinations may be very highly predictable from one of the component words – *foot the bill, mineral water, spring to mind*. Some "strong" collocations have the status of idioms – *shrug your shoulders* – they are not guessable and are non-generative. Some may be so common that they hardly seem worth remarking upon – *a big car, a nice flat, have lunch*. (Hill 2000: 51)

> Collocation is the way in which words co-occur in natural texts in statistically significant ways. It sounds an innocent definition, but one very important point needs to be made: collocation is about the way words naturally co-occur in what David Brazil brilliantly called 'used language'. (Lewis 2000: 132)

> Collocations exist in every language. The term itself denotes word combinations, consisting of two or more words, that repeatedly co-occur. (Osuchowska 2001: 7)

> What is a collocation? It can be said to be a set of two or more words that frequently occur in juxtaposition, and that seem to 'fit together'. (Douglas Kozłowska 2004: 9)

> As employed in this chapter, the term **collocation** refers to combinations of two lexical items each of which makes a distinct semantic contribution, belongs to a different word class and shows a restricted range (Gramley and Pätzold 2004: 51)

> Collocations are recurrent co-occurrences of words in texts. They certainly are statistically significant; but this is not enough. They also have to be semantically relevant. They have to have a meaning of their own, a meaning that isn't obvious from the meaning of the parts they are composed of. (Teubert: 2004: 188)

> 'Collocation is the co-ccurrence of two items in a text within a specified environment.' (Sinclair, Jones and Daley 2005: 10)

> Le collocazioni sono espressioni formate da due o più parole che per uso e consuetudine lessicale formano una unità fraseologica non fissa ma riconoscibile. (Tiberii 2012: 3)

Some of the definitions are quite elaborate and detailed (e.g. Cruse 1986, Hill 2000), whereas others, especially those included in dictionaries as opposed to theoretical linguistic literature, are relatively simple and general (e.g. Douglas-Kozłowska 2004, Osuchowska 2001, Tiberii 2012). Some of them may be perceived as relatively narrow (Cruse 1986: 40, Teubert 2004) whereas others are quite broad (Carter 1994, Hill 2000: 50–51). Even those relatively complex definitions make the impression that the notion of collocation deserves more detailed explanation (cf. Meer 1998, Fontenelle 1994). In fact, after formulating a definition of collocations, numerous researchers provide further information on the notion, and the information under discussion is frequently crucial. It can even be assumed that in order to describe properly the notion of collocation, one needs to go beyond its definition, since the above-mentioned notion cannot be accurately described in just few words or sentences. It is probably for this reason that numerous researchers who devote their attention to collocations resign from formulating any definition of the term and instead provide a detailed description of the concept.

Furthermore, while examining the definitions quoted above, it is not difficult to notice that there are several researchers who perceive collocations as word combinations which are recurrent or which occur repeatedly or frequently (Carter 1994, Osuchowska 2001, Douglas Kozłowska 2004). Nevertheless, Nation (2001: 324) notices that collocations cannot be satisfactorily defined solely in this way, as corpus-based frequency research returns many combinations such as *of the, although he* or *but if*. The combinations in question do have high frequency of occurrence, nonetheless intuition suggests that they are not collocations. According to Nation (2001: 324), the expressions which can be termed as collocations are 'closely structured' and demonstrate 'some element of grammatical or lexical unpredictability or inflexibility'. In addition, it should be pointed out that a number of researchers assume that collocations are statistically significant (Lewis 2000, Sag et al. 2002, Teubert 2004) or mutually selective word combinations (Cruse 1986, cf. Herbst 1996: 383).

Still, it should be highlighted that some authors may decide to employ relatively simple definitions of collocations for specific reasons. For the sake of example, the definitions by Osuchowska (2001), Douglas Kozłowska (2004) and Tiberii (2012) appear in collocational dictionaries which are presumably intended most of all for non-native users of English and Italian. It is probable that a significant part of dictionary users could find more complex definitions confusing. In fact, it can be assumed that all that they the need is only a general and basic understanding of what are collocations. Besides, the seemingly very simple definitions of collocations are often followed by more detailed description of the notion. For instance, Sinclair, Jones and Daley (2005: 9) immediately after their definition propose the distinction between significant collocations, whose component parts 'co-occur more often than their respective frequencies, and the length of text in which they appear, would predict', and casual collocations, which are non-significant collocations.

Besides, various definitions of collocations share the tendency to refer to lexical items. In this work we assume the definition of lexical item proposed by Sinclair, Jones and Daley (2005: 9), who postulate that 'a lexical item is a unit of language representing a particular area of meaning which has a unique pattern of co-occurrence with other lexical items'. Some lexical items can be identified with orthographic words. Others correspond to various senses of a polysemous word. Others again take the form of a group of words associated paradigmatically (e.g. *kick, kicked, kicking, kicks*) or syntagmatically (e.g. *to beat about the bush*). Lexical items are sometimes juxtaposed with grammatical items, i.e. units of language whose presence in a given text is related to their grammatical function and not their specific meaning (Sinclair, Jones and Daley 2005: 9). Besides, they are sometimes referred to as lexemes, though the term *lexeme* may also be understood as an uninflected word form (Carter 1994: 22, cf. Aprile 2005: 9–10).

Some authors assume that collocations may involve lexical items as well as grammatical items (Benson 1989, Carter 1994: 47–48). Accordingly, the researchers divide collocations into grammatical and lexical. Other authors, however, present collocations as combinations of lexical items rather than those grammatical (Cruse 1986, Hill 2000, Gramley and Pätzold 2004). Nevertheless, sometimes their examples of collocations include some grammatical words, such as prepositions (e.g. *completely obsessed with, moved to tears*, Hill 2000). Finally, it should be mentioned that collocation is sometimes juxtaposed with colligation. In such cases the former pertains to 'constrained lexical choice' (Bartsch 2004: 31), whereas the latter refers to what is elsewhere called grammatical collocation (e.g. *argument for, discrimination against,* Flowerdew 2009: 87).

In addition, various works devoted to collocations differ in the approach adopted with respect to idioms and free combinations. Let us firstly focus on the former of the two notions. In this work, idioms will be defined as multi-word items with holistic meanings which are not retrievable from the meanings of their component elements (e.g. the English *to kick the bucket,* or the Italian *darsi delle arie,* Moon 1997: 46). Hill (2000: 50–51) and Geller and Dąbrówka (2007: XIV) state that idioms constitute a kind of collocation (cf. Palmer 1976: 98, Moon 1997: 43), whereas Cruse (1986: 40), Benson (1989), Jędrzejko (ed., 1998: 74), Crowther et al. (2002: vii) and Rokicka (2007: 81) claim that they are a different type of word combination. Besides, Moon (1997) takes an intermediate approach assuming that multi-word items, such as idioms, phrasal verbs, compounds, fixed phrases and prefabs, 'in many respects can be seen as extreme cases of fixed collocations' (Moon 1997: 43). Finally, Palmer (1976: 96) criticises clear distinctions between collocations which are predictable from the meanings of their components and those which are unpredictable. He notices that 'co-occurrences are determined both by the meaning of the individual words and (…) by conventions about "the company they keep"'. In addition, the researcher postulates that the notion of collocation should not be restricted in any precise way, though understandably every researcher is allowed to limit their research to any items that they find interesting.

Let us now turn to the so-called free combinations, which are also termed as occasional or casual collocations (Roos 1976, Sinclair 1966: 418, Sinclair et al. 2005: 10). They are expressions of the smallest degree of restrictedness whose components combine with vast numbers of items, sometimes coming from different grammatical categories. For instance, the verb *to see* may be accompanied by a variety of nouns (for instance, *to see a car, a cat, a teacher, a flower,* etc.), prepositional phrases (*to see somebody on the street, in the park*) and adverbs (*to suddenly see, to see today*) (Roos 1976). Crowther et al. (2002: vii), Proost (2007: 165), Hausmann and Blumenthal (2006: 4), and McKeown and Radev (2000) distinguish between collocations and free combinations. Contrastingly, Howarth (1996: 33–34) assumes that free combinations constitute a kind of collocation and Hill (2000: 51) provides examples of collocations which are in fact free combinations (*a nice flat, a big car*).

Furthermore, some researchers who notice that the notion of collocation is problematic in terms of its definition approach the term in an unconventional way. To give an example, Meer (1998: 315) assumes that it is not possible to formulate a clear-cut definition of collocation, as the notion does not feature clear-cut distinctions in natural language. Thus, the researcher proposes to formulate a definition of the prototypical collocation (cf. Herbst 1996: 385). He tentatively defines the prototypical collocation as a combination:

1. of two or more lexical units, with meanings also occurring independently in other combinations;
2. of lexical units which are used non-metaphorically;
3. which appears normally, repeatedly and conventionally in a language;
4. which is available as a whole to the language user and serves to express conventional, established concepts;
5. whose constituents are in a modifier-modified relation;
6. whose constituents naturally select each other since the sense definition of the modifier includes the modified (and sometimes vice versa) in a non-banal way (semantic motivation).
7. which typically functions as part of a larger group and not as a complete utterance itself.

Meer (1998: 316) points out that the above-mentioned criteria eliminate a number of fixed expressions which are not prototypical collocations, such as proverbs, idioms, or catchphrases. Additionally, the researcher distinguishes collocations from free combinations, assuming that the former convey conventional concepts and are crucial to discuss some topics.

1.1.3. Collocational restrictions

Let us now turn to another notion which is crucial for understanding of the term *collocation*, i.e. the notion of collocational restrictions. Before their discussion, it should be stated that collocations are frequently divided into two parts, i.e. nodes and collocates. Nodes, which are also called bases (Spohr 2012) and headwords (Douglas Kozłowska 2004: 9), are modified by their collocates and constitute the most significant and meaningful element of a given collocation. For instance, provided that a collocation consists of a noun and adjective, the noun tends to be the node and the adjective its modifying collocate (e.g. *financial aid / pomoc finansowa / aiuto finanziario*). It should be added, however, that the identification of node and collocate is situation dependent. In some cases it is hardly possible to identify the more prominent part of a given expression (Malec 2010: 130). Besides, taking a different perspective, Sinclair (1991: 115) and Sinclair, Jones and Daley (2005: 10) assume that nodes are the lexical items subject to linguistic investigation, whereas collocates are the items which occur in their contexts. Finally, it should be mentioned that some researchers use the term *collocate* to refer to all of the components of a given collocation, including the node.

According to Palmer (1976: 97), collocational restrictions relate to the knowledge what kind of collocates can be used with a given node. To give an example, though one can say that *a rhododendron died*, they will not say that *a rhododendron passed away*, since the verb *to pass away* does not collocate with the names of shrubs. Similarly, in Italian the noun *caffè* (coffee) collocates with *forte* (strong), but not with *potente*, though the two adjectives can be perceived as synonyms. In other words, some collocations are rejected not because they have never been heard before, but because the language user knows the collocational range of a given node.

Palmer (1976) distinguishes three kinds of collocational restrictions, though he admits the existence of some borderline cases. Firstly, he postulates that some collocational restrictions are related to the meaning of a given lexical item, as in the case of the word pair **hot ice*. The second type of collocational restrictions pertains to the collocational range of a given item. As in the case of *rhododendron* which *dies* and not *passes away*, some nodes will not collocate with a set of items which share some semantic features. Finally, some restrictions are 'collocational in their straightest sense', i.e. they are not determined neither by the node meaning not by its range. To give an example, though one can say that *eggs* are *addled*, they would not say that they are *rancid* (Palmer 1976: 101, cf. Halliday 1966: 151).

1.2. The importance of collocations for linguistic competence

A number of researchers (Brown 1994, Ellis 1997, Hill 2000, Nation 2001, Crowther et al. 2002, Handl 2008, Jamrozik 2014) agree that collocational knowledge is a critical aspect of language knowledge. For the sake of example, Brown (1994: 27) states that collocations offer ample opportunities 'as a means of accessibility to the multifarious uses of language'. Ellis (1997: 129) observes that 'speaking natively is speaking idiomatically using frequent and familiar collocations, and the job of a language learner is to learn these familiar word sequences'. Nation (2001:318) states that 'language knowledge is a collocational knowledge' and 'all fluent and appropriate language use requires collocational knowledge'. Besides, the researcher claims that a myriad of lexical items are employed in restricted sets of collocations, hence a significant part of vocabulary cannot be correctly used unless one learns or acquires their collocations. Crowther et al. (2002: vii) point out that 'language which is collocationally rich is also more precise', since the exact meaning of a given word is frequently determined by its context. Thus, if one chooses the most suitable collocations, they can express their ideas more clearly. Finally, as Hill (2000: 55) notices, an individual who knows collocations that they need does not have to focus on the form and is able to concentrate better on what they intend to convey.

Furthermore, the importance of collocations has been confirmed by research on the human mind. As the research in question has demonstrated, recurring collocations are probably learnt, stored, and processed as wholes, which positively influences the speed and fluency of production and comprehension (Leśniewska 2002, Nation 2001: 321). Bringing together a number of units to form a larger unit, which is stored in the mind as a whole, is often referred to as chunking (Miller 1956, cited in Nation 2001, Newell 1990, cited in Ellis 1997). The process of chunking occurs not only at the level of words, but also at all the other levels of written and spoken language (see *Figure 1*).

Level	Type of chunking	Examples
Letters	Each letter is processed as a unit not as a set of separate strokes.	*p* is processed as a unit, not as a small circle and a descending stroke on the left hand side
Morphemes	Each morpheme is processed as a unit rather than a set of letters.	*play* is processed as a unit not as a combination of *p*, *l*, *a*, *y*
Words	Complex words are processed as a unit rather than several morphemes.	*player* is processed as a unit not as a combination of two units *play* and *-er*
Collocations	Collocations are processed as a unit not as a group of two or more words.	*a player with promise* is processed as a unit

Figure 1. Examples of chunking at different levels of written language (Nation 2001: 319).

The processing of chunks by human mind may consist in their use to form larger units or in the analysis of their component parts. In the case of non-native language users, the storage of multi-word chunks in long-term memory may be problematic, as the number of chunks is much greater than the number of their components. Additionally, the task of finding the required chunk in such a store may prove very challenging (Nation 2001: 319–321). An alternative to chunking is the so-called rule-based processing, which consists in recreating a given complex item each time when it is needed (Nation 2001: 320). According to Nation (2001: 321), previous research on the subject suggests that the process of chunking is typical of high-frequency complex units, whereas low-frequency complex items are re-created each time when they are needed (cf. Nation 2001: 321).

Lacks in collocational knowledge result in linguistic problems. If a language user knows the form of a given word but is unaware of its collocational restrictions, they are prone to committing language errors, such as lexical calques and semantic extensions (Gabryś-Barker 2005:102). Lexical calques occur when language users transfer to the target language collocations that are unique to another language, which is usually their mother tongue. In the case of Polish users of the English language, an example of lexical calque is saying **dense hair* instead of *thick hair* or **sincere field* instead of *open country* (Zybert 1999: 68–69). As for semantic extensions, they tend to occur when some interlingual equivalents are not exact synonyms. For instance, the French word *porte* is synonymous to the English word *door* when it comes to the door of a house or a room. Nevertheless, it is not used to refer to the door of a car, which is denominated as *portière*. The above-mentioned case of non-exact synonymy may trigger errors resulting from overgeneralisations (Swan 1997:168).

The differences between collocations in various languages give rise to numerous translation problems, which have been described Siepmann (2011: 70–76). The problems in question arise, for instance, in the case of polysemous collocations, interlingual collocational gaps and differences of frequencies between equivalent collocations in different languages. In addition, the problems under discussion may be due to some textual and stylistic factors. To give an example, due to textual factors, the French expression *jours heureux* is often translated into English as *happier days* and not *happy days*. As for stylistic factors, they may be related, for instance, to the tendency to synonymic variation which is typical of some languages (e.g. French) and less typical of others (e.g. English).

Despite the unquestionable importance of collocational knowledge, Bartsch (2004: 27) notices that collocations have been devoted scarce amount of academic research. One of the reasons is that the group of items which are termed as collocations is extremely heterogenous. Besides, the term in question is used to refer to a myriad of items which are 'to obvious and frequent to be ignored, yet defy explanation based on currently accepted paradigms of linguistic description' (Bartsch 2004: 27). Additionally, as collocations as a linguistic phenomenon lie on the borderline between grammar and lexis, they constitute a particularly problematic subject of linguistic research. Their investigation requires various types of linguistic analysis, which relate to syntactic, semantic, lexical, pragmatic, and even phonological description. Unfortunately, for practical reasons, collocational analysis is usually conducted at one level only. Nevertheless, despite numerous problems which are related to academic research on the subject, collocations definitely deserve more attention from linguists than they have so far received.

1.3. Typologies of collocations

The variety of word combinations which may be termed as collocations has generated the need of divisions within the notion. A number of researchers have attempted to classify collocations according to various criteria or have identified different types of collocations. This section aims at presenting the divisions that seem the most useful. Their review provides further insight into the nature of collocations. Besides, it has facilitated some decisions related to the content of the collocational dictionary comprised in the work.

First and foremost, collocations are often divided into grammatical and lexical (Benson 1989, Carter 1994). The latter type of collocation may consist, for instance, of a noun and an adjective (for example, the English *public function,* the Italian *atto illecito*) or a verb and a noun (for instance, the English *to mount resistance,* the Polish *udzielić kredytu*). As far as grammatical collocations are concerned, they consist of a dominant word and a grammatical word, which is usually a preposition. The dominant word may be a noun (for instance, *ambassador to, counselor to,* or the Polish *informacja o*), a verb (for example, *to abstain from, to hint at,* the Italian *partire per, riuscire a*) or an adjective (e.g. *typical of, adverse to).* Some linguists assume that grammatical collocations also include some syntactic structures which are typical of a given item. The structures in question may involve *that*-clauses (which, for instance, typically follow the adjective *adamant*) or *–ing* forms (e.g. required after the verb *to avoid*) (Fontenelle 1994).

So much for the distinction between grammatical and lexical collocations. Let us now turn to two independent divisions of collocations which are proposed by McCarthy (1994). Firstly, the researcher divides collocations into strong and weak (McCarthy 1994:12, cf. Hill 2000). The division in question hinges upon collocational range of lexical items which form a given collocation. A strong collocation is, for instance, the expression *blond hair,* since the adjective *blond* does not collocate with any noun except for *hair.* Contrastingly, the expression *brown hair* is an example of weak collocation, since both *brown* and *hair* collocate with many other lexical items (cf. the Italian *naso camuso* and *naso dritto*). Secondly, McCarthy (1994) divides collocations into marked and unmarked. The division is based on typicality or atypicality of a given collocation. For the sake of example, a very typical collocation, such as *a major problem,* is an unmarked collocation. In contrast, quite an original expression, such as *major amount,* is an example of marked collocation. Very marked collocations, such as *a major man*, are in most cases considered to be language errors (McCarthy: 1994: 12–13).

Furthermore, according to Carter (1994), collocations can be divided according to their degrees of restrictedness. The researcher postulates their division into unrestricted, semi-restricted, familiar, and restricted. Unrestricted collocations are typical of the simplest and the most rudimentary words, such as the verbs *to have, to make, to take* or *to run,* which collocate with a considerable number of lexical items. As for semi-restricted collocations, they differ from those unrestricted in that in their case 'the number of items which can be substituted in different syntactic roles is more determined'. To provide an example Carter (1994: 63) points to collocations of the verb *to harbour*, such as *to harbour a doubt, to harbour uncertainty* or *to harbour suspicion*. Contrastingly, familiar collocations consist of words which typically accompany each other, for instance *an innocent bystander, a lukewarm reception, an amicable divorce* or the Italian *pioggia torrenziale*. Last but not least, the category of restricted collocations encompasses fixed expressions, such as *pitch black* or *pretty sure*. Besides, it includes idioms (e.g. the English *to beat about the bush*, the Polish *spalić mosty*) and the so-called irreversible binomials, such as *swings and roundabouts, ups and downs,* or the Italian *sano e salvo* (cf. Benson 1989).

Carter's classification of collocations seems similar to the one proposed by Hill (2000: 63–64), who nevertheless does not refer to restrictedness, but to collocational strength. Firstly, Hill (2000) distinguishes unique collocations, such as to *foot the bill* or *to shrug one's shoulders*. The researcher points out that the verb *to shrug* does not collocate with other body parts, whereas the verb *to foot* does not collocate, for instance, with *invoice* or *coffee* (cf. the Italian *digrignare i denti*). The same type of collocation is termed by Cruse (1986: 41) as bound collocation. Secondly, Hill (2000: 63) refers to strong collocations. While describing them, he notices that 'predictably, we may talk of *trenchant criticism* or *rancid butter*, although this does not mean that other things cannot be *trenchant* or *rancid*'. Though the collocations in question are not unique, the knowledge of the adjectives *trenchant* or *rancid* would certainly not be complete without the knowledge of their most common collocates (cf. the Polish collocation *dosiadać konia*). As for the third type of collocations mentioned by Hill (2000), they are weak collocations, which are created, for instance, by the adjectives *long, cheap, good, bad*, etc. Finally, the researcher identifies medium-strength collocations, which are in between those strong and weak. Some examples of medium-strength collocations include the English expressions *to hold a conversation or to recover from a major operation*, the Polish *wykonywać pracę* or the Italian *raccogliere fiori*.

Let us now turn to a more complex division of collocations, which is proposed by Nation (2001). The researcher presents a set of ten scales for classifying items as collocations and for distinguishing their categories. The discussed scales, which were created based on previous research (e.g. Kennedy 1998, Kjellmer 1982, Renouf and Sinclair 1991, Sinclair 1991, all quoted in Nation 2001: 329–331), are presented in the table below (*Figure 2*). The left column shows the features of word combinations to be assessed on scales between two contrasting characteristics (e.g. *semantically opaque* and *semantically transparent, grammatically regular* and *grammatically unique* etc). As for the right column, it contains explanation and example collocations. According to Nation (2001: 332), it is possible to employ only some of the scales under discussion or prioritise them depending on the purpose for which they are used.

The feature	**Description**
the frequency of occurrence of a given pair or group of items	The scale goes from frequently co-occurring items to those co-occurring infrequently. According to Nation (2001), the criterion of co-occurrence entails numerous questions. It is not clear whether the co-occurring items need to adjacent, whether they can be inflected, whether they have to show strong grammatical relationships and whether frequent word pairs such as *and the* should be taken into account. Besides, collocation frequency needs to be considered alongside collocational range.
the adjacency of a given pair or group of items	The scale goes from items which co-occur immediately next to each other to those which are separated by one or more words.
grammatical connections	The scale goes from items which are grammatically connected to those unconnected. Collocating items usually show grammatical connections. Nevertheless, sometimes collocational status is granted to items which are grammatically unconnected but which stand in a 'lexical cohesion relationship' (Nation 2001: 330).
grammatical structure	Some collocations can be classified as 'well-structured' as opposed to 'loosely related'. The latter, such as *of the* or *although he*, show some grammatical connections but do not reflect the divisions that would take place while analysing a given clause.

Figure 2. A set of ten scales for classifying items as collocations and for distinguishing various collocational categories proposed by Nation (2001).

Figure 2. Continued

The feature	Description
grammatical uniqueness	Some collocations show grammatical uniqueness (e.g. *hell for leather*). Others constitute an exception to a rule (e.g. *to go to bed*, which does not require article). Still others are grammatically regular.
grammatical fossilisation	If a given collocation is grammatically fossilised, it allows no grammatical change and no change in word order (*e.g. law and order, by and large*). Nevertheless, there are also collocations which allow a variety of changes, such as passivisation, inflectional changes or changes in parts of speech. In between the extremes Nation (2001) locates collocations which allow small changes.
collocational specialisation	Some items occur only in one particular collocation (e.g. *kith* in *kith and kin* or *bubonic* in *bubonic plague*), whereas others have a significant number of possible collocates. The scales goes from items which always mutually co-occur to those which all appear in numerous collocations. In between the extremes there are collocations with one bound item.
lexical fossilisation	The scale ranges from collocations in which neither of the collocates can be replaced by their synonyms or words of related meanings (e.g. *a bird's eye view, no fear!)* to collocations which allow the replacements under discussion for all of the collocates.
semantic opaqueness	The scale goes from collocations which are semantically opaque, i.e. whose meaning cannot be deduced from the meaning of their parts (e.g. *to burn your bridges*), to collocations which are semantically transparent.
uniqueness of meaning	Some collocations have only one meaning, whereas other have multiple meanings.

The ranges in each of the scales presented by Nation (2001: 329–332) are ordered from the most lexicalised to the least. According to the researcher, an example of highly lexicalised collocation is *hocus pocus.* The collocation is frequent, grammatically unique and has only one meaning which cannot be deduced from its parts. The structure of the collocation under discussion allows neither grammatical nor lexical changes. The two collocates usually co-occur immediately next to each other, show grammatical connection, and rarely form other collocations.

Furthermore, taking a completely different perspective, Lewis (2000: 133–134, cf. Białek 2009: 22–26) provides a list of various types of collocations based on the parts of speech and structures of their collocates:

1. *A difficult decision* (adjective + noun)
2. *To submit a report* (verb + noun)
3. *Radio station* (noun + noun)
4. *To examine thoroughly* (verb + adverb)
5. *Extremenly inconvenient* (adverb + adjective)
6. *To revise the original plan* (verb + adjective + noun)
7. *The fog closed in* (noun + verb)
8. *To put it another way* (discourse marker)
9. *A few years ago* (multi-word prepositional phrase)
10. *Turn in* (phrasal verb)
11. *Aware of* (adjective + preposition)
12. *Fire escape* (compound noun)
13. *Backwards and forwards* (binomial)
14. *Hook, line and sinker* (trinomial)
15. *On the other hand* (fixed phrase)
16. *A sort of…* (incomplete fixed phrase)
17. *Not half!* (fixed expression)
18. *See you later / tomorrow / on Monday* (semi-fixed expression)
19. *Too many cooks…* (part of a proverb)
20. *To be or not to be…* (part of a quotation)

Still another view on collocations in reflected in the taxonomy by Spohr (2012: 71–73). The researcher divides collocations into simple and complex. The former may consist, for instance, of morphologically simple units, derivations, compounds, etc. As for complex collocations, they contain at least one other collocation (cf. Białek 2009: 24). Their further subdivision is schematically presented in *Figure 3.*

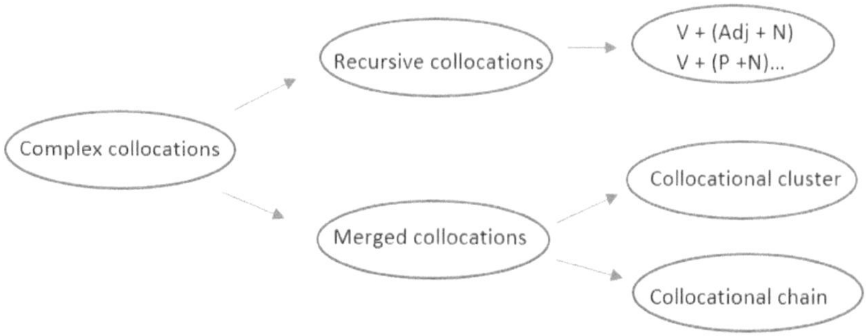

Figure 3. Subdivision of complex collocations proposed by Spohr (2012: 72).

Complex collocations are divided into merged collocations and recursive collocations. There are two types of merged collocations, which are referred to as collocational clusters and collocational chains. Collocational clusters share the same node. To give an example, *pay close attention* merges *pay attention* with *close attention.* In both of the collocations, the noun *attention* constitutes the node as opposed to collocate (cf. the Italian collocation *prestare un'attenzione particolare*). Contrastingly, in a collocational chain, the node of one of the collocations constitutes the collocate of the other one. For instance, the collocation *strongly recommended book* merges *strongly recommended,* where *recommended* constitutes the node, and *recommended book,* where *recommended* is the collocate. Finally, a recursive collocation is a combination of non-collocational component with a collocation which constitutes its node or collocate. For instance, in the collocation *to fall in love, fall* is a collocate, whereas the collocation *in love* constitutes its node (Spohr 2012: 73).

The review of various types of collocation presented in this work is far from being exhaustive. As for examples of some other typologies, Sinclair (1991: 115–116) distinguishes between upward, downward, and neutral collocations. As for downward collocations, their nodes are more frequently used in a given language than their collocates. Conversely, upward collocations consist of less frequently used nodes and more frequent collocates. Besides, neutral collocations constitute a 'buffer area' between the two above-mentioned types of collocations (cf. Handl 2008: 60–61). Furthermore, Fontenelle (1994) refers to delexical collocations, which are a type of restricted collocations consisting of a grammaticalised verb (such as *to have, to make, to do* or *to get*) and its direct object (cf. Jędrzejko 1998: 17–21, Nesselhauf 2005: 20, Vetulani 2005: 153–160). Lastly, Sinclair, Jones and Daley (2005) distinguish between significant collocations, whose component parts appear together more often than their respective frequencies would predict, and casual collocations, which are non-significant collocations.

Beyond any doubt, the differences between various typologies of collocations reflect different assumptions on what constitutes a collocation. They also demonstrate that collocations can be considered from various perspectives. Besides, though some typologies of collocations seem to be similar in terms of their content (e.g. McCarthy 1994, Hill 2000, Carter 1994), they differ in that some of them are more detailed (Hill 2000), whereas others are more general (McCarthy 1994). Additionally, given the collocations which are provided as examples of particular categories, it can be observed that the authors of the classifications under discussion seem to set different boundaries between various collocational types. In general, however, none of the presented typologies except for the one proposed by Lewis (2000) provides clear-cut boundaries between particular types of collocations. Accordingly, the typologies in question correspond to the recommendation by Bartsch (2004: 33), who postulates that the dispute over the status of various multi-word expressions is best resolved by their classification 'along a cline within a continuum without clearly definable borderlines' (cf. Carter 1994: 63).

1.4. Defining collocations for lexicographic purposes

In general, the notion of collocation is considered to be vague. Indeed, it is defined in different way depending on the context: a definition which is found in a learner's dictionary of collocations will differ from the definition concluding a linguistic article on what should be understood as a collocation. Given the variety of mutually exclusive assumptions on what constitutes a collocation, at present it seems impossible to formulate a definition of collocation which would suit all kinds of purposes. Even the definition of prototypical collocation proposed by Meer (1998) would have to be adjusted in the cases of some research. To give an example, the definition in question is not sufficient for the process of compilation of a collocational dictionary, as the above-mentioned process requires establishing what should be included in the dictionary and what should be omitted.

Accordingly, let us consider the notion of collocation focusing on the context, i.e. the dictionary making process. Our attention will be limited to the compilation of a multilingual dictionary of LSP collocations, which in this dissertation is compiled on the example of banking law. Understandably, if one undertakes the task of compiling a collocational dictionary of general language or a reference work including not only collocations, but also various other types of word combinations, they could need to adopt a completely different approach.

The inclusion of idioms (cf. subsection 1.1.2) in a collocational dictionary of banking law does not seem necessary, since they occur extremely rarely in the above-mentioned language for specific purposes (LSP). Nevertheless, they may be more frequent in some other LSPs, thus the compilers of other similar dictionaries should certainly consider their incorporation. In general, however, if one assumes that idioms constitute a kind of collocation, the creation a collocational dictionary seems to become an even more challenging enterprise. Idioms should be approached differently than other types of collocations, as they are not transparent in their meanings. Besides, their inclusion could contribute to an increase in the dictionary size, which in some cases constitutes an issue. Nevertheless, it should also be mentioned that Burkhanov (2003: 111–112) postulates the creation of a reference work which would encompass various types of multi-word items, such as collocations, phrasal verbs, idioms, etc. The researcher points out that spreading the items among separate dictionaries complicates the search for the information required.

Let us now consider the question whether the collocational dictionary of banking law should include free combinations. It seems that they are redundant, since potential dictionary users are advanced enough to deal with them with the aid of a traditional bilingual dictionary. Besides, their inclusion could lead to a significant increase in dictionary size, which in some cases constitutes a problem. In general, free combinations are believed not to pose serious problems neither to language learners nor to translators (Hatch and Brown 1995). Nevertheless, they could be included in a dictionary intended, for instance, to describe in detail possible contexts of occurrence of its headwords. Finally, it should be mentioned that the decision to include free combinations in a collocational dictionary may be related to the content of its headword list. To give an example, if a dictionary compiler intends to give headword status to adjectives such as *good* or *bad,* they will most probably create entries containing free combinations.

All things considered, numerous collocational dictionaries do not contain neither idioms nor free combinations and the approach will be adopted also in this work, at least at the present stage. Besides, what seems important for the definition of collocation in a collocational dictionary of LSP is statistical significance, habituality of occurrence in natural language and semantic cohesion. Furthermore, a collocational dictionary of banking law should include both lexical and grammatical collocations and should not be limited to collocations of only two words or collocations which are simple as opposed to complex (cf. Spohr 2012). It should also contain unique collocations, strong collocations and medium-strength collocations as understood by Hill (2000: 63–64).

Contrastingly, given the approach to idioms and free combinations, in this work it makes no sense to define collocations as any repeatedly occurring word combinations (cf. Nation 2001). Finally, collocations included in the dictionary will not be required to be semantically unpredictable as understood by Herbst (1996). The lack of semantic unpredictability does not seem to be a good reason to exclude any statistically significant and conventionally used collocation from the dictionary under discussion.

2. Law and language

The aim of this chapter is to present the basic characteristics of the language of law and to outline specific challenges posed by the LSP under discussion when it is chosen as the subject of lexicographic description. At the outset, however, we need to clarify what is language, what is LSP and what is the language of law. We will also explain the notions of term and terminology.

2.1. Language, LSP and LGP in the light of the anthropocentric theory of human languages

While attempting to explain what we understand under the term *language*, we will refer to the anthropocentric theory of human languages (cf. Grucza 1983, Grucza, S. 2010, Grucza 2013: 84–85). Accordingly, it will be assumed that in reality languages exist only in human minds and constitute their parts. The language in the primary meaning of the term is some knowledge of an individual which allows them to create oral and written texts. As Grucza (1993a: 29–31) notices, the language understood in this way may also encompass the abilities to use the above-mentioned knowledge in practice (cf. Grucza 1993b: 158, 163, Grucza 2013: 85, Utri 2013: 167).

By contrast, we frequently refer to languages of national groups (e.g. the English or the Polish language) and professional groups (e.g. the language of lawyers, technicians, etc.) (Utri 2013: 169). As Grucza (1993a: 40–41) explains, such a common language is not a *real* language, as such may exist only in human mind. Contrastingly, it constitutes an abstract, mental construction that should be understood either as the logical sum of languages of all the members of a given group, or as the common part of their languages. The common language under discussion is referred to as *polylect,* whereas the *real* language of an individual, i.e. the attribute of human mind, is called *idiolect* (Grucza 1993a: 41, Grucza 1993b: 158, cf. Grucza 2013: 85).

All things considered, it should be pointed out that the word *language* is by no means synonymous to the word *text,* as the latter is produced as a result of language abilities (Utri 2013: 167, cf. Grucza 2013: 131, Zmarzer 2008: 225–226). Besides, in the light of the assumptions above, we should avoid referring to 'the language of literature', 'the language of the movies' or 'the language of law', since literature, movies or law cannot have any languages themselves (Utri 2013: 167, 169). Nevertheless, the above-mentioned terms are in some cases the most concise and appropriate, for instance when used as cover terms by researchers making subdivisions within a given LSP (cf. section 2.3). Accordingly, the terms under discussion are commonly employed, also by linguists who assume the definition of language based on the anthropocentric theory of human languages (e.g. Olpińska 2009, Bartoszewicz 2011, Kielar 2011). In this work, the term *language of law* will be used due to its conciseness and will be devoted close attention in section 2.3. Nevertheless, it should be pointed out that some researchers would certainly prefer to refer, for instance, to *language(s) concerning the law.*

Let us now turn to LSP (language for special purposes), which is also referred to as specialised language. As Bowker and Pearson (2002: 25) succinctly explain:

> LSP is the language that is used to discuss specialized fields of knowledge. It is actually more accurate to talk about LSP in the plural (i.e. languages for special purposes) since different LSPs are used to describe different areas of specialized knowledge.

From the ontological perspective, a *real* LSP is the LSP of a really existing, specific specialist. Nevertheless, one can also refer to an LSP corresponding to the sum of languages of a given group of specialists, or to the common part of their languages related to a particular domain. Thus, LSP research should be divided into research devoted to *real* LSPs and research concerning some abstract, mental constructions, or the ideal models of LSPs. (Grucza, F. 2008: 12, Grucza 2009: 20, Grucza, S. 2010: 50, Grucza 2013: 86, 94). Grucza (1993a: 41, 2008: 13) calls LSPs understood as mental constructions *technolects* (technolekty). They are also referred to as polytechnolects, as opposed to idiotechnolects, which correspond to LSPs understood as specific attributes of human minds (Kierzkowska 2008: 15–16, Borkowski 2011: 225–226).

The concept of LSP is commonly contrasted with the concept of LGP (language for general purposes), which is also called general language or ordinary language. As Bowker and Pearson (2002: 25) explain, LGP 'is the language that we use every day to talk about ordinary situations'. It should be noted that general language should not be equated with national language, such as the Polish or the English language. National languages encompass a given general language as well as dialects, slangs and LSPs (Grucza, F. 2008: 14).

The key differences between an LSP and an LGP lay in their communicative and cognitive functions. Most obviously, the two types of language are employed in completely different communicative situations. Besides, unlike LGPs, LSPs are supposed to be strictly informative. Most of all, they are aimed at an objective, precise and unambiguous exchange of information (Warburton 2015: 371). Furthermore, LSPs typically differ from LGPs in terms of terminology, text patters and stylistic features. Nevertheless, they assume, among others, most of their grammatical, morphological, and phonological features (Grucza, S. 2010: 53–54).

2.2. Terms and terminology

2.2.1. Terms

For the purposes of this work, terms can be defined as words and word combinations whose meaning can be precisely defined and which can be classified as LSP vocabulary as opposed to general vocabulary (Grucza 1991: 15, Tryuk 1991: 103, Kornacka 2005a: 131). Still, it should be mentioned that various linguists tend to define the notion in other ways (cf. Jurkowski 1991: 49–53, Pearson 1998: 12, Lukszyn and Zmarzer 2001: 21–24, Pieńkoś 2003: 211–214).

All the domains of knowledge have their own systems of terms, which are more or less precise. Each system of terms is subject to constant development and partially intersects with some systems characteristic of other domains. The degree of precision of a given system of terms depends on the level of scientific development of the corresponding domain. Besides, it depends on the cognitive aims of the domain as well as on the branch of knowledge that it relates to (Grucza 1991: 39). There exist various types of terms, some of which are discussed by Jurkowski (1991: 49–50), Cabré (1999: 85–90), Lukszyn and Zmarzer (2001:29), and Kornacka (2005b: 151).

Terms differ from general language words and expressions in a number of respects. The most significant and obvious difference is that they belong to a specific conceptual field, which refers to a determined branch of knowledge or professional activity. Besides, terms are created in consequence of purposeful activity of a group of professionals, unlike general language words, which arise as a result of natural language evolution (Cabré 1999: 116, Kornacka 2005a: 131). Furthermore, given that terms are more specialised and more precise than general language vocabulary, the range of their applications is more limited (Grucza 1991: 35). Finally, terms tend to constitute emotionally neutral units, in which the relationship between the form and meaning tends towards unambiguity. By contrast, general vocabulary is quite often highly affective and ambiguous (Cabré 1999: 116). More details concerning typical features of terms and differences between terms and LGP vocabulary can be found in works by Jurkowski (1991: 51–53), Cabré (1999: 35–36), Lukszyn and Zmarzer (2001: 23–24) Kageura (2002: 14–15) and Pieńkoś (2003: 212–213).

When a new concept is established and a new term is needed, it is borrowed from another language or coined. Term coinage involves creating a new form or using an existing target language form (Schmitz 2007: 52). General language words and expressions become terms by means of a process which is referred to as terminologisation. In the course of the process, a given general language word receives a specific, specialised meaning, which can be conveyed in a definition. A process that is reverse to terminologisation also takes place. Some LSP terms become part of the general language lexicon and the phenomenon is referred to as de-terminologisation. To give an example, the terms *HIV* and *anorexia* once constituted LSP (medical) terms, but currently they are commonly understood and used by laymen. Apart from terms, LSP lexicons comprise words which are at the stage of transformation into terms, as well as a lot of general vocabulary which will never become terms (Lukszyn and Zmarzer 2001: 24; Bowker 2003: 156, Woźnicka 2004: 73; Górnicz 2005: 140; Kuratczyk 2005b: 95; Kuratczyk 2005c: 35).

2.2.2. Terminology

The term 'terminology' is employed to refer to at least three notions. Firstly, terminology is the discipline which is devoted to the study and compilation of terms (Cabré 1999: 1). Secondly, it is also 'the set of principles oriented toward term compilation'. Finally, the term is used to refer to 'the set of terms from a given subject field', i.e. the product of the term compilation practice (Cabré 1996: 16). It should be pointed out that only the first of the above-mentioned usages is congruent with the etymology of the term under discussion. The other two usages, though quite widespread, are often perceived as unacceptable (cf. Grucza 1991: 21).

As a discipline, terminology was born due to 'the need to facilitate specialised communication and translation, as well as knowledge transfer between text users belonging to different language communities and of similar as well as different knowledge levels' (Benitez 2009: 109). Terminology has been a subject of interest to linguists only since 1950s. Earlier, however, it had been devoted attention by scientists, technicians, and engineers. The founder of terminology, Eugen Wűster, is associated with the domain of engineering (Cabré 1999: 1–2).

Though in this work we assume that terminology constitutes a separate discipline, it should be mentioned that its status remains unclear. There are researchers who postulate that terminology is independent from other domains and that it should be viewed as a fully autonomous discipline. Numerous terminologists have elaborated on differences between terminology and other domains, including linguistics. Nonetheless, other researchers strongly relate terminology to linguistics, sociology, cognitive sciences, or other disciplines (cf.

Benitez 2009: 110). Still others claim that terminology should be perceived as 'an autonomous subject of an interdisciplinary nature' (Cabré 1999: 20). In other words, they affirm the autonomy of terminology, nevertheless they notice that it derives its elements from other domains, such as linguistics or particular subject fields (Cabré 1999: 20, cf. Lukszyn and Zmarzer 2001: 11).

The main aim of terminology is to identify, collect and describe terms. The fruits of these efforts can subsequently be used for the purposes of enhancing communication between specialists within a given domain, between specialists and laymen, or between specialists from various domains (Temmerman 2000: 2). Terms are collected and presented according to two approaches, which are often intentionally joined. In the first approach, which is called bottom-up or semasiological approach, the collector starts from a term to arrive at the designated concept. In the second, which is referred to as top-down or onomasiological approach, the collector starts from a concept to work out the denomination. (cf. Pozzi 1996:77, Bowker 2003: 155, Szemińska 2013: 16–17). Apart from term collection and description, terminological work often consists in attempts to choose a single term for a given concept and to make the chosen term widely accepted as the only correct (Pieńkoś 2003: 205). However, it should be mentioned that more and more linguists believe that full unambiguity in terminology is impossible (Benitez 2009: 110).

Despite the apparent focus on terms, as Sandrini (2014: 142, cf. Lukszyn and Zmarzer 2001: 103, Lerat 2014) notices, 'the basic unit of description in terminology is the concept' and not a term. The assumption constitutes the source of basic differences between terminology and lexicology as well as between terminography and lexicography. As Cabré (1996: 21) summarises:

> lexicology (…) does not conceive the meaning outside the word; terminology, on the contrary, regards the concept (…) as prior and conceives it as independent of the denomination or term that designates it.

The differences under discussion result, among others, in distinct methodologies of work of terminology and lexicology as well as in discrepancies between contents and layouts of various types of dictionaries (cf. Cabré 1996: 21, Lukszyn and Zmarzer 2001).

2.3. Law and the language of law

The term *law* is understood and defined in various ways. Its polysemy is illustrated by the variety of definitions included in Black's Law Dictionary (Garner 2004: 900):

law. 1. The regime that orders human activities and relations through systematic application of the force of politically organized society, or through social pressure, backed by force, in such a society; the legal system <respect and obey the law>. **2.** The aggregate of legislation, judicial precedents, and accepted legal principles; the body of authoritative grounds of judicial and administrative action; esp., the body of rules, standards, and principles that the courts of a particular jurisdiction apply in deciding controversies brought before them <the law of the land>. **3.** The set of rules or principles dealing with a specific area of a legal system <copyright law>. **4.** The judicial and administrative process; legal action and proceedings <when settlement negotiations failed, they submitted their dispute to the law>. **5.** A statute <Congress passed a law>. — Abbr. L. **6.** COMMON LAW <law but not equity>. **7.** The legal profession <she spent her entire career in law>.

Figure 4. Various senses of the term *law* in Black's Law Dictionary (Garner 2004: 900).

In this work the term *law* will be most often used to refer to an aggregate of normative acts which pertain to a specific area of legal systems, i.e. banking. As for the definition of law in the basic meaning of the term, we will assume the one proposed by Kielar (2009: 44), who perceives law as a collection of norms of conduct established or recognised by a suitable official authority. The authority is most often a state authority, nevertheless, it can be also a supranational authority, such as an institution of the European Union, or an authority of a given community, e.g. a self-government community (cf. Kielar 2011: 76).

It should be mentioned that from a worldwide perspective, there are two major legal families, i.e. the common law and the civil (continental) law. The former is applied in the English-speaking countries, whereas the latter is typical of Continental Europe and Latin America. The two legal families differ in terms of their basic concepts and divisions, the degree of generality of legal rules and the doctrine on sources of law. The differences under discussion, especially the first one, constitute a source of problems for translators and dictionary makers, as numerous common law terms do not have continental law equivalents and vice versa. Nevertheless, it should be pointed out that lacks interlingual equivalents in the domain of law are common also if the source and the target language are related to the same legal family, since legal concepts are in general particularly culture-specific (Garzone 2011: 225, Mattila 2012: 28, Mattila 2013: 138, 305–306, cf. section 2.5).

Let us now turn to the language concerning law, which in this work has to be devoted particular interest. It can be defined as 'the language used by persons qualified to practice law, i.e. lawyers involved in various professional activities, from the drafting of statutes to the drawing up of contracts' (Jopek-Bosiacka 2010: 18). It should be noted that as Mellinkoff (2004: 3) suggests, the term *the language of the law* is in a way preferable to the term *legal language*, since the adjective *legal* means also lawful, thus may easily become a source of confusion. Accordingly, though the term *legal language* is quite frequently employed, in this work it will be avoided, and the term *language of law* will be preferred. Nevertheless, the adjective *legal* will be used in various other contexts.

Various researchers notice the specificity of the language concerning law in comparison with ordinary language. Nevertheless, they point out that the language under discussion is not autonomous from general language. In the introduction to *The Oxford Handbook of Language and Law*, Solan and Tiersma (2012: 1) ask 'what is it about legal language that sounds so different, even though it must be some dialect of natural language or we would not understand it at all?' In turn, Kielar (2011: 79) postulates the existence of 'special idiolects or special polylects of law used in particular branches of the law'. Nevertheless, the researcher observes that in fact they should be considered *semi*-lects, since they are in a way supplementary to the basic nationlect (Kielar 2011: 79). Mattila (2012: 27) states that 'legal language is based on ordinary language', thus its grammar and the majority of its vocabulary do not differ from those of LGP. Nevertheless, the researcher admits that the language of law is one of the languages for special purposes, consequently it has certain features which make it markedly different from general language. It seems impossible not to agree with the above-mentioned views concerning both the status of the language of law as an LSP and its dependency from the LGP.

Furthermore, numerous researchers propose to divide the language of law into subfields. In Poland, it is the subdivision proposed by Wróblewski (1948) that is the most famous. Simultaneously, it seems perfectly suitable for the purposes of the present work. Wróblewski distinguished between *język prawny* and *język prawniczy*. We will employ the translations of the original terms which were proposed by Kielar (2011: 80), thus the former will be referred to as *the Legislator's language*, whereas the latter will be called *the lawyers' language* (cf Jopek-Bosiacka 2010: 19). The Legislator's language is the language in which various normative acts, such as statutes, decrees, or regulations, are formulated.

By contrast, the lawyers' language refers, for instance, to the language of legal theorists, public prosecutors, judges, notaries, etc. (Wróblewski 1948: 54, Jopek-Bosiacka 2010: 19, Kielar 2011: 80). It should be mentioned, however, that the division by Wróblewski (1948), though frequently referred to and employed, is sometimes criticised for being excessively schematic. As Olpińska (2009: 79) points out, it turns particularly problematic when it comes to texts which do not constitute normative acts but contain their fragments.

In this work it is the Legislator's language, i.e. the language in which various normative acts are formulated, that deserves our particular attention. As Hiltunen (2012: 37) notices:

> statutes (…) constitute a focal point for examining the characteristics of legal texts, since they embody the functions of control and regulation of the law in a maximally clear, explicit and precise wording. They can therefore be regarded as representing the law at its most prototypical.

Legislative texts are created not by individual persons, but by certain groups of legislators. The Legislator's language that is the central focus of this dissertation constitutes a polytechnolect, i.e. the logical sum of languages of all the members of groups of legislators who formulate normative acts pertaining to banking (cf. Kierzkowska 2008: 16). For obvious reasons, in this work it would be impossible to characterise idiotechnolects of particular members of the groups under discussion, though they constitute the Legislator's languages in the primary meaning of the term *language* (cf. section 2.1).

Within the past few years, Polish linguists have appreciated the significance of the Legislator's language and have devoted quite a lot of attention to texts of normative acts. They were analysed from the perspective of terminological lexicography by Borkowski (2008, 2011). Kielar (2003, 2007, 2011) and Rosner (2007) investigated various aspects of their translation. Besides, the texts under discussion were explored from other points of view by Malinowski (2006, 2012), Petzel (2006), Jadacka (2007), Śliwiński (2008), Choduń (2009), Niewiadomski (2009), Biel (2012), Malinowska (2012), Wiltos (2014), and Woźniak (2014). Interestingly, F. Grucza (2010) has even postulated the creation of a subfield of linguistics that he calls legislative linguistics. The principal aims of legislative linguistics are to reconstruct LSPs in which normative acts are formulated, to establish criteria of their linguistic evaluation and to create methods of their enhancement (Grucza, F. 2010: 6, cf. Bartoszewicz 2011). When it comes to research on the Legislator's language in Italy, it was conducted by Venturi (2010), who compared legislative corpora of Italian and English with general language corpora of those languages. Besides, Mattiello (2010) investigated nominalisations in the English and Italian

Legislator's language (cf. Gualdo and Telve 2011: 417–418). Finally, as for British research, Robinson (2014) devotes attention to the translation of legislative texts and Langton (2006) presents a way of accessing and reformulating them 'so as to make the content, scope and intended purposes clearer without losing content or scope or ignoring traditional drafting methods' (2006: 381).

Last but not least, it should be mentioned that the language of law is also divided according to various branches of law. Accordingly, some researchers may decide to explore, for instance, the language of criminal law, the language of family law or the language of international law. Understandably, as Mattila (2013: 3) notices, the various languages of particular branches of law share a significant amount of universal, legal terminology. Nevertheless, they also contain a multitude of items which are typical of other LSPs. To give a few examples, the language of tax law will certainly contain a myriad of terms which are absent from the language of constitutional law, and some terms which are typical of banking law will not be common in family law (cf. Mattila 2013: 3).

2.4. Characteristics of the language of law

The present section will be devoted to the most significant, typical, and distinctive features of the language of law. In this work, it is the description of its terminological, lexical, and collocational characteristics that deserves more attention. The grammatical, syntactic, and stylistic features cannot be totally neglected, nevertheless they have to be discussed in a more concise way. Understandably, given the purpose of this work, we will focus our attention on the features which seem especially typical of legislative texts.

The language of law, be it the English, Polish or Italian language of law, contains lexical items of various kinds. Firstly, it contains terms which are typical solely of the language of law, i.e. terms of art (e.g. *felony* and *plaintiff* in English, *zachowek* and *wokanda* in Polish or *legittimario* and *enfiteusi* in Italian) (Jopek-Bosiacka 2010: 106–107, Mellinkoff 2004: 16, Pronińska 2005: 271). Besides, it includes lexical items which are employed also for general purposes. Moreover, it encompasses vocabulary characteristic of other LSPs, such as the language of commerce, technology, or banking, as well as items typical of literary style – for instance, Latin expressions (Mattila 2012: 31–32, 2013: 121–122, Pronińska 2005: 271).

Before we briefly characterise the language of law, it should be highlighted that all the texts of normative acts constitute parts of a system, be it legislation or the entire legal order. In general they should not be perceived as separate entities, since they are always related to other texts. If a new law is enacted, usually some others need to be amended or repelled (Mattila 2013: 101–104) The revisions and updates are relatively common and entail linguistic changes, thus the language of law is subject to constant development (Hiltunen 2012: 40, 50).

2.4.1. The English language of law

The English legal system, unlike the Polish and Italian, is a common law system. It is based on case law, originally developed by judicial organs, which typically devote much attention to particulars of individual cases. Accordingly, the rules of law are relatively precise and English legal texts, including legislation, are typically long, wordy, and remarkably detailed (Mattila 2013: 308).

Mellinkoff (2004: 11, cf. 12–23) succinctly states that the English language of law is characterised by:

1) Frequent use of Old English and Middle English vocabulary which is currently rare in general language (e.g. *thenceforth, heretofore*)
2) Common presence of Latin words and phrases (e.g. *in forma pauperis, malum in se*)
3) Use of Old French and Anglo-Norman words, some of which are not used in general language (e.g. *estoppel, demurrer, chose in action*).
4) Use of terms of art (*lessee, libellant, tort*), formal words (*deceased, decedent*), and argot, understood as specialised vocabulary which is common to a particular group of language users and which is used within the group for communicative purposes (e.g. *legal conclusion, without prejudice)* (Mellinkoff 2004: 17–19)
5) Deliberate use of words and expressions with ambiguous meanings (e.g. *adequate, excessive, incidental, malice, objectionable, satisfactory*)
6) Attempts at extraordinary precision of expression, consisting, for instance, in the use of the so-called absolute expressions (e.g. *none, all, never, whoever…*) as well as expressions to keep the broad broad (*including but not limited to, or other similar and dissimilar causes…*) or, conversely, to keep the restricted restricted (*and no more, and no other purpose…*) (Mellinkoff 2004: 22–23).
7) frequent use of general language vocabulary with uncommon meanings. Mellinkoff (2004) provides the following examples of lexical items whose meanings in general English differ from their meanings in the language of law:

action	law suit
alien	transfer
assigns	assignees
avoid	cancel
consideration	benefit to promisor or detriment to promiseo
counterpart	duplicate of a document
covenant	sealed contract
demise	to lease
demur	to file a demurrer
executed	signed and delivered
hand	signature
instrument	legal document
letters	document authorizing one to act
master	employer
motion	formal request for action by a court
of course	as a matter of right
party	person contracting or litigating
plead	file pleadings
prayer	form of pleading request addressed to court
presents	this legal document
provided	word of introduction to a proviso
purchase	to acquire realty by means other than descent
said	mentioned before
save	except
serve	deliver legal papers
specialty	sealed contract
tenement	estate in land
virtue	force or authority, as in "by virtue of"
without prejudice	without loss of any rights

Figure 5. Some particularly confusing legal terms and their meaning in the language of law (Mellinkoff 2004: 12).

Let us now focus on points 2–3 in the list of characteristics above. When it comes to Latin words and expressions, as Mattila (2013: 315) notices, they are particularly frequent in legislative texts (e.g. *affidavit*, *certiorari*, *pendente lite*, *non compos mentis*). Besides, the influence of Latin is also visible in the sentence structure, for instance in multiple negatives (as in the sentence *innocent misrecollection is not uncommon*) (Mattila 2013: 317–318, Tiersma 2000: 66). As for the impact of French, Mattila (2013: 318) claims that 'most of the technical vocabulary of legal English goes back to Old French' in terms of the meaning, even though their equivalents in modern legal French frequently have other roots (e.g.

agreement, in French *accord, convention, contrat*; *arrest*, in French *garde à vue*; or *crime*, in French *infraction*). Moreover, the researcher notices that the influence of French is also visible in word formation (e.g. *trustee, acquittal*) as well as phrase structure (e.g. *attorney general, court martial, fee simple*) (cf. Bázlik, Ambrus and Bęcławski 2010: 28–30). Last but not least, it should be mentioned that the English language of law also contains some Scandinavian loanwords, such as *ombudsman* and *quisling*, as well as items of Anglo-Saxon (Germanic) origin, e.g. *abet, deed, manslaughter, to smuggle* (Bázlik, Ambrus and Bęcławski 2010: 22–30).

Furthermore, a feature which is particularly typical of English legal texts is the presence of pleonasms, such as *new and novel, false and untrue, act and deed*, or *terms and conditions* (Gotti 2012: 11). Their usage aims at ensuring solemnity, precision, and all-inclusiveness of legal texts (Jopek-Bosiacka 2010: 110–111). Mattila (2013: 321) mentions that the expressions under discussion usually consist of one word of Latin-Romance origin and the other of Anglo-Saxon origin. Moreover, the researcher points out that the English language of law in general demonstrates particular tendency to repetition. The tendency under discussion results in increased text length and quite frequently constitutes a source of translation problems.

Besides, as Bázlik, Ambrus and Bęcławski (2010: 26–27, 40) state, the English language of law is characterised by frequent nominalisations (e.g. *proceedings, pleadings*), as well as verb-support constructions, such as the expression *to make a delivery* used instead of the verb *to deliver* (cf. Jopek-Bosiacka 2010: 114–115). Moreover, the same researchers point to frequent use of conversions, in particular nouns converted into adjectives, as in the expressions *common-law marriage* or *community service order*. Finally, Bázlik, Ambrus and Bęcławski (2010) mention another relatively common feature of the English language of law, i.e. the presence of collocations forming special naming units, such as, for instance, *days of grace, natural person*, or *writ of summons*.

When it comes to sentence structures which are typical of the English language of law, Tiersma (2000: 65) states that it is characterised by the presence of constructions originating from Latin and relatively unusual in LGP. For instance, one of the structures typical of English legal texts consists of a verb (V) followed by a prepositional phrase (PP) and subsequently by a noun phrase (NP), whereas the usual word order in general English would be V-NP-PP. Another example is non-finite clauses that follow nouns, as in *rent hereinbefore reserved and agreed to be paid*. In LGP, the clauses of this type are typically placed before the nouns that they modify. By the same token, dependent clauses in English legal texts tend to be placed in a way atypical of LGP, i.e. next to the word that they modify or between the auxiliary and the main verb. The tendency under discussion is illustrated by the examples below:

> The defendant or the prosecutor, *if dissatisfied with the place of trial as fixed by the magistrates' court, or by the Crown Court,* may apply...

> The Lord Chancellor may, *with the concurrence of the Minister for the Civil Service as to numbers and salaries,* appoint... (Tiersma 2000: 66)

There are several other features of the English language of law that need to be at least briefly mentioned. Tiersma (2000: 67) points to the impersonality of the English language of law, which creates 'an aura of objectivity' (Tiersma 2000: 68) and sometimes even helps avoid ambiguity. It is illustrated, for instance, by the tendency to avoid first and second person pronouns. The researcher also notices that some types of legal texts (e.g. commands or orders) contain relatively high numbers of negatives, since 'the law is primarily about what people *cannot* do, and is logically phrased mainly in the negative' (Tiersma 2000: 66). Last but not least, Bázlik, Ambrus and Bęcławski (2010) state that English legal texts are characterised by particularly frequent use of subjunctives (e.g. *with the intent that it be uttered or published as true*), passive voice (such as in *this agreement is entered into*), coordinated prepositions (*on or before, under or in connection* with) and modals (e.g. *shall* and *may*, which are much less frequent in LGP) (cf. Langton 2006: 362).

2.4.2. The Polish language of law

The researchers who devote attention to the Polish language of law typically refer to its subdivision proposed by Wróblewski (1948), who distinguished between *język prawny* and *język prawniczy*. In this work we employ the translations of the original terms which were proposed by Kielar (2011: 80), thus the former is referred to as *the Legislator's language*, whereas the latter is called *the lawyers' language* (cf. Jopek-Bosiacka 2010: 19). The Legislator's language is the language in which various normative acts, such as statutes, decrees, or regulations, are formulated. By contrast, the lawyers' language refers, for instance, to the language of legal theorists, public prosecutors, judges, notaries, etc. (Wróblewski 1948: 54, Jopek-Bosiacka 2010: 19, Kielar 2011: 80).

Let us consider the Polish language of law from the lexical perspective. Its development has been influenced by several other languages, most of all Latin, but also Greek, Italian, English, German, and French. Example borrowings from the languages under discussion include *republika, senat, konstytucja, klauzula* (Latin), *monarchia, dekokracja, hipoteka* (Greek), *bank, konto* (Italian), *budżet, czek* (English), *rada, burmistrz* (German), or *arbitraż* (French) (Pieńkoś 1999: 61–62, Grzelak 2010: 203–204, cf. Jopek-Bosiacka 2008: 34–35, Gołąb 2012: 109–110). Grzelak (2010: 204) notices that the lawyer's language, as opposed to the Legislator's language, is characterised by the presence of numerous Latin terms and expressions in their original forms, such as *ad probationem, culpa in contrahendo* or *de lege.* As for other lexical features of the Polish language of law, Jopek-Bosiacka (2008: 31, 33–34) points to the high frequency of multiword terms. Besides, Malinowski (2006: 238–239), who devotes attention to the Legislator's language, mentions the relative frequency of nouns and infrequency of verbs. Another feature typical of the Polish language of law is the presence of verb-support constructions, such as the expressions *dokonać naprawy* or *dokonać oceny* used insead of the verbs *naprawiać* and *oceniać* (Kłodawski 2012: 131).

Furthermore, Malinowski (2006: 238) states that one of the characteristics of the Polish language of normative acts is its pursuit of precision. The characteristic is especially visible in numerous legislative definitions. Nevertheless, despite the attempts at precision, Polish legal texts happen to contain ambiguous vocabulary, such as the expressions *rażąca obraza czci, stosowne wynagrodzenie* or *czynność niecierpiąca zwłoki* (Jopek-Bosiacka 2008: 32, Malinowski 2012: 43). Interestingly, Jopek-Bosiacka (2008: 32) also notices that some terms happen to have different meanings in various branches of law. To give an example, the meaning of the noun *wina* in civil law is different from its meaning in criminal law. The differences of meaning can also be found between the language of law and the LGP. To give an example, Jopek-Bosiacka (2008) states that the conjunctions *albo* and *lub,* which are usually used interchangeably in LGP, are not synonymous in the language of law (cf. Nepelski 2012: 196).

As far as stylistic features are concerned, Jopek-Bosiacka (2008: 28–29) notices that the Polish language of law is characterised by a tendency to conciseness, which is in a way related to its postulated precision. To give an example, the research notices that the absolute expression *każdy* is frequently omitted in legal texts, nevertheless they are habitually interpreted as if it were present. Besides, Wojtak (2001: 160) and Malinowski (2006: 238) point to the impersonality of legal texts, mentioning that their institutional addressees are frequently implicit and that the first and second person pronouns are not employed. Nevertheless, the texts under discussion contain references to addressees of particular norms, who are referred to with the aid of pronouns such as *kto* or terms such as *pracownik górnictwa, osoba posiadająca stopień górniczy*, etc.

Finally, as for syntactic features, Malinowski (2006: 238–239) points to the frequent use of passive voice in the Legislator's language. Contrastingly, Boleszczuk and Szczepański (2011), who explore the lawyers' language, observe that the use of passive voice is not much more frequent than in LGP. Besides, the researchers pay attention to high frequency of nominalisations, such as *niewykonanie, posiadanie* or *dysponowanie,* whereas Choduń (2007: 92–93) mentions the rarity of anaphors. Last but not least, Jopek-Bosiacka (2008: 23) pays attention to a particularly interesting syntactic property of Polish legal texts related to subject and object position. The property under discussion is illustrated by the sentence fragments below:

1. minister wyda wykaz
2. wykaz wyda minister

The word order in the first of the examples implies a certain competence or duty of the subject (i.e. a minister), whereas in the second it suggests that it is the subject (and not anyone else) that has a given competence. Accordingly, the two sentence fragments could be translated into English in the following way:

1. the minister shall issue a list
2. the minister is authorised to issue a list.

2.4.3. The Italian language of law

Let us now turn to characteristics of the Italian language of law. As far as its terminological and lexical features are concerned, the language under discussion is characterised by a limited number of terms or lexical items which would not be typical of other domains or LGP. Cavagnoli (2007: 100) notices that 'il linguaggio giuridico (...) fa un uso limitato di lessico specialistico suo proprio, attinge sempre ad altre discipline, come per esempio la disciplina medica, ingegneristica, o edile; non ha un oggetto specifico, ma viene usato per scrivere o parlare di tutti gli argomenti'. Similarly, Gualdo and Telve (2011: 411) claim that 'tra i LSP il linguaggio giuridico è forse quello che più si 'sporca' con la lingua comune, capace come una spugna di assorbire linfa da ogni fonte terminologica'. Interestingly, however, Cavagnoli (2007: 100) also points out that general language synonyms frequently differ in their meanings in Italian legal texts (e.g. *reclusione* e *arresto, affitto* e *locazione*). Furthermore, the language under discussion is characterised by high frequency of ambiguous expressions (e.g. *danno ingiusto* o *normale tollerabilità*, Gualdo and Telve 2011) as well as the presence of lexical and morphological archaisms (e.g. *evincere, obliterare, optare, ivi, altresì*).

The historical development of the Italian language of law has been influenced by several other languages, most of all Latin, but also French and German (Caterina and Rossi 2008: 187, Gualdo and Telve 2011: 417, 433–434). Visconti (2012) and Gualdo and Telve (2011: 416) provide examples of calques from

German (e.g. *negozio giuridico, fattispecie)* as well as French (*procedura civile, a norma di, a tutti gli effetti*) identified in Italian legal texts. Contemporarily, the Italian language of law is also influenced by the English language of law, some of whose terms are transferred without any change in the form (for instance *leasing, rating, forfaiting*) or give rise to calques (e.g. *informazioni privilegiate, controesame)* (Caterina and Rossi 2008: 187, Gualdo and Telve 2011: 417, 433–434, Pozzo 2012: 10–11, Bambi 2013: 12–13, Cavagnoli 2013: 85).

As for collocational features, Caterina and Rossi (2008: 187) point out that the Italian language of law is characterised by the presence of collocations which are not typical of general language (e.g. *prestare il consenso, immune da vizi, produrre un testimone*). Besides, Venturi (2013) mentions that Italian legal texts are particularly rich in verb-support constructions. To give an example, in the corpus of Italian legal texts explored by the researcher the verb *obbligare* is relatively rare in comparison with collocations such as *prescrivere l'obbligo, stabilire l'obbligo, prevedere l'obbligo, fare obbligo, avere l'obbligo*, etc. Furthermore, as for verbal collocations typical of the Italian language of law, Caterina and Rossi (2008: 186) notice that some of them are semantically opaque (e.g. *far luogo, dar atto, portare a conoscenza*).

Last but not least, at the morphosyntactic level, the language under discussion is characterised by the presence of means which allow to maintain its precision, such as anaphors, cataphors, connectives, defining expressions (e.g. *il sottoscritto, il detto terreno, i seguenti immobili*), deictic words and expressions (e.g. *codesto, testè, peraltro*) and relative pronouns (e.g. *il cui figlio, in conformità ai quali*). In general, the syntax of Italian language of law can be described as complex and rather inflexible. The sentences are frequently long and contain numerous subordinate clauses introduced with the aid of relative pronouns or expressions such as *premesso che* and *preso atto di*. Besides, Venturi (2013: 66) notices that a typical feature of Italian legal texts is the frequent use of long prepositional complements, such as the one in the example below:

> *Si intendono nella piena ed esclusiva disponibilità dell'impresa le attrezzature di proprietà, in usufrutto, con patto di riservato dominio o prese in leasing.*

Prepositional complements such as the one in the sentence above are preferred to predicative complements in the form of adjectival phrases (e.g. *pienamente e unicamente disponibili*) (Venturi 2013: 66). Finally, other syntactic features of the Italian language of law include frequent nominalisations, impersonal verbal forms, passivisations, and the presence of numerous verbs in participial forms (Caterina and Rossi 2008: 186–187, Cavagnoli 2013: 85, cf. Garzone 2011, Cavagnoli 2013: 85).

2.4.4. Differences between the English, Polish and Italian language of law

The present section will be devoted to differences between the English, Polish and Italian language of law identified in the course of previous research. Let us firstly focus on lexical differences, which are partially related to discrepancies between common law and civil law traditions. There are numerous civil law terms and concepts which are absent in common law systems and vice versa (e.g. the Italian *dolo, forza maggiore* the English *bail, trespass*). Besides, the terms which seem equivalents frequently constitute false friends or only partially correspond in terms of their meanings (e.g. the English *contract* and the Italian *contratto,* or the English *common law* and the Italian *diritto commune*) (Garzone 2011: 225–226). It should be mentioned that in the civil law systems, it is the Legislator's language that should be granted the primary importance, whereas as for the common law systems, it is the lawyers' language that is in a way more important (Nepelski 2012: 199, cf. section 2.4.1.). Pozzo (2012: 12), referring to the context of European integration, states that:

> l'inglese, seppur goda dello *status* di lingua più parlata, è – al contempo – la lingua meno adatta ad esprimere concetti giuridici della maggior parte degli ordinamenti a base romanistica. Se si usa l'inglese è per comodità, senza intenti di veicolare istituti giuridici di quella lingua: anzi l'inglese viene via via forgiato per veicolare concetti di *civil law,* oppure concetti nouvi.

Nevertheless, despite the above-mentioned discrepancies and problems, it cannot be denied that English language of law exerts considerable influence on Italian language of law, in particular at the lexical level. Pozzo (2012: 12) provides examples of borrowings taken from English, such as for instance, *franchising, leasing, insider trading* or *dumping*. As for the Polish language of law, some of the borrowings from English, include, for example, *werdykt, budżet, czek* and *know-how* (Pieńkoś 1999: 61–62, Grzelak 2010 203–204).

Besides, as was demonstrated in the previous subsections, the Polish, English and Italian language of law have been influenced by several other languages, such as Latin, French, German, etc. The influence would certainly constitute an interesting subject for further research, especially comparative research. To give an example, the Latin suffix *-tio* corresponds to the English suffix *-tion,* and the Italian suffix *-zione* and the Polish suffix *-cja,* as in *cassatio* (Latin), *cassation* (English), *cassazione* (Italian) and *kasacja* (Polish) or *legislatio* (Latin), *legislation* (English), *legislazione* (Italian) and *legislacja* (Polish) (Gajda 1990: 102, Jopek-Bosiacka 2008: 34). Jopek-Bosiacka (2008: 35, 75; 2010: 122, 127) states that in comparison with the English language of law, the Polish language of law in characterised by a greater frequency of Latin terms and expressions, though its number of loanwords is in general smaller. The multitude of Latin terms and phrases is also typical of the Italian language of law (e.g. *ad quem, adversus omnes, contra jus, ex ante,* etc.) They are devoted detailed attention by Cavagnoli (2007: 95–97).

Furthermore, legal texts of all of the languages under discussion, in particular statutory texts, are supposed to be exceptionally accurate and precise. They should also be formulated without ambiguity, in a way that makes them understandable to non-lawyers (Kielar 2011: 81, Mattila 2013: 87). One of the means of ensuring the precision is definitions, which take various forms, and which are typical of English and Polish legal texts. The definitions in normative acts, called statutory definitions, are devoted meticulous attention by Niewiadomski (2007), Malinowski (2012: 57–70), Jopek-Bosiacka (2010: 96) and Mattila (2013: 89). It should be highlighted that according to Antelmi (2008: 95–96), legislative definitions are not typical of Italian legal texts, though at present they occur more and more often. The observation is in a way completed by Gualdo and Telve (2011), who state that legislative definitions are less frequent in civil law texts than in common law texts.

In addition, the texts of normative acts are supposed to be particularly concise, which in a way contributes to their internal logic, but which simultaneously entails high density of information (Mattila 2013: 95). One of the tools which helps make the texts more concise is nominalisations, i.e. nouns derived from verbs, such as *recovery (of damages)* or *payment (of debts),* or from adjectives (e.g. *liability (for damage)* or *invalidity (of a resolution),* Jopek-Bosiacka 2010: 114–115, Mattila 2012: 32). Frequent nominalisations are particularly common in legislative acts as opposed to other legal texts (cf. Jopek-Bosiacka 2010: 114–115, Marzec-Stawiarska and Loranc-Paszylk 2011: 34). Mattiello (2010), who investigated nominalisations in the English and Italian texts of normative acts, observed that they were more common in the Italian part of the corpus, though their frequency was relatively high for both of the languages. Similarly, Garzone (2011: 223) states that nominalisations are more frequent in Italian legal texts than in English legal texts. Nevertheless, the researcher admits that the English language of law, compared with other varieties of English, is characterised by frequent use of nominalisations.

As for the Polish language of law, the presence of nominalisations also constitutes its typical feature (Malinowski 2006: 66–67, Grzelak 2010: 171, Boleszczuk and Szczepański 2011). Moreover, it should be mentioned that the Polish language of law seems to be characterised by a particular tendency to conciseness in comparison with other languages of law which are devoted attention in this work. To give an example, Bázlik, Ambrus and Bęcławski

(2010: 109), who devote attention to coordinated prepositions typical of the English language of law (e.g. *on or before, under or in connection with*), notice that in Polish 'such coordination in rare and even considered as incorrect by prescriptivists'. Furthermore, a feature which is particularly typical of English legal texts is the presence of pleonastic collocations, such as *new and novel, false and untrue* or *terms and conditions* (Gotti 2012: 52). According to Caterina and Rossi (2008: 186), similar word combinations also appear in the Italian language of law (e.g. *entro e non oltre*). Contrastingly, Jopek-Bosiacka (2008: 28–29) points to the absence of pleonastic collocations in the Polish language of law. In addition, the researcher (2008: 28–29) notices that the absolute expression *każdy* is frequently omitted in Polish legal texts, which are nevertheless interpreted as if it were present. Given all of the above-mentioned observations, it can be preliminarily concluded that the Polish language of law is characterised by a particular tendency to conciseness if compared with the English and Italian language of law. The question undoubtedly deserves to be devoted further research.

Notwithstanding their supposed conciseness, legislative texts in all of the three languages under discussion tend to be rather complex at various levels (cf. Jopek-Bosiacka 2010: 109, Marzec-Stawiarska and Loranc-Paszylk 2011: 33). They frequently contain highly complex sentences with numerous paratactic and hypotactic clauses, such as those below:

> Tajemnicę zawodową, o której mowa w ust. 1, stanowią wszystkie uzyskane lub wytworzone w związku ze sprawowaniem nadzoru bankowego informacje, których udzielenie, ujawnienie lub potwierdzenie mogłoby naruszyć chroniony prawem interes podmiotów, których te informacje bezpośrednio lub pośrednio dotyczą lub utrudnić sprawowanie nadzoru bankowego. (Prawo Bankowe, Dz. U. 1997 nr 140 poz. 939, art. 10a)

> Se alle operazioni indicate nei commi 1, 2 e 3 partecipano soggetti appartenenti a Stati extracomunitari che non assicurano condizioni di reciprocità, la Banca d'Italia comunica la domanda di autorizzazione al Ministro dell'economia e delle finanze, su proposta del quale il Presidente del Consiglio dei Ministri può vietare l'autorizzazione. (Testo Unico Bancario, d.lgs. 1-09-1993, n. 385, art. 19 c. 8)

> Investment bank insolvency regulations may make the application of a provision depend—
> (a) on whether an investment bank is, or is likely to become, unable to pay its debts,
> (b) on whether the winding up of an investment bank would be fair, or
> (c) partly on those and partly on other considerations (Banking Act 2009, section 234 (3)).

Malinowski (2006: 203) observes that the mean sentence length in Polish normative acts is 40–44 words. Accordingly, the sentences in the above-mentioned texts contain nearly twice as many words as sentences in Polish scientific texts for general public (cf. Jopek-Bosiacka 2010: 112, Hiltunen 2012: 41). Furthermore, Venturi (2013), analysing a sub-corpus of legal texts enacted by the Italian state, mentions that the average sentence length is 28 tokens (cf. Cavagnoli 2007: 98–99). It should be highlighted, however, that sentences in Italian legal texts are also considered to be particularly long and complex in comparison with general language sentences (Cavagnoli 2007: 98–99). Finally, Gotti (2012: 58–59) claims that in the case of common law legislation, sentences tend to be even longer than in civil law legislation. The difference is related to the fact that common law texts tend to contain many details, whereas civil law texts are typically much more general (cf. Bázlik, Ambrus and Bęcławski 2010: 189–190, Mattila 2013: 308).

Furthermore, Gotti (2012) notices that in the case of the Italian language of law, legal provisions are stated in the present indicative, whereas in the English language of law, their presentation typically involves the application of the modal verb *shall* (cf. Garzone 2011: 224). When it comes to the Polish language of law, Boleszczuk and Szeczepański (2011) mention that it typically employs the present or future indicative forms in situations which entail the application of *shall* in English legal texts. Besides, the results of research by Boleszczuk and Szeczepański (2011) suggest that the English language of law is rich in passive sentences. As for the Polish language of law, it demonstrates preference for impersonal verbal constructions, in particular with the pronoun *się* (e.g. *stosuje się, wydaje się*). When it comes to the Italian language of law, it is characterised by frequent application of both passive voice and impersonal verbal forms (Cavagnoli 2013: 85).

Finally, it should be mentioned that according to Caterina and Rossi (2008: 186–187) another noteworthy feature of the Italian language of law is the presence of both anaphors and cataphors, whereas as stated by Bázlik, Ambrus and Bęcławski (2000: 48), the English language of law tends to avail itself only of anaphors. As for the Polish language of law, Choduń (2007: 92–93) observes that the application of anaphors is rare and limited to using pronouns such as *on, ona, one, ta, to, te*. Last but not least, it should be noticed that the English language of law is characterised by the presence of pronominal adverbs, such as *thereof* and *therein,* which in the Polish language of law would usually be replaced by ordinary adverbs or prepositional phrases such as, for instance, *wyżej wymieniony,* or *o którym mowa w*, etc. (Boleszczuk and Szeczepański 2011).

2.5. A multilingual dictionary of legal collocations

So far, legal dictionaries have not received much attention of linguists and legal researchers . A recent – and extensive – publication on the subject is the volume

Legal lexicography (2014) edited by Máirtín Mac Aodha and including, among others, contributions by Daniel Greenberg, Coen J. P. van Laer, Peter Sandrini and Pierre Lerat. The subject under discussion was also investigated by Groffier and Reed (1990), Šarčević (1988, 1990), Chromá (2004) and Preite (2012). In Poland, dictionaries devoted to law sparked the interest of Szemińska (2011, 2013) and Borkowski (2008, 2011). Besides, Pawelec (2007) examined legal vocabulary in general language dicitonaries. In addition, legal lexicography is sometimes referred to by those who explore the language of law (e.g. Pieńkoś 1999: 111–117, Mattila 2012: 37).

Legal dictionaries are typically aimed at defining legal terms or terms which are used by lawyers (Greenberg 2014: 59). The process of creation of such a dictionary is devoted attention by Garner (2014) and Greenberg (2014). In this work we are particularly interested in legal dictionaries of collocations, which, if available, constitute a real rarity. This is in a way surprising, since numerous researchers notice the specificity ad importance of LSP collocations, including those typical of the language of law. To give a few examples, Bowker and Pearson (2002: 26) notice that LSPs not only contain multiple terms but may also combine them in a special way (cf. Seretny 2011: 111). Moreover, Chromá (2004: 82) states that:

> The language of law is a highly formalized language using settled vocabulary, phrase and sentence patterns; the more vocabulary, phrase and sentence patterns firmly established in the target language and used in the process of translation of the source text, or production of the target legal text, the more natural and comprehensible may be the final product.

Besides, Garzone (2011: 218–219) notices that one of the characteristics of various languages of law is the presence of numerous word combinations such as collocations, fixed phrases and phraseological units. The researcher points out that they should be devoted assiduous attention by translators and translation teachers, since they frequently differ between various languages in terms of lexical and grammatical structures. For instance, the expression *unless otherwise provided* typical of English legal texts corresponds to the Italian expression *salvo disposizione contraria*, as opposed to *se non diversamente previsto* (Garzone 2011: 218–219).

Finally, a researcher who notices that legal collocations should be devoted attention by lexicographers is Szemińska (2013). She has elaborated an innovative model of system of dictionaries for translators of legal texts. The system includes a combinatorial dictionary (*słownik kombinatoryczny*). *Figure 6* demonstrates its model entry, whereas *Figure 7* is an example of how the entry could look like in practice (Szemińska 2013: 166):

wyraz hasłowy
(oznaczenie rodzaju ekwiwalentu, wyraz wyjściowy)
informacje gramatyczne
informacje leksykalne (m.in. ⇒ kolokacja, ⇒ synonim)
przykłady

Artykuł hasłowy 15: Wzór artykułu hasłowego w słowniku kombinatorycznym.

Figure 6. Model entry of a combinatorial dictionary of law (Szemińska 2013: 166)

Personenkennzahl (PKZ)
(≡†, numer PESEL)
f, -, -en
die ~ geben; jdm ~ zuteilen, zuerkennen; die Angabe der ~
Ab 1970 Geborenen wurde die Personenkennzahl beim Eintrag in das Melderegister zugeteilt, älteren Personen per Postkarte zugeschickt.

Artykuł hasłowy 16: Słownik kombinatoryczny
Rzeczpospolita Polska – Republika Federalna Niemiec.

Figure 7. An example entry of a combinatorial dictionary of law (Szemińska 2013: 166).

The collocational dictionary which is devoted attention in this work constitutes a multilingual dictionary. The creation of a multilingual dictionary of law is undoubtedly an arduous task, in particular if the dictionary entries are supposed to provide equivalents of headwords in all the dictionary languages. The stage of looking for equivalents is particularly challenging, since law as a domain is characterised by innumerable cross-cultural differences. Accordingly, the systems of terms and concepts within two distinct legal systems usually differ from one another in a multitude of respects. As Berns (2010: 146) puts it, 'legal terms from different cultures in principle do not mean the same (at least as long as no standardization has taken place)'. To make matters worse, as for interlingual equivalence in the domain of terminology, it requires all features of a given concept to overlap. In consequence, Šarčević (1988: 307) and Sandrini (2014: 147) perceive exact equivalence between concepts from different legal systems to be impossible, especially in its terminological understanding. Sandrini (2014: 147) admits exceptions only when a concept which is adopted from another legal system still functions in the same way in the target system, or in the case of partial unification of the legal systems involved. As the researcher notices:

> When we contrast concepts and their terms in law, we cannot identify a common defined subject field, since every legal system is a distinct reality. Furthermore, there can be no common concepts to identify, only idiosyncratic concepts to compare. Compilers of multilingual legal dictionaries are hard pressed to find substitutable equivalents (2014: 147).

In consequence, Sandrini (2014: 148) advises legal lexicographers to focus not on equivalence relations, but on the context of a given concept and its differences and similarities with respect to the concepts of another legal system. Nevertheless, the researcher states that such information is more easily included in electronic dictionaries than traditional dictionaries, since its inclusion seriously affects dictionary size (cf. Šarčević 1988: 308, Tarp 1995b: 64, Borkowski 2011: 230, Sandrini 2014: 150, cf. Tarp 1995b: 63, Pieńkoś 1999: 113–114, Szemińska 2011: 180–181). It should be highlighted that collocational information does constitute a sort of information on the typical contexts of a given item. This kind of contextual information is particularly useful to multilingual dictionary users, since the correct use of foreign language collocations is an enormous challenge. In the light of the considerations set forth above, the example dictionary presented in this work, though being a multilingual dictionary, will not provide headword equivalents, but rather their potential equivalents.

Despite the problems related to their compilation, multilingual legal dictionaries seem an essential tool. European integration creates the need for extremely effective international communication in the domain of law. The efficient communication is crucial for the coherence of international activities. Besides, more and more people, being not only lawyers and translators, use more than one language in their everyday professional life which requires them to create oral and written texts related to law. As a rule, those who are able to communicate efficiently in the domain of their interest get the opportunities of further development.

Admittedly, the efficiency of interlingual communication in specialised domains depends on the availability of resources which facilitate the abovementioned communication, such as LSP dictionaries. Though the language of law has already been devoted numerous publications, it still poses problems to translators, interpreters, LSP teachers and other professionals whose work is related to the domain. In some cases the problems can be attributed to constant evolution of the domain of law. Sometimes, however, they arise due to the lack of knowledge of the domain-specific collocations.

As was mentioned before, the present work is supposed to constitute a guide for those who aspire to create multilingual dictionaries of LSP collocations, in particular, though not only, those devoted to various branches of law. The creation of dictionaries, especially multilingual, LSP and collocational dictionaries, will be devoted detailed attention in the following chapter.

3. Lexicography and corpus linguistics

The aim of this chapter is to provide rudimentary information on dictionaries and the process of their creation. First and foremost, the chapter presents basic definitions related to the subject. Secondly, it provides a description of various types of dictionaries. Most of all, however, the chapter outlines the decisions and processes which are related to dictionary planning and compilation. Besides, assiduous attention is devoted to language corpora, which play a crucial role in modern lexicography.

3.1. The notion of lexicography

At the outset it should be mentioned that lexicography can be defined in various ways. The variety of definitions and the related controversies are well illustrated by Hartmann (2001: 32–34), Piotrowski (2001: 22–23), Żmigrodzki (2003: 14–19, 2008: 15–24) and Tarp (2008: 7). For the purpose of this work, I shall assume the definition proposed by Hartmann and James (1998: 85) who postulate that lexicography can be defined as 'the professional activity and academic field concerned with dictionaries and other reference works'. In the light of the definition, lexicography can be divided into theoretical and practical. The former is often referred to as metalexicography (cf. Piotrowski 2001: 25–27) or dictionary research (Hartmann 2001: 27–28) and can be defined as 'the academic study of such topics as the nature, history, criticism, typology and the use of dictionaries and other reference works' (Hartmann and James 1998: 43). In contrast, the latter is devoted to the dictionary making process (Gouws 2004: 193).

Practical lexicography was born in ancient China and India. The first dictionaries, which were compiled around two thousand years BC, were intended to facilitate reading and comprehension of old scriptures (Tarp 2009: 18). As for the European lexicographic tradition, it was born in the fifth century BC, when the first glossaries were compiled in the ancient Greece (Hartmann 2001: 6). Initially, the creation of glossaries and dictionaries was mostly an amateur activity. Lexicography in our understanding of the term was born in the twentieth century alongside the first academic research in the domain (Hartmann 2001: 7–8, Gao 2010: 285). A more detailed account of the history of lexicography can be found in Hartmann (1986), Green (1996), Hartmann (2001: 39–47), Jackson (2002: 31–74), or van Sterkenburg (2003: 8–17). As for the history of English lexicography, it is presented by Walker Read (1986), Landau (2001), Cowie (2009), and Adams (2010). Finally, the history of Polish lexicography is devoted attention by Żmigrodzki (2003), whereas the Italian is set forth by Marazzini (2009).

3.2. The notion of dictionary

Works which are referred to as dictionaries are immensely varied. To give a few examples, linguistic literature mentions monolingual and multilingual dictionaries, general and specialised dictionaries, synchronic and diachronic dictionaries, alphabetical and thematic dictionaries, dictionaries of synonyms and antonyms, dictionaries of pronunciation, collocations, idioms, proverbs, etc. The above-mentioned variety makes extraordinarily difficult the task of encompassing all the works referred to as dictionaries in one definition (van Sterkenburg 2003: 3). Various researchers approach the problem of defining a dictionary in different ways. For the sake of example, some of them propose definitions based on features of the prototypical dictionary (van Sterkenburg 2003: 3), whereas others focus on what distinguishes a dictionary from other reference books or other forms of language description (Piotrowski 2001: 32–43; Jackson 2002: 21–22, Żmigrodzki 2003: 20–21). A detailed review of various dictionary definitions is provided by Hartmann (2001: 12–14). For the purpose of this work, it will be sufficient to define a dictionary as a reference work which describes individual linguistic units of one or more languages, and which presents the linguistic units in an ordered way (cf. Piotrowski 2001: 41).

Dictionaries have been devoted extensive research, which has taken various points of focus. Different types of dictionary research are indicated in *Figure 8* (Hartmann 2001: 30):

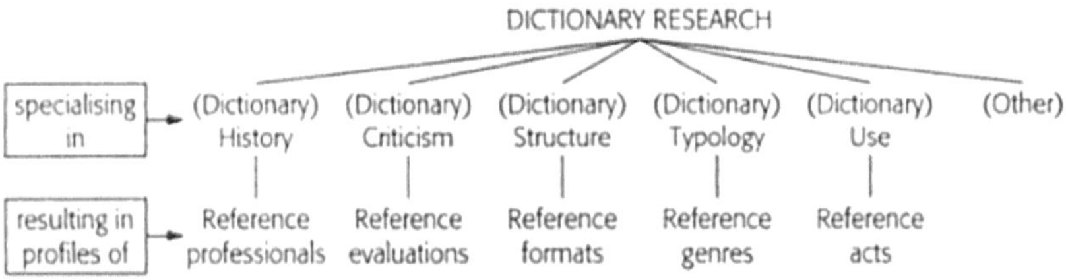

Figure 8. Types of dictionary research (Hartmann 2001: 30).

The parentheses in the names of the categories imply that the research types may concern not only dictionaries, but also other reference works. Hartmann (2001: 31) points out that the various types of research presented in the diagram can be variously combined. To give an example, the structure of a dictionary can be considered in the course of its critical evaluation. As for the category 'other', it may encompass, for instance, research on the relations between lexicographic production and economic or technological factors.

3.2.1. Dictionary types

The variety of works which are referred to as dictionaries has generated the need of divisions within the notion. Numerous researchers attempted to divide dictionaries into types and categories. The attempts resulted in the creation of typologies and classifications hinging on the formal features of dictionaries, such as size, shape, or the included information, or based on their pragmatic features, such as the situations when they are consulted (Hartmann 2001: 69). Dictionary typologies are proposed, for example, by Zgusta (1971: 198–220), Hartmann (2001: 68–79), Landau (2001: 7–42), Malkiel (2003), Swanepoel (2003: 44–69), and Żmigrodzki (2003: 23–27). As for the typologies of terminological dictionaries, they can be found in the works by Gajda (1990: 123), Lukszyn and Zmarzer (2001: 141–149), Zmarzer (2008), Łukasik (2007: 10–15), and Karpiński (2008: 59–66). Furthermore, Hannay (2003) presents a review of various types of bilingual dictionaries, whereas Hartmann (2001: 74–79) and Denisov (2003) propose a classification of pedagogical dictionaries.

Detailed description of all of the dictionary typologies is out of the scope of this dissertation. Instead, in order to demonstrate the variety of the available dictionary types, we will refer to the scheme of dictionary properties proposed by Atkins and Rundell (2008: 24–25). The scheme seems very simple and is perfectly suitable for the purpose of this work, despite being originally intended for trade dictionaries. Atkins and Rundell (2008: 24–25) postulate that those who aspire to create a dictionary should address the following questions:

1. **the dictionary's language(s):** is it…
   a. monolingual
   b. bilingual: if so, is it…
      (1) unidirectional or
      (2) bidirectional
   c. multilingual
2. **the dictionary's coverage:** is it…
   a. general language
   b. encyclopedic and cultural material
   c. terminology or sublanguages (e.g. a dictionary of legal terms, cricket, nursing)

   d. specific area of language (e.g. a dictionary of collocations, phrasal verbs, or idioms)
3. **the dictionary's size:** is it a…
   a. standard (or 'collegiate') edition
   b. concise edition
   c. pocket edition
4. **the dictionary's medium:** is it…
   a. print
   b. electronic (e.g. DVD or handheld)
   c. web-based
5. **the dictionary's organization:** is it…
   a. word to meaning (the most common)
   b. word to meaning to word (where looking up one word leads to other semantically related words)
6. **the users' language(s):** is the dictionary meant for…
   a. a group of users who all speak the same language
   b. two specific groups of language-speakers
   c. learners worldwide of the dictionary's language
7. **the users' skills:** are they…
   a. linguists and other language professionals
   b. literate adults
   c. school students
   d. young children
   e. language learners
8. **what they use the dictionary for:** is it for one or both of the following:
   a. decoding, which is …
      - understanding the meaning of a word
      - translating from a foreign language text into their own language
   b. encoding, which is …
      - using a word correctly
      - translating a text in their own language into a foreign language
      - language teaching

The presented set of dictionary properties constitutes a concise and reliable scheme for classification of most types of dictionaries. Every dictionary possesses one or more properties from each of the presented categories, though obviously the list of properties is not exhaustive and should be completed in the case of some less standard dictionaries. Besides, the scheme should be employed to describe dictionaries rather than to divide them into classes with clear borders (Atkins and Rundell 2008: 26).

3.2.2. Specialised dictionaries

Lexicographers use various terms to refer to dictionaries other than those devoted to general language. For the sake of example, the dictionaries under discussion are called specialised dictionaries, subject field dictionaries, terminological dictionaries, or special field dictionaries (Bowker 2003: 155). Let us discuss the above-mentioned dictionary types focusing most of all on their definitions provided by *Dictionary of Lexicography* (DL) by Hartmann and James (1998).

Specialised dictionaries are assumed to constitute the widest range of reference works. As opposed to general dictionaries, they focus either on a specific aspect of language, such as pronunciation, idioms, or collocations, or on the language of a given subject field (Harmann and James 1998: 128, 129). Cross-references in DL (1998: 119, 128–129) suggest that specialised dictionaries are in a way related to restricted dictionaries, special field dictionaries or special-purpose dictionaries (cf. Bowker 2003: 154–155). Besides, dictionaries which are specialised in terms of subject fields may be called subject dictionaries or subject field dictionaries (Hartmann and James 1998: 132–133). It should be noted that the dictionary whose creation is one of the purposes of this dissertation is specialised both in terms of an aspect of language and the subject field.

Let us now turn to technical dictionaries. Hartmann and James (1998: 137) assume that they are devoted to technical language, which is conceived as 'a language variety, especially its vocabulary, as used in a specialised field of activity such as a scientific or applied discipline'. A cross-reference in DL points to relations between the notions of technical dictionary and specialised dictionary (Hartmann and James 1998: 138). Additionally, the authors state that technical dictionaries can take various formats, which are dependent upon the level of expertise of their potential users. In turn, the users of the dictionaries under discussion may range from non-experts in a given subject field to qualified experts (cf. Aprile 2005: 156).

As far as the LSP dictionary is concerned, Hartmann and James (1998: 90) define it as 'a type of reference work intended to describe a variety of a language used by experts in a particular subject field'. The researchers assume that LSP dictionaries are intended for users who are specialists in the given subject field and who want to 'practice or further study it through the medium of the target language for specific purposes' (Hartmann and James 1998: 90). As for the term *language for specific (or special) purposes* (LSP), Hartmann and James (1998) state that it is used in the context of language teaching and lexicography. Accordingly, it seems in a way narrower than the term *technical language*. When it comes to LSP, the authors of DL define it as a variety of language used by experts in a given subject field. Such understanding of the term is reflected in their definition of the LSP dictionary (Hartmann and James 1998: 80, 137). Nevertheless, in the present work it is another definition of LSP that is assumed (cf. section 2.1). It was formulated by Bowker and Pearson (2002: 25), who understand LSP as 'the language that is used to discuss specialized fields of knowledge'. Consequently, we need to adjust the definition of LSP dictionary proposed in DL. LSP dictionaries will be understood as reference works describing a variety of language used to discuss a particular specialised field of knowledge. Besides, it will be assumed that target users of an LSP dictionary may be both experts and non-experts in a given subject field.

When it comes to terminological dictionaries, they are assumed to be reference works which contain information about the language of a subject field, particularly its vocabulary, 'as defined by its practitioners' (Hartmann and James 1998: 140). It should be mentioned that terminological dictionaries have been devoted particularly extensive attention in Polish linguistics (see, for instance, Lukszyn and Zmarzer 2001, Lukszyn 2008, Zmarzer 2008, Michałowski 2011, or Nasiadka 2011). Szemińska (2013: 10–11) suggests that terminological dictionaries differ from LSP dictionaries in that the former are focused on terms, whereas the latter are devoted to a wider range of items (Szemińska 2013: 11–12, cf. Lukszyn and Zmarzer 2001: 13). Besides, Lukszyn and Zmarzer (2001: 129–130, 133) state that the terminological dictionary typically aims to present relationships between the headword and other terminological units (cf. Lukszyn and Zmarzer 2001: 138–137).

The distinctions between various dictionary types that were presented in this subsetion happen to arouse doubts and are subject to controversies. To give an example, it is problematic that the presented definitions do not provide clear boundaries between the dictionary types concerned (cf. Szemińska 2013: 10–11). Besides, it should be highlighted that the definitions under discussion are not universally acknowledged. For the sake of example, some researchers such as Gajda (1990: 118), Bowker (2003: 154–55) and Kuratczyk (2005d: 155) use the terms *terminological dictionary* and *specialised dictionary* interchangeably (cf. Szemińska 2013: 9–12). All in all, however, it seems reasonable to infer that LSP dictionaries constitute a kind of specialised dictionaries. In turn, terminological dictionaries seem to constitute a kind of both LSP dictionaries and specialised dictionaries. As for the dictionary presented in this dissertation, it certainly constitutes a specialised dictionary, since it is simultaneously limited to one aspect of language (i.e. collocations) and devoted to one subject field (i.e. banking law). It will be referred to as a multilingual dictionary of LSP collocations.

3.3. Dictionary structures

The descriptions of dictionary structure virtually always refer to the macrostructure and microstructure. Other commonly applied terms are megastructure, mediostructure, access structure and distribution structure. All of the notions deserve attention, as their understanding allows to get an initial grasp of the decisions which have to be taken at the stage of dictionary planning. Accordingly, they will be briefly described in the present subsection. Besides, the macrostructure, the microstructure and the access structure decisions will be discussed in more detail in the section 3.4.

The broadest of the terms under discussion is the megastructure, which is also referred to as frame structure. It can be defined as the structure of the totality of components which constitute a dictionary (Hartmann and James 1998: 93, Hartmann 2001). The megastructure encompasses the dictionary outside matter, which consists of front matter, middle matter, and back matter. The front matter may comprise, for instance, a preface, an introduction, a table of contents, a user guide, or a list of the abbreviations employed. As for the middle matter, it may encompass not only dictionary entries, but also, for instance, illustrations, diagrams, tables, etc. Finally, as far as the back matter is concerned, it usually consists of appendices and bibliography (cf. Hartmann and James 1998: 92, Hartmann 2001: 61, Atkins and Rundell 2008: 177).

As for the macrostructure, in this work it will be perceived as the structure of the central list of dictionary entries which allows the dictionary user to find the information required. In the light of the definition, the macrostructure may be arranged, for instance, alphabetically, thematically, or chronologically (Hartmann and James 1998: 89, 91, Hartmann 2001: 64, cf. Gajda 1990: 121). It should be mentioned, however, that some researchers employ the term to refer to the overall design of a dictionary. Thus, in some works the term designates not only the list of entries, but also the front matter, the middle matter, and the back matter (Jackson 2002: 25, cf. Piotrowski 1993: 10).

Contrastingly, the dictionary microstructure can be defined as the internal design of individual dictionary entries. Each entry consists of a headword and some accompanying information. As far as the headwords are concerned, they are lexemes, compounds, derivational affixes, abbreviations, proper names, etc. which are devoted attention in a given entry. As for the accompanying information, its type and range are influenced by the type of headword as well as the type of dictionary. For the sake of example, in general purpose dictionaries it usually consists of headword definitions and some usage examples. Additionally, the dictionary entry may comprise, for instance, comments on pronunciation, etymology, spelling variants, irregularly inflected forms, idioms, collocations, etc. (Hartmann and James 1998: 94, 132, Jackson 2002: 25–27, cf. Aprile 2005: 165, Hausmann and Wiegand 2003, Hartmann 2001: 59, 64).

Let us now pass to the mediostructure, which is also referred to as cross-reference structure. It encompasses all the elements aimed at linking information located in different parts of a dictionary. The elements, called cross-references, may have the form of words, numbers, or symbols, such as arrows or punctuation marks. They are usually placed within a dictionary entry and link the given entry with another entry, with an illustration or with information placed in the front or back matter. In some works, however, cross-references may be located also in spaces between entries and even outside the entry list (Hartmann and James 1998: 32, Hartmann 2001: 65, 176, cf. Nielsen 2003).

As for the access structure, it can be defined as the aspects of dictionary design which allow the user to successfully search for the information required. The access structure can be divided into external, which is also called outer, and internal, which is also referred to as inner. The external access structure enables the dictionary user to find the required dictionary entry. Its typical device is the alphabetical macrostructure, which can be made more user-friendly by the use of bold print, capital letters or running heads indicating the first and the last headword on each page. The dictionaries which have only one type of external access structure, for instance the alphabetical ordering, are referred to as monoaccessible dictionaries. In contrast, the dictionaries with additional external access structures, such as indexes, are called polyaccessible dictionaries. Furthermore, as far as the internal access structure is concerned, its aim is to facilitate the search for information within the dictionary entry. Example devices of the structure under discussion include varied fonts, italic or bold types, frames, blocks, and other symbols which separate different information categories (Hartmann and James 1998: 3, Louw 1999, Hartmann 2001: 66, 169, Luna 2004, cf. Karpiński 2008: 230–235).

Finally, let us turn to the distribution structure, which relates to the distribution of linguistic and encyclopaedic information in different dictionary parts (Tarp 1995a: 188). The separation of linguistic and encyclopaedic (or technical) information frequently proves problematic for some dictionary makers. If all the information types are placed within one entry, the dictionary user does not have to perform several searches, nevertheless in some cases the entry may prove extremely cumbersome. Thus, numerous dictionary compilers decide to place some information in framed articles between entries or in a separate dictionary component, such as an encyclopaedic or grammatical section. It should be pointed out that the decisions related to the distribution structure should be taken bearing in mind the reference skills and needs of target dictionary users (Tarp 1995a: 188–189, Hartmann 2001: 67).

3.4. Dictionary planning

The section will comprise general advice on dictionary planning which seems particularly valid for the purpose of this work. The advice is intended to be useful most of all to those who aspire to compile LSP collocations dictionaries. It is assumed that all the work related to dictionary creation is performed by a single author and that the dictionary is in printed form.

3.4.1. Historical development of dictionary design

The practice of designing dictionaries has evolved over the centuries. Initially, lexicographers tended to concentrate on semantic information. Monolingual dictionaries contained most of all headword definitions, whereas bilingual dictionaries provided target language equivalents of the source language headwords. With the passing of time, the entry content began to be enriched with other information, concerning, for instance, pronunciation or grammatical categories. Nonetheless, lexicographers continued to concentrate on recommended language use and tended to ignore actual language use.

The approach was altered with the development of modern linguistics, particularly descriptive linguistics, which revolutionised the perception of dictionary functions and which gradually led to lexicographic focus on actual language use. Nowadays, the descriptive approach is still widely accepted in lexicography. Since 1960s, however, it has been modified with a trend to compile dictionaries which can be referred to as user oriented. The dictionaries in question are aimed most of all at responding to the needs of their potential users. To give some practical examples, they may describe lexical items as interrelated constituents of lexical systems or contain a myriad of linguistic and sociocultural contexts to facilitate not only text comprehension, but also text production (Yong and Peng 2007: 18–20). Besides, their compilers of such reference works seriously take into account the range of dictionary consultation skills which could have been developed by the intended users. Regardless of the adopted means, as Atkins and Rundell (2008: 176) state, at present a good dictionary can be defined as the one which responds to the needs and aims of its intended users.

3.4.2. Dictionary planning

The decisions taken at the stage of dictionary planning exert profound impact on the nature of the final product. The first issues for consideration include the target user group and their linguistic and reference skills as well as the predicted dictionary size. The above-mentioned questions should be considered at the starting point, as they exert marked effects on many other decisions taken at the planning stage, concerning, for instance, dictionary layout or coverage (cf. Jackson 2002: 161–163, Atkins and Rundell 2008: 28–30).

Secondly, the compiler needs to choose resources which will be used in the dictionary compilation process. The resources can be divided into primary and secondary. The former group includes language corpora, archives, citations, etc. As for the latter, they encompass, for instance, previous dictionaries, indexes, encyclopaedias, and materials obtained as a result of fieldwork activities, such as interviews or questionnaires. Contemporarily, the most important primary resource is language corpora, which will be devoted careful attention in sections 3.5–3.7. They provide the lexicographer with 'a quantity of material regarding syntactic structures, collocations, compounds, derived forms and different meanings related to the headword' (Royle et al. 2009: 528). The analysis of language corpora permits to determine which information from the secondary resources needs to be included in the new dictionary and which important patterns of usage have been hitherto unnoticed (Royle et al. 2009: 528).

As for the secondary resources, they are consulted, for instance, for information on different word meanings, typical syntactic and morphological structures, or common collocations and compounds. Particular importance should be admitted to previous dictionaries, which are virtually always used by lexicographers in order to identify changes and omissions. Another immensely popular secondary resource is Internet websites, which can be consulted, for instance, to gain information on a lexical item which is only briefly mentioned in other resources (Čermák 2003: 18–19, Kuratczyk 2007: 205–210, Royle et al. 2009: 523, 527–529). Finally, in the case of LSP dictionaries, the compilers particularly appreciate the role of reference books and textbooks. The resources under discussion are useful in the process of compilation of the headword list and constitute an important source of term definitions (Landau 2001: 347).

Besides, while planning a dictionary, the lexicographer needs to consider some external factors, such as the available budget or time (Jackson 2002: 163–169, cf. Zgusta 1971: 348). As far as the budget is concerned, it should be noted that the cost of dictionary production is not high in comparison with the cost of dictionary preparation. As for the dictionary scheduling, the compiler should bear in mind that it usually proves to be inaccurate, particularly in the case of scholarly dictionaries. Timely work completion is affected by multitudinous factors which cannot be fully evaluated at the planning stage, as they may include, for instance, unforeseen hardware or software issues or long duration of fund gathering. In fact, the scheduling is sometimes perceived as the most challenging aspect of dictionary planning (Landau 2001: 347–348). As far as smaller dictionary projects are concerned, Zgusta (1971: 349) recommends making time estimates based on samples of lexicographic work accompanied by corresponding time calculations. The calculations should be performed taking into account every aspect of the work predicted. Nevertheless, as the researcher states, that precise scheduling is more realistic when the project is nearly half-completed, since some factors, such as the compiler's abilities, cannot be adequately assessed earlier.

Last but not least, at the planning stage the compiler takes some rudimentary decisions regarding the dictionary structures which were presented in the previous section. Most of all, they need to form an idea of the dictionary macrostructure, i.e. to determine the order of the entry list. Besides, they need to decide what kind of information categories will be placed within an entry and how the entry content will be arranged. Finally, at the planning stage the compiler takes some primary decisions regarding the access structure. The abovementioned aspects of dictionary planning will be given more detailed attention in the following three subsections.

3.4.3. Macrostructure decisions

When designing the dictionary macrostructure, the compiler should firstly consider what kind of lexical items should be treated as headwords. The choice of headwords depends on the needs of dictionary users, the size and type of the dictionary, the available budget and time, etc. (cf. Atkins and Rundell 2008: 179). Some problematic headword candidates may include, among others, affixes, plural nouns, compounds, proper names, abbreviations, participial adjectives, derived forms, or fixed phrases (Landau 2001: 358–359, Atkins and Rundell 2008: 119, 180–181). What is more, one should consider whether all the items which will be treated as headwords should be presented in the headword list. Alternatively, some of them, such as proper names or abbreviations, may be placed in the back matter (cf. Steyn 2004: 281, Atkins and Rundell 2008: 179, see subsection 3.4.5).

Another important macrostructural decision concerns the approach to homographs and polysemous words. Homographs are words which are spelled identically but which differ in other crucial respects, such as meaning, etymology or pronunciation. An example pair of homographs is the noun *lead*, referring to the chemical element, and the verb *to lead*, meaning *to guide*. In most dictionaries, such lexical items are treated as separate headwords. Contrastingly, as for polysemous words, they share the form and grammatical functions and differ only in meaning, as in the case with the adjective *funny*, which means both *amusing* and *strange*. Polysemous words are most often treated as various senses of one headword. This is, however, merely a trend and sometimes the headword status is accorded to both homographs and polysemous words, or, conversely, both of them are treated as various senses of the corresponding headwords (Landau 2001: 100–101, Atkins and Rundell 2008: 191–193, see subsection 3.4.4.).

Furthermore, the dictionary compiler needs to bear in mind that the list of headwords needs to be balanced. For the sake of example, in the case of alphabetically ordered wordlists, one should avoid having a disproportionate number of headwords starting with a given letter. There are some systems aimed at facilitating the task, such as the Thorndike's block system. Regrettably, though the systems are useful in the case of large and medium-sized general language dictionaries, they are said not to work well for specialised dictionaries or relatively small dictionaries (cf. Jackson 2002: 163, Landau 2001: 360–362).

Let us now turn to the most classic macrostructural decision, which concerns the arrangement of entries. Typically, dictionary entries are arranged alphabetically. The alphabetical ordering is highly appreciated, since it enables dictionary users to easily find the entry needed. Nevertheless, it is sometimes criticised, as it is associated with presenting lexical items in isolation instead of demonstrating how they are connected. (Jackson 2002: 144–145, cf. Aprile 2005: 158–159).

If some headwords consist of multi-word units, dictionary entries may be alphabetised letter by letter or word by word. In the case of letter by letter arrangement, two separate or hyphenated words which constitute one headword are treated as if they were one word, i.e. the space or hyphen between them is not taken into account. The arrangement under discussion is more popular, as it does not require the dictionary user to know whether the given lexical item is written as a single word, as two separate words, or as a hyphenated word. Thus, the headwords *home, homebody* and *home cinema* will be most often ordered in the presented way rather than *home, home cinema* and *homebody* (Landau 2001: 107). Contrastingly, in the case of word by word alphabetisation, the correct order would be *home, home cinema* and *homebody*. Thus, the space between words would be taken into account and would take precedence over the subsequent letter of the following word. As for hyphenated words, they would most probably place after the items written as two words and before those written as one word (e.g. *star, star turn, star-struck, starfish*) (Atkins and Rundell 2008: 191).

Some dictionaries with alphabetical macrostructures use a supplementary ordering system, which is referred to as horizontal ordering or sinuous lemma file. The overall arrangement of headwords is alphabetical, i.e. vertical, nevertheless some entries additionally contain lemmata which are arranged horizontally and which could be granted the headword status. There exist two types of horizontal ordering, i.e. niching and nesting (Gouws 2009). An example of niching is presented in *Figure 9*, taken from Gouws (2009: 6):

date[2], (n) datum, dagtekening; afspraak; jaartal; tydperk; *BEAR the* ~, gedateer wees; *BRING up to* ~, (boeke) bywerk; *BLIND* ~, onbeplande afspraak, lukraak afspraak, toe-oë-afspraak, molafspraak; ~ *of EXPIRY*, vervaldatum; *FIX the* ~, jaar en dag bepaal; ~ *of ISSUE*, datum van uitgifte; *KEEP up to* ~, byhou; ~ *of MATURITY*, vervaldag; *OUT of* ~, verouder; ouderwets, uit die mode; *UP to* ~, nuwerwets, byderwets, modern; by (tot op) datum; op hoogte van die tyd; in die mode; (v) dateer, dagteken; reken; die datum vasstel; afspraak maak (met 'n meisie); ~ *from*, dagteken van; reken van; met ingang van; ~**d**, gedateer, verouderd; *be* ~*d*, genooi word (deur 'n man), geskiet word *(stud.)*; ~**less**, ongedateer, sonder datum; ~ **line**, datumgrens; datering;… ~ **loaf**, dadelbrood; ~ **mark**, jaarmerk, datummerk; datumstempel; ~ **oil**, dadelolie; ~ **palm**, dadelpalm; ~ **plum**, dadelpruim; ~ **press**, stempelmasjien, datummasjien; ~**r**, stempelmasjien; ~ **stamp**, datumstempel; ~ **stone**, dadelpit; ~ **wine**, dadelwyn.

Figure 9. An example entry from Groot woordeboek/Major dictionary (Eksteen et al. 1997, cf. Gouws 2009: 6).

Niching is often employed to present derivations and compounds related to a given headword. The lexical items involved usually share the first stem as well as semantic relations, though it is not an unbreakable rule. Lemmata within a niche are typically ordered alphabetically. Besides, the first lemma niched follows alphabetically the immediately preceding lemma of the primary, vertical order. Similarly, the last lemma in a niche is followed by the subsequent lemma arranged vertically in accordance with the alphabetical order (Gouws 2009: 5–6).

As for the second type of horizontal ordering, i.e. nesting, it is divided into first level nesting and second level nesting. The former differs from niching in that it adheres to the alphabetical order only internally. Thus, the lemmata ordered vertically which immediately precede and follow the nest will not be ordered alphabetically with the first and the last lemma in the nest respectively (Gouws 2009: 7–8). As for the secondary nesting, it does not follow the alphabetical order neither internally nor externally. The breach of the alphabetical order may be motivated, for instance, morpho-semantically, i.e. derivations may be presented before compounds or vice versa.

The horizontal ordering never acts as an independent entry ordering system. It is always applied as an addition to the alphabetical, i.e. vertical ordering, and should be perceived as a kind of 'deviation from the default' (Gouws 2009: 5). Accordingly, the application of niching or nesting should be motivated by 'its contribution within the domain of the envisaged functions of the given dictionary' (Gouws 2009: 5). In practice, however, the horizontal ordering is often applied due to the need to save space. A decisive factor is that lemmata ordered horizontally are usually accompanied by less information than lemmata ordered vertically (Gouws 2009: 5, 9, 10). It should be pointed out that niched and nested entries are in a way dependent upon the 'primary' entry, whose place in the dictionary is determined based on the vertical order. In fact, they are perceived by some researchers as ordinary entry components and not as separate entries ordered in a different way (Gouws 2009: 8–9, cf. Gouws 2003: 39–43).

Last but not least, the alphabetical ordering of entries is not the only possible solution. For the sake of example, numerous dictionaries are arranged thematically, i.e. 'according to classes of topics' (Hartmann and James 1998: 142). The thematic macrostructure enables the presentation of concepts in their natural contexts and gives a better insight into the structure of a given set of vocabulary, especially in the case of some LSP dictionaries or learner's dictionaries. Nevertheless, it is frequently accompanied by alphabetical indexes, since numerous dictionary users prefer searching for information with the aid of alphabetical lists. Besides, the alphabetical ordering is also often applied within particular thematic sections of the dictionaries under discussion (Bowker 2003: 157–158, Jackson 2002: 150–151, 155, cf. Stark 2011: 95). Finally, apart from the alphabetical or thematic ordering, dictionary macrostructure can be also arranged, for instance, chronologically or by frequency (Hartmann and James 1998: 91, cf. Gajda 1990: 121, Żmigrodzki 2003: 53–54).

3.4.4. Microstructure decisions

The entries, which are also referred to as articles or records, constitute basic devices for presenting information in a dictionary (Hartmann and James 1998: 50, 67, 117 cf. Gouws 2003). Their contents depend on the type of headword, which is most commonly a lexical word, but may also be, for instance, a grammatical word, a proper name or an abbreviation (Atkins and Rundell 2008: 193–199). Besides, the entry content and structure depend on the needs and skills of potential dictionary users (Atkins and Rundell 2008: 200). Accordingly, the entries in learner's dictionaries differ from the entries in terminological dictionaries or general purpose dictionaries for native-speakers.

Dictionary entries typically consist of headwords (lemmata), semantic comments and/or formal comments. The headwords allow dictionary users to find a given entry in the wordlist. The sematic comments encompass definitions, translations, or information on word usage or etymology. As for formal comments, they consist, for instance, of information on pronunciation, spelling, or grammar (Hartmann and James 1998: 50, 67, Atkins and Rundell 2008: 162, cf. Gouws 2003: 35). In the case of polysemous words, some entry components convey information on the headword, whereas others relate to its particular senses. The former class includes, for instance, information on pronunciation, frequency markers or inflected forms, whereas the latter encompasses translations, definitions, illustrations, style labels or collocations. (Atkins and Rundell 2008: 205–235). Last but not least, it should be mentioned that dictionary entries also contain navigational elements, such as homograph numbers or sections markers, which are intended to 'structure the entry and help users find their way around all the information it contains' (Atkins and Rundell 2008: 203–204).

When designing the microstructure, the dictionary compiler needs to consider what components will be included in the entries. Secondly, they need to decide how to how to arrange the components to make the entry user-friendly. The user-friendliness crucially depends on the consistency of approach to the entry content. Various entry components should be presented in an order which is not only logical, but also fixed. Besides, the lexicographer should apply consistent domain and style labels as well as consistent symbols and abbreviations used for presenting grammatical information or making cross-references. Furthermore, in the case of bilingual or multilingual dictionaries, the compiler should handle consistently the translations. Thus, at the dictionary planning stage they should consider how to deal with lexical items which have no target language equivalent and whether to translate, for instance, collocations or usage examples. Finally, the dictionary compiler should also decide what font will be used for each type of entry component. For instance, the bold font may be applied to grammatical information whereas capital letters may be used for making cross-references. It should be mentioned, however, that though consistency in lexicography is in most cases highly appreciated, sometimes the compiler should be flexible and break some rules provided that it contributes to creating a good dictionary entry instead of an odd one (Atkins and Rundell 2008: 118–120, 247–250, Żmigrodzki 2003: 68–70, cf. Karpiński 2008: 223–239, Żmigrodzki 2008: 38–44).

Furthermore, planning the microstructure, the dictionary compiler usually needs to decide how to handle polysemous headwords. If they are devoted single entries the entries under discussion can be internally divided based on meaning, i.e. particular word senses, or based on grammar, i.e. word classes. In the first case, all the lexical items which have similar meaning are grouped together regardless of their grammatical properties. Such division is surely 'modern and innovative', nevertheless it may pose problems to dictionary users who do not know the meaning of the lexical items they search for (Atkins and Rundell 2008: 249, cf. 3.3.3.). In addition, the meaning-based division may sometimes force the lexicographer to take subjective decisions. Contrastingly, the division based on word classes seems more objective and is chosen more often, thus it is familiar to the majority of dictionary users. Nonetheless, its application may result in placing items of similar meaning at a large distance from each other, since one meaning is often realised by more than one word class (Atkins and Rundell 2008: 248–250).

Having chosen the meaning-based or grammar-based order, the dictionary compiler still needs a more detailed internal division of entries with polysemous headwords. There are three main alternatives to consider. Firstly, various headword senses may be ordered based on the sequence in which they came into the language. The method is easy and objective provided that the compiler has sufficient knowledge of the process of historical development of language. Secondly, the headword senses may be arranged according to their frequencies of occurrence in the corpus which is used in the dictionary compilation process. Unfortunately, it is not always easy to determine the frequencies in question in an objective and precise way. Nonetheless, the advantage of the above-mentioned order is that the senses which occur frequently are particularly likely to be searched for by dictionary users, especially in the case of learner's dictionaries. Thirdly, the arrangement under discussion may be based on core meaning, i.e. the most intuitive meaning of a given headword. The core meaning is presented in the entry as the first. As for marginal meanings, they are placed at the end of the entry. The order under discussion, based on intuition and arguably the least scientific, is nonetheless widely applied, as it is the most straightforward and as it is believed to arrange the senses of polysemous headwords in quite a user-friendly way (Atkins and Rundell 2008: 250–251, cf. Żmigrodzki 2003 71–80).

Last but not least, when designing the microstructure, the dictionary compiler should consider whether the entries will contain some examples of usage. If this is the case, the examples should be natural and thought-provoking. What is more, they should demonstrate contexts which are typical of a given headword (Fox 1987). The compiler should decide in which cases the examples will be provided and whether they will consist of sentence fragments, complete sentences, or both. Besides, they should determine whether the examples will be composed of authentic or modified corpus fragments, or whether they will be created using the corpus as a guideline. If the examples are to contain modified corpus fragments, the lexicographer should precise the nature of the modifications introduced (Atkins and Rundell 2008: 119, Laufer 2008: 214, cf. Rudnicka 2010: 113–114).

In the case of learner's dictionaries, usage examples taken from the corpus are sometimes perceived as superior to examples created by lexicographers. The former fully show all the features of authentic texts, such as typical contexts and grammatical or collocational patterns. Accordingly, they help learners create natural sentences in a given language. As for the latter, they often differ from sentences in authentic texts, as they are created in order to be presented in isolation. Thus, they tend to contain more information than real language sentences, which makes them in a way unnatural (Fox 1987). Nevertheless, an opposite view can be taken in the light of the research by Laufer (2008), whose results suggest that made-up examples are more helpful to language learners than authentic examples. The researcher observes that examples created by lexicographers facilitate comprehension and use of new vocabulary more than authentic examples. Besides, their usefulness seems to be less affected by overall lexical knowledge of a given learner (cf. Landau 2001: 305–308, Rudnicka 2010: 116).

3.4.5. Access structure decisions

So far, we have been focussed on the dictionary macrostructure and microstructure. Now it is time to devote attention to the access structure. As Gouws (2009: 12) rightly states, 'in the planning and compilation of any dictionary it has to be a priority to ensure successful access to data by the intended target users'. Ensuring the successful access to information can be perceived as one of the basic functions of every dictionary. Nevertheless, dictionary users want not only the successful access, but also less time-consuming searches for what they need. In the case of dictionaries for professionals, the time needed to find what is required contributes to commercial success of a given dictionary. It should be noted, however, that quick access to information, unlike successful access, cannot be considered to be a basic function of every dictionary (Gouws 2009: 12).

When designing the access structure, the lexicographer should most of all take into account the predicted skills of potential dictionary users. There are cases in which some access devices, particularly those motivated linguistically, should be avoided. To give an example, numerous users of general purpose dictionaries may not understand the notion of semantic transparency, thus they may prefer a similar search path for *frogspawn* and *frogman*. Similarly, in some cases the access structure may prove less user-friendly if horizontal ordering is employed or if homographs or various word senses are ordered chronologically and not according to their frequency or core meaning (cf. Louw 1999: 112, Steyn 2004: 285, Gouws 2007: 64–65, Atkins and Rundell 2008: 250–251).

As was mentioned in the section 3.4., the access structure can be further divided into external and internal. Let us firstly turn to the external access structure. The first decision which closely relates to the structure under discussion is the choice of a macrostructure type, which has been devoted attention in subsection 3.4.3. The primary external access structure can be accompanied by some additional devices. For the sake of example, the lexicographer may decide to employ a thumb index, i.e. a series of notches indicating the pages which are devoted to a particular letter or a given subject field. They may also use running heads, i.e. they can place at the top of each page the first and the last headword which occurs on it. Finally, the dictionary compiler may decide to mark on each page the lemmata which have the greatest frequency of occurrence (Nielsen 1995: 221, Louw 1999: 110–111).

As was mentioned before, some dictionaries have more than one external access structure. The additional access structure may be placed in the back matter, in the front matter or even on the dictionary margins. It may be arranged, for instance, based on word usage, word frequency or semantic fields (Louw 1999: 110–111, Bowker 2003: 158, Steyn 2004: 281). Most typically, the structure under discussion takes the form of an index in the back matter. The index refers the user to a relevant page or entry in the main body of a given dictionary. Additionally, the front or back matter may also contain entries which are not included in the central list. The entries in question may be presented in sections devoted, for instance, to grammatical information, abbreviations, or geographical names (Steyn 2004: 281). Nevertheless, as Haas (1978: 107) states, 'a good dictionary is one in which you can find the information you are looking for – preferably in the very first place you look'. Accordingly, it is better to refrain from creating too many sections with entries independent of the central list, as it is the central list that is usually consulted as the first.

Let us now turn to the internal access structure, which relates to the ordering of information within dictionary entries (cf. section 3.4.). Firstly, it should be noted that various information categories within an entry should be clearly separated (Gouws 1996: 22). The devices which serve this purpose, called structural markers, 'indicate the borders between information categories as well as the position and scope of different search areas' (Gouws 1996: 23). Structural markers can be divided into typographic and non-typographic. The former group includes, for example, different font types and sizes, italics, capital letters, seriffed and sanseriffed typefaces, etc. Contrastingly, the latter encompass, for instance, frames, coloured blocks, asterisks, or diamonds (cf. Louw 1999: 115–116). The use of structural markers is common among lexicographers. They are employed not only to save space and to separate different types of information, but also for emphasis purposes. Their variety helps avoid ambiguity and allows for showing simultaneously two statutes of one word. For the sake of example, a given word in an entry may constitute a typical collocation of the headword, hence it may be displayed in italics. At the same time, however, the word may also constitute a cross-reference, accordingly it may be presented in capital letters (Louw 1999, Luna 2004: 852–853). Despite the numerous advantages of the devices under discussion, it should be pointed out the arrangement of data based on font variation is less user-friendly than spatial arrangement of information within entries (Luna 2004: 852–853). Dictionary users frequently find it difficult to interpret information conveyed by means of various fonts, particularly if the reliance on font variation is strong (cf. Hartmann and James 1998: 3, Atkins and Rundell 2008: 33–34, 246, Gouws 2009: 12). Accordingly, as Luna (2004: 852–853) postulates, the lexicographers should resist the temptation to create typographical oddities without valid reasons.

3.5. Corpus linguistics and language corpora

Last but not least, in order to complete planning the access structure, the lexicographer needs to address two more points. Firstly, they need to devote some attention to the dictionary layout, which exerts influence on successful access to data. In order to design a user-friendly layout, it is crucial to avoid placing too much information on a tiny space. Some white space and neatly ordered entries contribute to a more accessible look of the dictionary page (Atkins and Rundell 2008: 33–34). Secondly, the lexicographer needs to bear in mind that both the internal and external access structure ought to be described in the user's guide of the dictionary. The description should be detailed and illustrated with examples or sample entries (Louw 1999: 112, Steyn 2004: 278, 283, 285).

3.5.1. The notion of corpus linguistics

Though corpus linguistics has been present on linguistic arena for years, it is not altogether clear whether it should be treated as a methodology or a separate branch of linguistics. There are linguists who believe that corpus linguistics cannot be considered to be merely a research methodology, as its role is too important (e.g. Leech 1992: 106, Tognini-Bonelli 2001: 1). Consequently, they assume that corpus linguistics constitutes a separate discipline. Other linguists, however, express opposing views. For instance, McEnery, Xiao and

Tono (2006: 8) consider corpus linguistics to be 'a methodology with a wide range of applications'. They postulate that corpus linguistics should not be perceived as a branch of linguistics, as it is not limited to 'a particular aspect of language', such as, for instance, syntax or semantics (McEnery, Xiao and Tono 2006: 7, cf. Meyer 2002). Furthermore, McEnery and Wilson (2004: 2) state that corpus linguistics simultaneously is and is not a branch of linguistics. On the one hand, the researchers believe that corpus linguistics should be viewed as a methodology, as it does not require linguistic description or explanation, unlike, for instance, syntax or semantics. On the other hand, the researchers admit that in a sense corpus linguistics defines an area or a number of areas of linguistics, as it permits 'to differentiate between approaches taken to the study of language' (McEnery and Wilson 2004: 2). To give an example, one may refer to 'corpus based syntax' and 'non-corpus based syntax' or 'corpus based semantics' and 'non-corpus based semantics' (McEnery and Wilson 2004: 2).

To sum up the above considerations, apparently the notion of corpus linguistics breeds controversy among linguists and is not yet altogether clear. For the purpose of this work, it will be assumed that corpus linguistics is a methodology of research based on the analysis of data contained in language corpora. There are, however, two assumptions on corpus linguistics which are generally acknowledged. Firstly, corpus linguistics in its modern sense is strongly associated with the use of computers, which significantly contributed to its development (McEnery and Gabrielatos: 2006: 33–34). Secondly, corpus linguistics unarguably falls into the empirical domain, i.e. corpus based research concerns real language use as opposed to intuitive assumptions about language use (McEnery and Gabrielatos: 2006: 33–34). The involvement of real language data does not, however, exclude the use of intuition, which is sometimes crucial in the process of data interpretation (Leech 2004: 85).

3.5.2. The notion of language corpora

Language corpora can be defined as collections of 'texts or parts of texts upon which some general linguistic analysis can be conducted' (Meyer 2002: xi, cf. Cresti and Panunzi 2013: 52). Contemporarily, the notion of language corpora is usually associated with the collections of texts which are stored and processed with the aid of computers (O'Keeffe, McCarthy and Carter 2007). Nevertheless, the Latin word *corpus*, which signifies *body*, has also been used to refer to collections of linguistic examples gathered in paper form. As such collections were assembled for the purpose of linguistic analysis before the computer era, it may be assumed that language corpora were created in some form already before their invention (Francis 1992, Lindquist 2009: 3).

The first language corpus in the modern understanding of the term was most probably the Brown University Standard Corpus of Present-Day American English, which is usually referred to as the Brown corpus. It was created at the beginning of 1960s and was supposed to give 'a balanced and representative picture of printed, edited American English' (Lindquist 2009: 3, cf. Francis 1992). The corpus, totalling 1 million words, represented various genres, such as press reportages, academic texts, government documents, humour texts, biographies, or love stories (Lindquist 2009: 3–4) Its compilation was followed by the creation of many other corpora, which finally lead to the present popularity of corpus linguistics.

The first dictionary constructed with the aid of a language corpus was the *American Heritage Dictionary*, compiled in 1969. Nevertheless, it is the COBUILD dictionary, published in 1987 by Collins Publishers and the University of Birmingham, that can be referred to as the first truly corpus-based dictionary (Walter 2010: 428–429, cf. Rundell 2012: 21–22). Nowadays language corpora are undeniably an indispensable tool for lexicographers. As Čermák (2003: 20) points out, 'there is hardly any alternative to corpora as the primary and main resource for lexicographers now'. Most of all, lexicographers consult language corpora at the stage of word meaning and word frequency identification. Besides, the resources under discussion constitute a source of information on idioms, collocations, metaphors, verbs patterns, etc. They are also consulted in order to determine the commonness of different word senses or uses as well as their distribution across various registers. Last but not least, they allow to explore differences between seemingly synonymous words. The differences may concern, for instance, register, patterns, or typical collocations (cf. Biber et al 1998: 23–24).

In general, language corpora make the process of dictionary creation indisputably quicker, easier, and more effective. Nevertheless, lexicographic work carried out with their aid is often full of challenges. For the sake of example, the amount of corpus data is often excessive for some lexical items and insufficient for others. The results of corpus research are often affected by the presence of spelling and typographical errors as well as by poor quality of tools, such as pre-analysis tools, tools for data retrieval or tools for statistics. Besides, regardless of the tools employed, corpus data need to be interpreted by the lexicographer. The interpretation is frequently far from being an easy task, thus its results happen to be purely subjective or erroneous (Moon 1998, cf. Kuratczyk 2007: 206).

3.5.3. Types of language corpora

Language corpora are divided into numerous overlapping types and their divisions are based on multiple criteria. For the sake of example, various researchers distinguish between written and spoken language corpora, general and specialised corpora, unilingual and multilingual corpora, synchronic and diachronic corpora, sample and monitor corpora, or ready-made and DIY corpora etc (cf. Waliński 2005, Tognini-Bonelli 2001, Sinclair 1991, McEnery, Xiao and Tono 2006). This section will briefly describe some of the above-mentioned types of corpora. The description will provide additional information on the notion of language corpus itself. Besides, a review of the available corpus types permits to understand what kind of resource is the most adequate in the case of a specific project.

First and foremost, some language corpora are referred to as *general language corpora*. They are supposed to 'give a picture of the whole language' (Lindquist 2009: 18) and to be balanced with respect to different genres and language domains (McEnery, Xiao and Tono 2006: 9). Not surprisingly, they typically reach enormous sizes. A number of general corpora are available on the Internet and allow to restrict the queries to subcorpora of particular genres or registers (Lindquist 2009: 18). Some examples of general corpora include the British National Corpus (BNC), the Corpus of Contemporary American English (COCA) and the Polish National Corpus (PNC).

Let us now turn to *specialised corpora*, such as the Bononia Legal Corpus (BoLC) and the Michigan Corpus of Academic Spoken English (MICASE). The corpora of this kind are designed to reflect a non-standard variety of a given language, for instance the language of economy, law or politics, or the language employed by children or teenagers (Waliński 2005: 30). Specialised corpora are also referred to as *terminological corpora* (Laviosa 2002: 35), *special purpose corpora* and *LSP corpora* (Bowker and Pearson 2002: 11–12). The process of their compilation is particularly significant for the purpose of this work, which is why it will be discussed in a separate subsection.

As far as *sample corpora* are concerned, they are typically aimed at presenting 'the normal linguistic features of a language or variety in approximately the proportions found in general use' (Tognini-Bonelli 2010: 20). In order to meet the aim, the corpora under discussion contain fragments of various texts instead of their full versions (Sinclair 1991: 23–24. Waliński 2005: 30). The fragments usually come from texts of various types or genres and are selected in a way which is virtually random (Sinclair 1991). An example of the sample corpus is the Brown corpus, which has already been mentioned in the former subsection.

Another resource that we should mention are *monitor corpora*. They are supposed to reflect constant changes undergone by a given language, therefore they can be employed, for instance, to identify neologisms and changes in word usage. The uniqueness of monitor corpora consists in that they are regularly enriched with new texts. Their updates may take place annually, monthly, or even daily. Obviously, due to the regularly added data, monitor corpora constantly grow in size and the new materials need to be chosen in a way which allows to preserve the corpus balance. An example of the monitor corpus is the Bank of English corpus (BoE) (Dash 2005: 11, McEnery, Xiao and Tono 2006: 67, Cresti and Panunzi 2013: 55).

Furthermore, some researchers divide language corpora into *ready-made corpora* and *DIY corpora*. The former, such as the British National Corpus, are widely available and can be used by any individual. Contrastingly, the latter are prepared by individual researchers or groups of researchers for the purposes of particular research projects (McEnery, Xiao and Tono 2006: 71). The decision to make use of a ready-made corpus undeniably contributes to saving much time. Nevertheless, every corpus is designed for a specific purpose, thus it is suitable only for some types of research. Therefore, before deciding to use a ready-made corpus, each researcher ought to consider whether the corpus in question is truly adequate for their research needs (Xiao 2009: 383).

Last but not least, language corpora are divided into *unilingual corpora*, which contain texts in one language, and *multilingual corpora*, which consist of texts in two or more languages (Waliński 2005: 32). Unilingual corpora need not detain us further. As for multilingual corpora, they can be further divided into subtypes, which will be discussed in more detail in the following subsection.

3.5.4. Types of multilingual corpora

Fundamentally, multilingual corpora can be divided into *translation corpora* and *comparable corpora*. Translation corpora consist of texts which are in 'a translational relationship to each other' (Tognini-Bonelli 2001: 6). Their most significant advantage is that they offer great opportunities of observing crosslinguistic similarities and differences (Tognini-Bonelli 2001: 6). As for comparable corpora, they contain collections of 'original texts in two or more languages matched by criteria such as genre, time of publication, etc.' (Johansson 2007b: 9). Given the fact that comparable corpora are made up of original texts, they reflect ordinary language use better than corpora consisting of translated texts (Johansson 2007b: 9–10).

As far as translation corpora are concerned, they can be further divided into *parallel corpora* and *free translation corpora* (Tognini-Bonelli 2001). In the case of parallel corpora, source language texts and target language texts correspond virtually sentence by sentence and can be aligned with the aid of proper software (e.g. *Coral, Multiconcord*). As for free translation corpora, they can be said to float somewhere in between parallel corpora and comparable corpora. Their component texts are in a translation relationship, nevertheless, the translation is prevailingly not literal, thus the corpora cannot be subject to sentence-by-sentence alignment (Tognini-Bonelli 2001: 6–7, cf. Lee 2010: 119–120).

The presented subdivision of multilingual corpora has been chosen for the purposes of this work as it seems the most logical and complete. Nevertheless, it is not unanimously acknowledged. For the sake of example, Kűbler and Aston (2010: 510) and Kenning (2010: 487) use the term 'parallel corpus' to refer to what we call 'translation corpus'. Consequently, the researchers postulate the division of multilingual corpora into parallel and comparable corpora. Contrastingly, McEnery and Wilson (2004: 70–71) divide multilingual corpora into parallel corpora, corresponding to what we call translation corpora, and translation corpora, corresponding to what we call comparable corpora. Additionally, Johansson (2007a: 51) assumes that a parallel corpus is simply a multilingual corpus. The above-mentioned problems of nomenclature will not be, however, discussed in more detail in this work.

3.6. The creation of language corpora for lexicographic purposes

The previous section focussed on the notion of corpus linguistics and devoted attention to various types of language corpora. Now it is time to present advice on how to create language corpora. Given the nature of this work, it is assumed that the corpus is compiled by one individual for the purposes of a lexicographic project. The first of the following subsections will be devoted to the creation of DIY corpora. As for the subsections 3.6.2 and 3.6.3, they will concern the creation of multilingual corpora and specialised corpora respectively.

3.6.1. The creation of DIY language corpora

The process of corpus creation usually consists of three major stages, i.e. corpus design stage, text collection stage and corpus preparation stage (Kenning 2010: 489). In this subsection we will focus principally on the design stage. It deserves particular attention, as the quality of design exerts profound impact on corpus representativeness, which in turn constitutes a major criterion for assessing language corpora. (O'Keeffe, McCarthy and Carter 2007: 1–5, cf. McEnery and Wilson 2004: 77–80).

DIY corpora are created in the cases when neither of the corpora available publicly is adequate to a given task. They are created for specific purposes, thus, in the first place, the compiler needs to realise what they want to achieve with the aid of their corpus (Nelson 2010: 53). Provided that the corpus is created for the purposes of particular research, the compiler should start their work by specifying the research aims. Once they have their research aims in view, they should consider what kind of research questions will allow them to achieve the aims. For the sake of example, in the case of the corpus created for the purpose of this dissertation, the final research aim is the creation of a multilingual dictionary of LSP collocations. Thus, the general research question is 'what collocations are habitually employed in the domain of banking law?' It should be pointed out that all the further decisions regarding corpus design should be taken bearing in mind the research aims and the research questions (cf. McEnery, Xiao and Tono 2006: 71–76).

Having formulated the research questions, the compiler should decide what kind of corpus will allow them to answer the questions and to fulfil the research aims. Firstly, they should choose the most adequate corpus type (see subsections 3.5.3 and 3.5.4.). Secondly, they should determine the criteria for material selection. Understandably, if the corpus is compiled for lexicographic purposes, the criteria depend on the language variety that is supposed to be covered by the dictionary as well as on the needs and abilities of target dictionary users (Landau 2001: 323–324, McEnery and Wilson 2004: 77–78, O'Keffee, McCarthy and Carter 2007: 3).

The process of material selection is affected by some issues related to ethics and law (O'Keeffe, McCarthy and Carter 2007: 5). In particular, attention needs to be devoted to copyright issues. The corpus compiler may make use of a text only if they have obtained permission from the copyright holders. Failing to comply with this duty may trigger legal problems. Besides, it burdens the reputation of both the compiler and the institution they represent (Sinclair 1991: 15, cf. Landau 2001: 327–330, Cresti and Panunzi 2013: 69–71). Finally, it should be mentioned that if the texts included in the corpus undergo any modifications, the compiler is obliged to preserve all the original versions (cf. Sinclair 2003a: 169).

Besides, while selecting materials to be included in the corpus, the compiler should take steps to ensure corpus representativeness, which acts as an important factor in distinguishing language corpora from random text collections and which assures the validity of corpus research results (McEnery and Wilson 2004: 77–78, McEnery, Xiao and Tono 2006: 13, O'Keffee, McCarthy and Carter 2007: 3). It should be pointed out that the representativeness is a relative quality, which should be considered in the light of not only research questions, but also the availability of data. In other words, a corpus needs to be only 'as representative as possible of the language variety under consideration' (McEnery, Xiao and Tono 2006: 73).

In order to make a corpus representative, the compiler should ensure the balance of texts representing different genres and categories. In some cases they should also analyse regional distribution of the texts included. To give an example, if one compiles a corpus of the language of newspapers in the United States, they should bear in mind that the language may be different in various parts of the country. Finally, if a corpus covers a period of time, the texts included should be distributed throughout the period in a fairly even way (Landau 2001: 324–325, 331–333, McEnery and Wilson 2004: 77–78, Tognini-Bonelli 2001: 57, Čermák 2003: 21–22, McEnery, Xiao and Tono 2006: 13–19).

Moreover, the corpus compiler should carefully choose the most suitable sampling technique. Most of all, they ought to bear in mind that the corpus, unless it is exceptionally large, may be easily skewed by the inclusion of very long texts in their entirety. Besides, if the research concerns frequent linguistic features, it should be noted that they can be investigated with the aid of short text fragments, as they are distributed in texts in a relatively stable way. As for rare features, their exploration requires longer text chunks, since they show more variety in terms of distribution (Biber 1993a: 252, Landau 2001: 324–325, 331–333, McEnery and Wilson 2004: 77–78, Tognini-Bonelli 2001: 57, Čermák 2003: 21–22, McEnery, Xiao and Tono 2006: 19–21).

Furthermore, corpus representativeness is closely related to corpus size. The size is in turn affected by various other factors, such as the availability of data, copyright-related issues, and various practical aspects (such as the necessity of large-scale annotation) (McEnery, Xiao and Tono 2006: 71–73). When it comes to corpora created for lexicographic purposes, their size ultimately depends on the predicted dictionary size as well as on the available budget and human resources (cf. Landau 2001: 323–324). In general, lexicographic projects tend to require particularly large corpora featured by a diversity of texts, which ensure sufficient information even on low-frequency items (Hanks 1990: 36, Biber et al. 1998: 249). Besides, large language corpora are also considered to be the most suitable for investigating collocations (cf. Maniez 2001: 544–555).

Still, it should be highlighted that according to Bowker and Pearson (2002: 45–46) and Landau (2001: 323), bigger corpora are not always better than those smaller. In some cases a smaller but well-designed corpus satisfies the research needs better than a larger corpus designed for different purposes. In addition, Maniez (2001: 558) observes that a greater number of concordance lines does not necessarily trigger a proportional increase in the number of identified collocations. Still, Sinclair (2003b: 188–189) postulates that the small size of a corpus always limits research opportunities. Nevertheless, the researcher admits that some language corpora are inevitably small, for instance the corpora of dead languages or corpora devoted to works by a single author (cf. McEnery, Xiao and Tono 2006: 72–73, Grucza, S. 2008: 206).

Another important decision at the design stage concerns enriching the corpus with *annotation*. Annotation usually consists of notes on some linguistic features of words or phrases (Wilcock 2009: 1) and can be added to the corpus automatically or manually. The corpus compiler may also decide to combine both options (cf. Sinclair 2003b: 187). In practice, annotation may consist, for instance, in dividing the texts into words (tokens) or sentences. At a deeper level, it may refer, for example, to labelling (or tagging) words with the corresponding parts of speech or with some aspects of their meaning (Landau 2004: 337, Kuratczyk 2007: 201, Wilcock 2009: 19–20, Cresti and Panunzi 2013: 84–86). Besides, sentence parts may be labelled with their syntactic functions of subjects, objects, complements, etc. This type of annotation is often referred to as parsing. Last but not least, language corpora can also be enriched with extralinguistic annotation, which usually consists in indicating the authors, sources, genres, or media of texts included in a given corpus (Čermák 2003: 23–24).

Languae corpora are annotated with the aid of specially designed software, which is widely available on the Internet (e.g. *Annotate*). The use of annotation facilitates and quickens the retrieval of information from language corpora; therefore, it is highly popular among linguists (McEnery and Wilson 2004: 32). Nevertheless, its introduction to a corpus usually requires a massive amount of time-consuming work. To make matters worse, annotation conventions often undergo changes and become quickly outdated. Accordingly, before one decides to annotate their corpus, they should focus on their priorities and consider whether the additional work cannot be avoided, especially in the case of corpora which are constructed for the purpose of one particular piece of research. Additionally, if one opts to use an annotated corpus, they should bear in mind that annotation sometimes constitutes a kind of 'filter' which conceals some information from the user. Thus, in numerous cases it is reasonable to consult both annotated and unannotated version of the same corpus in order to ensure truly reliable research results (cf. Sincair 2003b: 183, 187 McEnery, Xiao and Tono 2006: 33). Finally, it should be mentioned that annotation can be added to a corpus not only at the stage of its preparation, but also at the stage of its analysis in order to respond to arising research needs (cf. Sinclair 2003b: 187–189).

More advice on the design and creation of language corpora is provided by Sinclair (1991), Edwards (1992), McEnery, Xiao and Tono (2006), O'Keeffe, McCarthy and Carter (2007), Adolphs and Knight (2010), Clancy (2010), Reppen (2010), Nelson (2010), and Kilgarriff and Kosem (2012).

3.6.2. The creation of multilingual corpora

As was mentioned before, the process of any corpus compilation can be divided into three main stages: corpus design stage, text collection stage and corpus preparation stage (Kenning 2010: 489). In this respect multilingual corpora are not an exception. The vast majority of advice on corpus creation which was presented in the previous subsection applies also in their case. Nevertheless, some issues are typical of the compilation of multilingual corpora, and it is them that will be devoted attention in this subsection.

Provided that a given multilingual corpus is created for the purposes of a particular research project, the compiler needs to start their work by determining the research aims and posing the research questions. The aims and questions under discussion constitute the governing factor in all the decisions taken at the corpus design stage. Inter alia, they deeply influence the choice of a given corpus type. As mentioned in the subsection 3.5.4., multilingual corpora are principally divided into translation corpora and comparable corpora. The most significant advantage of translation corpora is that they significantly facilitate the observation of crosslinguistic similarities and differences (Tognini-Bonelli 2001: 6–7). As for comparable corpora, they do not demonstrate the similarities and differences in question as easily and convincingly as translation corpora. Nevertheless, it can be argued that they allow for making more reliable observations, since they more often contain original texts and not their translations (Johansson 2007b: 9–10). Given the advantages and drawbacks of comparable and translation corpora, Peters, Picchi, and Biagini (2000: 74) postulate that the former are more suitable for proficient language users, whereas the latter should satisfy the needs of language learners. Contrastively, Maniez (2001) suggests a complementary use of both types of multilingual corpora.

Furthermore, the compiler a multilingual corpus should be particularly careful at the stage of text collection. In the case of translation corpora, the stage under discussion may bring some issues which are not common for other types of corpora. The first of the issues concerns the availability of translated texts, the second is related to the quality of translation, the third pertains to the lack of balance in translation flows between languages (Kenning 2010: 489–490). Translated texts are in general not as numerous as original texts. They are impacted by individual choices made by translators and contain translation errors (Johansson 2007b: 9–10). Besides, the number of translated texts is often different for one of the possible directions of translation, particularly in the case of languages which are less widely used (Kenning 2010: 490). Furthermore, as far as a comparable corpus is concerned, the collection of texts may also prove far from being straightforward. For the sake of example, some types of texts, particularly some scientific texts, may be difficult to find in languages other than English. Besides, if already found, the texts in question often contain large numbers of errors (cf. Kűbler and Aston 2010: 510).

Finally, it should be mentioned that the compilers of multilingual corpora may encounter additional problems also at the corpus preparation stage. For the sake of example, if one decides to tag texts in different languages, it frequently turns out that some annotation schemes are language specific. Additionally, in the case of parallel corpora, the compilers are frequently confronted with problems related to text alignment. Sentence by sentence translations are relatively rare and the source text order is not always respected in the translation. Accordingly, a part of the alignment work is usually performed manually despite the existence of alignment software, such as *Bilingual Sentence Aligner* (Kenning 2010: 490–491).

3.6.3. The creation of specialised corpora

Language corpora may be qualified as specialised based on various parameters. To give a few examples, some language corpora will be considered to be specialised due to the represented language variety, such as learner English. Others will be perceived as specialised because of their subject matter, e.g. economy or politics. Others again will be specialised on account of the text genre, such as, for instance, film review (cf. Flowerdew 2004: 21). The variety of parameters implies that specialised corpora are extremely varied and differ from each other in numerous respects. The differences are partially due to the fact that specialised corpora are most often created for the purposes of particular research projects (cf. Paltridge 2006: 157).

Before the creation of a specialised corpus, the compiler needs to carefully plan its content to make sure that the corpus will be suitable for their particular aims. Firstly, they should decide if the corpus will consist of oral, written, or both oral and written material. If the corpus contains written resources, one should consider including whole texts rather than their fragments given the fact that specialised texts may contain definitions in any of their parts. Nevertheless, as was mentioned before, the decision to include long texts in their entirety entails the risk of skewing the corpus (see subsection 3.6.1).

Moreover, in the case of specialised corpora, the compiler should pay particular attention to the quality of the included texts (Baker 2006: 28–29). Understandably, the texts under discussion should be written by experts in the domain in question. They should also be written in the first language of their authors (Goźdź-Roszkowski 2005: 182–183). Besides, it is recommended to choose texts which have been published, since they constitute a more reliable source of information (Pearson 1998: 59–60). The compiler should also take into account the date of text publication. To give an example, if the corpus is intended to represent the current state of knowledge in a given domain, it should consist of texts written recently (Goźdź-Roszkowski 2005: 183). Moreover, in the case of specialised parallel corpora, the compiler should take into consideration the degree of sentence-by-sentence correspondence between the original texts and their translations (Kűbler and Aston 2010: 508). Last but not least, while creating a specialised corpus, one should take steps to ensure a rich diversity of authors. If all the texts included are written by one or two individuals, the corpus will not be representative of a given language variety (Goźdź-Roszkowski 2005: 180–182).

Additionally, when selecting material, the compiler should decide which texts are likely to contain genuinely useful information. For instance, if a given corpus is created with the aim to explore terms in a given domain, the compiler should consider which texts will be a reliable source of the terms in question. It should be mentioned that in some cases older texts contain explanations of concepts which are unknown to corpus users, although they are perfectly obvious to contemporary experts in the domain in question (Goźdź-Roszkowski 2005: 183). Similarly, texts written for non-experts may prove to be a source of useful definitions and explanations. Nevertheless, if the texts under discussion are included in a given corpus, the compiler should consider dividing the content into 'authoritative' and 'explanatory'. They can also take steps to enable the extraction of the respective sub-corpora (Kűbler and Aston 2010: 508).

Furthermore, when one decides to create a specialised corpus, they should pay particular attention to the issue of corpus size. Some specialised corpora are extremely large. For instance, the PERC corpus of professional English amounts to 17 million words. In general, however, specialised corpora tend to be smaller than general language corpora. Lee (2010: 114) postulates that they may contain less material than general corpora and still be representative due to relative homogeneity of texts within specialised domains. Similarly, Bowker and Pearson (2002: 48) suggest that even a corpus of ten thousand words may be sufficient to investigate the language of some specialised domains. The researchers also postulate that bigger corpora are not always better than those smaller. Nevertheless, they admit that too small a corpus may not contain all the terms of a given domain and may not capture all the typical linguistic patterns. It may also lead to making invalid generalisations and may be justly criticised for the lack of representativeness (Bowker and Pearson 2002: 45–46).

Last but not least, it should be mentioned that in some cases it is possible to extract a representative corpus of specialised texts from a larger, general corpus (Walter 2010). Understandably, the researcher who decides to extract and use such a corpus should carefully analyse its content in terms of various criteria, such as corpus size, sampling techniques, balance, and quality of the included texts, etc. They cannot take for granted that the corpus is truly representative and suitable for the planned research. Nevertheless, it is always worthwhile to check whether a corpus which is totally adequate for one's needs is not waiting to be used on the Internet.

More information on the design and compilation of specialised corpora is provided by Bowker and Pearson (2002), Goźdź-Roszkowski (2005) or Koester (2010). Besides, Thompson (2010) devotes attention to the compilation of specialised audio-visual corpora, i.e. specialised spoken-language corpora enriched with recordings of the corresponding communicative events.

3.7. The analysis of language corpora

Corpus linguistics is usually associated with quantitative analysis of data, conducted with the aid of statistical tools. In a nutshell, quantitative corpus analysis consists in classification of linguistic features followed by their counting and construal of some statistical models which are used to present the observed trends. Thus, provided that the corpus is truly representative, quantitative analysis results in generalizable findings which can be further compared with observations based on other corpora. Unfortunately, the greatest dangers in this type of analysis are misinterpretations and overgeneralisations (McEnery and Wilson 2004: 76–77, McEnery and Gabrielatos: 2006: 35). To avoid making overgeneralisations, the researcher should establish reliable methods of analysing, classifying, and describing the data in the corpus (Asmussen 2006: 34–41).

Though corpus data are most often examined with the aid of quantitative analysis, language corpora also offer considerable opportunities of qualitative analysis (cf. McEnery and Gabrielatos: 2006: 35). It may consist in identifying and describing some specific aspects of usage or in finding examples of some linguistic phenomena (McEnery and Wilson 2004: 76). As the criterion of frequency is not considered significant in qualitative analysis, linguistic phenomena occurring rarely are as likely to be examined as those very common. In comparison with quantitative analysis, qualitative analysis offers greater precision of results. Hence, it carries definitely less danger of misinterpretations and allows for relatively quick identification of ambiguities. Nevertheless, its results are not extendable to wider populations with the degree of certitude offered by quantitative analysis, since they are not tested in terms of statistical significance and may be affected by coincidence (McEnery and Wilson 2004: 76–77).

3.7.1. Software for corpus analysis

Nowadays the analysis of language corpora is usually performed with the aid of software developed for this purpose (cf. Kilgarriff and Kosem 2012: 33–35). Some software is created to be used with monolingual corpora, whereas other is aimed to facilitate the analysis of translation corpora. As for comparable corpora, their users can employ software designed for the analysis of monolingual corpora and run it for each collection of texts separately (Kenning 2010: 491). Nevertheless, they have to choose a piece of software that is able to handle various languages, such as, for instance, *Wordsmith tools*, which is additionally enriched with functions facilitating the identification of equivalents (Kenning 2010: 491).

The most basic processes which are typical of corpus analysis software include *lemmatisation* and *tokenisation*. The former consists in identification of basic word forms, such as infinitive forms of verbs and singulars of nouns. As for the latter, it allows for identification of items which are likely to be sought by corpus users, such as single words, which need to be separated from punctuation marks (cf. Landau 2001: 299, 336, Kilgarriff and Kosem 2012: 32). Besides, the software under discussion typically offers other opportunities of annotating the corpus (cf. section 3.7.1.).

Furthermore, one of the most rudimentary operations performed by software for corpus analysis is *concordancing*, i.e. research and display of all the occurrences of a given lexical item or grammatical form. The item or form in question is frequently referred to as *node*. Each of its occurrences is usually displayed in the middle of a concordance line, between the words which constitute its immediate context. This format of display is termed as Key Word in Context (or KWIC) (Meyer 2002: 16–17, O'Keeffe, McCarthy and Carter 2007: 8, McEnery and Hardie 2012: 245, Cresti and Panunzi 2013: 119). *Figure 10* demonstrates several KWIC concordance lines from Bononia Legal Corpus:

```
[ 969 ] Supreme Court ] or any <court> consisting of three or more j
ains the age of 18 , the youth <court> may , at any time after convi
to any proceedings in a county <court> ( " the principal proceedings
y of that other offence if the <court> is satisfied as mentioned in
ed by a court ( " the original <court> " ) under section 1 above , t
issue in proceedings , and the <court> orders the release , then the
o this section and to rules of <court> , be admissible as evidence o
 As it is I consider that this <court> is in as good a position as t
ork are taking Mrs Fradkina to <court> seeking possession of the pro
```

Figure 10. Extract from a KWIC concordance from Bononia Legal Corpus.

In addition, corpus analysis software may have a myriad of other features which significantly facilitate linguistic analysis and are crucial to dictionary compilers. For instance, some pieces of software, such as *Sketch Engine*, offer the opportunity of summarising data, which allows to quickly identify truly significant collocations (Rundell 2012: 21–22, Kilgarriff and Kosem 2012: 32). Others allow for word sense disambiguation, which facilitates the grouping of homographs and polysemous words (McEnery, Xiao and Tono 2006: 81). Others again offer the opportunity to limit the number of hits which are displayed for one search. The selection of hits is randomised to ensure that they do not come from one source only. Nevertheless, in the case of rarely occurring items, the hits may come from a limited number of sources despite the randomisation technique. Thus, the lexicographer using the technique should pay careful attention to bibliographical data, especially in the case of items with low frequencies of occurrence (Landau 2001: 296). Finally, modern software for corpus analysis often allows for application of statistical tests, which will be devoted attention in the following subsection.

3.7.2. Statistical analysis of language corpora

Language corpora are often examined with the aid of the so-called descriptive statistics, which aims to describe the data as opposed to investigating their significance. The tools of descriptive statistics which are most widely applied by corpus research pertain to word and chunk frequency (O'Keffee, McCarthy and Carter 2007: 12–14, cf. McEnery and Hardie 2012: 49).

Most of all, corpus analysis is frequently carried out with the aid of frequency counts, which have a wide range of applications in lexicography. First and foremost, they facilitate the task of choosing lexical items to be included in the dictionary. Besides, in some cases they help identify correct spellings. To give an example, they can be used to verify whether a given compound is usually written in the closed, open, or hyphenated form. Additionally, in the case of polysemous words, frequency counts are sometimes employed to determine the frequencies of particular word senses (Landau 2001: 302–303). Finally, Royle et al. (2009) postulate that the tools under discussion can help identify collocations of high frequency words, as they permit 'to sift quickly through a large amount of data and to pinpoint potentially important, relevant and interesting structures' (Royle et al.: 528). Nevertheless, the researchers point out that frequency counts do not distinguish collocations from other types of word combinations. Therefore, their output needs to be carefully analysed (cf. O'Keffee, McCarthy and Carter 2007: 12–14, Gajek 2006: 315–317).

Furthermore, corpus data can be explored with the aid of the so-called *key word analysis* and *cluster analysis*, which are also based on word and chunk frequency. The former consists in identification of words whose frequency in a given corpus, e.g. a specialised corpus, is unusually high or unusually low in comparison with a reference corpus, such as a general corpus (O'Keffee, McCarthy and Carter 2007: 12–14 Kohnen 2009: 74, Scott 2013, McEnery and Hardie 2012: 49). Contrastingly, the latter relates to identification of the most frequently occurring word combinations (O'Keffee, McCarthy and Carter 2007: 12–14). It is frequently employed in the course of research on lexical co-occurrence, such as research concerning collocations, colligations or collostructions (Gries 2009b: 14).

Apart from descriptive statistics, language corpora are also examined with the aid of inferential statistics, which enables the researcher to assess whether the observed trends are not due to coincidence. The tools of inferential statistics include, among others, the so-called *association measures*, which are often employed in the course of corpus-based collocational research (Bartsch 2004, Dash 2005: 205–208, Biber and Jones, 2009: 1300–1303).

One of the most commonly used association measures is the *Mutual Information* test (MI) (Lenci, Montemagni and Pirelli 2005: 198). In a nutshell, it compares the probability of co-occurrence of two items with the probabilities of observing them separately. The higher the result of MI, the more statistically significant the relationship between the items in question. Contrastingly, if the result is roughly equal to zero, there is probably no association between the items under study. Finally, negative results of the test suggest their complementary distribution (Church and Hanks 1990: 23). MI is highly useful for exploring collocations, idioms, phrasal verbs, and open compounds (Landau 2001: 309–311). Nevertheless, it should be mentioned that it tends to give high scores to word pairs which show little variation, such as low-frequency collocations or technical vocabulary collocations (Bartsch 2004, Gries 2010).

Besides, the results of MI test are affected by corpus size, which should be taken into account at the stage of assessing their significance (McEnery, Xiao and Tono 2006: 56).

Another well-known association measure is the *t-score* test. It differs from MI in that it does not measure 'the strength of association' between items, but rather 'the confidence with which we can claim that there is some association' (Clear 1993: 280–281). Accordingly, if the t-score result is very high for a given pair of words, the researcher can be confident that the words are associated, since they occur together too often to attribute their co-occurrence to pure chance (Clear 1993: 281). It should be mentioned, however, that the test under discussion often returns high results for the most frequent items, such as function words. Contrastingly, the results of MI test tend to be high for low frequency vocabulary (Bartsch 2004: 103, McEnery, Xiao and Tono 2006: 57). Besides, the results of t-score are not affected by corpus size, unlike the results of MI (McEnery, Xiao and Tono 2006: 56). As for common features of the two association measures, the results of both t-score and MI are often problematic with respect to rare collocations (Bartsch 2004: 104).

Let us now turn to the *z-score* test, which is another association measure frequently employed in collocational research. The test measures statistical significance of the difference between the actual frequency of occurrence of a given word combination and its expected frequency of occurrence should the distribution be affected only by chance (McEnery, Xiao and Tono 2006: 57, Seretan 2011: 39, cf. Oakes, Krakowian and Uzar 2005). The higher the z-score result, the greater the degree of collocability of the items. As for the procedure of computation, z-score seems to resemble t-score. Nevertheless, in terms of the nature of the output, the test under discussion has more in common with MI test (McEnery, Xiao and Tono 2006: 57), since it typically gives high scores to collocations of infrequent words (Dunning 1993: 62, cf. McEnery, Xiao and Tono 2006: 216–217).

Now it is time to devote attention to an association measure whose results seem to be less dependent on word frequency. It is referred to as *log-likelihood* score. The computation involves testing two hypotheses. In the first of the hypotheses, the co-occurrence of a given pair of items is due to pure chance. Contrastingly, the second hypowork assumes the existence of association between the two items (Metin and Karaoğlan 2010: 242). The results of the test under discussion demonstrate 'how much more likely one hypowork is than the other' (Metin and Karaoğlan 2010: 243). Some researchers (Dunning 1993: 65–66) state that the test does not give precedence to neither frequent nor infrequent lexical items. Accordingly, they recommend *log-likelihood* for research based on smaller corpora or research comparing statistical significance of collocations which consist of both rare and frequent items (Dunning 1993: 65–66). Nonetheless, other researchers assume that the test in question favours high frequency items (Baker 2010: 108).

All things considered, it should be highlighted that the presented association measures tend to return results which are influenced by word frequency. Accordingly, they give precedence to some types of collocations. The tendency is not particularly worrying provided that one's research is based on a really huge language corpus or is limited to either only rare or only very frequent items (cf. McEnery, Xiao and Tono 2006: 216). In other cases, the researcher needs to take into account the features of a given association measure while they analyse their data (Lindquist 2009: 78). Besides, it should be mentioned that the results of collocational research are believed to be more reliable if the researcher employs several association measures and compares the obtained results (Bartsch 2004).

Statistical analysis of language corpora is devoted more detailed analysis by Oakes (1998), Oakes, Krakowian and Uzar (2005) and Gries (2009a and 2010). As for general information on statistics and its applications in linguistics, it is provided, for instance, by Okulska (2006) and Johnson (2008). Last but not least, further examples of association measures can be found in Liebetrau (1983), Biber et al (1998) and McEnery, Xiao and Tono (2006).

3.8. Planning and creating a collocational dictionary

When creating a dictionary of collocations, one should firstly precise how they understand the term *collocation*, which is highly ambiguous. As Nuccorini (2003: 386) states, 'the linguistic definition and classification of 'collocations', together with terminological issues, constitute a major problem and they inevitably affect the criteria for the selection and treatment of both headwords and their collocates in collocational dictionaries'. The assumed definition of collocations and the overall dictionary policy with respect to the notion should be subsequently presented in some part of the dictionary, for instance in the front matter.

There are two major strategies for presenting collocations in a dictionary. First of all, each collocation may constitute a headword and may be devoted a separate entry. The technique is based on presupposition that collocations constitute lexical items and should be treated in the same way as lexemes. As for the second strategy, it consists in presenting collocations in entries headed by one of their lexical constituent parts. The strategy is based on assumption that collocations constitute 'realizations of syntagmatic potentials of their components' (Burkhanov 2003: 110, cf. Żmigrodzki 2003: 103).

In a typical dictionary of collocations, the majority of headwords are single words, and the microstructure contains information on their combinational properties, i.e. collocations. By contrast, dictionaries of idioms frequently feature entries headed by idioms, whereas the microstructure provides information on their meaning, use and syntactic properties. Nevertheless, it should be pointed out that sometimes dictionaries of collocations also include idioms and dictionaries of idioms happen to contain some collocations. What is more, some dictionaries explicitly define idioms as a kind of collocation (Nuccorini 2003: 368, 374, 385).

3.8.1. Looking inside a collocational dictionary

Collocational dictionaries are most often intended for encoding purposes of advanced language users (Nuccorini 2003: 367, 385). Compared with general language dictionaries, they offer more direct and systematised access to collocations and contain their larger numbers (Tutin 2005: 40–41, 47, cf. Osuchowska 2007). Despite numerous common features, various collocational dictionaries differ from each other in a number of respects. In this subsection we will explore the above-mentioned differences.

Firstly, various collocational dictionaries include different types of collocations. For the sake of example, apart from fixed collocations, they may also incorporate free combinations. Aside from lexical collocations, they may contain grammatical collocations, such as prepositions following verbs or adjectives (cf. Nuccorini 2003: 375, 378, Coffey 2011: 339). Moreover, collocations included in the dictionaries under discussion may differ in terms of their frequencies as well as in terms of the frequencies of particular collocates. The compiler of a collocational dictionary should bear in mind that high frequency of a word or collocation is not always the sign of its high value. It is possible for a rare collocation to be more valuable than a high-frequency one, though in general collocational dictionaries should contain both high-frequency and low frequency collocations (Douglas Kozłowska 2004: 14). Last but not least, the dictionaries in question also differ from each other in that they contain collocations of different parts of speech as well as collocations which consist of various numbers of components (Nuccorini 2003: 375, 378, cf. Coffey 2011: 339).

Secondly, collocational dictionaries differ from each other in that they give headword status to different kinds of items. For instance, the entries in the dictionaries by Douglas Kozłowska and Dzierżanowska (1993) and Jędrzejko (1998) are headed by nouns. As for the dictionaries by Osuchowska (2001) and Crowther et al. (2002), they comprise entries headed by nouns, verbs and adjectives. Besides, Douglas Kozłowska (2004) includes in the headword list of her dictionary adjectives, verbs, some phrasal verbs and adverbs. It should be pointed out that according to Burkhanov (2003: 110) numerous collocational dictionaries have excessively limited headword lists. The restrictions in the choice of headwords are often imposed by dictionary authors themselves and often additionally complicate the task of dictionary compilation (cf. Tutin 2005: 47). If, however, the headword list of a given dictionary needs to remain short of necessity, some lexical items, such as compounds, may be devoted subentries instead of separate entries (Nuccorini 2003: 379).

Furthermore, collocational dictionaries contain different types of optional information. They include various grammatical and syntactic data, concerning, for instance, verb patterns, grammatical cases, or gender. In the case of adverbs, they sometimes provide information on their pre-modifying or post-modifying position or predominant use in the active or passive voice or in the positive or negative form. Besides, the entries of a collocational dictionary may include frequency or register information. They may also contain cross-references to other entries or pages in which the given headword occurs as a collocate or appears in the examples of usage (e.g. Nuccorini 2003: 377–378, 383, Douglas Kozłowska 2004: 17, 21, 29, Przybylska 2007: 72, Tutin 2010: 1085, Coffey 2011: 329, 332, Lo Cascio 2012: ix, cf. Osuchowska 2002: 83). Last but not least, some collocational dictionaries provide definitions or translations of headwords and collocates. The inclusion of such information is, however, not common, probably for time and space reasons. Besides, the headwords and collocates are simply assumed to be known to dictionary users and their meaning can be easily guessed with the aid of usage examples. Nevertheless, an example of dictionary which does provide definitions of more difficult collocates is *Dizionario Combinatorio Compatto Italiano* (Lo Cascio 2012). Moreover, the dictionary entitled *Słownik polskich zwrotów werbo-nominalnych* contains rough definitions of the majority of entire collocations (Jędrzejko 1998: 70, see *Figure 10* in the following subsection). As for translations of collocations, they can be found in *English at Work. An English-Polish Dictionary of Selected Collocations* (EPDC) by Osuchowska (2001, see *Figure 11*).

At the end, let us turn to one particularly interesting common feature of various collocational dictionaries. They often share the tendency to present noun-verb, verb-noun and adjective-noun collocations in the entries headed by nouns and not by verbs or adjectives. The practice is based on the assumption that language users are most likely to think of nouns when phrasing their messages and in most cases consult noun-headed entries to find collocating verbs and adjectives (Nuccorini 2003: 372–376, 380, Coffey 2011: 334, cf. Douglas Kozłowska and Dzierżanowska 1993: 8, Douglas Kozłowska 2004: 15, Tutin 2010: 1080–1083). Nevertheless, it should be mentioned that according to Coffey (2011: 335), the assumption is dangerous if the dictionary is perceived 'as a more general learning aid' and not 'just as an instrument to help with on-going production tasks'. Additionally, the researcher mentions that if the verb-headed entries do contain noun collocations, they can be placed in a separate dictionary section, which would make them easily visible and maximise their learning potential (Coffey 2011: 339).

3.8.2. Planning the entry

While planning the entry of a collocational dictionary, the compiler should bear in mind that the more types of information it includes, the more difficult the task of preserving clarity and accessibility, especially if the dictionary is not intended for the electronic medium (cf. Coffey 2011: 340). Nevertheless, as Osuchowska (2001: 9, 2002: 82) points out, the additional information may make the dictionary more interesting and can prove genuinely useful to dictionary users. To provide an example, the entries of EPDC contain headword synonyms, which can be used by dictionary users in order to avoid repetition (Osuchowska 2001: 9, see *Figure 11*). Besides, the dictionary entitled *English Adverbial Collocations* (EAC) provides information on collocations which occur only in negative sentences. Accordingly, it warns the users against possible errors. (Douglas Kozłowska 2004: 17). To give an example, the entry for the verb *to think* indicates that the adverbs *properly* and *straight* modify the verb only in negative sentences (see *Figure 12*).

acknowledge *verb syn.* admit, recognize, accept, endorse, certify
uznać, potwierdzić, poświadczyć
~ obligation — uznać zobowiązania
~ preferences — uznać preferencje
~ receipt of a letter — potwierdzić odbiór listu
~ a signature — poświadczyć/uznać, zatwierdzić podpis

Figure 11. An example entry of *English at Work. An English-Polish Dictionary of Selected Collocations* (Osuchowska 2001: 13).

THINK (use one's brain)
Adv. aloud, clearly, constructively, fast, in a muddled way, logically, lucidly, properly (*with neg*), straight (*with neg*)
THINK (about a problem)
Adv. afresh, along the right/the same lines, carefully, coolly, deeply, disjointedly, dispassionately, dully, earnestly, feverishly, furiously, hard, idly, intensively, judiciously, long and hard, quickly, rapidly, seriously

Figure 12. Example entries of *English Adverbial Collocations* (Douglas-Kozłowska 2004: 150).

The inclusion of various types of information within the entry generates the need for its subdivisions. In a typical collocational dictionary, the basic division into sub-entries is based on parts of speech of the collocates. Besides, the subdivision may also acknowledge the position taken by the headword in a sentence. (Nuccorini 2003: 379, Przybylska 2007: 72, cf. Tutin 2010: 1084–1085). For the sake of example, the entry for *night* in *Oxford Collocations Dictionary for Students of English* (OCD) contains sub-entries VERB + NIGHT and NIGHT +VERB (see *Figure 13,* Crowther et al. 2002: 524). Finally, the basic entry division may be also based on other types of information, such as verb patterns or collocability with animate or inanimate nouns (Nuccorini 2003: 383).

night *noun*

1 when it is dark and most people sleep
• ADJ. **last, tomorrow | Friday, Saturday, etc. | early, late** *I think I'll have an early night* (= go to bed early). **| long | winter, etc. | bad, restless, sleepless | black, dark | clear, moonlit, starlit, starry | cold, stormy | wedding**
• VERB + NIGHT **have | spend** *They spent the night in Bristol.* **| stay** *Ask your Mum if you can stay the night.*
• NIGHT + VERB **fall** *When it came the night fell quickly.* **| progress, wear on** *As the night wore on it grew colder.*
• NIGHT + NOUN **air, sky | duty, shift**
• PREP. **at~** *lying awake at night* **by~** *Paris by night* **during/in the~** *I woke in the night.* **for a/the~, on Friday, etc. ~, per~** *The hotel costs £65 per person per night.* **through/throughout the~**
• PHRASES **all night long, at this time of night, day and night/night and day** (= all the time), **a good night's sleep, good night** *She kissed him good night.* **in the dead of night** (= in the middle of the night), **morning, noon and night** (= all the time)

2 time between late afternoon and when you go to bed
• ADJ. **last, tomorrow | Friday, Saturday, etc. | the other** *I saw her the other night* (= a few nights ago).
• NIGHT + NOUN **school**
• PREP. **at~** *She doesn't like to walk home late at night.* **by~, on Friday, etc.~**

3 evening when a special event happens
• ADJ. **first, opening | last** *the last night of the play's run* **| big, great, memorable | dance, election, quiz**
• PHRASES **make a night of it** *They decided to make a night of it and went on to a club.* **a night out** *Fancy a night out?*

Figure 13. An example entry of *Oxford Collocations Dictionary for Students of English* (Crowther et al 2002: 524).

Furthermore, various collocational dictionaries differ in the approach to collocations of more than two words, such as preposition-centred phrases (e.g. *a decline in numbers, absent without leave*) or coordinated expressions (e.g. *toss and turn, law and order).* If the collocations under discussion are included in a given dictionary, they may be placed in separate subentries reflecting their structures (Coffey 2011: 334). *Figure 14* demonstrates the entry for the noun *impatience* from *Macmillan Collocations Dictionary for Learners of English* (MCD), which contains a subentry devoted to the category *noun+of+noun* (Rundell 2010). Alternatively, the collocations of more than two words can be placed all in one subentry. This is the case in OCD, where subentries of the type under discussion are labelled *phrases* (see *Figure 13,* cf. Coffey 2011: 334).

impulse N
a sudden strong feeling that you must do something

- adj+N sudden **sudden** *On a sudden impulse, I rode after him.*
- ▸ first **first, initial** *My first impulse was to go out and buy a whole new set of clothes.*
- ▸ strong **irresistible, powerful, strong** *There came to him an irresistible impulse to pray.*
- ▸ natural **natural, primitive, spontaneous** *Our natural impulses can be altruistic and cooperative as well as selfish.*
- ▸ violent, destructive **aggressive, anarchic, destructive, murderous, sadistic, self-destructive, suicidal, violent** *His life is a constant struggle to control his destructive impulses.*
- ▸ generous **charitable, generous** *On a generous impulse he gave the man his coat.*
- ▸ creative **artistic, creative** *The exhibition is a celebration of the creative impulse, which we all possess but which is so often stifled.*
- ▸ not rational **contradictory, irrational** *She will always be a woman of contradictory impulses.*
- ▸ not expressed **repressed** *Hidden motives, repressed impulses, and secret passions are revealed in the course of the play..*
- v+N have an impulse **feel, have** *He felt an impulse to assist her.*
- ▸ fight an impulse **control, fight, repress, resist, restrain** *She resisted the impulse to give him a hug.*
- ▸ obey an impulse **follow, obey** *What I really want to do is just obey my own impulses.*

impatience N
the annoyed feeling you have when something does not happen as quickly as you would like

- adj+N **growing, mounting** *His growing impatience with Robert began to show.*
- v+N show impatience **display, express, reveal, show** *Maintain normal eye contact and do not show impatience.*
- ▸ control impatience **conceal, control, curb, restrain** *I could no longer control my impatience at the delay; I climbed the stairs and opened the door.*
- n+of+N **feeling, gesture, sign** *I detect a feeling of growing public impatience.*

Figure 14. Example entries of *Macmillan Collocations Dictionary for Learners of English* (Rundell 2010: 388, 393).

Figure 14 permits to make some interesting observations regarding the order of collocates within subentries. In numerous collocational dictionaries the subentries contain collocates presented in the alphabetical order. Unfortunately, such ordering does not convey any useful information to dictionary users. As for MCD, it presents collocates in semantic sets. The semantic sets are preceded by labels which suggest the meaning of a given group of collocates (Coffey 2011: 329, Przybylska 2007: 74, Tutin 2010: 1084–1085). For instance, in the case of V+N category for the headword *impatience*, the semantic labels are *to show impatience* and t*o control impatience* (see *Figure 14*). Coffey (2011: 331) points out that the entries in MCD never contain 'very many collocates in a set, and sometimes there is only one'. Such presentation of collocates may make the dictionary very accessible in comparison with other dictionaries with medium-length or long entries (Coffey 2011).

A similar innovative approach has been taken by the authors of *Selected English Collocations,* who decided to group some collocates according to contexts (Douglas Kozłowska and Dzierżanowska 1993: 10). Nevertheless, in the dictionary under discussion the particular groups of collocates are presented in separate entries. For the sake of example, the three entries for *source* (see *Figure 15*) segregate collocations depending on whether they concern something positive, something negative, or *source of information*. The solution seems perfectly suitable for small collocational dictionaries. Incidentally, an analogous system of collocate grouping is adopted in EAC, which has already been mentioned at the beginning of the subsection (see *Figure 12*).

SOURCE (of information)
V. be based on/derived from, (re)check, come from, give, have, quote, refer to, stem from, use ~
V. ~ confirm sth, dry up, tell sb
Adj. authoritative, dependable, (in)direct, excellent, external, first-class, fruitful, impartial, impeccable, independent, obscure, official, prejudiced, private, (un)reliable, unattested, unbiased, unnamed ~
SOURCE (of sth negative, e.g. worry, infection, trouble, etc)
V. constitute ~
Adj. big, common, constant, continual, frequent, inevitable, perennial, recent, unavoidable ~
SOURCE (of sth positive, e.g. happiness, satisfaction)
V. provide ~
Adj. deep, great, lasting, potent, tremendous, unfailing, unique, wonderful ~

Figure 15. Example entries from *Selected English Collocations* (Douglas Kozłowska and Dzierżanowska 1993: 207).

Besides, the order of collocates within entries or subentries may be based on other criteria. For instance, in the article devoted to Polish lexicography, Przybylska (2007: 72–73) recommends grouping noun and prepositional collocates according to grammatical cases. Furthermore, provided that the dictionary comprises idiomatic expressions, the researcher postulates presenting collocates in the order from the most transparent and frequent to the least. In addition, she mentions that idioms should be kept graphically isolated from other collocates. Incidentally, Przybylska (2007) also points out that in the case of noun-headed entries, the compiler needs to consider whether verb collocates will be presented in the infinitive form or in the inflected form. The inflected form is sometimes more natural, especially if the noun is in the subject position (cf. e.g. *fatigue sets in / to set in*).

Last but not least, when planning the entry of a collocational dictionary, the compiler should devote special attention to usage examples. As Nuccorini (2003: 381) states, 'long lists of collocates (…) with no examples could prove challenging to the average student user'. The examples may, however, prove useful even to professional translators, as they are often indispensable for demonstrating subtle differences of meaning between various word senses (cf. Vetulani 2000: 180–182). If the dictionary compiler decides to enrich the entries with usage examples, they may decide to highlight some of their parts. The highlighted parts may include: the entire collocations; only the collocates which are presented; or some additional collocates, such as prepositions (Coffey 2011: 331). Unfortunately, the inclusion of usage examples significantly increases the dictionary volume and makes the task of dictionary compilation even more complicated. Thus, numerous collocational dictionaries do not contain usage examples (e.g. *Dizionario delle collocazioni*, Tiberii 2012, see *Figure 16*).

occasione *nf opportunità*
AGGETTIVI clamorosa, concreta, cruciale, favorevole, formidabile, giusta, imperdibile, importante, irripetibile, mancata, preziosa, rara, straordinaria
• buona, grande, prossima *o.*
• *o.* ideale, propizia, sprecata, unica
VERBO+COMPLEMENTO afferrare, approfittare di, aspettare, attendere, cercare, cogliere, dare, fornire, lasciarsi sfuggire, offrire, perdere, sciupare, sfruttare, sprecare
SOGGETTO+VERBO arriva, capita, si presenta

Figure 16. An example entry from *Dizionario delle collocazioni* (Tiberii 2012: 386).

A dictionary whose entries do contain rich usage examples is *Słownik polskich zwrotów werbo-nominalnych* (SPZ, Jędrzejko 1998, see *Figure 17*). The majority of examples included in the dictionary consist of authentic corpus fragments, which are accompanied by information on their source. Besides, some example sentences, presented in square brackets, are created by the dictionary author. They seem less numerous, shorter, and more intuitive than the authentic examples.

WSKAZÓWKA

dawać wskazówki // dać // podać wskazówkę ⟨komu⟩ *oficj.* **udzielić // udzielać wskazówki** ⟨komu⟩ ⟨żeby ... // jak ...⟩ *'mówić, wskazywać, jak należy postąpić, jak robić coś; pouczać; radzić'*: Nie dał mi żadnej wskazówki, co zrobić na wypadek awarii. Dała mi na drogę wiele cennych wskazówek. *TP 16-96.* „Niedziela" pragnie ułatwić im sprawowanie tej liturgii, podając wskazówki, jak każdego dnia ją odmawiać. *N 48-96.* Poprawiał artykuły słownikowe, a właściwie nie poprawiał, tylko udzielał bezbłędnych wskazówek, jak należy je skorygować [...] *GK 181196.*

nieos; **coś jest wskazówką // stanowi wskazówkę** ⟨dla kogo⟩ *'wskazuje'*: Słowa te stanowią klucz i główną wskazówkę pracy ks. Wojtyły na wikariacie w Niegowici. *N 46-96.*

conv. **otrzymać // uzyskać wskazówkę** ⟨od kogo⟩ *'dowiedzieć się, jak postąpić'*; **trzymać się wskazówek** *'postępować zgodnie z tym, co ktoś radzi // wskazuje'*; *coll.* **korzystać // skorzystać ze wskazówki // wskazówek**; *pot.* **szukać wskazówek**: Wskazówki i bezpłatne mapy można uzyskać w punktach informacji turystycznej. *GK 130496.* Studenci ćwiczą [...] korzystając z oceny i wskazówek prowadzących zajęcia. *N 23-96.* Wówczas odruchowo szukamy pomocy, wskazówek, rad pozwalających wybrać skuteczne rozwiązania. *N 33-96.* [Trzymaj się moich wskazówek, a dobrze na tym wyjdziesz].

por. RADA, PORADA, NAUKA

[Pdic; f (x,y,z); Ag – pers; Adr – pers; Ob – prop]

Figure 17. An example entry from *Słownik polskich zwrotów werbo-nominalnych* (Jędrzejko 1998: 138).

3.8.3. Extracting collocations for lexicographic purposes

The extraction of collocations for lexicographic purposes may involve various procedures. If the dictionary compilation process is approached in a traditional way, the lexicographer may analyse their corpus lemma by lemma. In this case, they start their work with extracting from the corpus an appropriate number of phrases in which a given lemma appears. The task may be carried out with the aid of a concordance programme. In the next step, the dictionary compiler analyses the phrases, 'deciding in each individual case whether the lemma forms a collocation with one of the items in the context' and dividing the collocations into types (Wanner et al. 2005: 143). Understandably, the procedure under discussion is time-consuming and its results are affected by a number of factors, including general well-being of the lexicographer. Thus, more and more researchers devote attention to automatic extraction of collocations and automatic dictionary compilation (Wanner et al. 2005: 143).

The first way to quicken the extraction of collocations from the corpus is to make use of statistical models. The models enjoy high popularity, since they do not omit any significant collocations and are efficient regardless of the text type or the language involved. Besides, they do not require much linguistic preprocessing of language corpora. Nevertheless, despite their popularity, statistical models are not free from disadvantages. Most of all, they tend to return results which include free combinations, or which are devoid of any semantic information, given that they are based on the assumption that collocations are words which habitually co-occur (Čermák 2003: 24, Nerima, Seretan and Wehrli 2003: 132, Wanner et al. 2005: 165, Buczyński 2006: 434, see subsection 3.7.2.).

Let us now turn to more complex recommendations concerning automatic extraction of collocations. Firstly, Wanner et al. (2005: 143) propose an elaborate automated method of extracting collocations from language corpora. The method under discussion, based on the Lexical Function theory, is recommended for the compilers of dictionaries of LSP collocations. The procedure involves the application of machine learning techniques as wells as parsing or morpho-topological filtering. Accordingly, it seems more suitable for lexicographic projects which are larger than the one described in this dissertation.

Another method of extracting collocations for lexicographic purposes is proposed by Nerima, Seretan and Wehrli (2003). The researchers compile a dictionary in the form of a database. They make use of a corpus coming from the World Trade Organisation and including parallel texts in Spanish, French and English. Firstly, the corpus is parsed by means of a multilingual parsing system called *Fips* (cf. Wehrli 2007). Subsequently, collocations are identified with the aid of the Log-likelihood ratio and the sentences which contain collocations are aligned across languages. The results are displayed in the dictionary. The strategy under discussion is recommended for projects which involve the use of large, parsed language corpora.

Still another method of machine-assisted extraction of collocations is described by Vetulani, Vetulani and Obrębski (2008) and Vetulani (2012: 54–67). The method is employed in the process of creation of a dictionary of Polish verb-noun collocations for NLP applications. The first part of the dictionary was already published. It was compiled based on IPI PAN Corpus, totalling 200 million words (Przepiórkowski 2004). The lexicographers made use of a package of language processing tools called *UAM Text Tools,* which permitted to automatically extract contexts most likely to contain verb-noun collocations. Besides, the tools under discussion were used to add morphological tagging to the corpus. Apart from *UAM TextTools*, the researchers employed some software developed specifically for the purposes of the project under discussion (Vetulani 2012: 60–61).

Last but not least, while searching for a technique for extracting collocations for lexicographic purposes, one may find inspiration in works devoted to investigating collocations in general. For the sake of example, Noël (1992) presents a three-step corpus-based procedure for investigating collocations in bilingual texts. Biber (1993b) describes a corpus-based collocational analysis aimed at the identification of single word senses and uses. Baker (2006: 119–120) presents a step-by-step procedure for exploring collocations for the purposes of corpus-based discourse analysis. Bini, Pernas and Pernas (2007) provide detailed advice on how to effectively extract collocations from Newsgroups UseNet Corpora (NUNC). Royle et al. (2009) devote attention to corpus-based search for collocations in the process of creating a general language dictionary. Furthermore, some linguists explore the opportunities of collocational research offered by corpus analysis software. For example, Buczyński (2006) demonstrates how to conduct collocational research with the aid of *Kolokacje*. The free application permits to quickly download the content of websites and can be used to create a language corpus. Additionally, it offers the opportunity to detect two-word collocations with the aid of fourteen statistical tests.

3.9. The creation of LSP dictionaries

The compilers of LSP dictionaries frequently face the same problems as the compilers of general dictionaries. Nevertheless, there are some aspects of LSP dictionary compilation which are in a way distinctive (cf. Bowker 2003: 154). They will be devoted attention in the present section.

3.9.1. LSP dictionary size and content

The size and content of an LSP dictionary are assessed in a slightly different way than the size and content of a general language dictionary. The tendency is not surprising given that the former type of dictionary describes linguistic units of a language variety, whereas the latter is aimed at 'a comprehensive description of the whole language' (Hartmann and James 1998: 61). Besides, understandably, various LSP dictionaries differ between themselves in respect of their sizes and contents, which are affected by a number of factors.

To give an example, the size of an LSP dictionary depends on whether a given dictionary is devoted to one or more subject fields or sub-fields. A multi-field dictionary is typically large, whereas a dictionary devoted to a small sub-field can contain only several hundred terms (Gajda 1990:120). Moreover, the size of an

LSP dictionary is affected by its maximising or minimising aim. If a dictionary has a maximising aim, it attempts to cover the vocabulary of a given specialised domain as comprehensively as possible. In contrast, in the case of minimising aim, the dictionary is supposed to cover a part of the domain's vocabulary, for instance the most frequent terms. In general, LSP dictionaries devoted to narrow subfields or intended as translation resources usually have maximising aims. Contrastingly, dictionaries with a wider scope or dictionaries intended for pedagogical purposes tend to have minimising aims (Gajda 1990: 120, Bowker 2003: 156). Furthermore, the size of an LSP dictionary is affected by factors which also influence the size of a general purpose dictionary, such as the available budget, time and other resources, as well as the corpus size.

As for the contents of LSP dictionaries, it crucially depends on target dictionary users. They may be divided into experts, i.e. specialists in a given domain, semi-experts, that is students in the domain or specialists in related domains, and non-experts, such as technical writers or translators. The level of expertise of target dictionary users exerts impact on the amount of encyclopaedic knowledge and linguistic information provided in the dictionary. In general, dictionaries for experts contain less information than dictionaries for non-experts (Bowker 2003: 156–157). In addition, dictionary content is also affected by potential users' level of competence in the languages covered by the dictionary. The predicted level of competence influences the explication language as well as the linguistic and encyclopaedic information included (Tarp 1995c: 20–21). If the profile of potential dictionary users is not clear at the outset of a project, it can be ascertained it with the aid of a suitable user survey, which may be designed for either qualitative or quantitative analysis (Duva and Laursen 1995: 77–78).

Furthermore, LSP dictionary content is dependent upon the intended function of a given dictionary, which may be text production, text reception or text translation. Some LSP dictionaries are designed to be used in the process of native language text production. Others are aimed at native language text reception. Others again are created for the purposes of foreign language text production or reception. Still others are designed to be used for translation into the native language or into a foreign language (Tarp 1995c: 22–24, cf. Gajda 1990: 120). It is not altogether clear whether a good LSP dictionary should serve only one or more of the functions under discussion. On the one hand, Tarp (1995b: 50–52) recommends that a comprehensive LSP dictionary should fulfil a number of functions, though it is reasonable to assign them different priorities. On the other hand, Gajda (1990: 118) claims that the assignment of different functions to one dictionary should be perceived as a drawback, since it complicates both lexicographer's work and the process of dictionary consultation. The functions of a given dictionary deeply influence the decisions taken by its authors regarding the inclusion of various information categories. Tarp (1995c: 24) elaborates on various types of dictionary information which is useful in the case of each dictionary function (see *Figure 18).*

Native-language production:	a) orthography, gender, pronunciation, irregularity, collocations, usage information
	b) standard, field label or brief explanation
Native-language reception:	a) word class, gender, pronunciation, irregularity
	b) encyclopedic note
Foreign-language production:	a) orthography, gender, pronunciation, irregularity, collocations, usage information
	b) standard, field label or brief explanation
Foreign-language reception:	a) word class, gender, pronunciation, irregularity
	b) translation equivalent
	c) encyclopedic note
Translation into the foreign language:	a) on the native language: word class, gender, pronunciation, irregularity
	b) on the foreign language: orthography, gender, pronunciation, irregularity, collocations, usage information
	c) ranslation equivalent
	d) degree of equivalence
	e) standard, field label or brief explanation
Translation from the foreign language:	a) on the foreign language: word class, gender, pronunciation, collocations, irregularity
	b) on the native language: orthography, gender, pronunciation, irregularity, collocations, usage information
	c) translation equivalent
	d) degree of equivalence
	e) standard, field label or brief explanation

Figure 18. Basic functions of LSP dictionaries and the relevant information categories (Tarp 1995c: 24).

3.9.2. Compiling an LSP dictionary

The authors of LSP dictionaries typically take onomasiological approach, i.e. they begin their work by identifying a concept and its features and at a later stage arrive at the corresponding term. An alternative is the semasiological approach, which consists in beginning with forms, such as words or terms, and proceeding to arrive at their meanings (Bowker 2003: 155). In this subsection we describe a procedure of the LSP dictionary compilation which is grounded in the former of the two approaches. The procedure is mostly based on the proposals by Bowker (2003).

First and foremost, if the lexicographer who wants to create an LSP dictionary is not an expert in the given subject field, they should start their work with background reading on the subject. It permits to get to know the domain, to identify its boundaries and to make some rough subdivisions. The preliminary subdivisions within the domain provide an outline of its structure and permit to identify its relations with other domains of knowledge. Besides, they help to choose the most suitable working approach (Bowker 2003: 161).

Subsequently, the lexicographer needs to select the resources which will be used in the project and, if necessary, compile their language corpus (cf. section 3.6, Gajda 1990: 120). Having gathered the resources, they scan them for potential headwords. In the case of language corpora, they take advantage of corpus analysis tools, such as concordancers, word lists and extraction tools using statistical methods. The stage permits the lexicographer to broaden the knowledge gained at the stage of background reading (Bowker 2003: 161–162).

Afterwards, the lexicographer needs to analyse their data. The analysis requires them to understand well the subject field to be covered in the dictionary. Essentially, the work at this stage consists in compiling the headword list and analysing various contexts of each term (or a different item under consideration) in order to identify typical features of each concept. In the case of the most typical LSP dictionaries, the features under discussion are subsequently used to form definitions or to identify interlingual equivalents (Bowker 2003: 162).

The choice of headwords poses multiple problems. For the sake of example, in the case of terminological dictionaries, the lexicographer needs to separate terms of a given subject field from non-terms, professional jargon and terms of other subject fields (Gajda 1990: 120). In some cases, more than one term is used to refer to the same concept and it is controversial which* of the terms is better. In order to identify the preferable term, the lexicographer should take into account various criteria, which are summarised as follows by Landau (2001: 106):

1. Usage, as in textbooks, (…) dictionaries, and other reference works
2. Recommendations of authoritative specialist organizations
3. Self-descriptiveness, i.e. giving preference to terms that describe the nature of the concept, as opposed to eponymous terms (terms named after people, such *as Bright's disease*). However, some eponymous terms are so well established by usage that they should be retained.
4. Specificity, i.e., not vague or ambiguous
5. Specificity, i.e., as short as possible

6. Conceptual relationships, i.e., related concepts should ideally be related in terminology (…).
7. Linguistic relationships, i.e., ideally the translations of a term into other major languages should be similar in all languages, so that one can more easily recognize that the two terms are the same.

Having analysed their data, the lexicographer turns to preparing dictionary entries. The entries may contain various types of information depending on dictionary functions and target users (see subsections 3.4.4 and 3.8.1., Bowker 2003: 163). In the case of terminological dictionaries, the composition of entries should be particularly homogenous and the entries devoted to related terms should be regularly cross-referenced (Gajda 1990: 118–119). Besides, as for bilingual dictionaries for translation purposes, the lexicographer should attempt to select the best translation equivalent rather than provide several possible equivalents. A significant part of dictionary users may experience difficulties while choosing from a number of alternatives (Gajda 1990: 118–119, 123).

Furthermore, if an LSP dictionary is not intended for experts in the given subject field, it should be enriched with a systematic introduction. The dictionary component is usually placed in the front or in the back matter. It can be either cognitively oriented or communication oriented. In the former case, systematic introduction provides general information on the subject field covered by the dictionary. In the latter case, it can contain some linguistic information, for instance on collocations, or some example texts in the LSP in question. Systematic introduction should be written in the users' native language if the dictionary is supposed to help understand the given specialised domain. Contrastingly, if the dictionary purpose is to assist foreign language translation or production, systematic introduction should be written in the target language. In the case of bilingual dictionaries, it is recommended to include systematic introductions in both languages. As for multilingual dictionaries, they frequently do not contain systematic introductions due to space limitations (Fuertes-Olivera 2009: 162–164).

Last but not least, numerous LSP dictionaries are enriched with illustrations, charts, and tables, which are particularly common in technical and scientific dictionaries. Their usefulness is closely related to the level of expertise of dictionary users. A student user may perceive illustrations and charts to be a valuable aid, whereas an advanced user may find them simplistic and may prefer additional entries instead. In general, if a dictionary is designed for a broad market, the illustrations are a helpful addition. As for tables and charts, they are usually recommended (Landau 2001: 147, Karpiński 2008: 236–237). Nevertheless, in general they should not be perceived as a way to reduce the number of entries, but rather as a 'convenient reorganization' of some terms included in the dictionary (cf. Landau 2001: 147, Karpiński 2008: 236–237).

3.10. The creation of multilingual LSP dictionaries

3.10.1. Looking inside a multilingual LSP dictionary

In this work, a multilingual dictionary is understood as a dictionary which describes linguistic units of at least three languages. The role of multilingual dictionaries devoted to particular subject fields was appreciated already in 1970s, when modern lexicography was still in its infancy. To give an example, Zgusta (1971: 297) claims that 'the multilingual dictionaries of different technical terminologies have a high, if limited, usefulness within their own field: they usually have a strong encyclopedic component and help much to guarantee the precise use of terms in different languages'.

Contemporarily, multilingual LSP dictionaries are relatively common (cf. Łukasik 2007, Klejnowska-Borowska 2014). As for the Polish market, the majority of the dictionaries under discussion link the local language with the dominant language of a given domain, with a language of special international importance or with a language dominant in the part of the world concerned (Karpiński 2008: 175). Multilingual LSP dictionaries are divided into three main types. The first takes a leading language as a point of departure and proceeds in one direction to other languages. The second proceeds in either direction between its leading language and the remaining languages. As for the third type, it has no leading language and proceeds in either direction between all of its languages. This kind of dictionary is most suitable for culture-independent subject fields, whereas dictionaries of the first and second kind are suitable for all subject fields (Tarp 1995b: 54–55, cf. Karpiński 2008: 175–180, Boguslavsky, Cardeňosa and Gallardo 2008: 72).

Multilingual LSP dictionaries are most often arranged alphabetically, tough it is possible to find some arranged thematically (e.g. Wrzosek 1995, Pieńkoś 2004). In the case of thematic dictionaries, the alphabetical ordering is sometimes employed within chapters devoted to particular themes (e.g. Wrzosek 1995). Furthermore, multilingual LSP dictionaries are frequently provided with alphabetical indexes which enable multidirectional searchers. The index may indicate the number of a page on which a given item occurs. Alternatively, it may indicate the item translation into one of the dictionary languages (see, for instance, Pieńkoś 2004).

The entry of a multilingual LSP dictionary usually contains equivalents of a given lexical item in all the languages covered by the dictionary (see *Figure 19*). In some cases, as illustrated in *Figure 20*, the main body of a dictionary is divided into columns in which the equivalents are juxtaposed, which facilitates comparison (cf. Tarp 1995b: 55–56).

1388. Granat właściwy
s. granatowiec właściwy, granatowe drzewo, granatowy krzew r. granatowcowate, *Punicaceae* l. *Punica granatum* L. a. pomegranate, common pomegranate f. grenadier n. Granatapfelbaum

Figure 19. An example entry of *Wielojęzyczny słownik florystyczny* (Anioł-Kwiatkowska 2003: 69).

badać zgłoszenie patentowe (patrz PCT, art. 1(1))	prüfen eine Patentanmeldung -	examine (to) a patent application	examiner une demande de brevet

Figure 20. An example entry of *Wielojęzyczny słownik terminów z zakresu własnościprzemysłowej* (Broszkiewicz et al. 1991: 69).

As *Figure 19* and *Figure 20* demonstrate, multilingual dictionaries tend to contain scarce information which can be perceived as optional, such as grammar tips, pronunciation details or illustrations. In general, the more languages a dictionary is devoted to, the less information is presented for each equivalent. The tendency may be attributed to various reasons, such as space limitations, high level of linguistic competence of target dictionary users, or the unwillingness of lexicographers to additionally complicate the task of multilingual dictionary compilation (Bowker 2003: 159–160, Klejnowska-Borowska 2014, cf. Łukasik 2007).

Furthermore, some authors of multilingual LSP dictionaries seek more imaginative solutions when arranging their data. For the sake of example, in the dictionary by Dąbkowski (2004), the headwords coming from seven languages are put on one alphabetical list. In the case of Polish headwords, the entries contain equivalents in the remaining six languages. Contrastingly, if a given headword does not come from the Polish language, the entry indicates its source language and its Polish equivalent. Additionally, the lexemes which take the same form in all the languages covered by the dictionary are marked with the equal sign (e.g. =bolero=). *Figure 21* presents several entries of the dictionary under discussion:

frequence F częstotliwość drgań
frequency A częstotliwość drgań
Frequenz N częstotliwość drgań
frequenza W częstotliwość drgań
Frequenzanalyse N analiza
dźwięku
from memory A na pamięć
front A prospekt (organów)
Front N prospekt (organów)
= **frottola** =
F-Schlüssel N klucz f
F sharp A fis
F sharp major A Fis-dur
F sharp minor A fis-moll
fuga
W fuga
F fugue
A fugue
N Fuge
R фуга
C fuga
fuga a due parti W fuga
dwugłosowa

Figure 21. The arrangement of entries in the dictionary by G. Dąbkowski (2004: 95).

Besides, the dictionary by Broszkiewicz et al (1991), which presents vocabulary of industrial property in Polish, German, English and French, is divided into four parts, each arranged alphabetically. The entries of the first part consist of Polish headwords and their equivalents in the remaining three languages (see *Figure 20*). The second, third, and fourth part of the dictionary contain, respectively, German, English, and French headwords juxtaposed with their Polish equivalents. To sum up, it seems that the dictionary under discussion encompasses one unidirectional multilingual part and three unidirectional bilingual parts. Each of the four parts is printed on paper of another colour, which facilitates dictionary consultation. Incidentally, a similar arrangement of data was proposed by Okoń, Dembska and Niemierko (1990) in their multilingual dictionary of pedagogical terms.

Last but not least, let us turn to the quadrilingual dictionary by Chmielewska-Gorczyca (1999), which is devoted to civil law, and which follows a particularly interesting organisational scheme. It should be mentioned that the dictionary under discussion constitutes a part of a series of dictionaries which is referred to as STEBIS (System Tezaurusów Biblioteki Sejmowej). In general, the dictionary by Chmielewska-Gorczyca (1999) seems to be a combination of alphabetical dictionary and thematic dictionary. It is divided into five parts. The main part, ordered alphabetically, consists of a list of entries with the headwords in Polish. The entries include detailed information on items related to the headwords, for instance their synonyms, hyponyms or hyperonyms. Besides, they comprise headword equivalents in English, French and German. *Figure 22* below demonstrates an example entry coming from the main part of the dictionary under discussion.

adopcja
TT: 03.1 PRAWO RODZINNE
UF: adopcja dziecka
przysposobienie
przysposobienie dziecka
BT: prawo rodzinne
NT: adopcja zagraniczna
RT: dom dziecka
dzieci
dziecko adoptowane
Europejska Konwencja o Adopcji Dzieci 1967
Europejska Konwencja o Wykonywaniu Praw Dzieci 1996
nazwisko
ochrona dziecka
opiekuństwo
prawa dziecka
rodzice
rodzina zastępcza
sierota
stosunki w rodzinie
FT: adoption of a child * (*ang.*)
adoption d'enfant * (*fr.*)
Adoption * (*niem.*)

adopcja dziecka
USE: **adopcja (03.1)**

adopcja zagraniczna
TT: 03.1 PRAWO RODZINNE
UF: przysposobienie zagraniczne
BT: adopcja
RT: dziecko adoptowane
Europejska Konwencja o Uznawaniu i Wykonywaniu Orzeczeń dotyczących Pieczy nad Dzieckiem 1980
handel ludźmi
małżeństwo mieszane
międzynarodowe prawo prywatne
obywatel-cudzoziemiec
obywatelstwo
przyjmowanie cudzoziemców
FT: intercountry adoption (*ang.*)
Auslandsadoption (*niem.*)

Agreement on Trade-Related Aspects of Intellectual Property Rights
USE: **Porozumienie w sprawie Handlowych Aspektów Praw Własności Intelektualnej (03.2)**

Figure 22. A fragment of the alphabetical part of the dictionary by Chmielewska-Gorczyca (1999: 16).

As for the remaining four parts of the dictionary by Chmielewska-Gorczyca (1999), each of them is devoted to one of the four dictionary languages and is further divided into smaller parts. First of all, each of the four parts presents the vocabulary of civil law in a given language in hierarchical order, subsequently in thematic order. *Figures 23* and *24* below come from the dictionary part which is devoted to the Polish language. They present the hierarchical and thematic arrangement of entries within the Polish part:

03.1 PRAWO RODZINNE

adopcja
- adopcja zagraniczna

kodeks rodzinny

małżeństwo
- małżeństwo mieszane
- młode małżeństwo

nazwisko

obowiązek alimentacyjny

pokrewieństwo
- małżonkowie
- wstępni
-- rodzice
--- matka
--- ojciec
- zstępni
-- dzieci
--- dziecko adoptowane
--- dziecko jedyne
--- dziecko porzucone
--- dziecko pozamałżeńskie
--- sierota

powinowactwo

prawo małżeńskie
- umowa majątkowa

prawo opiekuńcze
- nieletność
- opiekuństwo
- pełnoletność

rozwód

separacja sądowa

stan małżeński
- osoba owdowiała
- osoba rozwiedziona
- osoba stanu wolnego
- osoba w separacji
- osoba zamężna

usamodzielnienie

władza rodzicielska
- odpowiedzialność rodziców
- pozbawienie praw rodzicielskich

wspólne pożycie

Figure 23. Dictionary by Chmielewska-Gorczyca (1999: 47). A fragment of the part devoted to the Polish language with the entries ordered hierarchically.

03.1 PRAWO RODZINNE

adopcja
adopcja zagraniczna
dzieci
dziecko adoptowane
dziecko jedyne
dziecko porzucone
dziecko pozamałżeńskie
kodeks rodzinny
małżeństwo
małżeństwo mieszane
małżonkowie
matka
młode małżeństwo
nazwisko
nieletność
obowiązek alimentacyjny
odpowiedzialność rodziców
ojciec
opiekuństwo
osoba owdowiała
osoba rozwiedziona
osoba stanu wolnego
osoba w separacji
osoba zamężna
pełnoletność
pokrewieństwo
powinowactwo
pozbawienie praw rodzicielskich
prawo małżeńskie
prawo opiekuńcze
rodzice
rozwód
separacja sądowa
sierota
stan małżeński
umowa majątkowa
usamodzielnienie
władza rodzicielska
wspólne pożycie
wstępni
zstępni

Figure 24. Dictionary by Chmielewska-Gorczyca (1999: 52). A fragment of the part devoted to the Polish language with the entries ordered thematically.

Figure 23 demonstrates that in the section arranged hierarchically, the order of entries which are placed on the same level is alphabetical, and the entries on the highest level of the hierarchy are printed in bold. As for the part that is arranged thematically, the entries assigned to one thematic section are put in the alphabetical order (see *Figure 24*).

Besides, within the dictionary parts devoted to particular languages, what follows the hierarchical and thematic part is a type of multilingual microdictionary. It is organised alphabetically and contains headwords and their equivalents in the remaining three languages. In each of the four dictionary parts the headwords of the microdictionary come from another language. *Figure 25* presents a fragment of the microdictionary comprised in the part devoted to the Polish language:

Polski	Angielski	Francuski	Niemiecki
adopcja	adoption of a child *	adoption d'enfant *	Adoption *
adopcja zagraniczna	intercountry adoption		Auslandsadoption
Akt Paryski Konwencji Berneńskiej o Ochronie Dzieł Literackich i Artystycznych 1971		Convention de Berne pour la protection des oeuvres littéraires et artistiques 1971	Berner Übereinkunft zum Schutze von Werken der Literatur und Kunst
akta stanu cywilnego	population register *	registre d'état civil *	Standesamtsregister *
darowizna	gift *	donation *	Schenkung *
dobra wiara	good faith	bonne foi	guter Glaube
dokument dotyczący własności intelektualnej	document on intellectual property	document sur la propriété intellectuelle	Dokument betr. das geistige Eigentum
dzieci	children	enfants	Kinder
dziecko adoptowane	adopted child *	enfant adopté *	adoptiertes Kind *
dziecko jedyne	only child *	enfant unique *	Einzelkind *
dziecko porzucone	abandoned child *	enfant abandonné *	ausgesetztes Kind *
dziecko pozamałżeńskie	natural child *	enfant naturel *	nichteheliches Kind *
dziedziczenie	inheritance *	héritage *	Erbschaft *
dzieło sztuki	work of art *	oeuvre d'art *	Kunstwerk *
dzierżawa	farm lease *	bail rural *	Landpachtvertrag *

Figure 25. Dictionary by Chmielewska-Gorczyca (1999: 56–57). A fragment of the microdictionary in the part devoted to the Polish language.

The dictionary by Chmielewska-Gorczyca (1999) constitutes an interesting example of how various macrostructural and microstructural solutions can be applied in one lexicographic resource. Moreover, it demonstrates that when it comes to the macrostructural and microstructural choices, the compilers of multilingual dictionaries can show their imagination and search for completely new ideas instead of sticking to standard solutions.

3.10.2. Looking for interlingual equivalents

In this dissertation, we assume the view that an interlingual equivalent is 'a word or phrase in one language which corresponds in meaning to a word or phrase in another language' (Hartmann and James 1998: 51). Typically, the initial stage of compilation of a multilingual LSP dictionary consists in working separately for each of the languages concerned. The equivalents are usually identified at a more advanced stage (Bowker 2003: 159–160). While searching for the equivalents, the dictionary compiler should most of all make use of language corpora. Alternatively, they may recur to introspection or consult the available reference books. Nevertheless, the latter resources should be approached in a critical way as they sometimes provide erroneous information (cf. Piotrowski 1993: 119–120).

The identification of equivalent terms across languages is not an easy task. Even with mere one language the lexicographer often needs to perform extensive work to identify the best term for a given concept, given the terminological differences between various researchers, technical writers, and scientists (Zgusta 1971: 297–298). Besides, broadly speaking, exact interlingual equivalence is not a common phenomenon. It is frequently impossible to match equivalent lexical items on one-to-one basis, as they are usually largely indeterminate, and it is their context that makes them more precise. Accordingly, the lexicographer is most often faced with a group of lexemes and a group of their equivalents. The problems related to equivalence are especially acute in the case of onomasiological (lexical) gaps, culture-specific lexical items, and non-designative items, such as prepositions (Zgusta 1971, Piotrowski 1993: 126, 146–147). All in all, the lexicographer should decide how to proceed with items which lack a single and full equivalent.

First and foremost, they may attempt to find an approximate equivalent. Nevertheless, it will differ to some extent from the headword in terms of meaning and uses. Ideally, the above-mentioned differences should be described as comprehensively as possible in every bilingual and multilingual dictionary. Unfortunately, their complete description is most often impossible for space and time reasons. Furthermore, the identification of one fully acceptable approximate equivalent is frequently a problem in itself. If this is the case, the lexicographer may find several partial equivalents which together convey the meaning of a given problematic item. Nevertheless, they should bear in mind that all the equivalents added to a dictionary entry should be generally applicable, as they become in a way fixed and decontextualised once they are placed in the dictionary (cf. Zgusta 1971: 306, Piotrowski 1993: 126, 146–147, Tarp 1995b: 62, Hall, Smith and Wicaksono 2011: 261).

Alternatively, the lexicographer may decide to paraphrase the meaning of a lexical item which lacks the equivalent. Besides, in some cases they may coin a new expression or transfer the source language item into the target language without changing its form (Zgusta 1971: 306, Tarp 1995b: 62). Additionally, in some dictionaries it is possible not to provide any equivalent if the full one is not found, though the lexicographer may not resign from including a given headword. For the sake of example, in the dictionary by Parowenko (2007), whose main body has the form of a table, the corresponding cells are left empty in the case of missing equivalents (cf. Parowenko 2007: 159).

The presence or absence of interlingual equivalents is closely related to similarities and differences between cultures of the languages concerned. The more two cultures are similar, the easier the task of bilingual dictionary production (Piotrowski 1993: 126). Tarp (1995b: 63) recommends that in the case of very culture-dependent subject fields, such as law, multilingual dictionaries should take the form of a number of bilingual dictionaries. Besides, the researcher (1995b: 64–65) postulates that bilingual dictionaries of law should comprise encyclopaedic and comparative information which would enable their users to grasp the differences between the two legal systems. If the information under discussion is placed in a separate section, dictionary entries may contain cross-references to some of its parts (Tarp 1995b: 64–65).

4. The corpus of Polish, English and Italian language of banking law

Banking law as a domain of law has no clear-cut boundaries. Various researchers provide different lists of legislative acts pertaining to the domain. To give an example, Ofiarski (2011: 31) considers Polish normative acts *Prawo dewizowe* (Dz.U. 2002 nr 141 poz. 1178) and *Ustawa o przeciwdziałaniu praniu pieniędzy oraz finansowaniu terroryzmu* to be banking law, whereas Kaszubski and Tupaj-Cholewa (2010: 21–22) assume that the acts in question are only partially referring to the domain. The indication of a borderline between banking law and other domains is not the purpose of this work, since, if possible at all, it would be a task of legal theorists. By contrast, our task is to collect a corpus to be used in the process of creating a dictionary of banking law collocations. The dictionary needs to be large and varied enough to be used by those who aspire to create texts related to law and banking. Simultaneously, it has to be in a way limited so that it does not become a dictionary devoted to several domains of law.

The corpus used in this work consists of primary as well as secondary legislation. The former is parliamentary legislation, whereas the latter are acts which 'have the status and force of law but which are subordinate to primary legislation in the normative hierarchy' (Cane 2011: 51). The legislative acts included in the corpus were in force at the time of corpus compilation, which took place between January and October 2015. They were enacted not earlier than in 1989.

The corpus contains entire legislative acts which seem sufficiently related to banking law to be taken into account. In other words, the acts included in the corpus are devoted only or in majority to banking law. As for legislative acts which are largely devoted to other domains and which contain some banking law dispositions, they are not included in the corpus. Thus, the selection of normative acts could be easily narrowed or broadened, since most legislative acts pertaining to banking law are also referring to other domains of law. Besides, the corpus could be enlarged by various other acts, such as non-legislative acts adopted by executive bodies or international acts, such as EU acts (Mattila 2013).

The selection of normative acts is, therefore, partially subjective, which is in a way understandable given that banking law as a domain of law has no clear-cut boundaries. The subjectivity is, however, rather partial than full, since the choice of acts is also based on lexical criterion. The titles of all the legislative acts included in the corpus contain a key word or term related to banking. They are demonstrated in *Figure 26*:

The Polish part	The English part	The Italian part
Bank	Bank	Banca
Złoty	Banking	Materia bancaria
Waluta	Credit institution	Credito
Kredyt		Usura
Pożyczka		Euro
*Dewiza		Risparmio
*Poręczenie		Servizio di pagamento
Prawo bankowe		Moneta elettronica
System płatności		
Bankowy Fundusz Gwarancyjny		
Instrument płatniczy		
Stosunki kredytowe		
Komitet Stabilności Finansowej		
Instytucja finansowa		
Finansowe wsparcie		

Figure 26. Key words related to banking in the titles of the legislative acts included in the corpus

It should be noted that, in the case of the Polish part, the key terms are much more varied and their classification to the domain of banking may seem less obvious. Besides, the Polish part of the corpus contains two legislative acts whose titles contain no key terms, i.e. *Ustawa o niektórych formach popierania budownictwa mieszkaniowego oraz o zmianie niektórych ustaw* and *Ustawa o niektórych formach wspierania działalności innowacyjnej* (Ofiarski 2011). The first reason is that the Polish part of the corpus consists of the largest number of legislative acts, accordingly their titles are varied. Another reason is that the compilation of the Polish part of the corpus was to a large extent based upon banking law manuals (Kaszubski and Tupaj-Cholewa 2010: 21–23, Mikos-Sitek and Zapadka 2011: 14–20 and Ofiarski 2011: 15–26), whereas the Italian and English parts were created most of all based on personal research of the corpus compiler. The decision to include in the corpus some legislative acts which do not meet the lexical criterion seems acceptable if the linguist relies on the opinion of experts in a given branch law, who in turn postulate that the acts in question are devoted to the domain.

The three parts of the corpus were compiled in a way to make them similar in size and balanced. To give an example, the English part, which was compiled as the last, could include much more secondary legislation. Nevertheless, only the three acts were chosen bearing in mind not only their content, but also their total size, which could not differ radically from the size of the Polish and the Italian part of the corpus. The whole corpus contains 541 561 tokens. The sizes of its component parts are presented in *Figure 27:*

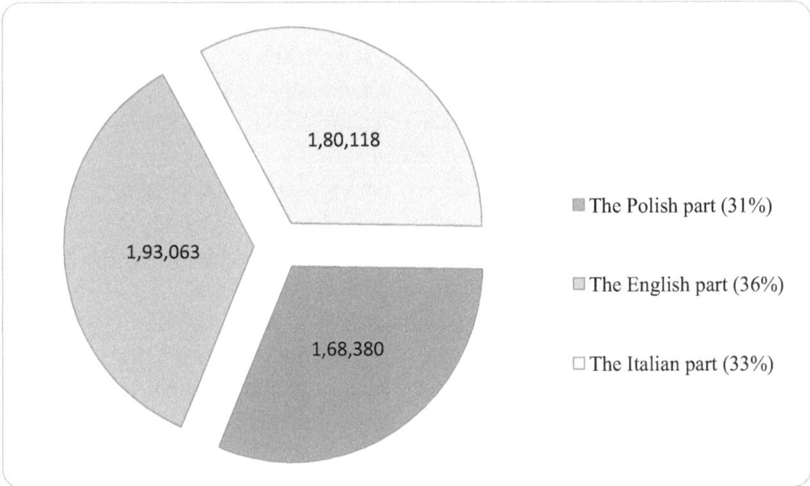

Figure 27. The sizes of the Polish, English and Italian part of the corpus.

As for the Polish part of the corpus, consisting of 168 380 tokens, it encompasses revised texts of the legislative acts listed below, chosen based on Kaszubski and Tupaj-Cholewa (2010: 21–23), Mikos-Sitek and Zapadka (2011: 14–20), and Ofiarski (2011: 15–26). It was assumed that tokens, which were counted automatically with the aid of AntConc, may consist only of letters, and not, for instance, of numbers, punctuation, and other symbols (e.g. @).

1. Ustawa z dnia 28 grudnia 1989 r. o uporządkowaniu stosunków kredytowych, available at http://isap.sejm.gov.pl/DetailsServlet?id=WDU19890740440, access on 25.01.2015, Dz.U. 1989 nr 74 poz. 440
2. Ustawa z dnia 3 lutego 1993 r. o restrukturyzacji finansowej przedsiębiorstw i banków oraz o zmianie niektórych ustaw, available at http://isap.sejm.gov.pl/DetailsServlet?id=WDU19930180082, access on 25.01.2015, Dz.U. 1993 nr 18 poz. 82
3. Ustawa z dnia 7 lipca 1994 r. o denominacji złotego, available at http://isap.sejm.gov.pl/DetailsServlet?id=WDU19940840386, access on 27.01.2015, Dz.U. 1994 nr 84 poz. 386

4. Ustawa z dnia 14 grudnia 1994 r. o Bankowym Funduszu Gwarancyjnym, available at http://isap.sejm.gov.pl/DetailsServlet?id=WDU19950040018, access on 26.01.2015, Dz.U. 1995 nr 4 poz. 18
5. Ustawa z dnia 5 stycznia 1995 r. o dopłatach do oprocentowania niektórych kredytów bankowych, available at http://isap.sejm.gov.pl/DetailsServlet?id=WDU19950130060, access on 26.01.2015, Dz.U. 1995 nr 13 poz. 60
6. Ustawa z dnia 26 października 1995 r. o niektórych formach popierania budownictwa mieszkaniowego oraz o zmianie niektórych ustaw, available at http://isap.sejm.gov.pl/DetailsServlet?id=WDU19951330654, access on 25.01.2015, Dz.U. 1995 nr 133 poz. 654
7. Ustawa z dnia 30 listopada 1995 r. o pomocy państwa w spłacie niektórych kredytów mieszkaniowych, refundacji bankom wypłaconych premii gwarancyjnych oraz zmianie niektórych ustaw, available at http://isap.sejm.gov.pl/DetailsServlet?id=WDU19960050032, access on 26.01.2015, Dz.U. 1996 nr 5 poz. 32
8. Ustawa z dnia 14 czerwca 1996 r. o łączeniu i grupowaniu niektórych banków w formie spółki akcyjnej, available at, http://isap.sejm.gov.pl/DetailsServlet?id=WDU19960900406, access on 25.01.2015, Dz.U. 1996 nr 90 poz. 406
9. Ustawa z dnia 8 maja 1997 r. o poręczeniach i gwarancjach udzielanych przez Skarb Państwa oraz niektóre osoby prawne, available at http://isap.sejm.gov.pl/DetailsServlet?id=WDU19970790484, access on 26.01.2015, Dz.U. 1997 nr 79 poz. 484
10. Ustawa z dnia 29 sierpnia 1997 Prawo bankowe, available at http://isap.sejm.gov.pl/DetailsServlet?id=WDU19971400939, access on 20.01.2014, Dz.U. 1997 nr 140 poz. 939
11. Ustawa z dnia 29 sierpnia 1997 r. o Narodowym Banku Polskim, available at http://isap.sejm.gov.pl/DetailsServlet?id=WDU19971400938, access on 20.01.2015, Dz.U. 1997 nr 140 poz. 938
12. Ustawa z dnia 29 sierpnia 1997 o listach zastawnych i bankach hipotecznych, available at http://isap.sejm.gov.pl/DetailsServlet?id=WDU20030990919, access on 20.01.2015, Dz.U. 2003 nr 99 poz. 919
13. Ustawa z dnia 17 lipca 1998 r. o pożyczkach i kredytach studenckich, available at http://isap.sejm.gov.pl/DetailsServlet?id=WDU19981080685, access on 25.01.2015, Dz.U. 1998 nr 108 poz. 685
14. Ustawa z dnia 8 lipca 1999 r. o dopłatach do oprocentowania kredytów bankowych udzielonych na usuwanie skutków powodzi, available at http://isap.sejm.gov.pl/DetailsServlet?id=WDU19990620690, access on 26.01.2015, Dz.U. 1999 nr 62 poz. 690

15. Ustawa z dnia 29 listopada 2000 r. o objęciu poręczeniami Skarbu Państwa spłaty kredytów mieszkaniowych, available at http://isap.sejm.gov.pl/DetailsServlet?id=WDU20001221310, access on 26.01.2015, Dz.U. 2000 nr 122 poz. 1310
16. Ustawa z dnia 7 grudnia 2000 r. o funkcjonowaniu banków spółdzielczych, ich zrzeszaniu się i bankach zrzeszających, available at http://isap.sejm.gov.pl/DetailsServlet?id=WDU20001191252, access on 20.01.2015, Dz.U. 2000 nr 119 poz. 1252
17. Ustawa z dnia 25 maja 2001 r. o skutkach wprowadzania w niektórych państwach członkowskich Unii Europejskiej wspólnej waluty euro, available at http://isap.sejm.gov.pl/DetailsServlet?id=WDU20010630640, access on 27.01.2015, Dz.U. 2001 nr 63 poz. 640
18. Ustawa z dnia 8 czerwca 2001 r. o dopłatach do oprocentowania kredytów eksportowych o stałych stopach procentowych, available at http://isap.sejm.gov.pl/DetailsServlet?id=WDU20010730762, access on 26.01.2015, Dz.U. 2001 nr 73 poz. 762
19. Ustawa z dnia 24 sierpnia 2001 r. o ostateczności rozrachunku w systemach płatności i systemach rozrachunku papierów wartościowych oraz zasadach nadzoru nad tymi systemami, available at http://isap.sejm.gov.pl/DetailsServlet?id=WDU20011231351, access on 27.01.2015, Dz.U. 2001 nr 123 poz. 1351
20. Ustawa z dnia 27 lipca 2002 r. Prawo dewizowe, available at http://isap.sejm.gov.pl/DetailsServlet?id=WDU20021411178, access on 8.10.2015, Dz.U. 2002 nr 141 poz. 1178
21. Ustawa z dnia 12 września 2002 r. o elektronicznych instrumentach płatniczych, available at http://isap.sejm.gov.pl/DetailsServlet?id=WDU20021691385, access on 27.01.2015, Dz.U. 2002 nr 169 poz. 1385
22. Ustawa z dnia 5 grudnia 2002 r. o dopłatach do oprocentowania kredytów mieszkaniowych o stałej stopie procentowej, available at http://isap.sejm.gov.pl/DetailsServlet?id=WDU20022301922, access on 26.01.2015, Dz.U. 2002 nr 230 poz.
23. Ustawa z dnia 14 marca 2003 r. o Banku Gospodarstwa Krajowego, available at http://isap.sejm.gov.pl/DetailsServlet?id=WDU20030650594, access on 25.01.2015, Dz.U. 2003 nr 65 poz. 594
24. Ustawa z dnia 8 września 2006 r. o finansowym wsparciu rodzin w nabywaniu własnego mieszkania, available at http://isap.sejm.gov.pl/DetailsServlet?id=WDU20061831354, access on 26.01.2015, Dz.U. 2006 nr 183 poz. 1354

25. Ustawa z dnia 30 maja 2008 r. o niektórych formach wspierania działalności innowacyjnej, available at http://isap.sejm.gov.pl/DetailsServlet?id=WDU20081160730, access on 25.01.2015, Dz.U. 2008 nr 116 poz. 730
26. Ustawa z dnia 7 listopada 2008 r. o Komitecie Stabilności Finansowej, available at http://isap.sejm.gov.pl/DetailsServlet?id=WDU20082091317, access on 25.01.2015, Dz.U. 2008 nr 209 poz. 1317
27. Ustawa z dnia 12 lutego 2009 r. o udzielaniu przez Skarb Państwa wsparcia instytucjom finansowym, available at http://isap.sejm.gov.pl/DetailsServlet?id=WDU20090390308, access on 25.01.2015, Dz.U. 2009 nr 39 poz. 308
28. Ustawa z dnia 5 listopada 2009 r. o spółdzielczych kasach oszczędnościowo-kredytowych, available at http://isap.sejm.gov.pl/DetailsServlet?id=WDU20120000855, access on 25.01.2015, Dz.U. 2012 poz. 855
29. Ustawa z dnia 19 czerwca 2009 r. o pomocy państwa w spłacie niektórych kredytów mieszkaniowych udzielonych osobom, które utraciły pracę, available at http://isap.sejm.gov.pl/DetailsServlet?id=WDU20091150964, access on 25.01.2015, Dz.U. 2009 nr 115 poz. 964
30. Ustawa z dnia 12 maja 2011 r. o kredycie konsumenckim, available at http://isap.sejm.gov.pl/DetailsServlet?id=WDU20111260715, access on 25.01.2015, Dz.U. 2011 nr 126 poz. 715

Let us now turn to the English part of the corpus, amounting to 193 063 tokens, which consists of the following legislative acts regulating the banking law in the United Kingdom:

1. The Credit Institutions (Protection of Depositors) Regulations 1995 no. 1442, available at http://www.legislation.gov.uk/uksi/1995/1442/contents/made, access on 28.09.2015
2. Bank of England Act 1998 c. 11, available at http://www.legislation.gov.uk/ukpga/1998/11/contents, access on 5.09.2015
3. The Credit Institutions (Reorganisation and Winding up) Regulations 2004 no 1045, available at http://www.legislation.gov.uk/uksi/2004/1045/contents/made, access on 28.09.2015
4. Banking Act 2009 c. 1, available at http://www.legislation.gov.uk/ukpga/2009/1/contents, access on 5.09.2015
5. Financial Services (Banking Reform) Act 2013 c. 33, available at http://www.legislation.gov.uk/ukpga/2013/33/contents, access on 5.09.2015
6. The Bank Recovery and Resolution Order 2014 no. 3329, available at http://www.legislation.gov.uk/uksi/2014/3329/contents/made, access on 28.09.2015.

Three of the acts, i.e. Bank of England Act 1998, Banking Act 2009, and Financial Services (Banking Reform) Act 2013 are included in the corpus in their revised versions. The remaining acts, i.e. secondary legislation, are included in the corpus in their original versions, since at the time corpus compilation the revised versions have not been available on the website which constitutes the official source of UK legislation. The acts to be included in the English part of the corpus were chosen based on Ellinger, Lomnicka and Hare (2011) and personal research of the dictionary author.

As far as the Italian part of the corpus is concerned, it contains around 180 118 tokens and it has been compiled, among others, based on *Elementi di diritto e legislazione bancaria* (2007), Bontempi (2009) and personal research of the dictionary author. It consists of the revised texts of the following legislative acts:

1. Decreto legislativo 27 gennaio 1992, n. 87, Attuazione della direttiva 86/635/CEE, relativa ai conti annuali ed ai conti consolidati delle banche e degli altri istituti finanziari, e della direttiva 89/117/CEE, relativa agli obblighi in materia di pubblicità dei documenti contabili delle succursali, stabilite in uno Stato membro, di enti creditizi ed istituti finanziari con sede sociale fuori di tale Stato membro, available at http://www.normattiva.it/atto/caricaDettaglioAtto?atto.dataPubblicazioneGazzetta=1992-02-14&atto.codiceRedazionale=092G0133&currentPage=1, access on 7.02.2015, GU n.37 del 14–2–1992 – Suppl. Ordinario n. 27.
2. Decreto legislativo 1 settembre 1993, n. 385, Testo unico delle leggi in materia bancaria e creditizia, available at http://www.normattiva.it/atto/caricaDettaglioAtto?atto.dataPubblicazioneGazzetta=1993-09-30&atto.codiceRedazionale=093G0428&currentPage=1, access on 27.01.2015, GU n.230 del 30–9–1993 – Suppl. Ordinario n. 92.
3. Decreto legge 4 gennaio 1994, n. 1, Misure a garanzia del credito agrario, available at http://www.normattiva.it/atto/caricaDettaglioAtto?atto.dataPubblicazioneGazzetta=1994-01-07&atto.codiceRedazionale=094G0007&currentPage=1, access on 9.09.2015, GU n.4 del 7–1–1994.
4. Legge 7 marzo 1996, n. 108, Disposizioni in materia di usura, available at http://www.normattiva.it/uri-res/N2Ls?urn:nir:stato:legge:1996-03-07;108, access on 7.02.2015, GU n.58 del 9–3–1996 – Suppl. Ordinario n. 44.
5. Decreto legislativo 10 marzo 1998, n. 43, Adeguamento dell'ordinamento nazionale alle disposizioni del trattato istitutivo della Comunita' europea in materia di politica monetaria e di Sistema europeo delle banche centrali, available at http://www.normattiva.it/atto/caricaDettaglioAtto?atto.dataPubblicazioneGazzetta=1998-03-14&atto.codiceRedazionale=098G0096&currentPage=1, access on 8.09 2015, GU n.61 del 14–3–1998.

6. Decreto legislativo 24 giugno 1998, n. 213, Disposizioni per l'introduzione dell'EURO nell'ordinamento nazionale, a norma dell'articolo 1, comma 1, della legge 17 dicembre 1997, n. 433, available at http://www.normattiva.it/atto/vediMenuExport?atto.dataPubblicazioneGazzetta=1998-07-08&atto.codiceRedazionale=098G0261, access on 8.09.2015, GU n.157 del 8–7–1998 – Suppl. Ordinario n. 116.
7. Legge 30 aprile 1999, n. 130, Disposizioni sulla cartolarizzazione dei crediti, available at http://www.normattiva.it/atto/caricaDettaglioAtto?atto.dataPubblicazioneGazzetta=1999-05-14&atto.codiceRedazionale=099G0212&currentPage=1, access on 7.02.2015, GU n.111 del 14–5–1999.
8. Legge 28 dicembre 2005, n. 262, Disposizioni per la tutela del risparmio e la disciplina dei mercati finanziari, available at http://www.normattiva.it/atto/vediMenuExport?atto.dataPubblicazioneGazzetta=2005-12-28&atto.codiceRedazionale=005G0295, access on 9.09 2015, GU n.301 del 28–12–2005 – Suppl. Ordinario n. 208.
9. Decreto legislativo 18 aprile 2006, n. 171, Ricognizione dei principi fondamentali in materia di casse di risparmio, casse rurali, aziende di credito a carattere regionale, enti di credito fondiario e agrario a carattere regionale, available at http://www.normattiva.it/atto/caricaDettaglioAtto?atto.dataPubblicazioneGazzetta=2006-05-12&atto.codiceRedazionale=006G0196&currentPage=1, access on 9.09.2015, GU n.109 del 12–5–2006.
10. Decreto legislativo 13 agosto 2010, n. 141, Attuazione della direttiva 2008/48/CE relativa ai contratti di credito ai consumatori, nonche' modifiche del titolo VI del testo unico bancario (decreto legislativo n. 385 del 1993) in merito alla disciplina dei soggetti operanti nel settore finanaziario, degli agenti in attività finanziaria e dei mediatori creditizi (10G0170), available at http://www.normattiva.it/atto/caricaDettaglioAtto?atto.dataPubblicazioneGazzetta=2010-09-04&atto.codiceRedazionale=010G0170&currentPage=1, access on 9.09.2015, GU n.207 del 4–9–2010 – Suppl. Ordinario n. 212.
11. Decreto legislativo 27 gennaio 2010, n. 11, Attuazione della direttiva 2007/64/CE, relativa ai servizi di pagamento nel mercato interno, recante modifica delle direttive 97/7/CE, 2002/65/CE, 2005/60/CE, 2006/48/CE, e che abroga la direttiva 97/5/CE, available at http://www.normattiva.it/atto/caricaDettaglioAtto?atto.dataPubblicazioneGazzetta=2010-02-13&atto.codiceRedazionale=010G0027&currentPage=1, access on 10.10.2015, GU n.36 del 13–2–2010 – Suppl. Ordinario n. 29.

12. Decreto legislativo 16 aprile 2012, n. 45, Attuazione della direttiva 2009/110/CE, concernente l'avvio, l'esercizio e la vigilanza prudenziale dell'attività degli istituti di moneta elettronica, che modifica le direttive 2005/60/CE e 2006/48/CE e che abroga la direttiva 2000/46/CE, available at http://www.normattiva.it/atto/caricaDettaglioAtto?atto.dataPubblicazioneGazzetta=2012-04-28&atto.codiceRedazionale=012G0065&currentPage=1, access on 10.09.2015, GU n.99 del 28–4–2012 - Suppl. Ordinario n. 86.

The corpus presented in this chapter could obviously be modified in various ways, for instance by adding acts which pertain to banking law to a smaller extent. It was designed and created to be used in the process of compilation of a particular dictionary. The following chapter will be devoted to the creation of the above-mentioned dictionary. Thus, it will demonstrate how the corpus was employed in practice.

5. Polish-English-Italian dictionary of banking law collocations

At the outset it should be reminded that the aim of the dictionary presented in this dissertation is to provide information on collocations pertaining to law and banking. The information is supposed be useful to legal translators, LSP learners and teachers and those who need the language of law and banking in their everyday professional life which requires them to communicate in at least two of the dictionary languages. The dictionary in question is a typical production oriented dictionary, which means that it is intended to facilitate the creation of correct and natural LSP texts. Accordingly, it contains numerous usage examples, which consist of sentences or sentence fragments taken from the corpus. By contrast, it is not the purpose of this dictionary to define legal terms. The information of this kind can be found in numerous other dictionaries devoted to law. Similarly, the provision of interlingual equivalents constitutes a secondary rather than primary aim of the dictionary under discussion. In fact, given that the dictionary is most of all a collocational dictionary, interlingual equivalents can be even perceived as a kind of supplementary information.

As was decided in the first chapter of this work, the dictionary in question includes lexical and grammatical collocations as well as simple and complex collocations which are statistically significant. The decision on statistical significance is taken based on the Mutual Information (MI) test and T-score test (cf. subsection 3.7.2.). Besides, collocations comprised in the dictionary can be classified as unique, strong or medium-strength as understood by Hill (2000: 63–64). By contrast, the dictionary is not -supposed to contain free combinations, since the target users are advanced enough to create them by themselves. Still, it should be pointed out that the borderline between a collocation and a free combination is often vague. In the case of such vagueness, any word combination that results to be statistically significant and seems potentially useful to dictionary users is treated as worth including in the dictionary. Besides, the dictionary under discussion does not include idioms, as they are not present in legislative acts which are comprised in the corpus.

5.1. The process of compilation

The collocational research undertaken in the process of dictionary compilation is conducted with the aid of AntConc 3.4.3 toolkit by Laurence Anthony, available at http://www.antlab.sci.waseda.ac.jp/antconc_index.html. The first step of the research involves the creation a frequency list for each of the three parts of the corpus. Subsequently, the frequency lists are scanned for nouns of over 80 occurrences. In this way a list of possible headwords is prepared. It contains the following nouns:

POTENTIAL HEADWORDS					
English part of the corpus		**Italian part of the corpus**		**Polish part of the corpus**	
TOTAL: 115		**TOTAL: 127**		**TOTAL: 104**	
act	liability	agente	impresa	akcja	prezes
action	liquidation	albo	informazione	bank	przedsiębiorca
activity	liquidator	ambito	interesse	brzmienie	przepis
agreement	management	amministrazione	intermediario	cel	przypadek
amendment	market	ammontare	iscrizione	część	rachunek
amount	matter	applicazione	istituto	członek	rada
annotation	member	articolo	Italia	czynność	ramy
appeal	notice	attività	legge	dane	realizacja
appointment	objective	atto	lettera	decyzja	rok
approval	obligation	attuazione	liquidazione	dzień	rozdział
arrangement	offence	autorità	materia	droga	rozporządzenie
article	office	autorizzazione	mese	działalność	rozumienie
asset	order	azione	ministro	finanse	Rzeczpospolita
authority	paragraph	banca	modalità	forma	sejm
bail	parent	base	modificazione	fundusz	Skarb
bank	parliament	beneficiario	moneta	gospodarstwo	spłata
board	part	bilancio	norma	gwarancja	sposób
body	payment	cambio	obbligo	gwarantowanie	sprawa
bridge	penalty	capitale	oggetto	informacja	środek
business	person	capo	operazione	instytucja	stopa
circumstance	power	capogruppo	organismo	kancelaria	stosunek
committee	procedure	caso	organo	kasa	system
company	proceeding	cliente	pagamento	komisja	szczególność
compensation	property	codice	pagatore	konsument	tekst
condition	protection	comma	parola	kontrola	termin
connection	provision	commissario	parte	koszt	terytorium
credit	purpose	comunicazione	partecipazione	kredyt	tryb
copy	reference	condizione	patrimonio	kwota	tytuł
country	reform	consiglio	periodo	likwidacja	udzielanie
creditor	regard	consumatore	potere	lokal	umowa
date	regulator	conto	presidente	miesiąc	usługa
day	relation	contratto	prestatore	minister	ustawa
decision	report	controllo	prestazione	mowa	wartość
deposit	requirement	conversione	procedura	nadzór	warunek
direction	resolution	credito	provvedimento	oddział	wierzytelność
directive	respect	criterio	rapporto	odnośnik	wniosek
document	right	data	regolamento	odsetek	wykonanie
draft	ring	dato	relazione	okres	wykonywanie
effect	scheme	decreto	repubblica	oprocentowanie	wyplata

Figure 28. Potential nominal headwords in the Polish, English and Italian part of the corpus.

Figure 28. Continued

POTENTIAL HEADWORDS					
enactment end England extent failure force function help house information insolvency institution instrument interest investigation investment Ireland kingdom law	Scotland section security service share society stabilisation statement term transfer transferee treasury undertaking virtue way winding word year	direttiva diritto disciplina disposizione documento economia elemento elenco ente entrata esecuzione esercizio euro finanze finanziamento finanziatore fine fondo forma funzione gestione giorno gruppo importo	requisito revisione riferimento rimborso rispetto sanzione sede servizio sezione sistema società somma spesa stato strumento succursale termine territorio Tesoro testo titolo utilizzatore valore vigilanza vigore	osoba otrzymanie państwo papier podmiot podstawa pomoc poręczenie postępowanie pożyczka praca prawo premia	wysokość zabezpieczenie zadanie zakres zarząd zasada zastrzeżenie zezwolenie zgoda zmiana zobowiązanie związek życie

It should be mentioned that the identification of headwords based solely on their frequency in the corpus results in disproportionate numbers of headwords starting with a given letter. To give an example, as for the Polish part of the corpus, there is only one potential headword starting with the letter *a*. The disproportion, is however, acceptable, given that the dictionary presented in this work is relatively small and is devoted to only one out of numerous domains of law.

The subsequent steps involve exploration of collocations of the potential headwords. The collocational research is carried out starting from the MI test, whose results are then compared with results of the t-score test. The procedure is motivated by the fact that MI is likely to give high scores to low-frequency collocates, whereas t-score tends to return high results for high-frequency items (cf. section 3.7.2). Once one of the tests is used for a given headword and the list of potential collocates is generated by AntConc, it is analysed in order to exclude items whose occurrences are accidental or which are useless to dictionary users, such as, for instance, articles.

While analysing the potential collocates of a given headword candidate, the author of the dictionary takes into account items which occur in the span of five words to the left and to the right of the headword. Besides, the analysis is limited to collocates of frequency of at least 5, which got an MI score of at least 3 or a t-score of at least 2 (see *Figure 29*, Hunston 2002: 72, McEnery et al. 2006: 56). The author does not analyse, however, more than 120 collocates for one headword.

As the corpus is not tagged, the potential headwords are investigated in their various forms. To give an example, when analysing the headword *action,* the researcher extracts a single list of potential collocates for two search terms, i.e. *action* and *actions.* In the case of the Polish *akcja,* one list of collocates is extracted for *akcja, akcji, akcje, akcjami* and all the other forms of the noun. A fragment of an example list of potential collocates, extracted for the noun *document(s)* with the aid of AntConc, can be seen in *Figure 29* below:

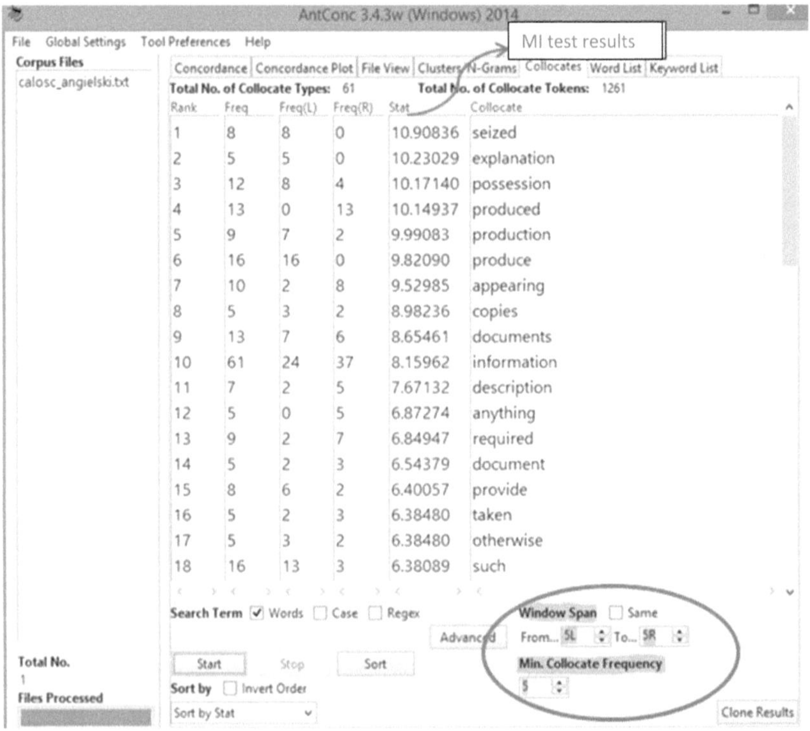

Figure 29. A fragment of list of potential collocates extracted for the noun *document(s).*

Once the list of potential collocates is generated for a given headword, the collocates are analysed one by one with the aid of advanced search options, which allow to search for concordances in which a given collocate appears in the context of the headword. *Figure 30* demonstrates how the advanced search options were used to find concordances, including the headword *document(s)* and its most significant potential collocate, i.e. *seized*. As for *Figure 31*, it demonstrates the output of the search under discussion, i.e. concordances in which the headword *document(s)* is accompanied by the participle *seized*.

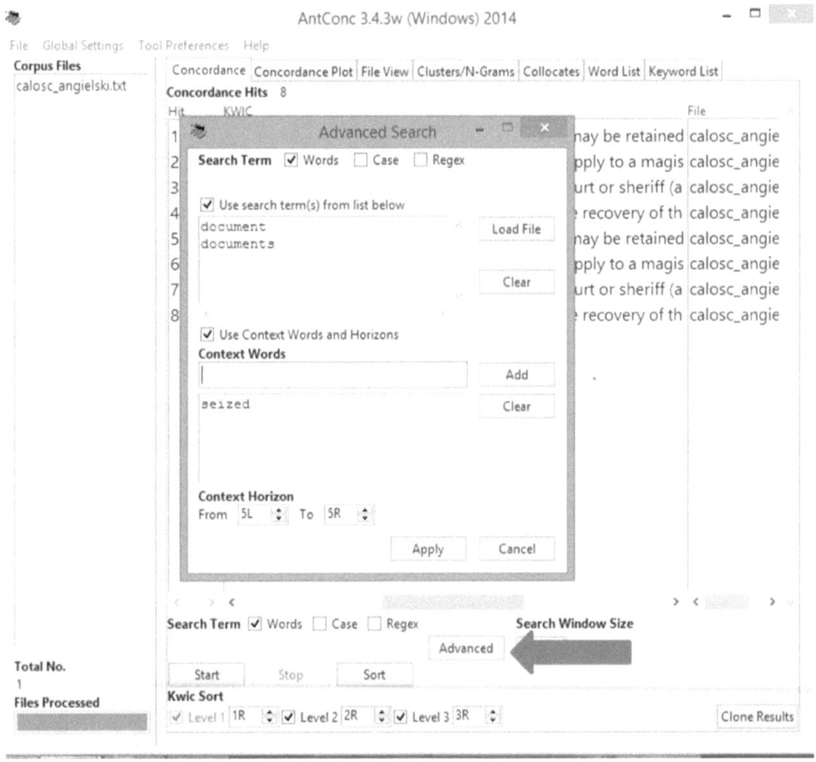

Figure 30. The search for concordances including the headword *document(s)* and one of its potential collocates, i.e. *seized*.

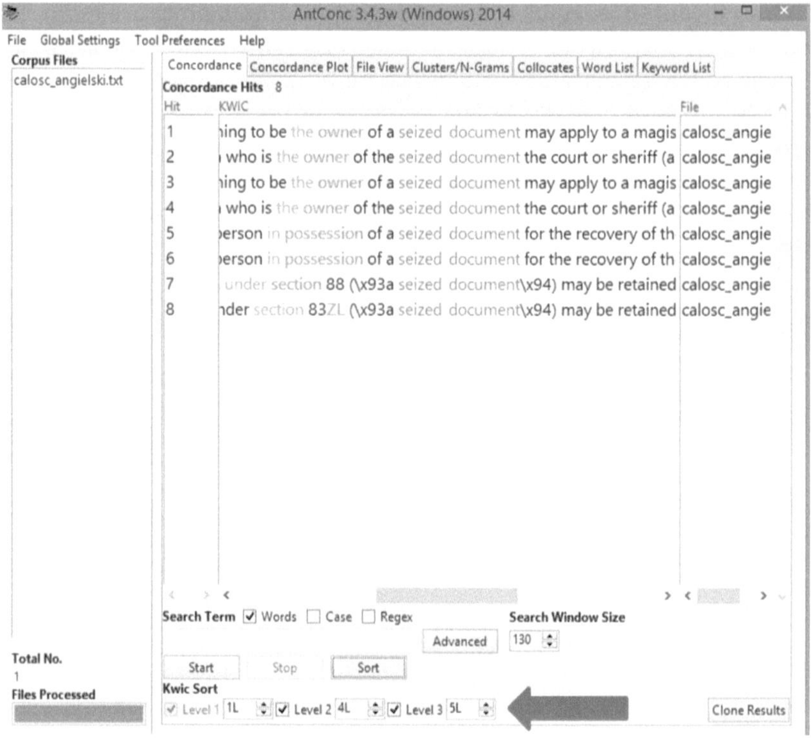

Figure 31. The output of the search for concordances including the headword *document(s)* and one of its potential collocates, i.e. *seized*.

Let us now focus on *Figure 31*, which shows concordances in which a given headword (*document(s)*) is accompanied by its collocate *seized*. In general, collocates are included in a given dictionary entry provided that they occur at least five times as logically related to the headword. Therefore, in the case of the example under discussion, it is next to no doubt that the collocation *seized document* should be included in the dictionary. It is, however, not only the collocate *seized* that needs to be analysed in the concordances under discussion. Wider context also needs to be considered to make sure that the collocation *seized document* is not a part of another, longer collocation, which could also be included in the dictionary entry. At this stage one may make use of the option of sorting (see the arrow in *Figure 31*) as the sorted data show best that there are no other collocations to include in this case. Nevertheless, to provide further example, the expression *owner of a / the seized document* (see *Figure 31*) would also be added to the dictionary entry should it appear in the concordances five times instead of four.

The decisions at the stage of collocate analysis are taken bearing in mind that collocations included in a dictionary should be habitual, typical for the domain in question and, most of all, potentially useful to dictionary users (cf. Meer 1998). If seven or more valid collocates are identified for a given headword, it is incorporated in the dictionary. In the opposite case, it is rejected. As far as polysemous headwords are concerned, their various senses are presented in one entry. If, however, each of the senses has at least seven collocates (e.g. *periodo, part*), they are devoted separate entries, ordered based on the intuitiveness of particular senses. In other words, the most intuitive meaning of a given polysemous headword is devoted the first of the entries under discussion. Finally, it should be mentioned that some potential headwords proved to constitute parts of multiword terms, which also possessed more than seven collocates. In such cases, the terms under discussion were granted the status of dictionary headwords. Some examples are the entries for *payment, payment system* and *payment systems regulator* or *państwo* and *państwo członkowskie*. The above-mentioned entries are linked with the aid of cross-references, which are placed among collocates and marked by bold font, underlining and capital letters (e.g. **PAYMENT SYSTEM** in the entry for *payment*).

Besides, should the choice of headwords be based solely on the frequency criterion, some terms that are intuitively expected to be found in a dictionary devoted to a given domain may not be included. Therefore, the generated list of potential headwords should be verified by the lexicographer and, if necessary, completed at their discretion. The choice of the additional headwords, their collocates and the corresponding examples should recommendably be based also on resources other than the corpus. In this work, however, the headwords that were added regardless of the frequency criterion were chosen with the aid of the frequency lists initially generated for each of the corpus parts. This time, however, the lists were scanned for nouns of less than 80 occurrences that seemed crucial for the domain of banking law. They are presented in *Figure 32*:

English part of the corpus	**Italian part of the corpus**	**Polish part of the corpus**
account	assegno	akcjonariusz
amendment	beneficiario	aktywa
banknote	cliente	banknot
client	creditore	deponent
contract	debitore	depozyt
currency	denaro	dłużnik
debt	finanza	emisja
debtor	ipoteca	finanse
depositor	mutuo	hipoteka
fee	pagatore	klient
fund	rate	konto
holder	tasso	kredytobiorca
loan	titolare	kredytodawca
money	valuta	książeczka
		lokata
		moneta
		nieruchomość
		niewypłacalność
		opłata
		pieniądz
		pieniądz elektroniczny
		instytucja pieniądza elektronicznego
		płatność
		posiadacz
		prowizja
		przedsiębiorstwo
		raty
		spółka
		uchwała
		waluta
		wierzyciel
		własność
		właściciel
TOTAL NUMBER OF HEADWORDS:		
113 + 14 = 127	115 + 14 = 129	98 + 33 = 131

Figure 32. Potential headwords considered regardless of the frequency criterion, intuitively crucial for the domain of banking law.

The choice of collocates that are presented in the entries devoted to the listed headwords was dependent on individual decisions of the lexicographer, but still it was made based on the corpus. If it was not possible to identify at least five collocates, the headword was rejected (e.g. the English *charge*, *finance*, *president* or the Polish *audyt* and *pasywa*). The number of the added headwords could be larger to further expand the dictionary and consequently to create an even more complete resource. For the purposes of this work, which aims at the creation a model and is supposed to provide an example of its practical application, but still remains to a large extent theoretical, the list presented in *Figure 32* was deemed to be sufficient. Still, undoubtedly, its further expansion would positively influence the dictionary quality, especially if it contributed to a larger number of equivalent headwords present in all the three parts devoted to different languages. Nevertheless, it should be highlighted that it is the frequency-based choice of headwords that ensures the best information on items which are actually often used in the language of banking law in a given area. The above-mentioned information is extremely significant to dictionary users, which constitutes an important argument against the inclusion of additional headwords and should be considered before taking decision in this respect.

5.2. Dictionary structure

Up to now, we have focussed on a general step-by-step description of the dictionary creation process. Now it is time to focus in detail on the dictionary macrostructure and microstructure. As for the macrostructure, it was decided that it should be as simple as possible hoping that the decision will contribute to the dictionary user-friendliness, the more so as the entries in the dictionary under discussion are typically rather long and complex. Accordingly, the macrostructure consists of three headword lists arranged alphabetically and devoted to the three dictionary languages. The author of this dissertation believes that such macrostructural solution can be adopted also in dictionaries covering a larger number of languages.

Let us now go on to the dictionary microstructure. First of all, each entry contains the headword followed by the information on the corresponding language, which is abbreviated and given in brackets (e.g. (en)). Besides, the top right corner of some entries contains a frame with information on the headword preference for singular or plural form. The frame under discussion, inserted in entries whose headwords occurred in singular or plural in at least 90 % of cases, is visible in the entry for *document* below. Furthermore, the entries are divided into subentries based on parts of speech of the collocates, which are indicated with the aid of the following abbreviations in brackets:

(Aff) – affix
(Adj) – adjective
(Adv) – adverb
(N) – noun
(P) – preposition
(V) – verb

The collocates are marked in bold type face, whereas the usage examples are printed in italics, as one can see in the example entry below:

DOCUMENT (en)

Usually singular

(Adj) **seized document** *any document of which possession is taken under section 88 ('a seized document') may be retained so long as it is necessary to retain it (rather than copies of it) in the circumstances* **specified document** ✂ **document relating to**

(N) **document or information, instrument or document** *a share transfer instrument or order may modify references (express or implied) in an instrument or document to a transferor* ✂ **document of a description** *an investigator may also require any person to produce at a specified time and place any specified documents or documents of a specified description* ✂ **possession, production of a document**

(V) **to produce a document** ✂ **document + to be produced**

to provide an explanation of a document *any person to whom a relevant document is produced may (b) require the person producing the document, or any relevant person (see subsection (4)), to provide an explanation of the document*

Possible equivalents: DOCUMENTO (it), dokument (pl)

As far as the usage examples are concerned, they consist of sentences or sentence fragments taken from the corpus and shortened, if needed. If some text which is omitted in a usage example was originally situated in its middle, the omission is marked with the symbol of ellipsis in brackets (…).

If a collocate occurs in plural in more than 90 % of cases, it is included in the entry in its plural form. The collocates within subentries are typically ordered alphabetically. Nevertheless, in some cases they are divided into categories which are separated by the symbol of scissors (✂). The categories are distinguished, for instance, based on the position taken by a given headword (e.g. *seized document* vs. *document relating to*). Moreover, they can be established based on grammatical criteria. For instance, passive infinitives are separated from those active within the subentry devoted to verbs (e.g. *to produce a document* vs. *document + to be produced*). Besides, past and present participles, which are placed in subentries devoted to adjectives and not verbs in order to make their presentation more intuitive, are also separated from ordinary adjectives by means of the symbol of scissors (e.g. *competent person vs. authorised person*). Finally, a subentry may be divided into categories if a number of collocates form a semantic set or if some collocates differ from the others in that they are accompanied by pronouns, conjunctions, etc. The division into categories may also be applied due to the length of a particular collocation or even for punctuation reasons. All in all, the reasons for the division under discussion were quite often specific to a particular case.

As for the symbol of pencil (✎) which is placed at the end of the entry, it opens a section devoted to collocations of more than two words. In the case of particularly complex entries with numerous multi-word collocations, several sections of this type may be created. They are established based on parts of speech and semantic or syntactic criteria. Where possible, the criteria are indicated by labels in brackets, for instance:

- *(NOMINAL)* indicates a section devoted to nominal group collocations
- *(VERBAL)* indicates a section including verbal group collocations
- *(THEMATIC)* indicates a section for collocations related thematically
- *(SYNTACTIC)* indicates a section created based on the position of headword in a given collocation

It should be mentioned that some sections are established based on more than one criterion, which is reflected in their labels (e.g. *(SYNTACTIC NOMINAL)* or *(THEMATIC NOMINAL)*). An example entry with two such sections, one of which is created based on the semantic criterion, is demonstrated below:

MANAGEMENT (en) | Always singular |

(N) **management body** *'management body' means the board of directors, or if there is no such board, the equivalent body responsible for the management of the undertaking concerned*

✎ *(NOMINAL)* **day to day management** ✂ **asset management vehicle** *an 'asset management vehicle' is an undertaking which (…) (c) is created for the purpose of receiving some or all of the assets, rights, and liabilities of one or more banks or of* *one or more bridge banks (or both)* **claims management services** *power to impose penalties on persons providing claims management services*

✎ *(THEMATIC NOMINAL)* **(designated) senior management function in relation to the carrying on of a regulated activity** *a function is a 'senior management function', in relation to the carrying on of a regulated activity by an authorised person, if (a) the function will require the person performing it to be responsible for managing one or more aspects of the authorised person's affairs, so far as relating to the activity, and (b) those aspects involve, or might involve, a risk of serious consequences* **function designated as a senior management function under section 1, relevant senior management function** *in subsection (1A) 'relevant senior management function' means a function which the PRA is satisfied is a senior management function as defined in section 59ZA (whether or not the function has been designated as such by the FCA)* **senior management function as defined in section 1** ✂ **to perform a designated senior management function**

📖 Possible equivalents: AMMINISTRAZIONE, direzione, GESTIONE (it), kierownictwo, zarządzanie, ZARZĄD (pl)

While discussing the sections devoted to collocations of more than two words, it should be mentioned, however, that collocations consisting of two words and one or more prepositions, conjunctions or numerals are treated as two-word collocations. In other words, they are placed in subentries devoted to particular parts of speech and not in the sections marked with the symbol of pen. Furthermore, it should be noted that the content of prepositional subentries (marked with *(P)*) is approached in a less strict way. They happen to include some collocations which, apart from prepositions and headwords, contain some nouns or verbs, such as *information about a matter* or *information in a form* in the entry for *information*.

Besides, the entry above demonstrates that some of the collocations included in the dictionary consist of a surprisingly high number of components. Indeed, no limit was set to the number of components of a collocation apart from the assumption that it cannot exceed sentence boundaries. The decision not to set a stricter limit results from the fact that its setting would contribute to the exclusion of various word combinations which are potentially very useful to dictionary users.

Furthermore, dictionary entries contain additional sections devoted to potential headword equivalents in the two other dictionary languages (cf. section 2.5). The sections are placed at the end of the entries and marked with the symbol of a book (🕮). Some of the equivalents presented in the sections simultaneously constitute cross-references to other dictionary entries. The cross-references are marked by capital letters (e.g. AMMINISTRAZIONE in the entry for *management* above). The potential equivalents sections were created with the aid of the dictionaries by Grelewicz-La Mela and Nuzzo (2003), Ożga (2006, 2009), Kwiatkowska (2011), Picchi (2011) and de Palma (2012). Subsequently, they were confronted with the content of IATE (Interactive Terminology for Europe), which is the terminology database of the European Union. If, based on the above-mentioned resources, it was not possible to identify any possible equivalent for a given headword, the equivalent was provided by the author of the dissertation.

As was mentioned in section 2.5. and subsection 3.10.2, the search for interlingual equivalents is not a straightforward task, in particular when it comes to the domain of law. In the case of a collocational dictionary, the task is additionally complicated by the fact that collocations within one entry frequently require different equivalents of one and the same headword. To give an example, as for the Italian headword *amministrazione*, it is usually translated into Polish as *administracja*, *kierownictwo* or *zarząd*. Nevertheless, some collocations require its translation into the adjective *administracyjny* (e.g. *attività di amministrazione*). Moreover, some of the headwords, such as the English *virtue* or the Polish *droga* or *tytuł*, constitute parts of complex prepositions (e.g. *by virtue of*, *w drodze*). Ideally, their equivalents should be target language nouns which are parts of functionally analogous complex prepositions, but in some cases their nominal translation is not possible at all. It should be mentioned that the presentation of potential equivalents belonging to various parts of speech may be confusing to dictionary users, especially in the case of a dictionary limited to nominal headwords. Accordingly, it is avoided as much as possible in the dictionary presented in this work.

Last but not least, it should be mentioned that several entries contain tables which allowed for a more user-friendly presentation of longer collocations. An example entry of this type is presented below:

DROGA (pl)

(N) **w drodze decyzji, rozporządzenia** *minister właściwy do spraw instytucji finansowych, po zasięgnięciu opinii Prezesa NBP, określa, w drodze rozporządzenia, sposób, zakres i terminy realizacji obowiązku, o którym mowa w ust. 2a* **w drodze uchwały, umowy, zarządzenia**

określać/ określić	⟹	**w drodze**	⟹	**rozporządzenia uchwały zarządzenia**	**sposób / szczegółowe warunki i tryb / szczegółowy zakres/ szczegółowe zasady / termin / wysokość**

* * *

In this chapter, we have focused on the dictionary of banking law collocations which is presented in this work. In particular, we elaborated on its structures as well as the process of its creation. Besides, it should be reminded that the first three chapters of this work devoted attention to the notion of collocation (see Chapter 1), explored the language of law (see Chapter 2), and presented the problems of lexicography and corpus linguistics (see Chapter 3). As for Chapter 4, it offered a description of the corpus which was employed in the dictionary compilation process.

The dictionary under discussion, which constitutes the most practical part of this work, is presented in the subsequent pages, and is followed by conclusions, which are comprised in Chapter 6.

POLISH-ENGLISH-ITALIAN DICTIONARY OF BANKING LAW COLLOCATIONS

THE POLISH PART

A

AKCJA (pl)

Usually plural

(Adj) **objęta, posiadana akcja**

(N) **akcje i udziały** *akcje i udziały w spółkach stanowiące własność Skarbu Państwa* ✂ **akcje banku** ✂ **nabycie, nabywanie, obejmowanie, objęcie akcji** *nabycie albo objecie akcji lub praw z akcji banku krajowego* **zbycie akcji** ✂ **ceny akcji, prawa z akcji, wartość akcji** *ogólna wartość nabytych i objętych akcji i udziałów nie może przekroczyć 10 % wysokości funduszy własnych banku hipotecznego*

(V) **nabyć, obejmować, posiadać akcje** *bank zależny, który w dniu zawiązania grupy bankowej posiada akcje banku dominującego, jest zobowiązany do ich zbycia*

✎ **prawo głosu z akcji** *Komisja Nadzoru Finansowego może, w drodze decyzji, zakazać wykonywania prawa głosu z akcji banku krajowego* **zamiana wierzytelności na akcje**

📖 Possible equivalents: SHARE, stock (en), azione, TITOLO, valore (it)

AKCJONARIUSZ (pl)

(N) **akcjonariusz banku** ✂ **udziałowiec albo akcjonariusz** *NBP nie może być udziałowcem albo akcjonariuszem innych osób prawnych, z wyjątkiem prowadzących działalność usługową na rzecz instytucji finansowych lub Skarbu Państwa, lub mających dla NBP istotne znaczenie w zakresie działania na rzecz stabilności krajowego systemu finansowego*

(V) **być akcjonariuszem** *bank zależny nie może być akcjonariuszem banku dominującego*

✎ **akcjonariusz banku krajowego, akcjonariusz banku zrzeszającego** *bank spółdzielczy będący akcjonariuszem banku zrzeszającego jest reprezentowany na walnym zgromadzeniu akcjonariuszy tego banku przez pełnomocnika* ✂ **walne zgromadzenie akcjonariuszy** ✂ **być akcjonariuszem banku** *Komisja Nadzoru Finansowego może, w drodze decyzji, zakazać wykonywania prawa głosu z akcji banku krajowego*

📖 Possible equivalents: shareholder, stockholder (en), azionista (it)

AKTYWA (pl)

Always plural

(Adj) **aktywa bilansowe** *banki są obowiązane do wnoszenia wpłat z tytułu nadzoru bankowego, stanowiących iloczyn sumy aktywów bilansowych banków i stawki nieprzekraczającej 0,024 %* **aktywa finansowe**

(N) **aktywa banku** ✂ **wartość aktywów** ✂ **zarządzanie aktywami** ✂ **aktywa i pasywa** *bank przejmujący działalność wstępuje, z mocy prawa, w prawa i obowiązki strony umów o kredyt kontraktowy. Jednocześnie przechodzą na niego zobowiązania i wierzytelności oraz inne aktywa i pasywa związane z przejętą działalnością* **aktywa i zobowiązania**

✎ **stosunek funduszy własnych do wartości aktywów** *minimalna kwota pomocy powinna zapewnić kasie utrzymanie wyrażonego procentowo stosunku funduszy własnych do wartości aktywów powyżej poziomu określonego w ust. 1* ✂ **aktywa stanowiące pokrycie funduszy ochrony środków gwarantowanych** *banki spółdzielcze – członkowie zrzeszeń – obowiązane są deponować aktywa stanowiące pokrycie funduszy ochrony środków gwarantowanych zrzeszenia na wyodrębnionym rachunku w banku zrzeszającym*

📖 Possible equivalents: ASSET (en), attività, attivo (it)

B

BANK (pl)

(Adj) **bank centralny** *Narodowy Bank Polski, zwany dalej 'NBP', jest bankiem centralnym Rzeczypospolitej Polskiej* **hipoteczny** *dochód banku hipotecznego z tytułu odsetek od wierzytelności zabezpieczonych hipoteką (…) nie może być niższy od kosztów z tytułu odsetek od znajdujących się w obrocie hipotecznych listów zastawnych* **krajowy, kredytujący, państwowy, polski, spółdzielczy, zagraniczny, zależny** ✂ **bank przejęty, przejmowany, przejmujący, zrzeszający, zrzeszony** ✂ **zatrudniony w banku**

(N) **akcjonariusz, oddział, przedstawicielstwo banku** *zakres działania przedstawicielstwa banku zagranicznego i instytucji kredytowej może obejmować wyłącznie prowadzenie działalności w zakresie reklamy i promocji banku zagranicznego lub instytucji kredytowej w zakresie ustalonym w zezwoleniu* ✂ **akcje, pracownicy, wierzytelności banku** *bank hipoteczny prowadzi i przechowuje rejestr zabezpieczenia listów zastawnych, do którego wpisywane są w odrębnych pozycjach wierzytelności banku hipotecznego oraz prawa i środki, o których mowa w art. 18 ust. 3* ✂ **grupa banków** ✂ **działalność, likwidacja, tworzenie, utworzenie banku** ✂ **łączenie się, połączenie (się), zrzeszanie się banków** ✂ **rachunek w banku**

(V) **reprezentować bank** *prezes zarządu banku państwowego reprezentuje bank, przewodniczy zarządowi banku oraz organizuje działalność banku* ✂ **bank + być obowiązanym** *bank jest obowiązany do utrzymywania płynności płatniczej dostosowanej do rozmiarów i rodzaju działalności, w sposób zapewniający wykonanie wszystkich zobowiązań pieniężnych zgodnie z terminami ich płatności* **bank + być tworzonym**

(P) **na wniosek banku, za pośrednictwem banku** *przedsiębiorca, za pośrednictwem banku kredytującego, składa do Banku Gospodarstwa Krajowego wniosek o przyznanie premii technologicznej, do którego dołącza warunkową umowę kredytu technologicznego albo promesę kredytu technologicznego*

✎ *(NOMINAL)* **instytucja kredytowa lub bank, podmiot dominujący (wobec) banku krajowego** *Komisja Nadzoru Finansowego może ustalić termin nabycia albo objęcia akcji lub praw z akcji albo uzyskania uprawnień podmiotu dominującego banku krajowego* ✂ **Europejski System Banków Centalnych** ✂ **członkowie zarządu banku, osoba zajmująca stanowisko kierownicze w banku, prezes zarządu banku, walne zgromadzenie akcjonariuszy banku, zarząd i rada nadzorcza banku** ✂ **wpisanie banku do rejestru przedsiębiorców, zabezpieczenie wierzytelności banku** *zabezpieczenie wierzytelności banku może być dokonane w drodze przeniesienia na bank przez dłużnika lub osobę trzecią, do czasu spłaty zadłużenia wraz z należnymi odsetkami i prowizją, prawa własności rzeczy ruchomej lub papierów wartościowych* **zezwolenie na utworzenie banku** ✂ **akcje lub prawa z akcji banku krajowego, fundusze podstawowe / własne banku** *bank spółdzielczy, który zrzeszył się z bankiem zrzeszającym, jest obowiązany uzyskać zwiększenie sumy funduszy własnych* **sprawozdanie finansowe banku, środki gromadzone w banku, umowa zawarta z bankiem** ✂ **ustawa o funkcjonowaniu banków spółdzielczych, ich zrzeszaniu się i bankach zrzeszających**

✎ *(THEMATIC NOMINAL)* **bank należący do grupy bankowej** *bieżąca płynność płatnicza każdego banku należącego do grupy bankowej jest gwarantowana przez wszystkie pozostałe banki tej grupy* **bank udzielający kredytu, bank w formie spółki akcyjnej, zrzeszone banki spółdzielcze** *bank zrzeszający utrzymuje rezerwę obowiązkową zrzeszonych banków spółdzielczych na swoim rachunku w Narodowym Banku Polskim* ✂ **Bank Gospodarki Żywnościowej, Bank Gospodarstwa Krajowego, Narodowy Bank Polski**

✎ *(VERBAL)* **bank + udzielać kredytu**

Possible equivalents: BANK (en), BANCA (it)

BANKNOT (pl)

Always plural

(N) **banknoty i monety** *przepis ust. 1 stosuje się odpowiednio do fałszywych banknotów i monet opiewających na waluty obce*

✎ **banknoty i monety nominowane w euro / w walutach narodowych, banknoty i monety opiewające (na)** *znakami pieniężnymi Rzeczypospolitej Polskiej są banknoty i monety opiewające na złote i grosze* ✂ **wymiana banknotów i monet**

📖 Possible equivalents: BANKNOTE (en), banconota (it)

C

CEL (pl)

(Adj) **cele mieszkaniowe, rolnicze** ✂ **mający na celu**

(N) **kredyt na cel** ✂ **cel działalności, nadzoru** *celem nadzoru nad rynkiem finansowym jest zapewnienie prawidłowego funkcjonowania tego rynku* ✂ **w celu dokonania, realizacji** *w celu realizacji kontroli, o której mowa w ust. 1, Funduszowi udostępniane są dane dotyczące deponentów zawarte w zbiorach prowadzonych przez podmioty lub osoby trzecie* **w celu ustalenia, usunięcia, utrzymania, uzyskania, wykonania, zabezpieczenia, zapewnienia**

(Adv) **wyłącznie w celu** *podmioty, oraz osoby w nich zatrudnione, którym (…) udzielono lub ujawniono informacje objęte tajemnicą bankową, mogą wykorzystać te informacje wyłącznie w celu zawarcia i wykonania umów, o których mowa w ust. 2 pkt 1, 2 oraz 4–6*

(P) **na cel** *adaptacja budynku lub lokalu o innym przeznaczeniu na cele mieszkalne* **w celu**

✎ **cel określony w art. 1** ✂ **fundusz (własny) tworzony w celu zapewnienia środków (na finansowanie zadań)** *fundusz kas jest tworzony w celu zapewnienia środków na finansowanie zadań Funduszu w zakresie wypłaty środków gwarantowanych* **kredyt na cele, o których mowa w art. 1, środki podjęte w celu usunięcia nieprawidłowości** ✂ **w celu realizacji programów rządowych** *BGK w celu realizacji programów rządowych, o których mowa w ust. 1 pkt 3, 5 i 7, może również pozyskiwać środki z innych źródeł, w szczególności zaciągać kredyty i pożyczki oraz emitować obligacje w kraju i za granicą* **w celu realizacji zadań, w**

celu uzyskania lokalu mieszkalnego stanowiącego odrębną nieruchomość, w celu zabezpieczenia wierzytelności

Possible equivalents: aim, goal, intent, object, OBJECTIVE, PURPOSE, target (en), finalità, FINE, intenzione, obiettivo, oggetto, scopo (it)

CZĘŚĆ (pl)

Only singular

(Adj) **zorganizowana część** *nabycie przedsiębiorstwa bankowego lub jego zorganizowanej części przez bank wymaga zezwolenia Komisji Nadzoru Finansowego*

(N) **całość lub część** ✂ **część kredytu, kwoty** *bank nie ma obowiązku zwrotu części kwoty przyjętej na własność, równej niespłaconej sumie zadłużenia wobec banku* **część środków, wierzytelności** *wierzyciele zachowują prawo do nie spłaconej przez dłużnika części wierzytelności istniejącej przed zawarciem ugody bankowej* **część zadłużenia**

(P) **w całości lub części**

budynki, budowle lub ich części *zakup robót i materiałów budowlanych w celu budowy lub rozbudowy budynków, budowli lub ich części* ✂ **spłata części kredytu**

Possible equivalents: component, PART (2), piece, portion (en), ELEMENTO, PARTE (it)

CZŁONEK (pl)

(Adj) **nowy członek** ✂ **będący, niebędący członkiem** *wysokość spłat wnoszonych przez członka spółdzielni lub osobę niebędącą członkiem spółdzielni, której przysługuje spółdzielcze własnościowe prawo do lokalu* ✂ **poszczególni, pozostali członkowie**

(N) **funkcja członka** *dostęp do tajemnicy, o której mowa w ust. 1, mają wyłącznie członkowie organów kasy, niezależnie od podstawy prawnej pełnienia funkcji członka organu kasy* **mandat członka** *mandat członka rady nadzorczej wygasa z*

dniem powołania nowego członka rady nadzorczej **odwołanie, powołanie członka ✂ członek kasy, komitetu, organu, spółdzielni, zarządu**

(V) **odwołać członka** *Komisja Nadzoru Finansowego odwołuje członka zarządu kasy lub Kasy Krajowej w przypadku prawomocnego skazania go za przestępstwo umyślne lub przestępstwo skarbowe* **powołać członka**

(P) **spośród członków ✂ na rzecz członka** *kasy oraz Kasa Krajowa są uprawnione do wydawania pieniądza elektronicznego na rzecz członków kas, na zasadach określonych w ustawie z dnia 19 sierpnia 2011 r. o usługach płatniczych*

✎ **członek banku spółdzielczego, członek Kasy Krajowej, członek Rady Nadzorczej, członek Unii Europejskiej, członek zarządu banku, członek zarządu kasy lub Kasy Krajowej ✂ objęcie stanowisk członków zarządu, osoby przewidziane do objęcia stanowisk członków zarządu** *założyciele oraz osoby przewidziane do objęcia w banku stanowisk członków zarządu, w tym prezesa, dają rękojmię ostrożnego i stabilnego zarządzania bankiem* **✂ zawiesić w czynnościach członka zarządu**

📖 Possible equivalents: affiliate, MEMBER (en), affiliato, membro, socio (it)

CZYNNOŚĆ (pl)

(Adj) **czynność bankowa, prawna, czynności faktyczne** *Pośrednik kredytowy w reklamach dotyczących kredytu konsumenckiego podaje konsumentowi w sposób jednoznaczny, zrozumiały i widoczny 1) zakres umocowania do dokonywania czynności faktycznych lub prawnych* **czynności kontrolne ✂ wszystkie czynności ✂ czynność dokonana, czynności określone (w), podejmowane (przez), powierzone, wykonywane, wynikające (z), związane (z)**

(N) **dokonanie, dokonywanie, wykonywanie czynności ✂ zakres czynności** *Dysponent Funduszu zawiera z Bankiem Gospodarstwa Krajowego umowę określającą w szczególności: 1) zakres czynności wykonywanych przez Bank Gospodarstwa Krajowego* **✂ czynności z zakresu**

(V) **wykonywać czynność, zawiesić w czynnościach** *Rada Nadzorcza może, z ważnych powodów, zawiesić w czynnościach poszczególnych lub wszystkich członków Zarządu, na okres nie dłuższy niż 3 miesiące* ✂ **czynności są wykonywane**

✎ **wszystkie lub niektóre czynności** *działalność transgraniczna – wykonywanie przez instytucję kredytową na terytorium Rzeczypospolitej Polskiej (...) wszystkich lub niektórych czynności w zakresie wynikającym z udzielonego zezwolenia* ✂ **czynności, o których mowa w art. 1, czynności obrotu dewizowego** *przedsiębiorcy wykonujący działalność kantorową oraz rezydenci i nierezydenci dokonujący czynności obrotu dewizowego* **czynności wynikające z zezwolenia** *Bank krajowy może wykonywać na terytorium państwa goszczącego czynności wynikające z zezwolenia, o którym mowa w art. 34 ust. 1* **czynności związane z działalnością** ✂ **powierzeni**e **wykonywania czynności, wykonywanie innej czynności, niż czynność bankowa** ✂ **w związku z wykonywaniem czynności bankowych** *wierzytelność, powstająca w związku z wykonywaniem czynności bankowych, nie będzie chroniona przez system gwarantowania* ✂ **wykonywać czynności na terytorium państwa, zawiesić w czynnościach członka zarządu** ✂ **bank + wykonywać czynności**

🕮 Possible equivalents: ACTION, ACTIVITY, FUNCTION, operation (en), atto, ATTIVITÀ, azione, FUNZIONE, OPERAZIONE (it)

D

DANE (pl)

Always plural

(Adj) **indywidualne** *dane indywidualne, o których mowa w ust. 2, 2a i 3, mogą być wykorzystywane wyłącznie do sporządzania zestawień statystycznych* **dane niezbędne (do), osobowe** ✂ **dane dotyczące, umożliwiające, zawarte**

(N) **przekazanie, przekazywanie, sporządzanie** *banki (…) są obowiązane do sporządzania i przekazywania danych umożliwiających identyfikację współposiadacza (współposiadaczy) rachunku wspólnego, na który zostały przekazane świadczenia lub uposażenia za okres po śmierci świadczeniobiorcy* **udostępnienie danych** ✂ **nośniki danych, zbiór danych** *jeżeli kredytodawca odmówi konsumentowi udzielenia kredytu konsumenckiego na podstawie informacji zawartych w bazie danych lub zbiorze danych kredytodawcy, kredytodawca niezwłocznie przekazuje konsumentowi bezpłatną informację o wynikach tego sprawdzenia oraz wskazuje bazę danych, w której tego sprawdzenia dokonano*

(V) **podać, przekazywać, zawierać dane**

✎ **dane indywidualne, o których mowa w ust. 2, dane określone w art. 1 ust. 1 pkt 1, dane umożliwiające identyfikację, dane ze zbiorów meldunkowych, dane zawarte / znajdujące się w systemie wyliczania** *odpowiedzialność za zgodność danych zawartych w systemie wyliczania z zapisami w księgach rachunkowych banku oraz z rzeczywistym stanem prawnym ponosi zarząd podmiotu objętego systemem gwarantowania* ✂ **informatyczne nośniki danych** *rozliczenia pieniężne przeprowadza się gotówkowo lub bezgotówkowo za pomocą papierowych lub informatycznych nośników danych* ✂ **podać / przekazać konsumentowi dane**

Possible equivalents: data (en), DATO (it)

DECYZJA (pl)

(Adj) **decyzja wydana** ✂ **określony w decyzji** *zarządca komisaryczny wykonuje również zadania określone w decyzji Komisji Nadzoru Finansowego o ustanowieniu zarządcy komisarycznego*

(N) **doręczenie, podejmowanie, podjęcie, wydanie, wykonanie decyzji**

(V) **podejmować, podjąć, wydać decyzję (o)** ✂ **decyzja + dotyczyć, wygasać**

(P) **decyzja o** *w przypadku gdy decyzja o likwidacji kasy została podjęta przez jej członków, likwidacja prowadzona jest zgodnie z zasadami obowiązującymi przy likwidacji spółdzielni* ✂ **decyzja o ustanowieniu, decyzja w przedmiocie** *Komisja Nadzoru Finansowego wydaje decyzję w przedmiocie zezwolenia na utworzenie kasy w terminie 3 miesięcy od daty otrzymania wniosku lub jego uzupełnienia* **decyzja w sprawie** ✂ **w drodze decyzji** *Komisja Nadzoru Finansowego, w drodze decyzji, na wniosek kasy, w uzasadnionych przypadkach może zwolnić ją z obowiązków określonych w ust. 1 lub ograniczyć ich zakres*

(SYNTACTIC) **decyzja Komisji Nadzoru Finansowego, decyzja o której mowa w ust. 1, decyzja o przejęciu kasy, decyzja o przejęciu lub likwidacji, decyzja o przejęciu wybranych praw majątkowych lub wybranych zobowiązań** *w przypadku decyzji o przejęciu wybranych praw majątkowych lub wybranych zobowiązań kasy przez inną kasę przejęcie powinno obejmować wszystkie prawa majątkowe i zobowiązania wobec członka kasy oraz wartość jego prawa do funduszu udziałowego* **decyzja o ustanowieniu zarządcy komisarycznego, decyzja o zawieszeniu działalności, decyzja w przedmiocie sprzeciwu** *Komisja Nadzoru Finansowego doręcza decyzję w przedmiocie sprzeciwu, o którym mowa w art. 25h ust. 1, w terminie 60 dni roboczych od dnia otrzymania zawiadomienia i wszystkich wymaganych informacji i dokumentów*

dzień wydania decyzji ✂ **uchwała lub decyzja; orzeczenie, postanowienie lub decyzja** ✂ **podjąć decyzję o likwidacji, wniesienie skargi nie wstrzymuje wykonania decyzji** ✂ **Kasa, w stosunku do której podjęto decyzję (o)** ✂ **w terminie 7 dni od daty doręczenia decyzji** *od decyzji, o której mowa w ust. 1, rada* *nadzorcza kasy lub Kasy Krajowej może wnieść skargę do sądu administracyjnego w terminie 7 dni od daty doręczenia decyzji*

Possible equivalents: DECISION, RESOLUTION (en), decisione, deliberazione, risoluzione (it)

DEPONENT (pl)

(N) **roszczenia, tożsamość, wierzytelność deponenta** ✂ **interesy, rachunki deponentów** ✂ **lista deponentów** *zarząd komisaryczny banku lub podmiot uprawniony do reprezentacji niezwłocznie, nie później niż w terminie 3 dni roboczych od dnia spełnienia warunku gwarancji, przekazuje Funduszowi listę deponentów* ✂ **identyfikacja deponentów** *podmiot objęty systemem gwarantowania przekazuje Funduszowi na każde jego żądanie dane znajdujące się w systemie wyliczania pozwalające na identyfikację deponentów oraz wysokości środków gwarantowanych należnych poszczególnym deponentom*

(V) **być deponentem** ✂ **być uznanym za deponenta** *osoby korzystające oraz zainteresowane korzystaniem z ich usług nie mogą być uznane za deponenta*

następca prawny deponenta ✂ **ochrona interesów deponentów** *przy wyborze trybu wypłaty środków gwarantowanych Zarząd Funduszu powinien uwzględnić konieczność zapewnienia ochrony interesów deponentów* ✂ **dane pozwalające na identyfikację deponentów** ✂ **środki gwarantowane na rachunkach deponentów, środki gwarantowane należne poszczególnym deponentom** *kasa przekazuje Funduszowi na każde jego żądanie dane znajdujące się w systemie wyliczania pozwalające na identyfikację deponentów oraz wysokości środków gwarantowanych należnych poszczególnym deponentom* ✂ **udostępniać dane dotyczące deponentów**

Possible equivalents: DEPOSITOR (en), depositante (it)

DEPOZYT (pl)

(Adj) **depozyt bankowy** *przepis ust. 1 nie dotyczy zmiany oprocentowania depozytów bankowych istniejących w dniu wejścia w życie ustawy*

(N) **gwarantowanie depozytów** *tej samej karze podlega członek zarządu lub rady banku objętego ustawowym systemem gwarantowania depozytów bankowych, który doprowadza do powstania straty po stronie Funduszu* **oprocentowanie depozytu**

✎ **depozyt papierów wartościowych** *emisja skarbowych papierów wartościowych następuje z dniem zarejestrowania skarbowych papierów wartościowych w depozycie papierów wartościowych* **Krajowy Depozyt Papierów Wartościowych S.A.** *w*

📖 Possible equivalents: DEPOSIT (en), deposito (it)

DŁUŻNIK (pl)

Usually singular

(Adj) **dłużnik zobowiązany (do)** *w tytule wykonawczym należy oznaczyć (...) dłużnika zobowiązanego do zapłaty*

(N) **dłużnik banku** ✂ **majątek, niewypłacalność, siedziba dłużnika** *sprzeciw wraz z uzasadnieniem wnosi się za pośrednictwem banku, o którym mowa w art. 15, w formie pisemnej do sądu rejonowego - sądu gospodarczego, właściwego dla siedziby dłużnika* **zobowiązania dłużnika** ✂ **dłużnik i wierzyciel** *na wniosek dłużnika, który zaprzestał spłacania długu wobec banku lub nie będzie w stanie spłacać długu w przyszłości – bank, z zastrzeżeniem art. 7, 8 i art. 37, może wszcząć bankowe postępowanie ugodowe w celu doprowadzenia do ugody między dłużnikiem i wierzycielami.*

✎ **dłużnik zobowiązany do zapłaty** ✂ **części składowe majątku dłużnika** *w przypadku egzekucji przeciwko kilku osobom lub z kilku części składowych majątku dłużnika można wystawić dalsze tytuły wykonawcze.* ✂ **ogólna kwota zobowiązań dłużnika, wysokość zobowiązań dłużnika wraz z odsetkami i terminami ich płatności** ✂ **dłużnik lub osoba trzecia** *w celu zabezpieczenia wierzytelności banku dłużnik lub osoba trzecia może przenieść określoną kwotę w złotych lub w innej walucie wymienialnej na własność banku.*

📖 Possible equivalents: bankrupt, borrower, DEBTOR, obligor (en), DEBITORE, obbligato (it)

DROGA (pl)

(N) **w drodze decyzji, rozporządzenia** *minister właściwy do spraw instytucji finansowych, po zasięgnięciu opinii Prezesa NBP, określa, w drodze rozporządzenia, sposób, zakres i terminy realizacji obowiązku, o którym mowa w ust. 2a* **w drodze uchwały, umowy, zarządzenia**

określać/ określić	⟹	**w drodze**	⟹	**zarządzenia/ uchwały / rozporządzenia**	⟹	**sposób / szczegółowe warunki i tryb / szczegółowy zakres/ szczegółowe zasady / termin / wysokość**

Possible equivalents: means (en), mezzo (it)

DZIAŁALNOŚĆ (pl)

(Adj) **działalność bankowa, gospodarcza, innowacyjna, kantorowa, transgraniczna** *działalność transgraniczna – wykonywanie przez instytucję kredytową na terytorium Rzeczypospolitej Polskiej lub przez bank krajowy na terytorium państwa goszczącego wszystkich lub niektórych czynności w zakresie wynikającym z udzielonego zezwolenia, bez uczestnictwa oddziału tej instytucji lub banku* ✂ **zamierzona działalność** ✂ **działalność określona (w)** *Kasa Krajowa nie może prowadzić działalności innej niż działalność określona w niniejszej ustawie lub ustawach odrębnych* **działalność polegająca (na), prowadzona, wykonywana** ✂ **prowadzący działalność, związany z działalnością**

(N) **działalność banku, kasy, oddziału** ✂ **koszty, program, rodzaj, zakres działalności** ✂ **podjęcie, prowadzenie, rozpoczęcie, wspieranie, wykonywanie, zaprzestanie, zawieszenie działalności** ✂ **nadzór nad działalnością, sprawozdanie z działalności**

(V) **prowadzić działalność** ✂ **działalność + naruszać** *Komisja Nadzoru Finansowego odmawia wydania zezwolenia na utworzenie kasy, jeżeli 2) zamierzona działalność naruszałaby przepisy prawa*

(P) **działalność na terenie** *bank spółdzielczy prowadzi działalność na terenie powiatu, w którym znajduje się jego siedziba* **działalność w zakresie**

✐ *(NOMINAL)* **część działalności lub cala działalność** *Komisja Nadzoru Bankowego może, na wniosek banku państwowego, wyłączyć część działalności lub całą działalność tego banku (…) z obowiązku spełniania niektórych wymogów i norm* ✂ **działalność instytucji kredytowej, działalność instytucji pieniądza elektronicznego, działalność kasy lub Kasy Krajowej, działalność, o której mowa w art. 1** ✂ **instytucja kredytowa prowadząca działalność na terytorium Rzeczypospolitej Polskiej, unijna dominująca finansowa spółka holdingowa o działalności mieszanej** ✂ **czynności związane z działalnością, normy dopuszczalnego ryzyka w działalności, przepisy regulujące działalność** *sprawowanie nad bankiem nadzoru skonsolidowanego nie wyłącza stosowania odpowiednich przepisów ustawy regulujących działalność banku jako podmiotu podlegającego nadzorowi indywidualnemu* **ryzyko występujące w działalności banku, ryzyko związane z działalnością** ✂ **ustawa z dnia 2 lipca 2004 r. o swobodzie działalności gospodarczej, ustawa z dnia 29 lipca 2005 r. o niektórych formach wspierania działalności innowacyjnej**

✐ *(SYNTACTIC NOMINAL)* **podejmowanie i prowadzenie działalności, podjęcie i zaprzestanie działalności** *banki oraz oddziały i przedstawicielstwa banków zagranicznych w kraju są obowiązane: 1) zawiadomić Komisję Nadzoru Finansowego o podjęciu i zaprzestaniu działalności* **prowadzenie działalności bankowej / gospodarczej, prowadzenie działalności przez instytucje pieniądza elektronicznego, wykonywanie działalności kantorowej** *czynności bezpośrednio związane z wykonywaniem działalności kantorowej mogą być wykonywane tylko przez osoby, które nie zostały skazane prawomocnie za przestępstwa określone w art. 12* **zakres działalności banku, zakres działalności banku, zawieszenie działalności banku / kasy, zgodność działalności z przepisami** ✂ **decyzja o zawieszeniu działalności, zezwolenie na prowadzenie / rozpoczęcie / wykonywanie działalności** ✂ **przepisy o niektórych formach wspierania działalności innowacyjnej**

✐ *(VERBAL)* **sprawować nadzór nad działalnością, udzielić zezwolenia na prowadzenie / wykonywanie działalności, uzyskać zezwolenie na wykonywanie działalności** *państwo członkowskie, w którym dana instytucja kredytowa uzyskała zezwolenie na wykonywanie działalności i na terenie którego ma swoją siedzibę*

🕮 Possible equivalents: ACTIVITY, business, FUNCTION, operation (en), ATTIVITÀ, ESERCIZIO, FUNZIONE, OPERAZIONE (it)

DZIEŃ (pl)

(Adv) **licząc od dnia** *kwota podlegająca zwrotowi płatna jest jednorazowo w ciągu 30 dni, licząc od dnia zatwierdzenia sprawozdania finansowego Kasy Krajowej za rok, w którym zgłoszono żądanie zwrotu*

(Adj) **ostatni dzień** ✂ **dzień roboczy, sprawozdawczy** *fundusz ochrony środków gwarantowanych jest tworzony w ostatnim sprawozdawczym dniu miesiąca, w którym podmiot objęty systemem gwarantowania uzyskał zezwolenie na rozpoczęcie działalności* ✂ **dzień poprzedzający** ✂ **sporządzony na dzień** *sprawozdanie finansowe sporządzone na dzień otwarcia likwidacji*

(N) **dzień dokonania, doręczenia, ogłoszenia, otrzymania, powołania, przejęcia, przekształcenia, spełnienia, umorzenia, wejścia, wydania, zakończenia, zatwierdzenia, zawarcia, zbycia, złożenia** ✂ **dzień miesiąca** ✂ **okres od dnia** *konsument nie ponosi kosztów związanych z odstąpieniem od umowy o kredyt konsumencki, z wyjątkiem odsetek za okres od dnia wypłaty kredytu do dnia spłaty kredytu*

(V) **wygasać z dniem** *poręczenie Skarbu Państwa, o którym mowa w ust. 1, wygasa z dniem 31 grudnia 2010 r.*

(P) **w okresie od dnia** ✂ **po upływie 7 dni, w terminie 7 dni**

✎ *(NOMINAL)* **dzień konsolidacji sprawozdań finansowych** *za zobowiązania banku należącego do grupy bankowej, w przypadku określonym w art. 108 ust. 1 i 2 ustawy – Prawo bankowe, pozostałe banki należące do tej grupy odpowiadają jak poręczyciele, od dnia konsolidacji sprawozdań finansowych* **dzień uzyskania przez Rzeczpospolita Polska członkostwa w Unii Europejskiej, dzień wydania decyzji, dzień zawarcia umowy kredytu preferencyjnego** ✂ **średni kurs ogłaszany przez NBP obowiązujący w dniu** ✂ **obwieszczenia Marszalka Sejmu Rzeczypospolitej Polskiej z dnia 1 stycznia 2015r. w sprawie ogłoszenia jednolitego tekstu ustawy** ✂ **dyrektywa 2000/12/WE z dnia 10 marca 2000 r.; ustawa z dnia 1 stycznia 2015r.**

✎ *(VERBAL)* **wnieść skargę do sądu administracyjnego w terminie 7 dni od daty doręczenia decyzji** ✂ **termin + wynosić 7 dni** *Termin ważności formularza wynosi co najmniej 1 dzień roboczy* ✂ **Ustawa wchodzi w życie po**

upływie 14 dni/ 2 miesięcy od dnia ogłoszenia; Ustawa weszła w życie z dniem 1 stycznia 2015r

✎ **w dniu zawarcia umowy ✂ po upływie 2 lat/miesięcy od dnia, przed dniem wejścia w życie ustawy** *do spraw wszczętych i niezakończonych, w tym wniosków o przyznanie statusu centrum badawczo-rozwojowego złożonych przed dniem wejścia w życie ustawy i nierozpatrzonych, mają zastosowanie przepisy niniejszej ustawy* **w ciągu 7 dni od dnia, w okresie 2 miesięcy od dnia, w terminie nie dłuższym niż 7 dni, w terminie 7 dni po upływie ✂ według stanu na dzień**

nie dłużej niż w terminie/ nie później (jednak) niż w terminie	⟹	**7 dni (roboczych) od dnia / 2 miesięcy od dnia**	⟹	**doręczenia decyzji otrzymania informacji/ kopii / wezwania/ wniosku spełnienia warunku gwarancji wejścia w życie ustawy złożenia wniosku**

📖 Possible equivalents: DATE, DAY (en), DATA, giornata, GIORNO, TERMINE (it)

E

EMISJA (pl)

Always singular

(N) **emisja obligacji** ✂ **data, dzień emisji** *w przypadku gdy termin wykupu listu zastawnego jest dłuższy niż 5 lat od dnia emisji, bank hipoteczny (…) może dokonać umorzenia listów zastawnych przed terminem wykupu, jednak nie wcześniej niż po upływie 5 lat od dnia emisji* ✂ **podstawa, waluta, warunki emisji** *warunki emisji skarbowych papierów wartościowych oraz sposób realizacji wynikających z nich świadczeń określi minister właściwy do spraw instytucji finansowych przez wydanie listu emisyjnego*

(V) **emisja + następować** *list emisyjny zawiera w szczególności (…) cenę zbycia lub sposób jej ustalenia, o ile emisja nie następuje w celu, o którym mowa w art. 3 ust. 1 pkt 2*

✎ **emisja (dłużnych / skarbowych) papierów wartościowych, emisja (hipotecznych) listów zastawnych** ✂ **podstawa prawna emisji** ✂ **środki (pochodzące) z emisji obligacji** ✂ **waluta, w której może następować emisja** *list emisyjny zawiera w szczególności (…) walutę, w której może następować emisja, lub sposób określenia waluty emisji* ✂ **stanowić podstawę emisji** *nie mogą stanowić podstawy emisji hipotecznych listów zastawnych wierzytelności zabezpieczone hipotekami ustanowionymi na nieruchomościach, których eksploatacja zgodnie z przeznaczeniem nie posiada trwałego charakteru*

📖 Possible equivalents: issuance, issue, offering (en), emissione, offerta (it)

F

FINANSE (pl)

Always plural

(Adj) **finanse publiczne** *Bankowy Fundusz Gwarancyjny nie jest państwową osobą prawną i nie jest jednostką sektora finansów publicznych*

(N) **minister finansów** *w uzasadnionych przypadkach Minister Finansów może dokonywać lokat, o których mowa w ust. 1, w dowolnie wybranym banku*

(P) **z zakresu finansów** *RADĘ nadzorczą powołuje się na okres 3 lat spośród osób posiadających odpowiednie kwalifikacje z zakresu finansów*

✎ **minister właściwy do spraw finansów publicznych** *minister właściwy do spraw finansów publicznych udziela, w drodze rozporządzenia, ogólnych zezwoleń dewizowych* **przepisy o finansach publicznych** *obowiązkowe opłaty roczne, o których mowa w ust. 1, dotacje na potrzeby funduszu kas udzielone na wniosek Funduszu z budżetu państwa na zasadach określonych w przepisach o finansach publicznych, oraz dotacje udzielone przez Kasę Krajową zwiększają fundusz kas* **ustawa z dnia 27 sierpnia 2009 r. o finansach publicznych**

Possible equivalents: finance (en), FINANZA (it)

FORMA (pl)

(Adj) **forma pisemna** *umowa sprzedaży wierzytelności powinna być zawarta w formie pisemnej pod rygorem nieważności* **forma prawna** *W przypadku utworzenia banku krajowego, o którym mowa w ust. 1, stosuje się przepisy ustawy z dnia 29*

września 1994 r. o rachunkowości (Dz. U. z 2009 r. Nr 152, poz. 1223, z późn. zm.19) dotyczące zmiany formy prawnej jednostki.

(N) **forma dokumentu** *rezydenci będący osobami fizycznymi mogą przekazywać dane, o których mowa w ust. 1, również w formie dokumentu papierowego według ustalonego wzoru*

✎ **bank w formie spółki akcyjnej** ✂ **przepisy o niektórych formach wspierania działalności innowacyjnej, ustawa z dnia 29 lipca 2005 r. o niektórych formach wspierania działalności innowacyjnej** ✂ **być zawartym w formie pisemnej** ✂ **w formie reprezentatywnego przykładu** *kredytodawca lub pośrednik kredytowy jest zobowiązany przekazać konsumentowi co najmniej (…) rzeczywistą roczną stopę oprocentowania przedstawioną w formie reprezentatywnego przykładu wraz z założeniami przyjętymi do jej obliczenia*

🕮 Possible equivalents: form, mode (en), FORMA (it)

FUNDUSZ (pl)

(Adj) **fundusz rezerwowy, sekurytyzacyjny, stabilizacyjny, statutowy** *fundusze podstawowe banku obejmują: 1) fundusze zasadnicze banku, które stanowią: a) w banku państwowym – fundusz statutowy, fundusz zapasowy i fundusz rezerwowy* **fundusz udziałowy, własny, założycielski, zasobowy** *funduszami własnymi kasy są: 1) fundusz udziałowy – powstający z wpłat udziałów członkowskich; 2) fundusz zasobowy – powstający z wpłat wpisowego wnoszonego przez członków oraz nadwyżki bilansowej* ✂ **fundusze podstawowe, uzupełniające** *minister właściwy do spraw finansów publicznych może udzielić BGK pożyczki ze środków budżetu państwa (…) na zwiększenie funduszy podstawowych lub uzupełniających* ✂ **fundusz tworzony, utworzony**

(N) **fundusz innowacyjności** *fundusz innowacyjności tworzy się z comiesięcznego odpisu wynoszącego nie więcej niż 20 % przychodów uzyskanych przez centrum badawczo-rozwojowe w danym miesiącu* ✂ **Fundusz Pracy** *minister właściwy do spraw pracy przekazuje środki Funduszu Pracy z przeznaczeniem na pomoc państwa w spłacie niektórych kredytów mieszkaniowych udzielonych osobom, które utraciły pracę, na zasadach określonych w odrębnych przepisach* ✂ **dysponent, rada funduszu** *organami Funduszu są: Rada Funduszu i Zarząd Funduszu* **środki, tworzenie, zadania, zarząd** ✂ **pomniejszenie, wysokość, zasilenie, zwiększenie**

funduszu ✂ **suma funduszy** *bank spółdzielczy, który zrzeszył się z bankiem zrzeszającym, jest obowiązany uzyskać zwiększenie sumy funduszy własnych*

(V) **fundusz + obejmować** *fundusz może nabyć i obejmować akcje banku w celu przejęcia lub nabycia przedsiębiorstwa kasy, w przypadku której powstało niebezpieczeństwo niewypłacalności* ✂ **tworzyć fundusz**

(P) **fundusze na poziomie** *bank jest obowiązany utrzymywać: 1) fundusze własne na poziomie nie niższym niż równowartość w złotych kwoty określonej w art. 32 ust. 1*

✎ *(SYNTACITC NOMINAL)* **aktywa stanowiące pokrycie funduszu ochrony środków gwarantowanych, członek zarządu funduszu, dysponent Funduszu Pracy, finansowanie zadań funduszu w zakresie udzielania pomocy podmiotom objętym systemem gwarantowania, jednostki uczestnictwa funduszy rynku pieniężnego** *wolne środki pieniężne funduszu stabilizacyjnego mogą być inwestowane wyłącznie w obligacje i inne papiery wartościowe emitowane, poręczone lub gwarantowane przez Skarb Państwa lub Narodowy Bank Polski, a także w jednostki uczestnictwa funduszy rynku pieniężnego* **komisja/środki funduszu stabilizacyjnego, plan finansowy funduszu, rachunek bankowy funduszu, suma/zwiększenie funduszy własnych, wysokość funduszu ochrony środków gwarantowanych, wysokość funduszy własnych banku, zadania funduszu (w zakresie)** *do zadań Funduszu w zakresie gromadzenia i analizowania informacji o kasach należy w szczególności opracowywanie analiz i prognoz dotyczących sektora kas*

✎ *(NOMINAL)* **fundusz kas do wykorzystania** *dla celów ewidencyjnych fundusz kas dzieli się na fundusz kas do wykorzystania i fundusz kas wykorzystany* **Fundusz Kredytu Technologicznego** *tworzy się państwowy fundusz celowy w formie rachunku bankowego o nazwie 'Fundusz Kredytu Technologicznego', zwany dalej 'Funduszem'* **fundusz ochrony środków gwarantowanych, fundusz oszczędnościowo-pożyczkowy, fundusz własny tworzony w celu zapewnienia środków na finansowanie zadań, fundusze podstawowe/ uzupełniające / własne banku, fundusze własne kasy** ✂ **Bankowy Fundusz Gwarancyjny** *Bankowy Fundusz Gwarancyjny nie jest państwową osobą prawną i nie jest jednostką sektora finansów publicznych* ✂ **ustawa z dnia 14 grudnia 1994 r. o Bankowym Funduszu Gwarancyjnym, ustawa z dnia 27 maja 2004 r. o funduszach inwestycyjnych**

✎ *(VERBAL)* **przekazywać funduszowi informacje, przekroczyć 10 % funduszy własnych** ✂ **funduszowi przysługuje roszczenie** *z tytułu udzielenia wsparcia, o którym mowa w art. 20g ust. 2 pkt 3 i 4, Funduszowi przysługuje roszczenie w stosunku do kasy, wobec której Komisja Nadzoru Finansowego podjęła decyzję o przejęciu wybranych praw majątkowych* **środki funduszu przeznacza się (na)** ✂ **fundusz dokonuje wypłat** *fundusz dokonuje wypłat deponentom ze środków, o których mowa w art. 38r*

🕮 Possible equivalents: fund (en), fondo (it)

G

GWARANCJA (pl)

(Adj) **gwarancja bankowa, rekapitalizacyjna** *Fundusz może udzielić gwarancji rekapitalizacyjnej wyłącznie na wniosek, o którym mowa w art. 6 ust. 2a ustawy z dnia 12 lutego 2010 r. o rekapitalizacji niektórych instytucji finansowych* ✂ **udzielona gwarancja** ✂ **gwarancje udzielane / udzielone (przez)**

(N) **poręczenie i/ lub gwarancja** ✂ **gwarancja spłaty** ✂ **udzielanie, udzielenie gwarancji** *udzielenie kredytu, pożyczki pieniężnej, gwarancji lub poręczenia może być uwarunkowane w statucie banku koniecznością zadeklarowania i wpłacenia przez kredytobiorcę, pożyczkobiorcę, osobę, której ma być udzielone poręczenie lub gwarancja, co najmniej jednego udziału w tym banku*

(V) **udzielać, udzielić gwarancji** ✂ **gwarancja jest udzielana / udzielona**

✎ *(NOMINAL)* **gwarancja dla Narodowego Banku Polskiego, gwarancja Skarbu Państwa, gwarancja udzielana / udzielona pod warunkiem przeznaczenia kredytu (na), gwarancja za instytucję finansową** *Skarb Państwa może udzielić gwarancji spłaty kredytów oraz linii kredytowych, zwanej dalej 'gwarancją za instytucję finansową'* ✂ **dzień spełnienia warunku gwarancji** *środki gwarantowane – środki pieniężne zgromadzone w banku przez deponenta na rachunkach imiennych oraz jego należności wynikające z innych czynności bankowych, w walucie polskiej lub walutach obcych, według stanu na dzień spełnienia warunku gwarancji* **roszczenia z tytułu gwarancji**

✎ *(THEMATIC NOMINAL)* **gwarancje objęte poręczeniem** ✂ **poręczenia i gwarancje, o których mowa w ust. 1, poręczenia i gwarancje udzielane przez Bank Gospodarstwa Krajowego / przez Skarb Państwa, udzielone poręczenie i/**

lub gwarancja ✂ kredyty, pożyczki pieniężne, gwarancje bankowe i poręczenia *suma kredytów, pożyczek pieniężnych, gwarancji bankowych i poręczeń, o których mowa w ust. 1 i 3, nie może przekroczyć: 1) w banku w formie spółki akcyjnej i w banku państwowym – 10 % sumy funduszy podstawowych* **udzielenie kredytu, pożyczki pieniężnej, gwarancji bankowej lub poręczenia ✂ kwota poręczenia i/lub gwarancji, udzielanie poręczeń i gwarancji, udzielenie poręczenia lub gwarancji, umowa poręczenia lub gwarancji, zobowiązanie objęte poręczeniem lub gwarancją** *poręczenie lub gwarancja są udzielane do wysokości 60 % pozostającej do spłaty kwoty zobowiązania objętego poręczeniem lub gwarancją wraz z 60 % należnych odsetek od tej kwoty i innych kosztów bezpośrednio związanych z tym zobowiązaniem* ✂ **ustawa z dnia 8 maja 1997 r. o poręczeniach i gwarancjach udzielanych przez Skarb Państwa oraz niektóre osoby prawne**

✎ *(PREPOSITIONAL)* **w przypadku którego / której nastąpiło spełnienie warunku gwarancji, w przypadku spełnienia warunku gwarancji, z tytułu poręczeń i gwarancji udzielanych przez Skarb Państwa, z tytułu udzielonych poręczeń i gwarancji** *kwota, o której mowa w ust. 1, nie obejmuje poręczeń i gwarancji Skarbu Państwa udzielonych na wykonanie zobowiązań objętych już poręczeniem lub gwarancją Skarbu Państwa, w zakresie, w jakim nie powoduje to zwiększenia zobowiązań Skarbu Państwa z tytułu udzielonych poręczeń i gwarancji*

✎ *(VERBAL)* **udzielać poręczenia i/lub gwarancji ✂ nastąpiło spełnienie warunku gwarancji** *z tytułu wypłat środków gwarantowanych Funduszowi przysługuje roszczenie do podmiotu objętego obowiązkowym systemem gwarantowania, co do którego nastąpiło spełnienie warunku gwarancji o zapłatę kwot odpowiadających wartości sumy środków gwarantowanych, z wyłączeniem środków, o których mowa w art. 16a*

📖 Possible equivalents: guarantee, guaranty, warranty (en), garanzia, guarentigia (it)

GWARANTOWANIE (pl)

Always singular

(N) **system gwarantowania**

✎ **obowiązkowy system gwarantowania środków pieniężnych, ustawowy system gwarantowania** *wierzytelność, powstająca w związku z wykonywaniem* *czynności bankowych, nie będzie chroniona przez ustawowy system gwarantowania* ✂ **funkcjonowanie systemu gwarantowania środków pieniężnych, uczestnictwo w systemie gwarantowania** *informacje o uczestnictwie w systemie gwarantowania nie mogą być wykorzystywane w celach reklamowych i powinny być ograniczone wyłącznie do informacji określonych w ust. 1a i 1b* ✂ **podmiot objęty obowiązkowym systemem gwarantowania, obowiązkowe wpłaty podmiotów objętych systemem gwarantowania** *środki pochodzące z obowiązkowych wpłat podmiotów objętych systemem gwarantowania przechodzą na własność Funduszu* **udzielanie pomocy podmiotom objętym systemem gwarantowania**

📖 Possible equivalents: guarantee, insurance, underwriting (en), assicurazione, garanzia (it)

H

HIPOTEKA (pl)

Usually singular

(Adj) **hipoteka ustanowiona (na)** *okres pomocy przyznanej kredytobiorcom na spłatę kredytu mieszkaniowego, zabezpieczonego hipoteką ustanowioną na tym samym przedmiocie kredytowania, nie może przekroczyć 12 miesięcy* **hipoteka zabezpieczająca** ✂ **niezabezpieczony, zabezpieczony hipoteką**

(N) **ustanowienie, wpis hipoteki** *dokumenty, o których mowa w ust. 1, są podstawą wpisu hipoteki do księgi wieczystej nieruchomości stanowiącej własność dłużnika banku lub innej osoby ustanawiającej hipotekę na rzecz banku w celu zabezpieczenia wierzytelności dłużnika banku* ✂ **zabezpieczenie hipoteką** *bank hipoteczny przed zabezpieczeniem hipoteką wierzytelności z tytułu udzielonego kredytu może oddać do dyspozycji kredytobiorcy określoną w umowie kredytowej kwotę środków pieniężnych* ✂ **zastaw lub hipoteka**

✎ **hipoteka zabezpieczająca wierzytelność** *w przypadku ustanowienia hipoteki zabezpieczającej wierzytelność banku hipotecznego wpisaną do rejestru zabezpieczenia hipotecznych listów zastawnych, należy uczynić o tym wpis w księdze wieczystej* **kredyt niezabezpieczony hipoteką, wierzytelności zabezpieczone (zastawem lub) hipoteką** ✂ **umowa o kredyt zabezpieczony hipoteką** *umowa o kredyt zabezpieczony hipoteką powinna zawierać co najmniej dane określone w art. 69 ust. 2 ustawy z dnia 29 sierpnia 1997 r. – Prawo bankowe*

📖 Possible equivalents: mortgage (en), IPOTECA (it)

I

INFORMACJA (pl)

(Adj) **informacja niejawna** ✂ **informacje niezbędne (do), sprawozdawcze** *kasa przekazuje Komisji Nadzoru Finansowego informacje sprawozdawcze obejmujące w szczególności dane o 1) strukturze organizacyjnej kasy, liczbie zatrudnionych, liczbie członków oraz liczbie wkładów członkowskich zadeklarowanych i wkładów członkowskich wpłaconych* ✂ **wszelkie informacje** ✂ **informacja chroniona** ✂ **informacje dotyczące, uzyskane** ✂ **wymagane informacje**

(N) **nośniki informacji** *na żądanie inspektora wykonującego czynności kontrolne kasa oraz Kasa Krajowa są obowiązane sporządzić kopie dokumentów i nośników informacji oraz opartych na tych dokumentach opracowań, zestawień i obliczeń* **zakres informacji** ✂ **gromadzenie, przekazanie, przekazywanie, udostępnienie, udzielenie, wymiana informacji** *osoby, o których mowa w art. 5 i art. 8 ust. 1 mogą dokonywać wzajemnej wymiany informacji, w tym informacji chronionych na podstawie odrębnych ustaw, niezbędnych do prawidłowej realizacji celów Komitetu* ✂ **informacje i/lub dokumenty**

(V) **przekazywać (sobie) informacje, udzielać informacji**

(P) **informacje o warunkach** *w treści bankowego papieru wartościowego, jak również w podanej przez emitenta do publicznej wiadomości informacji o warunkach emisji, nie mogą być zamieszczane porównania z warunkami emisji papierów wartościowych innych emitentów* **informacje w zakresie** *w celu dokonania oceny prawidłowości funkcjonowania systemu pod względem spełniania kryteriów, o których mowa w ust. 2, podmiot prowadzący system jest obowiązany do przedstawienia, na żądanie organu wydającego zgodę na prowadzenie tego systemu, niezbędnych informacji w zakresie objętym art. 17 ust. 2*

✏ **informacje o możliwości żądania w dowolnym momencie spłaty pełnej kwoty kredytu przez konsumenta** *kredytodawca lub pośrednik kredytowy przed zawarciem umowy o kredyt w rachunku oszczędnościowo-rozliczeniowym, który jest spłacany przez konsumenta na żądanie jest zobowiązany podać konsumentowi, na trwałym nośniku, dane, o których mowa w ust. 2, oraz informację o możliwości żądania w dowolnym momencie spłaty pełnej kwoty kredytu przez konsumenta* **informacje o opłatach stosowanych w czasie obowiązywania umowy oraz warunki ich zmiany, informacje o prawie konsumenta (do)** *kredytodawca lub pośrednik kredytowy przed zawarciem umowy o kredyt konsumencki jest zobowiązany podać konsumentowi, na trwałym nośniku 15) informację o prawie konsumenta do odstąpienia od umowy* **informacje stanowiące tajemnicę bankową ✂ przepisy o ochronie informacji niejawnych ✂ sposób, w jaki podawane są informacje o świadczonych usługach ✂ udzielenie informacji objętych tajemnicą bankową ✂ dokumenty i/lub inne nośniki informacji ✂ informacja + mieć charakter opcjonalny ✂ do/ od dnia otrzymania informacji**

📖 **Possible equivalents**: INFORMATION (en), COMUNICAZIONE, INFORMAZIONE (it)

INSTYTUCJA (pl)

(Adj) **instytucja finansowa, kredytowa, płatnicza ✂ instytucja dominująca** *w celu dokonania uzgodnienia, o którym mowa w ust. 8, właściwe władze nadzorcze mogą zasięgnąć opinii unijnej instytucji dominującej* **instytucja kredytująca** *pomoc polega na przekazywaniu przez Bank Gospodarstwa Krajowego instytucji kredytującej kwoty środków pieniężnych określonej w decyzji, o której mowa w art. 6 ust. 1, z przeznaczeniem na spłatę zobowiązań uprawnionego z tytułu kredytu mieszkaniowego, przez okres nie dłuższy niż 12 miesięcy* **instytucja upoważniona (do) ✂ instytucje utworzone** *banki, inne instytucje ustawowo upoważnione do udzielania kredytów oraz instytucje utworzone na mocy art. 105 ust. 4 mogą przetwarzać i wzajemnie udostępniać informacje objęte tajemnicą bankową, w przypadkach 1) uzasadnionych podejrzeń, o których mowa w art. 106a ust. 3; 2) przestepstw dokonywanych na szkode bankow, instytucji kredytowych, oraz instytucji finansowych*

(N) **oddział instytucji**

✎ **instytucja kredytowa lub instytucja finansowa, INSTYTUCJA PIENIĄDZA ELEKTRONICZNEGO ✂ instytucja kredytowa działająca na podstawie zezwolenia udzielonego w państwie** *podmiot dominujący w holdingu finansowym w państwie członkowskim – podmiot dominujący w holdingu finansowym lub hybrydowym, który nie jest podmiotem zależnym w stosunku do instytucji kredytowej działającej na podstawie zezwolenia udzielonego w tym samym państwie* **instytucja kredytowa prowadząca działalność na terytorium Rzeczypospolitej Polskiej (poprzez), instytucja ustawowo upoważniona do udzielania kredytów, międzynarodowa instytucja finansowa, zewnętrzne instytucje oceny wiarygodności kredytowej ✂ fundusze własne instytucji, minister właściwy do spraw instytucji finansowych, oddział instytucji kredytowej, podmiot zależny w stosunku do instytucji kredytowej ✂ bank krajowy, bank zagraniczny lub instytucja kredytowa**

📖 Possible equivalents: institute, INSTITUTION, BODY (en), agenzia, ENTE, ISTITUTO, istituzione (it)

INSTYTUCJA PIENIĄDZA ELEKTRONICZNEGO (pl)

(Adj) **krajowa instytucja pieniądza elektronicznego** *obowiązek dokonywania rozliczeń zgodnie z ust. 1 nie dotyczy przypadków, w których stroną rozliczenia jest uprawniony bank, krajowa instytucja płatnicza, oddział unijnej instytucji płatniczej, krajowa instytucja pieniądza elektronicznego lub oddział unijnej instytucji pieniądza elektronicznego* **zagraniczna instytucja pieniądza elektronicznego**

(N) **działalność instytucji pieniądza elektronicznego** p*rzedstawiony przez założycieli plan działalności instytucji pieniądza elektronicznego na okres co najmniej 3 lat powinien wskazywać, ze instytucja ta będzie w stanie wywiązywać się ze swoich zobowiązań wobec klientów* **klient instytucji pieniądza elektronicznego**

(V) **instytucja pieniądza elektronicznego jest obowiązana** *w przypadku niespełnienia wymogów, o których mowa w ust. 1, instytucja pieniądza elektronicznego obowiązana jest niezwłocznie powiadomić o tym KNF*

✎ **oddział zagranicznej instytucji pieniądza elektronicznego** *instytucja pieniądza elektronicznego i oddział zagranicznej instytucji pieniądza elektronicznego mogą przetwarzać dane informatyczne za granica na podstawie zezwolenia KNF*

fundusze własne instytucji pieniądza elektronicznego ✂ ochrona interesów klientów instytucji pieniądza elektronicznego ✂ prowadzenie działalności przez instytucję pieniądza elektronicznego *zezwolenie na utworzenie i prowadzenie działalności przez instytucję pieniądza elektronicznego może ustalać warunki, na jakich ono obowiązuje*

🕮 Possible equivalents: electronic money institution (en), istituto di moneta elettronica (it)

K

KASA (pl)

(Adj) **kasa mieszkaniowa** *w rozumieniu ustawy określenie 'kasa mieszkaniowa' oznacza finansowo wyodrębnioną działalność banków polegającą na prowadzeniu imiennych rachunków oszczędnościowo-kredytowych i udzielaniu kredytów kontraktowych* ✂ **kasa przejmowana**

(N) **aktywa, członek, działalność, likwidacja, przejęcie, statut kasy** *statut kasy, oprócz spraw określonych w art. 5 § 1 ustawy z dnia 16 września 1982 r. – Prawo spółdzielcze, powinien określać w szczególności 1) zasady funkcjonowania kontroli wewnętrznej* **upadłość, zarząd kasy, zarządzanie kasą** ✂ **restrukturyzacja, fundusz kas** ✂ **kasa w likwidacji**

(V) **zobowiązać kasę (do)** *w przypadku gdy kwota udzielonych kredytów płynnościowych, pomniejszona o wartość środków, o których mowa w art. 38 ust. 12, przekracza 60 % środków, o których mowa w art. 38 ust. 3 pkt 2, Kasa Krajowa może zobowiązać kasy do przeznaczenia dodatkowych środków na rezerwę płynną, określając jednocześnie ich wysokość* ✂ **kasa jest obowiązana**

✎ *(SYNTACTIC NOMINAL)* **badanie sprawozdań finansowych kasy, fundusz kas do wykorzystania** *dla celów ewidencyjnych fundusz kas dzieli się na fundusz kas do wykorzystania i fundusz kas wykorzystany* **fundusz własny kasy, księgi rachunkowe kasy, ogłoszenie upadłości kasy, organ kasy, rada nadzorcza kasy, zaangażowanie kapitałowe kasy, zawieszenie działalności kasy** ✂ **członek zarządu kasy lub Kasy Krajowej, działalność Kasy Krajowej, statut Kasy Krajowej** ✂ **decyzja o przejęciu kasy albo przejęciu wybranych praw majątkowych lub wybranych zobowiązań kasy, rezerwa obowiązkowa spółdzielczych kas oszczędnościowo-kredytowych**

✎ **kasa albo/lub bank krajowy przejmujący** *kasa albo bank krajowy przejmujący złoży do właściwego rejestru sądowego wniosek o wykreślenie z rejestru przejmowanej kasy* **kasa przejmowana lub kasa w likwidacji, spółdzielcza kasa oszczędnościowo-kredytowa lub/oraz Krajowa Spółdzielcza Kasa Oszczędnościowo-Kredytowa ✂ ostrożne i stabilne zarządzanie kasą, środki gromadzone w kasie, wykonywanie czynności kontrolnych w kasach ✂ bank prowadzący kasę mieszkaniową ✂ kasa, w stosunku do której podjęto decyzję** *zarządca komisaryczny kasy, w stosunku do której podjęto decyzję o przejęciu wybranych praw majątkowych lub wybranych zobowiązań, zgłosi do właściwego rejestru sądowego przejęcie wybranych praw majątkowych lub wybranych zobowiązań wraz ze sprawozdaniem finansowym zbadanym przez podmiot uprawniony do badania sprawozdań finansowych* ✂ **ustawa z dnia 5 listopada 2009 r. o spółdzielczych kasach oszczędnościowo kredytowych**

📖 Possible equivalents: association, credit union, fund, SOCIETY (en), cassa, cooperativa, SOCIETÀ (it)

KLIENT (pl)

Usually plural

(N) **klient banku** *kto, będąc obowiązany do podania uprawnionym organom informacji dotyczących banku i klientów banku w zakresie ustalonym w ustawie, podaje nieprawdziwe lub zataja prawdziwe dane, podlega grzywnie i karze pozbawienia wolności do lat 3* **klient instytucji, oddziału ✂ interes klienta** *Komisja Nadzoru Finansowego odmawia wydania zezwolenia, o którym mowa w ust. 1, jeżeli połączenie prowadziłoby do naruszenia przepisów prawa, interesów klientów banku biorącego udział w połączeniu*

✎ **klient instytucji pieniądza elektronicznego ✂ ochrona / naruszenie / zagrożenie interesu klienta, szkody wyrządzone klientom** *odpowiedzialności banku za szkody wyrządzone klientom wskutek niewykonania lub nienależytego wykonania umowy, o której mowa w art. 6a ust. 1 i 7, nie można wyłączyć ani ograniczyć.*✂ **naruszać interes klienta, działać na zlecenie klienta**

📖 Possible equivalents: CLIENT, customer (en), CLIENTE (it)

KOMISJA NADZORU FINANSOWEGO (pl)

Always singular

(N) **decyzja Komisji Nadzoru Finansowego, Przewodniczący Komisji Nadzoru Finansowego, Urząd Komisji Nadzoru Finansowego** *czynności kontrolne podejmowane w kasach oraz w Kasie Krajowej przez pracowników Urzędu Komisji Nadzoru Finansowego, zwanych dalej 'inspektorami', są wykonywane po okazaniu upoważnienia wydanego przez Przewodniczącego Komisji Nadzoru Finansowego oraz legitymacji służbowej* **zgoda Komisji Nadzoru Finansowego** *każda zmiana umowy wymaga zgody Komisji Nadzoru Finansowego*

(V) **informować, zawiadamiać, zawiadomić Komisję Nadzoru Finansowego (o)** ✂ **Komisja Nadzoru Finansowego + informować (o), nałożyć, odmawiać, odmówić, określić** *Komisja Nadzoru Finansowego może określić, w drodze uchwały, szczegółowe zasady dotyczące wyposażenia banków hipotecznych w kapitał założycielski* **Komisja Nadzoru Finansowego + powiadamiać, powiadomić, przekazać, przekazywać, sprawować** *nadzór nad prawidłowością funkcjonowania systemów wyliczania sprawuje Komisja Nadzoru Finansowego* **Komisja Nadzoru Finansowego + ustalać, wzywać, zobowiązać (do), żądać**

(P) **na żądanie Komisji Nadzoru Finansowego** *Kasa Krajowa sporządza i przekazuje na żądanie Komisji Nadzoru Finansowego plan czynności kontrolnych w kasach na dany rok* **za zgodą Komisji Nadzoru Finansowego**

✎ **uzyskanie zgody Komisji Nadzoru Finansowego** *zarządca komisaryczny działa nie dłużej niż do chwili powołania nowego zarządu kasy lub Kasy Krajowej oraz uzyskania zgody Komisji Nadzoru Finansowego na powołanie prezesa zarządu* ✂ **po uzyskaniu zezwolenia Komisji Nadzoru Finansowego, po zasięgnięciu opinii Komisji Nadzoru Finansowego, po zasięgnięciu opinii Prezesa Narodowego Banku Polskiego i Przewodniczącego Komisji Nadzoru Finansowego**

✎ *(VERBAL)* **być obowiązanym niezwłocznie powiadomić Komisję Nadzoru Finansowego, być obowiązanym zawiadomić Komisję Nadzoru Finansowego, następować za zgodą Komisji Nadzoru Finansowego** *powołanie prezesa zarządu oraz jednego członka zarządu następuje za zgodą Komisji Nadzoru Finansowego* **niezwłocznie zawiadomić Komisję Nadzoru Finansowego, składać Komisji Nadzoru Finansowego sprawozdanie, wymagać zezwolenia Komisji Nadzoru Finansowego** ✂ **Komisja Nadzoru Finansowego + odmawiać wydania**

zezwolenia / wyrażenia zgody, określać zasady, powiadamiać właściwe władze nadzorcze *w przypadku gdy instytucja finansowa przestanie spełniać warunki, o których mowa w ust. 1, Komisja Nadzoru Finansowego powiadamia o tym właściwe władze nadzorcze* ✂ **Komisja Nadzoru Finansowego + podejmować / podjąć / wydać / wydawać decyzję (o)**

Possible equivalents: Financial Supervision Authority (en), Commissione di Vigilanza Finanziaria (it)

KONSUMENT (pl)

Usually singual

(N) **prawo konsumenta (do)** *informacja o prawie konsumenta do odstąpienia od umowy*

całkowita kwota do zapłaty przez konsumenta, informacje o prawie konsumenta (do), spłata pełnej kwoty kredytu przez konsumenta ✂ **koszty, które konsument jest zobowiązany ponieść, kredyt w rachunku oszczędnościowo-rozliczeniowym, który jest spłacany przez konsumenta** ✂ **być zobowiązanym podać konsumentowi dane** ✂ **konsument + być w zwłoce** *umowa o kredyt konsumencki przewidująca odroczenie płatności lub zmianę sposobu spłaty w przypadku gdy konsument jest w zwłoce w związku ze spłatą zadłużenia wynikającego z umowy o kredyt, powinna zawierać co najmniej 1) dane określone w art. 30* **konsument + mieć prawo (do), pośrednik kredytowy + przekazywać konsumentowi dane**

Possible equivalents: consumer (en), CONSUMATORE (it)

KONTO (pl)

Usually plural

(Adj) **indywidualne konto** ✂ **konto emerytalne** *rezerwę obowiązkową banków stanowi wyrażona w złotych część (…) innych środków przyjętych przez bank podlegających zwrotowi, z wyjątkiem (…) środków pozyskanych na podstawie umów o prowadzenie indywidualnych kont emerytalnych oraz indywidualnych kont zabezpieczenia emerytalnego*

(N) **prowadzenie konta**

konto depozytowe papierów wartościowych ✂ **przepisy o indywidualnych kontach emerytalnych oraz indywidualnych kontach zabezpieczenia emerytalnego** *o w rozumieniu przepisów o indywidualnych kontach emerytalnych oraz indywidualnych kontach zabezpieczenia emerytalnego* **umowy o prowadzenie indywidualnych kont emerytalnych**

Possible equivalents: ACCOUNT (en), CONTO (it)

KONTROLA (it)

Usually singular

(Adj) **kontrola skarbowa** *zakres oraz zasady udzielania informacji przez kasy organom podatkowym, Generalnemu Inspektorowi Informacji Finansowej oraz organom kontroli skarbowej regulują odrębne przepisy* **kontrola wewnętrzna** *celem systemu kontroli wewnętrznej jest wspomaganie procesów decyzyjnych przyczyniające się do zapewnienia 1) skuteczności i efektywności działania banku* ✂ **bieżąca kontrola**

(N) **kontrola prawidłowości** *Funduszowi przysługuje prawo kontroli prawidłowości danych zawartych w systemach wyliczania* ✂ **przeprowadzenie kontroli**

(V) **sprawować kontrolę** *rada nadzorcza wybierana spośród pełnomocników reprezentujących kasy na walnym zgromadzeniu Kasy Krajowej sprawuje kontrolę i nadzór nad działalnością Kasy Krajowej*

(P) **kontrola nad** *Rada Funduszu sprawuje kontrolę i nadzór nad działalnością Funduszu*

system kontroli wewnętrznej *system kontroli wewnętrznej obejmuje 1) mechanizmy kontroli ryzyka; 2) badanie zgodności działania banku z przepisami prawa i regulacjami wewnętrznymi; 3) audyt wewnętrzny* ✂ **Najwyższa Izba Kontroli** ✂ **Funduszowi przysługuje prawo kontroli** *Funduszowi przysługuje prawo kontroli otrzymanych danych, w tym kontroli w siedzibie kasy* ✂ **kontrola, o której mowa w ust. 1**

Possible equivalents: audit, control, inspection (en), CONTROLLO, ispezione, REVISIONE, VIGILANZA (it)

KOSZT (pl)

(Adj) **koszty związane (z)** *koszty związane z wykonywaniem funkcji kuratora obciążają koszty działalności kasy lub Kasy Krajowej*

(N) **koszt badania, kredytu ✂ koszty budowy, czynności** *koszty czynności związanych z przygotowaniem i dokonaniem wypłat środków gwarantowanych obciążają kasę, w przypadku której nastąpiło spełnienie warunku gwarancji* **koszty działalności, finansowania** *Minister właściwy do spraw finansów publicznych, w porozumieniu z ministrem właściwym do spraw gospodarki, określi, w drodze rozporządzenia, sposób obliczania kosztów finansowania i przyjmowania rynkowej stawki oprocentowania krótkoterminowego dla poszczególnych walut* **koszty realizacji** *źródłem finansowania pomocy oraz kosztów jej realizacji jest Fundusz Pracy* **koszty usług ✂ pokrycie kosztów**

(V) **ponosić koszt**

całkowity koszt kredytu, koszt budowy domu jednorodzinnego / lokalu mieszkalnego, ✂ (inne) koszty bezpośrednio związane (z) *poręczenie lub gwarancja mogą być także udzielane pod warunkiem przeznaczenia objętego nimi kredytu na 4) spłatę, objętego już poręczeniem lub gwarancją Skarbu Państwa, zobowiązania wraz z odsetkami i innymi kosztami bezpośrednio związanymi z tym zobowiązaniem* **koszty, które konsument jest zobowiązany ponieść, koszty związane z kredytem ✂ umowa w sprawie partycypacji w kosztach budowy lokalu ✂ ponosić koszt badania** *jeżeli w wyniku badania zleconego przez Komisję Nadzoru Finansowego stwierdzono nieprawidłowości w kasie albo w Kasie Krajowej, koszty badania ponosi odpowiednio kasa albo Kasa Krajowa* **✂ koszty, o których mowa w ust. 7**

Possible equivalents: charge, cost, expense, rate (en), costo, SPESA (it)

KREDYT (pl)

(Adj) **kredyt eksportowy, indeksowany, konsumencki, krótkoterminowy, mieszkaniowy, odnawialny, płynnościowy, preferencyjny, refinansowy** *NBP może udzielać bankom kredytu refinansowego w złotych w celu uzupełnienia ich zasobów pieniężnych* **kredyt studencki, technologiczny** *kredyt technologiczny – kredyt udzielany przedsiębiorcy przez bank kredytujący na realizację inwestycji technologicznej, który jest częściowo spłacany ze środków Funduszu Kredytu Technologicznego w formie premii technologicznej, do wysokości i na warunkach określonych w ustawie* ✂ **udzielane kredyty** ✂ **kredyt spłacany, udzielony, wiązany, zaciągnięty**

(N) **koszt, kwota, oprocentowanie, rata, umowa kredytu** ✂ **SPŁATA KREDYTU, UMOWA O KREDYT** ✂ **pożyczka lub kredyt, pożyczki i kredyty** ✂ **przeznaczenie kredytu (na)** *poręczenia i gwarancje udzielane pod warunkiem przeznaczenia kredytu lub środków z emisji obligacji na cele, o których mowa w art. 7 ust. 2 pkt 2 i 5, oraz poręczenia, o których mowa w art. 23 ust. 1, są wolne od opłaty prowizyjnej* **udzielanie / udzielenie kredytu**

(V) **udzielać, udzielić kredytu, zwracać kredyt** *w przypadku naruszenia przez kredytodawcę art. 29 ust. 1 (…), konsument, po złożeniu kredytodawcy pisemnego oświadczenia, zwraca kredyt bez odsetek i innych kosztów kredytu należnych kredytodawcy w terminie i w sposób ustalony w umowie*

(P) **kredyt na cele** ✂ **przy wykorzystaniu kredytu** *lokale mieszkalne wybudowane przy wykorzystaniu kredytu, o którym mowa w art. 15a ust. 1, nie mogą być, pod rygorem nieważności, wyodrębnione na własność, a także nie może być do nich ustanowione spółdzielcze własnościowe prawo do lokalu*

(SYNTACTIC NOMINAL) **bank lub inna instytucja ustawowo upoważniona do udzielania kredytów, bank udzielający kredytu, całkowita kwota kredytu, całkowity koszt kredytu, dopłaty ze środków budżetu państwa do oprocentowania kredytów, dzień zawarcia umowy kredytu preferencyjnego, formularz informacyjny dotyczący kredytu, kwota kredytu preferencyjnego, poręczenie i / lub gwarancja udzielane pod warunkiem przeznaczenia kredytu (na), pozostająca do spłaty kwota kredytu, promesa kredytu technologicznego** *w terminie 60 dni od dnia złożenia wniosku, o którym mowa w ust. 1, bank kredytujący zawiera z przedsiębiorcą warunkową umowę kredytu technologicznego*

albo przyznaje promesę kredytu technologicznego **przejściowe wykupienie odsetek od kredytu** *pomoc państwa w spłacie kredytów mieszkaniowych, o których mowa w art. 1 ust. 2, polega na 2) przejściowym wykupieniu ze środków budżetu państwa odsetek od kredytów mieszkaniowych* **stopa procentowa kredytu eksportowego, udzielanie / udzielenie kredytu technologicznego / kredytów i pożyczek pieniężnych, wysokość stopy oprocentowania kredytu ✂ umowa kredytu mieszkaniowego, umowa ubezpieczenia kredytu eksportowego, warunkowa umowa kredytu technologicznego ✂ Fundusz Kredytu Technologicznego**

✎ **kredyt, pożyczka pieniężna, gwarancja (bankowa) i/lub poręczenie** *Udzielenie kredytu, pożyczki pieniężnej, gwarancji lub poręczenia może być uwarunkowane w statucie banku koniecznością zadeklarowania i wpłacenia przez kredytobiorcę, pożyczkobiorcę, osobę, której ma być udzielone poręczenie lub gwarancja, co najmniej jednego udziału w tym banku* **kredyt studencki i/lub pożyczka studencka ✂ kredyt niezabezpieczony hipoteką, kredyt o stałej stopie procentowej, kredyt udzielony przez Bank Gospodarstwa Krajowego, kredyt w rachunku oszczędnościowo-rozliczeniowym ✂ realizacja inwestycji technologicznej finansowanej kredytem technologicznym, ✂ ustawa z dnia 12 maja 2011 r. o kredycie konsumenckim ✂ kredyt (preferencyjny) + zostać udzielonym** *kredytobiorca może spłacić kredyt o stałej stopie procentowej przed upływem okresu, na jaki ten kredyt został udzielony, jeżeli 1) łączna kwota nadwyżek, o których mowa w art. 8 ust. 3, przekroczy łączną kwotę zastosowanych dopłat* **konsument + zwracać kredyt**

📖 Possible equivalents: credit, LOAN (en), CREDITO, MUTUO, prestito (it)

KREDYTOBIORCA (pl)

Usually singular

(Adj) **docelowy kredytobiorca** *docelowy kredytobiorca ubiegający się o kredyt preferencyjny równocześnie z zawarciem umowy kredytu preferencyjnego składa pisemne oświadczenie o spełnieniu warunków, o których mowa w ust. 1*

(N) **zadłużenie kredytobiorcy** *zadłużenie kredytobiorcy wobec Skarbu Państwa, z tytułu wykonania umów poręczenia, podlega oprocentowaniu, z zastrzeżeniem ust. 3* ✂ **pożyczkobiorca lub kredytobiorca** *wysokość raty spłat kredytu studenckiego*

lub pożyczki studenckiej nie może przekroczyć 20 % miesięcznego dochodu pożyczkobiorcy lub kredytobiorcy

(V) **kredytobiorca + być obowiązanym** *kredytobiorca jest obowiązany umożliwić podejmowanie przez bank czynności związanych z oceną sytuacji finansowej i gospodarczej oraz kontrolę wykorzystania i spłaty kredytu*

(P) **na wniosek kredytobiorcy** *instytucja kredytującą wydaje na wniosek kredytobiorcy, w terminie 3 dni roboczych od dnia złożenia wniosku, oświadczenie według ustalonego wzoru*

✎ **dochód gospodarstwa domowego kredytobiorcy** ✂ **dokonywanie spłat przez kredytobiorcę** *z budżetu państwa są przekazywane bankom środki w wysokości oprocentowania naliczonego według stopy procentowej określonej w art. 5a, pod warunkiem dokonywania przez kredytobiorcę spłat w wysokości wynikającej z przepisów art. 7 i 8, z zastrzeżeniem art. 8a ust. 3* **spłata zadłużenia kredytobiorcy** *środki zaliczone na spłatę zadłużenia kredytobiorcy wobec Skarbu Państwa z tytułu wykonania przez Skarb Państwa umów poręczenia, o których mowa w ust. 1, nie stanowią nadwyżki, o której mowa w art. 10 ust. 1 pkt 4* ✂ **oddać kwotę do dyspozycji kredytobiorcy** *bank hipoteczny może również oddać do dyspozycji kredytobiorcy określoną w umowie kredytowej kwotę środków pieniężnych przed zabezpieczeniem hipoteką wierzytelności z tytułu udzielonego kredytu, pod warunkiem ustanowienia zabezpieczenia, o którym mowa w ust. 4* ✂ **kredytobiorca + dokonać wpłaty**

📖 Possible equivalents: borrower, credited party, DEBTOR (en), beneficiario del credito, DEBITORE, mutuatario (it)

KREDYTODAWCA (pl)

Usually singular

(N) **adres, należności kredytodawcy** *kredytodawca lub pośrednik kredytowy przed zawarciem umowy o kredyt zabezpieczony hipoteką jest zobowiązany podać konsumentowi, na trwałym nośniku (...) zasady i terminy spłaty kredytu, w szczególności kolejności zaliczania rat na poczet należności kredytodawcy* **obowiązki kredytodawcy**

(V) **kredytodawca + być zobowiązanym do** *kredytodawca przed zawarciem umowy o kredyt konsumencki jest zobowiązany do dokonania oceny zdolności kredytowej konsumenta*

✎ **obowiązki kredytodawcy i pośrednika kredytowego, zaliczanie rat na poczet należności kredytodawcy ✂ kredytodawca + przekazać konsumentowi dane** *kredytodawca lub pośrednik kredytowy może przekazać konsumentowi dane, o których mowa w art. 17 ust. 2–4 i art. 18 ust. 1*

📖 Possible equivalents: creditor, lender, (en), creditore, mutuante, prestatore (it)

KSIĄŻECZKA (pl)

(Adj) **książeczka mieszkaniowa** *premię gwarancyjną oblicza i wypłaca bank prowadzący obsługę rachunków wkładów oszczędnościowych na książeczkach mieszkaniowych wystawionych do dnia 23 października 1990 r.*

(N) **likwidacja książeczki** *warunkiem udzielenia premii gwarancyjnej na zasadach określonych w ust. 1 pkt 1 i 2 jest złożenie przez właściciela książeczki mieszkaniowej dokumentów potwierdzających spełnienie warunków, o których mowa w ust. 1 pkt 1 i 2, na dzień złożenia wniosku o likwidację książeczki mieszkaniowej i wypłatę premii gwarancyjnej* ✂ **właściciel książeczki**

✎ **książeczka wystawiona w 1986 r. ✂ właściciel książeczki mieszkaniowej** *w przypadkach, o których mowa w art. 3 ust. 1 pkt 11 i 12, uprawnienie do złożenia wniosku o likwidację książeczki mieszkaniowej i wypłatę premii gwarancyjnej właściciel książeczki mieszkaniowej uzyskuje od dnia określonego zależnie od roku, w jakim wystawiono książeczkę mieszkaniową* **złożenie wniosku o likwidację książeczki mieszkaniowej i wypłatę premii gwarancyjnej**

📖 Possible equivalents: book, passbook (en), libretto (it)

KWOTA (pl)

(Adj) **całkowita, łączna, maksymalna, pełna kwota ✂ określona, wyegzekwowana kwota** *wynagrodzenie potrącane jest z wyegzekwowanej*

kwoty **wypłacona kwota** ✂ **kwota odpowiadająca** *refinansowanie nie może jednak przekroczyć kwoty odpowiadającej 60 % bankowo-hipotecznej wartości nieruchomości.* **kwota stanowiąca, uzyskana**

(N) **kwota kredytu, odsetek, partycypacji** *kwota partycypacji w kosztach budowy lokalu mieszkalnego uzyskana od osób, o których mowa w ust. 1, nie może przekroczyć 30 % kosztów budowy tego lokalu* **kwota poręczenia, pożyczki, rezerwy** *na potrzeby ustalenia limitu, o którym mowa w ust. 1, do funduszy własnych dolicza się kwotę rezerwy na ryzyko ogólne, o której mowa w art. 130* **kwota zobowiązania** ✂ **obciążenie kwotą, odzyskanie kwot** *banki przed wystąpieniem o realizację poręczenia są obowiązane do podjęcia działań zmierzających do odzyskania kwot niespłaconych kredytów* **równowartość, spłata, zwrot kwoty**

(P) **kwota wraz z** *poręczenia i gwarancje, o których mowa w ust. 1, mogą być udzielane do wysokości 100 % kwoty zobowiązań wynikających z emisji obligacji lub kredytu, objętych poręczeniem albo gwarancją, oraz do 100 % odsetek od tej kwoty wraz z innymi kosztami bezpośrednio związanymi z emisją obligacji lub obsługą tego kredytu*

całkowita kwota do zapłaty przez konsumenta, całkowita kwota kredytu, kwota kredytu preferencyjnego, kwota określona w art. 1, kwota polecenia zapłaty, kwota rezerwy obowiązkowej, kwota środków pieniężnych, nominalna kwota umorzenia kredytu *spółdzielnia mieszkaniowa przekazuje do banku środki wpłacone przez członków spółdzielni z tytułu zwrotu nominalnych kwot umorzeń kredytu, o których mowa w ust. 1 pkt 3 i 5, w terminie 14 dni od dnia ich otrzymania* **pozostająca do spłaty kwota kredytu** *Rada Ministrów lub minister właściwy do spraw finansów publicznych mogą udzielać poręczenia lub gwarancji do wysokości 50 % pozostającej do spłaty kwoty kredytu objętego poręczeniem lub gwarancją wraz z 50 % należnych odsetek od tej kwoty i innych kosztów bezpośrednio związanych z tym kredytem* ✂ **możliwość żądania w dowolnym momencie spłaty pełnej kwoty kredytu przez konsumenta**

Possible equivalents: AMOUNT, sum (en), AMMONTARE, IMPORTO, somma (it)

L

LIKWIDACJA (pl)

Always singular

(N) **likwidacja banku, instytucji, kasy, przedsiębiorstwa** ✂ **decyzja o likwidacji** *w decyzji o likwidacji kasy Komisja Nadzoru Finansowego ustanawia także likwidatora* **otwarcie, program likwidacji** *bilans otwarcia likwidacji, program likwidacji oraz sprawozdanie z przeprowadzonej likwidacji podlegają zatwierdzeniu przez Komisję Nadzoru Finansowego* ✂ **kasa w likwidacji** ✂ **przejęcie lub likwidacja**

(P) **w likwidacji**

kasa przejmowana lub kasa w likwidacji ✂ **decyzja o przejęciu lub likwidacji, złożenie wniosku o likwidację książeczki mieszkaniowej i wypłatę premii gwarancyjnej** *w przypadkach, o których mowa w art. 3 ust. 1 pkt 11 i 12, uprawnienie do złożenia wniosku o likwidację książeczki mieszkaniowej i wypłatę premii gwarancyjnej właściciel książeczki mieszkaniowej uzyskuje od dnia określonego zależnie od roku, w jakim wystawiono książeczkę mieszkaniową* ✂ **podjąć decyzję o likwidacji**

Possible equivalents: LIQUIDAZIONE, risoluzione (it), liquidation, resolution, WINDING UP (en)

LOKAL (pl)

(Adj) **lokal mieszkalny**

(N) **budynek lub lokal ✂ budowa, powierzchnia, własność, zakup lokalu** *ustawa określa zasady stosowania dopłat do oprocentowania kredytów udzielanych na zakup lokalu mieszkalnego, budowę i zakup domu jednorodzinnego albo wniesienie wkładu budowlanego do spółdzielni mieszkaniowej* **✂ prawo do lokalu** *lokale mieszkalne wybudowane przy wykorzystaniu kredytu, o którym mowa w art. 15a ust. 1, nie mogą być, pod rygorem nieważności, wyodrębnione na własność, a także nie może być do nich ustanowione spółdzielcze własnościowe prawo do lokalu*

✏ **budynek lub lokal o innym przeznaczeniu, dom jednorodzinny lub lokal mieszkalny ✂ lokal mieszkalny w budynku wielorodzinnym ✂ koszt budowy lokalu, powierzchnia użytkowa lokalu mieszkalnego** *premia gwarancyjna jest naliczana w odniesieniu do sumy wniesionych wpłat nieprzekraczających kosztów budowy 1) 55 m2 powierzchni użytkowej lokalu mieszkalnego w budynku wielorodzinnym* **prawo odrębnej własności lokalu mieszkalnego, spółdzielcze własnościowe/lokatorskie prawo do lokalu** *lokale mieszkalne wybudowane przy wykorzystaniu kredytu, o którym mowa w art. 15a ust. 1, nie mogą być, pod rygorem nieważności, wyodrębnione na własność, a także nie może być do nich ustanowione spółdzielcze własnościowe prawo do lokalu mieszkalnego* **umowa w sprawie partycypacji w kosztach budowy lokalu, uzyskanie lokalu mieszkalnego stanowiącego odrębną nieruchomość, własność lokalu mieszkalnego** *przeniesienie własności lokalu mieszkalnego przez towarzystwo budownictwa społecznego może nastąpić wyłącznie na rzecz osoby fizycznej, będącej jednocześnie najemcą lokalu mieszkalnego i stroną umowy w sprawie partycypacji w kosztach budowy tego lokalu* **zakup lokalu mieszkalnego ✂ ustawa z dnia 24 czerwca 1994 r. o własności lokali ✂ przypadający na dany lokal** *Jeżeli kredyt został zaciągnięty, z zastrzeżeniem ust. 3, do dnia 31 maja 1992 r., wysokość obciążających kredytobiorcę miesięcznych spłat przypadających na dany lokal nie może być niższa od iloczynu powierzchni użytkowej lokalu oraz normatywu spłaty kredytu ustalanego w przeliczeniu na 1 m2 powierzchni użytkowej lokalu*

📖 Possible equivalents: dwelling, housing, premise (en), abitazione, alloggio, locale (it)

LOKATA (pl)

(Adj) **lokata terminowa** *środki Funduszu są gromadzone na rachunkach bieżących, wyodrębnionych oraz rachunkach lokat jednodniowych i innych lokat terminowych w Narodowym Banku Polskim*

(N) **lokata środków** *przychodami kasy mieszkaniowej są (…) odsetki od lokat środków kasy na rachunkach terminowych w bankach* ✂ **rachunek lokaty** *NBP może (…) otwierać rachunki lokat terminowych banków* ✂ **lokaty w bankach, odsetki od lokat**

✏ **rachunki lokat terminowych, rachunek terminowej lokaty oszczędnościowej** *bank może wydać posiadaczowi rachunku oszczędnościowego oraz posiadaczowi rachunku terminowej lokaty oszczędnościowej imienną książeczkę oszczędnościową lub inny imienny dokument potwierdzający zawarcie umowy*

📖 Possible equivalents: DEPOSIT, investment (en), investimento, deposito (it)

M

MIESIĄC (pl)

(Adj) **miesiąc następujący (po)** *Bank Gospodarstwa Krajowego składa ministrowi właściwemu do spraw gospodarki, w terminie do końca miesiąca następującego po każdym kwartale, sprawozdanie z realizacji planu finansowego Funduszu* **miesiąc poprzedzający**

(P) **do końca miesiąca, na koniec miesiąca, po upływie miesiąca** ✂ **miesiąc od daty** *banki spółdzielcze zrzeszone z bankiem przejętym mogą wypowiedzieć tę umowę w okresie jednego miesiąca od daty połączenia, z zachowaniem trzymiesięcznego okresu wypowiedzenia* **miesiąc od dnia**

✏ *(NOMINAL)* **dwa miesiące od dnia otrzymania informacji, miesiąc następujący po miesiącu (w którym)** *dniem konsolidacji sprawozdań finansowych jest pierwszy dzień miesiąca następującego po miesiącu, w którym właściwy organ banku dominującego zatwierdził pierwsze skonsolidowane sprawozdanie finansowe* ✂ **oświadczenie o niezaleganiu z zapłatą podatku akcyzowego / składek na ubezpieczenia społeczne i zdrowotne na koniec miesiąca poprzedzającego miesiąc złożenia wniosku** *wniosek o częściową wypłatę premii technologicznej powinien zawierać: oświadczenie o niezaleganiu z zapłatą podatku akcyzowego na koniec miesiąca poprzedzającego miesiąc złożenia wniosku o częściową wypłatę premii technologicznej*

✏ **być spłacanym przez konsumenta w terminie do dwóch miesięcy** *kedytodawca lub pośrednik kredytowy przed zawarciem umowy o kredyt w rachunku oszczędnościowo-rozliczeniowym, który jest spłacany przez konsumenta w terminie do trzech miesięcy jest zobowiązany podać konsumentowi, na trwałym nośniku 1) dane określone w art. 13* **wchodzić w życie po upływie 2 miesięcy od**

dnia ogłoszenia ✂ **do końca miesiąca następującego (po), w terminie dwóch miesięcy od dnia wejścia w życie ustawy**

📖 Possible equivalents: month (pl), MESE (it)

MINISTER (pl)

(Adj) **minister właściwy (do)** *Bank Gospodarstwa Krajowego zawiera umowę z bankiem kredytującym, określającą zasady współpracy, zgodną z wzorem zatwierdzonym przez ministra właściwego do spraw gospodarki, w terminie 30 dni od dnia jej otrzymania*

(N) **Minister Finansów, Sprawiedliwości** ✂ **Rada Ministrów** *Rada Ministrów dokona, w drodze rozporządzenia, w terminie 30 dni od dnia wejścia w życie ustawy, zmian w statucie Bankowego Funduszu Gwarancyjnego*

(P) **na wniosek ministra, w porozumieniu z ministrem** *minister właściwy do spraw szkolnictwa wyższego w porozumieniu z ministrem właściwym do spraw finansów publicznych, określi, w drodze rozporządzenia, zasady zawierania umów, o których mowa w ust. 1, mając na uwadze konieczność zapewnienia sprawnego udzielania kredytów*

✏ **Minister Przekształceń Własnościowych** *ugodę zawieraną na warunkach określonych w art. 17 ust. 1 podpisuje w imieniu Skarbu Państwa Minister Przekształceń Własnościowych lub osoba przez niego upoważniona* **minister właściwy do spraw budownictwa, lokalnego planowania i zagospodarowania przestrzennego oraz mieszkalnictwa** *Bank Gospodarstwa Krajowego, w porozumieniu z ministrem właściwym do spraw budownictwa, lokalnego planowania i zagospodarowania przestrzennego oraz mieszkalnictwa oraz ministrem właściwym do spraw finansów publicznych, przygotowuje plan rzeczowo-finansowy związany z realizacją programów, o których mowa w art. 15a* **minister właściwy do spraw finansów publicznych / gospodarki / instytucji finansowych / Skarbu Państwa / szkolnictwa wyższego** ✂ **Prezes Rady Ministrów, przedstawiciel ministra właściwego (do spraw)** ✂ **minister + określić w drodze rozporządzenia** *minister właściwy do spraw instytucji finansowych określi, w drodze rozporządzenia, po zasięgnięciu opinii Komisji Nadzoru Finansowego, szczegółowy tryb wykonywania czynności kontrolnych w kasach i w Kasie Krajowej, uwzględniając konieczność skutecznego sprawowania nadzoru* **Rada Ministrów + określić w drodze**

rozporządzenia ✂ na wniosek ministra właściwego do spraw finansów publicznych, w porozumieniu z Ministrem Finansów

📖 Possible equivalents: minister (en), MINISTRO (it)

MONETA (pl)

Always plural

(N) **banknoty i monety** *przepis ust. 1 stosuje się odpowiednio do fałszywych banknotów i monet opiewających na waluty obce*

✎ **banknoty i monety nominowane w euro / w walutach narodowych, banknoty i monety opiewające (na)** *znakami pieniężnymi Rzeczypospolitej Polskiej są banknoty i monety opiewające na złote i grosze* ✂ **wymiana banknotów i monet**

📖 Possible equivalents: coin (en), MONETA, moneta metallica (it)

MOWA (pl)

Always singular

✎ **emisja skarbowych papierów wartościowych, o których mowa w ust. 1; jednostki uczestnictwa funduszy rynku pieniężnego, o których mowa w art. 1; kredyty na cele, o których mowa w art. 1; poręczenie Skarbu Państwa, o którym mowa w ust. 1; program postepowania naprawczego, o którym mowa w ust. 1 ✂ w brzmieniu ustalonym przez art. 1 pkt 1 ustawy, o której mowa w odnośniku 1; w przypadku, o którym mowa w ust.1** *w przypadku, o którym mowa w ust. 1 lub 2, Komisja Nadzoru Finansowego może, w drodze decyzji, nakazać zbycie akcji banku krajowego w wyznaczonym terminie* **w terminie, o którym mowa w ust. 1 ✂ spełniać warunki, o których mowa (w) ✂ ilekroć w ustawie jest mowa (o)** *ilekroć w ustawie jest mowa o fakturach, należy przez to rozumieć także inne dowody księgowe o równoważnej wartości dowodowej*

bank krajowy, o którym
działania, o których
holdingi, o których
metody statystyczne, o których
(obowiązkowa) opłata roczna, o której ⟹ **mowa w art. 1**
opłata ostrożnościowa, o której
przestępstwo, o którym
rozporządzenie, o którym
zgłoszenie sprzeciwu, o którym

dane indywidualne, o których
decyzja, o której
działania, o których
kara, o której
limit, o którym
obowiązek, o którym
okoliczności, o których
poręczenia i gwarancje, o których ⟹ **mowa w ust. 1**
porozumienie, o którym
powołanie osoby, o której mowa
rozporządzenie, o którym
uchwała, o której
upoważnienie, o którym
wymóg, o którym
wniosek, o którym

czynność bankowa, o której
dane, o których
decyzja, o której
dokument, o którym
fundusz stabilizacyjny, o którym obowiązek,
o którym ⟹ **mowa w art. 1 ust. 1**
podmiot, o którym
termin, o którym
wsparcie, o którym
wydatki, o których
zawiadomienie, o którym

Possible equivalents: referred (to) (en), di cui (a), previsto (da) (it)

N

NADZÓR (pl)

Usually singular

(Adj) **efektywny nadzór** ✂ **nadzór skonsolidowany (nad)** *w przypadku, o którym mowa w ust. 7, właściwe władze nadzorcze uzgadniają, która z władz sprawuje nadzór skonsolidowany* **nadzór sprawowany (przez), nadzór uzupełniający**

(N) **nadzór nad bankiem, działalnością** *nadzór nad działalnością banku krajowego, prowadzącego działalność na terytorium państwa goszczącego poprzez oddział lub w ramach działalności transgranicznej, sprawuje Komisja Nadzoru Finansowego* **nadzór nad kasami, podmiotami, systemami** ✂ **sprawowanie nadzoru** *Komisja Nadzoru Finansowego obowiązana jest do sprawowania nadzoru nad oddziałami instytucji kredytowych w zakresie przestrzegania obowiązku określonego w art. 8* **zasady nadzoru**

(V) **sprawować nadzór** *w przypadku, o którym mowa w ust. 7, właściwe władze nadzorcze uzgadniają, która z władz sprawuje nadzór skonsolidowany*

(P) **nadzór nad** ✂ **w ramach nadzoru** *Minister Finansów lub Minister Skarbu Państwa może wystąpić do Komisji Nadzoru Finansowego o podjęcie czynności lub środków w ramach nadzoru, o których mowa w art. 133 i art. 138*

✎ **nadzór nad rynkiem finansowym, nadzór skonsolidowany nad bankiem** ✂ **Europejski Urząd Nadzoru Bankowego, KOMISJA NADZORU FINANSOWEGO** ✂ **środki, jakie zostaną podjęte w celu usunięcia nieprawidłowości stwierdzonych w ramach nadzoru** *banki oraz oddziały i przedstawicielstwa banków zagranicznych w kraju są obowiązane 3) niezwłocznie zawiadomić Komisję Nadzoru Finansowego o środkach, jakie zostaną podjęte w celu* *usunięcia nieprawidłowości stwierdzonych w ramach nadzoru, oraz stosować się do wydanych decyzji i zaleceń* ✂ **ustawa o nadzorze nad rynkiem finansowym**

📖 Possible equivalents: charge, control, supervision, surveillance (en), controllo, sorveglianza, supervisione, vigilanza (it)

NIERUCHOMOŚĆ (pl)

(Adj) **nieruchomość wspólna** *większość właścicieli lokali wyodrębnionych na własność w budynku lub budynkach położonych w obrębie danej nieruchomości, obliczana według wielkości udziałów w nieruchomości wspólnej, może dokonać zmiany, ustalonego w trybie ust. 1, sposobu zarządu nieruchomością wspólną* ✂ **odrębna nieruchomość**

(N) **właściciel nieruchomości** *podstawę wpisu w księdze wieczystej hipoteki zabezpieczającej kredyt lub pożyczkę udzielaną przez kasy stanowi oświadczenie właściciela nieruchomości o ustanowieniu hipoteki na rzecz kasy* **wartość nieruchomości**

✏ **nieruchomość stanowiąca własność** *dokumenty, o których mowa w ust. 1, są podstawą wpisu hipoteki do księgi wieczystej nieruchomości stanowiącej własność dłużnika banku lub innej osoby ustanawiającej hipotekę na rzecz banku w celu zabezpieczenia wierzytelności dłużnika banku* ✂ **bankowo-hipoteczna wartość nieruchomości** *wysokość pojedynczego kredytu zabezpieczonego hipoteką nie może przekroczyć bankowo-hipotecznej wartości nieruchomości* **lokal mieszkalny stanowiący odrębną nieruchomość**

📖 Possible equivalents: estate, real estate, real estate property, premises (en), bene immobile, immobile (it)

NIEWYPŁACALNOŚĆ (pl)

Usually singular

(N) **niewypłacalność banku, dłużnika** ✂ **niebezpieczeństwo, ryzyko niewypłacalności** *umowa, o której mowa w ust. 1 pkt 2, nie może zwiększać ryzyka niewypłacalności lub pogarszać płynności banku*

powstanie / usunięcie niebezpieczeństwa niewypłacalności *w razie powstania straty bilansowej bądź groźby jej nastąpienia albo powstania niebezpieczeństwa niewypłacalności lub utraty płynności, zarząd banku niezwłocznie zawiadamia o tym Komisję Nadzoru Finansowego* **ubezpieczenie od ryzyka niewypłacalności** ✂ **niebezpieczeństwo niewypłacalności + powstać** *ustawa określa (…) zasady udzielania wsparcia w celu restrukturyzacji kas, w których powstało niebezpieczeństwo niewypłacalności*

Possible equivalents: bankruptcy, INSOLVENCY (en), insolvenza (it)

O

ODDZIAŁ (pl)

(Adj) **istotny oddział** *decyzję, o której mowa w ust. 13, otrzymuje instytucja kredytowa prowadząca działalność na terytorium Rzeczypospolitej Polskiej poprzez istotny oddział, istotny oddział instytucji kredytowej oraz właściwe władze nadzorcze zainteresowanych państw członkowskich*

(N) **oddział banku, instytucji** ✂ **dyrektor oddziału** *za wdrożenie i utrzymywanie prawidłowo funkcjonującego systemu wyliczania jest odpowiedzialny zarząd banku, a w przypadku oddziału banku zagranicznego lub oddziału instytucji kredytowej – dyrektor oddziału* ✂ **utworzenie oddziału**

(V) **utworzyć oddział**

✎ **oddziały i przedstawicielstwa banków** *ustawa określa zasady prowadzenia działalności bankowej, tworzenia i organizacji banków, oddziałów i przedstawicielstw banków zagranicznych, a także oddziałów instytucji kredytowych oraz zasady sprawowania nadzoru bankowego, postępowania naprawczego, likwidacji i upadłości banków* ✂ **oddział banku krajowego, oddział banku zagranicznego, oddział instytucji kredytowej, oddział zagranicznej instytucji pieniądza elektronicznego** ✂ **poprzez oddział lub w ramach działalności transgranicznej** *instytucja kredytowa może prowadzić działalność na terytorium Rzeczypospolitej Polskiej poprzez oddział lub w ramach działalności transgranicznej*

📖 Possible equivalents: branch, OFFICE (en), filiale, succursale (it)

ODSETKA (pl)

Always plural

(Adj) **należne, skapitalizowane odsetki** *z budżetu państwa przeznacza się środki finansowe na spłatę wierzytelności banków z tytułu zmniejszenia zadłużenia z tytułu skapitalizowanych odsetek, o których mowa w art. 11b* ✂ **odsetki wykupione**

(N) **kwota odsetek** ✂ **wykupienie odsetek** ✂ **kredyt wraz z odsetkami**

(P) **odsetki od** ✂ **odsetki w wysokości** ✂ **z tytułu odsetek** *dochód banku hipotecznego z tytułu odsetek od wierzytelności zabezpieczonych hipoteką, o których mowa w ust. 1, nie może być niższy od kosztów z tytułu odsetek od znajdujących się w obrocie hipotecznych listów zastawnych*

odsetki od kredytów mieszkaniowych, odsetki przejściowo wykupione ze środków budżetu państwa *odsetki przejściowo wykupione ze środków budżetu państwa są oprocentowane w wysokości stopy oprocentowania kredytu, o której mowa w art. 5a, z zastrzeżeniem art. 10 ust. 3* ✂ **spłata kredytu wraz z odsetkami, o których mowa (w); zadłużenie z tytułu przejściowego wykupienia odsetek od kredytu** *pomoc państwa w spłacie kredytów mieszkaniowych, o których mowa w art. 1 ust. 2, polega na 3) umorzeniu części zadłużenia kredytobiorców z tytułu przejściowego wykupienia odsetek od kredytów mieszkaniowych* ✂ **wraz z należnymi odsetkami** *bank jest zobowiązany do zwrotu tej kwoty po uzyskaniu spłaty zadłużenia wraz z należnymi odsetkami i prowizją*

Possible equivalents: interest (en), INTERESSE (it)

OKRES (pl)

(Adj) **okres kwartalny** *kredyt o stałej stopie procentowej jest spłacany w równych ratach kapitałowo-odsetkowych w okresach miesięcznych lub kwartalnych*

(N) **okres oszczędzania** *w okresie oszczędzania może nastąpić przeniesienie praw i obowiązków posiadacza rachunku oszczędnościowo-kredytowego na osobę bliską, która nie posiada takiego rachunku* **okres pracy, spłaty, studiów, urlopu, zawieszenia** *w okresie zawieszenia w stosunku do banku nie może zostać wszczęte postępowanie egzekucyjne, a wszczęte wcześniej ulega zawieszeniu*

(P) **okres o którym mowa (w)** ✂ **na okres, w okresie, za okres (od / po)** ✂ **po upływie okresu, przed upływem okresu, przez okres dwóch lat** *dopłaty stosuje się przez okres 8 lat od dnia pierwszej spłaty odsetek, o których mowa w art. 7 ust. 1* **w okresie do dnia** *bank zrzeszający posiadający fundusze własne w wysokości co najmniej równowartości 20 000 000 euro w okresie do dnia 31 grudnia 2007 r.*

okres dwóch miesięcy od dnia, okres nie dłuższy niż dwa lata, okres obowiązywania umowy, okres spłaty kredytu, okres urlopu bezpłatnego ✂ **zaliczać się do okresów pracy oraz innych okresów, od których zależy nabycie uprawnień pracowniczych** *okres pełnienia funkcji powiernika i jego zastępcy zalicza się do okresów pracy oraz innych okresów, od których zależy nabycie uprawnień pracowniczych* ✂ **na okres co najmniej dwóch lat**

Possible equivalents: period, term, time (en), PERIODO, tempo, TERMINE (it)

OPŁATA (pl)

(Adj) **obowiązkowa opłata, ewentualne opłaty** *pośrednik kredytowy jest zobowiązany poinformować kredytodawcę o wysokości ewentualnych opłat pobranych od konsumenta w celu obliczenia przez kredytodawcę rocznej stopy oprocentowania* ✂ **opłata lokalna, notarialna, ostrożnościowa** *przy określaniu wysokości stawki obowiązkowej opłaty rocznej, o której mowa w art. 13 ust. 1, oraz stawki opłaty ostrożnościowej, o której mowa w art. 14a, Rada Funduszu uwzględnia w szczególności sytuację w sektorze finansowym oraz jego otoczeniu makroekonomicznym* **opłata prowizyjna, roczna** ✂ **wolny od opłat** *otwarcie i prowadzenie rachunku, o którym mowa w art. 69 ust. 3, jest wolne od opłat w przypadku, gdy kredytobiorcą jest konsument w rozumieniu ustawy z dnia 23 kwietnia 1964 r. – Kodeks cywilny*

(N) **naliczanie, pobieranie opłaty** *Rada Ministrów określi, w drodze rozporządzenia, sposób naliczania i pobierania opłaty prowizyjnej od poręczenia i gwarancji oraz wysokość tej opłaty* **wnoszenie opłaty** ✂ **stawka, wysokość opłaty** ✂ **opłaty i prowizje** *przepis ust. 1 nie narusza prawa banku do ustalenia własnych opłat i prowizji związanych z wcześniejszą spłatą kredytu* ✂ **podatki i opłaty**

(V) **zwalniać z opłaty, wnosić opłatę** *od poręczeń i gwarancji, o których mowa w ust. 1 i 2, nie wnosi się opłaty prowizyjnej* ✂ **opłata jest pobierana** *od gwarancji dla*

Narodowego Banku Polskiego oraz gwarancji za instytucję finansową jest pobierana opłata prowizyjna.

opłata prowizyjna od poręczeń i gwarancji, opłaty z tytułu zaległości w spłacie kredytu ✂ **informacje o opłatach stosowanych od chwili zawarcia umowy** *jeżeli zgodnie z umową rachunku oszczędnościowo-rozliczeniowego konsumenta możliwe jest przekroczenie salda na tym rachunku, umowa powinna zawierać co najmniej dane określone w art. 30 ust. 1 pkt 6 oraz informację o opłatach stosowanych od chwili zawarcia umowy oraz warunkach ich zmiany* **informacje o opłatach stosowanych w czasie obowiązywania umowy** ✂ **oświadczenie o niezaleganiu z zapłatą podatków i opłat lokalnych** ✂ **podstawa naliczania opłaty rocznej, stawki obowiązkowej opłaty rocznej, wysokość stawki opłaty rocznej** *wydając rozporządzenie, minister właściwy do spraw instytucji finansowych określi dzień, na który oblicza się wysokość stawki opłaty rocznej, oraz termin jej wniesienia*

Possible equivalents: charge, fee, PAYMENT (en), contributo, SPESA, tassa (it)

OPROCENTOWANIE (pl)

Always singular

(N) **oprocentowanie kredytu, pożyczki, środków** *bank obowiązany jest ogłaszać w miejscu wykonywania czynności, w sposób ogólnie dostępny 1) stosowane stawki oprocentowania środków na rachunkach bankowych, kredytów i pożyczek* **oprocentowanie zadłużenia** *oprocentowanie zadłużenia, o którym mowa w ust. 1, jest równe stopie oprocentowania kredytów, określonej w art. 5a ustawy o pomocy państwa, powiększonej o 2 punkty procentowe* ✂ **stopa oprocentowania, wysokość oprocentowania** ✂ **dopłata do oprocentowania**

oprocentowanie kredytów udzielanych (na), rzeczywista roczna stopa oprocentowania, zmiana wysokości stopy oprocentowania *w przypadku zmiany wysokości stopy oprocentowania w czasie obowiązywania umowy o kredyt konsumencki, konsument przed jej dokonaniem otrzymuje od kredytodawcy, na trwałym nośniku, informację o tej zmianie* ✂ **dopłaty do oprocentowania kredytów bankowych** *dopłaty do oprocentowania kredytów bankowych na cele rolnicze, dla krajowych przedsiębiorców prowadzących produkcję rolniczą, udzielane są na jednakowych zasadach, bez względu na obszar użytków rolnych i formę ich własności* **dopłaty ze środków budżetu państwa do oprocentowania kredytów**

Possible equivalents: interest, interest rate, rate (en), INTERESSE, tasso d'interesse (it)

OSOBA (pl)

(Adj) **osoba fizyczna, osoba prawna, osoba trzecia** ✂ **osoby zagraniczne** *wpłacony w walutach obcych kapitał akcyjny banków utworzonych przez osoby zagraniczne lub z udziałem osób zagranicznych zostaje przeliczony na złote, według kursu średniego ogłaszanego przez Narodowy Bank Polski w dniu wejścia w życie ustawy* ✂ **osoba uprawniona (do)** ✂ **osoby korzystające (z), zatrudnione (w), osoby przewidziane (do), osoby upoważnione**

(N) **egzekucja przeciwko osobie** *bankowy tytuł egzekucyjny może być także podstawą egzekucji przeciwko osobie trzeciej, gdy osoba ta przejmie dług wynikający z czynności bankowej, o której mowa w art. 97 ust. 1* **powołanie osoby** *decyzja, o której mowa w ust. 1, może określać termin, do którego powinno nastąpić powołanie osoby, o której mowa w ust. 1* **wynagrodzenie osoby** *wysokość miesięcznego wynagrodzenia osób wchodzących w skład Rady Funduszu ustala się jako wielokrotność przeciętnego miesięcznego wynagrodzenia w sektorze przedsiębiorstw bez wypłat nagród z zysku w czwartym kwartale roku poprzedniego, ogłoszonego przez Prezesa Głównego Urzędu Statystycznego*

następcy prawni oraz osoby, o których mowa w art. 1 ust. 1 *wysokość świadczenia zostaje określona bez uwzględnienia środków gwarantowanych, jakie mogą przysługiwać następcom prawnym oraz osobom, o których mowa w art. 55 ust. 1 oraz art. 56 ust. 1 ustawy – Prawo bankowe, z tytułu czynności dokonanych odrębnie od czynności będących podstawą powstania środków gwarantowanych poprzednika prawnego* ✂ **osoba niebędąca członkiem, osoba zajmująca stanowisko kierownicze w banku** ✂ **osoby korzystające oraz zainteresowane korzystaniem z usług, osoby pełniące funkcję, osoby przewidziane do objęcia stanowisk członków zarządu, osoby wchodzące w skład** ✂ **podatek dochodowy od osób fizycznych** ✂ **ustawa z dnia 15 lutego 1992 r. o podatku dochodowym od osób prawnych, ustawa o pomocy państwa w spłacie niektórych kredytów mieszkaniowych udzielonych osobom, które utraciły pracę, ustawa z dnia 8 maja 1997 r. o poręczeniach i gwarancjach udzielanych przez Skarb Państwa oraz niektóre osoby prawne** ✂ **na rzecz osoby fizycznej** *tej samej karze podlega,* *kto dopuszcza się czynu określonego w ust. 1, działając w imieniu lub na rzecz osoby fizycznej, osoby prawnej lub jednostki organizacyjnej nieposiadającej osobowości prawne*

📖 Possible equivalents: PERSON (en), persona (it)

OTRZYMANIE (pl)

Always singular

(N) **otrzymanie informacji** *Bank Gospodarstwa Krajowego zaprzestaje przekazywania rat pomocy z dniem otrzymania informacji, o których mowa w ust. 1, z zastrzeżeniem art. 10 pkt 1* **otrzymanie kredytu, wniosku** *Komisja Nadzoru Finansowego wydaje decyzję w przedmiocie zezwolenia na utworzenie kasy w terminie 3 miesięcy od daty otrzymania wniosku lub jego uzupełnienia* **otrzymanie zawiadomienia**

(P) **od dnia otrzymania** *w przypadku, o którym mowa w ust. 6, Prezes NBP może żądać przedstawienia dokumentów, o których mowa odpowiednio w art. 17 ust. 2 lub w art. 17a ust. 1, w terminie 2 tygodni od dnia otrzymania żądania*

✎ **otrzymanie świadczenia pieniężnego** *informacje dotyczące trybu i warunków otrzymania świadczenia pieniężnego powinny zostać udostępnione na wniosek osoby korzystającej oraz zainteresowanej korzystaniem z usług oddziału banku zagranicznego* ✂ **dwa miesiące od dnia otrzymania** ✂ **w terminie dwóch dni (roboczych) od dnia otrzymania** *Komisja Nadzoru Finansowego doręcza decyzję w przedmiocie sprzeciwu, o którym mowa w art. 25h ust. 1, w terminie 60 dni roboczych od dnia otrzymania zawiadomienia i wszystkich wymaganych informacji i dokumentów, nie później niż w terminie 2 dni roboczych od dnia jej wydania*

📖 Possible equivalents: collection, receipt (en), ottenimento, ricezione, ricevimento (it)

P

PAŃSTWO (pl)

(Adj) **PAŃSTWO CZŁONKOWSKIE, goszczące, macierzyste** *państwo macierzyste – państwo członkowskie, w którym dana instytucja kredytowa uzyskała zezwolenie na wykonywanie działalności i na terenie którego ma swoją siedzibę*

(N) **budżet państwa** *środki gromadzone na rachunku, o którym mowa w ust. 1, mogą być wykorzystywane na sfinansowanie potrzeb pożyczkowych budżetu państwa oraz w związku z zarządzaniem długiem Skarbu Państwa* **SKARB PAŃSTWA, terytorium państwa**

dopłaty ze środków budżetu państwa do oprocentowania kredytów, odsetki przejściowo wykupione ze środków budżetu państwa *odsetki przejściowo wykupione ze środków budżetu państwa są oprocentowane w wysokości stopy oprocentowania kredytu, o której mowa w art. 5a, z zastrzeżeniem art. 10 ust. 3* **terytorium państwa goszczącego, właściwe władze nadzorcze państwa goszczącego / macierzystego** *Komisja Nadzoru Finansowego niezwłocznie powiadamia właściwe władze nadzorcze państwa goszczącego o utracie przez bank krajowy, prowadzący działalność na jego terytorium, zezwolenia na jego utworzenie* ✂ **Ustawa o pomocy państwa w spłacie niektórych kredytów mieszkaniowych udzielonych osobom, które utraciły pracę** ✂ **powiadamiać właściwe władze nadzorcze państwa** *Komisja Nadzoru Finansowego niezwłocznie powiadamia właściwe władze nadzorcze państwa goszczącego o utracie przez bank krajowy, prowadzący działalność na jego terytorium, zezwolenia na jego utworzenie*

Possible equivalents: COUNTRY, state (en), STATO (it)

PAŃSTWO CZŁONKOWSKIE (pl)

(N) **prawo, terytorium państwa członkowskiego** ✂ **władze państwa członkowskiego** ✂ **działalność w państwie członkowskim** *właściwe władze nadzorcze mogą uzgodnić, że kryteriów, o których mowa w ust. 6 pkt 1–6, nie stosuje się, jeżeli są one niewłaściwe z uwagi na specyfikę banku, instytucji kredytowych lub względną istotność ich działalności w państwach członkowskich*

państwo członkowskie Unii Europejskiej, państwo niebędące państwem członkowskim *udzielenie właściwym władzom nadzorczym państwa niebędącego państwem członkowskim informacji stanowiących tajemnicę zawodową (...) może nastąpić jedynie wówczas, gdy zapewniona będzie ochrona tych informacji co najmniej równoważna określonej w niniejszym artykule* ✂ **bank centralny państwa członkowskiego, siedziba na terytorium państwa członkowskiego** *zawarcie umowy, o której mowa w art. 6a ust. 1 lub 7 (...) lub umowy przewidującej, że powierzone czynności będą wykonywane poza terytorium państwa członkowskiego, wymaga zezwolenia Komisji Nadzoru Finansowego udzielonego na wniosek banku* **właściwe władze nadzorcze państwa członkowskiego** ✂ **podlegający prawu innego państwa** *podmiot prowadzący system interoperacyjny koordynuje moment wprowadzenia zlecenia rozrachunku do systemu (...) z zasadami funkcjonowania systemów, z którymi prowadzony przez niego system współpracuje, w tym także systemów podlegających prawu innego państwa członkowskiego*

Possible equivalents: member state (en), stato membro (it)

PAPIER WARTOŚCIOWY (pl)

Always plural

(Adj) **dłużne papiery wartościowe** *NBP może 1) emitować i sprzedawać papiery wartościowe* **skarbowe papiery wartościowe** ✂ **papiery wartościowe emitowane, wyemitowane (przez)** *gwarancja nie może obejmować spłaty kredytu wraz z odsetkami, którego zabezpieczenie stanowią skarbowe papiery wartościowe oraz papiery wartościowe wyemitowane przez Narodowy Bank Polski – do wysokości ich wartości nominalnej*

(N) **depozyt papierów wartościowych**

✏ **papiery wartościowe emitowane przez Skarb Państwa** ✂ **emisja skarbowych papierów wartościowych, o których mowa w ust. 1, sprzedaż skarbowych papierów wartościowych, uczestnik systemu płatności lub systemu rozrachunku papierów wartościowych, zarejestrowanie skarbowych papierów wartościowych w depozycie papierów wartościowych** *emisja skarbowych papierów wartościowych następuje z dniem zarejestrowania skarbowych papierów wartościowych w depozycie papierów wartościowych oraz w kwocie równej wartości nominalnej wyemitowanych papierów wartościowych* ✂ **Krajowy Depozyt Papierów Wartościowych S.A.**

📖 Possible equivalents: SECURITY (en), TITOLO (it)

PIENIĄDZ (pl)

Usually singular

(Adj) PIENIĄDZ ELEKTRONICZNY

(N) **podaż pieniądza** ✂ **pranie pieniędzy** *w przypadku gdy środki zdeponowane na rachunku zostały zablokowane na podstawie przepisów o przeciwdziałaniu praniu pieniędzy oraz finansowaniu terroryzmu, zawiesza się wypłatę deponentowi środków gwarantowanych, na czas trwania blokady*

✏ **przepisy o przeciwdziałaniu praniu pieniędzy oraz finansowaniu terroryzmu, Ustawa z dnia 16 listopada 2000 r. o przeciwdziałaniu praniu pieniędzy oraz finansowaniu terroryzmu** ✂ **kształtowanie podaży pieniądza** *w celu kształtowania podaży pieniądza i działalności kredytowej NBP gromadzi rezerwy obowiązkowe banków, spółdzielczych kas oszczędnościowo-kredytowych oraz Krajowej Spółdzielczej Kasy Oszczędnościowo-Kredytowej*

📖 Possible equivalents: money (en), DENARO, MONETA (it)

PIENIĄDZ ELEKTRONICZNY (pl)

Always singular

(N) **instrument pieniądza elektronicznego** *Banki i instytucje pieniądza elektronicznego przekazują do NBP dane dotyczące (…) liczby i wartości operacji zasilenia instrumentów pieniądza elektronicznego* **INSTYTUCJA PIENIĄDZA ELEKTRONICZNEGO** *nabycie* ✂ **wydanie, wydawanie pieniądza**

elektronicznego *kasy oraz Kasa Krajowa są uprawnione do wydawania pieniądza elektronicznego na rzecz członków kas, na zasadach określonych w ustawie z dnia 19 sierpnia 2011 r. o usługach płatniczych*

umowa o wydanie pieniądza elektronicznego *w okresie obowiązywania umowy o wydanie pieniądza elektronicznego, posiadacz może żądać od wydawcy wykupienia posiadanego pieniądza elektronicznego w każdym czasie i według wartości nominalnej* **świadczenie usług płatniczych oraz wydawanie pieniądza elektronicznego**

Possible equivalents: electronic money (en), MONETA ELETTRONICA (it)

PŁATNOŚĆ (pl)

(Adj) **odroczona płatność** *kredytodawca lub pośrednik kredytowy przed zawarciem umowy o kredyt wiązany lub w formie odroczonej płatności jest zobowiązany podać konsumentowi, na trwałym nośniku, dane, o których mowa w ust. 1, oraz opis i cenę towaru lub usługi*

(N) **płatność raty** *informacja, o której mowa w ust. 1, zawiera szczegółowe określenie stopy oprocentowania, wysokości raty kredytu po dokonaniu zmiany stopy oprocentowania oraz informację o liczbie i częstotliwości płatności rat, o ile ulegają one zmianie* ✂ **odroczenie, system, termin płatności** *starosta może odroczyć termin płatności, rozłożyć na raty lub umorzyć w całości albo w części należności, o których mowa w art. 13, 14 i 16.*

płatność rat pomocy *Bank Gospodarstwa Krajowego informuje właściwego starostę o wysokości środków przekazanych z tytułu dokonywanych płatności rat pomocy oraz terminach ich przekazania na rachunek instytucji kredytującej* ✂ **systemy płatności, rozliczeń i rozrachunku** *Obowiązku ochrony tajemnicy, o której mowa w ust. 1, nie narusza udzielenie bankowi centralnemu wchodzącemu w skład Europejskiego Systemu Banków Centralnych informacji niezbędnych do realizacji przypisanych mu prawem zadań, w tym zadań dotyczących polityki monetarnej i zapewnienia związanej z tym płynności, zadań związanych z nadzorem nad systemami płatności, rozliczeń i rozrachunku oraz zadań realizowanych na rzecz stabilności systemu finansowego* **uczestnik systemu płatności** ✂ **umowa**

(o kredyt) przewidująca odroczenie płatności lub zmianę sposobu spłaty, umowa o kredyt wiązany lub w formie odroczonej płatności ✂ wysokość zobowiązań dłużnika wraz z odsetkami i terminami ich płatności ✂ ustawa z dnia 24 sierpnia 2001 r. o ostateczności rozrachunku w systemach płatności i systemach rozrachunku papierów wartościowych oraz zasadach nadzoru nad tymi systemami

📖 Possible equivalents: PAYMENT, remittance (en), PAGAMENTO (it)

PODMIOT (pl)

(Adj) **PODMIOT DOMINUJĄCY, podmiot objęty, prowadzący, składający** *podmiot składający zawiadomienie, o którym mowa w art. 25 ust. 1, mający miejsce zamieszkania lub siedzibę poza granicami Rzeczypospolitej Polskiej, obowiązany jest ustanowić na terytorium Rzeczypospolitej Polskiej pełnomocnika do doręczeń w toku postępowania w przedmiocie zawiadomienia* **podmiot uprawniony, zależny ✂ zagrożone podmioty** *w przypadku, o którym mowa w ust. 1 pkt 3, Przewodniczący Komisji Nadzoru Finansowego przedstawia Komitetowi opinię dotyczącą wypłacalności zagrożonych podmiotów*

(N) **upadłość podmiotu** *Funduszowi przysługuje roszczenie także po ogłoszeniu upadłości podmiotu* **uprawnienia podmiotu**

✏ **zarząd komisaryczny lub podmiot uprawniony do reprezentacji** *zarząd komisaryczny banku lub podmiot uprawniony do reprezentacji są odpowiedzialni za sporządzenie listy deponentów zgodnie z przepisami wydanymi na podstawie art. 38j* ✂ **podmiot mający siedzibę na terytorium Rzeczypospolitej Polskiej, podmiot posiadający bliskie powiązania z bankiem, podmiot prowadzący system** *podmiot prowadzący system – partner centralny, agent rozrachunkowy oraz izba rozliczeniowa, w tym w szczególności izba rozliczeniowa lub izba rozrachunkowa działająca na podstawie ustawy z dnia 29 lipca 2005 r. o obrocie instrumentami finansowymi, lub inny podmiot określający wspólne dla uczestników systemu zasady realizacji ich zleceń rozrachunku* **podmiot składający zawiadomienie, podmiot uprawniony do badania sprawozdań finansowych, podmiot zależny w stosunku do instytucji kredytowej ✂ ogłoszenie upadłości podmiotu, ryzyko jednego podmiotu lub podmiotów powiązanych kapitałowo lub organizacyjnie,**

zapewnienie środków na finansowanie zadań Funduszu w zakresie udzielania pomocy podmiotom objętym systemem gwarantowania

Possible equivalents: subject (en), soggetto (it)

PODMIOT DOMINUJĄCY (pl)

Usually singular

(Adj) **pierwotny podmiot dominujący** *zgłoszenie holdingu do właściwego wykazu i aktualizację zgłoszenia składa do Komisji Nadzoru Finansowego 1) bank krajowy, jeżeli jest podmiotem dominującym w holdingu lub jeżeli pierwotny podmiot dominujący w holdingu, w którym działa bank krajowy, ma siedzibę za granicą* **unijny podmiot dominujący** ✂ **dominujący podmiot nieregulowany** *w przypadku gdy bank krajowy wchodzi w skład konglomeratu finansowego, którego podmiotem dominującym jest dominujący podmiot nieregulowany w rozumieniu ustawy o nadzorze uzupełniającym, stosuje się przepisy ustawy o nadzorze uzupełniającym*

(N) **podmiot dominujący banku** *przepisy ust. 1–6 i 9 stosuje się odpowiednio w przypadku, w którym dwa lub więcej podmiotów działa w porozumieniu, którego przedmiotem jest wykonywanie prawa głosu z akcji na poziomach określonych w ust. 1 lub wykonywanie uprawnień podmiotu dominującego banku krajowego* ✂ **uprawnienia podmiotu dominującego**

✎ **unijny podmiot dominujący w holdingu finansowym** *unijny podmiot dominujący w holdingu finansowym – podmiot dominujący w holdingu finansowym w państwie członkowskim, który nie jest podmiotem zależnym w stosunku do instytucji kredytowej lub banku krajowego ani w stosunku do instytucji finansowej lub dominującego podmiotu nieregulowanego w rozumieniu art. 3 pkt 5 ustawy o nadzorze uzupełniającym mających siedzibę na terytorium państwa członkowskiego* ✂ **uprawnienia podmiotu dominującego banku krajowego, wykonywanie uprawnień podmiotu dominującego** ✂ **stać się podmiotem dominującym banku krajowego**

Possible equivalents: parent company, parent entity, parent undertaking (en), impresa madre, società madre (it)

PODSTAWA (pl)

Usually singular

(Adj) **stanowiący podstawę** *bank dokonujący wypłat z rachunku bankowego jest obowiązany sprawdzić autentyczność i prawidłowość formalną dokumentu stanowiącego podstawę do wypłaty oraz tożsamość osoby dającej zlecenie* ✂ **działający, utworzony, wydany na podstawie**

(N) **podstawa naliczenia** *do podstawy naliczenia dopłaty nie wlicza się kwot skapitalizowanych odsetek* ✂ **ochrona na podstawie** *fundusz przekazuje Narodowemu Bankowi Polskiemu informacje niezbędne do oceny stabilności i ryzyka systemu bankowego, w tym dotyczące poszczególnych podmiotów objętych systemem gwarantowania, podlegające ochronie na podstawie odrębnych przepisów* ✂ **na podstawie art. 1, przepisów, umowy, ustawy, zezwolenia**

(V) **następować na podstawie** *powierzenie przez bank wykonywania czynności, o których mowa w ust. 1 pkt 1 lit. a–j, następuje na podstawie umowy agencyjnej.*

✎ **biegły rewident upoważniony do badania sprawozdań finansowych banku na podstawie zawartej umowy, Fundusz Kredytu Technologicznego utworzony na podstawie ustawy z dnia 29 lipca 2005 r., instytucja kredytowa działająca na podstawie zezwolenia udzielonego (w), przepisy wydane na podstawie art. 10 ust. 2** *Przepisy art. 9a ust. 2–11 oraz przepisy wydane na podstawie art. 9h stosuje się odpowiednio* ✂ **na podstawie odrębnych przepisów/ustaw** *obowiązek przekazywania do NBP danych niezbędnych do wykonywania zadań NBP wynikających z ustawy oraz uczestnictwa w Europejskim Systemie Banków Centralnych, obejmuje również dane objęte ochroną na podstawie odrębnych ustaw, w tym informacje objęte tajemnicą bankową* **na podstawie przepisów ustawy, na podstawie zezwolenia dewizowego** *dozwolone jest odstępowanie od ograniczeń określonych w art. 9 oraz obowiązków określonych w art. 18 i art. 25 ust. 1, na podstawie ogólnego albo indywidualnego zezwolenia dewizowego, w zakresie i na warunkach określonych w takim zezwoleniu* ✂ **działający na podstawie ustawy** ✂ **opracowano na podstawie: t.j. Dz. U. z 2013**

📖 Possible equivalents: base, basis (en), base, fondamento (it)

POMOC (pl)

Always singular

(Adj) **pomoc finansowa, publiczna** *w przypadku gdy umorzenie dotyczy kredytu technologicznego udzielonego na inwestycje technologiczne w sektorze budownictwa*

okrętowego, maksymalny limit pomocy publicznej wynosi 22,5 % wydatków, o których mowa w ust. 7

(N) **raty pomocy** *w przypadku gdy uprawniony zawarł umowę, o której mowa w art. 6 ust. 2 pkt 2 lit. b, przekazywanie rat pomocy rozpoczyna się po upływie okresu wypłaty świadczenia z tytułu tej umowy* ✂ **udzielanie pomocy**

(P) **pomoc de minimis** *premia technologiczna przeznaczona na pokrycie wydatków, o których mowa w ust. 6, wraz z wszelką inną pomocą, w tym pomocą de minimis, udzielaną na pokrycie tych samych wydatków, nie może przekroczyć 50 % wartości tych wydatków.*

✎ **pomoc finansowa, o której mowa w ust. 1** ✂ **płatność rat pomocy, udzielanie pomocy finansowej** ✂ **Ustawa z dnia 19 czerwca 2009 r. o pomocy państwa w spłacie niektórych kredytów mieszkaniowych udzielonych osobom, które utraciły pracę** ✂ **w celu zapewnienia środków na finansowanie zadań funduszu w zakresie udzielania pomocy podmiotom objętym systemem gwarantowania** *nadwyżka bilansowa Funduszu w danym roku powiększa jego fundusz własny, tworzony w celu zapewnienia środków na finansowanie zadań Funduszu w zakresie udzielania pomocy podmiotom objętym systemem gwarantowania, fundusz kas oraz fundusz stabilizacyjny, z zastrzeżeniem ust. 2a i 2b* ✂ **pomoc jest przyznana** *pomoc nie może być przyznana na spłatę kredytu mieszkaniowego, jeżeli jeden z kredytobiorców uzyskał pomoc na zasadach określonych w ustawie, chyba że pomoc nie jest już udzielana, a okres udzielonej pomocy nie przekroczył 11 miesięcy* ✂ **zakup nie był współfinansowany (...) z krajowych środków pomocy publicznej lub pomocy de minimis**

🕮 Possible equivalents: aid, assistance, support (en), aiuto, assistenza, patrocinio, soccorso, sostegno (it)

PORĘCZENIE (pl)

(Adj) **udzielane / udzielone poręczenie** *łączna kwota pożyczek i kredytów udzielonych jednemu członkowi kasy oraz zobowiązań tego członka wynikających z udzielonych poręczeń, nie może przekraczać 10 % funduszu oszczędnościowo-pożyczkowego, o którym mowa w art. 25, z zastrzeżeniem ust. 2 i art. 34*

(N) **poręczenie i/ lub gwarancja** ✂ **kwota poręczenia** *Rada Ministrów udziela poręczenia lub gwarancji, jeżeli kwota poręczenia lub gwarancji przekracza równowartość 30 000 000 euro* **udzielanie / udzielenie poręczenia umowa poręczenia** *Skarb Państwa, w drodze umowy poręczenia, udziela bankom poręczeń spłaty kredytów mieszkaniowych, spłacanych na zasadach określonych w ustawie o pomocy państwa, zwanych dalej 'poręczeniami'*

(V) **udzielać poręczenia**

(P) **z tytułu poręczenia** *wykonanie zobowiązań z tytułu poręczenia następuje na wniosek kredytodawcy w przypadku utraty przez kredytobiorcę zdolności kredytowej, po przedstawieniu przez kredytodawcę dokumentów i informacji potwierdzających brak tej zdolności*

✏ *(NOMINAL)* **udzielone poręczenie i/lub gwarancja** ✂ **poręczenia i gwarancje, o których mowa w ust. 1** ✂ **poręczenie Skarbu Państwa, o którym mowa w ust. 1** ✂ **kwota poręczenia i/lub gwarancji, opłata prowizyjna od poręczenia i/lub gwarancji, udzielanie poręczeń i gwarancji, udzielenie poręczenia lub gwarancji, umowa poręczenia lub gwarancji, zobowiązanie objęte poręczeniem lub gwarancją** *poręczenie lub gwarancja są udzielane do wysokości 60 % pozostającej do spłaty kwoty zobowiązania objętego poręczeniem lub gwarancją wraz z 60 % należnych odsetek od tej kwoty i innych kosztów bezpośrednio związanych z tym zobowiązaniem* ✂ **udzielenie kredytu, pożyczki pieniężnej, gwarancji bankowej i poręczenia** ✂ **zobowiązania z tytułu poręczenia** ✂ **ustawa o objęciu poręczeniami Skarbu Państwa spłaty niektórych kredytów mieszkaniowych, ustawa z dnia 8 maja 1997 r. o poręczeniach i gwarancjach udzielanych przez Skarb Państwa oraz niektóre osoby prawne**

✏ **z tytułu poręczeń i gwarancji udzielanych przez Skarb Państwa, z tytułu udzielonych poręczeń i gwarancji** *kwota, o której mowa w ust. 1, nie obejmuje poręczeń i gwarancji Skarbu Państwa udzielonych na wykonanie zobowiązań objętych już poręczeniem lub gwarancją Skarbu Państwa, w zakresie, w jakim nie powoduje to zwiększenia zobowiązań Skarbu Państwa z tytułu udzielonych poręczeń i gwarancji* **z tytułu wykonania przez Skarb Państwa umów poręczania, o których mowa w ust. 1, z tytułu wykonania umowy poręczenia** ✂ **udzielać poręczenia i/lub gwarancji**

📖 Possible equivalents: bail, bond, guarantee (en), fideiussione, garanzia (it)

POSIADACZ (pl)

(N) **posiadacz czeku** *czek rozrachunkowy może być przedstawiony do rozrachunku ze skutkami zapłaty bezpośrednio u trasata lub w banku, w którym posiadacz czeku ma rachunek* **posiadacz rachunku** *posiadacz rachunku bankowego dysponuje swobodnie środkami pieniężnymi zgromadzonymi na rachunku*

✎ **posiadacz rachunku bankowego / oszczędnościowego / oszczędnościowo-kredytowego / powierniczego** ✂ **śmierć posiadacza rachunku, spadek po posiadaczu rachunku** *w przypadku śmierci posiadacza rachunku powierniczego zgromadzone na tym rachunku kwoty nie wchodzą do spadku po posiadaczu rachunku* ✂ **dane umożliwiające identyfikację posiadacza rachunku** *banki, na pisemne zadanie Zakładu Ubezpieczeń Społecznych, są obowiązane do sporządzania i przekazywania informacji dotyczących numerów rachunków bankowych płatników składek oraz przekazywania danych umożliwiających identyfikacje posiadaczy tych rachunków*

📖 Possible equivalents: bearer, HOLDER, owner, possessor, proprietor (en), detentore, possessore, portatore, TITOLARE (it),

POSTĘPOWANIE (pl)

Usually singular

(Adj) **postępowanie administracyjne, cywilne, egzekucyjne, karne, naprawcze, przygotowawcze, ugodowe, upadłościowe** *po uprawomocnieniu się ugody zawieszone postępowania układowe, upadłościowe i egzekucyjne, w odniesieniu do wierzytelności objętych ugodą, ulegają umorzeniu, a wydane w toku tych postępowań tytuły wykonawcze pozbawia się z mocy prawa wykonalności* ✂ **toczące się postępowanie** *z dniem wszczęcia postępowania ugodowego do czasu jego umorzenia, uprawomocnienia się ugody lub uchylenia ugody bankowej przez sąd 1) ulegają zawieszeniu toczące się postępowania układowe i upadłościowe* ✂ **objęty postępowaniem**

(N) **program postępowania** *zarząd komisaryczny opracowuje i uzgadnia z Komisją Nadzoru Finansowego program postępowania naprawczego, kieruje jego realizacją oraz nie rzadziej niż co 3 miesiące informuje Komisję Nadzoru Finansowego i radę nadzorczą o wynikach realizacji programu* **tryb postępowania** *tryb postępowania*

kasy i Kasy Krajowej w razie wystąpienia okoliczności, o których mowa w ust. 1, określa odrębna ustawa ✂ **prowadzenie, wszczęcie postępowania**

(V) **prowadzić postępowanie** *jeżeli dłużnik nie wykonuje wynikających z ugody bankowej zobowiązań, bank, który prowadził postępowanie ugodowe, z własnej inicjatywy lub na wniosek innego wierzyciela, o którym mowa w pkt 2 1) występuje do sądu rejonowego – sądu gospodarczego, właściwego dla siedziby dłużnika, z wnioskiem o rozwiązanie ugody bankowej*

(P) **postępowanie w sprawie** ✂ **w toku postępowania** *w razie niedopełnienia obowiązku, o którym mowa w ust. 1, pisma w toku postępowania pozostawia się w aktach sprawy ze skutkiem doręczenia, z wyłączeniem decyzji kończącej postępowanie w przedmiocie zawiadomienia*

egzekucja w trybie przepisów o postępowaniu egzekucyjnym w administracji *należności z tytułu wpłat na finansowanie kosztów nadzoru, o których mowa w ust. 1, podlegają egzekucji w trybie przepisów o postępowaniu egzekucyjnym w administracji* **opracowanie programu postępowania naprawczego, o którym mowa w ust. 1, organ uprawniony do prowadzenia postępowania przygotowawczego, realizacja programu postępowania naprawczego, zagraniczne postępowanie upadłościowe** ✂ **Kodeks postępowania administracyjnego, Kodeks postępowania cywilnego (ugodowego)** ✂ **objęty bankowym postępowaniem ugodowym** *wierzytelności zabezpieczone zastawem lub hipoteką wyłączone na podstawie art. 11 pkt 4 i 5 mogą zostać objęte bankowym postępowaniem ugodowym tylko za zgodą wierzycieli* ✂ **prowadzić postępowanie karne lub postępowanie w sprawie o przestępstwo skarbowe (przeciwko)**

Possible equivalents: ACTION, INVESTIGATION, procedure, PROCEEDINGS (en), procedimento, PROCEDURA, processo (it)

POŻYCZKA (pl)

(Adj) **pożyczka studencka, pieniężna** *przepisy ustawy stosuje się do umów kredytu i pożyczki pieniężnej, zawieranych przez bank zgodnie z przepisami ustawy z dnia 12 maja 2011 r. o kredycie konsumenckim, w zakresie nieuregulowanym w tej ustawie* ✂ **pożyczka udzielona**

(N) **oprocentowanie pożyczki** *stopa oprocentowania pożyczki studenckiej wynosi nie mniej niż połowę stopy redyskontowej Narodowego Banku Polskiego* **spłata pożyczki** ✂ **udzielanie, udzielenie pożyczek**

✏ **kredyt studencki i/lub pożyczka studencka** ✂ **spłata kredytu i/lub pożyczki** *wysokość raty spłat kredytu studenckiego lub pożyczki studenckiej nie może przekroczyć 20 % miesięcznego dochodu pożyczkobiorcy lub kredytobiorcy* ✂ **udzielenie kredytu, pożyczki pieniężnej, gwarancji bankowej lub poręczenia** *udzielenie kredytu, pożyczki pieniężnej, gwarancji bankowej lub poręczenia członkowi zarządu albo rady nadzorczej banku lub osobie zajmującej stanowisko kierownicze w banku następuje zgodnie z regulaminem uchwalonym przez radę nadzorczą*

📖 Possible equivalents: borrowing, LOAN (en), CREDITO, prestito (it)

PRACA (pl)

(N) **Fundusz Pracy, stosunek pracy** *osoby, o których mowa w ust. 2, są obowiązane do zachowania tajemnicy, zarówno w trakcie pełnienia funkcji lub pozostawania w stosunku pracy, jak również po zakończeniu pełnienia funkcji lub ustaniu stosunku pracy* **urząd pracy**

(V) **utracić pracę** *pomoc może być przyznana kredytobiorcy zobowiązanemu do spłaty kredytu mieszkaniowego, który po dniu 1 lipca 2008 r. utracił pracę rozumiana jako 1) zatrudnienie lub inna pracę zarobkowa lub 2) prowadzenie działalności gospodarczej*

✏ **dysponent Funduszu Pracy** *Dysponent Funduszu Pracy przekazuje środki, o których mowa w ust. 1, na wyodrębniony rachunek w Banku Gospodarstwa Krajowego w terminie 7 dni od dnia złożenia zapotrzebowania na te środki* **powiatowy urząd pracy** ✂ **pomoc państwa w spłacie niektórych kredytów mieszkaniowych udzielonych osobom, które utraciły pracę** ✂ **zaliczać się do okresów pracy oraz innych okresów, od których zależy nabycie uprawnień pracowniczych** *okres urlopu bezpłatnego zalicza się do okresów pracy oraz innych okresów, od których zależy nabycie uprawnień pracowniczych*

📖 Possible equivalents: employment, job, labour, work (en), impiego, lavoro, occupazione (it)

PRAWO (pl)

(Adj) **prawo bankowe, dewizowe, majątkowe, naprawcze, polskie, spółdzielcze, upadłościowe** ✂ **podlegający prawu** *przepis ust. 1 stosuje się odpowiednio do podmiotów mających siedzibę na terytorium Rzeczypospolitej Polskiej, będących uczestnikami systemów płatności lub systemów rozrachunku papierów wartościowych podlegających prawu innego państwa członkowskiego*

(N) **prawo głosu, własności** ✂ **prawo konsumenta (do)** ✂ **prawo do lokalu** *w przypadku spółdzielczego lokatorskiego prawa do lokalu członkowi spółdzielni przysługuje roszczenie o przekształcenie tego prawa do lokalu na własnościowe prawo do lokalu albo o przeniesienie przez spółdzielnię mieszkaniową na rzecz członka prawa własności lokalu mieszkalnego* ✂ **przepisy prawa**

(V) **prawo + przysługiwać** *kuratorowi przysługuje prawo uczestniczenia w posiedzeniach organów banku oraz prawo do uzyskiwania wszelkich informacji niezbędnych do wykonywania jego funkcji* ✂ **mieć prawo**

(P) **z mocy prawa** *na Fundusz przechodzą, z mocy prawa, wierzytelności przysługujące deponentowi w stosunku do masy upadłości, w wysokości środków gwarantowanych*

✎ **prawo upadłościowe i naprawcze** ✂ **akcje lub prawa z akcji banku krajowego** ✂ **prawo do lokalu, którego przedmiotem jest lokal mieszkalny, prawo odrębnej własności lokalu, przejmowane prawa majątkowe, spółdzielcze lokatorskie prawo do lokalu mieszkalnego, spółdzielcze własnościowe prawo do lokalu** ✂ **decyzja o przejęciu wybranych praw majątkowych lub wybranych zobowiązań, informacje o prawie konsumenta (do), nabycie albo objęcie akcji lub praw z akcji, przepisy prawa polskiego, składanie oświadczeń w zakresie praw i obowiązków majątkowych, system rozrachunku papierów wartościowych** *przepis ust. 1 stosuje się odpowiednio do podmiotów mających siedzibę na terytorium Rzeczypospolitej Polskiej, będących uczestnikami systemów płatności lub systemów rozrachunku papierów wartościowych podlegających prawu innego państwa członkowskiego* **wykonywanie prawa głosu z akcji** *w przypadku, o którym mowa w ust. 4, obowiązek złożenia zawiadomienia powstaje przed przystąpieniem do wykonywania prawa głosu z akcji albo wykonywania uprawnień podmiotu dominującego wobec banku krajowego* ✂ **podlegający prawu polskiemu** ✂ **w przypadku przejęcia wybranych praw majątkowych**

lub wybranych zobowiązań kasy ✂ prowadzić do naruszenia przepisów prawa ✂ konsument ma prawo, Funduszowi przysługuje prawo

📖 Possible equivalents: LAW, POWER, RIGHT (en), DIRITTO, LEGGE (it)

PREMIA (pl)

(Adj) **premia gwarancyjna, technologiczna ✂ przekazana premia** *do czasu upływu terminu, o którym mowa w ust. 5 lub 5a, zwrócona równowartość przekazanej premii gwarancyjnej jest przechowywana na nieoprocentowanym rachunku bankowym w banku, o którym mowa w art. 3 ust. 3* **wypłacane premie**

(N) **promesa, przyznanie, równowartość, wypłata premii** *wypłata premii technologicznej następuje na wniosek przedsiębiorcy złożony do Banku Gospodarstwa Krajowego, za pośrednictwem banku kredytującego*

✎ **wypłacane premie gwarancyjne ✂ promesa premii technologicznej** *Bank Gospodarstwa Krajowego przyznaje promesę premii technologicznej nie później niż do końca miesiąca następującego po miesiącu, w którym został złożony kompletny wniosek, albo po miesiącu, w którym usunięto nieprawidłowości* **równowartość przekazanej premii gwarancyjnej** *inwestor na podstawie upoważnienia, o którym mowa w ust. 3 pkt 2, dokonuje zwrotu równowartości przekazanej premii gwarancyjnej* **wniosek o likwidację książeczki mieszkaniowej i wypłatę premii gwarancyjnej, wniosek o przyznanie / wypłatę premii technologicznej, złożenie wniosku o częściową wypłatę premii technologicznej**

📖 Possible equivalents: bonus, premium (en), premio (it)

PREZES (pl)

Usually singular

(Adj) **ogłaszany przez prezesa** *wysokość miesięcznego wynagrodzenia osób wchodzących w skład Rady Funduszu ustala się jako wielokrotność przeciętnego miesięcznego wynagrodzenia w sektorze przedsiębiorstw bez wypłat nagród z zysku w czwartym kwartale roku poprzedniego, ogłoszonego przez Prezesa Głównego Urzędu Statystycznego*

(N) **powołanie prezesa** *powołanie prezesa zarządu kasy następuje za zgodą Komisji Nadzoru Finansowego* ✂ **prezes zarządu** *wynagrodzenie kuratora ustala Komisja Nadzoru Finansowego, z tym że w kasach, w których w statutach przewidziano wynagrodzenie dla prezesa zarządu, wynagrodzenie kuratora nie może być wyższe niż wynagrodzenie prezesa zarządu kasy, w której ustanowiono kuratora*

✎ **Prezes Głównego Urzędu Statystycznego, Prezes Narodowego Banku Polskiego, Prezes Rady Ministrów, prezes zarządu banku, prezes zarządu kasy** ✂ **po zasięgnięciu opinii Prezesa Narodowego Banku Polskiego i Przewodniczącego Komisji Nadzoru Finansowego** *przewodniczącego Rady Funduszu powołuje i odwołuje minister właściwy do spraw instytucji finansowych, po zasięgnięciu opinii Prezesa Narodowego Banku Polskiego i Przewodniczącego Komisji Nadzoru Finansowego* ✂ **prezes + określać w drodze rozporządzenia** *Prezes Rady Ministrów określa, w drodze rozporządzenia, terminy uiszczania, wysokość i sposób obliczania wpłat, o których mowa w ust. 1, uwzględniając zapewnienie skuteczności sprawowanego nadzoru*

📖 Possible equivalents: chairman, governor, president (en), presidente (it)

PROWIZJA (pl)

(Adj) **należna prowizja**

(N) **pobieranie prowizji** ✂ **odsetki i prowizje, opłaty i prowizje, prowizje i opłaty** *warunki udzielania kredytu technologicznego, w szczególności prowizje i opłaty, nie mogą być mniej korzystne niż warunki proponowane przy udzielaniu przez bank kredytujący innych kredytów inwestycyjnych*

(P) **prowizja z tytułu** *Bankowi Gospodarstwa Krajowego przysługuje prowizja z tytułu realizacji zadań wynikających z przepisów ustawy*

✎ **prowizja za spłatę kredytu przed terminem** *prowizja za spłatę kredytu przed terminem nie może przekraczać 1 % spłacanej części kredytu, jeżeli okres między datą spłaty kredytu a terminem spłaty kredytu przekracza jeden rok* ✂ **opłaty, prowizje, marże oraz koszty usług dodatkowych** *kredytodawca lub pośrednik kredytowy przed zawarciem umowy o kredyt zabezpieczony hipoteką jest zobowiązany podać konsumentowi, na trwałym nośniku (…) informację o kosztach, które konsument* *jest zobowiązany ponieść w związku z umową o kredyt, w szczególności odsetkach, opłatach, prowizjach, marżach oraz kosztach usług dodatkowych*

📖 Possible equivalents: fee, commission (en), commissione (it)

PRZEDSIĘBIORCA (pl)

(Adj) **przedsiębiorca zagraniczny** ✂ **mały przedsiębiorca, średni przedsiębiorca** ✂ **krajowi przedsiębiorcy** *ze środków budżetu państwa udzielane są dopłaty do oprocentowania kredytów bankowych dla krajowych przedsiębiorców na 1) cele rolnicze*

(N) **rejestr przedsiębiorców** *NBP nie podlega wpisowi do rejestru przedsiębiorstw państwowych*

(V) **powierzyć coś przedsiębiorcy** ✂ **przedsiębiorca jest obowiązany** *przedsiębiorca jest obowiązany zapewnić kontrolującym 1) swobodny dostęp do urządzeń i pomieszczeń, za pomocą których realizowana jest inwestycja technologiczna*

(P) **przedsiębiorca w rozumieniu** *kredytodawca – przedsiębiorca w rozumieniu przepisów ustawy z dnia 23 kwietnia 1964 r. – Kodeks cywilny, który w zakresie swojej działalności gospodarczej lub zawodowej, udziela lub daje przyrzeczenie udzielenia konsumentowi kredytu*

✎ **mikroprzedsiębiorca, mały i/lub średni przedsiębiorca** *kredyt technologiczny jest udzielany przez bank kredytujący mikroprzedsiębiorcy, małemu lub średniemu przedsiębiorcy posiadającemu zdolność kredytową* ✂ **krajowi przedsiębiorcy prowadzący produkcję rolniczą** ✂ **wpisanie do rejestru przedsiębiorców** ✂ **powierzyć coś przedsiębiorcy lub przedsiębiorcy zagranicznemu** *kasa może, w drodze umowy agencyjnej, powierzyć przedsiębiorcy lub przedsiębiorcy zagranicznemu pośrednictwo w zawieraniu i zmianie umów o wykonywanie czynności, o których mowa w art. 3 ust. 1*

📖 Possible equivalents: contractor, entrepreneur, operator, trader (en), imprenditore, operatore (it)

PRZEDSIĘBIORSTWO (pl)

(Adj) **małe, średnie przedsiębiorstwo** ✂ **przedsiębiorstwo bankowe** *nabycie przedsiębiorstwa bankowego lub jego zorganizowanej części przez bank wymaga zezwolenia Komisji Nadzoru Finansowego* ✂ **przedsiębiorstwo utworzone (przez)**

(N) **mienie przedsiębiorstwa** ✂ **nabycie, nabywca przedsiębiorstwa** ✂ **komercjalizacja, prywatyzacja, restrukturyzacja przedsiębiorstw, sektor przedsiębiorstw** *wysokość miesięcznego wynagrodzenia osób wchodzących w skład Rady Funduszu ustala się jako wielokrotność przeciętnego miesięcznego wynagrodzenia w sektorze przedsiębiorstw*

zlikwidowane państwowe przedsiębiorstwo gospodarki rolnej ✂ **sektor małych i średnich przedsiębiorstw** *wsparcie stanowi regionalną pomoc inwestycyjną w rozumieniu art. 13 rozporządzenia Komisji (WE) nr 800/2008 oraz pomoc na usługi doradcze dla małych i średnich przedsiębiorstw* ✂ **restrukturyzacja przedsiębiorstw przemysłu lekkiego** ✂ **przeciętne miesięczne wynagrodzenie w sektorze przedsiębiorstw** ✂ **oddziały, przedstawicielstwa i przedsiębiorstwa**

Possible equivalents: COMPANY, concern, enterprise, establishment, UNDERTAKING (en), compagnia, IMPRESA, ditta, azienda, SOCIETÀ (it)

PRZEPIS (pl)

(Adv) **zgodnie z przepisami** *Kasa Krajowa przeprowadza lustrację zrzeszonych kas zgodnie z przepisami ustawy z dnia 16 września 1982 r. – Prawo spółdzielcze*

(Adj) **przepisy dotychczasowe, końcowe, ogólne, przejściowe** *przepisy przejściowe, zmiany w przepisach obowiązujących i przepisy końcowe* ✂ **odrębne przepisy** *przepisów ust. 2 nie stosuje się do przedsiębiorstw państwowych, których prywatyzacja wymaga zgody Rady Ministrów na podstawie odrębnych przepisów, chyba że Rada Ministrów wyrazi zgodę na prywatyzację, oraz do państwowych przedsiębiorstw gospodarki rolnej* ✂ **przepisy dotyczące, określające** ✂ **wynikający z przepisów** *w sprawozdaniu finansowym na dzień 31 grudnia 2003 r. BGK uwzględni zmiany wynikające z przepisów ustawy*

(N) **przepisy Kodeksu, prawa, rozdziału, ustawy ✂ przepisy o ochronie, o rachunkowości ✂ naruszenie przepisów** *Komisja Nadzoru Finansowego odmawia zatwierdzenia zmiany statutu Kasy Krajowej, jeżeli zmiana ta mogłaby prowadzić do naruszenia przepisów prawa, bezpieczeństwa środków gromadzonych w kasach lub bezpieczeństwa lokat kas gromadzonych przez Kasę Krajową*

(V) **stosować przepisy** *do zlecenia biegłemu rewidentowi badania sprawozdania finansowego kasy albo Kasy Krajowej, o którym mowa w ust. 2, nie stosuje się przepisów ustawy z dnia 29 stycznia 2004 r. – Prawo zamówień publicznych (Dz. U. z 2010 r. Nr 113, poz. 759, z późn. zm.18)*

(P) **z naruszeniem przepisu, z wyjątkiem przepisów ✂ w rozumieniu przepisów** *dom jednorodzinny – budynek mieszkalny jednorodzinny w rozumieniu przepisów ustawy z dnia 7 lipca 1994 r. – Prawo budowlane* **w trybie przepisów** *kara, o której mowa w ust. 1, podlega egzekucji w trybie przepisów o postępowaniu egzekucyjnym w administracji*

(NOMINAL) **przepisy niniejszego rozdziału, przepisy niniejszej ustawy, przepisy o niektórych formach wspierania działalności innowacyjnej, przepisy o ochronie informacji niejawnych, przepisy Prawa bankowego** *do zasad tworzenia, organizacji i działania banków hipotecznych nieuregulowanych w niniejszej ustawie stosuje się odpowiednio przepisy Prawa bankowego oraz przepisy o Narodowym Banku Polskim* **przepisy prawa polskiego, przepisy przejściowe i końcowe, przepisy wydane na podstawie art. 1 ✂ zmiany w przepisach obowiązujących**

na podstawie odrębnych przepisów, na zasadach określonych w przepisach *gospodarka finansowa środkami gromadzonymi na rachunku, o którym mowa w ust. 2, prowadzona jest przez ministra właściwego do spraw finansów publicznych, w imieniu Skarbu Państwa, na zasadach określonych w przepisach ustawy* ✂ **w rozumieniu przepisów ustawy z dnia 1 stycznia 2010r., w trybie przepisów o postępowaniu egzekucyjnym w administracji** *egzekucję należności z tytułu zwrotów pomocy, o których mowa w art. 13, 14 i 16, prowadzi starosta w trybie przepisów o postępowaniu egzekucyjnym w administracji* ✂ **zgodnie z odrębnymi przepisami, zgodnie z przepisami ustawy z dnia 1 stycznia 2010 r. ✂ prowadzić do naruszenia przepisów prawa ✂ przepisy + mieć zastosowanie ✂ przepisy art. 1 ust. 1 stosuje się odpowiednio** *do poręczenia Skarbu Państwa, o którym mowa w ust. 1, stosuje się odpowiednio przepisy art. 31, 43 ust. 1 i 2, art. 43a, 44–44b, 45 pkt 1 i art. 47*

Possible equivalents: DIRECTION, PROVISION, rule, regulation (en), DISPOSIZIONE (it)

PRZYPADEK (pl)

(Adj) **w uzasadnionych przypadkach** *w 1990 r. w szczególnie uzasadnionych przypadkach, w okresie nie przekraczającym 6 miesięcy, bank może na żądanie kredytobiorcy dopisać do jego zadłużenia więcej niż 60 % oprocentowania kredytu* ✂ **w przypadku określonym (w)**

(N) **w przypadku braku, nabycia, niedotrzymania, niespełnienia, ogłoszenia, przejęcia, spełnienia, stwierdzenia, wystąpienia, zagrożenia** *w terminie 6 miesięcy od dnia wejścia w życie niniejszej ustawy, w przypadku zagrożenia płynności spółdzielczej kasy oszczędnościowo-kredytowej Narodowy Bank Polski może udzielić bezpośrednio tej kasie kredytu w celu uzupełnienia jej zasobów pieniężnych* ✂ **w przypadku banków, oddziału** *w przypadku oddziału instytucji kredytowej przystępującego do systemu gwarantowania dzień utworzenia funduszu ochrony środków gwarantowanych określa Zarząd Funduszu w trybie określonym w art. 2b ust. 3*

(P) **w przypadku gdy** *w przypadku gdy zastosowanie ma kwota 150 mln euro, o której mowa w ust. 1a, Komisja Nadzoru Finansowego może zezwolić na przekroczenie limitu, o którym mowa w ust. 1b, powyżej 100 % funduszy własnych banku* ✂ **w przypadku, o którym mowa (w)** ✂ **w szczególności w przypadku** *osoby inne niż wymienione w ust. 1, które zapoznały się z informacjami stanowiącymi tajemnicę zawodową, w szczególności w przypadkach, o których mowa w ust. 4 pkt 2 i ust. 7 i 8, obowiązane są do zachowania tajemnicy zawodowej, o ile z przepisów odrębnych nie wynika obowiązek dalszego udzielania tych informacji*

✎ **w przypadku, o którym mowa w ust. 1, w przypadku określonym w art. 1** ✂ **w przypadku banków spółdzielczych, w przypadku umowy o kredyt** ✂ **w przypadku ogłoszenia upadłości, w przypadku przejęcia wybranych praw majątkowych lub wybranych zobowiązań kasy, w przypadku spełnienia warunku gwarancji** *w przypadku spełnienia warunku gwarancji zarządca komisaryczny, po ustaleniu stanu ksiąg rachunkowych kasy na dzień spełnienia* *warunku gwarancji, sporządza listę deponentów* **w przypadku stwierdzenia nieprawidłowości** ✂ **w szczególnie uzasadnionych przypadkach** *Komisja Nadzoru Finansowego może w szczególnie uzasadnionych przypadkach wyrazić zgodę na przekroczenie limitu, o którym mowa w ust. 2*

Possible equivalents: case (en), CASO (it)

R

RACHUNEK (pl)

(Adj) **rachunek bankowy, bieżący, oszczędnościowy, powierniczy** *na rachunku powierniczym mogą być gromadzone wyłącznie środki pieniężne powierzone posiadaczowi rachunku – na podstawie odrębnej umowy – przez osobę trzecią* **rachunek wspólny** *w przypadku prowadzenia przez bank jednego rachunku dla kilku osób (rachunek wspólny), deponentem jest każda z tych osób – w granicach określonych w umowie rachunku, a w przypadku braku postanowień umownych lub przepisów w tym zakresie – w częściach równych* ✂ **własny rachunek** *Komisja Nadzoru Finansowego odmawia wyrażenia zgody na powołanie członka zarządu Kasy Krajowej, jeżeli: 3) został wobec niego orzeczony zakaz prowadzenia działalności gospodarczej na własny rachunek oraz pełnienia funkcji reprezentanta lub pełnomocnika przedsiębiorcy, członka rady nadzorczej lub komisji rewizyjnej w spółce akcyjnej, spółce z ograniczoną odpowiedzialnością lub w spółdzielni* **wyodrębniony rachunek** ✂ **gromadzony na rachunku** *umowa o powołaniu umownego funduszu gwarantowania środków pieniężnych może stanowić o objęciu ochroną także środków pieniężnych gromadzonych na rachunkach bankowych innych niż te, o których mowa w art. 2 pkt 2*

(N) **rachunek dłużnika, wierzyciela** ✂ **rachunki deponentów** ✂ **numer, obciążenie rachunku** *dyspozycja wierzyciela oznacza równocześnie jego zgodę na cofnięcie przez bank dłużnika obciążenia rachunku dłużnika i cofnięcie uznania rachunku wierzyciela w przypadku dokonanego przez dłużnika odwołania polecenia zapłaty, o którym mowa w ust. 6* **posiadacz, umowa, współposiadacz rachunku** ✂ **obsługa rachunków**

✏ *(SYNTACTIC NOMINAL)* **rachunek budżetu państwa** *zakres działania BGK może obejmować również 1) obsługę bankową rachunków budżetu państwa*

rachunek oszczędnościowo-rozliczeniowy konsumenta, rachunek papierów wartościowych *w celu nabywania lub zbywania papierów wartościowych, o których mowa w ust. 3 pkt 2, Fundusz może również posiadać rachunki papierów wartościowych w zagranicznej izbie rozliczeniowej i posiadać rachunek bankowy do przeprowadzania rozliczeń z tym związanych* **rachunek zysków i strat** ✂ **rachunek w Narodowym Banku Polskim** ✂ **rachunki wymienione w ust. 1**

✏ **rachunek oszczędnościowy, rachunek oszczędnościowo-rozliczeniowy lub rachunek terminowej lokaty oszczędnościowej** ✂ **posiadacz rachunku oszczędnościowo kredytowego, posiadacz rachunku powierniczego** ✂ **blokada środków na rachunku, śmierć posiadacza rachunku, środki gromadzone na rachunku, środki gwarantowane na rachunkach deponentów, środki pieniężne zgromadzone na rachunku, środki zdeponowane na rachunku** *likwidator prowadzi likwidację w taki sposób, aby zapewnić zaspokojenie lub przejęcie zobowiązań kasy w likwidacji z tytułu środków gwarantowanych zdeponowanych na rachunkach deponentów, o których mowa w art. 38l pkt 1 ustawy z dnia 14 grudnia 1994 r. o Bankowym Funduszu Gwarancyjnym* **umowa o kredyt w rachunku oszczędnościowo-rozliczeniowym** ✂ **w imieniu i na rachunek Skarbu Państwa, we własnym imieniu i na własny rachunek** *kredytów, o których mowa w art. 15a, Bank Gospodarstwa Krajowego udziela we własnym imieniu i na własny rachunek*

📖 Possible equivalents: ACCOUNT (en), CONTO (it)

RADA (pl)

(Adj) **rada nadzorcza** *od decyzji, o której mowa w ust. 1, rada nadzorcza kasy lub Kasy Krajowej może wnieść skargę do sądu administracyjnego w terminie 7 dni od daty doręczenia decyzji*

(N) **Rada Funduszu, Rada Ministrów** *Rada Funduszu i Zarząd Funduszu wykonują swoje funkcje przy pomocy Biura Funduszu, którego strukturę organizacyjną oraz zasady działania określa Zarząd Funduszu w uzgodnieniu z Radą Funduszu* ✂ **członek rady, skład rady** *uprawnienia osób wchodzących w skład rady wierzycieli, o której mowa w ust. 3 pkt 1, w zakresie należności przysługujących im z tytułu pełnienia tych funkcji, określa akt powołania.*

✏ **rada nadzorcza banku, rada nadzorcza kasy, Rada Polityki Pieniężnej** *Rada Polityki Pieniężnej, zwana dalej 'Radą', ustala corocznie założenia polityki* *pieniężnej i przedkłada je do wiadomości Sejmowi równocześnie z przedłożeniem przez Radę Ministrów projektu ustawy budżetowej* ✂ **członek rady nadzorczej, członek zarządu lub rady** *udział osób będących członkami zarządu lub rady banku dominującego albo członkami zarządu lub rady banku zależnego oraz osób zajmujących stanowiska kierownicze w organach banków należących do grupy bankowej – nie stanowi działalności konkurencyjnej niedozwolonej na podstawie odrębnych przepisów* **mandat członka rady** ✂ **Prezes Rady Ministrów** ✂ **Rada Ministrów + określić w drodze rozporządzenia** *Rada Ministrów określi, w drodze rozporządzenia, tryb i warunki rozliczeń z bankami z tytułu poręczeń Skarbu Państwa spłaty niektórych kredytów mieszkaniowych*

Possible equivalents: BOARD, COMMITTEE, council (en), comitato, CONSIGLIO, giunta (it)

RAMY (pl)

Always plural

(P) **w ramach działalności, nadzoru, systemu** *w ramach systemu zarządzania w banku funkcjonuje co najmniej 1) system zarządzania ryzykiem 2) system kontroli wewnętrznej*

w ramach działalności transgranicznej, w ramach programów rządowych, w ramach realizacji programów rządowych popierania budownictwa mieszkaniowego *Bank Gospodarstwa Krajowego udziela kredytów w ramach realizacji programów rządowych popierania budownictwa mieszkaniowego* ✂ **nieprawidłowości stwierdzone w ramach** *Kasa jest obowiązana 3) niezwłocznie zawiadomić Komisję Nadzoru Finansowego i Kasę Krajową o środkach, jakie zostaną podjęte w celu usunięcia nieprawidłowości stwierdzonych w ramach kontroli oraz nadzoru*

Possible equivalents: under (en), ambito, quadro (it)

RATA (pl)

(Adj) **miesięczna rata / rata miesięczna** ✂ **równe raty** ✂ **raty kapitałowe** *wysokość pomocy określa się w złotych jako równowartość 12 miesięcznych rat kapitałowych i odsetkowych kredytu mieszkaniowego*

(N) **raty kredytu, pomocy, spłaty** *wysokość raty spłat kredytu studenckiego lub pożyczki studenckiej nie może przekroczyć 20 % miesięcznego dochodu pożyczkobiorcy lub kredytobiorcy* ✂ **wysokość raty** ✂ **płatność raty, spłata rat**

kolejność zaliczania rat *kredytodawca lub pośrednik kredytowy przed zawarciem umowy o kredyt konsumencki jest zobowiązany podać konsumentowi, na trwałym nośniku (…), zasady i terminy spłaty kredytu oraz w odpowiednich przypadkach kolejność zaliczania rat kredytu konsumenckiego na poczet należności kredytodawcy* ✂ **płatność, przekazywanie rat pomocy** *w przypadku gdy uprawniony zawarł umowę, o której mowa w art. 6 ust. 2 pkt 2 lit. b, przekazywanie rat pomocy rozpoczyna się po upływie okresu wypłaty świadczenia z tytułu tej umowy* ✂ **spłata rat kapitałowych, wysokość miesięcznej raty kapitałowej, wysokość rat kapitałowo-odsetkowych**

Possible equivalents: instalment, repayment (en), RATA (it)

REALIZACJA (pl)

(N) **realizacja obowiązku** *minister właściwy do spraw instytucji finansowych, po zasięgnięciu opinii Prezesa NBP, określa, w drodze rozporządzenia, sposób, zakres i terminy realizacji obowiązku, o którym mowa w ust. 2a, kierując się potrzebą zapewnienia NBP dostępu do informacji niezbędnych do wykonywania jego obowiązków wynikających z ustawy oraz odrębnych przepisów* **realizacja programu, zadań, zleceń, wypłat** ✂ **sposób realizacji**

(P) **w celu realizacji, w ramach realizacji** *Bank Gospodarstwa Krajowego udziela kredytów w ramach realizacji programów rządowych popierania budownictwa mieszkaniowego* **w związku z realizacją** *w celu realizacji programów rządowych minister właściwy do spraw finansów publicznych przekazuje środki na zwiększenie funduszu statutowego Banku Gospodarstwa Krajowego, mając na względzie konieczność pokrycia ryzyka działalności bankowej ponoszonego przez Bank Gospodarstwa Krajowego w związku z realizacją tych programów*

realizacja inwestycji technologicznej finansowanej kredytem technologicznym *środki trwałe, o których mowa w ust. 5, muszą być powiązane ze sobą funkcjonalnie i służyć do realizacji inwestycji technologicznej finansowanej kredytem technologicznym* **realizacja programu postępowania naprawczego** *Zarząd NBP może zwolnić bank, spółdzielczą kasę oszczędnościowo-kredytową* *oraz Krajową Spółdzielczą Kasę Oszczędnościowo-Kredytową, z obowiązku utrzymywania rezerwy obowiązkowej w okresie realizacji programu postępowania naprawczego* **realizacja programów rządowych popierania budownictwa mieszkaniowego, realizacja zleceń rozrachunku** ✂ **realizacja zadań, o których mowa w art. 1** ✂ **w celu realizacji programów rządowych, w ramach realizacji programów rządowych**

Possible equivalents: execution, exercise, implementation (en), ATTUAZIONE, effettuazione, esecuzione, realizzazione, raggiungimento (it)

ROK (pl)

(Adj) **rok budżetowy, kalendarzowy, obrotowy, poprzedni** ✂ **rok poprzedzający** ✂ **ostatni rok** ✂ **lata ubiegłe** *zarząd komisaryczny może dokonać zamknięcia ksiąg rachunkowych banku i sporządzić sprawozdanie finansowe banku na dzień wyznaczony przez Komisję Nadzoru Finansowego oraz podjąć uchwałę o pokryciu straty za okres kończący się w tym dniu oraz straty za lata ubiegłe* ✂ **nie dłuższy niż 2 lata** *pożyczki studenckie i kredyty studenckie są udzielane także na okres studiów doktoranckich, nie dłuższy jednak niż 4 lata*

(N) **okres 2 lat** *powiernika i jego zastępcę powołuje na okres 6 lat, na wniosek rady nadzorczej banku hipotecznego, Komisja Nadzoru Finansowego* ✂ **2 lata trwania**

(P) **na dany rok, w danym roku, za rok** *należności banków z tytułu zmienionego, stosownie do przepisów niniejszej ustawy, oprocentowania kredytów za rok 1990 podlegają spłacie w 40 % kwoty odsetek, a w pozostałej części są dopisywane do zadłużenia kredytobiorcy* ✂ **rok od daty, od dnia** *uprawnienie, o którym mowa w ust. 1, wygasa po upływie roku od dnia wykonania umowy* ✂ **po upływie roku, przed upływem roku, w okresie roku**

ostatni rok obrotowy *przeznaczenie do podziału między akcjonariuszy kwoty przekraczającej zysk za ostatni rok obrotowy, pomniejszony o niepokryte straty, akcje własne oraz o kwoty, które nie mogą być przeznaczone na wypłatę dywidendy, wymaga zgody Komisji Nadzoru Finansowego* **poprzedni rok obrotowy, rok osiągnięcia wymaganego progu kapitałowego** ✂ **kara pozbawienia wolności do 2 dwóch, okres co najmniej 2 lat, zysk z lat ubiegłych** ✂ **do dnia 30 czerwca każdego roku, do końca roku kalendarzowego, po upływie roku od dnia** *uprawnienie, o którym mowa w ust. 1, wygasa po upływie roku od dnia wykonania umowy* ✂ **na koniec każdego roku w ciągu ostatnich 2 lat trwania umowy**

📖 Possible equivalents: YEAR (en), ANNO (it)

ROZDZIAŁ (pl)

Usually singular

(Adj) **niniejszy rozdział** ✂ **rozdział dodany (przez)** ✂ **określony w rozdziale** *oświadczam, że 2) znane mi są i spełniam szczególne warunki wykonywania działalności kantorowej określone w rozdziale 4 ustawy z dnia 27 lipca 2002 r. – Prawo dewizowe*

(N) **przepisy rozdziału** *przy udostępnianiu osobom trzecim akcji banku zależnego stosuje się odpowiednio przepisy rozdziału 3 ustawy, o której mowa w art. 19 ust. 2, z wyłączeniem art. 24 tej ustawy*

✏ **rozdział dodany przez art. 1 pkt 10 ustawy, o której mowa w odnośniku 1** ✂ **przepisy niniejszego rozdziału** ✂ **stosować przepisy rozdziału** *do realizacji zadań, o których mowa w ust. 2, stosuje się przepisy rozdziału 3a ustawy zmienianej w art. 4*

📖 Possible equivalents: chapter (en), capitolo, CAPO (it)

ROZPORZĄDZENIE (pl)

Usually singular

(Adv) **wydając rozporządzenie** *jeżeli podmiotem prowadzącym obsługę centralnego rachunku bieżącego budżetu państwa jest Narodowy Bank Polski, Minister Finansów, wydając rozporządzenie, o którym mowa w ust. 5, zasięga opinii Prezesa Narodowego Banku Polskiego*

(N) **załącznik do rozporządzenia** *mikroprzedsiębiorca – mikroprzedsiębiorstwo w rozumieniu Załącznika I do rozporządzenia Komisji (WE) nr 800/2008*

(P) **w drodze rozporządzenia** *Minister Finansów określa, w drodze rozporządzenia, szczegółowe zasady obsługi rachunków bankowych wymienionych w ust. 1 oraz zakres informacji wymienionej w ust. 5 pkt 1 i sprawozdań wymienionych w ust. 5 pkt 2, z zastrzeżeniem ust. 7.*

✏ **rozporządzenie, o którym mowa w ust. 1** ✂ **art. 1 ust.1 rozporządzenia** *kredyt technologiczny nie może być udzielany 1) na realizację dużego projektu* *inwestycyjnego w rozumieniu art. 2 pkt 12 oraz art. 13 ust. 10 rozporządzenia Komisji (WE) nr 800/2008* **załącznik I do rozporządzenia Komisji (WE)** ✂ **minister właściwy do spraw instytucji finansowych + określić w drodze rozporządzenia, Rada Ministrów + określić w drodze rozporządzenia**

Possible equivalents: decree, ENACTMENT, regulation (en), DECRETO, DISPOSIZIONE, REGOLAMENTO (it)

RZECZPOSPOLITA POLSKA (pl)

Always singular

(N) **Sejm Rzeczypospolitej Polskiej, terytorium Rzeczypospolitej Polskiej** *przynajmniej jedna z instytucji, których powiązania prawne tworzą system, powinna posiadać siedzibę na terytorium Rzeczypospolitej Polskiej*

Dziennik Urzędowy Rzeczypospolitej Polskiej *założenia polityki pieniężnej, sprawozdanie z wykonania założeń polityki pieniężnej oraz akty normatywne organów NBP – z wyjątkiem aktów, o których mowa w art. 54 ust. 1 – ogłaszane są w Dzienniku Urzędowym Rzeczypospolitej Polskiej 'Monitor Polski'* **instytucja kredytowa prowadząca działalność na terytorium Rzeczypospolitej Polskiej, obwieszczenie Marszałka Sejmu Rzeczypospolitej Polskiej z dnia 1 stycznia 2010 r. (w sprawie), podmiot mający siedzibę na terytorium Rzeczypospolitej Polskiej, uzyskanie przez Rzeczpospolitą Polską członkostwa w Unii Europejskiej** *dane dotyczące ogłoszenia aktów prawa Unii Europejskiej, zamieszczone w niniejszej ustawie – z dniem uzyskania przez Rzeczpospolitą Polską członkostwa w Unii Europejskiej – dotyczą ogłoszenia tych aktów w Dzienniku Urzędowym Unii Europejskiej – wydanie specjalne*

Possible equivalents: Republic of Poland (en), Repubblica di Polonia (it)

S

SKARB PAŃSTWA (pl)

Usually singular

(Adj) **gwarantowany, udzielany/udzielony przez Skarb Państwa** *tworzy się zasób majątkowy Skarbu Państwa, zwany dalej 'zasobem', przeznaczony na zaspokojenie roszczeń z tytułu poręczeń i gwarancji udzielanych przez Skarb Państwa*

(N) **Minister Skarbu Państwa** *Minister Skarbu Państwa w porozumieniu z Ministrem Finansów, działając w imieniu Skarbu Państwa, może wnieść na pokrycie podwyższenia kapitału, o którym mowa w art. 14 pkt 2, należące do Skarbu Państwa akcje banków, o których mowa w art. 1 ust. 2 lub 3* **poręczenie, wierzytelność Skarbu Państwa** *ugodę obejmującą wierzytelności Skarbu Państwa podpisuje w imieniu Skarbu Państwa Minister Finansów lub osoba przez niego upoważniona.* **własność Skarbu Państwa** ✂ **zadłużenie wobec Skarbu Państwa**

(P) **w imieniu Skarbu Państwa** *Minister, w imieniu Skarbu Państwa, podejmuje działania zmierzające do odzyskania zadłużenia kredytobiorców wobec Skarbu Państwa z tytułu wykonania umów poręczenia, z zastrzeżeniem ust. 2*

✎ **Skarb Państwa lub Narodowy Bank Polski** ✂ **jednoosobowa spółka Skarbu Państwa** *jeżeli dłużnikiem jest przedsiębiorstwo państwowe: 1) Minister Przekształceń Własnościowych przekształci przedsiębiorstwo w jednoosobową spółkę Skarbu Państwa, w trybie i na zasadach przepisów ustawy o prywatyzacji przedsiębiorstw państwowych, najpóźniej w ciągu 30 dni od dnia podpisania ugody* **minister właściwy do spraw Skarbu Państwa, objęcie poręczeniami Skarbu Państwa spłaty niektórych kredytów mieszkaniowych, papiery wartościowe emitowane przez Skarb Państwa** ✂ **spłata zadłużenia kredytobiorcy wobec Skarbu Państwa z tytułu wykonania przez Skarb Państwa umowy poręczenia** ✂ **Agencja Własności Rolnej Skarbu Państwa** ✂ **ustawa z dnia 8 maja 1997**

r. o poręczeniach i gwarancjach udzielanych przez Skarb Państwa oraz niektóre osoby prawne ✂ stanowiący własność Skarbu Państwa ✂ w imieniu i na rachunek Skarbu Państwa, z tytułu poręczeń i gwarancji udzielanych przez Skarb Państwa *tworzy się zasób majątkowy Skarbu Państwa, zwany dalej 'zasobem', przeznaczony na zaspokojenie roszczeń z tytułu poręczeń i gwarancji udzielanych przez Skarb Państwa*

📖 Possible equivalents: TREASURY (en), tesoro (it)

SPŁATA (pl)

(Adj) **terminowa spłata** *dopłaty są przekazywane bankom pod warunkiem terminowej spłaty kredytu o stałej stopie procentowej wraz z odsetkami, z zastrzeżeniem ust. 2*

(N) **SPŁATA KREDYTU, spłata pożyczki, raty** *przez nieterminową spłatę kredytu o stałej stopie procentowej spłacanego w okresach miesięcznych lub kwartalnych należy rozumieć brak spłaty raty przez kolejne trzy miesiące* **spłata zobowiązań ✂ gwarancja, rata spłaty** *wysokość raty spłat kredytu studenckiego lub pożyczki studenckiej nie może przekroczyć 20 % miesięcznego dochodu pożyczkobiorcy lub kredytobiorcy* **sposób spłaty**

✎ **pozostająca do spłaty kwota kredytu, odroczenie płatności lub zmiana sposobu spłaty** *kredytodawca lub pośrednik kredytowy przed zawarciem umowy o kredyt przewidującej odroczenie płatności lub zmianę sposobu spłaty w przypadku gdy konsument jest w zwłoce ze spłatą zadłużenia wynikającego z umowy o kredyt jest zobowiązany podać konsumentowi, na trwałym nośniku 1) dane określone w art. 13 ust. 1* **✂ w związku ze spłatą zadłużenia wynikającego z umowy o kredyt ✂ informacje o możliwości żądania w dowolnym momencie spłaty pełnej kwoty kredytu przez konsumenta**

📖 Possible equivalents: discharge, PAYMENT, reimbursement, repayment (en) PAGAMENTO, RIMBORSO (it)

SPŁATA KREDYTU (pl)

(Adj) **spłata kredytu mieszkaniowego** *ustawa określa zasady przyznawania okresowej zwrotnej pomocy państwa osobom fizycznym zobowiązanym do spłaty kredytu mieszkaniowego, które utraciły pracę, zwanej dalej 'pomocą', oraz warunki korzystania z pomocy i jej zwrotu* **spłata kredytu studenckiego**

(N) **spłata kredytów i pożyczek** *czynności podejmowane przez Kasę Krajową w ramach kontroli działalności kas polegają w szczególności na 4) badaniu zabezpieczenia i terminowości spłaty kredytów i pożyczek kas* ✂ **okres, zabezpieczenie spłaty kredytu**

(P) **spłata kredytu przed terminem, spłata kredytu wraz z odsetkami** *NBP przy udzielaniu kredytu refinansowego kieruje się zdolnością banku do spłaty tego kredytu wraz z odsetkami w umownych terminach spłaty, z zastrzeżeniem, o którym mowa w ust. 3*

✎ **spłata kredytu, o którym mowa w ust. 1** ✂ **prowizja za spłatę kredytu przed terminem** *prowizja za spłatę kredytu przed terminem nie może przekraczać 1 % spłacanej części kredytu, jeżeli okres między datą spłaty kredytu a terminem spłaty kredytu przekracza jeden rok* ✂ **ustawa o objęciu poręczeniami Skarbu Państwa spłaty niektórych kredytów mieszkaniowych, ustawa z dnia 19 czerwca 2009 r. o pomocy państwa w spłacie niektórych kredytów mieszkaniowych udzielonych osobom, które utraciły pracę**

📖 Possible equivalents: credit repayment, loan repayment (en) rimborso del credito, rimborso del prestito, rimborso del mutuo (it)

SPOSÓB (pl)

Usually singular

(N) **termin i sposób** *kredytodawca lub pośrednik kredytowy przed zawarciem umowy o kredyt konsumencki jest zobowiązany podać konsumentowi, na trwałym nośniku 6) terminy i sposób wypłaty kredytu* ✂ **sposób dokonywania, obliczania, prowadzenia, realizacji, spłaty, zabezpieczenia** *do wierzytelności Funduszu związanych z udzieleniem pomocy, o której mowa w art. 4 ust. 2 pkt 1, stosuje się przepisy Kodeksu cywilnego oraz innych ustaw regulujących rodzaje i sposoby zabezpieczeń wierzytelności banków* ✂ **określenie, zmiana sposobu**

(P) **w sposób** *podmiot objęty systemem gwarantowania przechowuje dane w systemie wyliczania, w sposób zapewniający ich odtworzenie oraz dostęp do nich Komisji Nadzoru Finansowego oraz Funduszowi*

odroczenie płatności lub zmiana sposobu spłaty *kredytodawca lub pośrednik kredytowy przed zawarciem umowy o kredyt przewidującej odroczenie płatności lub zmianę sposobu spłaty w przypadku gdy konsument jest w zwłoce ze spłatą zadłużenia wynikającego z umowy o kredyt jest zobowiązany podać konsumentowi, na trwałym nośniku 1) dane określone w art. 13 ust. 1* ✂ **sposób, w jaki podawane są informacje o świadczonych usługach** ✂ **w sposób określony w art. 1** *wykonanie zobowiązania w sposób określony w art. 3 ust. 1 oraz wykonanie obowiązku określonego w art. 4 następuje z zastosowaniem kursów euro w stosunku do walut narodowych, wskazanych w tabeli zawartej w załączniku do ustawy*

Possible equivalents: manner, means, method, mode, way (en) FORMA, metodo, MODALITÀ, modo (it)

SPÓŁKA (pl)

(Adj) **spółka akcyjna, handlowa** *jeżeli podmiotem prowadzącym system jest spółka handlowa w rozumieniu Kodeksu spółek handlowych, na spółkę przejmującą lub spółkę nowo zawiązaną – powstałą w związku z połączeniem lub podziałem – nie przechodzi zgoda, o której mowa w art. 16* **spółka holdingowa, publiczna, zarządzająca**

(N) **statut spółki** *ilekroć w ustawie jest mowa o (…) statutach – należy przez to rozumieć statuty spółek akcyjnych oraz umowy i akty założycielskie spółek z ograniczoną odpowiedzialnością* ✂ **przekształcenie w spółkę**

spółka z ograniczoną odpowiedzialnością, (jednoosobowa) spółka Skarbu Państwa, unijna dominująca finansowa spółka holdingowa o działalności mieszanej *Komisja Nadzoru Finansowego informuje unijną instytucję dominującą, unijny podmiot dominujący w holdingu finansowym, unijną dominującą finansową spółkę holdingową o działalności mieszanej albo bank o najwyższej sumie bilansowej, o których mowa w ust. 6, o sprawowaniu przez siebie nadzoru skonsolidowanego* ✂ **spółka akcyjna, której kapitał akcyjny należy (do)** ✂ **bank w formie spółki akcyjnej, przekształcenie banku państwowego w spółkę akcyjną** ✂ **Kodeks**

spółek handlowych, ustawa z dnia 29 lipca 2005 r. o ofercie publicznej i warunkach wprowadzania instrumentów finansowych do zorganizowanego obrotu oraz o spółkach publicznych

📖 Possible equivalents: COMPANY, corporation, partnership (en), IMPRESA, SOCIETÀ (it)

SPRAWA (pl)

(P) **w sprawie ogłoszenia, wniosku, zastosowania, zatwierdzenia** *do decyzji Komisji Nadzoru Finansowego w sprawie zatwierdzenia prezesa zarządu kasy art. 21 ust. 1–3 stosuje się odpowiednio* ✂ **decyzja w sprawie** *w przypadku niedokonania płatności w terminie określonym w wezwaniu, starosta wydaje decyzję w sprawie zwrotu pomocy* **opinia, postępowanie, umowa w sprawie** ✂ **w sprawach dotyczących** *w sprawach dotyczących wpisu do rejestru, nieuregulowanych w niniejszym rozdziale, Prezes Narodowego Banku Polskiego stosuje przepisy Kodeksu postępowania administracyjnego*

✎ **minister właściwy do spraw finansów publicznych** *w celu zabezpieczenia wierzytelności wynikających z udzielonego wsparcia, o którym mowa w ust. 1, minister właściwy do spraw finansów publicznych żąda ustanowienia zabezpieczenia gwarantującego zwrot pełnej kwoty wsparcia wraz z odsetkami* **minister właściwy do spraw gospodarki / do spraw instytucji finansowych / do spraw Skarbu Państwa / do spraw szkolnictwa wyższego** ✂ **minister właściwy do spraw budownictwa, lokalnego planowania i zagospodarowania przestrzennego oraz mieszkalnictwa** ✂ **obwieszczenie Marszałka Sejmu Rzeczypospolitej Polskiej w sprawie ogłoszenia jednolitego tekstu ustawy, postępowanie w sprawie o przestępstwo skarbowe, umowa w sprawie partycypacji w kosztach budowy lokali** *powiat, gmina lub związek międzygminny, działając w celu podnajmowania lokali mieszkalnych osobom fizycznym, może zawierać z towarzystwem umowy w sprawie partycypacji w kosztach budowy lokali mieszkalnych, których będzie najemcą*

📖 Possible equivalents: MATTER (en), CASO, MATERIA (it)

STOPA (pl)

(Adj) **stopa referencyjna** *użyte w ustawie określenia oznaczają: 9) stopa referencyjna – zmienną stopę procentową, stanowiącą podstawę ustalenia wysokości dopłat do oprocentowania kredytów preferencyjnych, równą przeciętnej stopie WIBOR trzymiesięczny, obliczaną jako średnia arytmetyczna notowań w kwartale poprzedzającym dany kwartał, powiększoną o 2 punkty procentowe, publikowaną w Biuletynie Informacji Publicznej przez Bank Gospodarstwa Krajowego* **stopa procentowa**

(N) **stopa oprocentowania** *stopa oprocentowania pożyczki studenckiej wynosi nie mniej niż połowę stopy redyskontowej Narodowego Banku Polskiego*

(P) **według stopy** *dopłata stanowi równowartość 50 % kwoty odsetek naliczonych od podstawy naliczenia dopłaty, według stopy referencyjnej obowiązującej w dniu naliczenia dopłaty*

✎ **rzeczywista roczna stopa oprocentowania** *rzeczywista roczna stopa oprocentowania – całkowity koszt kredytu ponoszony przez konsumenta, wyrażony jako wartość procentowa całkowitej kwoty kredytu w stosunku rocznym* **stopa procentowa kredytu, stała stopa procentowa, stopa rezerwy obowiązkowej** *stopa rezerwy obowiązkowej może być zróżnicowana ze względu na umowny okres przechowywania środków pieniężnych, rodzaj waluty, a także rodzaj dokonywanych operacji finansowych stanowiących źródło pozyskania środków* ✂ **stopa redyskontowa weksli przyjmowanych od banków do redyskonta przez Narodowy Bank Polski** *dopłaty ze środków budżetu państwa do oprocentowania kredytów na cele, o których mowa w art. 3 ust. 1 pkt 4, przysługują w wysokości oprocentowania naliczonego według stopy równej stopie redyskontowej weksli przyjmowanych od banków do redyskonta przez Narodowy Bank Polski, powiększonego o marżę banku* ✂ **stopy CIRR** ✂ **kredyty o stałej stopie procentowej, wysokość stałej stopy procentowej kredytu eksportowego, zmiana wysokości stopy oprocentowania** ✂ **wysokość stopy oprocentowania kredytu uzależniona jest od wysokości stopy referencyjnej**

📖 <u>Possible equivalents:</u> rate, ratio (en) saggio, TASSO (it)

STOSUNEK (pl)

Usually singular

(Adj) **w stosunku rocznym** *kredyty kontraktowe są oprocentowane w wysokości nie większej niż 0,50 stopy redyskonta w Narodowym Banku Polskim, jednak w wysokości nie mniejszej niż 4 % w stosunku rocznym*

(N) **stosunek pracy** *osoby, o których mowa w ust. 2, są obowiązane do zachowania tajemnicy, zarówno w trakcie pełnienia funkcji lub pozostawania w stosunku pracy, jak również po zakończeniu pełnienia funkcji lub ustaniu stosunku pracy*

(P) **w stosunku do** ✂ **według stosunku** *obligacje i inne papiery wartościowe emitowane przed dniem 1 stycznia 1995 r. wyrażają po tej dacie wartość przeliczoną według stosunku, o którym mowa w art. 1*

✎ **stosunek, o którym mowa w art. 1 ust. 1** ✂ **w stosunku do banku krajowego / do instytucji finansowej / do oddziału** *przepis ust. 1 nie wyłącza uprawnień Komisji Nadzoru Finansowego w stosunku do oddziału instytucji kredytowej w przypadkach, o których mowa w art. 141a* ✂ **kasa, w stosunku której podjęto decyzję** *kasa, w stosunku do której podjęto decyzję o przejęciu wybranych praw majątkowych lub wybranych zobowiązań, na wniosek kasy albo banku przejmującego niezwłocznie zamieszcza ogłoszenie, o którym mowa w ust. 5* **podmiot zależny w stosunku do instytucji kredytowej**

📖 Possible equivalents: relation, relationship (en), RAPPORTO, RELAZIONE (it)

SYSTEM (pl)

(Adj) **system informatyczny** *działalność, o której mowa w ust. 1, polega na 5) opracowywaniu standardów świadczenia usług i prowadzenia dokumentacji przez kasy oraz systemów informatycznych dla kas*

(N) **system gwarantowania, obrotu, płatności, rozrachunku** *przepis ust. 1 stosuje się odpowiednio do podmiotów mających siedzibę na terytorium Rzeczypospolitej Polskiej, będących uczestnikami systemów płatności lub systemów rozrachunku papierów wartościowych podlegających prawu innego państwa członkowskiego*

system wyliczania *system wyliczania – system informatyczny podmiotu objętego systemem gwarantowania, przeznaczony do zapewnienia możliwości niezwłocznego uzyskania wszelkich danych pozwalających na identyfikację deponentów oraz określenie wysokości należnych poszczególnym deponentom środków gwarantowanych* ✂ **funkcjonowanie systemu** ✂ **rozrachunek, uczestnictwo w systemie** *w razie ogłoszenia upadłości uczestnika systemu do jego praw i obowiązków związanych z uczestnictwem w systemie stosuje się przepisy prawa polskiego, z zastrzeżeniem art. 12*

(V) **system + współpracować** *podmiot prowadzący system interoperacyjny koordynuje moment wprowadzenia zlecenia rozrachunku do systemu oraz moment, od którego zlecenie rozrachunku nie może zostać odwołane, z zasadami funkcjonowania systemów, z którymi prowadzony przez niego system współpracuje, w tym także systemów podlegających prawu innego państwa członkowskiego*

(P) **w odniesieniu do systemu** *podmioty prowadzące systemy, o których mowa w ust. 1, z wyjątkiem NBP i Krajowego Depozytu, przekażą odpowiednio NBP w odniesieniu do systemów płatności lub KPWiG w odniesieniu do systemów rozrachunku papierów wartościowych, w terminie 3 miesięcy od dnia wejścia w życie ustawy, dokumenty wskazane w art. 17 ust 2*

✎ **Europejski System Banków Centralnych, system autoryzacji i rozliczeń** *NBP prowadzi i ogłasza na swojej stronie internetowej listę podmiotów, które prowadza systemu autoryzacji i rozliczeń* **system kontroli wewnętrznej, system zarządzania ryzykiem** ✂ **funkcjonowanie systemu wyliczania, prawidłowość funkcjonowania systemu, zasady funkcjonowania systemu** ✂ **dane zawarte /znajdujące się w systemie wyliczania, moment wprowadzenia zlecenia rozrachunku do systemu** *moment wprowadzenia zlecenia rozrachunku do systemu oraz moment, od którego zlecenie rozrachunku nie może być odwołane, określają zasady funkcjonowania tego systemu* **podmiot prowadzący system, stabilność krajowego systemu finansowego, uczestnik systemu płatności lub systemu rozrachunku papierów wartościowych** ✂ **Ustawa z dnia 24 sierpnia 2001 r. o ostateczności rozrachunku w systemach płatności i systemach rozrachunku papierów wartościowych oraz zasadach nadzoru nad tymi systemami, Ustawa z dnia 29 lipca 2005 r. o ofercie publicznej i warunkach wprowadzania instrumentów finansowych do zorganizowanego systemu obrotu oraz o spółkach publicznych**

✎ *(THEMATIC NOMINAL)* **obowiązkowa wpłata podmiotów objętych systemem gwarantowania, system gwarantowania środków pieniężnych** *celem obowiązkowego systemu gwarantowania środków pieniężnych zgromadzonych w kasach, zwanego dalej 'systemem gwarantowania kas', jest zapewnienie deponentom wypłaty, do wysokości określonej ustawą, środków gwarantowanych w razie ich niedostępności* **ustawowy system gwarantowania** *podmioty objęte systemem gwarantowania obowiązane są poinformować osoby korzystające oraz zainteresowane korzystaniem z ich usług o braku ochrony gwarancyjnej w przypadku, gdy 1) wierzytelność, powstająca w związku z wykonywaniem czynności bankowych, nie będzie chroniona przez ustawowy system gwarantowania* ✂ **środki na finansowanie zadań Funduszu w zakresie udzielania pomocy podmiotom objętym systemem gwarantowania**

📖 Possible equivalents: system (en), SISTEMA (it)

SZCZEGOLNOŚĆ (pl)

(Adv) **uwzględniając w szczególności** *Rada Ministrów określi, w drodze rozporządzenia, sposób powiadamiania, o którym mowa w ust. 1, 2, 2a, w ust. 3 pkt 1 i 2 oraz w ust. 4, uwzględniając w szczególności właściwości postępowania, w którym wydano orzeczenie, postanowienie lub decyzję, oraz możliwość wykorzystania technicznych środków łączności* **wskazując w szczególności**

(V) **określać w szczególności, polegać w szczególności (na), zawierać w szczególności** *list emisyjny zawiera w szczególności: 1) datę emisji; 2) powołanie podstawy prawnej emisji; 3) jednostkową wartość nominalną* ✂ **należy w szczególności** *do zadań Funduszu w zakresie gromadzenia i analizowania informacji o podmiotach objętych systemem gwarantowania należy w szczególności opracowywanie analiz i prognoz dotyczących sektora bankowego*

(P) **w szczególności w przypadku** *Fundusz może odmówić udzielenia gwarancji rekapitalizacyjnej, w szczególności w przypadku istotnego zaangażowania środków Funduszu w stosunku do banku krajowego, w ramach zadań określonych w art. 4 ust. 1j pkt 1 lub ust. 2 pkt 1 lub pkt 1a*

📖 Possible equivalents: particular (en), particolare (it)

Ś

ŚRODEK (pl)

Usually plural

(Adj) **środek płatniczy** ✂ **środki finansowe, pieniężne, trwałe** *łączna wartość zakupionych przez kasę środków trwałych nie może przekroczyć 100 % funduszy własnych kasy* ✂ **ŚRODKI GWARANTOWANE** *środki gwarantowane – środki pieniężne zgromadzone w banku przez deponenta na rachunkach imiennych oraz jego należności wynikające z innych czynności bankowych, w walucie polskiej lub walutach obcych, według stanu na dzień spełnienia warunku gwarancji, potwierdzone dokumentami imiennymi wystawionymi przez ten bank lub imiennymi świadectwami depozytowymi* **środki gromadzone (w), określone (w)** *Komisja Nadzoru Finansowego może, bez konieczności uprzedniego upomnienia na piśmie, zastosować środki określone w art. 71 ust. 2, w przypadku gdy kasa nie doprowadzi, zgodnie z treścią decyzji, o której mowa w ust. 4, do zmiany albo rozwiązania umowy* **środki pochodzące (z), środki przekazane, przyjęte, uzyskane, wpłacone**

(N) **środki funduszu** *środki funduszu innowacyjności są gromadzone na odrębnym rachunku bankowym* ✂ **bezpieczeństwo, część, suma środków** ✂ **gwarantowanie środków** *do zadań Funduszu w zakresie funkcjonowania systemu gwarantowania środków pieniężnych w kasach należy wykonywanie obowiązków wynikających z gwarantowania środków pieniężnych na zasadach określonych w ustawie* **podjęcie, przeznaczenie, wyczerpanie, wykorzystanie, zapewnienie środków**

(V) **przekazywać środki** *w celu realizacji programów rządowych, o których mowa w ust. 1 pkt 3, 5 i 7, minister właściwy do spraw finansów publicznych przekazuje środki na zwiększenie funduszu statutowego BGK* **zastosować środki** *w przypadku braku*

realizacji zaleceń, o których mowa w ust. 4a, Komisja Nadzoru Finansowego13) może zastosować środki określone w art. 138 ustawy - Prawo bankowe

(P) **środki na rachunku** ✂ **z wykorzystaniem środków** *do podmiotu, którego udziały albo akcje zostały nabyte z wykorzystaniem środków pochodzących z pomocy finansowej Funduszu, przepisy ust. 1 stosuje się odpowiednio*

✏ **wartości dewizowe lub krajowe środki płatnicze** ✂ **prawny środek płatniczy** *znaki pieniężne, nieodpowiadające wskutek zużycia lub uszkodzenia warunkom ustalonym przez Prezesa NBP, przestają być prawnym środkiem płatniczym na obszarze Rzeczypospolitej Polskiej i podlegają wymianie* ✂ **środki funduszu stabilizacyjnego, środki pieniężne zgromadzone na rachunku** ✂ **środki, o których mowa w art. 1** ✂ **środki, jakie zostaną podjęte w celu usunięcia nieprawidłowości** ✂ **fundusz własny, tworzony w celu zapewnienia środków na finansowanie zadań Funduszu** ✂ **zastosować środki określone w art. 1** ✂ **środki + podlegać zwrotowi** *w przypadkach, o których mowa w ust. 4, środki podlegają zwrotowi na rachunek, o którym mowa w ust. 1, w wysokości i terminie umożliwiających ich przeznaczenie na cele określone w ust. 3*

✏ *(SYNTACTIC NOMINAL)* **dopłata ze środków budżetu państwa, odsetki przejściowo wykupione ze środków budżetu państwa** ✂ **bezpieczeństwo środków gromadzonych (w), blokada środków na rachunku, obowiązkowy system gwarantowania środków pieniężnych, przeznaczenie kredytu lub środków, suma środków pieniężnych, zakup rzeczowych środków obrotowych** *za kredyty na cele rolnicze, o których mowa w art. 3 ust. 1 pkt 1, uważa się kredyty 1) dla krajowych przedsiębiorców prowadzących produkcję rolniczą, przeznaczone na: a) zakup rzeczowych środków obrotowych do produkcji rolniczej* **zakup współfinansowany ze środków**

📖 Possible equivalents: funds, means, measure (en), fondi, mezzo (it)

ŚRODKI GWARANTOWANE (pl)

Always plural

(N) **suma, wypłata środków gwarantowanych** *członkowie Zarządu Funduszu działający z należytą starannością nie ponoszą odpowiedzialności za szkodę wynikłą z niewłaściwej realizacji wypłat środków gwarantowanych* **wysokość środków gwarantowanych** *na Fundusz przechodzą, z mocy prawa, wierzytelności*

przysługujące deponentowi w stosunku do masy upadłości, w wysokości środków gwarantowanych ✂ **deponenci środków gwarantowanych** *system wyliczania zapewnia gotowość do bieżącego sporządzania danych pozwalających na identyfikację deponentów, miejsca ich zamieszkania lub siedziby oraz na określenie wysokości należnych poszczególnym deponentom środków gwarantowanych, zwanych dalej 'danymi', według stanu na koniec każdego dnia*

✏ **środki gwarantowane na rachunkach deponentów** ✂ **środki gwarantowane, o których mowa w ust. 1** ✂ **dokonanie wypłat środków gwarantowanych, fundusz ochrony środków gwarantowanych** *podmiot objęty systemem gwarantowania obowiązany jest tworzyć fundusz ochrony środków gwarantowanych na zaspokojenie roszczeń deponentów w przypadku spełnienia warunków gwarancji przez którykolwiek podmiot objęty tym systemem* ✂ **wielkość zobowiązań z tytułu środków gwarantowanych + przewyższać sumę środków** *w przypadku gdy wielkość zobowiązań z tytułu środków gwarantowanych przewyższa sumę środków, o których mowa w ust. 1, Fundusz dokonuje wypłat środków gwarantowanych ze środków funduszu własnego Funduszu przeznaczonego do ewidencjonowania środków odzyskanych z mas upadłości banków*

📖 Possible equivalents: guaranteed funds (en), fondi garantiti (it)

T

TERMIN (pl)

(Adj) **termin określony (w)** *w okresie 14 dni od upływu terminu określonego w ust. 3 docelowy kredytobiorca informuje pisemnie instytucję ustawowo upoważnioną do udzielania kredytów o niewykonaniu zobowiązania, o którym mowa w tym przepisie*

(N) **termin i sposób, tryb i termin** ✂ **termin przekazywania** *umowa określa zasady, tryb i terminy naliczania, przekazywania i rozliczania dopłat, a także zakres i terminy składania przez instytucje ustawowo upoważnione do udzielania kredytów informacji o udzielonych kredytach preferencyjnych* **termin realizacji, uiszczenia, wykupu, wymagalności** *bank może potrącić ze swego długu wierzytelność, której termin wymagalności jeszcze nie nadszedł, jeżeli podmiot będący dłużnikiem został postawiony w stan likwidacji, oraz we wszystkich tych przypadkach, gdy służy bankowi prawo ściągnięcia swych wierzytelności przed nadejściem terminu płatności* **termin wypłaty, wypowiedzenia** ✂ **nadejście terminu**

(P) **przed terminem, w terminie** ✂ **przed upływem terminu, w wyznaczonym terminie** *w przypadku stwierdzenia braków w zawiadomieniu lub gdy nie zostały załączone do niego wymagane informacje lub dokumenty, Komisja Nadzoru Finansowego wzywa podmiot składający zawiadomienie do uzupełnienia tych braków w wyznaczonym terminie*

termin określony w umowie ✂ **spłata kredytu przed terminem** *prowizja za spłatę kredytu przed terminem nie może przekraczać 1 % spłacanej części kredytu, jeżeli okres między datą spłaty kredytu a terminem spłaty kredytu przekracza jeden rok* **upływ terminu, o którym mowa w ust. 1** ✂ **w terminie 10 dni (roboczych) od dnia otrzymania / zatwierdzenia / złożenia** *konsument zwraca niezwłocznie* *kredytodawcy kwotę udostępnionego kredytu wraz z odsetkami, o których mowa w ust. 1, nie później niż w terminie 30 dni od dnia złożenia oświadczenia o odstąpieniu od umowy* **w terminie miesiąca od dnia wejścia w życie ustawy, w terminie nie dłuższym niż 10 dni** ✂ **wnieść skargę do sądu administracyjnego w terminie 10 dni od dnia doręczenia decyzji** ✂ **być spłacanym przez konsumenta w terminie do jednego miesiąca** *kredytodawca lub pośrednik kredytowy przed zawarciem umowy o kredyt w rachunku oszczędnościowo-rozliczeniowym, który jest spłacany przez konsumenta w terminie do trzech miesięcy jest zobowiązany podać konsumentowi, na trwałym nośniku: 1) dane określone w art. 13; 2) informację o warunkach i sposobie rozwiązania umowy o kredyt*

📖 <u>Possible equivalents:</u> DATE, period (en), DATA, scadenza, TERMINE (it)

TERYTORIUM (pl)

Usually singular

(N) **terytorium państwa** *ograniczenie to nie dotyczy przypadków, w których informacje nie są objęte ochroną prawną na terytorium Rzeczypospolitej Polskiej lub na terytorium państwa, w którym funkcjonuje system gwarantowania przekazujący informacje* ✂ **działalność, siedziba na terytorium**

✏ **terytorium państwa członkowskiego, terytorium państwa goszczącego** *bank, o którym mowa w ust. 1, może wykonywać na terytorium państwa goszczącego czynności bankowe ustalone w statucie w zakresie, w jakim nie sprzeciwiają się temu przepisy ustawy* ✂ **instytucja kredytowa prowadząca działalność na terytorium Rzeczypospolitej Polskiej** *decyzję, o której mowa w ust. 13, otrzymuje instytucja kredytowa prowadząca działalność na terytorium Rzeczypospolitej Polskiej poprzez istotny oddział, istotny oddział instytucji kredytowej oraz właściwe władze nadzorcze zainteresowanych państw członkowskich* **podmiot mający siedzibę na terytorium Rzeczypospolitej Polskiej**

📖 <u>Possible equivalents:</u> area, territory (en), TERRITORIO (it)

TRYB (pl)

Always singular

(Adj) **szczegółowy tryb** *szczegółowy tryb działania Zarządu NBP określa regulamin uchwalony przez Zarząd*

(N) **tryb i terminy, warunki i tryb, zasady i tryb** *minister właściwy do spraw Skarbu Państwa określi, w drodze rozporządzenia, szczegółowe zasady i tryb podziału akcji, o których mowa w ust. 1, pomiędzy uprawnione osoby* ✂ **tryb działania, postępowania, przekazywania** *szczegółowy zakres i tryb przekazywania danych, o których mowa w ust. 10, określa umowa o wymianie informacji zawarta między Prezesem NBP i Prezesem Głównego Urzędu Statystycznego*

✎ **szczegółowe warunki i tryb** ✂ **zakres, tryb i terminy** *zakres, tryb i terminy przekazywania przez banki informacji, o których mowa w ust. 6, określa, w drodze zarządzenia, Prezes Narodowego Banku Polskiego, na wniosek Funduszu* ✂ **w trybie określonym w art. 1 ust. 1** *o uprawomocnieniu się ugody bankowej bank ogłasza w trybie określonym w art. 14 ust. 1* ✂ **podlegać egzekucji w trybie przepisów o postępowaniu egzekucyjnym w administracji** *należności z tytułu wpłat na finansowanie kosztów nadzoru, o których mowa w ust. 1, podlegają egzekucji w trybie przepisów o postępowaniu egzekucyjnym w administracji*

📖 Possible equivalents: mode, procedure (en), modo, procedimento, procedura (it)

TYTUŁ (pl)

Usually singular

(Adj) **tytuł egzekucyjny** *egzekucja należności pieniężnych od NBP może być prowadzona, gdy wierzyciel złożył w NBP tytuł egzekucyjny sądowy lub administracyjny i w ciągu miesiąca od daty złożenia tytułu objęte nim świadczenie nie zostało wykonane* **tytuł prawny** *przepis ust. 5 pkt 2 stosuje się odpowiednio, gdy najemca uzyskał tytuł prawny do innego lokalu mieszkalnego w tej samej miejscowości* **tytuł wykonawczy** *na podstawie dokumentów związanych z wierzytelnością Skarbu Państwa z tytułu wykonania umowy poręczenia lub gwarancji minister właściwy do spraw finansów publicznych może wystawić tytuł wykonawczy* ✂ **powstały z tytułu**

banki mogą udostępniać biurom, o których mowa w ust. 4a, dane o zobowiązaniach powstałych z tytułu umów związanych z dokonywaniem czynności bankowych, jeżeli umowy te zawierają klauzule informujące o możliwości przekazania danych do tych biur

(N) **z tytułu dopłat, gwarancji, kredytu, odsetek, oprocentowania** *środki pieniężne z tytułu oprocentowania rezerwy obowiązkowej przekazywane są bankom, spółdzielczym kasom oszczędnościowo-kredytowym oraz Krajowej Spółdzielczej Kasie Oszczędnościowo-Kredytowej* **z tytułu poręczeń ✂ należności, opłaty, roszczenia z tytułu** *roszczenia z tytułu gwarancji przedawniają się po upływie 5 lat od dnia spełnienia warunku gwarancji* **świadczenia, wierzytelności, zadłużenie, zobowiązania z tytułu**

bankowy tytuł egzekucyjny ✂ z tytułu poręczeń i gwarancji udzielonych przez Skarb Państwa, z tytułu przejściowego wykupienia odsetek od kredytu, z tytułu udzielonego kredytu, z tytułu udzielonych poręczeń i gwarancji *kwota, o której mowa w ust. 1, nie obejmuje poręczeń i gwarancji Skarbu Państwa udzielonych na wykonanie zobowiązań objętych już poręczeniem lub gwarancją Skarbu Państwa, w zakresie, w jakim nie powoduje to zwiększenia zobowiązań Skarbu Państwa z tytułu udzielonych poręczeń i gwarancji* **z tytułu wykonania przez Skarb Państwa umowy poręczenia ✂ zobowiązania z tytułu środków gwarantowanych** *w przypadku gdy wielkość zobowiązań z tytułu środków gwarantowanych przewyższa sumę środków, o których mowa w ust. 1, Fundusz dokonuje wypłat środków gwarantowanych ze środków funduszu własnego Funduszu przeznaczonego do ewidencjonowania środków odzyskanych z mas upadłości banków*

Possible equivalents: INSTRUMENT, ORDER, relation, title (en), relativo (a), TITOLO (it)

U

UCHWAŁA (pl)

(N) **odpis uchwały, podjęcie uchwały** *sprzeciw, o którym mowa w ust. 3, kurator wnosi do właściwego sądu okręgowego sądu gospodarczego w terminie 14 dni od daty podjęcia uchwały lub decyzji zarządu lub rady nadzorczej* ✂ **uchwała lub decyzja, uchwały i decyzje** *kuratorowi przysługuje prawo wniesienia sprzeciwu wobec uchwał i decyzji zarządu i rady nadzorczej odpowiednio kasy lub Kasy Krajowej*

(P) **uchwała w sprawie** ✂ **na podstawie uchwały** *wypłata środków z funduszu kas następuje na podstawie uchwały Zarządu Funduszu o udzieleniu pomocy lub wsparcia* **w drodze uchwały**

✏ **uchwała o zatwierdzeniu sprawozdania finansowego** ✂ **uchwała Komisji Nadzoru Finansowego / rady nadzorczej / walnego zgromadzenia banku / zarządu** *Rada Nadzorcza uchyla uchwały Zarządu niezgodne z przepisami prawa lub statutem BGK* ✂ **określać / określić w drodze uchwały** *Komisja Nadzoru Finansowego określi, w drodze uchwały, szczegółowe zasady funkcjonowania systemu zarządzania ryzykiem i systemu kontroli wewnętrznej*

📖 Possible equivalents: RESOLUTION (en), deliberazione, delibera, risoluzione, decisione (it)

UDZIELANIE (pl)

(N) **udzielanie i potwierdzanie** *udzielanie i potwierdzanie gwarancji bankowych* ✂ **udzielanie kredytów, pomocy, pożyczek** ✂ **tryb udzielania** *ustawa określa*

formy, warunki i tryb udzielania przez Skarb Państwa wsparcia instytucjom finansowym przeznaczonego na przedsięwzięcia mające na celu utrzymanie płynności płatniczej, w tym w związku z rozwojem akcji kredytowej banku krajowego **zasady udzielania**

udzielanie kredytu technologicznego *udzielanie kredytu technologicznego oraz premii technologicznej następuje zgodnie z przepisami rozporządzenia Komisji (WE) nr 800/2008* **udzielanie poręczeń i gwarancji** ✂ **instytucja ustawowo upoważniona do udzielania kredytów** *w okresie 14 dni od upływu terminu określonego w ust. 3 docelowy kredytobiorca informuje pisemnie instytucję ustawowo upoważnioną do udzielania kredytów o niewykonaniu zobowiązania, o którym mowa w tym przepisie*

Possible equivalents: granting, PROVISION (en), affidamento, aggiudicazione, concessione, prestazione (it)

UMOWA (pl)

(Adj) **umowa dodatkowa** *jeżeli do zawarcia umowy o kredyt konsumencki, na warunkach określonych w reklamie, niezbędne jest zawarcie umowy dodatkowej, w szczególności umowy ubezpieczenia, a kosztu takiej umowy nie można z góry określić, kredytodawca lub pośrednik kredytowy podaje konsumentowi w sposób jednoznaczny, zrozumiały i widoczny informację o tym obowiązku wraz z rzeczywistą roczną stopą oprocentowania* **umowa eksportowa** ✂ **umowa zawarta (między)** ✂ **zawarty w umowie** *kredytodawca lub pośrednik kredytowy zobowiązany jest (…) udzielić konsumentowi wyjaśnień dotyczących treści informacji przekazanych przed zawarciem umowy oraz postanowień zawartych w umowie, która ma zostać zawarta, w sposób umożliwiający konsumentowi podjęcie decyzji dotyczącej umowy o kredyt konsumencki*

(N) **umowa kredytu, leasingu, najmu, poręczenia, ubezpieczenia, zrzeszenia** *bank spółdzielczy, za zgodą banku zrzeszającego, z którym zawarł umowę zrzeszenia, może prowadzić działalność także na terenie powiatów sąsiadujących z terenem określonym w ust. 1 i ust. 1a* ✂ **UMOWA O KREDYT** ✂ **umowa o współpracy** *rachunek bankowy może być prowadzony dla kilku osób fizycznych, kilku jednostek samorządu terytorialnego albo stron umowy o współpracy w rozumieniu ustawy z dnia 9 czerwca 2011 r. – Prawo geologiczne i górnicze* ✂ **rodzaj, strona umowy** ✂ **postanowienia, warunki umowy** ✂ **obowiązywanie, podpisanie,**

rozwiązanie, wykonanie umowy *Komisja Nadzoru Finansowego nakazuje kasie, w drodze decyzji, zmianę albo rozwiązanie umowy, o której mowa w ust. 1, jeżeli 1) wykonanie umowy może zagrażać ostrożnemu i stabilnemu zarządzaniu kasą* **wypowiedzenie umowy** ✂ **zawarcie umowy, zawieranie umów** *do zawierania umów, o których mowa w ust. 2, nie mają zastosowania przepisy o zamówieniach publicznych* ✂ **odstąpienie od umowy**

(V) **wypowiedzieć umowę** *kredytodawca ma prawo, na trwałym nośniku, wypowiedzieć umowę o kredyt odnawialny* **zawrzeć umowę** ✂ **umowa + określać** ✂ **umowa powinna** *umowa powinna być zawarta pod rygorem nieważności w formie pisemnej*

(P) **na podstawie umów** *stała stopa procentowa ustalona na podstawie ust. 2 ma zastosowanie wyłącznie do kredytów o stałej stopie procentowej udzielanych na podstawie umów zawartych po dniu wejścia w życie rozporządzenia, o którym mowa w ust. 2*

✎ **umowa DOKE, umowa kredytu mieszkaniowego, umowa, o której mowa w ust. 1, umowa poręczenia lub gwarancji, umowa rachunku bankowego, umowa o subpartycypację, umowa ubezpieczenia kredytu eksportowego, umowa zawarta przez bank /z bankiem, umowa o zawiązaniu grupy bankowej, warunkowa umowa kredytu technologicznego** *bank kredytujący uzależnia zawarcie warunkowej umowy kredytu technologicznego albo wystawienie promesy kredytu technologicznego od posiadania przez przedsiębiorcę zdolności kredytowej na potrzeby kredytu technologicznego* ✂ **umowa w sprawie partycypacji w kosztach budowy lokali** ✂ **dzień zawarcia umowy kredytu preferencyjnego, nienależyte wykonanie umowy, oświadczenie o odstąpieniu od umowy** *termin do odstąpienia od umowy jest zachowany, jeżeli konsument przed jego upływem złoży pod wskazany przez kredytodawcę lub pośrednika kredytowego adres oświadczenie o odstąpieniu od umowy* **termin określony w umowie, wypowiedzenie umowy kredytu, zawieranie i zmiana umowy** ✂ **informacje o opłatach stosowanych w czasie obowiązywania umowy oraz warunki ich zmiany** ✂ **będący stroną umowy** ✂ **w dniu zawarcia umowy, z tytułu wykonania przez Skarb Państwa umowy poręczenia**

📖 Possible equivalents: AGREEMENT, ARRANGEMENT, contract (en), accordo, CONTRATTO (it)

UMOWA O KREDYT (pl)

(Adj) **umowa o kredyt konsumencki, kontraktowy** *przez zawarcie umowy o kredyt kontraktowy osoba fizyczna zobowiązuje się do systematycznego gromadzenia oszczędności w kasie mieszkaniowej przez czas oznaczony, a bank prowadzący kasę mieszkaniową – do przechowywania oszczędności i udzielenia po upływie tego okresu, z zastrzeżeniem art. 12 i 13, długoterminowego kredytu na cele mieszkaniowe* **umowa o kredyt odnawialny, wiązany**

(N) **obowiązywanie, zawarcie umowy o kredyt** *przez zawarcie umowy o kredyt kontraktowy osoba fizyczna zobowiązuje się do systematycznego gromadzenia oszczędności w kasie mieszkaniowej przez czas oznaczony, a bank prowadzący kasę mieszkaniową – do przechowywania oszczędności i udzielenia po upływie tego okresu, z zastrzeżeniem art. 12 i 13, długoterminowego kredytu na cele mieszkaniowe* ✂ **odstąpienie od umowy o kredyt**

(V) **wypowiedzieć umowę o kredyt** *kredytodawca ma prawo, na trwałym nośniku, wypowiedzieć umowę o kredyt odnawialny*

(P) **przed zawarciem umowy o kredyt, w przypadku umowy o kredyt, w związku z umową o kredyt** *trwały nośnik – materiał lub urządzenie służące do przechowywania i odczytywania informacji przekazywanych konsumentowi w związku z umową o kredyt, przez czas odpowiedni do celów jakim informacje te służą oraz pozwalające na odtworzenie tych informacji w niezmienionej postaci*

umowa o kredyt w rachunku oszczędnościowo-rozliczeniowym *kredytodawca lub pośrednik kredytowy przed zawarciem umowy o kredyt w rachunku oszczędnościowo-rozliczeniowym jest zobowiązany podać konsumentowi, na trwałym nośniku, dane, o których mowa w art. 13 ust. 1* **umowa o kredyt zabezpieczony hipoteką** ✂ **spłata zadłużenia wynikającego z umowy o kredyt** ✂ **odstąpienie od umowy o kredyt konsumencki, zawarcie umowy o kredyt konsumencki** ✂ **w czasie obowiązywania umowy o kredyt**

Possible equivalents: credit agreement (en), contratto di credito (it)

USŁUGA (pl)

(Adj) **usługa dodatkowa** ✂ **świadczone usługi** ✂ **usługi bankowe, płatnicze** *przepisu ust. 1 nie stosuje się do usług płatniczych uregulowanych w ustawie z dnia 19 sierpnia 2011 r. o usługach płatniczych*

(N) **towar lub usługa** ✂ **korzystanie z usług** *informacje dotyczące trybu i warunków otrzymania świadczenia pieniężnego na podstawie ustawy powinny zostać udostępnione na wniosek osoby korzystającej oraz zainteresowanej korzystaniem z usług* **świadczenie usług**

usługi badawczo-rozwojowe ✂ **informacje o świadczonych usługach, nabycie towaru lub usługi** *jeżeli konsument skorzystał z przyznanego mu, na podstawie odrębnych przepisów, prawa do odstąpienia od umowy na nabycie określonego towaru lub usługi, to odstąpienie konsumenta od tej umowy jest skuteczne także wobec umowy o kredyt wiązany* **osoba korzystająca oraz zainteresowana korzystaniem z usług** *informacje dotyczące trybu i warunków otrzymania świadczenia pieniężnego na podstawie ustawy powinny zostać udostępnione na wniosek osoby korzystającej oraz zainteresowanej korzystaniem z usług* **podatek od towarów i usług, świadczenie usług płatniczych** ✂ **wytwarzanie nowych lub znacząco ulepszonych towarów, procesów lub usług** *działalność innowacyjna – działalność polegającą na opracowaniu nowej technologii i uruchomieniu na jej podstawie wytwarzania nowych lub znacząco ulepszonych towarów, procesów lub usług* ✂ **ustawa z dnia 19 sierpnia 2011 r. o usługach płatniczych**

Possible equivalents: SERVICE (en), SERVIZIO (it)

USTAWA (pl)

(Adj) **niniejsza ustawa** ✂ **ustawa budżetowa** *łączną kwotę, do wysokości której mogą być udzielane przez Skarb Państwa poręczenia i gwarancje, określa ustawa budżetowa, z zastrzeżeniem ust. 2* ✂ **wymieniona ustawa** *zmiany tekstu jednolitego wymienionej ustawy zostały ogłoszone w Dz. U. z 2012 r. poz. 1385 i 1529* ✂ **ustawa wymieniona w** ✂ **określony w ustawie** *wszelkie wartości pieniężne określone w ustawach oraz uchwałach Sejmu Rzeczypospolitej Polskiej przyjętych do dnia 31 grudnia 1994 r., a ogłoszonych po tym dniu, podlegają z dniem ogłoszenia przeliczeniu z mocy prawa w stosunku, o którym mowa w art. 2 ust. 2*

(N) **rozdział, tekst, zmiana ustawy** *zmiany ustawy zostały ogłoszone w Dz. U. z 1998 r. Nr 160, poz. 1063, z 2000* ✂ **przepisy ustawy**

(V) **ustawa + określać** *ustawa określa zasady grupowania i łączenia się niektórych banków w formie spółki akcyjnej*

(P) **ustawa o** ✂ **na podstawie ustawy** *informacje dotyczące trybu i warunków otrzymania świadczenia pieniężnego na podstawie ustawy powinny zostać udostępnione na wniosek osoby korzystającej oraz zainteresowanej korzystaniem z usług* **w rozumieniu ustawy** *nazwa 'spółdzielcza kasa oszczędnościowo-kredytowa' może być używana wyłącznie przez podmioty zwane 'kasami' w rozumieniu ustawy*

✎ *(NOMINAL)* **ustawa wymieniona w lit. a / ust. 1** ✂ **dzień wejścia z życie niniejszej ustawy, ogłoszenie jednolitego tekstu ustawy, umowy zawarte przed dniem wejścia w życie ustawy, warunki określone w ustawie, zmiana niektórych ustaw** *traci moc ustawa z dnia 24 czerwca 1994 r. o restrukturyzacji banków spółdzielczych i Banku Gospodarki Żywnościowej oraz o zmianie niektórych ustaw* ✂ **rozdział dodany przez art. 1 pkt 10 ustawy, o której mowa w odnośniku 1**

✎ *(THEMATIC NOMINAL)* **ustawa o funkcjonowaniu banków spółdzielczych, ich zrzeszaniu się i bankach zrzeszających, ustawa o nadzorze uzupełniającym, ustawa o Narodowym Banku Polskim, ustawa o prywatyzacji przedsiębiorstw państwowych** ✂ **ustawa z dnia 27 sierpnia 2009 r. o finansach publicznych, ustawa z dnia 27 maja 2004 r. o funduszach inwestycyjnych, ustawa z dnia 12 maja 2011 r. o kredycie konsumenckim, ustawa z dnia 21 lipca 2006 r. o nadzorze nad rynkiem finansowym, ustawa z dnia 29 lipca 2005 r. o obrocie instrumentami finansowymi, ustawa z dnia 29 lipca 2005 r. o ofercie publicznej i warunkach wprowadzania instrumentów finansowych, ustawa z dnia 15 lutego 1992 r. o podatku dochodowym od osób prawnych, ustawa z dnia 30 listopada 1995 r. o pomocy państwa w spłacie niektórych kredytów mieszkaniowych, ustawa z dnia 29 września 1994 r. o rachunkowości, ustawa z dnia 2 lipca 2004 r. o swobodzie działalności gospodarczej, ustawa z dnia 19 sierpnia 2011 r. o usługach płatniczych, ustawa z dnia 24 czerwca 1994 r. o własności lokali, ustawa z dnia 30 kwietnia 2010 r. o zasadach finansowania nauki, ustawa z dnia 26 lipca 2013 r. o zmianie ustawy o Bankowym Funduszu Gwarancyjnym**

✎ *(VERBAL)* **przepisy ustawy + mieć zastosowanie** *odsetki skapitalizowane w okresie do dnia 31 grudnia 1999 r., przypadające od kredytów mieszkaniowych, do* *których mają zastosowanie przepisy ustawy, banki zaliczają do wyniku finansowego tego okresu, za który odsetki przypadają* **ustawa + określać zasady, tracić moc** *traci moc ustawa z dnia 28 października 1950 r. o zmianie systemu pieniężnego* **ustawa + wchodzić w życie po upływie 10 dni od dnia ogłoszenia / z dniem 1 stycznia 2000 r.** ✂ **ilekroć w ustawie jest mowa (o)** ✂ **stosuje się przepisy ustawy** *kasa jest spółdzielnią, do której w zakresie nieuregulowanym ustawą stosuje się przepisy ustawy z dnia 16 września 1982 r. – Prawo spółdzielcze* ✂ **użyte w ustawie określenia oznaczają** ✂ **zmiany (tekstu jednolitego) wymienionej ustawy zostały ogłoszone w Dz. U. z 2000 r. Nr 1, poz. 1**

dodany przez art. 1 pkt 1 lit. a ustawy, określony w art. 1 ustawy, określony w niniejszej ustawie ✂ **zgodnie z przepisami niniejszej ustawy** *podmioty objęte systemem gwarantowania, które wywiązują się z obowiązków nałożonych na nie zgodnie z przepisami niniejszej ustawy, mogą (...) zobowiązać się do rozszerzenia obowiązku gwarancji środków pieniężnych ponad minimum określone w obowiązkowym systemie gwarantowania środków pieniężnych* ✂ **na podstawie odrębnych ustaw** *minister właściwy do spraw Skarbu Państwa, nadając statut BGK, zasięga opinii ministrów właściwych ze względu na nadzór nad funduszami utworzonymi, powierzonymi lub przekazanymi BGK na podstawie odrębnych ustaw* **na podstawie przepisów ustawy, na zasadach określonych w ustawie** ✂ **w brzmieniu ustalonym przez art. 1 pkt 1 lit. a ustawy, w dniu wejścia w życie ustawy, w terminie 10 dni od dnia wejścia w życie ustawy, w zakresie określonym ustawą** *poręczenia i gwarancje, o których mowa w ust. 1 pkt 1 i 3, stanowią jedyne dopuszczalne formy, w jakich organy państwa oraz Bank Gospodarstwa Krajowego, w zakresie określonym ustawą, mogą ustanawiać, w drodze umowy, odpowiedzialność majątkową Skarbu Państwa za zobowiązania innych podmiotów* ✂ **w rozumieniu przepisów ustawy, w rozumieniu ustawy, w rozumieniu art. 1 pkt 1 ustawy**

Possible equivalents: ACT, law, statute (en), LEGGE (it)

W

WALUTA (pl)

(Adj) **wspólna waluta** ✂ **waluta narodowa, obca, polska** *kwoty wyrażone w ustawie w euro przelicza się na walutę polską według kursu średniego, ogłoszonego w danym roku budżetowym przez Narodowy Bank Polski w Tabeli nr 1 kursów średnich* **waluta wymienialna** *bankowy papier wartościowy służy gromadzeniu przez banki środków pieniężnych w złotych lub w innej walucie wymienialnej i zawiera w nazwie wyrazy 'bankowy papier wartościowy'* ✂ **nominowany w walucie** *hipoteczny list zastawny może być nominowany w złotych albo w walucie obcej w rozumieniu przepisów Prawa dewizowego* **wyrażony w walucie**

(N) **waluta emisji** *list emisyjny zawiera w szczególności (…) określenie waluty, w której może następować emisja, lub sposób określenia waluty emisji* **waluta kredytu** ✂ **kurs waluty** *kredytu preferencyjnego udziela się w walucie polskiej, a umowa kredytu preferencyjnego nie może uzależniać zmiany wysokości raty kapitałowo-odsetkowej, ani pozostającego do spłaty kredytu od zmiany kursów walut* ✂ **kwota i waluta**

waluta spłaty kredytu ✂ **kurs w stosunku do waluty** *zasady ustalania kursu złotego w stosunku do walut obcych ustala Rada Ministrów w porozumieniu z Radą* ✂ **środki pieniężne w złotych i w walutach obcych zgromadzone na rachunkach** ✂ **wymiana banknotów i monet nominowanych w walucie narodowej** ✂ **umowa o kredyt denominowany lub indeksowany do waluty innej niż waluta polska** *w przypadku umowy o kredyt denominowany lub indeksowany do waluty innej niż waluta polska, konsument może dokonywać spłaty rat kapitałowo-odsetkowych bezpośrednio w tej walucie*

Possible equivalents: CURRENCY, money (en), VALUTA, MONETA (it)

WARTOŚĆ (pl)

(Adj) **wartość bilansowa, wartość kosztorysowa, wartość nominalna, wartość pieniężna** ✂ **łączna wartość** ✂ **wartości dewizowe** *ustawa określa obrót dewizowy z zagranicą oraz obrót wartościami dewizowymi w kraju, a także działalność gospodarczą w zakresie kupna i sprzedaży wartości dewizowych oraz pośrednictwa w ich kupnie i sprzedaży*

(N) **liczba i wartość** *ogłoszenia powinny wymieniać w szczególności: 5) liczbę i wartość nominalną akcji banku dominującego* ✂ **wartość akcji** *łączna wartość akcji (udziałów) składających się na zasób nie może przekroczyć 15 % łącznej wartości wszystkich zobowiązań wynikających z udzielonych poręczeń i gwarancji według stanu na koniec ubiegłego roku* **wartość aktywów, wkładu**

wartości dewizowe lub krajowe środki płatnicze *organy celne oraz organy Straży Granicznej mogą, w celu sprawdzenia, czy przywóz do kraju wartości dewizowych lub krajowych środków płatniczych oraz ich wywóz za granicę odbywa się zgodnie z przepisami ustawy, podejmować czynności kontrolne na zasadach i w trybie określonych w przepisach o kontroli celnej lub kontroli granicznej* ✂ **wartości niematerialne i prawne** ✂ **bankowo-hipoteczna wartość nieruchomości** ✂ *do zadań powiernika nie należy sprawdzanie, czy bankowo-hipoteczna wartość nieruchomości odpowiada jej wartości rzeczywistej* ✂ **kupno i/lub sprzedaż wartości dewizowych** *banki oraz oddziały banków zagranicznych uprawnione, na mocy przepisów dotychchzasowych, do kupna i sprzedaży wartości dewizowych stają się bankami uprawnionymi do wykonywania czynności bankowej w tym zakresie, z zastrzeżeniem ust. 3 i 4*

Possible equivalents: value (en), VALORE (it)

WARUNEK (pl)

(Adj) **szczegółowe, następujące warunki** ✂ **na warunkach korzystniejszych (od)** *likwidatorowi przysługuje prawo żądania zmiany treści zobowiązania*

zaciągniętego przez kasę w okresie roku przed otwarciem likwidacji, jeżeli druga strona uzyskała wierzytelność na warunkach korzystniejszych od stosowanych w tym okresie przez kasę **na warunkach określonych (w)** ✂ **udzielany pod warunkiem** *poręczenia i gwarancje udzielane pod warunkiem przeznaczenia kredytu lub środków z emisji obligacji na cele, o których mowa w art. 7 ust. 2 pkt 2 i 5, oraz poręczenia, o których mowa w art. 23 ust. 1, są wolne od opłaty prowizyjnej*

(N) **warunek dokonywania** *warunek dokonywania przez kredytobiorcę spłat w wysokości wynikającej z art. 7 i 8, z zastrzeżeniem art. 8a ust. 3, uważa się za spełniony także wtedy, gdy spłaty za kredytobiorcę dokona Skarb Państwa na zasadach określonych w ustawie* **warunek gwarancji** ✂ **warunki umowy**✂ **informacje o warunkach**

(P) **pod warunkiem** *przepis ust. 7 stosuje się pod warunkiem złożenia przez spółkę wniosku w terminie 15 miesięcy od dnia przekształcenia* ✂ **warunki, o których mowa (w)**

✏ **szczegółowe warunki i tryb** *szczegółowe warunki i tryb przejęcia lub likwidacji banku oraz powołanie likwidatora określa decyzja, o której mowa w art. 147 ust. 1* ✂ **informacje o opłatach stosowanych w czasie obowiązywania umowy oraz warunki ich zmiany** ✂ **warunki, o których mowa w ust. 1** ✂ **ustawa z dnia 29 lipca 2005 r. o ofercie publicznej i warunkach wprowadzania instrumentów finansowych** ✂ **określić, w drodze rozporządzenia, szczegółowe warunki** *minister właściwy do spraw instytucji finansowych określi, w drodze rozporządzenia, szczegółowe warunki, zakres i tryb obrotu przez Fundusz wierzytelnościami, o których mowa w ust. 1d pkt 2 i ust. 2 pkt 1a*

✏ *(PREPOSITIONAL)* **na warunkach określonych w ustawie, pod warunkiem przeznaczenia kredytu lub środków (na), pod warunkiem ustanowienia odpowiedniego zabezpieczenia** *po wyczerpaniu środków, o których mowa w ust. 1–4, w sytuacji wystąpienia zagrożenia stabilności finansowej oraz w celu pokrycia pilnych potrzeb Funduszu Narodowy Bank Polski na wniosek Zarządu Funduszu może udzielić Funduszowi kredytu krótkoterminowego, o którym mowa w art. 15 pkt 6, pod warunkiem ustanowienia odpowiedniego zabezpieczenia.* ✂ **od dnia spełnienia warunku gwarancji, przed/z dniem spełnienia warunku gwarancji** *z dniem spełnienia warunku gwarancji przez kasę jest ona zwolniona -z obowiązku wnoszenia opłat rocznych, o których mowa w ust. 1* **w przypadku którego nastąpiło spełnienie warunku gwarancji** *koszty czynności związanych z przygotowaniem i dokonaniem wypłat środków gwarantowanych obciążają kasę, w* *przypadku której nastąpiło spełnienie warunku gwarancji* **w przypadku spełniania warunku gwarancji**

📖 Possible equivalents: CONDITION, TERM, REQUIREMENT (en), CONDIZIONE, MODALITÀ, REQUISITO (it)

WIERZYCIEL (pl)

(N) **wierzyciel banku** ✂ **rachunek wierzyciela** *polecenie przelewu stanowi udzieloną bankowi dyspozycję dłużnika obciążenia jego rachunku określoną kwotą i uznania tą kwotą rachunku wierzyciela* **rada wierzycieli** *uprawnienia osób wchodzących w skład rady wierzycieli, o której mowa w ust. 3 pkt 1, w zakresie należności przysługujących im z tytułu pełnienia tych funkcji, określa akt powołania* ✂ **dłużnik i wierzyciel** *na wniosek dłużnika, który zaprzestał spłacania długu wobec banku lub nie będzie w stanie spłacać długu w przyszłości – bank, z zastrzeżeniem art. 7, 8 i art. 37, może wszcząć bankowe postępowanie ugodowe w celu doprowadzenia do ugody między dłużnikiem i wierzycielami*

✏ **majątek pozostały po zaspokojeniu i zabezpieczeniu wierzycieli** *podział pomiędzy członków kasy majątku pozostałego po zaspokojeniu i zabezpieczeniu wierzycieli nie może nastąpić przed upływem roku od daty ostatniego ogłoszenia o otwarciu likwidacji*

📖 Possible equivalents: CREDITOR, promisee (en), CREDITORE (it)

WIERZYTELNOŚĆ (pl)

(Adj) **wierzytelność bankowa** ✂ **wierzytelności zabezpieczone** *przelewu wierzytelności z gwarancji bankowej można dokonać wraz z przeniesieniem wierzytelności zabezpieczonej gwarancją* ✂ **wierzytelności objęte** *brak odpowiedzi w terminie 21 dni od dnia otrzymania zawiadomienia oznacza odmowę objęcia bankowym postępowaniem ugodowym wierzytelności objętej zastawem lub hipoteką* **wierzytelności wynikające (z)** ✂ **sekurytyzowane wierzytelności** *bank może także przenieść w drodze umowy wierzytelności na, niebędącą towarzystwem funduszy inwestycyjnych tworzącym fundusz sekurytyzacyjny albo funduszem sekurytyzacyjnym, spółkę kapitałową (podmiot emisyjny) w celu emisji przez ten*

podmiot papierów wartościowych, których zabezpieczenie stanowią sekurytyzowane wierzytelności.

(N) **przelew wierzytelności** *przelewu wierzytelności z gwarancji bankowej można dokonać wraz z przeniesieniem wierzytelności zabezpieczonej gwarancją* **sprzedaż, suma wierzytelności** *bankiem właściwym do wszczęcia bankowego postępowania ugodowego jest 1) bank, którego suma wierzytelności wobec dłużnika jest największa spośród wszystkich wierzytelności bankowych* **zabezpieczenie wierzytelności** ✂ **wierzytelność banku**

(P) **wierzytelność wobec** *Minister Finansów określi, w drodze rozporządzenia, termin, w którym banki, o których mowa w ust. 1, zobowiązane są sprzedać niezaspokojone wierzytelności wobec dłużników, których kredyty były wyodrębnione zgodnie z art. 52 ust. 2 pkt 2, z zastrzeżeniem ust. 3* ✂ **wierzytelność z tytułu** *ogólna kwota wierzytelności z tytułu czynności, o których mowa w art. 12 pkt 1 i 3, w części przekraczającej 60 % bankowo-hipotecznej wartości nieruchomości nie może przekroczyć 30 % ogólnej kwoty wierzytelności banku hipotecznego zabezpieczonych hipoteką*

wierzytelność banku hipotecznego *jeżeli wierzytelność banku hipotecznego została wyrażona w walucie obcej, wpisu hipoteki zabezpieczającej tę wierzytelność dokonuje się w księdze wieczystej w tej samej walucie* **wierzytelność Skarbu Państwa** *jeżeli odzyskanie wierzytelności Skarbu Państwa, powstałych z tytułu udzielonego poręczenia lub gwarancji, nie jest możliwe w pełnej wysokości, Rada Ministrów może wyrazić zgodę na ich sprzedaż poniżej kwoty wynikającej z prawidłowego obliczenia* ✂ **wierzytelność powstająca w związku (z)** ✂ **wierzytelności zabezpieczone hipoteką, wierzytelności zabezpieczone zastawem** ✂ **w celu zabezpieczenia wierzytelności**

Possible equivalents: accounts receivable, amount receivable, claim, debt, RIGHT (en), CREDITO (it)

WŁAŚCICIEL (pl)

(N) **właściciel budynku, lokalu, nieruchomości** *do ustanowienia hipoteki, o której mowa w ust. 3, jest wymagane złożenie przez właściciela nieruchomości oświadczenia o ustanowieniu hipoteki na rzecz banku* ✂ **właściciel lub współwłaściciel** *W przypadku docelowego kredytobiorcy, o którym mowa w art. 3 ust. 1 pkt 3, dopłaty mogą być stosowane jeżeli do dnia zawarcia umowy*

kredytu preferencyjnego nie był on właścicielem lub współwłaścicielem budynku mieszkalnego lub lokalu mieszkalnego

✎ **właściciel książeczki mieszkaniowej** *warunkiem udzielenia premii gwarancyjnej na zasadach określonych w ust. 1 pkt 1 i 2 jest złożenie przez właściciela książeczki mieszkaniowej dokumentów potwierdzających spełnienie warunków, o których mowa w ust. 1 pkt 1 i 2* ✂ **właściciel lub współwłaściciel budynku mieszkalnego lub lokalu mieszkalnego**

📖 Possible equivalents: holder, keeper, owner, possessor, proprietor (en), detentore, proprietario, TITOLARE (it)

WŁASNOŚĆ (pl)

(Adj) **odrębna własność** ✂ **własność przemysłowa** ✂ **stanowiący własność, wyodrębniony na własność** *Bank Gospodarstwa Krajowego, w terminie 21 dni od dnia otrzymania wniosku, ustala wysokość zadłużenia przypadającego na wyodrębniony na własność lokal z tytułu udzielonego przez Bank Gospodarstwa Krajowego kredytu*

(N) **własność lokalu, rzeczy** ✂ **prawo własności** ✂ **przeniesienie własności** *przeniesienie własności lokalu mieszkalnego przez towarzystwo budownictwa społecznego może nastąpić wyłącznie na rzecz osoby fizycznej, będącej jednocześnie najemcą lokalu mieszkalnego i stroną umowy w sprawie partycypacji w kosztach budowy tego lokalu*

✎ **własność domu jednorodzinnego, własność Skarbu Państwa** ✂ **ustanowienie odrębnej własności** *w przypadku ustanowienia odrębnej własności lokalu, o którym mowa w art. 33e ust. 1, cena jego sprzedaży nie może być niższa niż jego wartość rynkowa* ✂ **prawo odrębnej własności lokalu mieszkalnego, wyodrębnienie na własność lokalu mieszkalnego** *Decyzję o wyodrębnieniu na własność lokalu mieszkalnego podejmuje zgromadzenie wspólników, walne zgromadzenie akcjonariuszy albo walne zgromadzenie* ✂ **przeniesienie przez spółdzielnię mieszkaniową na rzecz członka prawa własności lokalu mieszkalnego** ✂ **ustawa z dnia 24 czerwca 1994 r o własności lokali**

📖 Possible equivalents: ownership, possessions, PROPERTY (en), proprietà, titolarità (it)

WNIOSEK (pl)

Usually singular

(Adj) **wydany na wniosek** *Komisja Nadzoru Finansowego odstąpi, w drodze decyzji, wydanej na wniosek rady nadzorczej banku od wymogu udowodnionej znajomości języka polskiego, o którym mowa w art. 30 ust. 1 pkt 2, jeżeli nie jest to niezbędne ze względów nadzoru ostrożnościowego, biorąc w szczególności pod uwagę poziom dopuszczalnego ryzyka lub zakres działalności banku*

(N) **otrzymanie wniosku** *Komisja Nadzoru Finansowego w uzasadnionych przypadkach może przedłużyć do 6 miesięcy termin wydania decyzji, o której mowa w ust. 1 pkt 2, informując o tym założycieli przed upływem terminu 3 miesięcy od daty otrzymania wniosku lub jego uzupełnienia* **złożenie wniosku** ✂ **na wniosek banku, kasy, kredytobiorcy** *poręczenia i gwarancje, o których mowa w ust. 1 i 2, są udzielane na wniosek kredytobiorcy*

(P) **wniosek o** *w wypadku gdy naruszenie warunków systematycznego oszczędzania nastąpiło w okresie, o którym mowa w ust. 1, kasa mieszkaniowa nie może od umowy odstąpić, jeżeli posiadacz rachunku złoży wniosek o udzielenie kredytu* ✂ **w sprawie wniosku** *do postępowania w sprawie wniosku, o którym mowa w ust. 5, przepis art. 33 stosuje się odpowiednio.*

✎ **wniosek o ogłoszenie upadłości** *wniosek o ogłoszenie upadłości kasy może złożyć wyłącznie Komisja Nadzoru Finansowego* **wniosek o wydanie zezwolenia (na), wniosek o wypłatę premii technologicznej** ✂ **wniosek, o którym mowa w ust. 1, wniosek Zarządu Funduszu** *wysokość stawki, o której mowa w ust. 1, na kolejny rok określa na wniosek Zarządu Funduszu i przekazuje kasom Rada Funduszu, nie później niż do końca roku kalendarzowego poprzedzającego rok, w którym opłata ma być wniesiona* ✂ **złożenie wniosku o (częściową) wypłatę premii technologicznej, złożenie wniosku o likwidacje książeczki mieszkaniowej i wypłatę premii gwarancyjnej** ✂ **na wniosek ministra właściwego do spraw finansów publicznych, od dnia złożenia wniosku** *w przypadku nienależytego udokumentowania wniosku, bank, o którym mowa w ust. 3, wyznacza termin na uzupełnienie dokumentów, nie dłuższy niż 30 dni, licząc od dnia złożenia wniosku* ✂ **wystąpić z wnioskiem o wyrażenie zgody**

📖 Possible equivalents: application, claim, motion, proposal, petition (en), domanda, istanza, mozione, petizione, proposta (it)

WYKONANIE (pl)

Always singular

(N) **wykonanie czynności, decyzji** *jeżeli wykonanie decyzji lub innego rozstrzygnięcia właściwej władzy nadzorczej mogłoby zagrażać ostrożnemu i stabilnemu zarządzaniu bankiem, Komisja Nadzoru Finansowego może wypowiedzieć porozumienie, o którym mowa w ust. 3a, i zawiesza wykonanie decyzji lub innego rozstrzygnięcia* **wykonanie obowiązku, umowy, zobowiązań** *wykonanie zobowiązań z tytułu poręczenia następuje na wniosek kredytodawcy w przypadku utraty przez kredytobiorcę zdolności kredytowej, po przedstawieniu przez kredytodawcę dokumentów i informacji potwierdzających brak tej zdolności* ✂ **sprawozdanie z wykonania** *sprawozdanie z wykonania rocznego planu finansowego Funduszu sporządza dysponent Funduszu w terminach i na zasadach określonych w odrębnych przepisach*

zawarcie i wykonanie umowy *udzielenie informacji objętych tajemnicą bankową jest niezbędne do zawarcia i wykonania umów, o których mowa w art. 92a ust. 3 i art. 92d* ✂ **nienależyte wykonanie umowy, wykonanie zobowiązań wynikających (z)** ✂ **wykonanie przez Skarb Państwa umów poręczenia, o których mowa w ust. 1** *środki zaliczone na spłatę zadłużenia kredytobiorcy wobec Skarbu Państwa z tytułu wykonania przez Skarb Państwa umów poręczenia, o których mowa w ust. 1, nie stanowią nadwyżki, o której mowa w art. 10 ust. 1 pkt 4* ✂ **z tytułu wykonania umowy poręczenia** ✂ **wniesienie skargi nie wstrzymuje wykonania decyzji**

Possible equivalents: completion, enforcement, execution, exercise, fulfillment, implementation, performance (en), adempimento, ATTUAZIONE, compimento, effettuazione, esecuzione, esercizio (it)

WYKONYWANIE (pl)

Always singular

(Adj) **nienależyte wykonywanie** ✂ **uprawniony do wykonywania, związany z wykonywaniem** *kasa może, w drodze umowy zawartej w formie pisemnej, powierzyć przedsiębiorcy lub przedsiębiorcy zagranicznemu wykonywanie czynności faktycznych związanych z wykonywaniem czynności, o których mowa w art. 3 ust. 1*

(N) **wykonywanie czynności, działalności** *czynności bezpośrednio związane z wykonywaniem działalności kantorowej mogą być wykonywane tylko przez osoby,*

które nie zostały skazane prawomocnie za przestępstwa określone w art. 12 i które posiadają fachowe przygotowanie do wykonywania tych czynności **wykonywanie nadzoru** *sprawozdania dla potrzeb związanych z wykonywaniem nadzoru skonsolidowanego sporządza się, stosując odpowiednio przepisy o rachunkowości* **wykonywanie obowiązku, zadań**

(P) **w zakresie wykonywania** *Minister właściwy do spraw finansów publicznych (…) określi, w drodze rozporządzenia, niezbędne wyposażenie lokalu przeznaczonego do wykonywania działalności kantorowej, a także sposób prowadzenia ewidencji i wydawania dowodów kupna i sprzedaży wartości dewizowych, mając na uwadze zapewnienie bezpieczeństwa obrotu gospodarczego w zakresie wykonywania tej działalności* **w związku z wykonywaniem**

✎ **wykonywanie czynności bankowej** *banki oraz oddziały banków zagranicznych uprawnione, na mocy przepisów dotychczasowych, do kupna i sprzedaży wartości dewizowych stają się bankami uprawnionymi do wykonywania czynności bankowej w tym zakresie, z zastrzeżeniem ust. 3 i 4* **wykonywanie działalności kantorowej, wykonywanie innych czynności, wykonywanie prawa głosu z akcji, wykonywanie uprawnień podmiotu dominującego** *w przypadku, o którym mowa w ust. 4, obowiązek złożenia zawiadomienia powstaje przed przystąpieniem do wykonywania prawa głosu z akcji albo wykonywania uprawnień podmiotu dominującego wobec banku krajowego* ✂ **powierzenie wykonywania czynności, o którym mowa w ust. 1** ✂ **w związku z wykonywaniem czynności** ✂ **uzyskać zezwolenie na wykonywanie działalności**

📖 Possible equivalents: completion, enforcement, execution, fulfillment, implementation, performance (en), adempimento, ATTUAZIONE, compimento, effettuazione, esecuzione, esercizio (it)

WYPŁATA (pl)

(N) **wyplata premii, środków, świadczenia** *do wypłaty świadczeń pieniężnych, o których mowa w art. 22 ust. 2 ustawy wymienionej w art. 1, stosuje się przepisy dotychczasowe, jeżeli spełnienie warunku gwarancji nastąpiło przed dniem wejścia w życie niniejszej ustawy* ✂ **terminy wypłaty** ✂ **dokonanie wypłaty** *Wypłat środków gwarantowanych dokonuje w imieniu i na rachunek Funduszu zarząd komisaryczny, podmiot uprawniony do reprezentacji lub podmiot, z którym*

Zarząd Funduszu zawrze umowę o dokonanie wypłat środków gwarantowanych ✂ **realizacja wypłat** ✂ **wniosek o wypłatę**

✎ **dokonanie wypłat środków gwarantowanych, wniosek o częściową wypłatę premii technologicznej** *po zrealizowaniu co najmniej 25 % planowanej wartości inwestycji technologicznej przedsiębiorca może składać wnioski o częściową wypłatę premii technologicznej* **wniosek o likwidację książeczki mieszkaniowej i wypłatę premii gwarancyjnej, złożenie wniosku o wypłatę premii technologicznej** ✂ **fundusz + dokonywać wypłat** *w przypadku gdy wielkość zobowiązań z tytułu środków gwarantowanych przewyższa sumę środków, o których mowa w ust. 1, Fundusz dokonuje wypłat środków gwarantowanych ze środków funduszu własnego Funduszu przeznaczonego do ewidencjonowania środków odzyskanych z mas upadłości banków*

📖 Possible equivalents: disbursement, paying out, payout, PAYMENT, withdrawal (en), PAGAMENTO, prelevamento, prelievo, ritiro (it)

WYSOKOŚĆ (pl)

Always singular

(Adj) **maksymalna wysokość** *kwota, o której mowa w ust. 1, określa maksymalną wysokość roszczeń deponenta w stosunku do Funduszu, niezależnie od tego, w jakiej wysokości i na ilu rachunkach posiadał środki pieniężne lub z ilu wierzytelności przysługują mu należności w danym banku*

(N) **wysokość oprocentowania, wysokość raty, wysokość stawki** *wysokość stawki, o której mowa w ust. 1, na kolejny rok określa i przekazuje podmiotom objętym systemem gwarantowania Rada Funduszu, nie później niż do końca roku kalendarzowego poprzedzającego rok, w którym opłata ma być wniesiona*

✎ **wysokość, zakres i warunki** *Komisja Nadzoru Finansowego 2) może określić, w drodze uchwały b) wysokość, zakres i warunki pomniejszania funduszy podstawowych banku o pozycje, o których mowa w ust. 2 pkt 3 lit. a–e* ✂ **wysokość stałej stopy procentowej kredytu eksportowego** *na podstawie zawartej Umowy DOKE, w przypadku gdy wysokość stałej stopy procentowej danego kredytu eksportowego jest mniejsza od jego kosztów finansowania, Bank Gospodarstwa Krajowego jest obowiązany do przekazania bankowi kwoty dopłaty obliczonej zgodnie z Umowa DOKE* **wysokość stopy oprocentowania kredytu**

Possible equivalents: AMOUNT, level, rate (en), IMPORTO, AMMONTARE, quota, tasso (it)

Z

ZABEZPIECZENIE (pl)

Usually singular

(Adj) **odpowiednie zabezpieczenie** *podmiot objęty systemem gwarantowania stosuje odpowiednie zabezpieczenia, które zapewniają prawidłowe funkcjonowanie systemu wyliczania*

(N) **zabezpieczenie kredytu, wierzycieli, wierzytelności** *zabezpieczenie wierzytelności banku może być dokonane w drodze przeniesienia na bank przez dłużnika lub osobę trzecią, do czasu spłaty zadłużenia wraz z należnymi odsetkami i prowizją, prawa własności rzeczy ruchomej lub papierów wartościowych* ✄ **ustanowienie zabezpieczenia** *w przypadkach, o których mowa w ust. 1, konsument ponosi koszty ustanowienia zabezpieczenia kredytu przewidziane w umowie*

(P) **w celu zabezpieczenia** *w celu zabezpieczenia należności uznanych za zagrożone z tytułu udzielonych pożyczek, gwarancji i poręczeń, a także nabytych wierzytelności Fundusz tworzy odpisy aktualizujące zmniejszające stan funduszu kas do wykorzystania*

✎ **zaspokojenie i / lub zabezpieczenie wierzycieli** *po zaspokojeniu lub zabezpieczeniu wierzycieli przejętej kasy z jej majątku, kasa albo bank krajowy przejmujący dokonuje wypłat członkom przejętej kasy z jej pozostałego majątku w proporcji do funduszu udziałowego przejmowanej kasy ustalonego na dzień przejęcia* ✄ **zabezpieczenie spłaty kredytu, zabezpieczenie wierzytelności banku** ✄ **wpisany do rejestru zabezpieczenia listów zastawnych** *czynność rozporządzająca banku hipotecznego, której przedmiotem jest wierzytelność hipoteczna wpisana do rejestru zabezpieczenia listów zastawnych, wymaga uprzedniej pisemnej zgody powiernika* ✄ **pod warunkiem ustanowienia odpowiedniego zabezpieczenia, w celu zabezpieczenia wierzytelności**

Possible equivalents: collateral, guarantee, hedge, security (en), garanzia (it)

ZADANIE (pl)

(Adj) **ustawowe zadania** *Minister właściwy do spraw instytucji finansowych, po zasięgnięciu opinii Komisji Nadzoru Finansowego oraz Zarządu Funduszu, określi, w drodze rozporządzenia 5) tryb i sposób weryfikacji prawidłowości danych zawartych w systemie wyliczania – mając na względzie w szczególności potrzebę zapewnienia otrzymywania przez Fundusz należycie przygotowanych i zweryfikowanych danych na potrzeby realizacji ustawowych zadań Funduszu oraz warunki wykonywania czynności faktycznych związanych z działalnością bankową*

(N) **zadanie Funduszu** *realizując zadania Funduszu, o których mowa w art. 4 ust. 2 pkt 1, Fundusz może w szczególności udzielać podmiotom objętym systemem gwarantowania pożyczek, gwarancji lub poręczeń* ✂ **finansowanie, realizacja zadań** *do realizacji zadań, o których mowa w ust. 2, stosuje się przepisy rozdziału 3a ustawy zmienianej w art. 4, z zastrzeżeniem ust. 4–6* **wykonywanie zadań** *koszty działalności biura Funduszu oraz inne wydatki związane z wykonywaniem zadań Funduszu pokrywane są ze środków, o których mowa w art. 15 pkt 1, 1a i 3–7* **zakres zadań**

(P) **zadania związane (z)** *finansowanie zadań związanych z restrukturyzacją techniczną, technologiczną i organizacyjną, w tym zatrudnienia, dotyczy przedsiębiorstw, o których mowa w art. 3 ust. 1 pkt 4*

zadania, o których mowa w ust. 1, zadania określone w ustawie, zadania związane z restrukturyzacją *ustawa określa zasady udzielania dopłat ze środków budżetu państwa do oprocentowania kredytów bankowych na cele rolnicze, skup i przechowywanie zapasów ryb morskich oraz zadania związane z restrukturyzacją przedsiębiorstw przemysłu lekkiego* ✂ **zapewnienie środków na finansowanie zadań Funduszu w zakresie udzielania pomocy podmiotom objętym systemem gwarantowania** *Rada Funduszu (…) może przenieść całość lub część środków funduszu stabilizacyjnego na fundusz własny, tworzony w celu zapewnienia środków na finansowanie zadań Funduszu w zakresie udzielania pomocy podmiotom objętym systemem gwarantowania* ✂ **w celu realizacji zadań** *Narodowy Bank Polski udostępnia Ministrowi Finansów dane, w tym dane indywidualne oraz*

zestawienia i oceny, o których mowa w art. 23 ustawy o Narodowym Banku Polskim, niezbędne w celu realizacji zadań, o których mowa w art. 71 i 72
Possible equivalents: FUNCTION, OBJECTIVE, task (en), compito, FUNZIONE, incarico (it)

ZAKRES (pl)

Usually singular

(Adj) **szczegółowy zakres** *szczegółowy zakres czynności, o których mowa w ust. 1, określają odrębne przepisy lub umowy zawarte z właściwymi ministrami* ✂ **w zakresie dotyczącym** *bank, o którym mowa w ust. 6, niezwłocznie po złożeniu wniosku o wydanie zgody, przez właściwą władzę nadzorczą, o której mowa w ust. 6, przedstawia Komisji Nadzoru Finansowego wniosek w zakresie dotyczącym banku* **w zakresie nieregulowanym (w), niezbędnym dla/do, określonym (w)** ✂ **we własnym zakresie** *właściwe władze nadzorcze państwa macierzystego mogą przeprowadzać czynności kontrolne w oddziale, o którym mowa w ust. 1, we własnym zakresie lub poprzez osoby przez nie upoważnione, po uprzednim zawiadomieniu Komisji Nadzoru Finansowego o terminie i zakresie przeprowadzanej kontroli*

(N) **zakres działalności, działania, informacji** *Komisja Nadzoru Finansowego określi, w drodze uchwały, szczegółowe zasady i sposób ogłaszania informacji, o których mowa w ust. 1 i 3, oraz zakres informacji podlegających ogłaszaniu* **zakres zadań** ✂ **ograniczenie zakresu** ✂ **działalność, oświadczenie w zakresie** *do składania oświadczeń w zakresie praw i obowiązków majątkowych Funduszu upoważnieni są dwaj członkowie Zarządu Funduszu działający łącznie* ✂ **w zakresie czynności, danych** *Narodowy Bank Polski jest obowiązany do przestrzegania tajemnicy w zakresie danych jednostkowych uzyskanych od banków i rezydentów, w wykonaniu obowiązków określonych w art. 30 ust. 1, na zasadach określonych w art. 23 ust. 5–7 ustawy z dnia 29 sierpnia 1997 r.* **w zakresie działalności, w zakresie nadzoru, w zakresie polityki** *obejmując obowiązki członka Rady Polityki Pieniężnej przysięgam uroczyście, że będę działać z pełną bezstronnością, posiadaną wiedzą i doświadczeniem w zakresie polityki pieniężnej, zgodnie z celami działalności Narodowego Banku Polskiego* **w zakresie wykonywania**

(P) **w zakresie, w jakim** *potrącenie nie może być dokonane w zakresie, w jakim wierzytelność z rachunku bankowego została zajęta jako przedmiot egzekucji należności z tytułu zobowiązań podatkowych*

✎ **sposób, zakres i terminy** ✂ **wysokość, zakres i warunki** *Komisja Nadzoru Finansowego 2) może określić, w drodze uchwały b) wysokość, zakres i warunki pomniejszania funduszy podstawowych banku o pozycje, o których mowa w ust. 2 pkt 3 lit. a–e* ✂ **zakres działalności banku** ✂ **ograniczenie zakresu działalności** *decyzja Komisji Nadzoru Finansowego o ograniczeniu zakresu działalności banku może zawierać warunki i terminy* **składanie oświadczeń w zakresie praw i obowiązków majątkowych** *do składania oświadczeń w zakresie praw i obowiązków majątkowych Funduszu upoważnieni są dwaj członkowie Zarządu Funduszu działający łącznie* ✂ **zapewnienie środków na finansowanie zadań Funduszu w zakresie udzielania pomocy podmiotom objętym systemem gwarantowania** *Rada Funduszu (…) może przenieść całość lub część środków funduszu stabilizacyjnego na fundusz własny, tworzony w celu zapewnienia środków na finansowanie zadań Funduszu w zakresie udzielania pomocy podmiotom objętym systemem gwarantowania* ✂ **w zakresie nieuregulowanym w ustawie** *w zakresie nieuregulowanym w ustawie do prawa odrębnej własności lokalu stosuje się odpowiednio przepisy ustawy z dnia 24 czerwca 1994 r. o własności lokali* **w zakresie określonym ustawą, w zakresie określonym w ust. 1**
Possible equivalents: extent, limit, range, scope, span (en), ambito, campo, limite, portata, sfera (it)

ZARZĄD (pl)

Usually singular

(Adj) **zarząd komisaryczny** *członkowie zarządu komisarycznego otrzymują w razie potrzeby urlop bezpłatny w macierzystym zakładzie pracy na czas pełnienia tej funkcji*

(N) **członek, kadencja, prezes, skład zarządu** *w skład Zarządu Funduszu wchodzi od trzech do pięciu członków, w tym prezes i jego zastępca* **uchwała zarządu** ✂ **zarząd banku, Zarząd Funduszu, zarząd kasy** *za przekazywanie Funduszowi danych, o których mowa w art. 38zn ust. 1, znajdujących się w systemie wyliczania, w okresie do dnia spełnienia warunku gwarancji, jest odpowiedzialny zarząd kasy*

(V) **zarząd + określać** *zarząd NBP może określać wysokość zapasu gotówki w złotych, którego utrzymywanie w kasach bankowych, spółdzielczych kasach oszczędnościowo-kredytowych oraz w Krajowej Spółdzielczej Kasie Oszczędnościowo-Kredytowej, będzie równoznaczne z utrzymywaniem rezerwy obowiązkowej w NBP*

(P) **na wniosek zarządu** *wysokość stawki, o której mowa w ust. 1, na kolejny rok określa na wniosek Zarządu Funduszu i przekazuje kasom Rada Funduszu, nie później niż do końca roku kalendarzowego poprzedzającego rok, w którym opłata ma być wniesiona*

✎ **rada nadzorcza i/lub zarząd, zarząd i rada nadzorcza, zarząd kasy lub Kasy Krajowej, zarząd komisaryczny lub podmiot uprawniony do reprezentacji** *o nieprawidłowościach ujawnionych w toku kontroli, o której mowa w ust. 1, Fundusz zawiadamia Komisję Nadzoru Finansowego, wzywając zarząd komisaryczny lub podmiot uprawniony do reprezentacji do ich usunięcia* ✂ **zarząd banku spółdzielczego, Zarząd NBP** ✂ **członek zarządu lub rady, czynności członka zarządu, osoby przewidziane do objęcia stanowisk członków zarządu, pozostali członkowie zarządu** ✂ **powołanie prezesa zarządu, ustanowienie zarządu komisarycznego** *w związku z likwidacją w trybie art. 138 i art. 147, przejęciem lub upadłością banku albo ustanowieniem zarządu komisarycznego posiadane uprawnienia członków władz banku dotyczące wypłaty odpraw pieniężnych i wynagrodzeń za okres po rozwiązaniu stosunku pracy tracą moc*

📖 Possible equivalents: administration, BOARD, MANAGEMENT, management board (en), AMMINISTRAZIONE, consiglio di amministrazione, dirigenza, gestione (it)

ZASADA (pl)

Usually singular

(Adv) **zgodnie z zasadami** *w przypadku gdy decyzja o likwidacji kasy została podjęta przez jej członków, likwidacja prowadzona jest zgodnie z zasadami obowiązującymi przy likwidacji spółdzielni*

(Adj) **szczegółowe zasady** ✂ **zasady ogólne** ✂ **zasady określone (w)** *środki przeznaczane przez kredytobiorcę na spłatę kredytów mieszkaniowych według zasad określonych w art. 7 i 8 zaliczane są w pierwszej kolejności na zmniejszenie zadłużenia z tytułu kredytu wraz ze skapitalizowanymi odsetkami*

(N) **zasady i tryb** *minister właściwy do spraw instytucji finansowych (...) ustala regulamin określający organizację pracy oraz zasady i tryb działania Rady Funduszu, uwzględniając realizowane przez Fundusz zadania oraz specyfikę jego działalności* ✂ **zasady rachunkowości** *zasady rachunkowości NBP powinny odpowiadać*

standardom stosowanym w Europejskim Systemie Banków Centralnych ✂ **zasady dysponowania** *zasady dysponowania środkami pieniężnymi zgromadzonymi na rachunku wspólnym prowadzonym dla jednostek samorządu terytorialnego oraz zasady wypowiadania umowy tego rachunku określa umowa rachunku bankowego* **zasady funkcjonowania, stosowania, tworzenia, udzielania, zarządzania** ✂ **określenie zasad** ✂ **na zasadzie wzajemności** *NBP i Główny Urząd Statystyczny przekazują sobie nieodpłatnie, na zasadzie wzajemności, będące w ich posiadaniu odpowiednio dane indywidualne i dane statystyczne, w zakresie niezbędnym dla wykonywania ich ustawowo określonych zadań*

(V) **określać zasady** *ustawa określa zasady prowadzenia działalności bankowej, tworzenia i organizacji banków, oddziałów i przedstawicielstw banków zagranicznych, a także oddziałów instytucji kredytowych oraz zasady sprawowania nadzoru bankowego, postępowania naprawczego, likwidacji i upadłości banków*

(P) **według zasad** *środki przeznaczane przez kredytobiorcę na spłatę kredytów mieszkaniowych według zasad określonych w art. 7 i 8 zaliczane są w pierwszej kolejności na zmniejszenie zadłużenia z tytułu kredytu wraz ze skapitalizowanymi odsetkami* ✂ **w trybie i na zasadach** *udostępnianie informacji stanowiących tajemnicę zawodową, obejmujących swym zakresem tajemnicę bankową, jest możliwe wyłącznie w trybie i na zasadach określonych dla udostępniania informacji stanowiących tajemnicę bankową*

zasady i terminy spłaty kredytu *kredytodawca lub pośrednik kredytowy przed zawarciem umowy o kredyt konsumencki jest zobowiązany podać konsumentowi, na trwałym nośniku: 8) zasady i terminy spłaty kredytu oraz w odpowiednich przypadkach kolejność zaliczania rat kredytu konsumenckiego na poczet należności kredytodawcy* ✂ **zasady funkcjonowania systemu** *moment wprowadzenia zlecenia rozrachunku do systemu oraz moment, od którego zlecenie rozrachunku nie może być odwołane, określają zasady funkcjonowania tego systemu* ✂ **ustawa z dnia 30 kwietnia 2010 r. o zasadach finansowania nauki** ✂ **zgodnie z zasadami określonymi w art. 19** ✂ **na zasadach określonych w przepisach** *gospodarka finansowa środkami gromadzonymi na rachunku, o którym mowa w ust. 2, prowadzona jest przez ministra właściwego do spraw finansów publicznych, w imieniu Skarbu Państwa, na zasadach określonych w przepisach ustawy* ✂ **ustawa + określać zasady** *ustawa określa zasady udzielania dopłat ze środków budżetu państwa do oprocentowania kredytów bankowych na cele rolnicze, skup i przechowywanie zapasów ryb morskich oraz zadania związane z restrukturyzacją przedsiębiorstw przemysłu lekkiego*

Possible equivalents: law, rule, policy, principle (en), CRITERIO, legge, norma, principio, regola (it)

ZEZWOLENIE (pl)

Usually singular

(Adj) **zezwolenie dewizowe** *udzielone spółce zezwolenie dewizowe nie przechodzi na spółkę przejmującą lub spółkę nowo zawiązaną, gdy spółka, która otrzymała zezwolenie, została przejęta przez inną spółkę lub wraz z inną spółką albo spółkami zawiąże nową spółkę* ✂ **udzielone zezwolenie** ✂ **wynikający z zezwolenia**

(N) **zezwolenie na rozpoczęcie** *wpłata kapitału założycielskiego banku państwowego, jak również wydzielenie z majątku Skarbu Państwa innych środków na pokrycie kapitału założycielskiego powinno nastąpić przed złożeniem przez bank państwowy do Komisji Nadzoru Finansowego wniosku o zezwolenie na rozpoczęcie działalności* ✂ **uchylenie, wydanie zezwolenia**

(V) **udzielić zezwolenia** *indywidualne zezwolenie dewizowe jest wymagane na odstąpienie od ograniczenia lub obowiązku, o których mowa w art. 5, w zakresie których nie udzielono ogólnego zezwolenia dewizowego albo udzielono takiego zezwolenia, ale na innych warunkach niż te, na których ma nastąpić odstąpienie*

zezwolenie na wykonywanie działalności ✂ **instytucja kredytowa działająca na podstawie zezwolenia, uchylenie zezwolenia, o którym mowa w art. 1** *o uchyleniu zezwolenia, o którym mowa w ust. 6a, Komisja Nadzoru Finansowego powiadamia właściwe władze nadzorcze banku zagranicznego* **uchylenie zezwolenia na utworzenie banku, władza nadzorcza, która udzieliła zezwolenia na prowadzenie działalności, wniosek o wydanie zezwolenia, wydanie zezwolenia na utworzenie banku** *jeżeli z wnioskiem o wydanie zezwolenia na utworzenie banku występuje więcej niż 10 założycieli, są oni obowiązani ustanowić 1–3 pełnomocników, którzy będą ich reprezentować wobec Komisji Nadzoru Finansowego w okresie poprzedzającym wydanie zezwolenia na utworzenie banku. Pełnomocnictwo powinno być sporządzone w formie aktu notarialnego* ✂ **po uzyskaniu zezwolenia Komisji Nadzoru Finansowego** ✂ **wymagać zezwolenia Komisji Nadzoru Finansowego** ✂ **Komisja Nadzoru Finansowego + odmawiać wydania zezwolenia**

Possible equivalents: APPROVAL, authorisation, permission (en), AUTORIZZAZIONE, concessione, permesso (it)

ZGODA (pl)

Usually singular

(N) **uzyskanie zgody** *postępowanie w sprawie uzyskania zgody, o której mowa w art. 16 ust. 1, wszczyna się na wniosek podmiotu zamierzającego prowadzić system* **wydanie, wyrażenie zgody**

(V) **wyrazić zgodę** *Komisja Nadzoru Finansowego może w szczególnie uzasadnionych przypadkach wyrazić zgodę na przekroczenie limitu, o którym mowa w ust. 2*

(P) **zgoda na** ✂ **za zgodą** *za zgodą Komisji Nadzoru Finansowego bank może stosować metody statystyczne do obliczania wymogów kapitałowych.*

zgoda, o której mowa w ust. 1 *dłużnikowi przysługuje prawo do cofnięcia w każdym czasie zgody, o której mowa w ust. 2 pkt 2* ✂ **za zgodą banku przejmującego** ✂ **następować za zgodą Komisji Nadzoru Finansowego** *powołanie prezesa zarządu kasy następuje za zgodą Komisji Nadzoru Finansowego* **występować z wnioskiem o wyrażenie zgody** ✂ **Komisja Nadzoru Finansowego + odmówić wyrażenia zgody na powołanie**

Possible equivalents: AGREEMENT, APPROVAL, consent, permission (en), accordo, approvazione, assenso, AUTORIZZAZIONE, consenso (it)

ZMIANA (pl)

(N) **zmiana składu, statutu** *zmiana statutu Kasy Krajowej wymaga zatwierdzenia przez Komisję Nadzoru Finansowego* **zmiana stopy** *informacja, o której mowa w ust. 2, określa termin zmiany stopy oprocentowania* **zmiana ustawy (o)** ✂ **dokonanie zmiany** *Komisja Nadzoru Finansowego może zalecić Kasie Krajowej dokonanie zmian w metodyce i zasadach określających sposób i zakres przeprowadzania kontroli w kasach* **warunki zmiany**

(P) **zmiana w zakresie** *o zamiarze dokonania zmiany w zakresie wskazanym w art. 48c ust. 2 pkt 2–5 bank krajowy powiadamia, w formie pisemnej, Komisję Nadzoru Finansowego i właściwe władze nadzorcze państwa goszczącego, najpóźniej na miesiąc przed dokonaniem tej zmiany* ✂ **w przypadku zmiany** ✂ **po dokonaniu zmiany** *podjęcie przez bank działalności, o której mowa w art. 2 ust. 1, może nastąpić po dokonaniu zmiany statutu, polegającej na rozszerzeniu zakresu działania banku o tę działalność*

✎ **odroczenie płatności lub zmiana sposobu spłaty** *kredytodawca lub pośrednik kredytowy przed zawarciem umowy o kredyt przewidującej odroczenie płatności lub zmianę sposobu spłaty w przypadku gdy konsument jest w zwłoce ze spłatą zadłużenia wynikającego z umowy o kredyt jest zobowiązany podać konsumentowi, na trwałym nośniku 1) dane określone w art. 13 ust. 1 pkt 1–5* **zawieranie i zmiana umów** *kasa może, w drodze umowy agencyjnej, powierzyć przedsiębiorcy lub przedsiębiorcy zagranicznemu pośrednictwo w zawieraniu i zmianie umów o wykonywanie czynności, o których mowa w art. 3 ust. 1* **zmiany w przepisach obowiązujących i przepisy końcowe** ✂ **zmiana niektórych ustaw, zmiana stopy procentowej, zmiana wysokości stopy oprocentowania** ✂ **informacje o opłatach stosowanych w czasie obowiązywania umowy oraz warunki ich zmiany** ✂ **ustawa z dnia 23 października 2008 r. o zmianie ustawy o Bankowym Funduszu Gwarancyjnym** ✂ **ze zmianą wprowadzoną przez art. 1** ✂ **wprowadzać następujące zmiany** ✂ **zmiany (tekstu jednolitego) wymienionej ustawy zostały ogłoszone w Dz. U. z 2000 r. Nr 1, poz. 1**

📖 Possible equivalents: AMENDMENT, change, modification (en), cambiamento, modifica, MODIFICAZIONE (it)

ZOBOWIĄZANIE (pl)

(Adj) **zobowiązania finansowe, pieniężne, pozabilansowe** *w przypadku pożyczek i kredytów udzielanych na cele związane z działalnością gospodarczą łączna kwota takich pożyczek i kredytów udzielonych jednemu członkowi oraz udzielonych mu zobowiązań pozabilansowych nie może przekraczać 15 % funduszy własnych kasy* ✂ **zobowiązania wynikające (z)** ✂ **przejmowane zobowiązania** *jeżeli w przypadku przejęcia wybranych praw majątkowych lub wybranych zobowiązań kasy wartość przejmowanych praw majątkowych ustalonych zgodnie z ust. 1 jest wyższa niż wartość przejmowanych zobowiązań, przejmujący w terminie 14 dni od ustalenia wartości zgodnie z ust. 1 jest zobowiązany zapłacić nadwyżkę kasie,*

w stosunku do której podjęto decyzję o przejęciu wybranych praw majątkowych lub wybranych zobowiązań

(N) **zobowiązanie banku** ✂ **zobowiązania dłużnika** ✂ **kwota zobowiązania** *udzielenie gwarancji rekapitalizacyjnej następuje po wniesieniu przez bank krajowy na rzecz Funduszu opłaty prowizyjnej naliczonej od kwoty zobowiązania objętego tą gwarancją* ✂ **spłata zobowiązań** ✂ **wykonanie zobowiązania** *wykonanie zobowiązania w sposób określony w art. 3 ust. 1 oraz wykonanie obowiązku określonego w art. 4 następuje z zastosowaniem kursów euro w stosunku do walut narodowych, wskazanych w tabeli zawartej w załączniku do ustawy* ✂ **zaciąganie zobowiązań**

zobowiązanie, o którym mowa w art. 1, zobowiązanie Skarbu Państwa, zobowiązania z tytułu poręczenia *wykonanie zobowiązań z tytułu poręczenia następuje na wniosek kredytodawcy w przypadku utraty przez kredytobiorcę zdolności kredytowej, po przedstawieniu przez kredytodawcę dokumentów i informacji potwierdzających brak tej zdolności* ✂ **decyzja o przejęciu wybranych praw majątkowych lub wybranych zobowiązań, wielkość zobowiązań z tytułu środków gwarantowanych + przewyższać** *w przypadku gdy wielkość zobowiązań z tytułu środków gwarantowanych przewyższa sumę środków, o których mowa w ust. 1, Fundusz dokonuje wypłat środków gwarantowanych ze środków funduszu własnego Funduszu przeznaczonego do ewidencjonowania środków odzyskanych z mas upadłości banków* **wykonanie zobowiązań wynikających (z)**

Possible equivalents: accounts payable, amount payable, commitment, LIABILITY, OBLIGATION (en), impegno, obbligazione, OBBLIGO, passività (it)

THE ENGLISH PART

A

ACCOUNT (en)

(N) **account of an institution, of a society** ✂ **statement of account** ✂ **payments on account** *Regulations may make provision about payment including, in particular, provision for payments (a) on account subject to terms and conditions; (b) by instalment*

✏ **profit and loss account** *the Bank shall prepare for each of its financial years a statement of accounts consisting of (a) a balance sheet as at the last day of the year, and (b) a profit and loss account* ✂ **account held in a bank** *the regulations may, in particular, specify (…) funds in a specified kind of account held with the Bank of England or with another specified institution or class of institution*

📖 Possible equivalents: KONTO, RACHUNEK (pl), CONTO (it)

ACT (en)

Usually singular

(N) **act or any enactment** *an order may (a) amend the Building Societies Act 1986 or any other enactment which relates, or in so far as it relates, to building societies* ✂ **amendment of/to an act, part of an act, provision of an act, schedule to an act** *section 81BA was inserted by paragraph 7 of Schedule to the Financial Services (Banking Reform) Act 2013 (c.33)* **section of an act** ✂ **Banking Act 2009, Companies Act 2006, Compensation Act 2006, Competition Act 1998, Enterprise Act 2002, Insolvency Act 1986, Pensions Act 2005**

(V) **to amend an act** ✂ **act + to be amended** *the Legal Services Act 2007 is amended as set out in subsections (5) and (6)* **act + to be passed**

(P) **by or under an act** *in this section 'relevant requirement' means a requirement (a)imposed by or under this Act*

✏ **function / power / permission under part 1 / section 1 of an act** *anything done by the bank in connection with the exercise of a stabilisation power under Part 1 of this Act is not a transaction at an undervalue for the purposes of section 238* ✂ **Bank of England Act 1998, Building Societies Act 1986, Company Directors Disqualification Act 1986, Consumer Credit Act 1974, Court of Session Act 1988, Courts and Legal Services Act 1998, Credit Unions Act 1979, Criminal Justice Act 2003, Enterprise and Regulatory Reform Act 2013, European Communities Act 1972, Financial Services (Banking Reform) Act 2013, Human Rights Act 1998, Pension Schemes (Northern Ireland) Act 1993, Regulatory Reform Act 2013** ✂ **within the meaning of an act** *Objective 7 is to avoid interfering with property rights in contravention of a Convention right (within the meaning of the Human Rights Act 1998(f))* ✂ **to have the same meaning as in an act** ✂ **act + come into force, be amended as follows**

📖 Possible equivalents: akt, document, USTAWA (pl), ATTO, LEGGE (it)

ACTION (en)

(Adj) **specified action** ✂ **action required** *the Bank may take the action required by subsection (1)*

(N) **action or inaction** *the Treasury may by order confer immunity from liability in damages in respect of action or inaction* ✂ **part of action** *the Bank must make an instrument which (a) recognises the action, or (b) refuses to recognise the action, or (c) recognises part of the action and refuses to recognise the remainder* **recognition of action** ✂ **resolution action**

(V) **to recognise action** *article 103 inserts new provisions to require the Bank of England either to recognise or to refuse to recognise a resolution action of a third country* **to refrain from action, to take action** *if a regulator proposes to take action against a person under section 142S, it must give the person a warning notice*

(P) **action under** *before taking action under this Part in respect of a recognised inter-bank payment system the operator of which satisfies section 186(2), the Bank*

of England must consult the FSA ✂ **action in accordance with, in relation to, in respect of**

third-country resolution action *'third-country resolution action' means action under the law of a third country to manage the failure or likely failure of a third-country institution, third country parent undertaking or an EU institution*

Possible equivalents: CZYNNOŚĆ, działanie, POSTĘPOWANIE (pl), azione, OPERAZIONE, PROVVEDIMENTO (it)

ACTIVITY (en)

(Adj) **core activity** *the continuity of the provision of those services can more effectively be protected by treating the activity as a core activity* ✂ **excluded, regulated, specified activity**

(V) **to carry on an activity** *'insurer' means an institution which is authorised under this Act to carry on the regulated activity of effecting or carrying out contracts of insurance as principal.*

a mixed activity holding company ✂ **regulated activity of accepting deposits, regulated activity of dealing in investments as principal** *the regulated activity of dealing in investments as principal (…) is an excluded activity unless it is carried on in circumstances specified by the Treasury by order* ✂ **the carrying on of a regulated activity by a relevant authorised person**

Possible equivalents: CZYNNOŚĆ, DZIAŁALNOŚĆ, działania (pl), ATTIVITÀ, OPERAZIONE (it)

AGREEMENT (en)

(N) **agency agreement** *in this regulation 'agency agreement' means an agreement between the relevant Board and the authority responsible for the institution's home State scheme under which either agrees, whether or not for a consideration, to make on the other's behalf any payments falling to be made under the scheme for which the other is responsible* **information agreement** *'information agreement' means an agreement between the relevant Board and the authority responsible for the*

institutions home State scheme under which either agrees, whether or not for a consideration, to disclose to the other any information in its possession which would or might assist the other to discharge its functions **repurchase agreement** ✂ **party to an agreement** *'EEA State' means a State, other than the United Kingdom, which is a contracting party to the agreement on the European Economic Area*

(V) **to enter into an agreement, to make an agreement**

(P) **agreement between, under** *sum due and payable under an agreement*

contract or other agreement *subsection (6) applies where a contract or other agreement (a) is entered into by a bank, a third-country institution or a third-country parent undertaking* **rights or duties under an agreement** ✂ **Agreement on the European Economic Area, group financial support agreement** ✂ **to terminate, modify or replace an agreement** *if a specified event occurs or situation arises (a) the agreement is terminated, modified or replaced*

Possible equivalents: porozumienie, UMOWA (pl), accordo, consenso, CONTRATTO, convenzione (it)

AMENDMENT (en)

(Adj) **consequential amendments, minor amendments** ✂ **amendment made (by)** *the Treasury may by order make any provision they consider appropriate in consequence of the application to building societies of the amendments made by this Part* **amendment realting (to)**

(N) **amendment of/ to an act** *articles 123 and 124 make consequential amendments to the Corporation Tax Act 2009 and the Financial Services Act 2012* **amendments of provisions**

(V) **to make amendments** *part IV of the Regulations makes parallel amendments to the 1986 Act with similar effect*

Possible equivalents: nowelizacja, ZMIANA (pl), emendamento, modifica, MODIFICAZIONE, revisione (it)

AMOUNT (en)

(Adj) **principal, outstanding, payable, shortfall amount** *the Bank of England must allocate the losses represented by the shortfall amount equally between eligible liabilities of the same rank* ✂ **amount equal (to)**

(N) **amount of compensation, of an instrument** *the Bank may take the action required by subsection (1)(e) only if it converts or reduces the principal amount of any instruments referred to in subsection (1)* **amount of a penalty**

(V) **to determine an amount** ✂ **amount + to be calculated, to be owed, to be paid**

✏ **amount specified in a notice** *in this regulation 'unpaid contribution', in relation to an institution, means any amount specified in a notice served on the institution under subsection (2) of section 52 of the 1987 Act which remains unpaid after the period of 21 days mentioned in that subsection*

📖 Possible equivalents: ilość, KWOTA, liczba, suma, WARTOŚĆ, WYSOKOŚĆ (pl), AMMONTARE, IMPORTO, somma (it)

APPEAL (en)

(N) **appeal to a tribunal, appeal against a decision** ✂ **determination of appeal, notice of appeal** *the means of making an appeal is by sending the Tribunal a notice of appeal in accordance with Tribunal rules* **party to an appeal** *a person who gives oral evidence at the hearing may be cross-examined by or on behalf of any party to the appeal* ✂ **appeal rules**

(V) **to bring, to determine an appeal** *a group that determines an appeal must make an order requiring the payment to the CMA of the costs incurred by the CMA in connection with the appeal* **to make an appeal**

(P) **appeal under** *the Bank of England may not impose a sanction while an appeal under this section could be brought or is pending* ✂ **in connection with an appeal**

✏ **an application for permission to bring an appeal** *an application for permission to bring an appeal may be made only by sending a notice to the CMA requesting* *the permission* ✂ **appeal made in accordance with section 1** ✂ **Competition Appeal Tribunal** *this section applies where a person is appealing to the Competition Appeal Tribunal ('the Tribunal') against a decision to impose a penalty under section 73*

📖 Possible equivalents: apelacja, odwołanie (pl), appello, impugnazione, ricorso (it)

APPOINTMENT (en)

(Adj) **qualifying appointment** *a qualifying appointment means (i) the appointment of a provisional liquidator under section 135(1) of the 1986 Act* **relevant appointment**

(N) **appointment of an administrator, a liquidator, a person, a valuer** *the Bank of England must make arrangements for the appointment of a person to act as independent valuer for the purposes of a valuation to be conducted under section 6E or 48X* ✂ **appointment instrument** *an appointment instrument or a Part 1 instrument may require a resolution administrator to make reports to the Bank of England (a) on any matter specified in the instrument, and (b) at the times or intervals specified in the instrument* ✂ **appointment under section / subsection 1**

(V) **appointment + be made**

(P) **appointment as** *a person is eligible for appointment as a bank liquidator if qualified to act as an insolvency practitioner*

✏ **a decision, order or appointment** *where the Authority is informed of a decision, order or appointment in accordance with regulation 9, the Authority must as soon as is practicable inform the relevant person (a) that the decision, order or appointment has been made*

📖 Possible equivalents: mianowanie, nominacja, powołanie (pl), nomina (it)

APPROVAL (en)

Usually singular

(N) **approval of the Treasury** ✂ **approval under section 1** ✂ **application for approval**

(V) **to give, to vary an approval** *where an application for approval under section 59 is granted subject to conditions, the authorised person concerned may apply to the appropriate regulator to vary the approval by (a) varying a condition, (b) removing a condition, or (c) imposing a new condition.*

(P) **with the approval (of)** *the Regulator may, with the approval of the FCA, vary the budget for a financial year at any time after its adoption* **without approval**

✎ **a period for which an approval is to have effect, a person in relation to whom an approval is given, a decision with respect to the approval of a voluntary arrangement** *a qualifying decision means a decision with respect to the approval of a voluntary arrangement where the voluntary arrangement includes a realisation of some or all of the assets of the credit institution with a view to terminating the whole or any part of the business of that credit institution*

Possible equivalents: zatwierdzenie, ZEZWOLENIE, ZGODA (pl), approvazione, AUTORIZZAZIONE, omologazione, visto (it)

ARRANGEMENT (en)

(Adj) **voluntary arrangement** ✂ **netting arrangement** *'netting arrangements' are arrangements under which a number of claims or obligations can be converted into a net claim or obligation* **protected arrangement** *'protected arrangements' means security interests, title transfer collateral arrangements, set-off arrangements, and netting arrangements*

(N) **compromise or arrangment, contract or other arrangement** ✂ **compensation arrangement, set-off arrangmenet** *'set-off arrangements' means arrangements under which two or more debts, claims or obligations can be set off against each other* ✂ **scheme of arrangement**

(V) **to enter into an arrangement, to make an arrangement**

(P) **arrangement between, under (which)** *'title transfer collateral arrangements' means arrangements under which Person 1 transfers assets to Person 2 on terms providing for Person 2 to transfer assets if specified obligations are discharged*

financial collateral arrangement *'financial collateral arrangements' are arrangements under which financial collateral is used as security in respect of a loan or other liability* **title transfer collateral arrangement** ✂ **company voluntary arrangement, qualifying voluntary arrangement** *'qualifying voluntary arrangement' means a voluntary arrangement whose purposes include a realisation of some or all of the assets of the UK credit institution to which the order relates with a view to terminating the whole or any part of the business of that credit institution* ✂ **a decision with respect to the approval of a voluntary arrangement**

Possible equivalents: porozumienie, UMOWA, uzgodnienie (pl), accordo, CONTRATTO, intesa (it)

ARTICLE (en)

(N) **article of a directive, order, regulation, treaty**

(V) **article + to amend** *articles 24 – 98 amend the procedural rules for the use of the stabilisation options to implement RRD requirements* **article + to insert** *Article 103 inserts new provisions to require the Bank of England either to recognise or to refuse to recognise a resolution action of a third country*

(P) **in accordance with article 1** *'EU resolution authority' means an authority designated by an EEA state other than the United Kingdom in accordance with Article 3 of the recovery and resolution directive.*

article compromise or arrangement *'article 418 compromise or arrangement' means a compromise or arrangement sanctioned by the court in relation to a UK credit institution under Article 418 of the Companies Order, but does not include a compromise or arrangement falling within Article 420 or Article 420A of that Order* ✂ **conditions set out in article 1** ✂ **to have the meaning given by / in article 1, within the meaning of article 1, within the meaning given by article 1** *'group' means a parent undertaking within the meaning given by Article 4.1(15)(a) of the capital requirements regulation* ✂ **as defined in / by article 1** *'consolidating* *supervisor' means a consolidating supervisor as defined in Article 4.1(41) of the capital requirements regulation* ✂ **section 1A is inserted by article 1 of this Order**

📖 Possible equivalents: artykuł (pl), ARTICOLO (it)

ASSET (en)

(N) **assets and liabilities** *the Bank may carry out a provisional valuation of the assets and liabilities of the bank for the purposes of subsection (1)* ✂ **assets of a bank** ✂ **backing assets** *'backing assets' means assets of a kind specified by banknote regulations* **client assets** ✂ **value of assets**

(V) **to transfer assets** ✂ **assets + to be held** *the regulations must (…) require backing assets held in the form of coins to be held at one or more locations approved by the Bank of England*

✏ **assets of a credit institution** ✂ **asset management vehicle** *an 'asset management vehicle' is an undertaking which (a) is wholly or partially owned (directly or indirectly) by the Bank of England or the Treasury (…) and (c) is created for the purpose of receiving some or all of the assets, rights, and liabilities of one or more banks or of one or more bridge banks (or both).*

📖 Possible equivalents: AKTYWA, majątek, ŚRODKI FINANSOWE (pl), attività, cespite, FONDO (it)

AUTHORITY (en)

(Adj) **appropriate, competent, monetary, relevant, supervisory authority** ✂ **authority responsible for** *the authority responsible for the supervision of the transferee's business in the place in which the transferee has its head office*

(N) **authority of an institution** ✂ **continuity authority** *a continuity authority may give guarantees or indemnities in respect of consideration for services or facilities provided or to be provided in pursuance of a continuity obligation*

(V) **to consult with the authority** *as soon as practicable after an EEA institution which is participating in a UK scheme becomes insolvent (…), the relevant Board*

shall (a) consult with the authority having responsibility for the institution's home State scheme **to inform the authority**

✎ **administrative or judicial authority, EU resolution authority, foreign resolution authority** *the Bank may decide that it will not exercise its investigative power unless the foreign resolution authority undertakes to make such contribution towards the cost of its exercise as the Bank considers appropriate* **relevant third-country authority** ✂ **the Competition and Markets Authority (CMA), the Financial Conduct Authority (FCA), The Financial Services Authority (FSA), the Prudential Regulation Authority (PRA)** *'qualifying company' means any company which is wholly owned by the Bank other than (a) the Prudential Regulation Authority* ✂ **authority having responsibility for**

📖 Possible equivalents: organ władzy, urząd, władza, zakres władzy (pl) AUTORITÀ, ENTE, istituzione, POTERE (it)

B

BANK (en)

Usually singular

(Adj) **central, residual bank** *'residual bank' means a bank that is a transferor under a property transfer instrument* ✂ **failing, transferred bank**

(N) **BRIDGE BANK, investment bank** ✂ **Bank of England** ✂ **agent of a bank, assets of a bank, business of a bank** *The first stabilisation option is to sell all or part of the business of the bank to a commercial purchaser* **director of a bank, functions of a bank, Governor of a bank, servant a bank** ✂ **bank administration, administrator, insolvency, liquidator** ✂ **Bank Notes** *In the Bank Notes (Scotland) Act 1845 (a) every section ceases to have effect except for sections 16, 18, 21 and 22* ✂ **with the bank's consent**

(V) **bank + to appoint, to consult, to determine, to inform, to notify, to operate, to publish, to require, to suspend, to think** *A resolution instrument may make any other provision the Bank of England may think it appropriate to make in exercise of specific powers under this Part* ✂ **bank + be satisfied (that)** ✂ **to notify a bank**

✎ *(NOMINAL)* **a bank or a banking group company** ✂ **the court of directors of a bank, Deputy Governor of a bank** ✂ **Common Equity Tier 1 instruments of a bank** *'Common Equity Tier 1 instruments' means capital instruments that meet the conditions laid down in Article 28(…) of the capital requirements regulation* **internet website of a bank, parent undertaking of a bank** *The Treasury may take a parent undertaking of a bank (the 'holding company') into temporary public ownership stabilisation power in respect of a bank* ✂ **a recognised inter-bank payment system** ✂ **bank insolvency order, bank insolvency procedure, investment bank insolvency regulations** ✂ **bank administration order,**

bank administration procedure, Investment Bank Special Administration Regulations 2011

✎ *(VERBAL)* **bank + be failing or likely to fail, enter insolvency, exercise stabilisation power** *Where the Treasury notify the Bank of England that they have provided financial assistance in respect of a bank for the purpose of resolving or reducing a serious threat to the stability of the financial systems of the United Kingdom, the Bank may exercise a stabilisation power in respect of the bank in accordance with section 11(2) or 12(2)* **bank + give directions, give notice** *the Bank of England has given an Objective 1 Achievement Notice* **bank + make a property transfer, publish information** ✂ **to make something with the bank's consent** ✂ **securities + to be issued by a bank, company + to be wholly owned by a bank** *'Qualifying company' means any company which is wholly owned by the Bank*

📖 Possible equivalents: BANK (pl), BANCA (it)

BANKNOTE (en)

(N) **destruction of banknotes** *the regulations may, in particular (a) provide for the destruction of banknotes which have not been issued; (b) provide for the destruction of banknotes which have been exchanged in accordance with section 217* **issue of banknotes** *nabycie* ✂ **banknote regulations, banknote rules** *banknote regulations may require or permit the Bank of England to make rules ('banknote rules') about any aspect of the treatment, holding or issuing of banknotes by authorised banks*

(V) **to issue banknotes** *this Part repeals existing provisions about permission to issue banknotes in Scotland and Northern Ireland*

✎ **banknote regulations or rules, provision of banknote regulations** *transitional provision of banknote regulations (…) may include provision for a case where a bank loses the right to rely on section 213* ✂ **to stop issuing banknotes**

📖 Possible equivalents: BANKNOT (pl), banconota (it)

BOARD (en)

Usually singular

(Adj) **relevant board** *in this regulation and regulation 7 below 'the relevant Board' (a) in relation to the deposit protection scheme, means the Deposit Protection Board; and (b)in relation to the investor protection scheme, means the Investor Protection Board*

(N) **decision of a board**

(V) **board + consult, determine** *a non-EEA institution shall be eligible not to participate in the deposit protection scheme ('the scheme') if the Deposit Protection Board ('the Board') determines under this regulation (...) that it is so eligible* ✂ **board + be satisfied (that)** *a deposit which the Board is satisfied was made in the course of a money-laundering transaction*

the CMA Board, Deposit Protection Board, Investor Protection Board ✂ **board + maintain a list of** ✂ **to appear to the Board to correspond as nearly as may be** *references to a liquidator or administrator include references to a person whose functions appear to the Board to correspond as nearly as may be to those of a liquidator or administrator*

Possible equivalents: dyrekcja, KOMISJA, RADA, ZARZĄD (pl), collegio, comitato, CONSIGLIO (it)

BODY (en)

(Adj) **designated, relevant, representative body** *'Designated representative body' means a body designated by the Treasury by order*

(N) **body corporate** *in this section 'UK institution' means a body corporate incorporated in the United Kingdom* ✂ **director, officer of a body** ✂ **management body** *'management body' means the board of directors, or if there is no such board, the equivalent body responsible for the management of the undertaking concerned*

(V) **to require a body (to)** *regulations under this section may not require ring-fenced bodies to achieve the results mentioned in subsection (1) before 1 January*

2026, but this does not prevent the regulations requiring steps to be taken at any time after the regulations come into force.

ring-fenced body, business of a ring-fenced body, a member of a ring-fenced body (body's group), parent undertaking of a ring-fenced body ✂ a ring-fenced body that is a PRA-authorised person

Possible equivalents: organ, OSOBA (pl), ENTE, entità, organizzazione, ORGANISMO, ORGANO (it)

BRIDGE BANK (en)

Usually singular

(Adj) **original bridge bank** *this section applies where the Bank of England (a) transfers all or part of the business of a bank ('the original bank') to a bridge bank ('the original bridge bank') by making a property transfer instrument in accordance with section 12(2),*

(N) **transfer to a bridge bank**

bank administration following transfer to a bridge bank *in the case of bank administration following transfer to a bridge bank, the bank administrator must co-operate with any request of the Bank of England to enter into an agreement for the residual bank to provide services or facilities to the bridge bank* ✂ **property, rights or liabilities of a bridge bank** ✂ **private sector purchaser or bridge bank** ✂ **to make a bridge bank (reverse) share transfer instrument** *section 26 applies where the Bank of England has made a bridge bank share transfer instrument*

Possible equivalents: bank pomostowy (pl), banca-ponte (it)

BUSINESS (en)

Usually singular

(Adj) **small business** ✂ **transferred business**

(N) **business or other interests, business and property** *the FMI administrator of a company must manage its affairs, business and property, and exercise and perform the FMI administrator's functions, so as to achieve the objective in section 115* **dealing or business** ✂ **business of a bank** ✂ **business day**

(V) **to carry on a business** ✂ **business + be transferred** *'residual bank' means a bank all or part of whose business has been transferred to a commercial purchaser in accordance with section 11 or to a bridge bank in accordance with section 12*

✎ **business of a building society, business of a ring-fenced body** ✂ **all or part of the business of a bank, the whole or any part of the business of a credit institution** ✂ **business reorganisation plan** ✂ **a reclaim fund business transfer scheme** ✂ **to operate business, or part of it, effectively** *the residual bank and each group company must provide such services and facilities as are required to enable a transferee to operate the transferred business, or part of it, effectively* ✂ **to transfer all or part of the business**

📖 Possible equivalents: DZIAŁALNOŚĆ (pl), ATTIVITÀ (it)

C

CIRCUMSTANCES (en)

Only plural

(Adj) **different, financial circumstances** *the regulations may in particular (c) require ring-fenced bodies to establish new occupational pension schemes in prescribed circumstances* **relevant circumstances** ✂ **prescribed, specified circumstances**

(P) **in circumstances where** *the PRA must also report in general terms on (d) the extent to which ring-fenced bodies are carrying on the regulated activity (…) in circumstances where as a result of an order under section 142D(2) that activity is not an excluded activity*

✎ **different/specified purposes, cases or circumstances** *provision under subsection (7) may apply subsection (8) or (9) (a) generally or only for specified purposes, cases or circumstances, or (b) differently for different purposes, cases or circumstances* ✂ **institution's financial circumstances**

📖 Possible equivalents: okoliczność, sytuacja (pl), circostanza, situazione (it)

CLIENT (en)

(N) **client account, client assets** *in this group of sections 'client assets' means assets which an institution has undertaken to hold for a client*

✎ **the protection of client assets** *Condition 2 is that the Bank of England is satisfied that the exercise of the power in respect of the banking group company is* *necessary, having regard to the public interest in (…) the protection of any client assets that may be affected* ✂ **a person representing a client** ✂ **to hold client assets**

📖 Possible equivalents: KLIENT (pl), cliente (it)

COMMITTEE (en)

Usually singular

(Aff) **sub-committee** *there shall be a sub-committee of the court of directors of the Bank (the 'Financial Stability Committee')*

(Adj) **delegated to a committee** *functions delegated to the Committee by the court of directors for the purpose of pursuing the Financial Stability Objective*

(N) **creditors' committee** *a creditors' meeting may not establish a creditors' committee in reliance on para. 57 until the Bank of England has given an Objective 1 Achievement Notice* **liquidation committee** ✂ **functions, meeting, member, proceedings of a committee**

(V) **committee + to decide** *if, at any meeting, the Committee decides that the Bank should intervene in financial markets, it shall also consider at the meeting whether immediate publication of the decision would be likely to impede or frustrate the achievement of the intervention's purpose* **committee + to determine**

✎ **Monetary Policy Committee, (Treasury) Committee of the House of Commons** *before appointing the members of the review panel, the Treasury must consult the chair of the Treasury Committee of the House of Commons* ✂ **committee constituted by section 1** ✂ **liquidation committee + to pass a full payment resolution** *a person aggrieved by any action of the liquidation committee before it has passed a full payment resolution may apply to the court, which may make any order (including an order for the repayment of money)*

📖 Possible equivalents: komisja, komitet, RADA (pl), comitato, commissione (it)

COMPANY (en)

(Adj) **new, old company** *the old company may (a) with the consent of the new company, and (b) for the purpose of giving effect to the proposed transfer, make a scheme under this Schedule for the transfer of property, rights and liabilities from the old company to the new company (an 'FMI transfer scheme')* ✂ **qualifying company** *if the Bank considers it necessary to do so having regard to the Financial Stability Objective, the Bank may by direction to a qualifying company exclude the application to the qualifying company of any of the relevant Companies Act requirements* ✂ **company subject to**

(N) **registrar of companies** *a person who obtains deferral under subsection (1) or (3) shall, within 7 days after the giving of the deferral direction, deliver a copy of the direction to the registrar of companies for registration* **reference to a company, subsidiary of a company, undertaking of a company** *the means by which transfers falling within subsection (5) may be effected include, in particular (a) a transfer of the undertaking of the company subject to the FMI administration order, or of part of its undertaking, to a wholly-owned subsidiary of that company* ✂ **group company, holding company, infrastructure company** *'Infrastructure company' means a company which is (a) the operator of a recognised inter-bank payment system* **resolution company** *In this Act 'resolution company' means a bridge bank or an asset management vehicle*

(P) **in relation to a company** *in this Part references to a person qualified to act as an insolvency practitioner in relation to a company are to be read in accordance with Part 13 of the 1986 Act*

✎ **the old company and the new company, the residual bank or a group company** *the Bank of England may (a) cancel a contract or other arrangement between the residual bank and a group company (whether or not rights or obligations under it have been transferred to a transferee)* ✂ **banking group company, financial holding company** *'Financial holding company' has the meaning given by Article 1(21) of Council Directive 2000/12/EC of the European Parliament and the Council* **former group company, mixed activity holding company, mixed financial holding company, third-country group company** ✂ **FMI administrator of a company** ✂ **company registered under the Companies Act 2006, company wholly owned by the Treasury / Bank of England** ✂ **company voluntary arrangement** *on the termination of a company voluntary arrangement the* *bank liquidator may apply to the court to lift the suspension of the bank insolvency order* ✂ **Companies Act 2006, Company Directors Disqualification Act 1986, Companies (Northern Ireland) Order 1986**

📖 Possible equivalents: firma, PRZEDSIĘBIORSTWO, SPÓŁKA, towarzystwo (pl), azienda, compagnia, IMPRESA, SOCIETÀ (it)

COMPENSATION (en)

(Adj) **eligible for compensation (under)** *in paragraph 15B 'eligible deposit' means a deposit in respect of which the person (…) to whom it is owed would be eligible for compensation under the Financial Services Compensation Scheme*

(N) **compensation arrangements, payments, compensation scheme** *where a bank insolvency order is made in respect of a bank, the fact that it later ceases to be an authorised person does not prevent the operation of the compensation scheme in respect of it* ✂ **amount of compensation**

(V) **to be paid compensation** *a 'bail-in compensation order' is an order establishing a scheme for determining, in accordance with section 52A, whether any transferors or others should be paid compensation*

✏ **bail-in compensation order, compensation scheme order** *a 'compensation scheme order' is an order (a) establishing a scheme for determining whether transferors should be paid compensation, or providing for transferors to be paid compensation, and (b) establishing a scheme for paying any compensation* **third party compensation order** ✂ **Financial Services Compensation Scheme, the scheme manager of the Financial Services Compensation Scheme** ✂ **the Compensation Act 2006** ✂ **compensation + to be payable**

📖 Possible equivalents: kompensacja, odszkodowanie, rekompensata, wynagrodzenie (pl), compensazione, compenso, indennità, indennizzo, retribuzione, risarcimento (it)

CONDITION (en)

(Adj) **general, specific condition** ✂ **following conditions** ✂ **conditions imposed, mentioned (in), set out** *any requirement in this Part to send a relevant*

notification to a creditor shall also be treated as satisfied if the conditions set out in paragraph (6) are satisfied **conditions specified in** ✂ **subject to conditions**

(N) **terms and conditions** ✂ **threshold conditions** *condition 1 is that the bank is failing, or is likely to fail, to satisfy the threshold conditions (within the meaning of section 41(1) of the Financial Services and Markets Act 2000 (permission to carry on regulated activities))* ✂ **set of conditions** ✂ **condition 1 in section 1**

(V) **to meet, to satisfy a condition, to impose a condition (on)** ✂ **condition + to be met, to be satisfied**

(P) **conditions for** *the conditions for applying for and making a bank administration order are set out in sections 143 and 144*

conditions for the exercise of power, condition for financial assistance, condition 1 of the general conditions ✂ **subject to conditions or for a limited period** *each regulator must prepare and issue a statement of its policy with respect to (a) its giving of approval under section 59 subject to conditions or for a limited period only* ✂ **condition + to be in addition to the conditions in section 1** *the condition in this section is in addition to the conditions in sections 7 and 8ZA* **(following / general) conditions + to be met (in respect of)** *the PRA is satisfied that the general conditions for the exercise of a stabilisation power set out in section 7 are met in respect of a bank in the same group* **to be satisifed that a condition is met** ✂ **before determining whether a condition is met** *before determining whether Conditions A and B are met, and if so how to react, the Bank of England must consult (a) the PRA, (b) the FCA, and (c) the Treasury*

Possible equivalents: WARUNEK (pl), CONDIZIONE, MODALITÀ, REQUISITO (it)

CONTRACT (en)

(N) **contract of insurance** ✂ **employment contract** *in this regulation, an employment contract is an EEA employment contract, and an employment relationship is an EEA employment relationship if it is subject to the law of an EEA State* **service contract** ✂ **provision, terms of contract** ✂ **one of the parties to the contract** *the Bank of England may suspend obligations to make a payment, or delivery, under*

a contract where one of the parties to the contract is a bank in respect of which the Bank is exercising a stabilisation power ✂ **contract or agreement**

(V) **to cancel, to terminate, to vary a contract** *share transfer instrument may enable the Bank of England (…) to vary the service contract of a director of a specified bank*

(P) **contract between** ✂ **under a contract** *subject to subsection (2), suspends all obligations to make a payment or delivery under the contract in question, whether the obligation concerned is that of the bank under resolution or of any other party to the contract* ✂ **contract under which** *the reference to cancelling a liability owed by the bank includes a reference to cancelling a contract under which the bank has a liability*

✎ **contract under which the bank has a liability** ✂ **restriction arising by virtue of contract or legislation** ✂ **the activity of effecting or carrying out contracts of insurance** *'insurer' means an institution which is authorised under FSMA 2000 to carry on the regulated activity of effecting or carrying out contracts of insurance as principal* ✂ **done under a contract or other agreement rights or obligations** *a thing is not done by virtue of a resolution instrument for the purposes of subsection (5)(b) merely by virtue of being done under a contract or other agreement rights or obligations under which have been affected by the instrument* ✂ **to have effect as if created by contract (between)** *the continuity authority may (…)confer and impose rights and obligations on a former group company and the transferred bank, which shall have effect as if created by contract between them* ✂ **to terminate / to vary the service contract of a director of a specified bank** ✂ **provision of a contract or (other) agreement + to take effect**

📖 Possible equivalents: kontrakt, UMOWA (pl), CONTRATTO (it)

COPY (en)

(Adj) **hard copy** *a document or information is sent or supplied in hard copy form if it is sent or supplied in a paper copy or similar form capable of being read*

(N) **copy of accounts** *the Regulator must send a copy of its annual accounts to the Comptroller and Auditor General and the Treasury as soon as is reasonably practicable* **copy of a notice, of a report, of a statement** *a regulator may charge*

a reasonable fee for providing a person with a copy of a statement published under this section

(V) **to lay a copy (before), to send a copy (to)**

in hard copy form *the society must send the document or information in hard copy form within 21 days of receipt of the request from the person* ✂ **the Treasury + to lay a copy of a report before Parliament, the Chancellor of the Exchequer + lay a copy of each report under subsection 1** *the Chancellor of the Exchequer must lay a copy of each report under subsection (2) before Parliament*

Possible equivalents: egzemplarz, kopia, odpis (pl), copia, esemplare (it)

COUNTRY (en)

Usually singular

(N) **country or territory** ✂ **third-country authority, institution, instrument** ✂ **law of a country** *in this section 'foreign law' means the law of a country or territory outside the United Kingdom*

relevant third-country authority, third-country credit institution, third-country group company, third-country parent undertaking, third-country resolution action *'third-country resolution action' means action under the law of a third country to manage the failure or likely failure of a third-country institution* ✂ **recognition of third-country resolution action** ✂ **country or territory outside the United Kingdom / the European Economic Area** ✂ **to be incorporated in or formed under the law of a country or territory outside the United Kingdom** *section 5(3) above shall have effect as if (a) the references in paragraph (a) to an authorised institution included references to a building society and to any credit institution which is incorporated in or formed under the law of a country or territory outside the United Kingdom*

Possible equivalents: kraj, PAŃSTWO (pl), paese, STATO (it)

CREDIT INSTITUTION (en)

(Adj) **relevant credit institution** ✂ **affected credit institution**

(N) **EEA, third-country, UK credit institution** ✂ **assets of a credit institution** *An EEA insolvency measure has effect in the United Kingdom in relation to (a) any branch of an EEA credit institution, (b) any property or other assets of that credit institution* **business of a credit institution** *'banking consolidation directive' means the directive of the European Parliament and the Council of 20 March 2000 relating to the taking up and pursuit of the business of credit institutions* **reorganisation, winding up of a credit institution** *Where a person has honoured a relevant obligation for the benefit of a relevant credit institution, he shall be deemed to have discharged that obligation if he was unaware of the winding up of that credit institution*

✎ *(NOMINAL)* **credit institution and / or investment firm** *The RRD requires EEA states to have powers to manage the failure of credit institutions and investment firms and their group companies ('banks') as an alternative to insolvency, in order to ensure that critical functions continue to be performed* ✂ **reorganisation and winding up of a credit institution, realisation of some or all of the assets of a credit institution** *the voluntary arrangement includes a realisation of some or all of the assets of the credit institution with a view to terminating the whole or any part of the business of that credit institution* ✂ **The Credit Institutions (Protection of Depositors) Regulations 1995**

✎ *(VERBAL)* **to have effect in relation to a credit institution** *'voluntary arrangement' means a voluntary arrangement which has effect in relation to a UK credit institution in accordance with section 4A of the 1986 Act* **to terminate the whole or any part of the business of a credit institution credit institution + to be subject to** *Regulations 9 and 10 apply where a third country credit institution is subject to a relevant measure, as if references in those regulations to a UK credit institution included a reference to a third country credit institution*

📖 Possible equivalents: instytucja kredytowa (pl), ente creditizio, istituto di credito, istituzione di credito (it)

CREDITOR (en)

(Adj) **known creditor** *the liquidator, provisional liquidator, or administrator (as the case may be) must send a report to every known creditor once in every 12 months beginning with the date when his appointment has effect*

(N) **shareholders and creditors** ✂ **EEA creditor** *'EEA creditor' means a creditor of a UK credit institution who (a) in the case of an individual, is ordinarily resident in an EEA State* **pre-transfer creditor** *'pre-transfer creditor' means a person who (i) is a creditor of a residual bank immediately before a property transfer instrument takes effect, and (ii) satisfies conditions specified by the regulations* ✂ **meeting of creditors, right of a creditor (or: creditors' meeting, creditors' rights)** ✂ **creditor of a bank (or: bank's creditors), creditor of an institution** ✂ **creditors' committee**

✎ **bank's creditors as a whole** *Objective 2 is to wind up the affairs of the bank so as to achieve the best result for the bank's creditors as a whole* ✂ **a legal act detrimental to creditors, creditors' voluntary winding up** *in the case of a creditors voluntary winding up, the liquidator is appointed in accordance with section 100 of the 1986 Act*

📖 Possible equivalents: kredytodawca, udzielający kredytu, WIERZYCIEL (pl), CREDITORE (it)

CURRENCY (en)

(N) **deposit in a currency** *the deposit base of an institution in relation to any contribution is the amount which the Board determines as representing the average (…) of deposits in EEA currencies with the United Kingdom offices of that institution*

✎ **EEA (European Economic Area) currency** *deposits in all EEA currencies and in ecus are protected* ✂ **deposit in an EEA currency, deposit made in another currency** *in calculating a depositors protected deposit for the purposes of subsection (1) above, the amount to be taken into account as regards any deposit made in another EEA currency shall be its sterling equivalent immediately before the time when the institution became insolvent* ✂ **the European currency unit**

📖 Possible equivalents: WALUTA (pl), VALUTA (it)

D

DATE (en)

(Adj) **relevant date ✂ specified date**

(N) **commencement, transfer date** *'transfer date' means the date or time on or at which a share transfer instrument or order (or the relevant part of it) takes effect*

(V) **to begin / end with a date** *the first report must be made as soon as is reasonably practicable after the end of one year beginning with the date of the first transfer to the bridge bank*

(P) **on or after a date** *on or after the relevant date, an administrator may not, in relation to an EEA credit institution, be appointed under paragraphs 14 or 22 of Schedule B1 of the 1986 Act.*

year-end date *the financial year of a building society established before the relevant day is the period of 12 months ending with the year-end date of the society*

Possible equivalents: data, DZIEŃ, TERMIN (pl), DATA, GIORNO (it)

DAY (en)

(Adj) **last, relevant day** *the financial year of a building society established before the relevant day is the period of 12 months ending with the year-end date of the society* ✂ **working day**

(N) **period of 2 days ✂ business day**

day on which this Act comes into force, day on which the notice is received by the Bank ✂ **period of 2 years beginning with the day (on which)** ✂ **before the end of 10 working days beginning with the first working day (after)** *the Payment Systems Regulator must make the representations or observations in writing before the end of 10 working days beginning with the first working day after the day on which it received a copy of the application under paragraph 3(5) or 4(4)* **first business day following the day (on which)** ✂ **day to day management of a bank or a banking group company** *in this section 'senior manager' means a person who (b) is responsible, and directly accountable to the directors, for the day to day management of that bank or banking group company*

Possible equivalents: data, DZIEŃ, TERMIN (pl), DATA, giornata, GIORNO (it)

DEBT (en)

(N) **debt instrument** *'debt instrument' means (a) a bond, (b) any other instrument creating or acknowledging a debt, or (c) an instrument giving rights to acquire a debt instrument* **debt security** *'debt security' means any instrument creating or acknowledging indebtedness (including a government or public security)* ✂ **proof of a debt**

(V) **to pay one's debts** *the court may make an FMI administration order in relation to an infrastructure company if satisfied (a) that the company is unable to pay its debts*

inability to pay debts ✂ **to be unable to pay one's debts** *for the purposes of this section a company is unable to pay its debts if it is treated as being so unable under section 123 of the 1986 Act*

Possible equivalents: dług, należność, zadłużenie, ZOBOWIĄZANIE (pl), debito, indebitamento (it)

DEBTOR (en)

(N) **debtor of a bank** *powers conferred by this Act, by the Insolvency Act 1986 (as applied) and the Companies Acts are in addition to, and not in restriction of, any existing powers of instituting proceedings against a contributory or debtor of a bank,*

or the estate of any contributory or debtor, for the recovery of any call or other sum **debtor of a company** ✂ **proceedings against a debtor** ✂ **contributory or debtor**

✎ **estate of a contributory or debtor** *powers conferred by this Part of this Act and by the 1986 Act (as applied) are in addition to, and not in restriction of, any existing powers of instituting proceedings against any contributory or debtor of an infrastructure company, or the estate of any contributory or debtor, for the recovery of any call or other sum*

📖 Possible equivalents: DŁUŻNIK, KREDYTOBIORCA, pożyczkobiorca (pl), DEBITORE (it)

DECISION (en)

(Adj) **relevant decision** ✂ **qualifying decision** *qualifying decision means a decision with respect to the approval of a voluntary arrangement where the voluntary arrangement includes a realisation of some or all of the assets of the credit institution with a view to terminating the whole or any part of the business of that credit institution*

(N) **Board's decision, decision of the Board** ✂ **publication of a decision** ✂ **decision notice** *if the regulator decides to exercise the group restructuring powers it must give each of the relevant persons a decision notice* ✂ **decision under regulation**

(V) **decision to intervene** *subsection (1) shall not apply to minutes of any proceedings relating to (a) a decision to intervene in financial markets, or (b) a decision about the publication of a decision to intervene in financial markets,* ✂ **to appeal against a decision, to make, to take a decision**

(P) **decision under** *an EEA institution which is aggrieved by a decision under regulation 3 (…) may, within 28 days after the day on which it received notice of the decision, appeal against the decision to the Chancellor of the Exchequer* **decision with respect to** *for the purposes of this regulation (a) a qualifying decision means a decision with respect to the approval of a proposed voluntary arrangement, in accordance with section 4A of the 1986 Act*

✐ **decision, order, or appointment** ✂ **CAT-appealable decision** *if the decision is a CAT-appealable decision, the appeal must be made to the Competition Appeal Tribunal in accordance with section 77* **decision to impose a requirement** ✂ **written notice of a decision** ✂ **decision + to have effect**

🕮 Possible equivalents: DECYZJA, postanowienie (pl), decisione (it)

DEPOSIT (en)

(Adj) **eligible, relevant deposit** ✂ **deposit made (with), protected deposit**

(N) **deposit advertisement** *in this regulation 'deposit advertisement' means any advertisement containing (a) an invitation to make a deposit* **deposit base** *in determining the percentage to be applied under subsection (4) above to the share and deposit bases of contributory institutions, the Board shall have regard to the factors specified in subsection (6) below* **deposit-taker** ✂ **reference to a deposit**

(V) **to accept deposits** *in its application to UK institutions or building societies which accept deposits at offices in EEA States other than the United Kingdom, paragraph (1) above shall have effect as if the reference to a United Kingdom office included a reference to an office in such a State* ✂ **deposits + to be protected**

(P) **deposit with** *a person claiming to be entitled to a payment under subsection (1) above in respect of a protected deposit with a participating institution shall make his claim in such form, with such evidence proving it, and within such period, as the Board directs*

✐ **deposit in an EEA currency, the most relevant deposits with the institution** ✂ **deposit-guarantee scheme, deposit protection scheme** *'the deposit protection scheme' means the scheme for the protection of depositors continued in force by that Part* **Deposit Protection Board** ✂ **Directive 9419EC on deposit-guarantee scheme** ✂ **to carry on the regulated activity of accepting deposits, to have a liability in respect of a deposit, to participate in the deposit protection scheme** *a non-EEA institution shall be eligible not to participate in the deposit protection scheme ('the scheme') if the Deposit Protection Board ('the Board') determines under this regulation, on an application made by the institution, that it is so eligible*

📖 Possible equivalents: DEPOZYT, LOKATA, wpłata (pl), deposito (it)

DEPOSITOR (en)

(Adj) **eligible depositor** *the amount of compensation that would have been payable does not include any compensation actually paid to an eligible depositor of the bank*

(N) **depositors of a bank** ✂ **protection of depositors** *any reference to an EEA institutions home State scheme includes a reference to any alternative permitted system or arrangement for the protection of depositors which is in force in the institutions home State and in which the institution participates* ✂ **depositors or investors**

✏ **compensation payments to depositors, protection afforded to depositors** *the Board shall not make a determination under this regulation unless (…) it is satisfied that (a) the scope of the protection afforded to depositors by the institutions home State scheme; and (b) the level of the protection so afforded are each not less than that afforded to depositors by the UK scheme in which the institution is participating* ✂ **depositors or intending depositors** *in these Regulations, unless the context otherwise requires, references to deposits include references to investments, and references to depositors or intending depositors shall be construed accordingly*

📖 Possible equivalents: DEPONENT, wpłacający (pl), depositante (it)

DIRECTION (en)

(Adj) **general direction** *a direction under this section that applies as mentioned in subsection (3)(a) or (b) is referred to in this Part as a 'general direction'* ✂ **direction requiring**

(N) **fees direction** *in this section 'a fees direction' means a direction given by the Treasury as a result of regulations under section 410A* ✂ **direction under paragraph 1 /section 1 / subsection (1)** ✂ **application for a direction**

(V) **to apply for directions, to comply with a direction** *a director must comply with a direction within the period of time specified in the direction, or if no period of time is specified, as soon as reasonably practicable* **to give a direction (to)**

(P) **in accordance with a direction** *the Treasury may by order confer immunity from liability in damages in respect of action or inaction in accordance with a direction*

✎ **power to give a direction**

📖 Possible equivalents: instrukcja, pouczenie, wskazówka, zalecenie (pl), DISPOSIZIONE, istruzione, ordine (it)

DIRECTIVE (en)

Usually singular

(N) **annex to directive** *'financial instrument' includes anything specified in Section C of Annex I to Directive 2004/39/EC of the European Parliament and of the Council of 21 April 2004 on markets in financial instruments* **article of directive ✂ Council Directive**

✎ **banking consolidation directive** *'banking consolidation directive' means the directive of the European Parliament and the Council of 20 March 2000 relating to the taking up and pursuit of the business of credit institutions (200012EC)(g)* **Banking Coordination (Second Council Directive) Regulations 1992, directive of the European Parliament and of the Council, recovery and resolution directive ✂ directive reorganisation measure** *'directive reorganisation measure' means a reorganisation measure as defined in Article 2 of the reorganisation and winding up directive which was adopted or imposed on or after the 5th May 2004* **directive winding-up proceedings**

📖 Possible equivalents: dyrektywa (pl), DIRETTIVA (it)

DOCUMENT (en)

Usually singular

(Adj) **seized document** *any document of which possession is taken under section 88 ('a seized document') may be retained so long as it is necessary to retain it (rather than copies of it) in the circumstances* **specified document ✂ document relating to**

(N) **document of a description** *an investigator may also require any person to produce at a specified time and place any specified documents or documents of a*

specified description ✂ **possession, production of a document** ✂ **document or information, instrument or document** *a share transfer instrument or order may modify references (express or implied) in an instrument or document to a transferor*

(V) **to produce a document** ✂ **document + to be produced**

to provide an explanation of a document *any person to whom a relevant document is produced may (b) require the person producing the document, or any relevant person (see subsection (4)), to provide an explanation of the document*

Possible equivalents: dokument (pl), ATTO, DOCUMENTO, STRUMENTO (it)

E

EFFECT (en)

Usually singular

(Adj) **adverse effect ✂ specified effect** *regulations may (a) require a resolution fund order (…) or a bail-in compensation order to include provision of a specified kind or to specified effect*

(N) **statement to the effect (that)** *a deposit advertisement may include (c) if it relates to a non-EEA institution which is participating in the deposit protection scheme, a statement to the effect that most relevant deposits with the institution are protected by that scheme*

(V) **to give effect (to)** *these Regulations give effect to Directive 9419EC on deposit-guarantee schemes* **to have an effect (on), to have effect (as if)** *the transfer of functions by this Part shall not affect the validity of anything done (or having effect as if done) by or in relation to the Bank before the day on which this Act comes into force* **to modify an effect of, to take effect**

adverse effect on the continuity of the provision in the United Kingdom of core services ✂ to cease to have effect, to take effect immediately, to take effect in accordance with, to take / to have effect only if ✂ to have effect as if a reference included *in its application to UK institutions, subsection (4) above shall have effect as if the reference to United Kingdom offices included a reference to offices in other EEA States* **to have effect for the purpose of / subject to** *paragraph (b) of subsection (8) above has effect subject to the provisions of Schedule 6 to this Act* **to have effect in relation to ✂ agreement, approval, section 1 of an Act + to have effect, instrument, scheme, transfer, variation + to take effect** *a variation may be expressed to take effect immediately (or on a specified date) only if the regulator concerned, (…) reasonably considers that it is necessary for the variation to take* *effect immediately (or on that date)* ✂ **for the purpose of giving effect to** *rules may also be made for the purpose of giving effect to Part 2 of the Banking Act 2009*

📖 Possible equivalents: moc obowiązująca, skutek, wynik (pl), conseguenza, effetto, efficacia, risultato (it)

ENACTMENT (en)

Usually singular

(Adj) **fiscal enactment** *an order may, in particular, amend or modify the effect of an enactment (including a fiscal enactment) passed before the commencement of this Part* **relevant enactment** ✂ **enactment amended, contained (in)** *'enactment' includes (a) an enactment contained in subordinate legislation* **enactment passed**

(N) **reference in an enactment** *a reference in an enactment or other document to anything done under a provision applied by this Part of this Act includes a reference to the provision as applied* ✂ **enactment about insolvency** *the Secretary of State and the Treasury may by order made jointly (a) provide for an enactment about insolvency to apply to bank insolvency (with or without specified modifications)*

(V) **to amend, to disapply an enactment** *an order may disapply, modify or apply (with or without modifications) any enactment which relates, or in so far as it relates, to credit unions* **to modify an enactment** ✂ **enactment + to relate**

(P) **enactment about** ✂ **under an enactment** *it is immaterial for the purposes of subsection (2) whether or not the information was received (a) as a result of a requirement to provide it imposed by or under any enactment*

✎ **act or any other enactment** *neither section 16 of the Banking (Special Provisions) Act 2008 (finance) nor any other enactment restricts the breadth of application of this section* ✂ **to disapply or modify an enactment**

📖 Possible equivalents: akt prawny, ROZPORZĄDZENIE, USTAWA (pl), ATTO, REGOLAMENTO (it)

END (en)

Usually singular

(N) **end of year, paragraph, period** *if the power to make investment bank insolvency regulations has not been exercised before the end of the period of 2 years beginning with the date on which this Act is passed, it lapses* **end of sub-paragraph**

(P) **at the end** ✂ **after, before the end**

✎ **year-end date** *the year-end date of a building society established on or after 25th August 1894 and before the relevant day is 31st December* ✂ **practicable after the end of one year** *The first report must be made as soon as is reasonably practicable after the end of one year beginning with the date of the first transfer to the bridge bank* ✂ **to insert something at the end** *in subsection (2), at the end insert 'or suspended'* **to substitute for the words from… to the end** *in subsection (4), for the words from 'appropriate' to the end substitute 'necessary to do so having regard to the Financial Stability Objective'* ✂ **before the end of a period, before the end of 15 working days (beginning with)**

📖 Possible equivalents: koniec, zakończenie (pl), fine (it)

F

FEE (en)

(N) **fees direction** *as soon as practicable after giving a fees direction, the Treasury must lay before Parliament a copy of the direction* ✂ **charging of fees** *the regulations must provide for the charging of fees in pursuance of a direction given under the regulations to the FCA or the PRA to be by rules made by that regulator* **payment of fees** ✂ **fee or charge** *The power under this section to vary any fee or charge includes power to specify a maximum fee or charge*

(V) **to charge a fee, to pay a fee** *regulations made under subsection (3) may, in particular, specify the consequences of failure to pay fees*

✎ **to charge a reasonable fee (for)** *a regulator may charge a reasonable fee for providing a person with a copy of the statement published under this section*

📖 Possible equivalents: OPŁATA, zapłata, honorarium, PROWIZJA (pl), canone, commissione, provvigione, onorario, tassa, SPESA (it)

FUNCTION (en)

(Adj) **public, relevant function** ✂ **concurrent functions** *the functions to which this subsection applies are to be concurrent functions of the Payment Systems Regulator and the Competition and Markets Authority ('the CMA')* **critical, exercisable, general functions** ✂ **controlled function** *if a function of a description specified in rules made by the PRA under subsection (3)(a) is a controlled function in relation to the carrying on of a regulated activity by a relevant authorised person, the PRA must designate the function in the rules as a senior management* **specified, transferred function** ✂ **function conferred (by or under)** *the relevant functions*

of the FCA or the PRA are (a) its functions conferred by or under FSMA 2000, other than its legislative functions **function conferred (on), functions referred to**

(N) **functions of the CMA, of a committee, of the FCA, of the office** *independent valuers (and their staff) are not liable for damages in respect of anything done in good faith for the purposes of or in connection with the functions of the office* ✂ **discharge of functions** *at least once a year, the Regulator must make a report to the FCA in relation to the discharge of its functions* **exercise, performance of functions** ✂ **functions under Part 1 / section 1 / subsection 1** *in particular, the court's functions under subsection (1) shall include determining the Bank's objectives (including objectives for its financial management) and strategy* ✂ **Regulator's functions**

(V) **to discharge, to perform a function** *the Bank of England may appoint more than one bail-in administrator to perform functions in relation to a bank* ✂ **to confer functions (on), to exercise functions** ✂ **functions + to be exercised**

(P) **function by virtue of** *section 49 (the Payment Systems Regulator's general duties) does not apply in relation to anything done by the Payment Systems Regulator in the carrying out of its functions by virtue of sections 59 to 63* **function in relation to** *despite the transfer to the Scottish Ministers of functions in relation to observing and implementing obligations under Community law, any function of a Minister of the Crown shall continue to be exercisable by him as regards Scotland for the purposes specified in section 2(2) of the European Communities Act* **function under** *this subsection applies to a request if the request is made by a foreign resolution authority in connection with the exercise by that authority of (a) functions under the recovery and resolution directive* ✂ **in connection with functions**

✎ **functions of the Payment Systems Regulator** ✂ **significant-harm function, (designated / relevant) senior management function as defined in section 1** ✂ **to be a fit and proper person to perform the function** *a relevant authorised person may issue a certificate to a person under this section only if the authorised person is satisfied that the person is a fit and proper person to perform the function to which the certificate relates* **to exercise any of the concurrent functions in relation to any matter, to perform a designated senior management function** ✂ **in the carrying out of functions**

Possible equivalents: CZYNNOŚĆ, DZIAŁALNOŚĆ, funkcja, ZADANIE (pl), carica, ATTIVITÀ, FUNZIONE (it)

H

HOUSE (en)

Usually singular

(Adj) **clearing house** *Where an FMI administrator is appointed in relation to the operator of a recognised inter-bank payment system or a securities settlement system, the objective of the FMI administration is (b) where the operator of the system is also a clearing house falling within section 285(1)(b)(ii) of FSMA 2000 (recognised clearing house that is not a recognised central counterparty), to ensure that the protected activities continue to be carried on*

(N) **House of Commons, of Parliament**

✎ **recognised clearing house** ✂ **committee of the House of Commons** ✂ **to be subject to annulment in pursuance of a resolution of either House of Parliament** *A statutory instrument containing an order or regulations under this Act is subject to annulment in pursuance of a resolution of either House of Parliament, unless (a) the instrument contains only provision made under section 148* ✂ **unless a draft has been laid before and approved by resolution of each House of Parliament** *An order under this section (a) is to be made by statutory instrument, and (b) may not be made unless a draft has been laid before and approved by resolution of each House of Parliament*
Possible equivalents: izba (pl), camera (it)

HOLDER (en)

(N) **holder of an instrument** ✂ **holder of shares** *losses are born by the holders of shares of the bank that are not within paragraph (a), (b) or (c) in accordance with the hierarchy of claims in normal insolvency proceedings* **holder of securities** ✂

office-holder *the office-holder referred to in subsection (4) above is (a) in England and Wales, the Official Receiver; (b) in Scotland, the liquidator; and (c) in Northern Ireland, the Official Receiver for Northern Ireland*

holder a capital instrument *where the principal amount of a relevant capital instrument is reduced under section 6B (…) no liability to the holder of the relevant capital instrument remains under, or in connection with, so much of the amount of the instrument as constitutes the reduction* **holder of a floating charge**

Possible equivalents: okaziciel, POSIADACZ, użytkownik (pl), detentore, portatore, possessore, TITOLARE (it)

I

INFORMATION (en)

(Adj) **confidential, false information** ✂ **restricted information** *restricted information shall not be disclosed (…) without the consent of the person from whom the Bank obtained the information and, if different, the person to whom the information relates* ✂ **information given, obtained (by), provided, received, relating (to), required (by), specified, supplied** *any information supplied in pursuance of paragraph (1) above shall be supplied in English except that, where the request is made at an office in an EEA State other than the United Kingdom, it shall be supplied instead in an official language of that State*

(N) **information of a kind** ✂ **disclosure, provision of information** ✂ **information agreement, information requirement** *in this section 'information requirement' means (a) a requirement imposed by the Payment Systems Regulator under section 81 or 86, or (b) a requirement imposed by an investigator under section 85 or 86* ✂ **document or information, information and documents**

(V) **to disclose information** *the Bank of England may disclose information that it thinks relevant to the financial stability of (a) individual financial institutions, or (b) one or more aspects of the financial systems of the United Kingdom* **to give, to obtain, to provide, to publish information** ✂ **information + to relate (to)** ✂ **information + to be provided** ✂ **bank + to publish information**

(P) **information on** ✂ **information about a matter** *subject to subsection (8), where the Bank gives a decision notice it may publish such information about the matter to which the notice relates as it considers appropriate* **information in a form** *the society may not make a charge for providing the document or information in that form*

information required by paragraph (1), insolvency practitioner information *Insolvency practitioner information is not subject to the restrictions on disclosure imposed by section 348(1) of the 2000 Act* **specially protected information** ✂ **disclosure of confidential information** *section 91 does not prevent a disclosure of confidential information which (a) is made for the purpose of facilitating the carrying out of a public function* ✂ **power to obtain information, regulatory information service, restriction on disclosure of information, to provide with information and assistance, to require information to be provided** ✂ **information requirement + to be imposed**

Possible equivalents: INFORMACJA (pl), INFORMAZIONE (it)

INSOLVENCY (en)

Always singular

(N) **bank insolvency** ✂ **insolvency law, insolvency practitioner** *'insolvency practitioner' means an insolvency practitioner, within the meaning of section 388 of the 1986 Act or Article 3 of the 1989 Order, who is appointed or acts in relation to a third country credit institution* **insolvency procedure, proceedings, treatment** *the insolvency treatment principles are that where an instrument includes special bail-in provision (a) the provision made by the instrument must be consistent with treating all the liabilities of the bank in accordance with the priority they would enjoy on a liquidation* ✂ **enactment about insolvency, law of insolvency** ✂ **Insolvency Act 1986, Insolvency Rules**

(V) **to enter insolvency** *in making regulations the Treasury shall, in particular, have regard to the desirability of ensuring that if a residual bank enters insolvency after transfer, pre-transfer creditors do not receive less favourable treatment than they would have received had it entered insolvency immediately before transfer*

application of insolvency law, general law of insolvency of the United Kingdom ✂ **EEA insolvency measure** *'EEA insolvency measure' means, as the case may be, a directive reorganisation measure or directive winding-up proceedings which have effect in relation to an EEA credit institution by virtue of the law of the relevant EEA State* **insolvency procedure to which the notice relates, insolvency treatment principles, investment bank insolvency regulations, normal insolvency proceedings** ✂ **the bank insolvency procedure and the bank administration procedure** ✂ **expenses attributable to the insolvency, group company entering insolvency** ✂ **Insolvency (Northern Ireland) Order 1989, Insolvency**

(Scotland) Rules, rule 1.11 of the Insolvency Rules ✂ **qualified to act as an insolvency practitioner** ✂ **to apply for a bank insolvency order** *in the case where (b) the FSA or the Bank of England applies for a bank insolvency order in the period of 2 weeks specified in Condition 3 in that section, the bank insolvency order is treated as having taken effect when the application or petition was made or presented*

📖 Possible equivalents: bankructwo, NIEWYPŁACALNOŚĆ, upadłość (pl), decozione, insolvenza, insolvibilità (it)

INSTITUTION (en)

(Adj) **central, contributory institution** *all UK institutions and participating institutions shall be liable to contribute to the Fund and are in this Part of this Act referred to as 'contributory institutions'* **eligible, financial, relevant institution** ✂ **authorised institution** *'UK institution' means an authorised institution (within the meaning of the 1987 Act) which is incorporated in or formed under the law of any part of the United Kingdom* **participating institution**

(N) **CREDIT INSTITUTION** ✂ **parent, third-country institution** ✂ **class of institution** *'bank' does not include (c) any other class of institution excluded by an order made by the Treasury* ✂ **liability of an institution (to)** *in determining the liability or total liability of an institution to a depositor for the purposes of subsection (1) above, no account shall be taken of any liability in respect of a deposit if (a) it is a secured deposit* ✂ **assets, creditor, office of an institution** ✂ **deposits with the institution, reference to an institution** *any reference in this regulation to an EEA institution includes a reference to an institution which was formerly an EEA institution and continues to have a liability in respect of any deposit for which it had a liability at a time when it was an EEA institution* ✂ **institution or society**

(V) **institution + to participate (in)** *'home State scheme' (a) in relation to an EEA institution, means a scheme for the protection of depositors which is in force in the institutions home State and in which the institution participates*

✎ *(SYNTACTIC NOMINAL)* **EU institution, European authorised institution** ✂ **former authorised / participating / UK institution** ✂ **participating EEA / non-EEA institution** *in its application to participating EEA institutions, subsection (2) above shall have effect as if the reference to a basis of equality were a reference to a basis of parity* ✂ **institution which is incorporated in or formed under the law of any part of the United Kingdom**

✏ *(NOMINAL)* **bank or other financial institution, third-country institution or third-country parent undertaking, UK institution or building society, UK institution or participating non-EEA institution ✂ authority responsible for the institution's home State scheme, contribution levied on an institution under section 1** *where an election ceases to have effect by virtue of this regulation, the amount of the initial contribution levied on the institution under section 53 of the 1987 Act shall be reduced* **notice served on an institution** *in this regulation 'unpaid contribution' (…) means any amount specified in a notice served on the institution under subsection (8) of section 26 of the 1986 Act which remains unpaid after the period of 21 days mentioned in that subsection* **supervisory authority in the institution's home State, United Kingdom office of an institution**

✏ *(VERBAL)* **to directly relate to the institution's financial circumstances** *for reasons which directly relate to the institutions financial circumstances, the institution (a) is unable to repay protected deposits which are due and payable* **to maintain a list of institutions ✂ institution + to be eligible (to), to commence or resume its participation in a scheme, to continue to have a liability in respect of a deposit, to have permission (under Part 1 of an Act), participating institution + to become insolvent ✂ most relevant deposits with the institution are protected (by)** *a deposit advertisement may include (c) if it relates to a non-EEA institution which is participating in the deposit protection scheme, a statement to the effect that most relevant deposits with the institution are protected by that scheme*

✏ *(PREPOSITIONAL)* **in relation to an EEA / third-country / UK institution** *'branch', in relation to an EEA or UK credit institution has the meaning given by Article 1(3) of the banking consolidation directive* **in the case of a UK institution (2)**

📖 Possible equivalents: INSTYTUCJA (pl), ENTE, ISTITUTO, istituzione, ORGANISMO, ORGANO (it)

INSTRUMENT (en)

(Adj) **initial instrument** *references in this section to the initial instrument are (a) in relation to compensation arrangements in the case of property transfer instruments under section 12(2), to the first instrument to be made under that provision with respect to the bank* **original instrument** *provision made by virtue of*

subsection (3) may include (b) where a previous mandatory reduction instrument ('the original instrument') has contained provision under paragraph (a), provision for the transfer of (i) securities which were transferred by the original instrument **relevant, statutory, supplemental instrument ✂ instrument containing, issued (by), providing (for)**

(N) **appointment instrument** *an appointment instrument or a Part 1 instrument may (a) authorise a resolution administrator to manage the banks business (or confer on a resolution administrator any other power with respect to the management of the banks business)* **capital, debt instrument, Part 1 instrument** *'Part 1 instrument' means (a) a mandatory reduction instrument, (b) a share transfer instrument, (c) a property transfer instrument, or (d) a resolution instrument* **RESOLUTION INSTRUMENT, third-country instrument ✂ Tier 1/2 instruments** *'Tier 2 instruments' means capital instruments or subordinated loans that meet the conditions laid down in Article 63 of the capital requirements regulation (or which qualify as Tier 2 instruments by virtue of Chapter 2 of Title I of Part Ten of that regulation)* **✂ capacity, conversion, holder of an instrument ✂ making of an instrument ✂ instrument or order**

(V) **to make an instrument ✂ instrument + to modify, to transfer ✂ instrument + to be reduced, to be converted ✂ to be transferred by an instrument** *a supplemental share transfer instrument is a share transfer instrument which (a) provides for the transfer of securities which were issued by the bank before the original instrument and have not been transferred by the original instrument or another supplemental share transfer instrument*

(NOMINAL) **Additional Tier 1 instruments** *'Additional Tier 1 instruments' means capital instruments that meet the conditions laid down in Article 52(1) of the capital requirements regulation* **an appointment instrument or a Part 1 instrument, Common Equity Tier 1 instruments of the bank, instrument containing provision, instrument providing for the transfer, Part 1 instrument or share transfer order, PROPERTY TRANSFER INSTRUMENT, relevant capital instrument** *'relevant capital instruments' means Additional Tier 1 instruments and Tier 2 instruments* **SHARE TRANSFER INSTRUMENT, statutory instrument containing an order (under) ✂ holder of a relevant capital instrument, mandatory write-down, conversion etc. of capital instrument, principal amount of an instrument** *where the principal amount of a relevant capital instrument is reduced under section 6B (a) the reduction must be permanent, subject to any provision made by virtue of section 48Y(1)(a)(a)*

✂ *(VERBAL)* **to make an instrument in accordance with section 1, to make a mandatory reduction instrument, to write down or convert an instrument** ✂ **to be converted into Common Equity Tier 1 instruments, to be done by virtue of an instrument** *in subsections (3) and (4) a reference to the resolution instrument is a reference to (b) anything that is done by the instrument or is to be, or may be, done under or by virtue of the instrument* ✂ **instrument + to be converted, to contain provision, to take effect** ✂ **order + to be made by statutory instrument** ✂ **the transfer has been or is to be effected by an instrument** *a property transfer instrument is an instrument which (b) makes other provision for the purposes of, or in connection with, the transfer of property, rights or liabilities of a specified bank (whether the transfer has been or is to be effected by that instrument, by another property transfer instrument or otherwise)*

📖 Possible equivalents: akt, dokument, instrument (pl), ATTO, DOCUMENTO, strumento (it)

INTEREST (en)

(Adj) **public interest (in)** *the Treasury have recommended the Bank of England to exercise the stabilisation power on the grounds that it is necessary to protect the public interest*

(N) **interest or right** ✂ **business or other interest** *this section applies if the Bank of England thinks that a compliance failure (b) has serious consequences for business or other interests throughout the United Kingdom*

(V) **to have an interest** *if a member of the Committee has any direct or indirect interest (including any reasonably likely future interest) in any dealing or business which falls to be considered by the Committee (a) he shall disclose his interest to the Committee when it considers the dealing or business*

(P) **interest in** *the Bank of England must have regard to the public interest in (a) the protection and enhancement of the stability of the financial system of the United Kingdom*

✏ **interests, rights or liabilities** *in this paragraph 'the transferee' means (b) in relation to interests, rights or liabilities created by such a scheme, the person in whose favour, or in relation to whom, they are created* ✂ **interest of those who use, or are likely to use, services** *the innovation objective is to promote the development* *of, and innovation in, payment systems in the interests of those who use, or are likely to use, services provided by payment systems* ✂ **having regard to the public interest (in)** *the exercise of the power in respect of the banking group company is necessary having regard to the public interest in the advancement of one or more of the special resolution objectives*

📖 Possible equivalents: interes, zainteresowanie (pl), interessamento, interesse (it)

INVESTIGATION (en)

(Adj) **relevant investigation** *a 'relevant investigation' is an investigation carried out on a reference made by the Payment Systems Regulator under section 131 of the Enterprise Act 2002 by virtue of section 59*

(N) **conduct, purpose, scope of the investigation** *if there is a change in the scope or conduct of the investigation and, in the opinion of the Payment Systems Regulator, the person who is the subject of the investigation is likely to be significantly prejudiced by not being made aware of it, that person must be given written notice of the change*

(V) **to carry out, to conduct an investigation**

(P) **investigation into** *the Payment Systems Regulator must carry out an investigation into the events and the circumstances surrounding them and report to the Treasury on the result of the investigation* ✂ **under investigation**

✏ **person connected with the person under investigation** *the investigator may require a person who is neither the person under investigation nor a person connected with the person under investigation (a) to attend before the investigator at a specified time and place and answer questions* **person who is the subject of the investigation** ✂ **to conduct an investigation on one's behalf** *if it appears to the Payment Systems Regulator that there are circumstances suggesting that there may have been a compliance failure, the Payment Systems Regulator may appoint one or more competent persons to conduct an investigation on its behalf*

📖 Possible equivalents: badanie, dochodzenie, KONTROLA, POSTĘPOWANIE, śledztwo (pl), inchiesta, indagine (it)

INVESTMENT (en)

(Adj) **protected investment** *subject to the following provisions of this section, if at any time a participating institution becomes insolvent, the Board (a) shall as soon as practicable pay out of the Fund to persons who have at that time protected investments in the institution which are due and payable amounts equal to 90 per cent of their protected investments* ✂ **investment made (with)**

(N) **investment bank, firm** *'investment firm' means an investment firm as defined in Article 4.1(2) of Regulation (EU) No 575/2013 of the European Parliament and of the Council that is subject to the initial capital requirement specified in Article 28(2) of Directive 2013/36/EU of the European Parliament and of the Council*

(P) **in respect of an investment** *there shall be deducted from any payment to be made by the Board under subsection (1) above in respect of a protected investment any payment already made in respect of that investment by a liquidator of the institution*

✎ **credit institution and / or investment firm** ✂ **regulated activity of dealing in investments as principal** *the regulated activity of dealing in investments as principal (whether carried on in the United Kingdom or elsewhere) is an excluded activity unless it is carried on in circumstances specified by the Treasury by order* ✂ **investment bank insolvency regulations, Investment Bank Special Administration Regulations 2011**

📖 Possible equivalents: inwestycja, inwestowanie (pl), collocamento, investimento (it)

L

LAW (it)

Uusally singular

(Adj) **foreign law** ✂ **law applicable (to)** *the effects of a relevant reorganisation or a relevant winding up on a netting agreement shall be determined in accordance with the law applicable to that agreement*

(N) **law of a country, a state** ✂ **insolvency law** ✂ **provision of the law, rule of law** *anything done by the bank in connection with the exercise of a stabilisation power under Part 1 of this Act is not a gratuitous alienation for the purpose of section 242 or any other rule of law*

(P) **under the law** *'appropriate authority' means the authority authorised, under the law of the EEA state mentioned in paragraph (d) of subsection (4), to enter into the joint determination mentioned in that paragraph,* **in accordance with the law**

✎ **general law of insolvency of the United Kingdom, law of an EEA State, law of the third country** ✂ **application of insolvency law, partnership constituted under the law of Scotland** *this section does not apply in relation to partnerships constituted under the law of Scotland* ✂ **institution which is incorporated in or formed under the law of a country or territory outside the United Kingdom, institution which is incorporated in or formed under the law of any part of the United Kingdom** *'UK institution' means an institution which is incorporated in, or formed under the law of any part of, the United Kingdom* ✂ **to be determined in accordance with the law of a state**

📖 Possible equivalents: PRAWO (pl), DIRITTO, LEGGE (it)

LIABILITY (en)

(Adj) **eligible liability** *the Treasury may by order define eligible liabilities for the purposes of this paragraph and make provision about the calculation of any description of eligible liability, including provision for the amount of a liability of any description to be treated as reduced by the amount of an asset of any description* ✂ **excluded liability** *the following liabilities of the bank are 'excluded liabilities' (a) liabilities representing protected deposits; (b) any liability, so far as it is secured; (c) liabilities that the bank has by virtue of holding client assets* ✂ **liabilities arising** *a property transfer instrument may transfer any property, rights or liabilities including, in particular (b) rights and liabilities arising on or after the transfer date in respect of matters occurring before that date*

(N) **liability in damages** *for provision conferring immunity from liability in damages on the Bank of England in respect of its functions, see section 244 of the Banking Act 2009* **liability of a bank, of an institution** ✂ **pension liabilities** *'pension liabilities' means liabilities attributable to or associated with the provision under a relevant pension scheme of pensions or other benefits* ✂ **immunity from liability** ✂ **assets and liabilities, rights and liabilities**

(V) **to have a liability**

(P) **liability to** *subsection (5) does not apply in the case of a sum paid by the Treasury for indemnifying a person in respect of a liability to the infrastructure company* **liability under** *in subsection (1) 'foreign property' means (b) rights and liabilities under foreign law* ✂ **liability in respect of**

✎ **interests, rights and liabilities; property, rights or liabilities of a bank, transfer of property, rights and / or liabilities** ✂ **liability owed by a bank** *the reference to cancelling a liability owed by the bank includes a reference to cancelling a contract under which the bank has a liability* ✂ **contract under which the bank has a liability, immunity from liability in damages, limited liability partnership** *in subsection (2) 'officer', in relation to a limited liability partnership, means a member of the limited liability partnership* ✂ **to continue to have a liability in respect of a deposit** *any reference in this regulation to a UK institution includes a reference to an institution which was formerly a UK institution and continues to have a liability in respect of any deposit for which it had a liability at a time when it was a UK institution* **to give rise to a liability** *for the purposes of subsection (1)* *above no account shall be taken of any liability unless (a) proof of the debt, or a claim for repayment of the deposit, which gives rise to the liability has been lodged with a liquidator or administrator of the institution* ✂ **rights and / or liabilities + to be transferred**

📖 Possible equivalents: należność, odpowiedzialność, pasywa, ZOBOWIĄZANIE (pl), obbligazione, obbligo, passività, passivo, responsabilità (it)

LIQUIDATOR (en)

Usually singular

(Adj) **provisional liquidator** *paragraph (1)(b) does not prevent a provisional liquidator of an EEA credit institution appointed before the relevant date from acting in relation to that credit institution on or after that date*

(N) **liquidator or administrator** ✂ **bank liquidator** *where a bank liquidator vacates office the Bank of England must as soon as is reasonably practicable appoint a replacement bank liquidator* ✂ **appointment of a liquidator**

(V) **liquidator + to be appointed**

✏ **liquidator, provisional liquidator, or administrator** *the liquidator, provisional liquidator or administrator (as the case may be) must send a report to every known creditor once in every 12 months beginning with the date when his appointment has effect* ✂ **liquidator + to apply to court** *on the termination of a company voluntary arrangement the bank liquidator may apply to the court to lift the suspension of the bank insolvency order*

📖 Possible equivalent: likwidator (pl), commissario liquidatore, curatore del fallimento, liquidatore (it)

LOAN (en)

(V) **to make a loan (to)** *the Treasury may, out of money provided by Parliament, make loans to the company for achieving the objective in section 115* **to request a loan (from)** *the scheme manager may request a loan from the National Loans Fund for the purpose of funding expenses incurred or expected to be incurred under the scheme*

✎ **the rate of interest on a loan** *the Treasury shall determine (a) the rate of interest on a loan, and (b) other terms and conditions* ✂ **National Loans Fund** *sums received by the Treasury in respect of loans by virtue of this section shall be paid into the National Loans Fund* **borrowing from National Loans Fund, investing in National Loans Fund**

📖 Possible equivalents: KREDYT, POŻYCZKA (pl), prestito, MUTUO (it)

M

MANAGEMENT (en)

Always singular

(N) **management body** *'management body' means the board of directors, or if there is no such board, the equivalent body responsible for the management of the undertaking concerned*

✎ *(NOMINAL)* **day to day management** ✂ **asset management vehicle** *an 'asset management vehicle' is an undertaking which (…) (c) is created for the purpose of receiving some or all of the assets, rights, and liabilities of one or more banks or of one or more bridge banks (or both)* **claims management services** *power to impose penalties on persons providing claims management services*

✎ *(THEMATIC NOMINAL)* **(designated) senior management function in relation to the carrying on of a regulated activity** *A function is a 'senior management function', in relation to the carrying on of a regulated activity by an authorised person, if (a) the function will require the person performing it to be responsible for managing one or more aspects of the authorised person's affairs, so far as relating to the activity, and (b) those aspects involve, or might involve, a risk of serious consequences* **function designated as a senior management function under section 1, relevant senior management function** *in subsection (1A) 'relevant senior management function' means a function which the PRA is satisfied is a senior management function as defined in section 59ZA (whether or not the function has been designated as such by the FCA)* **senior management function as defined in section 1** ✂ **to perform a designated senior management function**

📖 Possible equivalents: ZARZĄD, zarządzanie (pl), AMMINISTRAZIONE, direzione, GESTIONE (it)

MARKET (en)

(Adj) **financial markets** *the Bank of England must have regard to the impact a suspension might have on the orderly functioning of the financial markets before exercising the power in subsection (1)*

(N) **market for services** ✂ **competition in a market**

(P) **market for** *the competition objective is to promote effective competition in (a) the market for payment systems*

✏ **trading on a regulated market** *securities issued by the bank have been admitted to trading on a regulated market* ✂ **Competition and Markets Authority (the CMA)** ✂ **Financial Services and Markets Act 2000** ✂ **to intervene in financial markets** *if, at any meeting, the Committee decides that the Bank should intervene in financial markets, it shall also consider at the meeting whether immediate publication of the decision would be likely to impede or frustrate the achievement of the intervention's purpose* ✂ **to have permission under Part 4 of the Financial Services and Markets Act 2000 to carry on a regulated activity**

📖 Possible equivalents: rynek (pl), mercato (it)

MATTER (en)

(Adj) **matter concerned** *this section applies where the Bank of England has required or could require a person to whom subsection (2) applies ('the person concerned') to provide information or produce documents with respect to any matter ('the matter concerned') under section 83ZA* **matter falling (within)** *'relevant information', in relation to a relevant investigation, is information (a) which relates to matters falling within the scope of the investigation* **matter mentioned (in)** ✂ **specified matter**

(N) **matter of law** *the transferor and the transferee must each take any necessary steps to ensure that the transfer is effective as a matter of foreign law (if it is not wholly effective by virtue of the property transfer instrument)* ✂ **report on a matter**

(P) **in relation to a matter, with respect to a matter** ✂ **as a matter of** *if the action is recognised, it becomes effective as a matter of United Kingdom law*

✎ **matter to which the notice relates** ✂ **report on the matter concerned** ✂ **to exercise any of the concurrent functions in relation to any matter** *before the CMA or the Payment Systems Regulator first exercises any of the concurrent functions in relation to any matter, it must consult the other* **to have regard to a matter, to refer a matter to the Tribunal** *if the regulator decides to take action against a person under section 142S, the person may refer the matter to the Tribunal*

📖 Possible equivalents: kwestia, SPRAWA (pl), CASO, oggetto, MATERIA, questione (it)

MEMBER (en)

(Adj) **member appointed (by)** *the Bank may, with the consent of the Chancellor of the Exchequer, remove a member appointed under section 13(2)(b) or (c) if it is satisfied (a) that he has been absent from the Committee's meetings for more than 3 months without the Committee's consent* ✂ **authorised member**

(N) **member or employee** *the references to a firm of which a person was a member or employee at a particular time include references to a firm which holds itself out to be the successor of a firm of which the person was a member or employee at that time* ✂ **member of a committee, of a court, of a group, of a partnership** *in subsection (2) 'officer', in relation to a limited liability partnership, means a member of the limited liability partnership* **member of staff**

✎ **an officer or a member of staff** *the function of issuing general guidance may not be discharged by an officer or member of staff of the Regulator or of the FCA* ✂ **authorised member of the CMA, member of a ring-fenced body's group, member of staff of the FCA, members of a review panel** *the members of the review panel must be persons (a) who appear to the Treasury to be independent of the PRA, the FCA, the Bank of England and the Treasury* ✂ **bank, person + to be a member** *in subsection (3)(a) 'existing group member' means a person who is a member of the ring-fenced body's group at the time when the requirement is imposed or the direction given* ✂ **subsection (1)(a) does not apply unless the bank has as a member of its immediate group a PRA-authorised person**

📖 Possible equivalents: CZŁONEK (pl), membro, socio (it)

MONEY (en)

Usually singular

(Adj) **electronic money** ✂ **money provided (by)** *expenditure of the Treasury under, by virtue of or in connection with a provision of this Act shall be paid out of money provided by Parliament*

(N) **money laundering** *in determining whether a person has a protected investment in a participating institution and the amount of it there shall be disregarded (…) any deposit or share which the Board is satisfied was made or acquired in the course of a money-laundering transaction*

(P) **out of money** *the Treasury may, out of money provided by Parliament, make loans to the company for achieving the objective in section 115*

✎ **money laundering transaction** ✂ **to issue electronic money** *'third country credit institution' means a person (…) who has permission under the 2000 Act to accept deposits or to issue electronic money as the case may be*

📖 Possible equivalents: PIENIĄDZ, środek płatniczy, WALUTA (pl), MONETA, DENARO, soldi (it)

N

NORTHERN IRELAND (en)

(N) **Scotland and Northern Ireland** *this Part (a) repeals existing provisions about permission to issue banknotes in Scotland and Northern Ireland*

(P) **in Northern Ireland**

Companies (Northern Ireland) Order 1986, Credit Unions (Northern Ireland) Order 1985, Insolvency (Northern Ireland) Order 1989, Pensions (Northern Ireland) Order ✂ Insolvency Rules (Northern Ireland) ✂ Pension Schemes (Northern Ireland) Act 1993 ✂ England and Wales and Northern Ireland

Possible equivalents Irlandia Północna (pl), Irlanda del Nord (it)

NOTICE (en)

Usually singular

(Adj) **final, further, preliminary notice ✂ warning, written notice ✂ notice given (under)** *a notice given under subsection (5)(b) of a decision by the Bank to give a different direction must comply with subsection (1)* ✂ **specified in a notice**

(N) **call notice** *notice under this paragraph ('a call notice') shall be in writing and shall specify (a) the period to which it relates, and (b) the amount which, in relation to that period, is the institution's depositable amount* **decision notice ✂ notice of appeal ✂ notice under paragraph 1 / section 1 / subsection (1) ✂ copy of a notice** *condition 2 is that a copy of the notice complying with Condition 1 has been filed with the court (and made available for public inspection by the court)*

(V) **to give notice (of) (to)** ✂ **notice + to relate (to)** *subject to subsection (8), where the Bank gives a decision notice it may publish such information about the matter to which the notice relates as it considers appropriate* **notice + to require, to specify** ✂ **notice + to be given, to be received** ✂ **to be specified in a notice** *the Bank may by notice in writing require an eligible institution to provide the Bank with such information as may be specified in the notice*

(P) **notice about** *a warning notice about a proposal to impose a penalty must state the amount of the penalty* **notice under** ✂ **by notice (to)** *the Treasury may by notice to the Bank of England disapply subsection (3) in respect of a bank*

✏ **notice given under subsection (1), written notice of a decision** ✂ **amount specified in a notice, insolvency procedure to which the notice relates, matter to which the notice relates, person who gave the notice** ✂ **to give a warning notice, to give written notice (of)** ✂ **to require by notice in writing** *the Bank of England may by notice in writing require a person to provide information (a) which the Bank thinks will help the Treasury in determining whether to make a recognition order* ✂ **Bank of England + to give an Objective 1 Achievement Notice** *in the case of bank administration following transfer to a bridge bank, until the Bank of England has given an Objective 1 Achievement Notice a bank administrator may make a distribution only with the Bank of England's consent*

📖 Possible equivalents: obwieszczenie, ogłoszenie, oświadczenie, nota, powiadomienie, wezwanie, zawiadomienie (pl), avviso, COMUNICAZIONE, notifica (it)

O

OBJECTIVE (en)

(Adj) **operational objectives** *the FCA may refuse an application under this section if it appears to the FCA that it is desirable to do so in order to advance one or more of its operational objectives*

(N) **continuity objective** *in relation to the matters mentioned in subsection (2), the continuity objective is protecting the continuity of the provision in the United Kingdom of core services* ✂ **objective in/ of / under section 1** ✂ **pursuit of objective** *a bank liquidator may do anything necessary or expedient for the pursuit of the Objectives in section 99*

(V) **to achieve an objective, to advance objectives** *the PRA may refuse an application under this section if it appears to the PRA that it is desirable to do so in order to advance any of its objectives*

✎ **Financial Stability Objective** *if the Bank considers it necessary to do so having regard to the Financial Stability Objective, the Bank may by direction to a qualifying company exclude the application to the qualifying company of any of the relevant Companies Act requirements* **objective in section 1 of an Act, objective of the FMI administration, special resolution objectives** *the Treasury may by order amend the law for the purpose of enabling the powers under this Part to be used effectively, having regard to the special resolution objectives* ✂ **to advance payment systems objectives, to prejudice pursuit of Objective 1** *the bank administrator may comply with a request under para. 56(1)(a) only if satisfied that it will not prejudice pursuit of Objective 1 in section 137* ✂ **the Bank of England + to give an Objective 1 Achievement Notice, the court + to have regard to an objective in section 1**

Possible equivalents: CEL, zamierzenie (pl), FINE, obiettivo, scopo (it)

OBLIGATION (en)

(Adj) **international, relevant obligation** *this regulation applies where, on or after 5th May 2004, a relevant obligation has been honoured for the benefit of a relevant credit institution by a relevant person* ✂ **obligation imposed (by or under)**

(N) **rights or obligations (under)** ✂ **continuity obligation** *the duty to provide services and facilities in pursuance of the continuity obligation is subject to a right to receive reasonable consideration* ✂ **obligation of confidence** *no person may be required under this Part to disclose information or produce a document in respect of which the person ('A') owes an obligation of confidence by virtue of carrying on the business of banking*

(V) **to comply with an obligation** *if the request has been made by an EU resolution authority in pursuance of any EU obligation, the Bank must, in deciding whether or not to exercise its investigative power, consider whether its exercise is necessary to comply with any such obligation* **to impose obligations (on)**

(P) **obligation under** ✂ **obligation by virtue (of)** *subsection (2) may be used to impose obligations (a) in addition to obligations under or by virtue of section 63 or 64*

EU obligation, general continuity obligation, obligation of the United Kingdom, obligation under section 1, special continuity obligation ✂ **international obligation notice** ✂ **in pursuance of a continuity obligation** *a continuity authority may give guarantees or indemnities in respect of consideration for services or facilities provided or to be provided in pursuance of a continuity obligation*

Possible equivalents: obowiązek, powinność, ZOBOWIĄZANIE (pl), obbligazione, OBBLIGO (it)

OFFENCE (en)

(Adj) **offence relating (to)** *offence relating to a decision causing a financial institution to fail*

(N) **offence under Part 1 / section 1/ subsection 1** ✂ **proceedings for an offence (under)** *proceedings for an offence may be instituted in England and Wales only (a) by the FCA, the PRA or the Secretary of State*

(V) **offence + to be committed**

✏ **person guilty of an offence under subsection 1** ✂ **to be charged with an offence, to be guilty of an offence and liable (to)** *a person who fails without reasonable excuse to comply with any requirement imposed on him under section 17(1) or paragraph 9 of Schedule 2 shall be guilty of an offence and liable on summary conviction to a fine not exceeding level 4 on the standard scale* ✂ **offence + to be committed before the commencement of section 1** ✂ **person guilty of an offence + to be liable on summary conviction**

📖 Possible equivalents: przestępstwo, wykroczenie (pl), illecito, infrazione, offesa, reato (it)

OFFICE (en)

(N) **office of an institution, of a society** ✂ **office-holder** *for the purposes of the application of section 7(3) of the Disqualification Act (disqualification order or undertaking) to a bank which is subject to a bank insolvency order, the responsible office-holder is the bank liquidator* ✂ **functions of the office** *a bail-in administrator must have regard, in performing any functions of the office, to any objectives that may be specified in a resolution instrument* **removal from office**

(V) **to hold, to vacate office** *an independent valuer is to hold and vacate office in accordance with the terms of his or her appointment*

✏ **office in an EEA state** *in its application to UK institutions or building societies which accept deposits at offices in EEA States other than the United Kingdom, paragraph (1) above shall have effect as if the reference to a United Kingdom office included a reference to an office in such a State* **United Kingdom offices of an institution**

📖 Possible equivalents: ODDZIAŁ, posada, stanowisko, urząd (pl), ufficio, SEDE, SUCCURSALE (it)

ORDER (en)

Usually singular

(Adj) **original order** ✂ **qualifying order** *a qualifying order means (i) a winding-up order under section 125 of the 1986 Act or Article 105 of the 1989 Order; or (ii) an administration order under paragraph 13 of Schedule B1 to the 1986 Act in the prescribed circumstances* **winding-up order** ✂ **order appointing, establishing, restraining, sanctioning** *for the purposes of paragraph (2), a relevant order means an order sanctioning a section 425 or Article 418 compromise or arrangement which (a) is intended to enable the credit institution, and the whole or any part of its undertaking, to survive as a going concern and which affects the rights of persons other than the credit institution or its contributories* ✂ **order made (by)**

(N) **instrument or order, order or appointment** *the Authority was represented at all hearings in connection with the application in relation to which the order or appointment is made* ✂ **administration, closure, designation, recognition order** *the Treasury may by order ('recognition order') specify an inter-bank payment system as a recognised system for the purposes of this Part* ✂ **Companies Order** *'the Companies Order' means the Companies (Northern Ireland) Order 1986(a)* ✂ **order of the court** ✂ **article, revocation of an order**

(V) **to make, to revoke an order** ✂ **to amend something by order** ✂ **order + to amend** *an order may amend sections 44C(4) and 48E(4)* **order + to include, to provide, to specify** *an order may specify the meaning of 'insolvency' for one or more purposes of the order* ✂ **order + to be made**

(P) **order under** *for procedural purposes an order under subsection (1) shall be treated in the same way as an order under section 420 of the Insolvency Act 1986 (partnerships)* ✂ **by order** *the Treasury may by order make provision about the procedure to be followed by independent valuers*

(SYNTACTIC NOMINAL) **bail-in compensation order** *a 'bail-in compensation order' is an order establishing a scheme for determining, in accordance with section 52A, whether any transferors or others should be paid compensation* **bank administration order, bank insolvency order, compensation scheme order** *a 'compensation scheme order' is an order (a) establishing a scheme for determining whether transferors should be paid compensation, or providing for transferors to be paid compensation, and (b) establishing a scheme for paying any compensation* **FMI administration order, property transfer order, resolution**

fund order, SHARE TRANSFER ORDER, third party compensation order ✂ Companies (Northern Ireland) Order 1986, Credit Unions (Northern Ireland) Order 1985, Insolvency (Northern Ireland) Order 1989, Pensions (Northern Ireland) Order

decision, order or appointment ✂ order for specific performance under section 45 of the Court of Session Act 1988 *an obligation imposed on a person as a result of the exercise of the powers conferred by subsection (1) is enforceable by injunction or, in Scotland, by an order for specific performance under section 45 of the Court of Session Act 1988* **order made by virtue of subsection 1 ✂ application for an administration order, statutory instrument containing an order ✂ subject to modifications set out in an order ✂ making an order in reliance (on)** *the possibility of making a supplemental share transfer order in reliance on subsection (2) is without prejudice to the possibility of making of a new order in accordance with section 13(2) (and not in reliance on subsection (2) above)*

(VERBAL) **to apply for a bank insolvency order, to make a designation / recognition order, to make an order in respect of, to make an order under section 1 ✂ administration order + to be in force, order + to be made by statutory instrument** *an order (a) is to be made by statutory instrument, and (b) may not be made unless a draft has been laid before and approved by resolution of each House of Parliament* **order + to include provision (for), order or appointment + to be made ✂ the court + to make an order restraining, section 1 + to be inserted by an article of an order, the Treasury + to amend / to make provision / to provide (for) by order** *the Treasury may by order amend this Schedule so as to make further modifications*

Possible equivalents: dyspozycja, instrukcja, nakaz, polecnie, zarządzenie, zlecenie (pl) ordinanza, ordine (it)

P

PARAGRAPH (en)

Usually singular

(Aff) **sub-paragraph** *in sub-paragraph (1) for 'once a month' substitute '7 times in each calendar year'*

(Adv) **paragraph above** *no initial contribution shall be levied (…) from an EEA institution which commences or resumes its participation in the deposit protection scheme in accordance with paragraph (1) above*

(Adj) **following paragraph** *the following paragraphs of Schedule B1 to the Insolvency Act 1986 (administration) apply to a bank insolvency order as to an administration order* ✂ **appointed under paragraph, falling within paragraph** *this sub-paragraph applies if the transferee is an EEA firm falling within paragraph 5(a) or (b) of Schedule 3* **mentioned in paragraph, required by paragraph**

(N) **paragraph 1 of a regulation, of Schedule 1 (to)** ✂ **application, direction, notice, order, scheme under paragraph 1** *a scheme under paragraph 3 may also contain provision (a) for rights and liabilities to be transferred so as to be enforceable by or against both the Bank and the Authority* ✂ **references in paragraph**

(V) **to omit paragraph, to comply with paragraph** ✂ **to insert something after / before paragraph** ✂ **paragraph + to apply, to modify, to preclude** *Paragraph 1 does not preclude the disclosure of information in any case in which disclosure is for the purpose of enabling or assisting the Bank to discharge (a) its functions as a monetary authority* ✂ **for paragraph + to substitute** *in the definition of 'banking institution' for paragraph (e), substitute '(e) a banking group company'* ✂ **to be amended / inserted by paragraph 1, to be transferred under paragraph** ✂ **after paragraph + to be inserted** *in subsection (3), after paragraph (h) there is inserted*

'(ha)the Financial Services Authority, other than in its capacity as a designated agency within the meaning of the Financial Services Act 1986' **for paragraph + to be substituted**

(P) **after, in paragraph ✂ in accordance with paragraph, at the end of paragraph, for the purposes of paragraph, by virtue of paragraph** *in respect of the exercise of a function under Part 1 of the Competition Act 1998, the power in sub-paragraph (1) is subject to provision in rules made under section 51 of that Act by virtue of paragraph 1A of Schedule 9 to that Act*

✎ **administration order under paragraph, condition mentioned in paragraph, information required by paragraph** *each of the following, namely, a UK institution, a building society, an EEA institution and a non-EEA institution, shall secure that the information required by paragraph (4) below is supplied to any depositor or intending depositor who requests it* ✂ **mentioned in paragraph above** ✂ **of a kind mentioned in paragraph** *in exercising the functions of the kind mentioned in paragraph (2), the competent offcer or qualifying agent (a) may not take any action which would constitute an unlawful use of force in the part of the United Kingdom in which he is exercising those functions* ✂ **Section 1 + to be amended by paragraph 1 of Schedule 1 to an Act** *section 1 was amended by paragraph 12 of Schedule 2 to the Financial Services (Banking Reform) Act 2013 (c.33), there are other amending instruments but none are relevant*

📖 Possible equivalents: ustęp (pl), COMMA (it)

PARENT (en)

Always singular

(N) **parent institution, parent undertaking** *the Treasury may take a parent undertaking of a bank (the 'holding company') into temporary public ownership, in accordance with section 13(2), if the following conditions are met*

✎ **bank or a parent undertaking, third-country institution or third-country parent undertaking** ✂ **qualifying parent undertaking** *a parent undertaking of a ring-fenced body by reference to which the group restructuring powers are exercisable is for the purposes of this Part a 'qualifying parent undertaking' if (a) it is a body corporate which is incorporated in the United Kingdom* **UK parent undertaking** ✂ **parent undertaking of a ring-fenced body** *this section also applies if a regulator is satisfied that a person ('P') who is or has been a parent undertaking* *of a ring-fenced body has contravened a provision of rules made by that regulator under section 192JA* ✂ **in relation to a parent undertaking** *a regulator may not exercise its general powers in relation to the ring-fenced body or parent undertaking so as to achieve either of the results in subsection (3)*

Possible equivalents: macierzysty, nadrzędny, założycielski (pl), controllante, madre (it)

PARLIAMENT (en)

Always singular

(Adj) **European Parliament** ✂ **laid before Parliament** *regulations to which subsection (2B) applies are not to be made unless a draft of the regulations has been laid before Parliament and approved by a resolution of each House*

(N) **House of Parliament** *regulations are to be made by statutory instrument and are subject to annulment in pursuance of a resolution of either House of Parliament*

Directive / Regulation of the European Parliament and of the Council ✂ **to be paid out of money provided by Parliament, to be subject to annulment in pursuance of a resolution of either House of Parliament** *a statutory instrument containing an order or regulations under this Act is subject to annulment in pursuance of a resolution of either House of Parliament, unless (a) the instrument contains only provision made under section 148 (commencement)* ✂ **the Treasury + to lay a copy of a report before Parliament** *the Treasury must (a) lay a copy of the report before Parliament, and (b) publish the report in such manner as they think fit* ✂ **draft + to be laid before and approved by resolution of each House of Parliament**

Possible equivalents: parlament (pl), parlamento (it)

PART 1

Usually singular

(N) **part of business** *purpose of the special resolution regime for banks is to address the situation where all or part of the business of a bank has encountered, or is likely to encounter, financial difficulties* ✂ **neglect on the part (of)**

(P) **on the part of** *where an offence under this Part committed by a body corporate is proved to have been committed with the consent or connivance of, or to be attributable to any neglect on the part of, any director, manager, secretary, or other similar officer of the body corporate, (...) he, as well as the body corporate, shall be guilty of that offence and be liable to be proceeded against and punished accordingly*

court in any part of the United Kingdom ✂ **institution which is incorporated in, or formed under the law of any part of, the United Kingdom** ✂ **with a view to terminating the whole or any part of the business of a credit institution** *a 'qualifying arrangement' means a voluntary arrangement which (b) includes a realisation of some or all of the assets of the credit institution, with a view to terminating the whole or any part of the business of that credit institution* ✂ **to be attributable to any neglect on the part (of), to transfer all or part of business** *the second stabilisation option is to transfer all or part of the business of the bank to a company which is wholly owned by the Bank of England (a 'bridge bank')*

Possible equivalents: CZĘŚĆ, strona (pl), PARTE (it)

PART 2 (en)

Usually singular

(Adj) **used in Part, established under Part** *in this Part a reference to 'the FSCS' is a reference to (a) the Financial Services Compensation Scheme (established under Part 15 of the Financial Services and Markets Act 2000)*

(N) **Part 1 of an Act, of Regulations, of Schedule 1** ✂ **Chapter 1 of Part I, Title I of Part One** *'Additional Tier 1 instruments' means capital instruments that meet the conditions laid down in Article 52(1) of the capital requirements regulation (or which qualify as Additional Tier 1 instruments by virtue of Chapter 2 of Title I of Part Ten of that regulation)* ✂ **Part 1 instrument** *'Part 1 instrument' means (a) a mandatory reduction instrument, (b) a share transfer instrument, (c) a property transfer instrument, or (d) a resolution instrument* ✂ **application of a Part** *section 89 allows the application of this Part to credit unions* **commencement of a Part** *an order may, in particular, amend or modify the effect of an enactment (including a fiscal enactment) passed before the commencement of this Part* **provision of a Part** ✂ **functions, permission under Part 1** ✂ **reference in a Part (to)**

(V) **to be referred to in this Part (as)** *a notice under subsection (1) is referred to in this Part as an 'Objective 1 Achievement Notice'* ✂ **Part + to apply**

(P) **under Part** ✂ **by virtue of Part** *nothing in this section applies to information received by a primary recipient for the purposes of, or in the discharge of, any functions of the FCA under the Competition Act 1998 or the Enterprise Act 2002 by virtue of Part 16A of this Act* **within the meaning of Part** *'recognised inter-bank payment system' means an inter-bank payment system (within the meaning of Part 5 of the Banking Act 2009)*

(NOMINAL) **Part 1 of the Banking Act 2009 / of the the Companies Act / of the Enterprise Act 2002 / of the Financial Services and Markets Act 2000 / of the Financial Services (Banking Reform) Act 2013** ✂ **application of a power under Part, exercise of a stabilisation power under Part 1 of an Act** *anything done by the bank in connection with the exercise of a stabilisation power under Part 1 of this Act is not a transaction at an undervalue for the purposes of section 238* **protective scheme provisions of Part, requirements imposed by or under Part, transfer of functions by Part** *the Treasury may by order make such amendments or revocations of any instrument made under an Act as they think necessary or expedient in consequence of the transfer of functions by this Part* ✂ **an appointment instrument or a Part 1 instrument, Part 1 instrument or share transfer**

in accordance with Chapter I of Part I of Regulations ✂ **to have permission under Part 1 to carry on the regulated activity (of), to have the same meaning as in Part, to modify provisions of Part** *the Lord Chancellor may, by order made with the concurrence of the Secretary of State and the Lord Chief Justice, modify provisions of this Part in their application to partnerships* ✂ **provision made under or by virtue of this Part + to make special provision in relation to the application of this Part to credit unions**

Possible equivalents: część (pl), PARTE (it)

PAYMENT (en)

Usually singular

(Adj) **payment made (by)** *payments made by the scheme manager in error may be provided for in setting a levy by virtue of section 213, 214A, 214B or 223B*

(N) **payment or delivery** *where a payment or delivery under the contract concerned first fell due within the period of the suspension, that payment or delivery is treated as being due immediately on the expiry of the suspension* ✂ PAYMENT SYSTEM, PAYMENT SYSTEMS REGULATOR ✂ **payment of a penalty**

(V) **to make a payment, to provide for payment** *a resolution instrument may provide for the payment of remuneration and allowances to a bail-in administrator* ✂ **payment + to be made**

✎ **to become a payment service provider in relation to** *the Payment Systems Regulator may by order require the operator of a regulated payment system to enable the applicant to become a payment service provider in relation to the system* ✂ **liquidation committee + to pass a full payment resolution** *a person aggrieved by any action of the liquidation committee before it has passed a full payment resolution may apply to the court, which may make any order (including an order for the repayment of money)* **payment + to fall to be made** *if, when a payment falls to be made under section 1(4) of this Act, the Bank's accounts for the previous financial year have not been audited, the payment shall be made on the basis of the Bank's estimate of the relevant amounts*

📖 Possible equivalents: PŁATNOŚĆ, SPŁATA, wpłata, WYPŁATA, zapłata (pl), PAGAMENTO (it)

PAYMENT SYSTEM (en)

Usually singular

(Adj) **regulated payment system** *the Treasury may by order (a 'designation order') designate a payment system as a regulated payment system for the purposes of this Part*

(N) **access to a payment system** *a person is a 'relevant person' for the purposes of subsection (1) if regulation 97 of the Payment Services Regulations 2009 (prohibition on restrictive rules on access to payment systems) applies in relation to access to, or participation in, a payment system by the person* **operator of a payment system, participation in a payment system** *'participant', in relation to a payment system, has the meaning given by section 42 (and references to participation in a payment system are to be read in accordance with that section)* **regulation of payment systems** ✂ **payment systems objectives, <u>PAYMENT SYSTEMS REGULATOR</u>**

(P) **in relation to a payment system** *'payment service provider', in relation to a payment system, has the meaning given by section 42(5)* **in respect of a payment system** *in considering whether to make a recognition order in respect of a payment system the Treasury may rely on information provided by the Bank of England or the FSA*

✎ **operator of a recognised inter-bank payment system** *the Treasury must consider any request by the operator of a recognised inter-bank payment system for the revocation of its recognition order* **operator of a regulated payment system, participant in a regulated payment system ✂ to use services provided by payment system**

📖 Possible equivalents: system płatniczy, system płatności (pl), sistema di pagamento, sistema salariale (it)

PAYMENT SYSTEMS REGULATOR (en)

Always singular

(N) **functions of the Payment Systems Regulator** *the functions to which this subsection applies are to be concurrent functions of the Payment Systems Regulator and the Competition and Markets Authority ('the CMA')*

(V) **Payment Systems Regulator + to publish, to require** *the Payment Systems Regulator may require a participant in a regulated payment system to pay a penalty in respect of a compliance failure.*

(P) **in the opinion of the Payment Systems Regulator, in relation to the Payment Systems Regulator** *no objection is to be taken to anything done under the Competition Act 1998 or Part 4 of the Enterprise Act 2002 by or in relation to the Payment Systems Regulator on the ground that it should have been done by or in relation to the Competition and Markets Authority*

✎ **Payment Systems Regulator + to exercise power/ functions** *before the CMA or the Payment Systems Regulator first exercises any of the concurrent functions in relation to any matter, it must consult the other* **Payment Systems Regulator + to have regard to, Payment Systems Regulator + to make representations or observations** *sub-paragraph (2) applies where the Payment Systems Regulator wishes to make representations or observations to the CMA in relation to (a) an application for permission to bring an appeal under paragraph 3*

📖 Possible equivalents: organ nadzorujący system płatności (pl), ente regolatore del sistema di pagamento (it)

PENALTY (en)

(Adj) **penalty imposed** *the regulations may also include, in particular (a) provision for a penalty imposed by the Regulator to be enforced as a debt*

(N) **amount of a penalty** *banknote regulations must establish a method for determining the maximum amount of a penalty* **payment of a penalty**

(V) **to impose a penalty (on)** *if the decision is a decision to impose a penalty on the person under section 73, the appeal must be made to the Competition Appeal Tribunal in accordance with section 78* **to pay a penalty**

(P) **penalty in respect of** *the Bank of England may require the operator of a recognised inter-bank payment system to pay a penalty in respect of a compliance failure* ✂ **penalty under section 1** *a penalty under this section (a) must be paid to the Bank of England, and (b) may be enforced by the Bank as a debt*

financial penalty scheme *the Regulator must prepare and operate a scheme ('the financial penalty scheme') for ensuring that the amounts that, as a result of the deduction for which paragraph 10(1) provides, are retained by the Regulator in respect of amounts paid to it by way of penalties imposed under section 73 are applied for the benefit of participants in regulated payment systems* ✂ **power to impose penalty** ✂ **to require an authorised person to pay a penalty** *regulations under sub-paragraph (1) may enable the Regulator to require an authorised person to pay a penalty*

Possible equivalents: kara, sankcja (pl), ammenda, multa, pena, penale, SANZIONE (it)

PERSON (en)

(Adj) **competent, relevant person** ✂ **approved, authorised person** *'approved person' (a) means a person in relation to whom (ii) the FCA has given its approval under section 59 in respect of the performance by the person of a relevant senior management function in relation to the carrying on by a PRA-authorised person of a regulated activity* ✂ **person guilty (of), likely (to)** ✂ **person appearing (to), appointed (as / under), entitled, qualified (to)** *in this Part references to a person*

qualified to act as an insolvency practitioner in relation to a company are to be read in accordance with Part 13 of the 1986 Act

(N) **person under investigation** ✂ **person of a description** *regulations under this section may, in particular, make provision permitting the disclosure of confidential information or of confidential information of a specified kind (b) by specified recipients, or recipients of a specified description, to specified persons, or persons of specified descriptions, for the purpose of enabling or assisting those persons to discharge specified public functions* ✂ **attention of a person** *as soon as is reasonably practicable after making a share transfer instrument the Bank of England shall publish a copy (b) in two newspapers, chosen by the Bank of England to maximise the likelihood of the instrument coming to the attention of persons likely to be affected* **conduct, employee of a person** ✂ **class of persons** *directions under this section (a) must be in writing, and (b) may be given with general effect or with respect to a particular relevant person or class of relevant persons*

(V) **to appoint a person (to), to indemnify persons** *the Treasury may agree to indemnify persons in respect of one or both of the following (a) liabilities incurred in connection with the exercise of powers and duties by the FMI administrator (b) loss or damage sustained in that connection* **to require a person (to)** ✂ **person + to know, to suspects, to wish (to)** ✂ **person + to be appointed, compelled** *no person is to be compelled under this paragraph to produce a document or supply an estimate, forecast, return or other information which the person could not be compelled to produce in civil proceedings in the High Court or Court of Session* **person + to be required**

authorised person concerned *'the authorised person concerned', in relation to an approved person, means the person on whose application approval was given* **person guilty of an offence under subsection 1, person likely to be affected, relevant PRA-authorised person** ✂ **carrying on by an authorised person of a regulated activity** ✂ **to appoint one or more competent persons, to be a fit and proper person to perform the function, to give a notice to a person, to impose a sanction on a person, to require an authorised person to pay a penalty, to require a person to produce a document** *an investigator may also require any person to produce at a specified time and place any specified documents or documents of a specified description* ✂ **bank + to have as a member of its immediate group a PRA-authorised person, Bank of England + to inform the person who gave notice (that), person + to fail to comply with, person + to know or suspect, regulator + to charge a reasonable fee for providing a person (with)**

a regulator may charge a reasonable fee for providing a person with a copy of the statement published under this section

Possible equivalents: OSOBA, podmiot (pl), persona, soggetto (it)

POWER (en)

(Adj) **power exercisable** *an order may, in particular (c) provide for any power exercisable as a result of the amendments made by this Part to be exercisable in relation to the company* ✂ **general powers** *the following provisions of this section provide for (a) general powers and duties of bank liquidators* ✂ **power conferred (by / on)** *no power conferred by section 3A may be exercised before the statement of policy in relation to the exercise of that power has been published*

(N) **powers and duties** *the following provisions of this section provide for (a) general powers and duties of bank administrators (by application of provisions about administrators)* ✂ **power of the Treasury** *any power of the Treasury to make an order under this Act shall be exercisable by statutory instrument* ✂ **stabilisation power** *the Bank of England may exercise a stabilisation power in respect of a bank in accordance with section 12A(2) only if satisfied that the condition in subsection (2) is met* ✂ **resolution powers** ✂ **application, exercise, use of a power**

(V) **to exercise, to have power** ✂ **power + to be exercised** ✂ **power to direct, to impose, to require, to vary** *this section applies to an exercise, by either regulator, of the power to vary an approval under section 63ZB*

(P) **power in / under Part 1, section 1, subsection (1)** *the power in subsection (2) must be exercised in accordance with section 12AA(b)* ✂ **powers in relation (to)**

(NOMINAL) **power conferred by section 1 / subsection (1), power of FCA, power to give a direction (under)** *the power to give a direction under this paragraph is exercisable only where (a) an application for its exercise has been made by the appellant at the same time as the appellant made an application in accordance with paragraph 3 for permission to bring an appeal against a decision of the Payment Systems Regulator* **power to impose a penalty / a requirement, power to make a mandatory reduction instrument, power to make provision / rules, power to obtain / require information** ✂ **exercise of a power conferred (by), exercise of a stabilisation power under Part 1 of an Act, use of stabilisation powers**

✎ **before exercising a power** ✂ **for all other purposes, including for the purposes of the application of a power under this Part** *sections 7 and 8A do not apply to a supplemental resolution instrument (but it is to be treated in the same way as a resolution instrument for all other purposes, including for the purposes of the application of a power under this Part)* ✂ **to exercise the group restructuring powers** *the appropriate regulator may exercise the group restructuring powers only if it is satisfied that one or more of Conditions A to D is met in relation to a ring-fenced body that is a member of a group* ✂ **Bank of England + to exercise a stabilisation power in respect of a bank, the exercise of power + to be necessary, Payment Systems Regulator + to exercise power**

📖 Possible equivalents: moc, prawo, władza (pl), capacità, competenza, diritto, facoltà, POTERE (it)

PROCEEDINGS (en)

Always plural

(Adj) **civil proceedings** *an obligation imposed by a provision included in a scheme by virtue of sub-paragraph (1)(d) or (e) shall be enforceable by civil proceedings by the Bank or the Authority for an injunction or for any other appropriate relief* **legal proceedings** ✂ **winding-up proceesings**

(N) **insolvency proceedings** ✂ **proceedings for an offence** *in exercising its power to institute proceedings for an offence under section 83ZN, the Bank must comply with any conditions or restrictions imposed in writing by the Treasury*

(V) **to participate in proceedings** *the FSCS is entitled to participate in proceedings for or in respect of a bank insolvency order*

(P) **proceedings against** ✂ **proceedings in respect of** *reorganisation measures and winding-up proceedings in respect of EEA credit institutions effective in the United Kingdom* ✂ **for the purposes of proceedings** *a communication or item falls within this subsection if it is made in connection with, or in contemplation of, legal proceedings and for the purposes of those proceedings*

✎ **directive winding-up proceedings** *'directive winding-up proceedings' means winding-up proceedings as defined in Article 2 of the reorganisation and winding up* *directive which were opened on or after the 5th May 2004* **normal insolvency proceedings** *'normal insolvency proceedings' has the meaning given by Article 2.1(47) of the resolution and recovery directive (and, in particular, includes the bank insolvency procedure and the bank administration procedure)*

Possible equivalents: POSTĘPOWANIE, procedura (pl) procedimento, PROCEDURA (it)

PROPERTY (en)

Always singular

(Adj) **foreign property** *in subsection (1) 'foreign property' means (a) property outside the United Kingdom, and (b) rights and liabilities under foreign law*

(N) **land or other property** *where a person is entitled (...) to possession of a document relating in part to the title to land or other property in England and Wales, or to the management of such land or other property (a) the scheme may provide for that person to be treated as having given another person an acknowledgement in writing of the right of that other person to production of the document and to delivery of copies of it* ✂ **property transfer**

✎ **onward / partial / reverse property transfer, (reverse) property transfer order** *the Treasury may make one or more reverse property transfer orders in respect of property, rights or liabilities of the transferee under the original order* ✂ **PROPERTY TRANSFER INSTRUMENT** ✂ **transfer of property subsequent to resolution instrument** ✂ **to make other provision for the purposes of, or in connection with, the transfer of property, rights or liabilities** *an onward property transfer instrument is a property transfer instrument which (b) makes other provision for the purposes of, or in connection with, the transfer of property, rights or liabilities of the bridge bank (whether the transfer has been or is to be effected by that instrument, by another property transfer instrument or otherwise)*

Possible equivalents: majątek, własność (pl) bene, PATRIMONIO, proprietà (it)

PROPERTY TRANSFER INSTRUMENT (en)

(Adj) **onward property transfer instrument** *an onward property transfer instrument is a property transfer instrument which (a) provides for property, rights or liabilities of the bridge bank to be transferred (whether accruing or arising before or after the original instrument); (b) makes other provision for the purposes of, or in connection with, the transfer of property, rights or liabilities of the bridge bank* **reverse, supplemental property transfer instrument** *where property, rights or liabilities are transferred to an asset management vehicle pursuant to the third stabilisation option, the Bank of England may make one or more supplemental property transfer instruments transferring any of that property, or those rights or liabilities, to one or more other asset management vehicles* ✂ **transferred by a property transfer instrument**

(V) **property transfer instrument + to provide (for)** *a property transfer instrument is an instrument which (a) provides for property, rights or liabilities of a specified bank to be transferred (b) makes other provision for the purposes of, or in connection with, the transfer of property, rights or liabilities of a specified bank* ✂ **to make a property transfer instrument**

✎ **bail-in reverse property transfer instrument** *a bail-in reverse property transfer instrument is a property transfer instrument which (a) provides for a transfer to the transferor under the original instrument (b) makes other provision for the purposes of, or in connection with, the transfer of property, rights or liabilities which are, or could be or could have been, transferred under paragraph (a)* ✂ **to make an onward / a reverse property transfer instrument** *this section applies where the Bank of England (a) transfers all or part of the business of a bank ('the original bank') to a bridge bank ('the original bridge bank') by making a property transfer instrument in accordance with section 12(2), and (b) later makes or proposes to make an onward property transfer instrument under section 43(2) from the bridge bank to a transferee ('the onward transferee')* ✂ **Bank of England + to make a property transfer instrument in accordance with section 1**

📖 Possible equivalents: akt przeniesienia własności (pl) atto di trasferimento di proprietà (it)

PROTECTION (en)

Always singular

(Adj) **protection afforded (by)** *any reference in paragraph (4) above to a summary of the provisions of a scheme is a reference to a summary of those provisions which includes (but is not limited to) details of the level and scope of the protection afforded by the Scheme*

(N) **protection of depositors** *'host State scheme', in relation to a UK institution or building society, means a scheme for the protection of depositors which is in force in an EEA State other than the United Kingdom and in which the institution or society participates* **protection of investors** ✂ **level, scope of protection**

(P) **protection for** *the Bank of England is providing adequate protection for the performance of the obligations of the subsidiary undertaking under the contract in any other way*

✎ **level of protection afforded (by), scheme for the protection of depositors** *'home State scheme' (a) in relation to an EEA institution, means a scheme for the protection of depositors which is in force in the institutions home State and in which the institution participates* ✂ **Deposit Protection Board** *an election by a non-EEA institution not to participate in the deposit protection scheme ('the scheme') shall cease to have effect if the deposit Protection Board ('the Board') determines under this regulation that it is no longer eligible not to participate in the scheme* **Investor Protection Board, investor protection scheme** ✂ **Credit Institutions (Protection of Depositors) Regulations 1995** ✂ **to participate in the deposit protection scheme** *a non-EEA institution shall be eligible not to participate in the deposit protection scheme ('the scheme') if the Deposit Protection Board ('the Board') determines under this regulation, on an application made by the institution, that it is so eligible*

📖 Possible equivalents: ochrona, zabezpieczenie (pl) difesa, protezione, tutela (it)

PROVISION (en)

(Adj) **consequential provision** *incidental or consequential provision of an order (included in reliance on section 259(1)(c)) may disapply or modify an enactment, whether by textual amendment or otherwise* **different, further, incidental, similar**

provision *section 172 is not applied to a bank liquidator–but section 108 makes similar provision* **special, supplemental provision** *an FMI transfer scheme may make incidental, supplemental, consequential and transitional provision in connection with the other provisions of the scheme* **supplementary provision** *part V of the Regulations contains miscellaneous and supplementary provisions* **transitional provision** ✂ **provision conferring** *for provision conferring immunity from liability in damages on the Bank of England in respect of its functions, see section 244 of the Banking Act 2009* **provison enabling, contained (in), made** *in these Regulations, references to the law of insolvency of the United Kingdom include references to every provision made by or under the 1986 Act or the 1989 Order as the case may be* **provision relating (to), requiring** ✂ **following, specified provisions** ✂ **subject to provision**

(N) **provision of a kind** *an order under or by virtue of this section may include any provision of a kind that may be made by order under section 90B of the Building Societies Act 1986* **provision of the law** ✂ **provision of Part I, of a Schedule** ✂ **application of provisions (about), summary of provisions** *any reference in paragraph (4) above to a summary of the provisions of a scheme is a reference to a summary of those provisions which includes (but is not limited to) details of the level and scope of the protection afforded by the Scheme*

(V) **to amend, to apply, to modify a provision** ✂ **to contain provision (about), to make provision** *the Treasury may by order make provision, in addition to the provisions of this group of sections, in consequence of the application of this Part to building societies* ✂ **provision + to apply**

(P) **provision about** *contingency fund regulations may make provision about the establishment and management of contingency funds*

✎ *(NOMINAL)* **transitional provisions and savings** ✂ **protective scheme provisions, ring-fencing provisions, provision of a contract or other agreement, provision made under or by virtue of this Part, special bail-in provision, (Type 1/2) default event provision** *a Type 1 default event provision is a provision of a contract or other agreement that has the effect that if a specified event occurs or situation arises (a) the agreement is terminated, modified, or replaced*

✎ *(VERBAL)* **to be disregarded in determining whether a default event provision applies** *if this subsection applies, the Part 1 instrument or share transfer order is to be disregarded in determining whether a default event provision applies*

to be exercised by way of provision in a share transfer instrument *the power under subsection (2) (c) must be exercised by way of provision in a share transfer instrument or order (or supplemental instrument or order)* **to make different provision for differerent purposes ✂ to make other provision for the purposes of, or in connection with, the transfer of property, rights or liabilities ✂ default event provision + to apply, order / regulation + to include provision** *an order may include provision for determining which arrangements are to be, or not to be, treated as protected arrangements* **regulations + to make provision ✂ provision made under or by virtue of this Part may make special provision in relation to the application of this Part (to)**

📖 Possible equivalents: klauzula, PRZEPIS (pl), clausola, DISPOSIZIONE, PROVVEDIMENTO (it)

PURPOSE (en)

(Adj) **necessary for the purposes (of) ✂ for procedural purposes** *for procedural purposes an order under subsection (1) shall be treated in the same way as an order under section 420 of the Insolvency Act 1986 (partnerships)* **✂ for specified purposes** *a resolution instrument (a) may make provision generally or only for specified purposes, cases or circumstances, and (b) may make different provision for different purposes, cases or circumstances* **✂ for the purpose specified (in) ✂ for a purpose connected with** *a share transfer instrument or order may provide for a transferee to be treated for any purpose connected with the transfer as the same person as the transferor*

(N) **for the purposes of functions** *the Bank of England may use information received in accordance with subsection (3) only for the purposes of its functions under or by virtue of this Part* **for the purposes of investigation, proceedings, regulation** *for the purposes of this regulation, rule 7.62 has effect as if there were substituted for paragraph (1)* **✂ for the purposes of paragraph (1), Part 1, section 1, subsection (1)**

(P) **for the purposes of, or in connection with** *so far as necessary for the purposes of, or in connection with, the provisions of subsections (1) and (2), references to the CMA in Part 1 of the Competition Act 1998 are to be read as including references to the FCA*

group ring-fencing purposes *the appropriate regulator may make such rules applying to bodies corporate falling within subsection (2) as appear to the regulator to be necessary or expedient for the group ring-fencing purposes* ✂ **generally or only for specified purposes, cases or circumstances** *in relying on subsection (1) a share transfer instrument or order (a) may make provision generally or only for specified purposes, cases or circumstances* ✂ **necessary for the purposes of, or in connection with** ✂ **necessary or desirable for the purposes of, necessary or expedient for the purpose of** *an order under subsection (4) may be made only if the Treasury are of the opinion that the making of the order is necessary or expedient for the purpose of protecting the continuity of the provision in the United Kingdom of core services* ✂ **for the purpose of enabling or assisting somebody (to)** *paragraph 1 does not preclude the disclosure of information in any case in which disclosure is for the purpose of enabling or assisting the Bank to discharge (a) its functions as a monetary authority* **for the purposes of giving effect (to)** ✂ **for all other purposes, including for the purposes of the application of a power under Part 1**

(VERBAL) **to be necessary for the purposes of, or in connection with** ✂ **to have effect for the purpose of** *section 78(2) and (3) have effect for the purposes of this section* **to make different provision for different purposes, cases or circumstances** ✂ **to make other provision for the purposes of, or in connection with** *a share transfer order is an order which (a) provides for securities issued by a specified bank to be transferred (b) makes other provision for the purposes of, or in connection with, the transfer of securities issued by a specified bank*

Possible equivalents: CEL (pl), FINE, obiettivo (it)

R

REFERENCE (en)

(Adj) **defined by reference (to)** *before making regulations under this section relating to a description of charges defined by reference to their being granted in favour of the Bank of England, or in connection with settlement arrangements provided by the Bank, the Secretary of State and the Treasury shall consult the Bank*

(N) **reference in an enactment** *a reference in an enactment or other document to anything done under a provision applied by this Part of this Act includes a reference to the provision as applied* **reference in Part 1, in section 1, in subsection (1)** ✂ **reference to an administrator, to a bank, to a committee, to a company, to a deposit, to insolvency, to an institution, to liquidation, to a liquidator** *the modifications are that (a) a reference to the liquidator is a reference to the bank liquidator, (b) a reference to winding up is a reference to bank insolvency* **reference to an office, to a provision**

(V) **to include a reference (to), to treat references (as)** *treat references to acting as an insolvency practitioner as references to acting as an FMI administrator* ✂ **to be treated as a reference (to)** *in the application of this section to Northern Ireland the reference to section 31 of the Credit Unions Act 1979 is to be treated as a reference to Article 2 of the Credit Unions (Northern Ireland) Order 1985*

✎ **reference to acting as an insolvency practitioner** *treat references to acting as an insolvency practitioner as references to acting as a bank liquidator* **reference to bank insolvency, to the FCA, to a holding company, to a justice of the peace** *in the application of this section to Scotland (a) for the reference to a justice of the peace substitute references to a justice of the peace or a sheriff* **reference to the official receiver** *in subsection (3), treat the second reference to the official receiver* *as a reference to the Secretary of State* **reference to a participating institution, to the PRA** ✂ **to be read as (including) references to** ✂ **to include a reference to functions conferred by** *a reference in this Part to functions of the scheme manager (including a reference to functions conferred by or under this Part) includes a reference to functions conferred by or under the Banking Act 2009* **to include a reference to a provision**✂

Possible equivalents: nawiązanie, odniesienie (pl), RIFERIMENTO, rinvio (it)

REGARD (en)

Usually singular

(V) **to have regard (to / in)** *the Bank of England may publish principles to which operators of recognised inter-bank payment systems are to have regard in operating the systems*

(P) **as regards** *'report' means a written report setting out the position generally as regards the progress of the winding up, provisional liquidation or administration (as the case may be)*

to have regard to a need *in appointing the members of the review panel, the Treasury (a) must have regard to the need to ensure that the review panel (considered as a whole) has the necessary experience to undertake the review* **to have regard to an objective** ✂ **to be necessary having regard to the public interest (in)** *the exercise of the power in respect of the banking group company is necessary having regard to the public interest in the advancement of one or more of the special resolution objectives.* ✂ **The Bank of England, the court, the Payment Systems Regulator + to have regard (to)** *in determining the appeal the CMA must have regard, to the same extent as is required of the Payment Systems Regulator, to the matters to which the Payment Systems Regulator must have regard in discharging its functions under this Part* ✂ **the Treasury + to have regard to the desirability (of)** *in making regulations the Treasury shall, in particular, have regard to the desirability of ensuring that if a residual bank enters insolvency after transfer, pre-transfer creditors do not receive less favourable treatment than they would have received had it entered insolvency immediately before transfer*

Possible equivalents: uwzględnienie, wzgląd (pl), considerazione, conto (it)

REGULATOR (en)

Usually singular

(Adj) **appropriate regulator** ✂ **issuing regulator** *before issuing a statement of policy under section 63ZD, a regulator ('the issuing regulator') must (a) consult the other regulator, and (b) publish a draft of the proposed statement in the way appearing to the issuing regulator to be best calculated to bring it to the attention of the public*

(N) **regulator's functions, reasons** *the draft must be accompanied by (c) an explanation of the Payment Systems Regulator's reasons for believing that imposing the requirement is compatible with its duties under section 49* ✂ **reference to the regulator** *subsections (5) and (10) of that section have effect as if any reference to the PRA were a reference to the appropriate regulator*

(V) **to consult, to direct the regulator (to)** *the Tribunal may not direct the Payment Systems Regulator to take any action which it would not otherwise have the power to take in relation to the decision* **to notify the regulator (of)** ✂ **regulator + to comply (with), to consider, to decide, to exercise, to prepare, to propose, to require, to vary** *a regulator may vary an approval by (a) imposing a condition, (b) varying a condition, (c) removing a condition, or (d) limiting the period for which the approval is to have effect* ✂ **regulator + to be required to,**

(P) **in the opinion of the regulator** *if there is a change in the scope or conduct of the investigation and, in the opinion of the Payment Systems Regulator, the person who is the subject of the investigation is likely to be significantly prejudiced by not being made aware of it, that person must be given written notice of the change*

EEA regulator, home state regulator *'home state regulator', in relation to an EEA credit institution, means the relevant EEA regulator in the EEA State where its head office is located* ✂ **officer or member of staff of the regulator** *the function of issuing general guidance may not be discharged by an officer or member of staff of the Regulator or of the FCA* ✂ **appropriate regulator + to make rules, regulator + to charge a reasonable fee for providing a person with a copy (of)** *a regulator may charge a reasonable fee for providing a person with a copy of the statement published under this section* **regulator + to issue a statement** *if a statement issued under this section is altered or replaced by a regulator, the regulator must issue the altered or replacement statement* **regulator + to require the authorised person (to)** *the appropriate regulator may require the authorised person (a) to provide* *information which the person is required to give under this section in such form as the appropriate regulator may direct* **regulator + to take action**

📖 Possible equivalents: organ nadzorujący, organ regulacyjny, organ regulacji (pl), autorità di regolamentazione, regolatore (it)

RELATION (en)

Usually singular

(N) **in relation to a company, a decision, an institution, a matter, a person, a provision, a requirement, securities, a system, winding up** *the provisions set out in the Table apply in relation to bank insolvency as in relation to winding up, with (a) the modifications set out in subsection (4)* ✂ **action in relation to** *a direction given to a participant in a regulated payment system may (a) require or prohibit the taking of specified action in relation to the system* **provision in relation to**

(V) **to apply in relation to** *Rule 7.62 of the Insolvency Rules or Rule 7.56 of the Insolvency Rules (Northern Ireland) applies in relation to a UK credit institution with the modification specified in paragraph (2) or (3)* ✂ **to be appointed in relation to** *'administrator' means an administrator, as defined by Article 2 of the reorganisation and winding up directive, who is appointed in relation to the EEA credit institution in relation to which the proposal is made* **to be exercised in relation to** *neither the CMA nor the Payment Systems Regulator may exercise any of the concurrent functions in relation to any matter if any of those functions have been exercised in relation to that matter by the other*

✏ *(NOMINAL)* **person in relation to whom an approval is given, performance of a senior management function in relation to the carrying on of a regulated activity by a relevant authorised person** *the FCA may vary an approval under section 59 given by the FCA or the PRA for the performance of a designated senior management function in relation to the carrying on of a regulated activity by a relevant authorised person if the FCA considers that it is desirable to do so in order to advance one or more of its operational objectives* ✂ **things done by, or in relation to** *without prejudice to subsection (3), an order under subsection (1) may contain (a) provision requiring things done by, or in relation to, the Director of Savings, to be treated as done by, or in relation to, the Bank*

✏ **to be in force in relation to** *such a scheme may be made only at a time when the FMI administration order is in force in relation to the old company* **to**

become a payment service provider in relation to *an order under this section may provide for the applicant to become a payment service provider in relation to a payment system (a) for a period specified in the order* **to exercise any of the concurrent functions in relation to any matter** *before the CMA or the Payment Systems Regulator first exercises any of the concurrent functions in relation to any matter, it must consult the other* **to have effect in relation to a credit institution** *the general law of insolvency has effect in relation to UK credit institutions subject to the provisions of this Part* ✂ **conditions + to be met in relation to, provisions, section / subsection + to apply in relation (to)** ✂ **provision made under or by virtue of this Part may make special provision in relation to the application of this Part (to)**

Possible equivalents: odniesienie, stosunek (pl), rapporto, RELAZIONE, riguardo (it)

REPORT (en)

(Adj) **annual report** *the annual report of each regulator must include the number of meetings that have taken place during the period to which the report relates between the regulator and auditors of PRA-authorised persons to which section 339C applies* ✂ **written report**

(N) **scheme report** *an application under section 106B in respect of a ring-fencing transfer scheme must be accompanied by a report on the terms of the scheme (a 'scheme report')* ✂ **copy of a report**

(V) **to lay, to make, to prepare, to publish a report** *if it considers that it is desirable to do so in order to advance any of its payment systems objectives, the Payment Systems Regulator may prepare and publish a report into any matter which it considers relevant to the exercise of its functions under this Part* ✂ **report + to relate (to)** ✂ **report + to be made**

(P) **report to** *the review must result in a report to the Treasury* ✂ **report on a matter** ✂ **report under section 1, subsection (1)**

report on a matter concerned ✂ **period to which the report relates** ✂ **the Chancellor of the Exchequer + to lay a copy of each report under subsection (1)** *the Chancellor of the Exchequer must lay a copy of each report under subsection*

(2) before Parliament **report + to be made as soon as (is) reasonably practicable (after)** *a report must be made as soon as reasonably practicable after the making of the resolution instrument to which it relates* **the Treasury + to lay a copy of the report before Parliament**

📖 Possible equivalents: protokół, raport, sprawozdanie (pl), RAPPORTO, RELAZIONE, rendiconto (it)

REQUIREMENT (en)

(Adj) **relevant requirement ✂ requirement imposed by or under ✂ proposed requirement** *before imposing the proposed requirement the Payment Systems Regulator must have regard to any representations made to it in accordance with subsection (3)(d)*

(N) **information requirement** *'information requirement' means a requirement imposed by an investigator under section 83ZG, 83ZH or 83ZJ* ✂ **compliance with a requirement, contravention of a requirement**

(V) **to comply with a requirement, to impose a requirement** *article 18 imposes further requirements on the use of the bridge bank option* ✂ **requirement + to be imposed**

(P) **requirement under section 1, subsection (1)** *a requirement under subsection (1)(c) or (d) may be general or specific.*

✏ **generally-imposed requirement** *in this section references to imposing a generally applicable requirement are to (a) giving a general direction under section 54, or (b) imposing a generally-imposed requirement under section 55,and references to the requirement are to be read accordingly* **requirement imposed under section 1 ✂ own funds requirements** *'own funds requirements' means the requirements laid down in Articles 92 to 98 of the capital requirements regulation (read with Title I of Part Ten of that regulation)* ✂ **decision / power to impose a requirement ✂ to have the meaning given by Article 1 of the capital requirements regulation ✂ to fail without reasonable excuse to comply with a requirement, to impose a requirement under section 1 ✂ information requirement + to be imposed**

📖 Possible equivalents: obowiązek, WARUNEK, wymaganie, wymóg (pl), OBBLIGO, CONDIZIONE, esigenza, REQUISITO (it)

RESOLUTION

Usually singular

(Aff) **pre-resolution** *in these Regulations, 'relevant persons' means the pre-resolution shareholders and creditors (within the meaning of section 60B(3) of the Act)*

(Adj) **negative resolution**

(N) **resolution action, administrator, authority, company** ✂ **<u>RESOLUTION INSTRUMENT</u>** ✂ **resolution powers** *in subsection (3)(b) 'transferee' means a person to whom all or part of the business of the parent undertaking or the subsidiary undertaking could be transferred as a result of the exercise of the resolution powers*

(V) **to pass a resolution** *where, on or after 5th May 2004, a UK credit institution ('the institution') intends to pass a resolution to wind up the institution under paragraph (b) or (c) (…) the institution must give written notice of the resolution to the Authority before it passes the resolution*

(P) **under resolution** *a contract is a 'qualifying contract' for the purpose of this section if (a) one of the parties to the contract is a bank in respect of which the Bank is exercising a stabilisation power (a 'bank under resolution') and all the obligations under the contract to make a payment, make delivery or provide collateral continue to be performed*

✎ **draft affirmative resolution** ✂ **EU / foreign resolution authority, recognition of a third-country resolution action** *the recognition of third-country resolution action (or any part of it) is without prejudice to any normal insolvency proceedings* **resolution fund order** *a 'resolution fund order' is an order establishing a scheme under which transferors become entitled to the proceeds of the disposal of things transferred (a) in specified circumstances, and (b) to a specified extent* **resolution for voluntary winding up** *a resolution for voluntary winding up of a bank under section 84 of the Insolvency Act 1986 shall have no effect without the prior approval of the court* **special resolution objectives / regime** ✂ **to be subject to annulment in pursuance of a resolution of either House of Parliament, to have the meaning given in Article 1 of the recovery and resolution directive** ✂ **draft + to be laid before and approved by resolution of each House of Parliament, liquidation committee + to pass a full payment resolution** *a person aggrieved by any action of the liquidation committee before it has passed a full payment resolution may apply to the court, which may make any order (including an order for the repayment of money)* **third country resolution action + to be taken**

Possible equivalents: postanowienie, rezolucja, rozstrzyganie, UCHWAŁA (pl), delibera, deliberazione, risoluzione (it)

RESOLUTION INSTRUMENT

(Adj) **supplemental resolution instrument** *the Bank of England may make, with respect to the bank, one or more resolution instruments designated by the Bank of England as supplemental resolution instruments*

(V) **to make a resolution instrument** ✂ **resolution instrument + to provide for, to require** *a resolution instrument may require a bail-in administrator, or one or more directors of the bank, to (a) draw up a business reorganisation plan with respect to the bank*

✎ **onward transfer resolution instrument** *an onward transfer resolution instrument is a resolution instrument which (a) provides for the transfer of (i) securities which were issued by the bank before the original instrument and have been transferred by the original instrument or a supplemental resolution instrument, or (ii) securities which were issued by the bank after the original instrument* **reverse transfer resolution instrument** *a reverse transfer resolution instrument is a resolution instrument which (a) provides for transfer to the transferor under the original instrument (b) makes other provision for the purposes of, or in connection with, the transfer of securities which are, or could be or could have been, transferred under paragraph (a)* **transfer of property subsequent to resolution instrument** ✂ **Bank of England + to make a resolution instrument**

Possible equivalents: postanowienie o środkach zaradczych (pl), atto di risoluzione, strumento di risoluzione (it)

RESPECT (en)

Usually singular

(P) **in respect of** *in paragraph 6B 'eligible deposit' means a deposit in respect of which the person, or any of the persons, to whom it is owed would be eligible for compensation under the Financial Services Compensation Scheme* **with respect to** *the Treasury, after consultation with the Governor of the Bank, may by order give*

the Bank directions with respect to monetary policy if they are satisfied that the directions are required in the public interest and by extreme economic circumstances

✎ **decision with respect to the approval ✂ to make provision with respect to, to take action in respect of ✂ the Bank of England + to exercise a stabilisation power in respect of a bank, condition + to be met in respect of a bank** *the PRA is satisfied that Condition 1 in section 7 is met in respect of a bank to which section 81D(1)(a) applies* **institution + to continue to have a liability in respect of any deposit for which it had a liability, the Treasury + to make a share transfer order in respect of securities issued by a bank ✂ action + to be taken in respect of** *condition 1 is that third-country resolution action has been taken in respect of a third-country institution, a third-country parent undertaking or another third-country group company, in the same group* **power + to be exercised in respect of a bank**

📖 Possible equivalents: tytuł, wzgląd, ZAKRES (pl), riguardo (it)

RIGHT (en)

(Adj) **specified right ✂ rights arising** *the compensation scheme may make provision (a) about the effect of a payment of compensation under the scheme on rights or obligations arising out of matters in connection with which the compensation was paid* **right attaching (to)** *a resolution instrument may (a) make provision with respect to rights attaching to securities issued by the bank*

(N) **interest or right, property or right ✂ rights or obligations ✂ right of a creditor, of a person ✂ termination right** *for the purposes of this section, 'termination right' means (a) a right to terminate a contract, (b) a right to accelerate, close out, set-off or net obligations, or any similar provision that suspends, modifies or extinguishes an obligation of a party to the contract, or (c) a provision that prevents an obligation from arising under the contract* ✂ **creation of a right** *sub-paragraphs (3) and (4) apply to the creation of an interest or right by an FMI transfer scheme as they apply to the transfer of an interest or right*

(V) **to confer a right, to exercise a right, to lose a right (to) ✂ right + to accrue** *a right accrues to terminate, modify, or replace rights or duties under the agreement*

(P) **right in rem** *a right, recorded in a public register and enforceable against third parties, under which a right in rem within the meaning of paragraph (1) may be obtained, is also to be treated as a right in rem for the purposes of this regulation* ✂ **right within the meaning (of)**

✏ **rights or duties under an agreement** ✂ **right to refer to the Tribunal** *the giving of consent for the purpose of subsection (4)(b) does not affect any right to refer to the Tribunal the matter to which any decision notice resulting from the warning notice relates* ✂ **rights attaching to securities** ✂ **Human Rights Act 1998** ✂ **to lose the right to rely on section 1** *if an authorised bank enters insolvency (within the meaning of section 217(6)) it loses the right to rely on section 213* **to make provision for the purposes of, or in connection with, the transfer of property, rights or liabilities** *a reverse property transfer instrument is a property transfer instrument which (a) provides for transfer to the transferor under the original instrument (…) (c) makes other provision for the purposes of, or in connection with, the transfer of property, rights or liabilities that are, could be or could have been transferred under paragraph (a)*

📖 Possible equivalents: PRAWO, uprawnienie (pl), DIRITTO (it)

S

SCHEME (en)

Usually singular

(Adj) **scheme established (by / under)** ✂ **establishing a scheme** *a 'compensation scheme order' is an order (a) establishing a scheme for determining whether transferors should be paid compensation, or providing for transferors to be paid compensation*

(N) **scheme of arrangement** ✂ **compensation scheme** ✂ **scheme manager, report** *an application under section 106B in respect of a ring-fencing transfer scheme must be accompanied by a report on the terms of the scheme (a 'scheme report')* ✂ **participation in a scheme** *if the default has not been remedied before the end of the period of 12 months referred to in paragraph (3) above the relevant Board may, with the consent of the supervisory authority, by notice to the institution exclude the institution from participation in the scheme* ✂ **provision of a scheme**

(V) **to participate in a scheme** ✂ **scheme + to include** *the compensation scheme may include provision about contingency funds provided that it is not inconsistent with contingency fund regulations* **scheme + to relate (to)**

(P) **scheme for** *a 'bail-in compensation order' is an order establishing a scheme for determining, in accordance with section 52A, whether any transferors or others should be paid compensation* ✂ **scheme under a paragraph** *the property, rights and liabilities capable of being transferred in accordance with a scheme under paragraph 3 shall include property, rights and liabilities that would not otherwise be capable of being transferred or assigned by the Bank* ✂ **in accordance with a scheme, in relation to a scheme** *'employer', in relation to a relevant pension scheme, means (a) a person who is for the purposes of Part 1 of the Pensions Act 1995 or Part 2 of the Pensions (Northern Ireland) Order 1995 an employer in relation*

to the scheme, and (b) any other person who has or may have any liability under the scheme

(SYNTACTIC NOMINAL) **financial penalty scheme** *the Regulator must prepare and operate a scheme ('the financial penalty scheme') for ensuring that the amounts that, as a result of the deduction for which paragraph 10(1) provides, are retained by the Regulator in respect of amounts paid to it by way of penalties imposed under section 73 are applied for the benefit of participants in regulated payment systems* **Financial Services Compensation Scheme, FMI transfer scheme** *the old company may (a) with the consent of the new company, and (b) for the purpose of giving effect to the proposed transfer, make a scheme under this Schedule for the transfer of property, rights and liabilities from the old company to the new company (an 'FMI transfer scheme')* **host state scheme, investor protection scheme, occupational pension scheme, reclaim fund business transfer scheme, ring-fencing transfer scheme** ✂ **scheme for the protection of depositors**

(NOMINAL) **authority responsible for the institutions home State scheme** *where an EEA institution commences or resumes its participation in a UK scheme, the relevant Board may enter into an agency or information agreement with the authority responsible for the institutions home State scheme* **compensation scheme order, Directive 9419EC on deposit-guarantee schemes, protection afforded by a scheme, protective scheme provisions** *for the purpose of the protective scheme provisions of this Part, a building society becomes insolvent (a) on the making by the Commission of a determination that, for reasons which directly relate to the society's financial circumstances, the society (i) is unable to repay investments which are due and payable; and (ii) has no current prospect of being able to do so* ✂ **Pension Schemes (Northern Ireland) Act 1993**

(VERBAL) **to be participating in a host State scheme** *where a UK institution or building society which is participating in a host State scheme becomes insolvent (within the meaning of the relevant Part), the relevant enactments (which enable the relevant Board to obtain information) shall have effect as if (a) any reference to the relevant Board included a reference to the authority having responsibility for the host State scheme* **to be payable under a scheme** *the regulations must ensure that payments required do not exceed the amount of compensation that would have been payable under the scheme if the stabilisation power had not been exercised and the bank had been unable to satisfy claims against it* **to participate in the deposit protection scheme** ✂ **EEA institution + to be participating in a UK scheme, most relevant deposits with the institution + to be**

protected by a scheme *a deposit advertisement may include d) if it relates to a non-EEA institution which is not participating in the deposit protection scheme, a statement to the effect that most relevant deposits with the institution are protected by its home State scheme*

📖 Possible equivalents: harmonogram, plan, program, projekt, SYSTEM (pl), piano, proposta, SISTEMA (it),

SECTION (en)

(Adv) **section above, below** *section 146 is not applied–but section 115 below makes similar provision*

(Adj) **inserted by a section** ✂ **ignoring a section** *this subsection applies in relation to the banking group company if (b) the Bank of England is satisfied that (ignoring section 6B) Condition 2 in section 7 is met in relation to that bank*

(N) **section of an Act** ✂ **contravention, heading, interpretation of a section** *the following provisions have effect for the interpretation of section 142W and this section* ✂ **entry for a section** *after the entry for section 81B insert Section 81ZBA (a) Treat the references to the PRA in subsections (2)(a) and (2A) as references to the FCA* ✂ **group of sections** *expressions used in this group of sections and in the Building Societies Act 1986 have the same meaning in this group of sections as in that Act* ✂ **order, powers, rules, statement, warrant under a section** *any person who intentionally obstructs the exercise of any rights conferred by a warrant under section 83ZL is guilty of an offence*

(V) **to rely on a section** *a right to rely on section 213 cannot be transferred by or acquired from an authorised bank* **to see a section** *for the meaning of 'relevant authorised person', see section 71A* ✂ **section + to apply (to)** ✂ **section + to be amended (by), to be inserted (by)**

(P) **by virtue of a section** *in subsections (1) and (2) 'the concurrent functions' means the functions which by virtue of section 59 are concurrent functions of the Payment Systems Regulator and the CMA* **in accordance with a section, in reliance on a section** *where the Bank of England imposes a sanction on a person without notice in reliance on section 201(3), the person may appeal to the Financial Services and Markets Tribunal* **within the meaning of a section**

(VERBAL) **to have the meaning as in section 1** *'the relevant persons' has the same meaning as in section 142M* **to have the meaning given by / in section 1 of an Act, to lose the right to rely on section 1, to see section 1 of an Act ✂ to be read in accordance with section 1 ✂ condition in section 1 + to be in addition to conditions in section 2, offence + to be committed before the commencement of section 1 of the Criminal Justice Act 2003** *any person who intentionally obstructs the exercise of any rights conferred by a warrant under section 88 is guilty of an offence and liable on summary conviction (a) in England and Wales, to imprisonment for a term not exceeding 51 weeks (or 3 months, if the offence was committed before the commencement of section 280(2) of the Criminal Justice Act 2003) or a fine, or both (b) in Scotland, to imprisonment for a term not exceeding 3 months or a fine not exceeding level 5 on the standard scale, or both* **section 1 + to apply in relation to, sections 1 to 3 + to contain provisions about, subsection (1) + to be inserted into section 1 (by)** *subsection (7A) is inserted into section 48B by article 48 of this Order* ✂ **section 1 + to be amended by an Order / by paragraph 1 of Schedule 1 to an Act / by Regulations / by section 2 of an Act ✂ section 1 + to be inserted by article 1 / paragraph 1 / section 2 of an Act 2012 ✂ after subsection (1) of that section there shall be inserted the following subsection**

section 1 or Article 1 compromise or arrangement *those conditions are (a) the person proposing the section 425 or Article 418 compromise or arrangement ('the proposal') has given (i) the administrator or liquidator, and (ii) the relevant administrative or judicial authority, reasonable notice of the details of that proposal* ✂ **code of practice under section 1, contravention of section 1 of an Act, contribution levied under section 1 of an Act** *the amount of the initial contribution levied on the institution under section 53 of the 1987 Act shall be reduced by the aggregate of (a) the amount of any previous initial contribution levied on the institution under that section; and (b) so much of any further contribution levied on the institution under section 54 of that Act as was attributable to an order under subsection (2) of that section* **order for specific performance under section 45 of the Court of Session Act 1988** *the obligation imposed by subsection (7) is enforceable, on the application of the Bank, by an injunction or, in Scotland, by an order for specific performance under section 45 of the Court of Session Act 1988(a)* **power / rules under section 1 of an Act, pursuit of Objective 1 in section 1, share transfer order under section 1, statement issued under a section ✂ ✂ (as) applied by section 1 below, within the meaning of section 1 of an Act**

Possible equivalents: sekcja (pl), SEZIONE (it)

SECURITY (en)

(Adj) **securities held (by)** *securities held by a bail-in administrator (in that capacity, and whether as a result of a resolution instrument or otherwise) are to be held in accordance with the terms of a resolution instrument that transfers those, or other, securities to the bail-in administrator* **securities issued (by)**

(N) **transfer of securities** ✂ **listing of securities** *a property transfer instrument may provide for the listing of securities, under section 74 of the Financial Services and Markets Act 2000(b), to be discontinued or suspended* ✂ **security interest** *in this section (a)'security interests' means arrangements under which one person acquires, by way of security, an actual or contingent interest in the property of another*

(V) **to hold securities** *the Bank of England may appoint more than one bail-in administrator to perform functions in relation to a bank (but no more than one of them may at any one time be authorised to hold securities as mentioned in subsection (2))* ✂ **securities + to be transferred**

✎ **securities issued by a specified bank, securities which were issued by a bank** ✂ **rights attaching to securities, securities settlement system** *'securities settlement system' means a computer-based system, and procedures, which enable title to units of a security to be evidenced and transferred without a written instrument, and which facilitate supplementary and incidental matters* ✂ **to make provision for the purposes of, or in connection with, the transfer of securities issued by a bank** *an onward share transfer order is a share transfer order which (b) makes other provision for the purposes of, or in connection with, the transfer of securities issued by the bank (whether the transfer has been or is to be effected by that order, by another share transfer order or otherwise)* **to make a share transfer order in respect of securities issued by a bank** *this section applies where the Treasury (a) make a share transfer order, in respect of securities issued by a bank (or a bank's holding company), in accordance with section 13(2)*

Possible equivalents: papier wartościowy (pl), TITOLO, valore (it)

SERVICE (en)

(*Adj*) **core services** *in relation to the matters mentioned in subsection (2), the continuity objective is protecting the continuity of the provision in the United Kingdom of core services (see section 142C)* **financial services** ✂ **banking services** *Objective 1 is to ensure the continuity of banking services in the United Kingdom and of critical functions* ✂ **services provided (by)**

(*N*) **services and / or facilities** ✂ **provision of services** ✂ **market for services** *the Treasury must have regard to the desirability of minimising any adverse effect that the ring-fencing provisions might be expected to have on competition in the market for services provided in the course of carrying on core activities, including any adverse effect on the ease with which new entrants can enter the market* ✂ **service-user** *a designated representative body may make a complaint to the Payment Systems Regulator that a feature, or combination of features, of a market in the United Kingdom for services provided by payment systems is, or appears to be, significantly damaging the interests of those who use, or are likely to use, those services ('service-users')*

(*V*) **to provide services** *the duty to provide services and facilities in pursuance of the continuity obligation is subject to a right to receive reasonable consideration* **to use services**

✏ **services and facilities as are required (to)** *each former group company must provide such services and facilities as are required to enable the transferred bank to operate effectively* ✂ **claims management services** *in determining the leviable OLC expenditure for the purposes of section 173, any expenditure incurred, or income received, by the OLC in connection with the exercise of its functions in relation to claims management services is to be disregarded* **regulatory information service** ✂ **adverse effect on the continuity of the provision in the United Kingdom of core services, service contract of a director of a specified bank** *a resolution instrument may enable the Bank of England (a) to remove a director of a specified bank (b) to vary the service contract of a director of a specified bank* **those who use, or are likely to use, services provided by payment systems** ✂ **Financial Services Authority, scheme manager of the Financial Services Compensation Scheme** *before issuing the code of practice the Treasury must consult (a) the FSA, (b) the Bank of England, and (c) the scheme manager of the Financial Services Compensation Scheme (established under Part 15 of the*

Financial Services and Markets Act 2000) ✂ **Courts and Legal Services Act 1990, Financial Services and Markets Act 2000, Financial Services (Banking Reform) Act 2013** ✂ **to become a payment service provider in relation to a system** *the Payment Systems Regulator may by order require the operator of a regulated payment system to enable the applicant to become a payment service provider in relation to the system*

Possible equivalents: DZIAŁALNOŚĆ, USŁUGA (pl), ATTIVITA, SERVIZIO (it)

SHARE (en)

(Adj) **deferred shares** *for the purpose of exercising the third stabilisation option in respect of a building society the Treasury may make one or more orders for the purposes of (a) arranging for deferred shares of a building society to be publicly owned*

(N) **share transfer** *where the Treasury take a bank's holding company into temporary public ownership in reliance on section 82 (d) a share transfer may be made in respect of securities which were issued by the bank or by another bank which is or was in the same group*

(P) **share in a society** *in this section investment (a) in relation to a building society or Irish building society, means a deposit with or a share in the society*

new deferred shares *if and in so far as an order under section 85 provides for the issue of new deferred shares, section 51(2) shall not apply* ✂ **SHARE TRANSFER INSTRUMENT, SHARE TRANSFER ORDER** ✂ **share in a building society**

Possible equivalents: AKCJA, udział (pl), azione, TITOLO (it)

SHARE TRANSFER INSTRUMENT (en)

(Adj) **supplemental share transfer instrument** *a supplemental share transfer instrument is a share transfer instrument which (a) provides for the transfer of securities which were issued by the bank before the original instrument and have not been transferred by the original instrument or another supplemental share transfer instrument*

(N) **share transfer instrument or order** *a share transfer instrument or order may include incidental, consequential or transitional provision*

✎ **bridge bank (reverse) share transfer instrument** *a bridge bank share transfer instrument is a share transfer instrument which (a) provides for securities issued by the bridge bank to be transferred* ✂ **to be exercised by way of provision in a share transfer instrument** *the power under subsection (1) must be exercised by way of provision in a share transfer instrument, property transfer instrument, resolution instrument or third-country instrument* **to be treated in the same way as any other share transfer instrument for all other purposes** *sections 7 and 8 do not apply to a supplemental share transfer instrument (but it is to be treated in the same way as any other share transfer instrument for all other purposes, including for the purposes of the application of a power under this Part)* ✂ **share transfer instrument or order + to provide (for)** *a share transfer instrument or order may provide for a transfer to take effect free from any trust, liability or other encumbrance* ✂ **the Bank of England + to make a share transfer instrument**

Possible equivalents: dokument zbycia akcji (pl), atto di cessione delle azioni, atto di trasferimento delle azioni (it)

SHARE TRANSFER ORDER (en)

Usually singular

(Adj) **onward, reverse share transfer order** *a reverse share transfer order is a share transfer order which (a) provides for transfer to the transferor under the original order (where subsection (2) applies) (b) provides for transfer to the original transferee (where subsection (3) applies) (c) makes other provision for the purposes of, or in connection with, the transfer of securities which are, could be or could have been transferred under paragraph (a) or (b)* **supplemental share transfer order** *a supplemental share transfer order is a share transfer order which (a) provides for the transfer of securities which were issued by the bank before the original order and have not been transferred by the original order or another supplemental share transfer order (b) makes provision of a kind that a share transfer order may make under section 16(1)(b), whether in connection with a transfer under the original order or in connection with a transfer under that or another supplemental order*

(V) **to make a share transfer order**

✐ **Part 1 instrument or share transfer order** *a Part 1 instrument or share transfer order may provide for subsection (8) or (9) to apply (but need not apply either) in circumstances where subsection (6) would not apply* ✂ **to make an onward share transfer order** ✂ **the Treasury + to make a share transfer order in respect of securities issued by a bank**

📖 Possible equivalents: polecenie przeniesienia akcji, umowa zbycia akcji (pl), ordine di cessione delle azioni, ordine di trasferimento delle azioni (it)

SOCIETY (en)

(Adj) **contributory, friendly society** *'friendly society' means (a) a society which is registered within the meaning of the Friendly Societies Act 1974; or (b) a society incorporated under the Friendly Societies Act 1992* ✂ **building society** ✂ **society established** *the year-end date of a building society established on or after 25th August 1894 and before the relevant day is 31st December*

(N) **institution or society** ✂ **office of a society** *where a UK institution or building society withdraws or is excluded from a scheme for the protection of depositors which is in force in an EEA State other than the United Kingdom, it shall as soon as practicable take all such steps as may be necessary to bring the withdrawal or exclusion to the notice of depositors whose deposits were made with offices of the institution or society in that State*

(P) **share in a society** *a property transfer instrument in respect of a bank which provides for transfer to a building society may confer rights and impose liabilities by way of actual or deemed shares in the building society*

✐ **UK institution or building society** *where a UK institution or building society commences or resumes its participation in a host State scheme, the relevant Board may enter into an agency or information agreement with the authority responsible for that scheme* ✂ **Irish building society** *'Irish building society' means an EEA institution which is incorporated in or formed under the law of the Republic of Ireland and whose characteristics correspond as nearly as may be to those of a building society* ✂ **business of a building society** *for the purpose specified in subsection (1)(c) an order may make any provision which the Treasury think desirable* *to facilitate the business of the building society after the making of provision in accordance with subsections (3) to (5)* **financial year of a society** ✂ **Building Societies Act 1986**

📖 Possible equivalents: spółka, towarzystwo, związek (pl), cooperativa, IMPRESA, istituto, SOCIETÀ (it)

STATEMENT (en)

(Adj) **false statement** *if the court is satisfied that the defaulter failed without reasonable excuse to comply with the notice or other requirement, or made the false statement, or provided the false information, it may deal with the defaulter (and in the case of a body corporate, any director or other officer of the body) as if that person were in contempt* ✂ **written statement** ✂ **statement issued (under)** *if a statement issued under this section is altered or replaced, the regulator must issue the altered or replacement statement* **statement relating (to)**

(N) **statement of affairs, of policy** *each regulator must prepare and issue a statement of policy with respect to (a) the imposition of penalties under section 142S* ✂ **clearance statement** *a 'clearance statement' is a statement issued by the Pensions Regulator under any of the following provisions (a) section 42 of the Pensions Act 2004 (clearance statements relating to contribution notice under section 38) (b) section 46 of that Act (clearance statements relating to financial support directions)* ✂ **copy, terms of a statement** *a decision notice about the publication of a statement must set out the terms of the statement*

(V) **to publish a statement** *if the decision is to publish a statement, the decision notice must set out the terms of the statement*

(P) **statement as to** *as soon as practicable after each meeting of the Monetary Policy Committee, the Bank shall publish a statement as to whether it was decided at the meeting that the Bank should take any action, other than action by way of intervening in financial markets, for the purpose of meeting its objectives under section 1* ✂ **statement to an effect** *except as provided for by paragraph 7(5), the Regulator is exempt from the requirements of Part 16 of the Companies Act 2006 (audit) and its balance sheet must contain a statement to that effect*

✎ **statement issued under a section** ✂ **summary financial statement** *if, at any time during the period beginning with the publication of the summary financial statement and ending with the publication of the next summary financial statement, an individual for the first time subscribes for shares in the society, the society shall at that time notify the individual of the information in subsection (8C)(c)(i) to (iii)* ✂ **to set out the terms of a statement**

📖 Possible equivalents: deklaracja, oświaczenie, sprawozdanie, zestawienie (pl), dichiarazione, enunciazione, informativa, prospetto, RELAZIONE, rendiconto (it)

T

TERM (en)

(N) **terms and conditions** ✂ **terms of a contract** ✂ **term of office** *a person appointed as director of the Bank in place of a person who ceased to hold office before the end of the term for which he was appointed shall be appointed for the remainder of that person's term of office*

(P) **on terms** *'title transfer collateral arrangements' means arrangements under which Person 1 transfers assets to Person 2 on terms providing for Person 2 to transfer assets if specified obligations are discharged* ✂ **in general terms** *the regulators must prepare and maintain a memorandum which describes in general terms (a) the role of each regulator in relation to the exercise of relevant functions which relate to matters of common regulatory interest* ✂ **in accordance with terms**

✂ **imprisonment for a term not exceeding 2 months / 10 years** *a person guilty of an offence under subsection (4), (5) or (6) is liable, on summary conviction to imprisonment for a term not exceeding 3 months or a fine not exceeding level 5 on the standard scale, or both*

Possible equivalents: okres, TERMIN, WARUNEK (pl), durata, CONDIZIONE, clausola, PERIODO, scadenza (it)

TRANSFER (en)

(Adj) **onward, original transfer** *subsection (2) may be relied on to impose obligations on (a) an original transferee (where the original transfer was a property transfer)* **partial transfer** ✂ **multiple transfers** ✂ **transfer falling (within)** *the means by which transfers falling within subsection (5) may be effected include,*

in particular (a) a transfer of the undertaking of the company subject to the FMI administration order, or of part of its undertaking, to a wholly-owned subsidiary of that company, and (b) the transfer to a company of securities of a wholly-owned subsidiary to which there has been a transfer falling within paragraph (a)

(N) **property, share transfer** ✂ **transfer date, scheme** *an FMI transfer scheme is to take effect in accordance with paragraph 7 at the time appointed by the court* ✂ **transfer of funds, shares** ✂ **pre-transfer creditor** *'pre-transfer creditor' means a person who (i) is a creditor of a residual bank immediately before a property transfer instrument takes effect*

(V) **to provide for a transfer** *a bail-in reverse property transfer instrument is a property transfer instrument which (a) provides for a transfer to the transferor under the original instrument (b) makes other provision for the purposes of, or in connection with, the transfer of property, rights or liabilities which are, or could be or could have been, transferred under paragraph (a)*

✏ *(NOMINAL)* **transfer falling within a subsection, transfer of property subsequent to resolution instrument** ✂ **PROPERTY TRANSFER INSTRUMENT, SHARE TRANSFER INSTRUMENT, SHARE TRANSFER ORDER** ✂ **FMI transfer scheme** *the old company may (a) with the consent of the new company, and (b) for the purpose of giving effect to the proposed transfer, make a scheme under this Schedule for the transfer of property, rights and liabilities from the old company to the new company (an 'FMI transfer scheme')* **onward / reverse transfer resolution instrument, reclaim fund business transfer scheme, (reverse) property transfer order, ring-fencing transfer scheme** *a scheme is a ring-fencing transfer scheme if it (a) is one under which the whole or part of the business carried on (i) by a UK authorised person, or (ii) by a qualifying body, is to be transferred to another body ('the transferee'), (b) is to be made for one or more of the purposes mentioned in subsection (3), and (c) is not an excluded scheme or an insurance business transfer scheme* **title transfer collateral arrangements** *'title transfer collateral arrangements' means arrangements under which Person 1 transfers assets to Person 2 on terms providing for Person 2 to transfer assets if specified obligations are discharged* ✂ **bank administration following transfer to a bridge bank**

✏ *(VERBAL)* **to make provision for the purposes of, or in connection with, the transfer of securities issued by a bank / the transfer of property, rights or liabilities** *a bail-in reverse property transfer instrument is a property transfer* *instrument which (a) provides for a transfer to the transferor under the original instrument (b) makes other provision for the purposes of, or in connection with, the transfer of property, rights or liabilities which are, or could be or could have been, transferred under paragraph (a)* ✂ **to make a reverse transfer resolution instrument** ✂ **transfer + to take effect**

📖 Possible equivalents: cesja, przekaz, przekazanie, transfer, zbycie (pl), cessione, trapasso, trasferimento (it)

TREASURY (en)

Always singular

(Adj) **specified by the Treasury** *the regulated activity of accepting deposits (whether carried on in the United Kingdom or elsewhere) is a core activity unless it is carried on in circumstances specified by the Treasury by order*

(N) **nominee of the Treasury** *the obligation to produce reports continues to apply in respect of each year until the first during which no securities issued by the bank are owned by (a) a company wholly owned by the Treasury, or (b) a nominee of the Treasury* **power of the Treasury** *any power of the Treasury, the Secretary of State or the Lord Chancellor to make an order or regulations under this Act is exercisable by statutory instrument* **report to the Treasury** *the review must result in a report to the Treasury*

(V) **to appear to the Treasury (to)** *subsection (3) also applies where the Treasury direct the Payment Systems Regulator that it appears to the Treasury that the conditions in subsection (1) are met in relation to specified events* ✂ **Treasury + to amend, to appoint, to consider, to consult, to direct, to receive, to require, to specify, to think** *a loan under this section may be made on such terms as the Treasury think fit*

(P) **with the approval / consent of the Treasury** *the Bank of England may act under or by virtue of subsection (2) only with the consent of the Treasury*

✏ **the Bank of England or the Treasury** *in determining an amount of compensation (whether or not in accordance with valuation principles) an independent valuer must disregard actual or potential financial assistance provided by the Bank of England or the Treasury* ✂ **company wholly owned by the Treasury** ✂ **Treasury + to have regard (to), to lay a copy of a report before Parliament, to**

make provision, to make regulations (about), to make a share transfer order
✂ **order + to be made only if the Treasury are of the opinion (that)** *an order under subsection (2) may be made only if the Treasury are of the opinion that it is not necessary for either of the following purposes that the regulated activity of accepting deposits should be a core activity when carried on in the specified circumstances*

📖 Possible equivalents: SKARB PAŃSTWA (pl), ministero del tesoro, tesoro (it)

U

UNDERTAKING (en)

(Adj) **subsidiary undertaking** *'subsidiary' means a subsidiary undertaking within the meaning given by section 1162 of the Companies Act 2006*

(N) **undertaking of a bank** ✂ **group undertaking** *'former group company' means anything which was a group undertaking in relation to the transferred bank immediately before the transfer (whether or not it is also a group undertaking in relation to the transferred bank immediately after the transfer)* **parent undertaking** *the Treasury may take a parent undertaking of a bank (the 'holding company') into temporary public ownership, in accordance with section 13(2)* ✂ **part of an undertaking** *the transfer of functions by this Part shall be regarded for the purposes of the M1Transfer of Undertakings (Protection of Employment) Regulations 1981 as the transfer of part of an undertaking, whether or not it would be so regarded apart from this provision*

✏ **third-country institution or third-country parent undertaking** *this section applies where the Bank of England is notified of third-country resolution action in respect of a third-country institution or third-country parent undertaking* ✂ **parent undertaking of a ring-fenced body, qualifying parent undertaking** *a parent undertaking of a ring-fenced body by reference to which the group restructuring powers are exercisable is for the purposes of this Part a 'qualifying parent undertaking' if (a) it is a body corporate which is incorporated in the United Kingdom and has a place of business in the United Kingdom, and (b) it is not itself an authorised person* **UK parent undertaking**

📖 Possible equivalents: PRZEDSIĘBIORSTWO (pl), azienda, IMPRESA (it)

UNITED KINGDOM (en)

(P) **outside the United Kingdom** *for this purpose property, or a right, interest, or liability, is 'foreign' if an issue relating to it arising in any proceedings would (in accordance with the rules of private international law) be determined under the law of a country or territory outside the United Kingdom*

✎ **EEA State other than the United Kingdom** ✂ **United Kingdom office of an institution** ✂ **general law of insolvency of the United Kingdom, stability of the financial system of the United Kingdom** *condition 2 is that the Bank of England is satisfied that the exercise of the power in respect of the third-country group company is necessary, having regard to the public interest in the stability of the financial systems of the United Kingdom and the third-country concerned* ✂ **institution which is incorporated in, or formed under the law of any part of, the United Kingdom** ✂ **adverse effect on the continuity of the provision in the United Kingdom of core services** ✂ **in the United Kingdom or elsewhere, under the law of a country or territory outside the United Kingdom** *for this purpose property, or a right, interest or liability, is 'foreign' if an issue relating to it arising in any proceedings would (in accordance with the rules of private international law) be determined under the law of a country or territory outside the United Kingdom*

📖 Possible equivalents: Zjednoczone Królestwo (pl), Regno Unito (it)

V

VIRTUE (en)

Always singular

(Adj) **done, obtained by virtue (of)** *the Bank may publish information obtained by virtue of this section*

(N) **by virtue of paragraph (a), section 1, subsection (2)** ✂ **(under or) by virtue of an instrument** *A transfer takes effect by virtue of the instrument or order (and in accordance with its provisions as to timing or other ancillary matters)* **under or by virtue of Part 1**

(V) **to apply by virtue of** *an order under para. 110 may amend a provision of the Schedule as it applies by virtue of this Act (whether or not in the same way as it amends the provision as it applies otherwise)*

(P) **by virtue of, under or by virtue of** *the Bank of England may use information received in accordance with subsection (3) only for the purposes of its functions under or by virtue of this Part*

✎ **order made by virtue of subsection (1), provision made under or by virtue of a Part** *provision made under or by virtue of this Part may make special provision in relation to the application of this Part to credit union*

📖 Possible equivalents: podstawa, wzgląd (pl), norma, virtù (it)

W

WINDING UP (en)

Always singular

(Adj) **relevant winding up** *for the purposes of paragraph (1)(c), a winding up is a relevant winding up if (a) in the case of a winding up by the court, the winding-up order is made on or after 5th May 2004; or (b) in the case of a creditors voluntary winding up, the liquidator is appointed in accordance with section 100 of the 1986 Act, Article 86 of the 1989 Order or paragraph 83 of Schedule B1 to the 1986 Act on or after 5th May 2004*

(N) **reorganisation and / or winding up** ✂ **winding up by the court** *'winding up' means (a) winding up by the court, or (b) a creditors voluntary winding up* ✂ **winding-up order, petition, proceedings** ✂ **reference to winding up**

✎ **a relevant reorganisation or a relevant winding up** *'relevant reorganisation' or 'relevant winding up' means any voluntary arrangement, administration, winding up, or order referred to in regulation 19(1) to which this Part applies* ✂ **winding up of a UK credit institution** ✂ **creditors voluntary winding up** ✂ **directive winding-up proceedings, opening of a relevant winding up, resolution for voluntary winding up** *a resolution for voluntary winding up of a bank under section 84 of the Insolvency Act 1986 shall have no effect without the prior approval of the court* ✂ **reorganisation and / or winding up directive** ✂ **the Credit Institutions (Reorganisation and Winding up) Regulations 2004** ✂ **winding-up order + to be made**

📖 Possible equivalents: LIKWIDACJA, rozwiązanie (pl), LIQUIDAZIONE (it)

Y

YEAR (en)

(Adv) **once a year** *at least once a year each relevant authorised person must, in relation to every person in relation to whom an* approval *has been given on the application of the authorised person (a) consider whether there are any grounds on which a regulator could withdraw the approval under this section*

(Adj) **financial, subsequent year** *a report must be made as soon as is reasonably practicable after the end of each subsequent year*

(N) **period of 5 years** *the review must be completed during the period of 2 years beginning with the date on which the regulations come into force*

✎ **current / previous / relevant / subsequent financial year** *the 'relevant financial year', in relation to any day by reference to which the value of X falls to be calculated for the purposes of subsection (1) in relation to a building society, means the last financial year ending before that day* ✂ **year-end date** ✂ **imprisonment for a term not exceeding 5 years, period of 5 years beginning with a day** *the initial period is the period of 2 years beginning with the first day on which section 142G of FSMA 2000 is fully in force*

📖 Possible equivalents: ROK (pl), ANNO (it)

THE ITALIAN PART

A

AGENTE (it)

(N) **attività di agente, collaboratore di agente, controllo su agenti, elenco di agenti**

(V) **avvalersi di agenti** *per l'attività di consulenza e gestione dei crediti (...) le banche e gli intermediari finanziari possono avvalersi di agenti in attività finanziaria*

✎ **agente insediato in Italia** *la Banca d'Italia esercita il controllo sugli agenti insediati in Italia per conto di istituti di moneta elettronica o istituto di pagamento comunitari* **elenco degli agenti in attività finanziaria e dei mediatori creditizi** ✂ **agente + prestare servizi** *gli agenti che prestano esclusivamente i servizi di pagamento sono iscritti in una sezione speciale dell'elenco*

📖 Possible equivalents: agent, pośrednik, przedstawiciel (pl), agent (en)

ALBO (it)

Usually singular

(Adj) **iscritto nell'albo (all'albo)** ✂ **albo previsto (da)** *i servizi indicati nel comma 3, lettera c), possono essere svolti da banche o da intermediari finanziari iscritti nell'albo previsto dall'articolo 106 del decreto legislativo 1 settembre 1993, n. 385*

(N) **iscrizione nell'albo** *gli altri soggetti che intendono prestare i servizi indicati nel comma 3, lettera c), chiedono l'iscrizione nell'albo*

✎ **albo degli istituti di pagamento** *la Banca d Italia può esentare i soggetti iscritti nell'albo degli istituti di pagamento dall'applicazione di alcune delle disposizioni previste dal presente titolo* **albo dei mediatori creditizi, albo unico dei promotori finanziari** ✂ **gruppo bancario iscritto nell'albo, confidi/intermediari finanziari iscritti nell'albo** ✂ **iscrivere in un apposito albo / nel relativo albo** *gli intermediari finanziari possono prestare servizi di pagamento, a condizione che siano a ciò autorizzati ai sensi dell'articolo 114 novies, comma 4, e iscritti nel relativo albo*

📖 Possible equivalents: lista, spis, rejestr (pl), list, register, roll (en)

AMMINISTRAZIONE (it)

(Adj) **amministrazione straordinaria** ✂ **pubblica amministrazione**

(N) **amministrazione della banca, della società, dello stato** ✂ **attività di amministrazione, consiglio di amministrazione, dipendenti di un'amministrazione, irregolarità nell'amministrazione** *qualora risultino gravi irregolarità nell'amministrazione (…) la Banca d'Italia può disporre che uno o più commissari assumano i poteri di amministrazione dell'intermediario finanziario iscritto all'albo di cui all'articolo 106* **poteri di amministrazione, procedura di amministrazione**

✎ **organi di amministrazione e di controllo** *la nomina dei membri degli organi di amministrazione e controllo spetta esclusivamente ai competenti organi sociali* ✂ **le pubbliche amministrazioni statali, regionali e locali** *possono emettere moneta elettronica (…) la Banca centrale europea, le banche centrali comunitarie, lo Stato italiano e gli altri Stati comunitari, le pubbliche amministrazioni statali, regionali e locali, nonché Poste Italiane* ✂ **sottoposto all'amministrazione straordinaria** *quando la capogruppo sia sottoposta ad amministrazione straordinaria o a liquidazione coatta amministrativa, per l'azione revocatoria (…) è competente il tribunale nella cui circoscrizione ha la sede legale la capogruppo* ✂ **svolgere funzioni di amministrazione, direzione e controllo** *i soggetti che svolgono funzioni di amministrazione, direzione e controllo presso banche devono possedere i requisiti di professionalità, onorabilità e indipendenza*

📖 Possible equivalents: administracja, kierownictwo, ZARZĄD (pl), administration, government, MANAGEMENT (en)

AMMONTARE (it)

Usually singular

(Adj) **ammontare inferiore (a)** *ammontare non inferiore a quello determinato dalla Banca d'Italia* **ammontare minimo, modesto** *i soggetti diversi dalle banche (…) i quali, senza fine di lucro, raccolgono tradizionalmente in ambito locale somme di modesto ammontare* **superiore (a)** *l'ammontare non superiore a euro 25.000,00* ✂ **ammontare complessivo** *l'ammontare complessivo degli elementi dell'attivo* **ammontare determinato**

(N) **ammontare del capitale** *moltiplicando il valore così ottenuto per il numero delle azioni si ottiene il nuovo ammontare del capitale sociale espresso in euro* **ammontare del patrimonio**

✎ **ammontare delle differenze cambio**

📖 Possible equivalents: KWOTA, suma, WYSOKOŚĆ (pl), AMOUNT (en)

ANNO (it)

(Adj) **anno precedente** ✂ **inferiore, superiore a un anno** *in casi eccezionali la procedura può essere prorogata per un periodo non superiore a un anno*

(N) **periodo di due anni, reclusione da uno a due anni** ✂ **in carica un anno** *ciascun consigliere rimane in carica cinque anni ed e rieleggibile* ✂ **un anno dalla data di** *l'incarico (…) non può essere rinnovato se non siano decorsi almeno tre anni dalla data di cessazione del precedente*

(V) **anno + decorrere** *l'agente in attività finanziaria e il mediatore creditizio cancellati ai sensi del comma 1 possono richiedere una nuova iscrizione purché siano decorsi cinque anni dalla pubblicazione della cancellazione.*

(P) **fino a un anno, entro un anno, da uno a due anni**

✎ tempo non inferiore a un anno

📖 Possible equivalents: ROK (pl), YEAR (en)

APPLICAZIONE (it)

Always singular

(N) **ambito di applicazione, provvedimento di applicazione** *il provvedimento di applicazione delle altre sanzioni previste dal presente titolo è pubblicato per estratto sul bollettino previsto dall'articolo 8* ✂ **applicazione dell'articolo, del comma** *le differenze cambio rilevate in applicazione del comma 2 sono incluse nel conto economico* **applicazione del decreto, della disciplina, delle disposizioni, delle norme, delle sanzioni**

(V) **trovare applicazione** *le previsioni di cui ai commi 1, 2 e 3 trovano applicazione soltanto ai casi e nei modi ivi indicati*

(P) **in applicazione (di)** *la Banca d'Italia emette banconote in applicazione di quanto previsto dagli articoli 105A, paragrafo 1, del trattato e 16 dello statuto del SEBC* ✂ **ai fini dell'applicazione** *ai fini dell'applicazione della disciplina della liquidazione coatta amministrativa all'istituto di moneta elettronica, i detentori di moneta elettronica sono equiparati ai clienti aventi diritto alla restituzione di strumenti finanziari*

✎ **data prevista per l'applicazione** *la modifica si intende approvata ove il cliente non receda, senza spese, dal contratto entro la data prevista per la sua applicazione* ✂ **l'applicazione resta ferma** *nei confronti dei soggetti inclusi nell'ambito della vigilanza consolidata resta ferma l'applicazione di norme specifiche in tema di controlli e di vigilanza*

📖 Possible equivalents: stosowanie, zastosowanie (pl), application, implementation (en)

ARTICOLO (it)

(Adj) **corrispondente, medesimo articolo** *si applicano le disposizioni dell'articolo 58 (…) anche quando il cessionario non sia una banca o uno degli altri soggetti previsti dal comma 7 del medesimo articolo* **presente, seguente articolo**

(N) **articolo 1, paragrafo 1** *quest'ultima opzione presenta un campo di applicazione più ristretto di quello consentito dall'articolo 39, paragrafo 1, della direttiva n. 86/635* ✂ **articolo 1 della Costituzione, del trattato** ✂ **attuazione, disposizione,**

disposto dell'articolo *alle medesime cessioni può altresì applicarsi, su espressa volontà delle parti, il disposto dell'articolo 5* **violazione dell'articolo, capoverso articolo ✂ albo, autorizzazione, disposizione, elenco, esame, intermediario, previsione, soggetto di cui all'articolo 1**

(V) **articolo + applicare** *alle cessioni effettuate nell'ambito di operazioni di cartolarizzazione non si applicano gli articoli 69 e 70 del regio decreto 18 novembre 1923, n. 2440* **articolo + fissare** *il presente articolo dà attuazione all'articolo 8 della legge delega e fissa i principi generali relativi all'adozione dell'euro quale moneta di conto* ✂ **articolo + essere abrogato, inserito, sostituito ✂ essere aggiunti all'articolo, essere definiti dall'articolo, essere indicati nell'/dall'/all'articolo, essere previsti dall'articolo, essere richiamati dall'articolo** *la violazione delle norme di cui al comma 1, in quanto richiamate dall'articolo 110, è punita con la sanzione amministrativa pecuniaria*

(P) **di cui all'articolo 1 ✂ a norma dell'articolo 1** *le informazioni pubblicizzate non costituiscono offerta al pubblico a norma dell'articolo 1336 del codice civile* **in deroga all'articolo 1** *il pagatore, in deroga all'articolo 17, non può revocare l'ordine di pagamento dopo averlo trasmesso al beneficiario* ✂ **visto l'articolo 1**

✎ **articolo 1, comma 1, lettera a) ✂ articolo 1 del codice civile, del codice penale, del decreto legislativo, della legge delega, della legge fallimentare, del regio decreto, del testo unico ✂ inosservanza delle norme contenute nell'articolo, entrata in vigore dell'articolo ✂ fatta eccezione per articolo 1, salvo quanto previsto dall/nell'articolo 1**

✎ *(VERBAL)* **articolo + dare attuazione a** *il presente articolo dà attuazione, per le imprese di assicurazione, all'articolo 9 della legge delega* ✂ **essere adottati, autorizzati, emanati ai sensi dell'articolo** *il Ministro dell'economia e delle finanze, sentita la Banca d'Italia, determina con regolamento emanato ai sensi dell'articolo 17, comma 3 (…) i requisiti di onorabilità dei titolari delle partecipazioni indicate all'articolo 19 (4)* ✂ **resta fermo quanto previsto / disposto dall'articolo 1 ✂ articolo si applica in quanto compatibile** *Il presente articolo si applica, in quanto compatibile, alle succursali italiane di banche comunitarie o extracomunitarie*

📖 Possible equivalents: artykuł (pl), ARTICLE (en)

ASSEGNO (it)

(Adj) **assegni circolari** *il titolare del conto corrente ha la disponibilità economica delle somme relative agli assegni circolari o bancari versati sul suo conto, rispettivamente emessi da o tratti su una banca insediata in Italia, entro i quattro giorni lavorativi successivi al versamento* **assegni bancari ✂ assegni tratti (su), assegni emessi (da)**

(N) **incasso di assegni** *il CICR può stabilire termini inferiori a quelli previsti nei commi 1 e 1-bis in relazione all'evoluzione delle procedure telematiche disponibili per la gestione del servizio di incasso degli assegni*

✎ **assegni tratti su una banca** *a decorrere dal 1° novembre 2009, la data di valuta per il beneficiario di assegni circolari e bancari tratti su una banca insediata in Italia non può superare, rispettivamente, uno e tre giorni lavorativi successivi alla data del versamento* ✂ **incasso di assegni bancari / circolari**

📖 Possible equivalents: czek (pl), cheque, check (en)

ATTIVITÀ (it)

(Adj) **attività abusiva, bancaria, commerciale, finanziaria, imprenditoriale, iniziale, necessaria per, professionale ✂ attività accessorie, connesse** *gli agenti in attività finanziaria possono svolgere esclusivamente l'attività indicata nel presente comma, nonché attività connesse o strumentali* **attività diverse da, strumentali ✂ relative, seguenti attività**

(N) **esercizio dell'attività, restrizione delle attività, riduzione delle attività, riserva di attività** *fatte salve le riserve di attività previste dalla legge, le fondazioni e le associazioni per la prevenzione del fenomeno dell'usura esercitano le altre attività previste dallo statuto* **svolgimento delle attività, volume di attività** *la Banca d'Italia stabilisce, con proprio provvedimento, gli elementi da prendere in considerazione per il calcolo del volume di attività finanziaria* ✂ **attività di consulenza, di vigilanza ✂ attività di cui all'articolo 1**

(V) **esercitare, svolgere attività ✂ regolare attività ✂ attività +essere esternalizzate a** *la Banca d'Italia può effettuare ispezioni presso gli istituti di moneta elettronica, i loro agenti o i soggetti a cui sono esternalizzate attività*

✎ **attività di assunzione di partecipazioni, attività di concessione di finanziamenti** *l'esercizio nei confronti del pubblico dell'attività di concessione di finanziamenti sotto qualsiasi forma è riservato agli intermediari finanziari autorizzati, iscritti in un apposito albo* **attività di emissione di moneta elettronica, attività di intermediazione mobiliare, attività di mediatore creditizio, di mediazione creditizia, attività di prestazione dei servizi di pagamento, attività di raccolta del risparmio** ✂ **attività ai sensi dell'articolo 1, indicata nell'articolo 1, prevista dall'articolo 1** ✂ **attività riservata ai sensi di legge** *i soggetti ivi indicati deliberano la liquidazione della società ovvero modificano il proprio oggetto sociale, eliminando il riferimento ad attività riservate ai sensi di legge* ✂ **agente in attività finanziaria, agenzia in attività finanziaria** *l'esercizio di agenzia in attività finanziaria comporta gli obblighi di contribuzione previdenziale previsti per i soggetti di cui all'articolo 1742 del codice civile* ✂ **esercizio abusivo dell'attività, legittimazione allo svolgimento dell'attività** ✂ **continuare a svolgere la propria attività, disporre la riduzione delle attività** *la Banca d'Italia può imporre agli intermediari il divieto di intraprendere nuove operazioni e disporre la riduzione delle attività* **iniziare l'esercizio dell' attività**

📖 Possible equivalents: CZYNNOŚĆ, DZIAŁALNOŚĆ (pl), ACTIVITY, BUSINESS, SERVICE (en)

ATTO (it)

(Adj) **atto costitutivo, normativo**

(N) **atto di surrogazione** *la quietanza rilasciata dal finanziatore originario e il contratto stipulato con il creditore surrogato sono forniti al notaio per essere prodotti unitamente all'atto di surrogazione* **atti di cui all'art. 1**

(V) **adottare un atto** *inosservanza del divieto, la deliberazione o il diverso atto, adottati con il voto o il contributo determinanti delle partecipazioni previste dal comma 1*

✎ **esibizione di documenti e atti, trasmissione di atti e documenti** ✂ **inserire un atto nella Raccolta ufficiale degli atti normativi della Repubblica italiana, ritenere necessari documenti e atti** *la Banca d'Italia può effettuare ispezioni presso gli istituti di moneta elettronica, i loro agenti o i soggetti a cui sono esternalizzate attività e richiedere a essi l'esibizione di documenti e gli atti che ritenga necessari*

Possible equivalents: akt, document, wdrażanie (pl), ACT, DOCUMENT, INSTRUMENT (en)

ATTUAZIONE (it)

Only singular

(N) **attuazione dell'articolo, della direttiva** *decreto legislativo 13 agosto 2010, n. 141, recante attuazione della direttiva 2008/48/CE* **attuazione della riforma, del titolo ✂ disciplina di attuazione** *fino al 31 dicembre 2013 la Banca d'Italia esercita il controllo sui mediatori creditizi per verificare l'osservanza delle disposizioni di cui al comma 1 e della relativa disciplina di attuazione* **disposizioni di attuazione, misure di attuazione, modalità di attuazione, norme di attuazione**

(P) **fino all'attuazione** *sono abrogati i commi 4, 5 e 6 dell'articolo 4 (…); tuttavia essi continuano a essere applicati fino all'attuazione dell'articolo 155, comma 5, del presente decreto legislativo*

(V) **dare attuazione a** *il presente articolo dà attuazione all'articolo 5 della legge delega*

✎ **decreto legislativo recante attuazione della direttiva ✂ entrata in vigore delle disposizioni di attuazione** *con riferimento agli istituti di pagamento (…) l'abrogazione ha effetto a decorrere dalla data di entrata in vigore delle disposizioni di attuazione dell'articolo 128-quater, comma 6*

Possible equivalents: WYKONANIE, zrealizowanie (pl), implementation (en)

AUTORITÀ (it)

(Adj) **autorità competente, creditizia, europea, giudiziaria, monetaria, pubblica**

(N) **autorità dello stato** *la Banca d'Italia notifica all'autorità competente dello Stato comunitario ospitante l'intenzione di effettuare ispezioni sul territorio di quest'ultimo* **autorità di vigilanza ✂ poteri delle autorità ✂ collaborazione tra autorità**

(V) **autorità + esercitare** *le autorità creditizie esercitano i poteri loro attribuiti in armonia con le disposizioni dell'Unione europea* **autorità + provvedere a** *le Autorità competenti provvedono all'emanazione delle disposizioni attuative* ✂ **informare le autorità (di)**

(P) **da parte dell'autorità** *la trasmissione di informazioni all'Organismo per le suddette finalità non costituisce violazione del segreto d'ufficio da parte delle Autorità di vigilanza.*

✎ **autorità garante della concorrenza e del mercato** ✂ **agire in veste di pubblica autorità, dare comunicazione all'autorità** *la Banca d'Italia può ordinare alla banca di porre termine a tali irregolarità, dandone comunicazione all'autorità competente dello Stato membro in cui la banca ha sede legale*

📖 Possible equivalents: organ, władza (pl), AUTHORITY, INSTITUTION (en)

AUTORIZZAZIONE (it)

Usually singular

(Adj) **previa autorizzazione** *gli istituti di moneta elettronica italiani possono operare (...) in uno Stato extracomunitario, anche senza stabilirvi succursali, previa autorizzazione della Banca d'Italia*

(N) **istanza, procedura, revoca di autorizzazione** *il Ministro dell'economia e delle finanze (2), su proposta della Banca d'Italia, può disporre con decreto la revoca dell'autorizzazione all'attività bancaria* ✂ **autotizzazione di cui all'articolo 1**

(V) **negare l'autorizzazione** *la Banca d'Italia nega l'autorizzazione quando dalla verifica delle condizioni indicate nel comma 1 non risulti garantita la sana e prudente gestione* ✂ **autorizzazione + essere rilasciata** *l'autorizzazione non può essere rilasciata in caso di fondato sospetto che l'acquisizione sia connessa ad operazioni di riciclaggio o di finanziamento del terrorismo.*

✎ **autotizzazione all'attività bancaria, autotizzazione della Banca d'Italia** ✂ **autorizzazione prevista dall'articolo 1** ✂ **presentare istanza di autorizzazione** *le società fiduciarie (...) presentano istanza di autorizzazione ai fini dell'iscrizione alla sezione separata dell'albo di cui all'articolo 106*

📖 Possible equivalents: pozwolenie, upoważnienie, ZEZWOLENIE, ZGODA (pl), APPROVAL, authorisation, consent, permission (en)

B

BANCA (it)

(Adj) **banca centrale, cooperativa, extracomunitaria, italiana** ✂ **singola banca** *la Banca d'Italia può autorizzare, per periodi determinati, le singole banche di credito cooperativo a una operatività prevalente a favore di soggetti diversi dai soci* ✂ **banche comunitarie, popolari** ✂ **banche costituite** *le banche di credito cooperativo costituite anteriormente al 1° gennaio 1993 possono mantenere l'originaria denominazione purché integrata dall'espressione «credito cooperativo»* **banche operanti (in)**

(N) **Banca d'Italia** ✂ **gestione di una banca, partecipazioni in banche** *la Banca d'Italia può richiedere alle banche ed alle società ed agli enti di qualsiasi natura che possiedono partecipazioni nelle banche medesime l'indicazione nominativa dei titolari delle partecipazioni* **statuto di una banca, succursali di una banca** ✂ **banca dati**

(V) **banca + autorizzare** *la Banca d'Italia autorizza all'emissione di moneta elettronica soggetti che esercitino anche altre attività imprenditoriali* **banca + comunicare, banca + convocare** *La Banca d'Italia può a) convocare gli amministratori, i sindaci e i dirigenti degli istituti di moneta elettronica per esaminare la situazione degli stessi* **banca + determinare, disporre, impartire, imporre, procedere (a), richiedere, stabilire** *le banche italiane possono stabilire succursali nel territorio della Repubblica e degli altri Stati comunitari* ✂ **comunicare qualcosa alla banca, essere riservati a una banca** *l'esercizio dell'attività bancaria da parte di società cooperative è riservato alle banche popolari e alle banche di credito cooperativo*

(P) **da parte di una banca** *la Banca d'Italia, in conformità delle deliberazioni del CICR, disciplina l'emissione da parte delle banche delle obbligazioni non convertibili o convertibili in titoli* **presso una banca**

✏ *(NOMINAL)* **una banca o un intermediario finanziario, banche e società finanziarie, soggetti diverse dalle banche ✂ banca a carattere regionale, banche autorizzate in Italia** *«banche autorizzate in Italia»: le banche italiane e le succursali in Italia di banche extracomunitarie* **Banca centrale europea, banche centrali nazionali, banche di credito cooperativo, banca insediata in Italia ✂ Sistema europeo di banche centrali, statuto del Sistema europeo di banche centrali ✂ assegni tratti su una banca, istruzioni emanate / impartite dalla Banca d'Italia ✂ Governatore della Banca d'Italia**

✏ *(VERBAL)* **banca + dettare disposizioni attuative, disciplinare la procedura** *La Banca d'Italia disciplina la procedura di autorizzazione, i casi di revoca, nonché di decadenza, quando l'intermediario autorizzato non abbia iniziato l'esercizio dell'attività* **banca + effettuare ispezioni (presso), emanare disposizioni di carattere generale, emanare istruzioni, esercitare i poteri / la vigilanza, negare autorizzazione**

✏ *(PREPOSITIONAL)* **dopo aver informato la Banca d'Italia, nel rispetto delle procedure fissate dalla Banca d'Italia, nel rispetto delle / secondo le modalità stabilite dalla Banca d'Italia, previa autorizzazione della Banca d'Italia** *Le banche italiane possono stabilire succursali in uno Stato extracomunitario previa autorizzazione della Banca d'Italia* **sentita la Banca d'Italia** *Il Ministro dell'economia e delle finanze, sentita la Banca d'Italia, specifica il contenuto delle attività indicate nel comma 1* **su proposta della Banca d'Italia**

📖 Possible equivalents: BANK (pl), BANK (en)

BENEFICIARIO (it)

Usually singular

(Adj) **disposto dal beneficiario** *quando tutte le condizioni previste dal contratto quadro sono soddisfatte, il prestatore di servizi di pagamento del pagatore non può rifiutare di eseguire un ordine di pagamento autorizzato, indipendentemente dal fatto che tale ordine sia disposto dal pagatore o dal beneficiario o per il tramite di quest'ultimo*

(N) **il pagatore e/o il beneficiario** *se un'operazione di pagamento non comporta conversioni valutarie da parte del prestatore di servizi di pagamento del pagatore, il pagatore e il beneficiario sostengono ciascuno le spese applicate dal rispettivo prestatore di servizi di pagamento*

(P) **a disposizione del beneficiario, su iniziativa del beneficiario** *nel caso in cui un'operazione di pagamento autorizzata disposta su iniziativa del beneficiario o per il suo tramite sia già stata eseguita, il pagatore ha diritto al rimborso dell'importo trasferito*

✏ **prestatore di servizi di pagamento del beneficiario** *il prestatore di servizi di pagamento del beneficiario assicura che l'importo dell'operazione di pagamento sia a disposizione del beneficiario non appena tale importo è accreditato sul conto del prestatore medesimo* ✂ **operazione di pagamento disposta su iniziativa del beneficiario o per il suo tramite**

📖 Possible equivalents: beneficjent, odbiorca, uprawniony (pl), beneficiary, owner, recipient, payee (en)

BILANCIO (it)

(Adj) **bilancio approvato, consolidato** ✂ **ultimo bilancio**

(N) **bilancio d'esercizio** *gli amministratori redigono un separato rendiconto per il patrimonio destinato, da allegare al bilancio d'esercizio dell'istituto di pagamento (1)* **bilancio d'impresa, bilancio dello Stato** ✂ **redazione del bilancio** *sono tenuti alla redazione del bilancio consolidato gli enti creditizi e finanziari che sono imprese capogruppo* **relazione al bilancio, revisione del bilancio**

(V) **pubblicare, redigere un bilancio, trasmettere i bilanci** *le banche (...) trasmettono anche i bilanci con le modalità e nei termini stabiliti dalla Banca d'Italia* ✂ **bilancio + riferirsi (a)**

✏ **bilancio della società estera controllata, bilancio della società italiana** *il bilancio della società estera controllata, allegato al bilancio della società italiana ai sensi del comma 1, è sottoposto a revisione ai sensi dell'articolo 165 da parte della società incaricata della revisione del bilancio della società italiana;* ✂ **in bilancio e 'fuori bilancio', le operazioni 'fuori bilancio'** *Gli elementi dell'attivo e del passivo* *e le operazioni 'fuori bilancio' nonché i proventi e gli oneri delle imprese incluse nel consolidamento sono ripresi integralmente nel bilancio consolidato* ✂ **nota integrativa di bilancio** *Nella nota integrativa del bilancio sono separatamente illustrati i criteri di rilevazione e di trattamento (…) l'ammontare complessivo delle differenze cambio positive e negative e gli importi iscritti nel conto economico e nello stato patrimoniale* **data di riferimento del bilancio** ✂ **Ministro del tesoro, del bilancio e della programmazione economica**

📖 Possible equivalents: bilans, budżet (pl), accounts, balance sheet, budget, (financial) statement (en)

C

CAMBIO (it)

(N) **rischio di cambio** *l'articolo si applica ai bilanci d'impresa redatti a far tempo da quelli chiusi o in corso al 31 dicembre 1998 e, a differenza dell'articolo 16, non riguarda tutte le imprese ma solo quelle che corrono rischi di cambio in una delle valute aderenti all'euro* **tasso di cambio** ✂ **intermediazione in cambi** *l'esercizio nei confronti del pubblico delle attività di assunzione di partecipazioni (…) e di intermediazione in cambi è riservato a intermediari finanziari iscritti in un apposito elenco tenuto dall'UIC* ✂ **differenze cambio** *se l'elemento monetario viene incassato, pagato o ceduto, la differenza cambio residua va per intero inclusa nel conto economico nel quale l'incasso, il pagamento o la cessione avvengono*

✎ **differenza cambio positiva e negativa, trattamento delle differenze cambio** ✂ **tassi di interesse o di cambio, tasso di cambio di riferimento** *'tasso di cambio di riferimento': il tasso di cambio che è utilizzato come base per calcolare un cambio valuta e che è reso disponibile dal fornitore di servizi di pagamento o proviene da una fonte accessibile al pubblico* ✂ **andamento dei tassi di cambio delle valute aderenti** *gli elementi monetari denominati nelle valute aderenti o comunque variabili in funzione dell'andamento dei tassi di cambio delle valute aderenti sono tradotti nella moneta di conto, anche ai fini della determinazione del reddito d'impresa* ✂ **Ufficio italiano dei cambi**

📖 Possible equivalents: kurs wymiany, kurs przeliczeniowy, wymiana (walut) (pl), exchange, exchange rate (en)

CAPITALE (it)

Usually singular

(Adj) **capitale minimo** *la lettera c) modifica rispettivamente i commi 1, 2 e 3 dell'articolo 2474 dei codice civile riguardante le società a responsabilità limitata il cui capitale minimo viene fissato in diecimila euro* **capitale sociale, versato**

(N) **riduzione del capitale** *le riduzioni del capitale sociale che vengono a determinarsi ai sensi del presente articolo configurano una fattispecie diversa rispetto a quelle 'canoniche' disciplinate dall'articolo 2445 del codice civile che tratta della riduzione del capitale esuberante* ✂ **società di capitali**

✎ **capitale espresso in euro, conversione in euro del capitale, le azioni e il capitale sociale** *se l'arrotondamento avviene per eccesso, si procede all'aumento del valore nominale delle azioni e del capitale sociale mediante l'utilizzo delle riserve* ✂ **capitale versato + essere di ammontare non inferiore (a)**

📖 Possible equivalents: kapitał (pl), capital (en)

CAPO (it)

Usually singular

(Adj) **presente capo** ✂ **disciplinato, previsto dal capo I** *le disposizioni del presente capo non si applicano ai servizi di pagamento disciplinati dal capo II-bis a meno che non siano espressamente richiamate da quest'ultimo*

(N) **disposizioni del capo I**

(P) **ai sensi del capo I** *la Banca d'Italia adotta i provvedimenti previsti dal presente capo avendo riguardo, per i servizi di pagamento regolati in conto corrente (…), alle disposizioni previste ai sensi del capo I* **di cui al capo I, di cui al presente capo**

(V) **capo + essere inserito**

✎ **libro I, titolo I, capo I, sezione I (del codice penale)** *salve le altre pene accessorie di cui al libro I, titolo II, capo III, del codice penale, la condanna importa l'inabilitazione all'esercizio di un'impresa commerciale* **parte I, titolo I, capo I** ✂ **disposizioni / norme del presente capo + applicarsi (a)**

📖 Possible equivalents: ROZDZIAŁ (pl), chapter (en)

CASO (it)

(Adv) **fuori del caso** *Chiunque, fuori dei casi previsti dall'articolo 643, si fa dare o promettere (…) in corrispettivo di una prestazione di denaro o di altra utilità, interessi o altri vantaggi usurari, è punito con la reclusione da uno a sei anni*

(N) **in caso di cessione, inosservanza (di), offerta, violazione** ✂ **caso di necessità, di urgenza** ✂ **casi di revoca** *la Banca d'Italia disciplina la procedura di autorizzazione, i casi di revoca e le ipotesi di decadenza quando l'istituto autorizzato non abbia iniziato l'esercizio dell'attività* ✂ **seguenti casi** *le disposizioni del presente capo si applicano ai contratti di credito comunque denominati, a eccezione dei seguenti casi*

(V) **applicarsi nel caso di** *il presente articolo non si applica nel caso di rettifica di operazioni di pagamento non autorizzate o eseguite in modo inesatto*

(P) **in ogni caso** *in ogni caso, l'indennizzo non può superare l'importo degli interessi che il consumatore avrebbe pagato per la vita residua del contratto* **in quest'ultimo caso, in tal(e) caso, nel caso di cui (a)** *nel caso di cui all'articolo 15, comma 2, l'utilizzatore puà revocare un ordine di pagamento non oltre la fine della giornata operativa precedente il giorno concordato* ✂ **in casi eccezionali** *se, in casi eccezionali, l'applicazione di una disposizione degli articoli seguenti è incompatibile con la rappresentazione veritiera e corretta, la disposizione non deve essere applicata*

✏ **nei casi e alle condizioni ivi previsti** *le disposizioni di cui al presente articolo (…) trovano applicazione, nei casi e alle condizioni ivi previsti, anche per i finanziamenti concessi da enti di previdenza obbligatoria ai loro iscritti* **nei casi previsti dall'articolo 1 / dal comma 1**

📖 Possible equivalents: PRZYPADEK, sytuacja (pl), case, CIRCUMSTANCES, situation (en)

CLIENTE (it)

(Agg) **singoli clienti ✂ favorevole, sfavorevole per il cliente** *le variazioni contrattuali per le quali non siano state osservate le prescrizioni del presente articolo sono inefficaci, se sfavorevoli per il cliente*

(N) **rapporti con i clienti**

(P) **a carico del cliente** *i contratti di apertura di credito possono prevedere, quali unici oneri a carico del cliente, una commissione onnicomprensiva, calcolata in maniera proporzionale rispetto alla somma messa a disposizione del cliente e alla durata dell'affidamento, e un tasso di interesse debitore sulle somme prelevate* **da parte del cliente** *in mancanza di opposizione scritta da parte del cliente, gli estratti conto e le altre comunicazioni periodiche alla clientela si intendono approvati trascorsi sessanta giorni dal ricevimento.*

✎ **clienti aventi diritto alla restituzione di strumenti finanziari** *i clienti aventi diritto alla restituzione degli strumenti finanziari relativi ai servizi previsti dal decreto legislativo 24 febbraio 1998, n. 58 sono iscritti in apposita e separata sezione dello stato passivo* ✂ **cliente + avere diritto ✂ pregiudicare per il cliente il ricorso a ogni altro mezzo di tutela** *le disposizioni di cui ai commi 1 e 2 non pregiudicano per il cliente il ricorso a ogni altro mezzo di tutela previsto dall'ordinamento.*

📖 Possible equivalents: CLIENT, consumer, customer (en), KLIENT (pl)

CODICE (it)

Usually singular

(Adj) **codice civile, penale**

(N) **codice di comportamento** *le società di cui al presente capo diffondono annualmente (…) informazioni sull'adesione a codici di comportamento promossi da società di gestione di mercati regolamentati o da associazioni di categoria degli operatori* **Codice del consumo** *salvo quanto previsto dai commi 1 e 2, ai contratti disciplinati dal presente capo non si applicano gli articoli 64, (…) e 67-ter decies del Codice del consumo* ✂ **articolo 1 del codice, disposizioni del codice**

✎ **codice di procedura civile ✂ articolo 1, primo comma, del codice civile ✂ il primo comma dell'articolo 1 del codice civile ✂ articolo 1 e seguenti**

del codice civile *gli oggetti non riscattati entro trenta giorni dalla scadenza del prestito sono venduti all'asta pubblica secondo le norme contenute negli articoli 529 e seguenti del codice di procedura civile* ✂ **libro I, titolo I, capo I, del codice penale** ✂ **a norma dell'articolo 1 del codice civile, ai sensi dell'articolo 1 del codice civile, in deroga all'articolo 1 del codice civile** *le operazioni di cui ai commi da 1 a 4 sono deliberate dagli amministratori in deroga agli articoli 2365 e 2376 del codice civile* ✂ **seguenti modificazioni + essere apportate al codice civile** *al codice civile sono apportate le seguenti modificazioni*

Possible equivalents: kodeks (pl), code (en)

COMMA (it)

(Adj) **medesimo comma** ✂ **presente, seguente comma** ✂ **comma precedente** ✂ **comma abrogato (da), modificato (da), sostituito (da)**

(N) **periodo del comma 1** *ai soggetti iscritti nella sezione speciale non si applicano il secondo periodo del comma 1 e il comma 4* ✂ **adempimenti di cui al comma 1** *La banca deve provvedere agli adempimenti di cui al comma 6 entro il termine di novanta giorni dalla data di ricevimento della richiesta di suddivisione del finanziamento in quote* **attività, disposizioni, società di cui al comma 1** ✂ **comma 1 del decreto, della legge**

(V) **comma + applicarsi, chiarire, fissare** *il comma fissa il principio che le imprese sono libere di adottare l'euro quale moneta di conto già a partire dal 1 gennaio 1999* **comma + precisare, prescrivere** *il comma 1 prescrive che i titoli obbligazionari emessi dalle regioni possano essere ridenominati se rispondono alle caratteristiche richieste per gli emittenti privati;* ✂ **comma + essere aggiunto, essere sostituito (da)**

(P) **ad eccezione del comma 1** *il D.lgs. 13 agosto 2010, n. 141 ha disposto (...) l'abrogazione del presente articolo, ad eccezione del comma 9* **ai sensi del comma 1, di cui al comma 1 (dell'articolo 1), in deroga al comma 1** *in deroga al comma 2, gli statuti possono fissare al 3 per cento la partecipazione delle fondazioni di origine bancaria di cui al decreto legislativo 17 maggio 1999, n. 153*

(NOMINAL) **comma 1 dell'articolo 1 del codice civile** ✂ **comma (così) modificato / sostituito dall'art. 1, comma inserito dall'art. 1** ✂ **comma abrogato dall'art. 1, comma 1, n. 1), dell'allegato 1 al D.Lgs.** ✂ **condizioni/disposizioni/materie indicate nel comma 1, regolamento adottato ai sensi del comma 1** *con il*

regolamento adottato ai sensi del comma 1, la CONSOB individua altresì i criteri per stabilire l'appartenenza di un'entità alla rete di una società di revisione **scandenza del termine indicato al comma 1, termine previsto dal comma 1** *i commissari, trascorso il termine previsto dal comma 5 e non oltre i trenta giorni successivi, presentano alla Banca d'Itali (...) l'elenco dei creditori ammessi e delle somme riconosciute a ciascuno*

✎ **art. 1, comma 1, capoverso articolo; articolo 1, comma 1 del decreto legislativo / del testo unico** *all'articolo 4, comma 2, capoverso articolo 117, i commi 5, 6 e 7 sono rinumerati, rispettivamente, come commi 6, 7 e 8* ✂ **esentato ai sensi del comma 1** *gli istituti di moneta elettronica esentati ai sensi del comma 1 non beneficiano delle disposizioni per il mutuo riconoscimento* **modificato / previsto dall'art. 1, comma 1, lettera a)** ✂ **come definito dall'articolo 1, comma 1, lettera a)** *imprese che esercitano, in via esclusiva o principale, attività strumentale come definita dall'art. 59, comma 1, lettera c)* **quanto previsto al comma 1** ✂ **comma 1 è sostituito dal seguente; dopo il comma 1 è aggiunto / inserito il seguente** ✂ **disporre (con l'art. 1, comma 1)** *il D.Lgs. 14 dicembre 2010, n. 218 ha disposto (con l'art. 6, comma 2) che 'All'articolo 9, comma 8, capoverso articolo 199, comma 1, dopo le parole: '23 luglio', la parola: '1966' e' sostituita dalla seguente: '1996''*

📖 Possible equivalents: ustęp (pl), PARAGRAPH (en)

COMUNICAZIONE (it)

(Adj) **comunicazione periodica** ✂ **comunicazioni sociali** ✂ **comunicazioni ricevute** ✂ **false comunicazioni**

(N) **invio, modalità della comunicazione, obblighi di comunicazione** *la violazione degli obblighi di comunicazione previsti dall'articolo 20, comma 2, nonché la violazione delle disposizioni dell'articolo 24 (...) sono punite con la sanzione amministrativa pecuniaria da 25.820 a 258.225 euro* **strumenti di comunicazione** ✂ **comunicazione all'autorità, comunicazione del provvedimento** *entro sessanta giorni dalla comunicazione del provvedimento di revoca, l'intermediario finanziario comunica alla Banca d'Italia il programma di liquidazione della società* ✂ **informazioni e/o comunicazioni** *le banche e gli intermediari finanziari non possono addebitare al cliente spese, comunque denominate, inerenti alle informazioni e alle comunicazioni previste ai sensi di legge trasmesse con strumenti di comunicazione telematica* ✂ **comunicazione di cui al comma 1**

(V) **chiedere, dare, richiedere comunicazione** *le banche possono intraprendere l'esercizio del credito su pegno di cose mobili (...) dotandosi delle necessarie strutture e dandone comunicazione alla Banca d'Italia*

(P) **entro due giorni dalla comunicazione**

✎ **Comunicazione alla Banca d'Italia, comunicazioni periodiche alla clientela, comunicazioni previste dall'articolo 1, comunicazione rivolta al pubblico** *l'uso, nella denominazione o in qualsivoglia segno distintivo o comunicazione rivolta al pubblico, delle parole «banca», «banco», «credito», «risparmio» ovvero di altre parole o locuzioni, anche in lingua straniera, idonee a trarre in inganno sulla legittimazione allo svolgimento dell'attività bancaria è vietato a soggetti diversi dalle banche* ✂ **chiedere la comunicazione di dati e notizie**

📖 Possible equivalents: INFORMACJA, komunikacja, wiadomość, zawiadomienie (pl) advice, communication, INFORMATION, NOTICE (en)

CONDIZIONE (it)

(Adj) **condizioni contrattuali, favorevoli** ✂ **condizioni previste (da), stabilite (da)** ✂ **seguenti condizioni**

(N) **condizione di reciprocità** *a condizione di reciprocità, la Banca d'Italia può concordare con le autorità competenti degli Stati extracomunitari modalità per l'ispezione di succursali di banche insediate nei rispettivi territori* **condizioni del rimborso** ✂ **trasparenza, variazione delle condizioni** *la Banca d'Italia stabilisce le procedure che i soggetti di cui al comma 1 seguono per comunicare ogni variazione delle condizioni di cui al comma 1* **verifica delle condizioni** ✂ **modalità e condizioni**

(V) **condizioni + ricorrere** *le disposizioni dell'articolo 15, comma 1, e dell'articolo 16, comma 1 si applicano anche alle società finanziarie con sede legale in Italia sottoposte a forme di vigilanza prudenziale, quando (...) ricorrono le condizioni stabilite dalla Banca d'Italia.*

(P) **condizione per** *l'autorizzazione può essere sospesa o revocata se vengono meno o si modificano i presupposti e le condizioni per il suo rilascio*

✎ **condizioni di cui all'articolo 1/ al comma 1** ✂ **modifica unilaterale delle condizioni contrattuali** *qualunque modifica unilaterale delle condizioni contrattuali deve essere comunicata espressamente al cliente* **verifica delle condizioni indicate in comma 1** *la Banca d'Italia nega l'autorizzazione quando dalla verifica delle condizioni indicate nel comma 1 non risulti garantita la sana e prudente gestione* ✂ **ricorrere delle seguenti condizioni** *la Banca d'Italia autorizza gli intermediari finanziari ad esercitare la propria attività al ricorrere delle seguenti condizioni* ✂ **nei casi e alle condizioni ivi previsti** *le disposizioni di cui al presente articolo e quelle contenute nell'articolo 40-bis trovano applicazione, nei casi e alle condizioni ivi previsti, anche per i finanziamenti concessi da enti di previdenza obbligatoria ai loro iscritti* ✂ **essere subordinato al ricorrere delle condizioni**

📖 Possible equivalents: CONDITION, REQUIREMENT, TERM (en), WARUNEK (pl)

CONSIGLIO (it)

Only singular

(Adj) **Consiglio superiore** *le attribuzioni del Consiglio superiore della Banca d'Italia in materia di banconote continuano a essere esercitate, nel rispetto di quanto previsto dal comma 1*

(N) **consiglio di amministrazione, gestione, sorveglianza** ✂ **Consiglio dei Ministri** ✂ **componente del consiglio** *il momento della nomina dei componenti del consiglio di amministrazione e prima dell'accettazione dell'incarico, sono resi noti all'assemblea gli incarichi di amministrazione e di controllo da essi ricoperti presso altre società* **membro del Consiglio** ✂ **deliberazione del Consiglio** ✂ **camera di consiglio** *il tribunale decide con sentenza in camera di consiglio sulla proposta di concordato, tenendo conto delle opposizioni e del parere su queste ultime reso dalla Banca d'Italia.*

✎ **proposta del Presidente del Consiglio dei Ministri** *la nomina del governatore è disposta con decreto del Presidente della Repubblica, su proposta del Presidente del Consiglio dei ministri, previa deliberazione del Consiglio dei ministri* ✂ **direttiva del Parlamento europeo e del Consiglio** ✂ **la preliminare deliberazione del Consiglio dei Ministri, adottata nella riunione del 1 gennaio 2000**

📖 Possible equivalents: KOMISJA, RADA, ZARZĄD (pl), BOARD, COMMITTEE, council (en)

CONSUMATORE (it)

(N) **recesso del consumatore**

(V) **fornire qualcosa al consumatore** *il finanziatore o l'intermediario del credito forniscono al consumatore il modulo di cui al comma 2 immediatamente dopo la conclusione del contratto di credito* ✂ **consumatore + essere informati** *il consumatore è informato della cessione del credito, a meno che il cedente, in accordo con il cessionario, continui a gestire il credito nei confronti del consumatore*

(P) **da parte del consumatore** *'sconfinamento' indica l'utilizzo da parte del consumatore di fondi concessi dal finanziatore in eccedenza rispetto al saldo del conto corrente in assenza di apertura di credito ovvero rispetto all'importo dell'apertura di credito concessa*

✎ **contratti di credito ai consumatori** *attuazione della direttiva 2008/48/CE relativa ai contratti di credito ai consumatori* **informazioni fornite dal consumatore** ✂ **consumatore + recedere dal contratto di credito, finanziatore + informare il consumatore** *se il rifiuto della domanda di credito si basa sulle informazioni presenti in una banca dati, il finanziatore informa il consumatore immediatamente e gratuitamente del risultato della consultazione e degli estremi della banca dati*

📖 Possible equivalents: KONSUMENT (pl), consumer (en)

CONTO (it)

Usually singular

(Adj) **conto economico** ✂ **conti annuali** *direttiva comunitaria n. 91/674 in materia di conti annuali e consolidati delle imprese di assicurazione* ✂ **conti consolidati**

(N) **conto del bilancio** *le voci, le sottovoci e i relativi dettagli informativi previsti dagli schemi di stato patrimoniale e di conto economico costituiscono i conti del bilancio, che sono redatti dagli enti creditizi e finanziari secondo le disposizioni*

del presente decreto ✂ **moneta di conto** *'moneta di conto': la moneta, lira o euro, che risulta in prevalenza utilizzata, a partire da un dato momento, per la rilevazione delle operazioni di gestione* **redazione del conto, situazione dei conti** *La Banca d'Italia trasmette mensilmente al Ministro del tesoro, del bilancio e della programmazione economica una situazione dei conti redatta secondo il modello approvato, su proposta della Banca, dallo stesso Ministro, con proprio decreto.*

✎ **stato patrimoniale e conto economico** ✂ **conto economico dell'esercizio** *Qualora si sia verificata una variazione notevole nella composizione delle imprese incluse nel consolidamento, sono fornite le informazioni che rendono significativo il confronto fra lo stato patrimoniale e il conto economico dell'esercizio e quelli dell'esercizio precedente* ✂ **soggetto incaricato della revisione legale dei conti** *Il soggetto incaricato della revisione legale dei conti comunica senza indugio alla Banca d'Italia gli atti o i fatti, rilevati nello svolgimento dell'incarico, che possano costituire una grave violazione delle norme disciplinanti l'attività bancaria* ✂ **adozione dell'euro quale moneta di conto, conversione in moneta di conto** ✂ **adottare l'euro quale moneta di conto, essere (per intero) inclusi nel conto economico, essere iscritti nel conto economico, essere tradotti nella moneta di conto**

📖 Possible equivalents: KONTO, RACHUNEK, sprawozdanie (pl), account, statement (en)

CONTRATTO (it)

(Adj) **contratto relativo (a)** ✂ **contratto concluso, stipulato** ✂ **contratti disciplinati (da)** *salvo quanto previsto dai commi 1 e 2, ai contratti disciplinati dal presente capo non si applicano gli articoli 64, 65, 66, 67-duodecies e 67-ter decies del Codice del consumo*

(N) **contratto di credito, di durata** *negli altri contratti di durata la facoltà di modifica unilaterale può essere convenuta esclusivamente per le clausole non aventi ad oggetto i tassi di interesse, sempre che sussista un giustificato motivo* **contratto di finanziamento, fornitura, locazione, mutuo, contratto quadro** *'contratto quadro': il contratto che disciplina la futura esecuzione di operazioni di pagamento singole e ricorrenti e che può dettare gli obblighi e le condizioni che le parti devono rispettare per l'apertura e la gestione di un conto di pagamento* ✂ **contratto con un preavviso (di)** ✂ **conclusione, condizioni, nullità, parte, risoluzione, scadenza di un contratto**

(V) **applicarsi ai contratti** *le disposizioni di cui ai commi 1 e 2 dell'articolo 120-ter si applicano ai contratti di mutuo per l'acquisto della prima casa stipulati a decorrere dal 2 febbraio 2007 concludere un contratto* ✂ **contratto + prevedere** ✂ **contratto + essere redatti** *i contratti sono redatti per iscritto e un esemplare è consegnato ai clienti* ✂ **essere previsti dal / nel contratto**

✎ **contratto a tempo indeterminato, contratto di credito ai consumatori, contratto di locazione finanziaria** ✂ **contratti relativi alla concessione di finanziamenti** ✂ **la vita residua del contratto** *l'indennizzo non può superare l'importo degli interessi che il consumatore avrebbe pagato per la vita residua del contratto* ✂ **comportare la nullità del contratto** *La nullità del patto non comporta la nullità del contratto* **recedre da un contratto con un preavviso di** *il prestatore di servizi di pagamento può recedere da un contratto quadro a tempo indeterminato se ciò è previsto dal contratto e con un preavviso di almeno due mesi* ✂ **contratto + essere nulli**

📖 Possible equivalents: kontrakt, UMOWA (pl), AGREEMENT, contract (en)

CONTROLLO (it)

(Adj) **controllo interno** ✂ **controlli previsti (da)**

(N) **funzione, organo, partecipazione di controllo** *le disposizioni dell'articolo 15, comma 3, e dell'articolo 16, comma 3, si applicano (...) -anche alle società finanziarie aventi sede legale in uno Stato comunitario quando la partecipazione di controllo è detenuta da una o più banche aventi sede legale nel medesimo Stato* ✂ **controllo della banca, società**

(V) **detenere il controllo** *i requisiti si applicano a coloro che svolgono funzioni di amministrazione, direzione e controllo e, limitatamente ai requisiti di onorabilità, anche a coloro che detengono il controllo* **esercitare il controllo (su)**

✎ *(NOMINAL)* **comitato per il controllo sulla gestione, organi di amministrazione e controllo, organi di gestione e controllo dell'Organismo** *la Banca d'Italia provvede agli adempimenti necessari alla ricostituzione degli organi di gestione e controllo dell'Organismo, assicurandone la continuità operativa, se necessario anche attraverso la nomina di un commissario* ✂ **organizzazione amministrativa e contabile, nonché i controlli interni e i sistemi di**

remunerazione e incentivazione *la Banca d'Italia emana disposizioni di carattere generale aventi a oggetto: il governo societario, l'adeguatezza patrimoniale, il contenimento del rischio nelle sue diverse configurazioni, l'organizzazione amministrativa e contabile, nonché i controlli interni e i sistemi di remunerazione e incentivazione*

✎ *(VERBAL)* **svolgere la funzione di controllo, svolgere funzioni di amministrazione, direzione e controllo (presso)** ✂ **essere sottoposti a comune controllo** *le disposizioni della presente sezione (...) si applicano altresì alle società che controllano società con azioni quotate e alle società sottoposte con queste ultime a comune controllo.*

📖 Possible equivalents: KONTROLA, NADZÓR (pl), control, scrutiny, supervision (en)

CONVERSIONE (it)

Usually singular

(N) **conversione del capitale, conversione in euro** ✂ **tasso di conversione, risultato della conversione** *la legge delega consente, appunto, di rettificare i risultati della conversione oltre il semplice arrotondamento ai centesimi di euro.*

✎ **conversione in euro del capitale sociale** *il comma detta la regola di conversione in euro del capitale sociale quando il valore nominale delle azioni è superiore alle duecento lire* **conversione in moneta di conto** ✂ **differenze derivanti dalla conversione del patrimonio netto** *l'articolo precisa che al bilancio consolidato sono applicabili le disposizioni previste per il bilancio d'esercizio e fissa la modalità di imputazione delle differenze derivanti dalla conversione del patrimonio netto denominato in una valuta aderente* ✂ **rispettivo tasso di conversione** *I riferimenti alle unità monetarie nazionali (...) vengono intesi come riferimenti all'unità euro, da calcolarsi in base ai rispettivi tassi di conversione* ✂ **applicare un tasso di conversione**

📖 Possible equivalents: konwersja, przeliczenie, wymiana (pl), conversion, swap (en)

CREDITO (it)

(Adj) **credito agrario, fondiario, peschereccio, crediti futuri** ✂ **credito ceduto** *in caso di cessione di crediti derivanti da aperture di credito, anche regolate in conto corrente, il diritto di rendere esigibile il credito ceduto è esercitato dalla società cessionaria in conformità alle previsioni del relativo contratto* **credito collegato, vantato (da)** *se le somme di denaro ricevute per l'emissione di moneta elettronica sono depositate presso terzi (…) non può essere pattuita la compensazione convenzionale rispetto ai crediti vantati dal depositario nei confronti dell'istituto di moneta elettronica* **crediti acquistati, derivanti (da)**

(N) **credito ai consumatori, al consumo, su pegno** ✂ **acquisto di crediti, apertura di credito, cartolarizzazione di crediti** *la presente legge si applica altresì alle operazioni di cartolarizzazione di crediti sorti dalla concessione di uno o più finanziamenti da parte della società emittente i titoli* **cessione del credito, concessione di credito, contratto di credito, operazioni di credito, rimborso di un credito, rischio di credito, titoli di credito, settore del credito** *è istituito, nell'ambito del Ministero dell'economia e delle finanze, un sistema pubblico di prevenzione, sul piano amministrativo, delle frodi nel settore del credito al consumo e dei pagamenti dilazionati o differiti, con specifico riferimento al furto di identità*

(V) **concedere, ottenere un credito**

(SYNTACTIC NOMINAL) **aperture di credito regolate in conto corrente, contrattO di credito ai consumatori, contratto di credito collegato costo totale del credito, finanziamenti di credito agragio e di credito peschereccio** *i finanziamenti di credito agrario e di credito peschereccio possono essere assistiti dal privilegio previsto dall'articolo 46* **importo totale del credito** ✂ **banche di credito cooperativo, Monti di credito su pegno** *entro il 1° gennaio 1996 le casse comunali di credito agrario e i monti di credito su pegno di seconda categoria che non raccolgono risparmio tra il pubblico devono assumere iniziative che portino alla cessazione dell'esercizio dell'attività creditizia ovvero alla estinzione degli enti stessi*

credito agrario e credito peschereccio, credito alle opere pubbliche ✂ **conclusione del contratto di credito, frodi nel settore del credito, risoluzione del contratto di credito, valutazioni del rischio di credito rilasciate da società o enti esterni** ✂ **Comitato interministeriale per il credito e il risparmio, il**

finanziatore e l'intermediario del credito *il finanziatore o l'intermediario del credito forniscono al consumatore chiarimenti adeguati, in modo che questi possa valutare se il contratto di credito proposto sia adatto alle sue esigenze e alla sua situazione finanziaria* ✂ **avere ad/per oggetto crediti** *se la cessione ha per oggetto crediti derivanti dalle operazioni indicate negli articoli 15, 16 e 19 (…) continuano ad applicarsi le agevolazioni previste nel citato articolo 15.*

📖 Possible equivalents: KREDYT, WIERZYTELNOŚĆ (pl), credit, loan (en)

CREDITORE (it)

(Adj) **creditori chirografari** *quando sia necessario per decidere sulle contestazioni, il giudice richiede ai commissari l'esibizione di un estratto dell'elenco dei creditori chirografari previsto dall'articolo 86, comma 6*

(N) **creditori di un cliente, di un soggetto** ✂ **elenco dei creditori, interesse dei creditori** *qualora ricorrano circostanze eccezionali i commissari, al fine di tutelare gli interessi dei creditori, possono sospendere il pagamento delle passività di qualsiasi genere da parte della banca* **azioni dei creditori** *le azioni dei creditori dei singoli clienti degli istituti di moneta elettronica sono ammesse nel limite di quanto registrato ai sensi del comma 1*

✏ **i creditori e i titolari dei diritti** *entro quindici giorni dal ricevimento della raccomandata, i creditori e i titolari dei diritti indicati nel comma 2 possono presentare o inviare, mediante raccomandata con avviso di ricevimento, i loro reclami ai commissari, allegando i documenti giustificativi*

📖 Possible equivalents: WIERZYCIEL (pl), CREDITOR (en)

CRITERIO (it)

(Adj) **criteri direttivi** ✂ **criteri indicati, stabiliti, utilizzati** ✂ **seguenti criteri**

(N) **criterio di economicità** *la Banca d'Italia vigila sull'Organismo secondo modalità, dalla stessa stabilite, improntate a criteri di proporzionalità ed economicità dell'azione di controllo* **criteri di proporzionalità, criteri di redazione** *i bilanci*

compilati in conformità del presente comma, con particolare riguardo ai criteri di redazione adottati, assumono rilevanza anche agli effetti tributari **criterio di valutazione** ✂ **criteri per la determinazione (di)** ✂ **principi e criteri** *l'organismo opera nel rispetto dei principi e dei criteri stabiliti con regolamento dalla CONSOB, e sotto la vigilanza della medesima*

(V) **stabilire criteri**

(P) **in base ai criteri, sulla base di criteri** *la Banca d'Italia può prescrivere che determinati contratti, individuati attraverso una particolare denominazione o sulla base di specifici criteri qualificativi, abbiano un contenuto tipico determinato* ✂ **secondo un criterio**

✎ **principi e criteri direttivi** *entro due anni dalla data di entrata in vigore del decreto legislativo di cui al comma 1, il Governo, nel rispetto dei principi e criteri direttivi previsti dal comma 3 (…), può emanare disposizioni correttive e integrative del medesimo decreto legislativo* **criteri di rilevazione delle operazioni** *l'articolo dà attuazione all'articolo 9 della legge delega per le imprese in genere e tratta sia dei criteri di rilevazione delle operazioni in corso soggette al rischio di cambio 'generato' da una delle valute aderenti all'euro, sia del trattamento delle relative differenze cambio*

🕮 Possible equivalents: kryterium, ZASADA (pl), criterion (en)

D

DATA (it)

Usually singular

(Adj) **medesima data** ✂ **data successiva** *tale data, comunque non successiva al 30 giugno 2012, è comunicata alla Banca d'Italia e pubblicata nella Gazzetta Ufficiale della Repubblica italiana* ✂ **corrente, pendente, vigente alla data di** *dalla data di entrata in vigore del presente decreto legislativo sono soppressi gli elenchi previsti dagli articoli 113 e 155, comma 5 del decreto legislativo 1° settembre 1993, n. 385, vigenti alla data del 4 settembre 2010*

(N) **data di costituzione, estinzione, notificazione, riferimento** *le differenze derivanti dalla conversione, al tasso di cambio corrente alla data di riferimento del bilancio consolidato, del patrimonio netto delle imprese controllate incluse nel consolidamento sono ricomprese nelle riserve consolidate* ✂ **data valuta** *'data valuta': la data di riferimento usata da un prestatore di servizi di pagamento per il calcolo degli interessi applicati ai fondi addebitati o accreditati su un conto di pagamento* ✂ **un anno dalla data di** *le monete metalliche si prescrivono a favore dell'erario decorsi dieci anni dalla data di cessazione del corso legale*

(V) **decorrere dalla data di** *per le domande relative a fatti verificatisi tra il 1 gennaio 1990 e il 2 novembre 1991, il termine fissato dal medesimo articolo 3 del citato decreto-legge n. 419 del 1991 decorre dalla data di entrata in vigore della presente legge*

(P) **alla data di** ✂ **a decorrere dalla data** *con riferimento agli istituti di pagamento e agli istituti di moneta elettronica autorizzati in Italia l'abrogazione ha effetto a decorrere dalla data di entrata in vigore delle disposizioni di attuazione dell'articolo 128-quater, comma 6* **fino alla data**

✎ *(NOMINAL)* **data di avvio della gestione dell'elenco** *la data di avvio della gestione degli elenchi da parte degli Organismi previsti dagli articoli 112-bis e 113 del decreto legislativo 1° settembre 1993, n. 385, è comunicata alla Banca d'Italia e pubblicata nella Gazzetta Ufficiale della Repubblica italiana* **data di chiusura dell'esercizio, data di iscrizione nell'elenco, data di riferimento del bilancio** *le differenze derivanti dalla conversione, al tasso di cambio corrente alla data di riferimento del bilancio consolidato, del patrimonio netto delle imprese controllate incluse nel consolidamento sono ricomprese nelle riserve consolidate* **data prevista per l'applicazione ✂ data di entrata in vigore dei corrispondenti articoli / delle disposizioni di attuazione / del presente decreto (legislativo) / della presente disposizione / della presente legge ✂ articolo del decreto legislativo vigente alla data di, documenti riferiti ad una data** *quando l'euro è utilizzato come moneta di conto, i documenti contabili obbligatori a rilevanza esterna riferiti ad una data compresa tra il 1 gennaio 1999 e il 31 dicembre 2001 possono essere ad ogni effetto redatti e pubblicati in euro* **tasso di cambio corrente alla data di, termine di 10 giorni dalla data di**

✎ *(PRESPOSTIONAL)* **entro 10 giorni / mesi dalla data di entrata in vigore, fino alla data di entrata in vigore**

✎ *(VERBAL)* **continuare ad applicarsi fino alla data di ✂ i termini pendenti alla data di + essere prorogati fino a 10 giorni successivi alla data di entrata in vigore del presente decreto** *i termini di conclusione dei procedimenti amministrativi, stabiliti da norme di legge o di regolamento, pendenti alla data del 19 settembre 2010, sono prorogati fino a 120 giorni successivi alla data di entrata in vigore del presente decreto* **le disposizioni modificate, introdotte o sostituite dal presente decreto si applicano a decorrere dalla data di entrata in vigore dei corrispondenti articoli**

📖 Possible equivalents: data, DZIEŃ, TERMIN (pl), DATE, DZIEŃ, day (en)

DATO (it)

Usually plural

(Adj) **dati falsi, personali, relativi (a) ✂ dati contenuti (in)** *per le finalità di cui alla presente lettera, il titolare dell'archivio si avvale anche delle elaborazioni dei dati contenuti nell'archivio informatizzato istituito ai sensi dell'articolo 1, comma 4*

(N) **autenticità dei dati** *la verifica dell'autenticità dei dati non può essere richiesta al di fuori dei casi e delle finalità previste per la prevenzione del furto di identità* **protezione dei dati** ✂ **banca dati** ✂ **dati e informazioni**

✏ **Garante per la protezione dei dati** *lo schema del decreto di cui al comma 1 viene trasmesso al Garante per la protezione dei dati personali affinché esprima il proprio parere entro venti giorni dalla trasmissione* ✂ **segnalazioni periodiche nonché ogni altro dato e documento richiesto** *le banche inviano alla Banca d'Italia, con le modalità e nei termini da essa stabiliti, le segnalazioni periodiche nonché ogni altro dato e documento richiesto* ✂ **chiedere la comunicazione di dati e notizie e la trasmissione di atti e documenti** *per lo svolgimento dei propri compiti, l'Organismo può chiedere agli iscritti la comunicazione di dati e notizie e la trasmissione di atti e documenti, fissando i relativi termini, e può effettuare ispezioni.*

📖 Possible equivalents: DANE (pl), DATA (en)

DEBITORE (it)

(Adj) **debitore ceduto** *nel caso di operazioni realizzate mediante sottoscrizione o acquisto di titoli, i richiami ai debitori ceduti si intendono riferiti alla società emittente i titoli*

(N) **fallimento del debitore** *l'azione esecutiva sui beni ipotecati a garanzia di finanziamenti fondiari può essere iniziata o proseguita dalla banca anche dopo la dichiarazione di fallimento del debitore* ✂ **tasso debitore** *in caso di sconfinamento consistente che si protragga per oltre un mese, il creditore comunica senza indugio al consumatore, su supporto cartaceo o altro supporto durevole: a) lo sconfinamento; b) l'importo interessato; c) il tasso debitore; d) le penali, le spese o gli interessi di mora eventualmente applicabili.*

✏ **somme corrisposte dai debitori** *sui crediti sorti e sulle somme corrisposte dai debitori sono ammesse azioni soltanto a tutela dei diritti di cui all' articolo 1, comma 1, lettera b)* ✂ **senza alcun onere per il debitore** *il conservatore procede d'ufficio alla cancellazione dell'ipoteca, senza alcun onere per il debitore, entro il giorno successivo a quello di ricezione della comunicazione*

📖 Possible equivalents: DŁUŻNIK (pl), borrower, DEBTOR, obligor (en)

DECRETO (it)

Usually singular

(Adj) **decreto legislativo, ministeriale ✂ decreto recante ✂ regio decreto ✂ presente, citato decreto ✂ approvato con decreto** *ai titoli di Stato appartenenti a prestiti vigenti non si applicano le norme speciali del testo unico approvato con decreto del Presidente della Repubblica 14 febbraio 1963, n. 1343* **introdotto, modificato, sostituito dal decreto**

(N) **decreto legge ✂ disposizioni, norme del decreto ✂ emanazione, pubblicazione del decreto ✂ integrazioni, modifiche al decreto** *modifiche ed integrazioni al decreto legislativo 13 agosto 2010, n. 141, recante attuazione della direttiva 2008/48/CE relativa ai contratti di credito ai consumatori*

(V) **essere nominati con decreto** *i primi componenti dell'organo di gestione dell'Organismo sono nominati con decreto del Ministro dell'economia e delle finanze, su proposta della Banca d'Italia, e restano in carica tre anni a decorrere dalla data di costituzione dell'Organismo*

(P) **ai sensi del decreto**

✎ *(NOMINAL/SYNTACTIC)* **decreto del Ministro dell'economia e delle finanze, decreto del Ministro del tesoro, del bilancio e della programmazione economica, decreto del Presidente della Repubblica, decreto legislativo del Capo provvisorio dello Stato, decreto vigente alla data di, regio decreto legge ✂ (regio) decreto legge convertito (con modificazioni) dalla legge** *sono fatti salvi i commi 4-bis, 4-ter e 4-quater dell'articolo 8 del decreto-legge 31 gennaio 2007, n. 7, convertito, con modificazioni, dalla legge 2 aprile 2007, n. 40* **✂ decreto legislativo e successive modificazioni / modifiche ✂ decreto munito del sigillo dello Stato** *il presente decreto, munito del sigillo dello Stato, sarà inserito nella Raccolta ufficiale degli atti normativi della Repubblica italiana*

✎ *(NOMINAL)* **articolo 1, comma 1, lettera a), del decreto; data di entrata in vigore del (presente) decreto legislativo, data di entrata in vigore dei corrispondenti articoli del decreto legislativo ✂ disposizioni di attuazione del Titolo I del decreto legislativo, disposizioni modificate, introdotte o sostituite dal presente decreto** *le disposizioni modificate, introdotte o sostituite dal presente decreto si applicano a decorrere dalla data di entrata in vigore dei corrispondenti articoli del decreto legislativo 13 agosto 2010, n. 141* **✂ albo previsto dall'articolo**

1 del decreto legislativo, testo unico di cui al decreto legislativo✂ come modificato dal presente decreto, con proprio decreto *ministro dell'economia e delle finanze provvede con proprio decreto alla nomina dei componenti del gruppo di lavoro*

📖 Possible equivalents: dekret, ROZPORZĄDZENIE (pl), decree, ORDER (en)

DENARO (it)

Always singular

(N) **riciclaggio di denaro, somma di denaro ✂ denaro o altra utilità** *chiunque (...) si fa dare o promettere, sotto qualsiasi forma, per se o per altri, in corrispettivo di una prestazione di denaro o di altra utilità, interessi o altri vantaggi usurari, è punito con la reclusione da uno a sei anni*

✏ **somme di denaro ricevute (per) ✂ somme di denaro + essere depositate** *se le somme di denaro registrate nei conti di pagamento sono depositate presso terzi non operano le compensazioni legale e giudiziale e non può essere pattuita la compensazione convenzionale rispetto ai crediti vantati dal depositario nei confronti dell'istituto di pagamento* ✂ **subire condanne per riciclaggio di denaro o finanziamento del terrorismo o altri reati finanziari** *coloro che svolgono funzioni di amministrazione, direzione e controllo nell'istituto di moneta elettronica non hanno subito condanne per riciclaggio di denaro o finanziamento del terrorismo o altri reati finanziari*

📖 Possible equivalents: PIENIĄDZ (pl), MONEY (en)

DIRETTIVA (it)

(Adj) **direttiva relativa a ✂ recante la direttiva** *direttiva 89/646/CEE, recante la seconda direttiva relativa al coordinamento delle disposizioni legislative, regolamentari e amministrative riguardanti l'accesso all'attività degli enti creditizi e il suo esercizio*

(N) **attuazione, recepimento della direttiva** *la normativa di recepimento della Direttiva 93/22/CEE, relativa ai servizi di investimento nel settore dei valori mobiliari, è attualmente contenuta nel D.Lgs. 24 febbraio 1998*

(V) **abrogare, modificare la direttiva** *attuazione della direttiva 2009/14/CE, che modifica la direttiva 94/19/CE, relativa ai sistemi di garanzia dei depositi* ✂ **direttiva + essere abrogata**

(P) **direttiva in materia (di)**

✎ **art. 1, paragrafo 1, lettera a), della direttiva (n.)** ✂ **direttiva del Parlamento europeo e del Consiglio**

📖 Possible equivalents: dyrektywa (pl), DIRECTIVE (en)

DIRITTO (it)

(Adj) **diritto italiano, privato** ✂ **diritti derivanti (da)** *i diritti previsti dal presente articolo possono essere fatti valere anche nei confronti del terzo al quale il finanziatore abbia ceduto i diritti derivanti dal contratto di concessione del credito*

(N) **diritto di recesso, voto** ✂ **diritto al rimborso** ✂ **esercizio del diritto, soddisfacimento dei diritti** *fino al completo soddisfacimento dei diritti dei soggetti a cui vantaggio la destinazione è effettuata, sul patrimonio destinato e sui frutti e proventi da esso derivanti sono ammesse azioni soltanto a tutela dei diritti dei predetti soggetti* **titolari dei diritti** *entro quindici giorni dal ricevimento della raccomandata, i creditori e i titolari dei diritti indicati nel comma 2 possono presentare (…) i loro reclami ai commissari, allegando i documenti giustificativi* **tutela dei diritti**

(V) **diritto di ottenere, recedere (da)** ✂ **avere diritto (a)**

✎ **diritti di voto e gli altri diritti che consentono di influire sulla società, diritti di voto esercitabili nell'assemblea ordinaria** ✂ **clienti aventi diritto alla restituzione di strumenti finanziari** ✂ **emesso a norma del diritto** *il 1 gennaio 1999 sono ridenominati in euro i titoli di Stato denominati in lire, emessi a norma del diritto italiano e negoziabili sui mercati regolamentati.*

📖 Possible equivalents: PRAWO (pl), LAW, RIGHT (en)

DISCIPLINA (it)

Usually singular

(Adj) **disciplina applicabile, relativa** ✂ **disciplina prevista (da)** *ove i finanziamenti di credito agrario siano garantiti da ipoteca su immobili, si applica la disciplina prevista dalla sezione I del presente capo per le operazioni di credito fondiario*

(N) **disciplina di attuazione** *fino al 31 dicembre 2013 la Banca d'Italia esercita il controllo sui mediatori creditizi per verificare l'osservanza delle disposizioni di cui al comma 1 e della relativa disciplina di attuazione* **disciplina delle crisi** *non rientra nell'ambito del presente decreto la regolamentazione in materia di vigilanza sulle banche, ivi compresa la disciplina delle crisi di cui al titolo IV del testo unico delle disposizioni in materia bancaria e creditizia* ✂ **applicazione della disciplina** *ai fini dell'applicazione della disciplina della liquidazione coatta amministrativa all'istituto di moneta elettronica, i detentori di moneta elettronica sono equiparati ai clienti aventi diritto alla restituzione di strumenti finanziari* **rispetto della disciplina**

(V) **essere sottoposti alla disciplina** *la Banca d'Italia tiene l'elenco previsto dall'articolo 111 e vigila sul rispetto da parte degli iscritti della disciplina cui essi sono sottoposti anche ai sensi dell'articolo 111, comma 5*

Possible equivalents: regulacja, zasady (pl), regulation, rules (en)

DISPOSIZIONE (it)

Usually plural

(Adj) **disposizioni amministrative, applicabili (a), attuative, compatibili, finali, generali, legislative, normative, particolari, regolamentari, relative (a), speciali (per), specifiche, statutarie, transitorie, urgenti (per), vigenti, volte (a)** *con riferimento a determinati tipi di attività la Banca d'Italia può inoltre dettare disposizioni volte ad assicurarne il regolare esercizio* ✂ **disposizione abrogata** ✂ **disposizioni concernenti, contenute (in), dettate (da), emanate, indicate, introdotte, modificate, previste (da), sostituite** ✂ **recante disposizioni** *la legge 1° marzo 2002, n. 39, recante disposizioni per l'adempimento di obblighi derivanti dall'appartenenza dell'Italia alle Comunità europee*

(N) **disposizioni del Titolo I, disposizioni di legge** *le disposizioni del presente decreto e gli atti di cui all'art. 5 si applicano anche alle situazioni dei conti infrannuali*

e ai bilanci consolidati la cui redazione è prevista da specifiche disposizioni di legge ✂ **applicazione, emanazione, osservanza, violazioni delle disposizioni**

(V) **adottare, dettare disposizioni** *la Banca d'Italia detta disposizioni attuative del presente articolo* **emanare disposizioni** ✂ **disposizioni + applicarsi**

(P) **in deroga alla disposizione, secondo disposizioni** *gli enti creditizi e finanziari redigono gli schemi dello stato patrimoniale e del conto economico secondo le disposizioni del presente decreto e degli atti di cui all'art. 5* ✂ **disposizioni in materia di**

✏ *(NOMINAL)* **disposizioni attuative del presente articolo, disposizioni del capo I, sezioni I e II; disposizioni dell'Unione europea** *le autorità creditizie esercitano i poteri loro attribuiti in armonia con le disposizioni dell'Unione europea* **disposizioni emanate ai sensi del comma 1, disposizioni generali o particolari impartite dalle autorità creditizie, disposizioni per l'adempimento di obblighi derivanti da, disposizioni previste dal presente titolo/dall'articolo 1, disposizioni transitorie e finali; disposizioni modificate, introdotte o sostituite dal presente decreto** *le disposizioni modificate, introdotte o sostituite dal presente decreto si applicano a decorrere dalla data di entrata in vigore dei corrispondenti articoli del decreto legislativo 13 agosto 2010, n. 141* ✂ **data di entrata di vigore delle disposizioni di attuazione, emanazione delle disposizioni attuative, gravi violazioni delle disposizioni legislative, amministrative o statutarie** ✂ **testo unico delle disposizioni in materia di intermediazione finanziaria**

✏ *(VERBAL)* **dettare, emanare disposizioni attuative, verificare l'osservanza delle disposizioni di cui al comma 1** ✂ **disposizioni + continuare ad applicarsi** *alle banche di credito cooperativo continuano ad applicarsi le disposizioni degli articoli 7 e 9 della legge 31 gennaio 1992, n. 59, in quanto compatibili* **disposizone + restare ferma/salva** *restano salve le disposizioni riguardanti gli enti e le società che abbiano emesso titoli quotati in borsa* ✂ **La Banca d'Italia + dettare disposizioni attuative del presente articolo, emanare disposizioni di carattere generale (aventi a oggetto)** ✂ **la disposizione abrogata così recitava; si applicano, in quanto copmpatibili, disposizioni contenute nell'articolo 1**

📖 Possible equivalents: PRZEPIS, ROZPORZĄDZENIE, zarządzenie (pl), DIRECTION, PROVISION, rule (en)

DOCUMENTO (it)

(Adj) **documenti contabili, obbligatori, societari** *la relazione è altresì sottoscritta dal direttore generale e dal dirigente preposto alla redazione dei documenti contabili societari* ✂ **documento richiesto**

(N) **esibizione, redazione, trasmissione di documenti** *per lo svolgimento dei propri compiti, l'Organismo può chiedere agli iscritti la comunicazione di dati e notizie e la trasmissione di atti e documenti, fissando i relativi termini, e può effettuare ispezioni*

✎ **documenti contabili obbligatori a rilevanza esterna** *i dati comparativi, originariamente espressi in lire, da includere nei documenti contabili obbligatori a rilevanza esterna espressi in euro sono convertiti in euro adottando il tasso di conversione con la lira* ✂ **trasmissione di atti e documenti** ✂ **ogni altro dato e documento richiesto** *gli intermediari finanziari inviano alla Banca d'Italia, con le modalità e nei termini da essa stabiliti, le segnalazioni periodiche nonché ogni altro dato e documento richiesto* ✂ **dirigente preposto alla redazione dei documenti contabili societari** ✂ **richiedere esibizione di documenti, ritenere necessari documenti e atti** *la Banca d'Italia può effettuare ispezioni presso le banche e richiedere a esse l'esibizione di documenti e gli atti che ritenga necessari*

📖 Possible equivalents: dokument (pl), DOCUMENT, INSTRUMENT (en)

E

ELEMENTO (it)

(Adj) **elemento monetario, non monetario** *'elementi monetari': le disponibilità di denaro, le attività e passività iscritte in bilancio e le restanti operazioni in corso (dette anche 'fuori bilancio') che comportano o comporteranno il diritto a incassare o l'obbligo a pagare a date future importi di denaro determinati o determinabili*

(N) **elementi dell'attivo** *gli elementi dell'attivo diversi dai crediti sono contabilizzati al costo di acquisto o di produzione maggiorato delle spese incrementative* **elementi del passivo, del patrimonio**

✎ **elementi dell'attivo e del passivo e le operazioni 'fuori bilancio'** ✂ **distribuire utili o altri elementi di patrimonio**

🕮 Possible equivalents: CZĘŚĆ, element, składnik (pl), component, item (en)

ELENCO (it)

(Adj) **elenco generale, speciale** ✂ **elenco previsto (da)** ✂ **apposito elenco** *le fondazioni e le associazioni riconosciute per la prevenzione del fenomeno dell'usura sono iscritte in apposito elenco tenuto dal Ministro del tesoro* ✂ **iscritto in un elenco** *per il contatto con il pubblico, gli agenti in attività finanziaria che siano persone fisiche o costituiti in forma di società di persone si avvalgono di dipendenti o collaboratori iscritti nell'elenco di cui all'articolo 128-quater, comma 2*

(N) **cancellazione dall'elenco, gestione dell'elenco, iscrizione nell'elenco, sezione dell'elenco ✂ elenco delle imprese, elenco di cui all'articolo 1**

(P) **elenco di ✂ in un elenco**

✏ **elenco degli agenti in attività finanziaria, elenco dei mediatori creditizi, elenco previsto dall'articolo 1, comma 1, elenco tenuto dall'Organismo ✂ data di avvio della gestione dell'elenco** *la data di avvio della gestione degli elenchi da parte degli Organismi previsti dagli articoli 112-bis e 113(…) è comunicata alla Banca d'Italia e pubblicata nella Gazzetta Ufficiale della Repubblica italiana* **data/istanza di iscrizione nell'elenco, requisiti per l'iscrizione nell'elenco, somme dovute per l'iscrizione nell'elenco ✂ confidi iscritti nell'elenco previsto dall'articolo 1, intermediari finanziari iscritti nell'elenco speciale, soggetti iscritti in un apposito elenco ✂ disporre la cancellazione dall'elenco** *l'Organismo può disporre la cancellazione dall'elenco: a) qualora vengano meno i requisiti per l'iscrizione* **svolgere attività necessaria per la gestione dell'elenco**

📖 Possible equivalents: lista, spis, wykaz (pl), directory, list (en)

ENTE (it)

(Adj) **ente creditizio, finanziario ✂ enti esterni, locali, pubblici, territoriali**

(N) **ente gestore** *il Ministero dell'economia e delle finanze è titolare dell'archivio e può avvalersi, per la gestione dell'archivio, di Consap S.p.A., di seguito denominato ente gestore* ✂ **enti di previdenza**

(V) **appartenere all'ente** *le banche, le società o gli enti ai quali appartengono i responsabili delle violazioni rispondono, in solido con questi, del pagamento della sanzione e delle spese di pubblicità previste dal primo periodo del comma 3*

✏ **enti creditizi e finanziari ✂ finanziamenti concessi da enti di previdenza obbligatoria, titoli emessi dall'ente** *le disposizioni di cui al comma 2 del presente articolo sono applicate ai titoli emessi dagli enti pubblici indicati dal decreto ministeriale di cui al comma 1* **valutazioni del rischio di credito rilasciate da società o enti esterni**

📖 Possible equivalents: INSTYTUCJA (pl), AUTHORITY, body, INSTITUTION (en)

ENTRATA IN VIGORE (it)

Always singular

(N) **data di entrata in vigore** *le disposizioni riguardanti le imprese di assicurazione si applicano decorsi dodici mesi dalla data di entrata in vigore del decreto di cui al comma 1* ✂ **entrata in vigore dell'articolo, del decreto, della disposizione, della legge**

✏ **entrata in vigore delle disposizioni attuative** ✂ **data di entrata in vigore della presente disposizione** ✂ **10 giorni successivi alla data di entrata in vigore del presente decreto** ✂ **a decorrere dalla data di entrata in vigore dei corrispondenti articoli del decreto legislativo** *le disposizioni modificate, introdotte o sostituite dal presente decreto si applicano a decorrere dalla data di entrata in vigore dei corrispondenti articoli del decreto legislativo 13 agosto 2010, n. 141* **entro due mesi dalla data di entrata in vigore della presente legge, fino alla data di entrata in vigore delle disposizioni di attuazione**

📖 Possible equivalents: wejście w życie (pl), coming into force / into effect, entry into force (en)

ESERCIZIO (it)

Usually singular

(Adj) **esercizio abusivo, effettivo, professionale** ✂ **esercizio chiuso (a)** *le disposizioni del presente articolo si applicano ai bilanci d'impresa redatti dalle imprese di assicurazione a partire da quelli relativi all'esercizio chiuso al 31 dicembre 1998* **esercizio precedente** *la situazione dei conti alla data di apertura dell'esercizio corrisponde a quella confluita nel bilancio approvato relativo all'esercizio precedente* ✂ **derivante dall'esercizio** *salvo che il fatto costituisca reato, la violazione degli obblighi derivanti dall'esercizio dei poteri attribuiti alla CONSOB dall'articolo 165-septies, comma 1, è punita con la sanzione amministrativa pecuniaria prevista dall'articolo 193* **relativo all'esercizio**

(N) **esercizio dell'attività, di un diritto, delle funzioni, dei poteri, della vigilanza** ✂ **esercizio di un'impresa, bilancio d'esercizio** *gli amministratori redigono un separato rendiconto per il patrimonio destinato, da allegare al bilancio d'esercizio dell'istituto di pagamento* **chiusura dell'esercizio, ostacolo all'esercizio**

(V) **consentire l'esercizio** *le società indicate nell'articolo 65 forniscono alla capogruppo ovvero alla singola banca le situazioni, i dati e le informazioni richiesti*

per consentire l'esercizio della vigilanza consolidata **iniziare, ostacolare l'esercizio** *non sussistano, tra gli istituti di moneta elettronica o i soggetti del gruppo di appartenenza e altri soggetti, stretti legami che ostacolino l'effettivo esercizio delle funzioni di vigilanza*

(P) **nel corso dell'esercizio, nell'esercizio (di)** *nell'esercizio dei poteri regolamentari previsti dal presente capo, la Banca d'Italia tiene conto anche della finalità di garantire un adeguato livello di affidabilità ed efficienza dei servizi di pagamento* ✂ **esercizio in corso (a)**

esercizio abusivo dell'attività, esercizio dell'attività bancaria, esercizio di agenzia in attività finanziaria, esercizio professionale nei confronti del pubblico dell'attività *l'esercizio professionale nei confronti del pubblico dell'attività di agente in attività finanziaria è riservato ai soggetti iscritti in un apposito elenco tenuto dall'Organismo previsto dall'articolo 128-undecies* ✂ **conto economico dell'esercizio, data di chiusura dell'esercizio, risultato economico di esercizio** *il bilancio dell'impresa e il bilancio consolidato sono redatti con chiarezza e rappresentano in modo veritiero e corretto la situazione patrimoniale, la situazione finanziaria e il risultato economico dell'esercizio* ✂ **iniziare l'esercizio dell'attività, ostacolare l'effettivo esercizio delle funzioni di vigilanza**

Possible equivalents: DZIAŁALNOŚĆ, sprawowanie, WYKONYWANIE (pl) exercise, operation, performance, practice, pursuit (en)

EURO (it)

(Adj) **inferiore, pari, superiore a 10 euro** *nelle società cooperative nessun socio può avere una quota superiore a cinquantamila euro, né tante azioni il cui valore nominale superi tale somma* ✂ **espresso in euro, ridenominato in euro** *il 1 gennaio 1999 sono ridenominati in euro i titoli di Stato denominati in lire, emessi a norma del diritto italiano e negoziabili sui mercati regolamentati*

(N) **adozione dell'euro, banconote in euro** *falsificazione di banconote e monete in euro non aventi corso legale* **conversione in euro, importo in euro, introduzione dell'euro, migliaia di euro, monete in euro, pagamento in euro, ridenominazione in euro (di), unità di euro, versamenti in euro** ✂ **multa, sanzione da 2 a 10 euro** ✂ **euro o multipli** *la lettera b) aggiunge all'articolo 2327*

del codice civile un secondo comma che stabilisce in euro o suoi multipli il valore nominale delle azioni delle società per azioni

(P) **fino a 10 euro** *nei confronti dei soggetti che svolgono funzioni di amministrazione o di direzione e dei dipendenti si applica la sanzione amministrativa pecuniaria fino a euro 258.225 per l'inosservanza delle norme contenute nell'articolo 128, comma 1*

✏ **importo inferiore a 10 euro, sanzione amministrativa pecuniaria da euro 2 a euro 10 per l'inosservanza delle norme, unità di euro senza cifre decimali** *il bilancio d'impresa va redatto alle unità di euro senza cifre decimali, con l'eccezione della nota integrativa che può essere redatta in migliaia di euro* ✂ **adozione dell'euro quale moneta di conto, arrotondamento al centesimo di euro** *Se l'arrotondamento ai centesimi di euro viene effettuato per eccesso (comma 2), il valore nominale unitario delle azioni e il capitale sociale sono aumentati mediante l'utilizzo di riserve* **conversione in euro del capitale sociale, ridenominazione in euro degli strumenti di debito** ✂ **adottare dell'euro quale moneta di conto, essere redatti e pubblicati in euro; bilancio consolidato, nota integrativa + essere redatti in migliaia di euro**

📖 Possible equivalents: euro (pl), euro (en)

F

FINANZA (it)

(Adj) **finanza pubblica** *dall'attuazione delle disposizioni del presente decreto non devono derivare nuovi o maggiori oneri, né minori entrate per la finanza pubblica*

(N) **Guardia di Finanza** *la Banca d'Italia può effettuare ispezioni presso l'agente in attività finanziaria, anche avvalendosi della Guardia di Finanza che agisce con i poteri ad essa attribuiti per l'accertamento dell'imposta sul valore aggiunto e delle imposte sui redditi*

✎ **Ministero / Ministro dell'economia e delle finanze** ✂ **Corpo della guardia di finanza** *tutte le notizie, le informazioni e i dati acquisiti dal Corpo della guardia di finanza nell'assolvimento dei compiti previsti dal comma 1 sono coperti dal segreto d'ufficio e vengono senza indugio comunicati esclusivamente alle Autorità competenti* ✂ **senza nuovi o maggiori oneri a carico della finanza pubblica / per la finanza pubblica** *il Governo è delegato ad adottare, entro diciotto mesi dalla data di entrata in vigore della presente legge, uno o più decreti legislativi per l'istituzione di un fondo di garanzia per i risparmiatori e gli investitori, senza nuovi o maggiori oneri per la finanza pubblica*

📖 Possible equivalents: FINANSE (pl), finance (en)

FINANZIAMENTO (it)

(Adj) **finanziamenti concessi (da), destinati (a), garantiti (da)** *finanziamenti garantiti da pegno su un bene mobile*

(N) **finanziamento del terrorismo ✂ contratto di finanziamento, erogazione di un finanziamento** *nel caso di operazioni realizzate diante erogazione di un finanziamento, i chiami al cedente e al cessionario devono intendersi riferiti, rispettivamente, al soggetto finanziato e al soggetto finanziatore.*

(V) **concedere, erogare finanziamenti**

✎ **finanziamenti di credito agrario ✂ finanziamenti concessi da enti di previdenza obbligatoria ai loro iscritti ✂ attività di concessione di finanziamenti sotto qualsiasi forma** *agli intermediari iscritti nell'elenco previsto dal comma 1 che esercitano l'attività di concessione di finanziamenti sotto qualsiasi forma si applicano le disposizioni dell'articolo 47* **contratti relativi alla concessione di finanziamenti**

📖 Possible equivalents: finansowanie (pl), financing, funding, LOAN (en)

FINE (it)

(N) **a fini di vigilanza, ai fini dell'applicazione** *con il regolamento previsto dal comma 1, il Ministro dell'economia e delle finanze stabilisce le soglie partecipative ai fini dell'applicazione del medesimo comma 1* **ai fini della costituzione, dell'iscrizione**

(V) **al fine di agevolare, assicurare, evitare, garantire, verificare** *la Banca d'Italia, al fine di verificare l'osservanza degli obblighi indicati nei commi 1 e 2, può chiedere informazioni ai soggetti comunque interessati*

(P) **ai fini di cui (a), a tal fine, a tali fini** *a tali fini, per portatori di titoli devono intendersi i portatori delle obbligazioni di cui al comma 1*

✎ **ai fini del presente decreto, ai fini della determinazione del reddito d'impresa, al fine di verificare il rispetto (di) ✂ presentare istanza di autorizzazione ai fini dell'iscrizione (a)** *almeno tre mesi prima della scadenza del termine indicato al comma 1, gli altri soggetti ivi indicati presentano istanza di autorizzazione ai fini dell'iscrizione all'albo di cui all'articolo 106*

📖 Possible equivalents: aim, goal, intent, OBJECTIVE, PURPOSE (en), CEL (pl)

FONDO (it)

(Adj) **fondo pubblico, speciale**

(N) **fondo di garanzia, fondo per rischi** *è ammessa la costituzione di un fondo per rischi bancari generali destinato alla copertura dei rischi propri delle operazioni bancarie* ✂ **fondi pensione** *'fondi pensione': le forme pensionistiche di cui al decreto legislativo 21 aprile 1993, n. 124 e successive modifiche e integrazioni* ✂ **disponibilità, gestione di un fondo** ✂ **ricezione di fondi** *non costituisce raccolta del risparmio tra il pubblico la ricezione di fondi connessa all'emissione di moneta elettronica*

(V) **erogare fondi**

(P) **fondo per** *il rimborso avviene mediante l'utilizzo delle disponibilità del Fondo per l'ammortamento dei titoli di Stato di cui alla legge 27 ottobre 1993, n. 432 e successive modifiche e integrazioni*

✎ **fondo con obbligo di rimborso** *Ai fini del presente decreto legislativo è raccolta del risparmio l'acquisizione di fondi con obbligo di rimborso, sia sotto forma di depositi sia sotto altra forma* **fondo per rischi ed oneri** *i fondi per rischi ed oneri sono destinati soltanto a coprire perdite, oneri o debiti di natura determinata, di esistenza probabile o certa, dei quali tuttavia alla data di chiusura dell'esercizio sono indeterminati o l'ammontare o la data di sopravvenienza* ✂ **gestione di un fondo pubblico di agevolazione** *l'assegnazione e la gestione di fondi pubblici di agevolazione creditizia previsti dalle leggi vigenti e la prestazione di servizi a essi inerenti, sono disciplinate da contratti stipulati tra l'amministrazione pubblica competente e le banche da questa prescelte* ✂ **gli impegni ad erogare fondi e le garanzie rilasciate**

📖 Possible equivalents: kapitał, FUNDUSZ, ŚRODKI, zasoby (pl), allowance, capital, fund (en)

FORMA (it)

(Adj) **forma giuridica, tecnica** *il Ministro dell'Economia e delle finanze, sentita la Banca d'Italia, emana disposizioni attuative del presente articolo,*

anche disciplinando: a) requisiti concernenti i beneficiari e le forme tecniche dei finanziamenti ✂ **forma scritta, forme stabilite** ✂ **costituito in forma (di)**

(N) **forme di collaborazione, di pubblicità, di tutela** *lo scopo della prevenzione del fenomeno dell'usura, anche attraverso forme di tutela, assistenza ed informazione, deve risultare dall'atto costitutivo e dallo statuto*

(V) **la forma + essere adottata**

(P) **in forma (di), nella forma, nelle forme** *al fine di agevolare il superamento di difficoltà finanziarie, I commissari possono disporre la sospensione dei pagamenti nelle forme e con gli effetti previsti dall'articolo 74* **sotto forma (di)** ✂ **in forma scritta**

✎ **forma di società per azioni** ✂ **attività di concessione di finanziamenti sotto qualsiasi forma** *agli intermediari iscritti nell'elenco previsto dal comma 1 che esercitano l'attività di concessione di finanziamenti sotto qualsiasi forma si applicano le disposizioni dell'articolo 47* ✂ **stabilire forme di pubblicità** *la Banca d'Italia può stabilire ulteriori forme di pubblicità allo scopo di rendere nota la scadenza dei termini per la presentazione delle domande di insinuazione ai sensi del comma 5* ✂ **la forma di società per azioni + essere adottata** *la Banca d'Italia autorizza l'attività bancaria quando ricorrano le seguenti condizioni: a) sia adottata la forma di società per azioni o di società cooperativa per azioni a responsabilità limitata;*

📖 Possible equivalents: FORMA (pl), form (en)

FUNZIONE (it)

(Adj) **funzioni decisorie, istruttorie** ✂ **rispettive funzioni** *la Banca d'Italia, la CONSOB, la COVIP e l'ISVAP collaborano tra loro, anche mediante scambio di informazioni, al fine di agevolare le rispettive funzioni*

(N) **funzione di controllo** ✂ **funzioni di amministrazione, di vigilanza** ✂ **funzioni degli organi** ✂ **esercizio delle funzioni** *i dipendenti della Banca d'Italia, nell'esercizio delle funzioni di vigilanza, sono pubblici ufficiali e hanno l'obbligo di riferire esclusivamente al Governatore tutte le irregolarità constatate*

(V) **svolgere funzioni**

(P) **con funzioni** *soggetti con funzioni di amministrazione, direzione e controllo*

✏ **distinzione tra funzioni istruttorie e funzioni decisorie** *le Autorità di cui al presente comma disciplinano le modalità organizzative per dare attuazione al principio della distinzione tra funzioni istruttorie e funzioni decisorie rispetto all'irrogazione della sanzione* ✂ **soggetti che svolgono funzioni di amministrazione, direzione e controllo (presso), soggetti che svolgono funzioni di di amministrazione o di direzione** ✂ **stretti legami che ostacolino l'effettivo esercizio delle funzioni di vigilanza** ✂ **svolgere la funzione di controllo** ✂ **i commissari, nell'esercizio delle loro funzioni, sono pubblici ufficiali**

📖 Possible equivalents: CZYNNOŚĆ, funkcja, ZADANIE (pl), FUNCTION, purpose, task (en)

G

GESTIONE (it)

(Adj) **gestione provvisoria** ✂ **gestione accentrata** *il 5 ottobre 1998 il sistema di gestione centralizzata della Banca d'Italia comunica a ciascun depositario l'ammontare dei titoli detenuti in gestione accentrata con riferimento ai saldi dell'ultimo giorno lavorativo precedente*

(N) **gestione della banca, di un elenco, di un'impresa** ✂ **consiglio di gestione, irregolarità nella gestione, operazioni di gestione, organi di gestione, relazione sulla gestione** ✂ **emissione e/o gestione (di)** *la Banca d'Italia detta specifiche disposizioni per la concessione di credito collegata all'emissione o alla gestione di carte di credito* **gestione e controllo**

✎ **gestione di un fondo pubblico** ✂ **comitato per il controllo sulla gestione, componenti degli organi di gestione e controllo, data di avvio della gestione di un elenco** *la data di avvio della gestione degli elenchi da parte degli Organismi previsti dagli articoli 112-bis e 113 (...) è comunicata alla Banca d'Italia e pubblicata nella Gazzetta Ufficiale della Repubblica italiana* **organi di gestione e controllo dell'Organismo, sistema di gestione accentrata, società di gestione del mercato, società di gestione di mercati regolamentati** ✂ **competente per la gestione di un elenco** ✂ **svolgere ogni attività necessaria per la gestione** ✂ **sana e prudente gestione + risultare garantita** *la Banca d'Italia nega l'autorizzazione quando dalla verifica delle condizioni indicate nel comma 1 non risulti garantita la sana e prudente gestione ovvero il regolare funzionamento del sistema dei pagamenti*

🕮 Possible equivalents: zarządzanie (PL), administration, MANAGEMENT (en)

GIORNO (it)

(Adj) **giorno lavorativo, successivo (a)** *il presente decreto entra in vigore il primo lunedì successivo al quindicesimo giorno successivo a quello della sua pubblicazione nella Gazzetta Ufficiale della Repubblica italiana*

(P) **entro 10 giorni, fino a 10 giorni** *i termini di conclusione dei procedimenti amministrativi, stabiliti da norme di legge o di regolamento, pendenti alla data del 19 settembre 2010, sono prorogati fino a 120 giorni successivi alla data di entrata in vigore del presente decreto* ✂ **10 giorni prima di** *le ipoteche a garanzia dei finanziamenti non sono assoggettate a revocatoria fallimentare quando siano state iscritte dieci giorni prima della pubblicazione della sentenza dichiarativa di fallimento* ✂ **nel termine di 10 giorni (di)**

(Adv) **almeno 10 giorni** *il creditore, anche attraverso il proprio prestatore di servizi di pagamento, deve comunicare per iscritto ai propri debitori, con un preavviso di almeno trenta giorni, la data dalla quale si avvarrà di nuovi servizi di addebito diretto*

giorno lavorativo successivo al versamento ✂ **il termine di 10 giorni dalla data (di)** ✂ **essere prorogati fino a 10 giorni successivi alla data di entrata in vigore del presente decreto** *i termini di conclusione dei procedimenti amministrativi, stabiliti da norme di legge o di regolamento, pendenti alla data del 19 settembre 2010, sono prorogati fino a 120 giorni successivi alla data di entrata in vigore del presente decreto* ✂ **fissandone l'ordine del giorno** *la Banca d'Italia può b) ordinare la convocazione degli organi collegiali degli istituti di moneta elettronica, fissandone l'ordine del giorno, e proporre l'assunzione di determinate decisioni* ✂ **entro 10 giorni dalla comunicazione (di) / dalla data (di) / dal ricevimento (di)**

Possible equivalents: data, DZIEŃ, termin (pl), DATE, DAY (en)

GRUPPO (it)

(Adj) **gruppo bancario, finanziario** ✂ **gruppo composto (da)** *la Banca d'Italia emana disposizioni volte a individuare, tra soggetti non sottoposti a vigilanza consolidata ai sensi del capo II, titolo III (...) il gruppo finanziario, composto da uno o più intermediari finanziari, dalle banche extracomunitarie e dalle società finanziarie come definite dall'articolo 59*

(N) **gruppo di lavoro (di cui a)** ✂ **componenti del gruppo, società del gruppo** *gli amministratori delle società del gruppo sono tenuti a fornire ogni dato e informazione per l'emanazione delle disposizioni e la necessaria collaborazione per il rispetto delle norme sulla vigilanza consolidata.*

✎ **società appartenenti a un gruppo bancario / finanziario, società finanziaria capogruppo di un gruppo bancario iscritto nell'albo previsto dall'articolo 1** *agli effetti dell'art. 24 è impresa capogruppo a) l'ente creditizio o la società finanziaria capogruppo di un gruppo bancario iscritto nell'albo previsto dall'art. 64 del testo unico delle leggi in materia bancaria e creditizia* ✂ **soggetti del gruppo di appartenenza** *la Banca d'Italia autorizza gli istituti di moneta elettronica quando (…)non sussistano, tra gli istituti di moneta elettronica o i soggetti del gruppo di appartenenza e altri soggetti, stretti legami che ostacolino l'effettivo esercizio delle funzioni di vigilanza*

📖 Possible equivalents: grupa (pl), group (en)

I

IPOTECA (it)

(Adj) **ipoteca iscritta** *l'ipoteca iscritta a garanzia di obbligazioni derivanti da contratto di mutuo stipulato o accollato a seguito di frazionamento (…), ancorché annotata su titoli cambiari, si estingue automaticamente alla data di estinzione dell'obbligazione garantita*

(N) **cancellazione dell'ipoteca ✂ ipoteca su immobili** *durante lo stesso periodo non possono essere iscritte ipoteche sugli immobili o acquistati altri diritti di prelazione sui mobili della banca se non in forza di provvedimenti giudiziali esecutivi anteriori all'inizio del periodo di sospensione*

(V) **essere garantito da ipoteca** *quando i finanziamenti siano garantiti da ipoteca su immobili, si applica la disciplina prevista dalla presente sezione per le operazioni di credito fondiario*

finanziamenti garantiti da ipoteca ✂ procedere d'ufficio alla cancellazione dell'ipoteca *il conservatore procede d'ufficio alla cancellazione dell'ipoteca, senza alcun onere per il debitore, entro il giorno successivo a quello di ricezione della comunicazione*

Possible equivalents: HIPOTEKA (pl), mortgage (en)

IMPORTO (it)

(Adj) **importo inferiore (a), pari (a), superiore (a), totale (di) ✂ importo dovuto, espresso (in)** *quando nei documenti contabili obbligatori è richiesta*

l'indicazione di dati comparativi riferiti a date precedenti l'adozione dell'euro quale moneta di conto, la conversione in euro degli importi originariamente espressi in lire va effettuata al tasso di conversione con la lira **importo rimborsato, trasferito** *i prestatori di servizi di pagamento che partecipano al trasferimento di fondi necessario all'esecuzione di un'operazione di pagamento trasferiscono la totalità dell'importo dell'operazione e non trattengono spese sull'importo trasferito*

(N) **importo dell'operazione** *quando l'operazione di pagamento è disposta su iniziativa del beneficiario o per il suo tramite, il prestatore di servizi di pagamento di cui egli si avvale garantisce che la totalità dell'importo dell'operazione sia ricevuto dal beneficiario* ✂ **importo in euro / lire**

(P) **di importo** *finanziamenti di importo inferiore a 200 euro o superiore a 75.000 euro* **per un importo** *finanziamenti a fronte dei quali il consumatore è tenuto a corrispondere esclusivamente commissioni per un importo non significativo*

importo dell'operazione di pagamento, importo totale del credito ✂ **importi in lire contenuti in norme vigenti** *l'articolo 6 della legge delega consente, ma non obbliga, di riesprimere sistematicamente in euro, fin dal 1 gennaio 1999, gli importi in lire contenuti in norme vigenti* **importi originariamente espressi in lire** ✂ **costituire autonomo importo** *quando un importo in euro non costituisce autonomo importo monetario da contabilizzare o da pagare è possibile trattarlo, anche elettronicamente, con un numero di cifre decimali a piacere*

Possible equivalents: KWOTA (pl) AMOUNT, value (en)

IMPRESA (it)

(Aff) **micro-impresa** *'micro-impresa': l'impresa che, al momento della conclusione del contratto per la prestazione di servizi di pagamento, è un'impresa che possiede i requisiti previsti dalla raccomandazione n. 2003/361/CE della Commissione, del 6 maggio 2003*

(Adj) **impresa controllata, sottoposta (a)** *gli elementi dell'attivo e del passivo e le operazioni 'fuori bilancio' nonché i proventi e gli oneri dell'impresa sottoposta a controllo congiunto sono ripresi nel bilancio consolidato secondo il criterio della proporzione con la partecipazione in essa posseduta* ✂ **imprese finanziarie** ✂

imprese associate *sono imprese associate quelle sulle quali l'impresa capogruppo o imprese da questa controllate esercitano un'influenza notevole*

(N) **impresa capogruppo** ✂ **imprese di assicurazione, di investimento** ✂ **bilancio dell'impresa, elenco delle imprese, esercizio dell'impresa** *la concessione di finanziamenti a medio e lungo termine da parte di banche alle imprese può essere garantita da privilegio speciale su beni mobili, comunque destinati all'esercizio dell'impresa, non iscritti nei pubblici registri* **gestione dell'impresa, reddito d'impresa / dell'impresa registro delle imprese** ✂ **partecipazione in un'impresa**

✎ **impresa capogruppo ai sensi dell'art. 1, imprese controllate incluse nel consolidamento** *le imprese controllate incluse nel consolidamento a norma dell'art. 28 (…) sono tenute a trasmettere tempestivamente all'impresa capogruppo le informazioni da questa richieste ai fini della redazione del bilancio consolidato* **imprese consorziate o socie, imprese in genere** *disposizioni per le imprese in genere* ✂ **il bilancio dell'impresa e il bilancio consolidato** *il bilancio dell'impresa e il bilancio consolidato sono costituiti dallo stato patrimoniale, dal conto economico e dalla nota integrativa* ✂ **iscrizione nel registro delle imprese** ✂ **ai fini della determinazione del reddito d'impresa**

📖 Possible equivalents: PRZEDSIĘBIORSTWO, SPÓŁKA, zakład (pl), BUSINESS, COMPANY, ENTERPRISE, SOCIETY, UNDERTAKING (en)

INFORMAZIONE (it)

(Adj) **informazione finanziaria, necessaria (per), relativa (a)** ✂ **informazioni precontrattuali** *il finanziatore assicura che il consumatore riceva comunque le informazioni precontrattuali* **informazioni supplementari** ✂ **informazioni fornite, previste** *la Banca d'Italia stabilisce modalità e termini per la trasmissione delle informazioni previste dai commi 1 e 2* **informazioni richieste**

(N) **scambio, trasmissione di informazioni** ✂ **informazioni di cui al comma 1**

(V) **fornire informazioni** *gli enti creditizi e finanziari possono fornire nella nota integrativa altre informazioni ad integrazione di quelle di cui al comma 1*

✎ **i dati e le informazioni, informazioni e / o comunicazioni, le informazioni e le condizioni** *le informazioni e le condizioni sono redatte in termini di facile* *comprensione e in forma chiara e leggibile* ✂ **collaborare mediante lo scambio di informazioni, la Banca d'Italia + scambiare informazioni (con)** *nel rispetto delle condizioni previste dalle disposizioni dell'Unione europea, la Banca d'Italia scambia informazioni con tutte le altre autorità e soggetti esteri indicati dalle disposizioni medesime*

📖 Possible equivalents: INFORMACJA (pl), INFORMATION (en)

INTERESSE (it)

(Adj) **interesse usurario** *per la determinazione del tasso di interesse usurario si tiene conto delle commissioni, remunerazioni a qualsiasi titolo e delle spese, escluse quelle per imposte e tasse, collegate alla erogazione del credito*

(N) **interessi di mora** *le banche e gli intermediari finanziari rendono noti in modo chiaro ai clienti i tassi di interesse, i prezzi e le altre condizioni economiche relative alle operazioni e ai servizi offerti, ivi compresi gli interessi di mora e le valute applicate per l'imputazione degli interessi* ✂ **calcolo dell'interesse, importo dell'interesse, tasso di interesse** ✂ **pagamento di interessi**

(V) **pagare interessi**

✎ **divieto di pagare interessi** *la Banca d'Italia può d) adottare (…) provvedimenti specifici nei confronti di singoli istituti di pagamento, riguardanti anche: la restrizione delle attività o della struttura territoriale; il divieto di effettuare determinate operazioni, anche di natura societaria, e di distribuire utili o altri elementi del patrimonio, nonché, con riferimento a strumenti finanziari computabili nel patrimonio a fini di vigilanza, il divieto di pagare interessi* **modifica dei tassi di interesse, tassi di interesse o di cambio** *le modifiche dei tassi di interesse o di cambio possono essere applicate con effetto immediato e senza preavviso* **variazioni del tasso di interesse** *le variazioni dei tassi di interesse adottate in previsione o in conseguenza di decisioni di politica monetaria riguardano contestualmente sia i tassi debitori che quelli creditori, e si applicano con modalità tali da non recare pregiudizio al cliente*

📖 Possible equivalents: ODSETKA, OPROCENTOWANIE, procent (pl), interest (en)

INTERMEDIARIO (it)

(Adj) **intermediario finanziario ✂ intermediario autorizzato ✂ singolo intermediario** *le disposizioni emanate dalla Banca d'Italia per esercitare la vigilanza su base consolidata possono tenere conto, anche con riferimento al singolo intermediario finanziario, della situazione dei soggetti indicate nel comma 2, lettere a) e b)*

(N) **intermediario del credito**

✎ **intermediario finanziario iscritto all'albo di cui all'articolo 1 ✂ intermediari finanziari di cui all'articolo 1, intermediari finanziari iscritti nell'elenco speciale, intermediari finanziari previsti dal Titolo I, intemediari iscritti nell'elenco di cui all'articolo 1 ✂ una banca e / o un intermediario finanziario, il finanziatore o l'intermediario del credito** *il finanziatore o l'intermediario del credito (...) forniscono al consumatore, prima che egli sia vincolato da un contratto o da un'offerta di credito, le informazioni necessarie per consentire il confronto delle diverse offerte di credito sul mercato* **l'intermediario finanziario o la società finanziaria**

📖 Possible equivalents: pośrednik (pl), agent, broker, intermediary (en)

ISCRIZIONE (it)

Usually singular

(N) **iscrizione alla/nella sezione, nell'albo, nell'elenco, nel registro ✂ istanza di iscrizione, obbligo di iscrizione, requisiti per l'iscrizione** *l'Organismo può disporre la cancellazione dall'elenco a) qualora vengano meno i requisiti per l'iscrizione*

(P) **iscrizione a** *almeno tre mesi prima della scadenza del termine indicato al comma 1, gli altri soggetti ivi indicati presentano istanza di autorizzazione ai fini dell'iscrizione all'albo di cui all'articolo 106* **iscrizione in**

✎ **iscrizione nell'albo di cui all articolo 1 / previsto (da)** *il Ministro dell'economia e delle finanze, sentita la Banca d'Italia, determina i criteri oggettivi, riferibili al volume di attività finanziaria in base ai quali sono individuati i confidi che sono tenuti a chiedere l'autorizzazione per l'iscrizione nell'albo previsto dall'articolo 106* **iscrizione nell'elenco degli agenti in attività finanziaria, iscrizione nell'elenco**

di cui all'articolo 1, iscrizione nel registro delle imprese ✂ data / istanza di iscrizione nell'elenco, requisiti per l'iscrizione nell'elenco ✂ presentare istanza di autorizzazione ai fini dell'iscrizione all'albo, riscuotere i contributi e le altre somme dovute per l'iscrizione nell'elenco *l'Organismo svolge ogni attività necessaria per la gestione dell'elenco, determina la misura dei contributi a carico degli iscritti (...) e riscuote i contributi e le altre somme dovute per l'iscrizione nell'elenco*

📖 Possible equivalents: rejestracja, wpis (pl), enrolment, entry, registration (en)

ISTITUTO (it)

(Adj) **istituto autorizzato** *la Banca d'Italia disciplina la procedura di autorizzazione, i casi di revoca e le ipotesi di decadenza quando l'istituto autorizzato non abbia iniziato l'esercizio dell'attività*

(N) **ISTITUTO DI PAGAMENTO, istituto per la vigilanza ✂ ispezioni presso gli istituti (di)** *la Banca d'Italia può effettuare ispezioni presso gli istituti di moneta elettronica, i loro agenti o i soggetti a cui sono esternalizzate attività e richiedere a essi l'esibizione di documenti e gli atti che ritenga necessari* **organi degli istituti** *la Banca d'Italia può b) ordinare la convocazione degli organi collegiali degli istituti di moneta elettronica, fissandone l'ordine del giorno, e proporre l'assunzione di determinate decisioni* **succursale di un istituto**

(P) **presso un istituto**

✏ **istituto di moneta elettronica con sede legale (in), ✂ Istituto per la vigilanza sulle assicurazioni private e di interesse collettivo (ISVAP) ✂ convocazione degli organi collegiali degli istituti** *la Banca d'Italia può b) ordinare la convocazione degli organi collegiali degli istituti di moneta elettronica, fissandone l'ordine del giorno, e proporre l'assunzione di determinate decisioni* **soggetti diversi dagli istituti (di) ✂ istituto + svolgere attività**

📖 Possible equivalents: INSTYTUCJA, organizacja (pl), BODY, INSTITUTION (en)

ISTITUTO DI PAGAMENTO (it)

(Adj) **istituto di pagamento comunitario** ✂ **istituti di pagamento italiani** *gli istituti di pagamento italiani possono stabilire succursali nel territorio della Repubblica e degli altri Stati comunitari nel rispetto delle procedure fissate dalla Banca d'Italia*

(N) **albo degli istituti di pagamento** *la Banca d'Italia può esentare i soggetti iscritti nell'albo degli istituti di pagamento dall'applicazione di alcune delle disposizioni previste dal presente titolo*

istituto di moneta elettronica o istituto di pagamento comunitario ✂ **le banche, gli istituti di moneta elettronica e gli istituti di pagamento** *le banche, gli istituti di moneta elettronica e gli istituti di pagamento aderiscono ai sistemi di risoluzione stragiudiziale delle controversie previsti dall'articolo 128-bis (…) per le controversie individuate dalle disposizioni attuative del medesimo articolo* ✂ **istituti di pagamento + stabilire succursali** ✂ **per conto di istituti di moneta elettronica o istituto di pagamento comunitari** *la riserva di attività prevista dal presente articolo non si applica agli agenti che prestano servizi di pagamento per conto di istituti di moneta elettronica o istituti di pagamento comunitari*

Possible equivalents: instytucja płatnicza (pl), payment institution (en)

ITALIA (it)

(Adj) **autorizzato in Italia** *con riferimento agli istituti di pagamento e agli istituti di moneta elettronica autorizzati in Italia l'abrogazione ha effetto a decorrere dalla data di entrata in vigore delle disposizioni di attuazione dell'articolo 128-quater comma 6* **insediato in Italia**

(N) **Banca d'Italia → BANCA** ✂ **succursale in Italia** *la Banca d'Italia iscrive in un apposito albo gli istituti di moneta elettronica autorizzati in Italia e le relative succursali nonché le succursali in Italia degli istituti di moneta elettronica con sede legale in uno Stato comunitario o extracomunitario*

(P) **in Italia o all'estero**

✎ **agenti insediati in Italia** *fino al 31 dicembre 2013 la Banca d'Italia esercita il controllo sugli agenti insediati in Italia per conto di istituti di moneta elettronica o istituto di pagamento comunitari per verificare l'osservanza delle disposizioni di cui al comma 1* ✂ **disposizioni per l'adempimento di obblighi derivanti dall'appartenenza dell'Italia (a)**

📖 Possible equivalents: Włochy (pl), Italy (en)

L

LEGGE (it)

Uusally singular

(Adj) **legge comunitaria, fallimentare** ✂ **legge recante** ✂ **presente legge** ✂ **vista una legge** *il Presidente della Repubblica (…) vista la legge 17 dicembre 1997, n. 433 (…) emana il seguente decreto legislativo* ✂ **previsto dalla legge**

(N) **legge delega** ✂ **decreto legge** ✂ **disposizione di legge** *le disposizioni del presente decreto e gli atti di cui all'art. 5 si applicano anche alle situazioni dei conti infrannuali e ai bilanci consolidati la cui redazione è prevista da specifiche disposizioni di legge* **norma di legge**

(V) **legge + applicarsi** ✂ **essere disciplinati da una legge** *in deroga a quanto previsto dall'articolo 95-bis, sono disciplinati dalla legge che regola il contratto gli accordi di compensazione e di novazione, nonché, fatto salvo quanto previsto alla lettera d) del comma 1, le cessioni con patto di riacquisto e le transazioni effettuate in un mercato regolamentato*

(P) **ai sensi di legge** *il prestatore dei servizi di pagamento non può richiedere all'utilizzatore spese inerenti all'informativa resa ai sensi di legge*

legge e successive modificazioni *sono trasferite all'ISVAP le funzioni del Ministro delle attività produttive previste dagli articoli 4, sesto comma, e 6, quarto comma, della legge 12 agosto 1982, n. 576, e successive modificazioni, nonché le altre analoghe competenze ministeriali in materia sanzionatoria previste da altre leggi* ✂ **decreto legge convertito, con modificazioni, dalla legge; regio decreto legge convertito dalla legge** ✂ **regolamento adottato ai sensi dell'articolo 1, comma 1, della legge** ✂ **attività riservate ai sensi di legge** *decorsi i termini stabiliti, i soggetti che non abbiano presentato istanza di autorizzazione, iscrizione o* *cancellazione (…) deliberano la liquidazione della società ovvero modificano il proprio oggetto sociale, eliminando il riferimento ad attività riservate ai sensi di legge* **autorizzazione di cui all articolo 2 della legge, riserve di attività previste dalla legge, società previste dalla legge ✂ termini di conclusione dei procedimenti amministrativi, stabiliti da norme di legge o di regolamento, pendenti alla data (di) ✂ testo unico delle leggi in materia bancaria e creditizia ✂ disciplinato dalla legge di uno stato, emanato ai sensi dell'articolo 1, comma 1, della legge ✂ entro diciotto mesi dalla data di entrata in vigore della presente legge**

📖 Possible equivalents: PRAWO, USTAWA (pl), ACT, LAW (en)

LETTERA (it)

(Adj) **lettera inserita, soppressa, sostituita ✂ indicato alla / nella lettera** *la CONSOB determina, con regolamento, i principi e i criteri relativi f) all'esame, da parte della stessa CONSOB, dei reclami contro le delibere dell'organismo di cui al comma 4, relative ai provvedimenti indicati alla lettera c)*

(P) **lettere da a) a c)** *nei casi indicati al comma 1 il numero di cifre decimali non può comunque essere inferiore a quello minimo richiesto dalle lettere da a) a d)* ✂ **(di cui) alla lettera, nella lettera** *per le differenze cambio di cui alla lettera b) del comma 4 la rilevanza fiscale si produce nell'esercizio di realizzo delle stesse a seguito della cessione, dell'ammortamento o della svalutazione degli attivi sottostanti.*

✎ **art. 1, paragrafo 1, lettera a) della direttiva; articolo 1, comma 1, lettera a) del decreto legislativo / testo unico ✂ lettera così sostituita dall'art. 1, comma 1, lett. a); lettera inserita dall'art. 1, comma 1, lett. a) ✂ articolo inserito dall'art. 1, comma 1, lettera a); comma così modificato / sostituito dall'art. 1, comma 1, lettera a); disposizioni di cui agli articoli 1, comma 1, lettere a) e b); soggetti di cui all'articolo 1, comma 1, lettera a); soggetti indicati nel comma 1, lettera a) ✂ collegato ai sensi dell articolo 121, comma 1, lettera a)** *in caso di offerta contestuale di più contratti da concludere per iscritto, diversi da quelli collegati ai sensi dell'articolo 121, comma 1, lettera d), il consenso del consumatore va acquisito distintamente per ciascun contratto attraverso documenti separati previsto dall'articolo 1, comma 1, lettera a)* ✂ **lettera + essere sostituita dalla seguente, organi competenti + ottemperare a quanto previsto dalla lettera a)** *la Banca d'Italia può: c) procedere direttamente alla convocazione degli organi collegiali degli intermediari finanziari quando gli organi competenti non abbiano* *ottemperato a quanto previsto dalla lettera b)* ✂ **come definito dall'articolo 1, comma 1, lettera a)**

📖 <u>Possible equivalents</u>: litera (pl), letter (en)

LIQUIDAZIONE (it)

Always singular

(Adj) **liquidazione ordinaria, volontaria** *entro sessanta giorni dalla comunicazione del provvedimento di cancellazione, l'organo amministrativo convoca l'assemblea per modificare l'oggetto sociale o per assumere altre iniziative conseguenti al provvedimento ovvero per deliberare la liquidazione volontaria della società* ✂ **liquidazione coatta** *la liquidazione coatta può essere disposta, con il medesimo procedimento indicato nel comma 1, su istanza motivata degli organiliquidationliquidatio amministrativi, dell'assemblea straordinaria, dei commissari straordinari o dei liquidatori*

(N) **risanamento e liquidazione** *i provvedimenti e le procedure di risanamento e liquidazione di banche comunitarie sono disciplinati e producono i loro effetti, senza ulteriori formalità, nell'ordinamento italiano secondo la normativa dello Stato d'origine* ✂ **liquidazione di una società** ✂ **procedura di liquidazione**

(P) **in liquidazione** *nei confronti della società in liquidazione restano fermi i poteri delle autorità creditizie previsti nel presente decreto*

✏ **procedura di liquidazione coatta** ✂ **deliberare la liquidazione di una società** *in caso di mancato accoglimento delle istanze di cui al comma 4, lettere b), c) ed e), i soggetti ivi indicati deliberano la liquidazione della società ovvero modificano il proprio oggetto sociale, eliminando il riferimento ad attività riservate ai sensi di legge* **capogruppo + essere sottoposta ad amministrazione straordinaria o a liquidazione coatta amministrativa**

📖 <u>Possible equivalents:</u> LIKWIDACJA, rozwiązanie (pl), liquidation, WINDING UP (en)

M

MATERIA (it)

(N) **competenza in materia di** *le competenze in materia di trasparenza e di correttezza dei comportamenti di cui all'articolo 1, comma 2, lettera h), della legge 23 agosto 2004, n. 243, sono esercitate dalla COVIP compatibilmente con le disposizioni per la sollecitazione del pubblico risparmio* **direttiva, disposizioni, norme in materia (di)**

(P) **in materia di**

✎ **informativa da rendere al pubblico sulle predette materie** *la Banca d'Italia emana disposizioni di carattere generale aventi a oggetto: il governo societario, l'adeguatezza patrimoniale, il contenimento del rischio nelle sue diverse configurazioni (...) nonché l'informativa da rendere al pubblico sulle predette materie* ✂ **testo unico delle disposizioni in materia di intermediazione finanziaria, testo unico delle leggi in materia bancaria e creditizia, di cui al decreto legislativo 1 settembre 1993, n. 385** ✂ **adottare per le materie indicate nel comma 1, ove la situazione lo richieda, provvedimenti specifici (nei confronti di)**

📖 Possible equivalents: dziedzina, SPRAWA (pl), domain, MATTER (en)

MESE (it)

Usually singular

(Avv) **almeno un mese**

(Adj) **mesi precedenti** ✂ **superiore a un mese** *in casi eccezionali la procedura può essere prorogata, per un periodo non superiore a sei mesi, con il medesimo procedimento indicato nel comma 1*

(N) **preavviso di due mesi** *i contratti di credito a tempo indeterminato possono prevedere il diritto del finanziatore a: a) recedere dal contratto con un preavviso di almeno due mesi, comunicato al consumatore su supporto cartaceo o altro supporto durevole* **termine di due mesi**

(P) **entro un mese (da)** *entro un mese dall'approvazione della Banca d'Italia, gli organi subentrati ai commissari presentano la dichiarazione dei redditi relativa a detto periodo secondo le disposizioni tributarie vigenti* ✂ **da due mesi a dieci anni** ✂ **due mesi prima (di)**

✐ **almeno due mesi prima della scadenza del termine indicato al comma 1** ✂ **titoli emessi nei due mesi precedenti** ✂ **entro due mesi dalla data di entrata in vigore della presente legge** *lo statuto della Banca d'Italia è adeguato alle disposizioni contenute nei commi da 1 a 7 entro due mesi dalla data di entrata in vigore della presente legge, con le modalità stabilite dal comma 2 dell'articolo 10 del decreto legislativo 10 marzo 1998, n. 43* ✂ **essere punito con la reclusione da due mesi a dieci anni** *chiunque svolge l'attività di mediazione creditizia senza essere iscritto nell'albo indicato al comma 1 è punito con la reclusione da sei mesi a quattro anni e con la multa da quattro a venti milioni di lire*

📖 Possible equivalents: MIESIĄC (pl), month (en)

MINISTRO (it)

(N) **Ministro della giustizia** ✂ **Consiglio dei Ministri, decreto del ministro** *il decreto del Ministro dell'economia e delle finanze (3) e la proposta della Banca d'Italia sono comunicati dai commissari liquidatori agli interessati, che ne facciano richiesta, non prima dell'insediamento (4) ai sensi dell'articolo 85*

(P) **di concerto con un ministro** *il Presidente della Repubblica (…) sulla proposta del Presidente del Consiglio dei Ministri e del Ministro per gli affari regionali, di concerto con i Ministri della giustizia e dell'economia e delle finanze emana il seguente decreto legislativo*

Ministro degli affari esteri, Ministro di grazia e giustizia ✂ decreto del Ministro dell'economia e delle finanze, del Ministro del tesoro, del bilancio e della programmazione economica ✂ proposta del Presidente del Consiglio dei Ministri ✂ (vista) la preliminare deliberazione del Consiglio dei Ministri, adottata nella riunione del 1 gennaio 2000 *Il Presidente della Repubblica (...) vista la deliberazione del Consiglio dei Ministri, adottata nella riunione del 18 giugno 1998 (...) emana il seguente decreto legislativo*

Possible equivalents: MINISTER (pl), minister (en)

MODALITÀ (it)

Usually plural

(Adj) **modalità indicate (in)** *il bilancio consolidato, la relazione sulla gestione e la relazione degli organi e dei soggetti incaricati della verifica di tale bilancio sono pubblicati in lingua italiana secondo le modalità indicate nell'art. 41* **modalità previste (da), stabilite (da) ✂ relative modalità** *il comma disciplina, mediante rinvio, la rilevanza tributaria delle differenze cambio analogamente a quanto previsto per la generalità delle imprese, e le relative modalità di iscrizione nello stato patrimoniale*

(N) **il contenuto e le modalità** *Il CICR indica il contenuto e le modalità della comunicazione* **le modalità e le condizioni, modalità e termini ✂ modalità di attuazione** *i termini e le modalità di attuazione dell'articolo 30-quinquies, comma 1, lettera b), sono definiti con decreto interdirettoriale del Dipartimento del Tesoro del Ministero dell'economia e delle finanze e del direttore dell'Agenzia delle entrate* **modalità di comunicazione, di rimbroso**

(V) **indicare, stabilire modalità** *la Banca d'Italia, in conformità alle deliberazioni del CICR, stabilisce le modalità di calcolo del TAEG, ivi inclusa la specificazione dei casi in cui i costi di cui al comma 2 sono compresi nel costo totale del credito*

(P) **con, secondo le modalità** *nei casi di cui al comma 2 il prestatore di servizi di pagamento informa il pagatore, secondo le modalità concordate, del blocco dello strumento motivando tale decisione* ✂ **modalità per** *la CONSOB stabilisce con regolamento modalità per l'elezione di un membro effettivo del collegio sindacale da parte dei soci di minoranza*

✎ **il contenuto e le modalità della comunicazione** *la Banca d'Italia, in conformità alle deliberazioni del CICR, fissa i contenuti e le modalità di tale comunicazione* ✂ **inviare alla Banca d'Italia, con le modalità e nei termini da essa stabiliti, le segnalazioni periodiche nonché ogni altro dato e document richiesto** *gli istituti di moneta elettronica inviano alla Banca d'Italia, con le modalità e nei termini da essa stabiliti, le segnalazioni periodiche nonché ogni altro dato e documento richiesto* **trasmettere bilanci con le modalità e nei termini stabiliti dalla Banca d'Italia** ✂ **nel rispetto delle / secondo le modalità stabilite dalla Banca d'Italia, secondo le modalità peviste (da)**

📖 Possible equivalents: SPOSÓB, WARUNEK (pl), CONDITION, means, method, REQUIREMENT (en)

MODIFICAZIONE (it)

Always plural

(Adj) **successive modificazioni** ✂ **modificazioni statutarie** *le deliberazioni assembleari sono assunte con le maggioranze previste dagli statuti per le modificazioni statutarie* ✂ **seguenti modificazioni**

(N) **modificazioni e integrazioni** *quando nelle norme statali e regionali sono richiamate le disposizioni del regio decreto-legge 29 luglio 1927, n. 1509 (1), convertito con modificazioni dalla legge 5 luglio 1928, n. 1760, e del decreto ministeriale 23 gennaio 1928, e successive modificazioni e integrazioni, dette disposizioni continuano a integrare le norme suddette che a esse fanno riferimento*

(P) **con modificazioni** *comma così sostituito dall'art. 1, comma 1, lett. h), n. 3, D.L. 27 dicembre 2006, n. 297, convertito, con modificazioni, dalla L. 23 febbraio 2007, n. 15*

✎ **successive modificazioni e integrazioni** ✂ **decreto legge convertito, con modificazioni, dalla legge** ✂ **decreto legislativo / legge / regio decreto e successive modificazioni, testo unico di cui al decreto legislativo e successive modificazioni** *nel testo unico di cui al decreto legislativo 24 febbraio 1998, n. 58, e successive modificazioni, alla parte IV, titolo III, capo II, dopo l'articolo 165-bis, introdotto dall'articolo 18, comma 1, lettera h), della presente legge, è aggiunta la seguente sezione* ✂ **seguenti modificazioni + essere apportate al codice civile /**

decreto legislativo *al decreto legislativo 21 novembre 2007, n. 231, sono apportate le seguenti modificazioni*

📖 Possible equivalents: nowelizacja, ZMIANA (pl), alteration, AMENDMENT, modification (en)

MONETA (it)

Usually singular

(Adj) **MONETA ELETTRONICA, moneta unica** *fino all'adozione da parte dell'Italia della moneta unica, secondo le previsioni del trattato, il Governatore della Banca d'Italia determina la misura dell'interesse dei depositi in conto corrente fruttifero presso la Banca stessa* ✂ **monete metalliche** *la coniazione e l'emissione delle monete metalliche in Euro sono effettuate nel rispetto delle misure adottate dal Consiglio dell'Unione europea a norma degli articoli 105A, paragrafo 2, e 109L, paragrafo 4, del trattato*

(N) **moneta di conto** ✂ **banconote e monete** *falsificazione di banconote e monete in euro non aventi corso legale*

✎ **adozione dell'euro quale moneta di conto** *il presente articolo dà attuazione all'articolo 8 della legge delega e fissa i principi generali relativi all'adozione dell'euro quale moneta di conto* **conversione in moneta di conto** ✂ **adottare l'euro quale moneta di conto, essere tradotti nella moneta di conto** *gli elementi monetari denominati nelle valute aderenti o comunque variabili in funzione dell'andamento dei tassi di cambio delle valute aderenti sono tradotti nella moneta di conto, anche ai fini della determinazione del reddito d'impresa, applicando i rispettivi tassi di conversione e nel rispetto degli articoli 4 e 5 del Regolamento (CE) n. 1103/97*

📖 Possible equivalents: moneta, PIENIĄDZ, waluta (pl), coin, currency, money (en)

MONETA ELETTRONICA (it)

Always singular

(N) **detentore di moneta elettronica** *il contratto tra l'emittente e il detentore di moneta elettronica indica chiaramente ed esplicitamente le modalità e le condizioni del rimborso* **emissione, emittente, istituto di moneta elettronica, rimborso della moneta elettronica**

(V) **emettere moneta elettronica** *possono emettere moneta elettronica, nel rispetto delle disposizioni ad essi applicabili, la Banca centrale europea, le banche centrali comunitarie, lo Stato italiano e gli altri Stati comunitari, le pubbliche amministrazioni statali, regionali e locali, nonché Poste Italiane*

✎ **attività di emissione di moneta elettronica, attività imprenditoriali diverse dall'emissione di moneta elettronica o dalla prestazione di servizi di pagamento** *agli istituti di moneta elettronica che non esercitano attività imprenditoriali diverse dall'emissione di moneta elettronica o dalla prestazione di servizi di pagamento, si applicano altresì gli articoli 78, 79, 82, 113-bis e 113-ter* **istituto di moneta elettronica con sede legale (in)** ✂ **nei confronti dell'istituto di moneta elettronica** *se le somme di denaro ricevute per l'emissione di moneta elettronica sono depositate presso terzi non operano le compensazioni legale e giudiziale e non può essere pattuita la compensazione convenzionale rispetto ai crediti vantati dal depositario nei confronti dell'istituto di moneta elettronica* **per conto di istituti di moneta elettronica o istituti di pagamento comunitari** *la riserva di attività prevista dal presente articolo non si applica agli agenti che prestano servizi di pagamento per conto di istituti di moneta elettronica o istituti di pagamento comunitari*

📖 Possible equivalents: PIENIĄDZ ELEKTRONICZNY (pl), electronic money (en)

MUTUO (it)

(Adj) **mutuo immobiliare** *per i mutui immobiliari estinti prima del 3 aprile 2007 e la cui ipoteca non sia stata cancellata alla medesima data, il termine di cui al comma 2 dell'articolo 40-bis decorre dalla data della richiesta della quietanza da parte del debitore*

(N) **mutuo per l'acquisto (di)** *ak* ✂ **concessione del mutuo, contratto di mutuo** ✂ **mutuo e/o provvisionale** *il Fondo procede alla revoca dei provvedimenti di erogazione del mutuo e della provvisionale ed al recupero delle somme già erogate*

✎ **mutuo stipulato o accollato a seguito di frazionamento** *l'ipoteca iscritta a garanzia di obbligazioni derivanti da contratto di mutuo stipulato o accollato a seguito di frazionamento (…), ancorché annotata su titoli cambiari, si estingue automaticamente alla data di estinzione dell'obbligazione garantita* ✂ **estinzione**

anticipata dei mutui immobiliari ✂ **somme erogate a titolo di mutuo** *le somme erogate a titolo di mutuo ai sensi del comma 2-bis non sono imputabili alla massa fallimentare né alle attività sopravvenute dell'imprenditore fallito*

🕮 Possible equivalents: KREDYT, POŻYCZKA (pl), credit, loan (en)

N

NORMA (it)

(Adj) **norme applicabili** *l'attività dell'Organismo, anche nei rapporti con i terzi, è disciplinata dal codice civile e dalle altre norme applicabili alle persone giuridiche di diritto privato* **norme finali, vigenti** ✂ **norma contenuta (in), norme indicate (in)** ✂ **contenuto in norme, stabilito da norme**

(N) **norme e disposizioni** ✂ **norme di attuazione** *le regioni a statuto speciale, alle quali sono riconosciuti, in base alle norme di attuazione dei rispettivi statuti, poteri nelle materie disciplinate dalla direttiva n. 89/646/CEE (2), provvedono a emanare norme di recepimento della direttiva stessa* ✂ **applicazione delle norme** *la Banca d'Italia può dettare disposizioni attuative ai fini dell'applicazione delle norme di cui al presente articolo* **inosservanza delle norme, violazione delle norme (di cui a)** ✂ **a norma dell'articolo 1 / di legge / del diritto** *il 1 gennaio 1999 sono ridenominati in euro i titoli di Stato denominati in lire, emessi a norma del diritto italiano e negoziabili sui mercati regolamentati.*

(V) **norme + applicarsi** *si applicano le norme procedurali del processo amministrativo, in quanto compatibili, compresa la sospensione (…) dell'esecutività del provvedimento impugnato per gravi motivi* **norme + disciplinare** *le banche e gli altri intermediari finanziari effettuano le operazioni valutarie e in cambi nel rispetto delle norme che li disciplinano* **norme + regolare** *norme legislative o amministrative che regolano l'attività di agenzia in attività finanziaria o di mediazione creditizia*

(P) **norme su** *gli amministratori delle società del gruppo sono tenuti a fornire ogni dato e informazione per l'emanazione delle disposizioni e la necessaria collaborazione per il rispetto delle norme sulla vigilanza consolidate* ✂ **norme di cui a** ✂ **norme in materia di** ✂ **a norma di**

✎ **norma contenuta nell'articolo 1, norme applicabili ai soggetti operanti nel settore finanziario, norme del decreto legislativo, norme del presente titolo, relative norme di attuazione** ✂ **grave violazione di norme** *la Banca d'Italia può disporre la cancellazione dall'elenco b) qualora risultino gravi violazioni di norme di legge e delle disposizioni emanate ai sensi del presente decreto legislativo* **importi in lire contenute in norme vigenti, sanzione amministrativa pecuniaria per l'inosservanza delle norme contenute nell'articolo 1** ✂ **termini di conclusione dei procedimenti amministrativi, stabiliti da norme di legge o di regolamento** *i termini di conclusione dei procedimenti amministrativi, stabiliti da norme di legge o di regolamento, pendenti alla data del 19 settembre 2010, sono prorogati fino a 120 giorni successivi alla data di entrata in vigore del presente decreto* ✂ **a norma dell'articolo 1, comma 1; a norma dell'articolo 1 del codice civile** *La deliberazione è depositata e iscritta a norma dell'articolo 2436 del codice civile*

📖 Possible equivalents: norma, ZASADA (pl), norm, rule, standard (en)

O

OBBLIGO (it)

(Adj) **obblighi informativi** ✂ **obbligo indicato** *spetta all'intermediario l'onere della prova di aver adempiuto agli obblighi indicati dal presente comma* **obbligo previsto (da)** ✂ **obblighi derivanti (da)**

(N) **obbligo di iscrizione** *i confidi tenuti ad iscriversi nell'albo di cui all'articolo 106 sono esclusi dall'obbligo di iscrizione nell'elenco tenuto dall'Organismo previsto all'articolo 112-bis* **obbligo di rimborso, verifica** ✂ **obblighi di comunicazione** *nei casi e nei modi previsti dalle disposizioni dell'Unione europea, le autorità creditizie adempiono agli obblighi di comunicazione nei confronti delle autorità e dei comitati che compongono il SEVIF* **obblighi di trasparenza** ✂ **violazione dell'obbligo** ✂ **adempimento, inosservanza di obblighi** ✂ *(V)* **adempiere all'obbligo** *spetta al prestatore dei servizi di pagamento l'onere della prova di aver correttamente adempiuto agli obblighi previsti dal presente capo* ✂ **comportare l'obbligo (di)**

(P) **obbligo di cui (a)** ✂ **con obbligo (di)** *sono ammessi al rimborso i crediti relativi ai fondi acquisiti dalle banche con obbligo di restituzione, sotto forma di depositi o sotto altra forma, nonché agli assegni circolari e agli altri titoli di credito ad essi assimilabili*

✎ **obbligo previsto dall'articolo 1, obbligo di pubblicare un prospetto** ✂ **legge recante disposizioni per l'adempimento di obblighi derivanti dall'appartenenza dell'Italia (a)** ✂ **è fatto obbligo a chiunque spetti di osservarlo e di farlo osservare** *Il presente decreto, munito del sigillo dello Stato, sarà inserito nella Raccolta ufficiale degli atti normativi della Repubblica italiana. È fatto obbligo a chiunque spetti di osservarlo e di farlo osservare* ✂ **fermo restando**

l'obbligo (di) *il presente articolo si applica anche ai prodotti finanziari diversi dagli strumenti finanziari e dai prodotti finanziari emessi dalle imprese di assicurazione, fermo restando l'obbligo di consegna del prospetto informativo*

Possible equivalents: obowiązek, powinność (pl), duty, OBLIGATION, REQUIREMENT (en)

OPERAZIONE (it)

(Adj) **nouve, singole operazioni** *il consenso ad eseguire un'operazione di pagamento o una serie di operazioni di pagamento è prestato nella forma e secondo la procedura concordata nel contratto quadro o nel contratto relativo a singole operazioni di pagamento* ✂ **operazioni finanziarie, passive** *i commissari possono contrarre mutui, effettuare altre operazioni finanziarie passive e costituire in garanzia attività aziendali* ✂ **relativo a un'operazione** ✂ **operazione effettuata, eseguita** ✂ **operazione non autorizzata** ✂ **operazioni realizzate (mediante)** *nel caso di operazioni realizzate mediante sottoscrizione o acquisto di titoli, i richiami ai debitori ceduti si intendono riferiti alla società emittente i titoli* ✂ **determinate operazioni** ✂ **derivante da operazioni** *qualora abbia agito in modo fra-udolento o non abbia adempiuto ad uno o più obblighi di cui all'articolo 7 con dolo o colpa grave, l'utilizzatore sopporta tutte le perdite derivanti da operazioni di pagamento non autorizzate e non si applica il limite di 150 euro di cui al comma 3*

(N) **operazioni e servizi** ✂ **operazione di conversione** *tale comma prescrive i requisiti minimi di informativa che occorre soddisfare relativamente alle operazioni di conversione e di trattamento contabile delle differenze cambio di cui ai precedenti commi 2, 3 e 4* OPERAZIONE DI PAGAMENTO ✂ **operazioni di cartolarizzazione, di credito, di gestione** ✂ **operazioni fuori bilancio** ✂ **categoria di operazione** ✂ **esecuzione, importo di un'operazione** *fatto salvo l'articolo 9, nel caso in cui un'operazione di pagamento non sia stata autorizzata, il prestatore di servizi di pagamento rimborsa immediatamente al pagatore l'importo dell'operazione medesima* ✂ **oggetto delle operazioni** *nel caso in cui i titoli oggetto delle operazioni di cartolarizzazione siano offerti ad investitori non professionali, l'operazione deve essere sottoposta alla valutazione del merito di credito da parte di operatori terzi* **rilevazione delle operazioni** *'moneta di conto': la moneta, lira o euro, che risulta in prevalenza utilizzata, a partire da un dato momento, per la rilevazione delle operazioni di gestione*

(V) **effettuare, eseguire un'operazione, intraprendere operazioni** ✂ **applicarsi alle operazioni** *la presente legge si applica alle operazioni di cartolarizzazione realizzate mediante cessione a titolo oneroso di crediti pecuniari, sia esistenti sia futuri*

(P) **operazioni in corso** *'elementi monetari': le disponibilità di denaro, le attività e passività iscritte in bilancio e le restanti operazioni in corso (dette anche 'fuori bilancio') che comportano o comporteranno il diritto a incassare o l'obbligo a pagare a date future importi di denaro determinati o determinabili* ✂ **nell'ambito di operazioni** *alle cessioni effettuate nell'ambito di operazioni di cartolarizzazione non si applicano gli articoli 69 e 70 del regio decreto 18 novembre 1923, n. 2440, nonché le altre disposizioni che richiedano formalità diverse o ulteriori rispetto a quelle di cui alla presente legge*

attività, passività e le operazioni 'fuori bilancio'; elementi dell'attivo e del passivo e le operazioni 'fuori bilancio' ✂ **operazioni denominate in valute aderenti, operazioni poste in essere** *il CICR stabilisce modalità e criteri per la produzione di interessi nelle operazioni poste in essere nell'esercizio dell'attività bancaria* ✂ **criteri di rilevazione delle operazioni** *l'articolo dà attuazione all'articolo 9 della legge delega per le imprese in genere e tratta sia dei criteri di rilevazione delle operazioni in corso soggette al rischio di cambio 'generato' da una delle valute aderenti all'euro, sia del trattamento delle relative differenze cambio* **informazione relativa all'operazione** ✂ **divieto di effettuare determinate operazioni, anche di natura societaria** ✂ **imporre un divieto di intraprendere nuove operazioni**

Possible equivalents: CZYNNOŚĆ, DZIAŁALNOŚĆ, działanie, operacja, transakcja (pl), ACTION, ACTIVITY, deal, operation, transaction (en)

OPERAZIONE DI PAGAMENTO (it)

(Adj) **singole operazioni di pagamento** *il consenso può essere revocato in qualsiasi momento, nella forma e secondo la procedura concordata nel contratto quadro o nel contratto relativo a singole operazioni di pagamento* ✂ **operazione di pagamento autorizzata, eseguita** *il rimborso corrisponde all'intero importo dell'operazione di pagamento eseguita*

(N) **esecuzione di un'operazione di pagamento** *il pagatore, in deroga all'articolo 17, non può revocare l'ordine di pagamento dopo averlo trasmesso al beneficiario o dopo avergli dato il proprio consenso ad avviare l'esecuzione dell'operazione di pagamento* **importo di un'operazione di pagamento**

(V) **eseguire un'operazione di pagamento** ✂ **operazione di pagamento + essere disposta** *fatto salvo quanto previsto all'articolo 5, comma 4, se l'operazione di pagamento è disposta su iniziativa del beneficiario o per il suo tramite, il pagatore non può revocare l'ordine di pagamento dopo averlo trasmesso al beneficiario o avergli dato il consenso ad eseguire l'operazione di pagamento*

✎ **consenso ad eseguire un'operazione di pagamento** *il consenso ad eseguire un'operazione di pagamento o una serie di operazioni di pagamento è prestato nella forma e secondo la procedura concordata nel contratto quadro o nel contratto relativo a singole operazioni di pagamento* **importo dell'operazione di pagamento eseguita** *il rimborso corrisponde all'intero importo dell'operazione di pagamento eseguita*

Possible equivalents: transakcja płatnicza, usługa płatnicza (pl), money transfer, payment transaction (en)

ORGANISMO (it)

(Adj) **organismo previsto (da)** *l'Organismo previsto dall'articolo 128-undecies individua forme di collaborazione e di scambio di informazioni con gli enti di previdenza.*

(N) **costituzione dell'organismo** *ai fini della costituzione dell'Organismo, i primi componenti sono nominati con decreto del Ministro dell'economia e delle finanze, su proposta della Banca d'Italia* ✂ **organismo di cui all'articolo 1**

(V) **organismo + essere istituito** *è istituito un Organismo, avente personalità giuridica di diritto privato (...), con autonomia organizzativa, statutaria e finanziaria competente per la gestione dell'elenco di cui all'articolo 112, comma 1*

✎ **organismi di investimento collettivo del risparmio** *'organismi di investimento collettivo del risparmio (OICR)': i fondi comuni di investimento aperti e chiusi e le società di investimento a capitale variabile* **organismi pubblici e privati** *ai fini del riscontro sull'autenticità dei dati contenuti nelle richieste di verifica inviate dagli aderenti, l'ente gestore autorizza di volta in volta la procedura di collegamento dell'archivio alle banche dati degli organismi pubblici e privati* ✂ **organi di gestione e di controllo dell'organismo, soggetti iscritti in un apposito elenco tenuto dall'organismo previsto dall'articolo 1** *l'esercizio professionale nei confronti del pubblico dell'attività di agente in attività finanziaria è riservato ai soggetti iscritti in un apposito elenco tenuto dall'Organismo previsto dall'articolo 128-undecies* ✂ **organismo + avere personalità giuridica**

📖 Possible equivalents: INSTYTUCJA, organ, PODMIOT, przedsiębiorstwo (pl), BODY, INSTITUTION, organisation, UNDERTAKING (en)

ORGANO (it)

(Adj) **organo amministrativo, liquidatore** *l'organo liquidatore trasmette alla Banca d'Italia riferimenti periodici sullo stato di avanzamento della liquidazione* ✂ **organi collegiali, competenti, straordinari**

(N) **organo di amministrazione, controllo, gestione** ✂ **organi della procedura** *gli organi della procedura possono trasferire o affidare in gestione a banche o altri intermediari autorizzati alla prestazione di servizi di pagamento, i beni e i rapport giuridici ricompresi nel patrimonio destinato e le relative passività* ✂ **componenti dell'organo** *componenti degli organi e coloro che prestano la propria attività nell'ambito dei sistemi di garanzia dei depositanti sono vincolati al segreto professionale in relazione a tutte le notizie, le informazioni e i dati in possesso* ✂ **convocazione, funzioni, membri degli organi**

(V) **organi + ottemperare** *la Banca d'Italia può c) procedere direttamente alla convocazione degli organi collegiali degli istituti di moneta elettronica quando gli organi competenti non abbiano ottemperato a quanto previsto dalla lettera b)*

✏ **organi di amministrazione e controllo** ✂ **componenti degli organi di gestione e (di) controllo dell'Organismo** *la Banca d'Italia può disporre la rimozione di uno o più componenti degli organi di gestione e controllo in caso di grave inosservanza dei doveri ad essi assegnati dalla legge, dallo statuto o dalle disposizioni di vigilanza* **convocazione degli organi collegiali degli istituti di pagamento** ✂ **ordinare la convocazione degli organi collegiali** *la Banca d'Italia* *può ordinare la convocazione degli organi collegiali degli istituti di pagamento, fissandone l'ordine del giorno, e proporre l'assunzione di determinate decisioni* **procedere direttamente alla convocazione degli organi collegiali ✂ organi competenti + ottemperare a quanto previsto dalla lettera a)**

Possible equivalents: INSTYTUCJA, organ (pl), AUTHORITY, body, entity, INSTITUTION, organisation (en)

P

PAGAMENTO (it)

Usually singular

(Adj) **mancato pagamento** *la cancellazione dall'elenco potrà essere disposta dall'Organismo anche per il mancato pagamento del contributo e delle altre somme dovute per l'iscrizione nell'elenco*

(N) **pagamento di un contributo, pagamento di interessi** ✂ **conto, dilazione di pagamento** *'contratto di credito' indica il contratto con cui un finanziatore concede o si impegna a concedere a un consumatore un credito sotto forma di dilazione di pagamento, di prestito o di altra facilitazione finanziaria* **ISTITUTO DI PAGAMENTO, mezzi di pagamento, OPERAZIONE DI PAGAMENTO, ordine di pagamento, SERVIZIO DI PAGAMENTO, sistema di pagamento, sospensione del pagamento** *la richiesta al fornitore determina la sospensione del pagamento dei canoni* **strumento di pagamento**

✏ **denominazione valutaria dei pagamenti, mancato pagamento del contributo, regolare funzionamento del sistema dei pagamenti** *la Banca d'Italia nega l'autorizzazione quando dalla verifica delle condizioni indicate nel comma 1 non risulti garantita la sana e prudente gestione ovvero il regolare funzionamento del sistema dei pagamenti* **sorveglianza sul sistema dei pagamenti, utilizzo di un determinato strumento di pagamento**

📖 Possible equivalents: PŁATNOŚĆ, SPŁATA, WYPŁATA, zapłata (pl), PAYMENT (en)

PAGATORE (it)

Always singular

(N) **il pagatore e /o il beneficiario** *il titolo II si applica ai servizi di pagamento prestati nella Comunità europea, a condizione che i prestatori di servizi di pagamento del pagatore e del beneficiario siano insediati nella Comunità europea*

✎ **il prestatore di servizi di pagamento del pagatore** *se un'operazione di pagamento non comporta conversioni valutarie da parte del prestatore di servizi di pagamento del pagatore, il pagatore e il beneficiario sostengono ciascuno le spese applicate dal rispettivo prestatore di servizi di pagamento* ✂ **il pagatore e il prestatore di servizi di pagamento** ✂ **rimborsare al pagatore l'importo di un'operazione** *nel caso in cui un'operazione di pagamento non sia stata autorizzata, il prestatore di servizi di pagamento rimborsa immediatamente al pagatore l'importo dell'operazione medesima* ✂ **pagatore + avere diritto al rimborso**

🕮 Possible equivalents: płatnik (pl), payer (en)

PARTE (it)

(N) **concessione da parte di** *il credito fondiario ha per oggetto la concessione, da parte di banche, di finanziamenti a medio e lungo termine garantiti da ipoteca di primo grado su immobili* **possesso, rispetto da parte (di)** ✂ **da parte dell'autorità, del consumatore, del debitore, della società** ✂ **da parte degli agenti, degli iscritti** ✂ **da parte di banche, di soggetti** *fermo quanto disposto dall'articolo 18, il Ministro dell'economia e delle finanze disciplina l'esercizio nel territorio della Repubblica, da parte di soggetti aventi sede legale all'estero, delle attività indicate nell'articolo 106*

(P) **da parte, in parte** *dalla data certa dell'avvenuta erogazione, anche in parte, del finanziamento relativo alle operazioni di cartolarizzazione di cui al comma 2-quater, sui crediti sorti e sulle somme corrisposte dai debitori sono ammesse azioni soltanto a tutela dei diritti di cui all' articolo 1, comma 1, lettera b)* ✂ **in tutto o in parte** *con riferimento alle fattispecie disciplinate in tutto o in parte da ordinamenti stranieri, la verifica dell'insussistenza delle condizioni previste dai commi l e 2 è effettuata sulla base di una valutazione di equivalenza sostanziale a cura dell'Organismo*

✎ **parte I, titolo I, capo I** *nel testo unico delle disposizioni in materia di intermediazione finanziaria, di cui al decreto legislativo 24 febbraio 1998, n. 58, e successive modificazioni, alla parte IV, titolo III, capo II, dopo l'articolo 147-bis, è inserita la seguente sezione* ✂ **vigilare sul rispetto da parte degli iscritti della disciplina cui (essi) sono sottoposti** *la Banca d'Italia tiene l'elenco previsto dall'articolo 111 e vigila sul rispetto da parte degli iscritti della disciplina cui essi sono sottoposti anche ai sensi dell'articolo 111, comma 5*

📖 Possible equivalents: CZĘŚĆ, strona (pl), PART (en)

PARTECIPAZIONE (it)

(N) **participazione di controllo** *le disposizioni dell'articolo 15, comma 3, e dell'articolo 16, comma 3, si applicano, in armonia con la normativa comunitaria, anche alle società finanziarie aventi sede legale in uno Stato comunitario quando la partecipazione di controllo è detenuta da una o più banche aventi sede legale nel medesimo Stato* ✂ **assunzione, gestione di partecipazioni** *la detenzione o la gestione di partecipazioni si considera esclusiva quando l'atto costitutivo o lo statuto preveda unicamente lo svolgimento di tali attività* **titolare di partecipazioni** *la Banca d'Italia può altresì richiedere agli amministratori delle società e degli enti titolari di partecipazioni in banche l'indicazione dei soggetti controllanti* ✂ **partecipazioni in banche, in imprese, in società**

(P) **participazione in** *le disposizioni del comma 2 si applicano anche alle partecipazioni in imprese controllate diverse da quelle indicate nell'art. 28 e alle partecipazioni in imprese sottoposte a controllo*

✎ **attività di assunzione di partecipazioni** *ai fini del presente decreto, l'attività di assunzione di partecipazioni al fine di successivi smobilizzi è in ogni caso considerata attività finanziaria* **società di partecipazione finanziaria mista capogruppo** *la Banca d'Italia può individuare le ipotesi in cui la società di partecipazione finanziaria mista capogruppo è esentata dall'applicazione di una o più disposizioni adottate ai sensi del presente capo*

📖 Possible equivalents: uczestnictwo, udział (pl), interest, SHARE, stake, stock (en)

PATRIMONIO (it)

Usually singular

(Adj) **patrimonio distinto** *le somme di denaro detenute nei conti di pagamento costituiscono, per ciascun cliente, patrimonio distinto a tutti gli effetti da quello dell'istituto di pagamento e degli altri clienti dello stesso* **patrimonio netto** ✂ **patrimonio destinato** *a tale patrimonio destinato si applica l'articolo 114-terdecies, anche con riferimento all'emissione di moneta elettronica*

(N) **elementi del patrimonio** *la Banca d'Italia può imporre agli intermediari il divieto di intraprendere nuove operazioni e disporre la riduzione delle attività, nonché vietare la distribuzione di utili o di altri elementi del patrimonio per violazione di norme di legge o di disposizioni emanate ai sensi del presente decreto*

(V) **costituire (un) patrimonio** *le somme di cui al comma 1 sono investite, nel rispetto delle modalità stabilite dalla Banca d'Italia, in attività che costituiscono patrimonio distinto a tutti gli effetti da quello dell'istituto di moneta elettronica.*

strumenti finanziari computabili nel patrimonio a fini di vigilanza ✂ **differenze derivanti dalla conversione del patrimonio netto, denominate in una valuta aderente** *la disposizione chiarisce che le differenze cambio derivanti dalla conversione del patrimonio netto, denominato in valute aderenti, delle imprese controllate incluse nel consolidamento devono essere imputate alle riserve consolidate, conformemente quindi a quanto prescritto dalla disciplina generale di settore* ✂ **costituire un patrimonio destinato, distribuire utili o altri elementi del patrimonio, azioni + essere ammesse su patrimonio** *fino al completo soddisfacimento dei diritti dei soggetti a cui vantaggio la destinazione è effettuata, sul patrimonio destinato e sui frutti e proventi da esso derivanti sono ammesse azioni soltanto a tutela dei diritti dei predetti soggetti*

Possible equivalents: majątek, mienie (pl), assets, estate, equity, PROPERTY (en)

PERIODO 1 (it)

Usually singular

(Adj) **periodo non inferiore (a), non superiore (a), transitorio** *ai documenti contabili obbligatori a rilevanza esterna redatti in euro nel periodo transitorio si applicano le disposizioni del comma 8*

(N) **periodo di tempo** ✂ **inizio di un periodo** *durante lo stesso periodo non possono essere iscritte ipoteche sugli immobili o acquistati altri diritti di prelazione sui mobili della banca se non in forza di provvedimenti giudiziali esecutivi anteriori all'inizio del periodo di sospensione*

(P) **durante, per un periodo** *il termine può essere prorogato dalla Banca d'Italia, in circostanze del tutto eccezionali per un periodo complessivo non superiore a 10 giorni lavorativi (3)* ✂ **nel periodo**

per un periodo non inferiore / superiore a due anni

Possible equivalents: OKRES (pl), period (en)

PERIODO 2 (it)

Usually singular

(Adj) **ultimo periodo** *nel caso in cui l'intermediario mandante rilevi nel comportamento dell'agente in attività finanziaria le violazioni previste dai commi 3, 3-bis e 4, l'inosservanza degli obblighi previsti dall'articolo 125-novies o la violazione dell'articolo 128-decies, comma 1, ultimo periodo, adotta immediate misure correttive e trasmette la documentazione relativa alle violazioni riscontrate (…) all'Organismo di cui all'articolo 128* ✂ **periodo inserito, sostituito (da)**

(N) **periodo del comma 1** *le banche, le società o gli enti ai quali appartengono i responsabili delle violazioni rispondono, in solido con questi, del pagamento della sanzione e delle spese di pubblicità previste dal primo periodo del comma 3 e sono tenuti a esercitare il regresso verso i responsabili*

(V) **periodo + essere aggiunto** *al comma 1-bis è aggiunto il seguente periodo: 'Nel caso in cui le notizie o i dati falsi siano forniti ad un intermediario finanziario, si applica la pena dell'arresto fino a un anno o dell'ammenda fino ad euro 10.000'*

articolo 1, comma 1, primo / secondo periodo ✂**periodo inserito dall'art 1, comma 1,** *periodo inserito dall'art. 9.14, comma 1, lett. a), D.Lgs. 17 gennaio 2003, n. 6* **periodo sostituito dall'art. 1**

Possible equivalents: zdanie (pl), sentence (en)

POTERE (it)

(Adj) **poteri attribuiti (a), conferiti (a)** *La Banca d'Italia partecipa all'esercizio dei poteri conferiti al SEBC in materia di sistemi di pagamento* **poteri indicati (a)** *nell'esercizio dei poteri indicati all'articolo 6, l'ISVAP può imporre che il bilancio consolidato sia redatto in migliaia di euro oppure consentire o imporre un grado di sintesi maggiore delle migliaia, sentita la Consob per le società quotate* ✂ **potere previsto (da)**

(N) **poteri delle autorità, degli organi** ✂ **poteri di controllo** *le disposizioni del codice civile, statutarie o convenzionali relative ai poteri di controllo dei titolari di partecipazioni non si applicano agli atti dei commissari.* ✂ **esercizio dei poteri**

(V) **agire con i poteri** *la Banca d'Italia può effettuare ispezioni presso i mediatori creditizi anche avvalendosi della Guardia di Finanza che agisce con i poteri ad essa attribuiti per l'accertamento dell'imposta sul valore aggiunto e delle imposte sui redditi, utilizzando strutture e personale esistenti in modo da non determinare oneri aggiuntivi* **esercitare i poteri**

(P) **nell'esercizio dei poteri** *nell'esercizio dei poteri regolamentari previsti dal presente capo, la Banca d'Italia tiene conto anche della finalità di garantire un adeguato livello di affidabilità ed efficienza dei servizi di pagamento* ✂ **poteri di cui all'articolo 1**

✎ **potere previsto dall'articolo 1** ✂ **esercitare i poteri di vigilanza** ✂ **avvalersi della Guardia di Finanza che agisce con i poteri ad essa attribuiti per l'accertamento di** *la Banca d'Italia può effettuare ispezioni presso l'agente in attività finanziaria, anche avvalendosi della Guardia di Finanza che agisce con i poteri ad essa attribuiti per l'accertamento dell'imposta sul valore aggiunto e delle imposte sui redditi, utilizzando strutture e personale esistenti in modo da non determinare oneri aggiuntivi*

📖 Possible equivalents: prawo, uprawnienie, kompetencja, władza (pl), AUTHORITY, POWER (en)

PRESTAZIONE (it)

Usually singular

(Adj) **autorizzato alla prestazione** *in caso di sottoposizione a procedura concorsuale del soggetto autorizzato alla prestazione di servizi di pagamento ai sensi dell'articolo 114-novies, comma 4, l'amministrazione del patrimonio destinato è attribuita agli organi della procedura, che provvedono con gestione separata alla liquidazione dello stesso secondo le regole ordinarie*

(N) **prestazione di garanzie (per)** *gli istituti di pagamento possono esercitare le seguenti attività accessorie alla prestazione di servizi di pagamento: b) prestare servizi operativi o strettamente connessi, come la prestazione di garanzie per l'esecuzione di operazioni di pagamento, servizi di cambio, attività di custodia e registrazione e trattamento di dati* **prestazione di servizi** ✂ **attività di prestazione**

✎ **attività di prestazione di servizi di pagamento, attività imprenditoriali diverse dall'emissione di moneta elettronica e/o dalla prestazione dei servizi di pagamento** *gli istituti di moneta elettronica che svolgano anche altre attività imprenditoriali diverse dall'emissione di moneta elettronica e dalla prestazione dei servizi di pagamento, autorizzati ai sensi dell'articolo 114- quinquies, comma 4, costituiscono un patrimonio destinato unico per l'emissione di moneta elettronica, la prestazione dei servizi di pagamento e per le relative attività accessorie e strumentali* **soggetto utorizzato alla prestazione di servizi di pagamento**

📖 Possible equivalents: świadczenie, UDZIELENIE (pl), PROVISION (en)

PROCEDURA (it)

(Adj) **procedure interne** *la Banca d'Italia vigila sull'Organismo secondo modalità, dalla stessa stabilite, improntate a criteri di proporzionalità ed economicità dell'azione di controllo e con la finalità di verificare l'adeguatezza delle procedure interne adottate dall'Organismo per lo svolgimento della propria attività* ✂ **procedure adottate, fissate (da)**

(N) **apertura, avvio, chiusura, svolgimento di una procedura** *ove la Banca d'Italia accerti la mancata sussistenza dei presupposti per un regolare svolgimento della procedura di liquidazione si applica il comma 6* ✂ **organi della procedura** *gli organi della procedura possono trasferire o affidare*

in gestione a banche o altri intermediary autorizzati alla prestazione di servizi di pagamento, i beni e i rapport giuridici ricompresi nel patrimonio destinato e le relative passività ✂ **adozione di procedure** ✂ **procedura di amministrazione, di autorizzazione, di liquidazione, di risanamento** *la Banca d'Italia, qualora ritenga necessaria l'applicazione in Italia di una procedura di risanamento nei confronti di una banca comunitaria, ne fa richiesta all'autorità di vigilanza dello Stato d'origine*

(V) **disciplinare la procedura** *la Banca d'Italia disciplina la procedura di autorizzazione, i casi di revoca e le ipotesi di decadenza quando l'istituto autorizzato non abbia iniziato l'esercizio dell'attività*

(P) **nel rispetto delle procedure, secondo la procedura** *il consenso ad eseguire un'operazione di pagamento o una serie di operazioni di pagamento è prestato nella forma e secondo la procedura concordata nel contratto quadro o nel contratto relativo a singole operazioni di pagamento* ✂ **procedura di cui (a)**

procedura di amministrazione straordinaria, procedura di liquidazione coatta *la pendenza di ricorsi e giudizi, ivi compreso quello di accertamento dello stato di insolvenza, non preclude l'effettuazione degli adempimenti finali previsti ai commi precedenti e la chiusura della procedura di liquidazione coatta amministrativa* ✂ **codice di procedura civile** ✂ **nel rispetto delle procedure fissate dalla Banca d'Italia** ✂ **la Banca d'Italia + disciplinare la procedura di autorizzazione** *la Banca d'Italia disciplina la procedura di autorizzazione, i casi di revoca, nonché di decadenza, quando l'intermediario autorizzato non abbia iniziato l'esercizio dell'attività, e detta disposizioni attuative del presente articolo*

Possible equivalents: postępowanie, procedura (pl) procedure, PROCEEDINGS, process (en)

PROVVEDIMENTO (it)

(Adj) **provvedimenti specifici** *la Banca d'Italia può adottare, ove la situazione lo richieda, provvedimenti specifici nei confronti di singoli intermediari per le materie in precedenza indicate* ✂ **provvedimento adottato, emanato, previsto** *la Banca d'Italia adotta i provvedimenti previsti dal presente capo avendo riguardo, per i servizi di pagamento regolati in conto corrente o commercializzati unitamente a un conto corrente, alle disposizioni previste ai sensi del capo I*

(N) **provvedimento di applicazione, di revoca, di risanamento** *gli effetti dell'adozione di un provvedimento di risanamento o dell'apertura di una procedura di liquidazione sulle cause pendenti relative a un bene o a un diritto del quale la banca è spossessata sono disciplinati dalla legge dello Stato comunitario in cui la causa è pendente* ✂ **adozione, comunicazione di un provvedimento** *entro sessanta giorni dalla comunicazione del provvedimento di cancellazione, l'organo amministrativo convoca l'assemblea per modificare l'oggetto sociale o per assumere altre iniziative conseguenti al provvedimento ovvero per deliberare la liquidazione volontaria della società*

(V) **provvedimento + essere pubblicati** *i provvedimenti sono pubblicati entro il secondo mese successivo a quello della loro adozione*

(P) **con provvedimento** *le sanzioni previste dai commi 3 e 3-bis si applicano quando le infrazioni rivestono carattere rilevante, secondo i criteri definiti dalla Banca d'Italia, con provvedimento di carattere generale, tenuto conto dell'incidenza delle condotte sulla complessiva organizzazione e sui profili di rischio aziendali*

provvedimento di applicazione delle sanzioni *il provvedimento di applicazione delle sanzioni previste dall'articolo 144, commi 3, 3-bis e 4, è pubblicato, per estratto, entro il termine di trenta giorni dalla data di notificazione, a cura e spese della banca, della società o dell'ente al quale appartengono i responsabili delle violazioni, su almeno due quotidiani a diffusione nazionale, di cui uno economico* **provvedimenti di carattere generale** ✂ **adottare, ove la situazione lo richieda, provvedimenti specifici nei confronti (di)** *la Banca d'Italia adotta, ove la situazione lo richieda, provvedimenti specifici nei confronti di singoli intermediari per le materie in precedenza indicate*

Possible equivalents: postanowienie, ŚRODEK, zarządzenie (pl) ACTION, INSTRUMENT, measure, remedy (en)

R

RAPPORTO (it)

(Adj) **rapporti giuridici** *la continuazione dell'esercizio dell'impresa disposta all'atto dell'insediamento degli organi liquidatori entro il termine indicato nell'articolo 83, comma 1, esclude lo scioglimento di diritto dei rapporti giuridici preesistenti previsto dalle norme richiamate dal comma 2 del medesimo articolo*

(N) **rapporto di lavoro** *in deroga a quanto previsto dall'articolo 95-bis, gli effetti di un provvedimento di risanamento o dell'apertura di una procedura di liquidazione a) su contratti e rapporti di lavoro, sono disciplinati dalla legge dello Stato comunitario applicabile al contratto di lavoro* ✂ **rapporti con la clientela** *la Banca d'Italia può stabilire ulteriori regole per garantire trasparenza e correttezza nei rapporti con la clientela* **rapporti con i clienti**

(P) **rapporto con, tra** *i rapporti tra il Ministero dell'economia e delle finanze e l'ente gestore sono disciplinati con apposita convenzione, dalla quale non devono derivare nuovi o maggiori oneri a carico della finanza pubblica.*

✎ **beni e rapporti giuridici** *la Banca d'Italia emana istruzioni per la cessione a banche di aziende, di rami d'azienda, di beni e rapporti giuridici individuabili in blocco* ✂ **trasparenza delle condizioni contrattuali e dei rapporti con i clienti**

📖 Possible equivalents: STOSUNEK (pl), RELATION, relationship (en)

RATA (it)

(Adj) **rate mensili, trimestrali** ✂ **rate già pagate, rate scadute** *nel caso di vendita in più lotti, ciascun aggiudicatario o assegnatario è tenuto a versare proporzionalmente alla banca le rate scadute, gli accessori e le spese*

(N) **ammontare, importo delle rate** *sull'importo delle rate successive sono dovuti gli interessi al saggio legale*

✎ **ammontare delle singole rate** ✂ **mutui a tasso variabile e a rata variabile** *per i mutui a tasso variabile e a rata variabile per tutta la durata del contratto, stipulati o accollati (...) per l'acquisto, la ristrutturazione o la costruzione dell'abitazione principale entro il 29 gennaio 2009, gli atti di consenso alla surrogazione di cui all'articolo 120-quater, comma 1, sono autenticati dal notaio senza l'applicazione di alcun onorario e con il solo rimborso delle spese*

📖 Possible equivalents: RATA (pl), instalment, repayment (en)

REGOLAMENTO (it)

Usually singular

(Adj) **(con) proprio regolamento** *la CONSOB emana, con proprio regolamento, le disposizioni per l'attuazione della presente sezione* ✂ **regolamento adottato, emanato** ✂ **stabilito con regolamento** *L'attestazione è resa secondo il modello stabilito con regolamento dalla CONSOB*

(N) **articolo 1 del Regolamento** *si parte dal valore nominale in lire di ciascuna azione, gli si applica il tasso di conversione e lo si arrotonda ai centesimi di euro secondo le regole dettate dall'articolo 5 del Regolamento (CE) n. 1103/97*

(V) **determinare con regolamento** *il Ministro dell'economia e delle finanze, sentita la Banca d'Italia, determina con regolamento emanato ai sensi dell'articolo 17, comma 3, della legge 23 agosto 1988, n. 400, i requisiti di onorabilità dei titolari delle partecipazioni indicate all'articolo 19 (4)* **stabilire con regolamento** *la CONSOB stabilisce con regolamento modalità per l'elezione di un membro effettivo del collegio sindacale da parte dei soci di minoranza*

✎ **regolamento adottato ai sensi dell'articolo 1, comma 1** *gli agenti che prestano esclusivamente i servizi di pagamento sono iscritti in una sezione speciale* *dell'elenco di cui al comma 2 quando ricorrono le condizioni e i requisiti stabiliti con regolamento adottato ai sensi dell'articolo 17, comma 3, legge 23 agosto 1988, n. 400, dal Ministro dell'economia e delle finanze* ✂ **procedimenti amministrativi, stabiliti da norme di legge o di regolamento, pendenti alla data (di)**

📖 Possible equivalents: ROZPORZĄDZENIE, zarządzenie (pl), ENACTMENT, regulation (en)

RELAZIONE (it)

(N) **relazioni o comunicazioni** ✂ **relazione sull'attività, sulla gestione** ✂ **relazione degli amministratori** *il bilancio dell'impresa e il bilancio consolidato sono corredati di una relazione degli amministratori* ✂ **relazione al bilancio**

(P) **relazione su** *la relazione sulla gestione consolidata e la relazione sulla gestione dell'impresa possono essere presentate in un unico documento* ✂ **in relazione a**

✏ **in relazione all'articolo 1, comma 1; in relazione al servizio di pagamento** *Per la violazione degli articoli 52, 61, comma 5, 110 in relazione agli articoli 52 e 61, comma 5, 114-quinquies.3, in relazione all'articolo 52, e 114-undecies, in relazione all'articolo 52, si applica la sanzione prevista dal comma 1 (2)*

📖 Possible equivalents: relacja, sprawozdanie, STOSUNEK, związek (pl), REPORT, STATEMENT, RELATION (en)

REPUBBLICA (it)

Always singular

(Adj) **Repubblica italiana** *la Banca d'Italia, banca centrale della Repubblica italiana, è parte integrante del SEBC*

(N) **Presidente, Senato della Repubblica** ✂ **territorio della Repubblica** *le autorità competenti di uno Stato comunitario, dopo aver informato la Banca d'Italia, possono ispezionare, anche tramite persone da esse incaricate, gli istituti di moneta elettronica comunitari, i loro agenti o i soggetti a cui sono esternalizzate attività che operano nel territorio della Repubblica*

✎ **la Camera dei deputati ed il Senato della Repubblica** ✂ **decreto del Presidente della Repubblica, stabile organizzazione nel territorio della Repubblica** *l'iscrizione nell'elenco di cui all'articolo 128-sexies, comma 2, è subordinata al ricorrere dei seguenti requisiti a) forma di società per azioni, di società in accomandita per azioni, di società a responsabilità limitata o di società cooperativa b) sede legale e amministrativa o, per i soggetti comunitari, stabile organizzazione nel territorio della Repubblica* ✂ **operare nel territorio della Repubblica, stabilire succursali nel territorio della Repubblica** ✂ **essere inseriti nella Raccolta ufficiale degli atti normativi della Repubblica italiana** *il presente decreto, munito del sigillo dello Stato, sarà inserito nella Raccolta ufficiale degli atti normativi della Repubblica italiana* **essere pubblicati (per estratto) nella Gazzetta Ufficiale della Repubblica italiana** ✂ **la sede legale e la direzione generale + essere situati nel territorio della Repubblica** *la Banca d'Italia autorizza gli istituti di pagamento quando ricorrano le seguenti condizioni: a) sia adottata la forma di società di capitali; b) la sede legale e la direzione generale siano situate nel territorio della Repubblica*

📖 Possible equivalents: republika (pl), republic (en)

REQUISITO (it)

Usually singular

(Adj) **requisiti patrimoniali** *il Ministro del tesoro, sentito il Ministro dell'industria, del commercio e dell'artigianato, determina con decreto i requisiti patrimoniali dei fondi speciali antiusura di cui al comma 2 e i requisiti di onorabilità e di professionalità degli esponenti dei fondi medesimi* ✂ **requisiti indicati (a), previsti (da), richiesti (per), stabiliti (da)** ✂ **seguenti requisiti**

(N) **requisiti di onorabilità, indipendenza, professionalità** *l'Organismo indice con cadenza almeno annuale, secondo modalità dallo stesso stabilite, un esame volto ad accertare i requisiti di professionalità di coloro che richiedono l'iscrizione negli elenchi degli agenti in attività finanziaria e dei mediatori creditizi* ✂ **determinazione, difetto dei requisiti** *nel caso di difetto dei requisiti di indipendenza stabiliti dal codice civile o dallo statuto della banca (6) si applica il comma 2* **possesso, rispetto, verifica dei requisiti**

(V) **possedere i requisiti (di)** *i soggetti che svolgono funzioni di amministrazione e direzione devono possedere i requisiti di onorabilità stabiliti per i membri degli*

organi di controllo con il regolamento emanato dal Ministro della giustizia ai sensi dell'articolo 148, comma 4

(P) **requisiti per l'iscrizione** *l'Organismo può disporre la cancellazione dall'elenco: a) qualora vengano meno i requisiti per l'iscrizione*

requisiti di professionalità, onorabilità e indipendenza ✂ **sistemi interni di misurazione dei rischi per la determinazione dei requisiti patrimoniali** *le disposizioni emanate ai sensi del comma 1 prevedono che gli intermediari finanziari possano utilizzare b) sistemi interni di misurazione dei rischi per la determinazione dei requisiti patrimoniali, previa autorizzazione della Banca d'Italia* ✂ **requisiti indicati al comma 1, requisiti per l'iscrizione nell'elenco, requisiti previsti ai sensi dell'articolo 1** ✂ **essere subordinati al ricorrere dei seguenti requisiti** *l'iscrizione nell'elenco di cui all'articolo 128-sexies, comma 2, è subordinata al ricorrere dei seguenti requisiti* ✂ **i titolari di partecipazioni di cui all' articolo 1 e gli esponenti aziendali + possedere, rispettivamente, i requisiti previsti ai sensi degli articoli 1 e 2** *la Banca d'Italia autorizza gli intermediari finanziari ad esercitare la propria attività al ricorrere delle seguenti condizioni a) sia adottata la forma di società per azioni, in accomandita per azioni, a responsabilità limitata e cooperativa b) la sede legale e la direzione generale siano situate nel territorio della Repubblica e) i titolari di partecipazioni di cui all'articolo 19 e gli esponenti aziendali possiedano, rispettivamente, i requisiti previsti ai sensi degli articoli 25 e 26* ✂ **difetto dei requisiti + determinare la decadenza dalla carica**

Possible equivalents: WARUNEK, wymóg (pl), CONDITION, REQUIREMENT (en)

REVISIONE (it)

Usually singular

(Adj) **revisione contabile** *la CONSOB dispone d'ufficio la revoca dell'incarico di revisione contabile qualora rilevi una causa di incompatibilità ovvero qualora siano state accertate gravi irregolarità nello svolgimento dell'attività di revisione*

(N) **attività, incarico di revisione** *la CONSOB stabilisce con regolamento a) i criteri generali per la determinazione del corrispettivo per l'incarico di revisione contabile* **società di revisione** *l'assemblea revoca l'incarico, previo parere dell'organo di controllo, quando ricorra una giusta causa, provvedendo contestualmente a conferire l'incarico ad altra società di revisione secondo le modalità di cui al comma*

1 **responsabile della revisione** *le società di revisione, in relazione a ciascun incarico di revisione loro conferito, comunicano alla CONSOB i nomi dei responsabili della revisione entro dieci giorni dalla data in cui essi sono stati designati*

✎ **società incaricata della revisione contabile** *alla società incaricata della revisione contabile della società capogruppo si applicano le disposizioni dell'articolo 165, comma 1-bis* **soggetto incaricato della revisione legale dei conti** *nell'interesse della procedura i commissari, sentito il comitato di sorveglianza, previa autorizzazione della Banca d'Italia, possono sostituire il soggetto incaricato della revisione legale dei conti per la durata della procedura*

📖 Possible equivalents: audyt, KONTROLA, korekta, przegląd, rewizja (pl), audit, review, revision (en)

RIFERIMENTO (it)

Usually singular

(Avv) **eliminando il riferimento (a)** *in caso di mancato accoglimento delle istanze di cui al comma 4, lettere b), c) ed e), i soggetti ivi indicati deliberano la liquidazione della società ovvero modificano il proprio oggetto sociale, eliminando il riferimento ad attività riservate ai sensi di legge*

(N) **data di riferimento** *nel periodo transitorio, dalla data di riferimento del primo documento contabile obbligatorio a rilevanza esterna redatto in euro, tutti i documenti riferiti a quella data e a date successive sono redatti in euro, salvo che ricorrano particolari ragioni da illustrare nei documenti anzidetti*

(V) **fare riferminento (a)** *se non diversamente disposto, le norme del presente decreto legislativo che fanno riferimento al consiglio di amministrazione, all'organo amministrativo e agli amministratori si applicano anche al consiglio di gestione ed ai suoi componenti*

(P) **con riferimento a** *con riferimento a determinati tipi di attività la Banca d'Italia può inoltre dettare disposizioni volte ad assicurarne il regolare esercizio*

✎ **data di riferimento del bilancio** *la data di riferimento del bilancio consolidato coincide con quella del bilancio d'esercizio dell'impresa capogruppo* **tasso di cambio di riferimento** *'tasso di cambio di riferimento': il tasso di cambio che è utilizzato come base per calcolare un cambio valuta e che è reso disponibile dal fornitore di* *servizi di pagamento o proviene da una fonte accessibile al pubblico* ✂ **disposizioni + fare riferimento (a)** *le quotazioni delle valute estere rilevate ai sensi dei commi 5 e 5-bis tengono luogo di quelle precedentemente rilevate, cui le disposizioni vigenti fanno riferimento, a qualsiasi titolo*

Possible equivalents: nawiązanie, odniesienie (pl), REFERENCE (en)

RIMBORSO (it)

(Adj) **rimborso anticipato** *in caso di rimborso anticipato, il finanziatore ha diritto ad un indennizzo equo ed oggettivamente giustificato per eventuali costi direttamente collegati al rimborso anticipato del credito*

(N) **rimborso del credito, dei titoli** *al fine di agevolare la ridenominazione dei titoli di Stato si dispone il rimborso dei titoli nominativi e al portatore di taglio inferiore a cinque milioni di capitale nominale, e delle eventuali frazioni di capitale inferiori a cinque milioni* ✂ **diritto al rimborso** ✂ **obbligo di rimbroso** ✂ **condizioni, modalità di rimborso** *la Banca d'Italia, avendo riguardo alla tutela dei risparmiatori e alla stabilità del sistema bancario c) disciplina le modalità di rimborso, anche con riferimento ai casi di cointestazione*

(V) **chiedere un rimborso** *il CICR individua i casi in cui la banca o l'intermediario finanziario possono chiedere al cliente un rimborso delle spese sostenute in relazione a servizi aggiuntivi da questo richiesti in occasione del recesso*

rimborso della moneta elettronica ✂ **fondi con obbligo di rimborso** *ai fini del presente decreto legislativo è raccolta del risparmio l'acquisizione di fondi con obbligo di rimborso, sia sotto forma di depositi sia sotto altra forma*

Possible equivalents: pokrycie, SPŁATA, WYPŁATA, zapłata, zwrot (pl), refund, reimbursement, repayment (en)

RISPETTO (it)

Always singular

(N) **rispetto di condizioni, di requisiti** *al fine di verificare il rispetto dei requisiti per l'iscrizione nell'elenco, l'UIC può chiedere agli intermediari finanziari dati, notizie, atti e documenti e, se necessario, può effettuare verifiche presso la sede degli*

intermediari stessi, anche con la collaborazione di altre autorità ✂ **rispetto della disciplina, delle disposizioni, delle previsioni** *l'istanza è corredata della sola documentazione attestante il rispetto delle previsioni di cui all'articolo 107, comma 1, lettere c), d), e)* **rispetto del principio, delle procedure**

(V) **verificare il rispetto (di), vigilare sul rispetto (di)** *la Banca d'Italia tiene l'elenco previsto dall'articolo 111 e vigila sul rispetto da parte degli iscritti della disciplina cui essi sono sottoposti anche ai sensi dell'articolo 111, comma 5*

(P) **nel rispetto di** ✂ **rispetto a (quanto)** *il prestatore di servizi di pagamento e l'utilizzatore possono concordare le spese relative a informazioni fornite su richiesta dell'utilizzatore se esse, rispetto a quanto previsto nel contratto quadro, sono supplementari o rese in modo più frequente o trasmesse con strumenti di comunicazione diversi* ✂ **rispetto da parte di** *l'Organismo verifica il rispetto da parte degli agenti in attività finanziaria e dei mediatori creditizi della disciplina cui essi sono sottoposti*

rispetto delle disposizioni del Titolo I ✂ **documentazione attestante il rispetto delle previsioni di cui all'articolo 1** *l'istanza è corredata della sola documentazione attestante il rispetto delle previsioni di cui all'articolo 107, comma 1, lettere c), d), e) ed f), del decreto legislativo 1° settembre 1993, n. 385, come modificato dal presente decreto legislativo* ✂ **al fine di verificare il rispetto (di)** *al fine di verificare il rispetto delle disposizioni del presente titolo, la Banca d'Italia può acquisire informazioni, atti e documenti ed eseguire ispezioni presso le banche, gli istituti di moneta elettronica, gli istituti di pagamento e gli intermediari finanziari* **nel rispetto delle disposizioni dettate da, nel rispetto delle modalità stabilite dalla Banca d'Italia, nel rispetto delle procedure fissate dalla Banca d'Italia** ✂ **vigilare sul rispetto da parte degli iscritti della disciplina cui sono sottoposti** *l'Organismo (…); riscuote i contributi e le altre somme dovute per l'iscrizione nell'elenco e vigila sul rispetto da parte degli iscritti della disciplina cui sono sottoposti anche ai sensi dell'articolo 111, comma 5*

Possible equivalents: przestrzeganie, wzgląd (pl), compliance, observance, regard, respect (en)

S

SANZIONE (it)

(Adj) **sanzione accessoria, amministrativa, pecuniaria, penale** *a decorrere dal 1 gennaio 2002 ogni sanzione penale o amministrativa espressa in lire nelle vigenti disposizioni normative è tradotta in Euro secondo il tasso di conversione irrevocabilmente fissato ai sensi del Trattato* ✂ **sanzione prevista (da)**

(N) **applicazione, importo, irrogazione della sanzione** *quando l'irregolarità consista nella violazione delle disposizioni dell'articolo 160, l'irrogazione della sanzione prevista dal comma 1-octies del medesimo articolo non pregiudica l'applicabilità dei provvedimenti indicati nel comma 1 del presente articolo nei riguardi della società di revisione*

(V) **sanzione + applicarsi** *la stessa sanzione si applica a chi, attraverso informazioni e comunicazioni in qualsiasi forma, induce in altri il falso convincimento di essere sottoposto alla vigilanza della Banca d'Italia ai sensi dell'articolo 108 o di essere abilitato all'esercizio delle attività di cui all'articolo 111*

sanzione prevista dall'articolo 1, comma 1 ✂ **sanzioni previste dal presente titolo** ✂ **sanzioni amministrative pecuniarie previste dal testo unico** ✂ **applicazione delle sanzioni previste (da)** ✂ **disporre il raddoppio delle sanzioni penali previste dal testo unico entro i limiti posti per ciascun tipo di pena** *cfr. l'art. 39, comma 1, L. 28 dicembre 2005, n. 262, citato in nota al presente Titolo, che dispone il raddoppio delle sanzioni penali previste dal testo unico entro i limiti posti per ciascun tipo di pena dal libro I, titolo II, capo II, del codice penale* **essere puniti con la sanzione amministrativa pecuniaria da euro 10 euro a euro 100** *Chiunque contravviene al disposto dei commi 1, 1-bis, 1-ter e 1- quater è punito con la sanzione amministrativa pecuniaria da euro 5.164 a euro 51.645* ✂ **sanzione**

amministrativa + essere applicabile *nei confronti di società, enti o associazioni tenuti a effettuare le comunicazioni previste dagli articoli 113, 114 e 115 è applicabile la sanzione amministrativa pecuniaria da cinquemila a cinquecentomila euro per l'inosservanza delle disposizioni degli articoli medesimi o delle relative disposizioni applicative* **sanzione amministrativa pecuniaria / sanzioni previste dall'articolo 1 + applicarsi**

📖 Possible equivalents: sankcja, kara (pl), fine, PENALTY, sanction (en)

SEDE (it)

Usually singular

(Adj) **sede legale** *«banca comunitaria»: la banca avente sede legale e amministrazione centrale in un medesimo Stato comunitario diverso dall'Italia*

(V) **avere (la) sede** *avverso i provvedimenti di cui primo comma, è ammesso ricorso dell'interessato alla giurisdizione esclusiva del Tribunale amministrativo regionale nella cui circoscrizione ha sede l'Organismo*

(P) **con sede** *le società con sede legale in Italia ricomprese nella vigilanza su base consolidata di competenza delle autorità di vigilanza degli altri Stati comunitari forniscono ai soggetti individuati dalle stesse le informazioni necessarie per l'esercizio della vigilanza consolidata* ✂ **sede all'estero**

✏ **sede legale e amministrativa** ✂ **società aventi sede legale in uno Stato, società con sede legale in Italia** ✂ **avente sede legale all'estero** *fermo quanto disposto dall'articolo 18, il Ministro dell'economia e delle finanze disciplina l'esercizio nel territorio della Repubblica, da parte di soggetti aventi sede legale all'estero, delle attività indicate nell'articolo 106* ✂ **sede legale e la direzione generale + essere situati nel territorio della Repubblica** *la Banca d'Italia autorizza gli istituti di pagamento quando ricorrano le seguenti condizioni: a) sia adottata la forma di società di capitali b) la sede legale e la direzione generale siano situate nel territorio della Repubblica*

📖 Possible equivalents: siedziba (pl), seat, OFFICE (en)

SERVIZIO (it)

Usually plural

(Adj) **servizio finanziario ✂ servizi accessori** *nel costo totale del credito sono inclusi anche i costi relativi a servizi accessori connessi con il contratto di credito, compresi i premi assicurativi, se la conclusione di un contratto avente ad oggetto tali servizi è un requisito per ottenere il credito, o per ottenerlo alle condizioni offerte* **servizi bancari ✂ servizi connessi** *il recesso disciplinato dal presente articolo si estende automaticamente, anche in deroga alle condizioni e ai termini eventualmente previsti dalla normativa di settore, ai contratti aventi a oggetto servizi accessori connessi col contratto di credito, se tali servizi sono resi dal finanziatore ovvero da un terzo sulla base di un accordo col finanziatore* **servizi disciplinati (da), indicati (in), offerti ✂ relativo a servizi** *analoga comunicazione viene inviata a coloro che risultino titolari di diritti reali sui beni e sugli strumenti finanziari relativi ai servizi previsti dal decreto legislativo 24 febbraio 1998, n. 58 in possesso della banca, nonché ai clienti aventi diritto alle restituzioni dei detti strumenti finanziari*

(N) **beni e / o servizi, operazioni e servizi, prodotti e / o servizi** *la CONSOB, previa consultazione con tutti i soggetti interessati e sentite le Autorità di vigilanza competenti, determina con proprio regolamento gli specifici obblighi di informazione e di rendicontazione cui sono tenuti i soggetti abilitati e le imprese di assicurazione che promuovono prodotti e servizi qualificati come etici o socialmente responsabili* ✂ **servizi di investimento, <u>SERVIZI DI PAGAMENTO</u> ✂ prestatore, prestazione di un servizio ✂ fornitore di servizi** *se al pagatore è offerto, prima di disporre un'operazione di pagamento, un servizio di conversione valutaria dal beneficiario ovvero presso il punto vendita da un venditore di merci o da un fornitore di servizi, colui che propone il servizio di conversione gli comunica tutte le spese e il tasso di cambio che sarà utilizzato per la conversione*

(V) **prestare servizi** *tutte le banche possono erogare finanziamenti o prestare servizi previsti dalle vigenti leggi di agevolazione, purché essi siano regolati da contratto con l'amministrazione pubblica competente e rientrino tra le attività che le banche possono svolgere in via ordinaria*

✎ **servizi indicati nel comma 1 ✂ direttiva relativa ai servizi** *attuazione della direttiva 2007/64/CE relativa ai servizi di pagamento nel mercato interno* **fornitore dei beni o dei servizi, libera prestazione di servizi**

📖 <u>Possible equivalents:</u> USŁUGA (pl), SERVICE (en)

SERVIZI DI PAGAMENTO (it)

Always plural

(N) **prestatore, prestazione, utilizzatore dei servizi di pagamento** ✂ **utenti di servizi di pagamento** *in caso di incapienza del patrimonio destinato l'istituto di pagamento risponde anche con il proprio patrimonio delle obbligazioni nei confronti degli utenti dei servizi di pagamento e di quanti vantino diritti derivanti dall'esercizio delle attività accessorie e strumentali*

(V) **prestare servizi di pagamento** *nei confronti dei soggetti che emettono o gestiscono strumenti di pagamento e di quelli che prestano servizi di pagamento resta fermo quanto previsto ai sensi degli articoli 51, 53, 54 (…) e del titolo VI*

✎ *(NOMINAL)* **agente che presta servizi di pagamento, attività di prestazione di servizi di pagamento, attività imprenditoriali diverse dall'emissione di moneta elettronica e dalla prestazione dei servizi di pagamento, prestatore di servizi di pagamento del beneficiario / pagatore** *il titolo II si applica ai servizi di pagamento prestati nella Comunità europea, a condizione che i prestatori di servizi di pagamento del pagatore e del beneficiario siano insediati nella Comunità europea ovvero l'unico prestatore di servizi di pagamento coinvolto nell'operazione di pagamento sia insediato nella Comunità* **soggetto autorizzato alla prestazione di servizi di pagamento**

✎ *(VERBAL)* **avvalersi di un prestatore di servizi di pagamento** *il momento della ricezione di un ordine di pagamento è quello in cui l'ordine, trasmesso direttamente dal pagatore o indirettamente dal beneficiario o per il suo tramite, è ricevuto dal prestatore di servizi di pagamento di cui si avvale il pagatore* **prestatore di servizi di pagamento + addebitare spese** *il prestatore di servizi di pagamento non può addebitare all'utilizzatore dei servizi di pagamento le spese sostenute per l'adozione di misure correttive e preventive ai sensi del presente Titolo, salvo quanto previsto negli articoli 16, comma 4, 17, comma 5, e 24, comma 2* **prestatore di servizi di pagamento + essere responsabili nei confronti (di)** *in tale caso, il prestatore di servizi di pagamento del beneficiario è responsabile nei confronti del beneficiario della corretta esecuzione dell'operazione di pagamento*

📖 Possible equivalents: usługa płatnicza (pl), payment service (en)

SEZIONE (it)

(Adj) **sezione speciale** ✂ **presente, seguente sezione** *nel testo unico di cui al decreto legislativo 24 febbraio 1998, n. 58, e successive modificazioni, alla parte IV, titolo III, capo II, dopo l'articolo 165-bis, introdotto dall'articolo 18, comma 1, lettera h), della presente legge, è aggiunta la seguente sezione* ✂ **sezione separata** ✂ **iscritto in una sezione**

(N) **sezione dell'albo, dell'enenco** *l'esercizio in via prevalente, non nei confronti del pubblico, delle attività indicate nell'articolo 106, comma 1, è riservato ai soggetti iscritti in un'apposita sezione dell'elenco generale* ✂ **disposizioni di una sezione**

(V) **in una sezione** *nella Sezione I, composta da quattro articoli (dall'articolo 5 all'articolo 8) si disciplina la ridenominazione in euro dei Titoli di Stato*

✎ **titolo I, capo I, sezione I** *dal termine indicato nel comma 1 si producono gli effetti previsti dagli articoli 42, 44, 45 e 66, nonché dalle disposizioni del titolo II, capo III, sezione II e sezione IV della legge fallimentare* ✂ **disposizioni del capo I, sezioni I e II, disposizioni della presente sezione** ✂ **iscritto in una sezione separata** *la Banca d'Italia esercita i poteri indicati all'articolo 108 del decreto legislativo 1° settembre 1993, n. 385, al fine di assicurare il rispetto da parte delle società fiduciarie iscritte nella sezione separata delle disposizioni contenute nel decreto legislativo 21 novembre 2007, n. 231* **previsto dalla presente sezione** ✂ **dopo l'articolo 1 è inserita la seguente sezione**

📖 Possible equivalents: część, dział, sekcja (pl) SECTION (en)

SISTEMA (it)

(Adj) **sistema finanziario** *le autorità creditizie, nei casi di crisi o di tensioni sui mercati finanziari, tengono conto degli effetti dei propri atti sulla stabilità del sistema finanziario degli altri Stati comunitari interessati*

(N) **sistema di garanzia, di gestione** *i titoli in essere presso il sistema di gestione accentrata della Banca d'Italia sono annullati e inviati al Tesoro a decorrere dal 5 ottobre 1998* **sistema di pagamento** *'sistema di pagamento' o 'sistema di scambio, di compensazione e di regolamento': un sistema di trasferimento di fondi con meccanismi di funzionamento formali e standardizzati e regole comuni per*

il trattamento, la compensazione e/o il regolamento di operazioni di pagamento **sistema dei pagamenti** *la Banca d'Italia nega l'autorizzazione quando dalla verifica delle condizioni indicate nel comma 1 non risulti garantita la sana e prudente gestione ovvero il regolare funzionamento del sistema dei pagamenti* **sistema di prevenzione** ✂ **adesione al sistema** *le autorità che hanno rilasciato l'autorizzazione all'attività bancaria revocano la stessa al venir meno dell'adesione ai sistemi di garanzia* **funzionamento del sistema**

(V) **aderire a un sistema** *le banche italiane aderiscono a uno dei sistemi di garanzia dei depositanti istituiti e riconosciuti in Italia*

(P) **nell'ambito del sistema** *nell'ambito del sistema di prevenzione, è istituito, presso l'ente gestore, un servizio gratuito, telefonico e telematico, che consente di ricevere segnalazioni da parte di soggetti che hanno subito o temono di aver subito frodi configuranti ipotesi di furto di identità*

✎ **sistema di scambio, di compensazione e di regolamento** ✂ **Sistema europeo di banche centrali, sistema di garanzia dei depositanti, sistema di garanzia italiano** ✂ **sistemi di remunerazione e incentivazione** *La Banca d'Italia emana disposizioni di carattere generale aventi a oggetto: il governo societario, l'adeguatezza patrimoniale, il contenimento del rischio nelle sue diverse configurazioni, l'organizzazione amministrativa e contabile, nonché i controlli interni e i sistemi di remunerazione e incentivazione* **sistemi di risoluzione stragiudiziale delle controversie** *le banche, gli istituti di moneta elettronica e gli istituti di pagamento aderiscono ai sistemi di risoluzione stragiudiziale delle controversie previsti dall'articolo 128-bis del decreto legislativo 1° settembre 1993, n. 385, per le controversie individuate dalle disposizioni attuative del medesimo articolo* ✂ **sistemi interni di misurazione dei rischi per la determinazione dei requisiti patrimoniali** ✂ **sorveglianza sul sistema dei pagamenti** ✂ **sana e prudente gestione ovvero il regolare funzionamento del sistema dei pagamenti** *la Banca d'Italia nega l'autorizzazione quando dalla verifica delle condizioni indicate nel comma 1 non risulti garantita la sana e prudente gestione ovvero il regolare funzionamento del sistema dei pagamenti*

📖 Possible equivalents: SYSTEM (pl), system (en)

SOCIETÀ (it)

(Adj) **società cessionaria** *le disposizioni di cui al titolo V del decreto legislativo 1° settembre 1993, n. 385, non si applicano alle società cessionarie, o alle società emittenti titoli, se diverse dalle società cessionarie, nell'ambito di operazioni di cartolarizzazione.* **società cooperativa, estera, fiduciaria, finanziaria, italiana, soggetta (a)** ✂ **società bancarie, diverse (da), strumentali** *per 'società strumentali' si intendono le società che esercitano, in via esclusiva o prevalente, attività che hanno carattere ausiliario dell'attività delle società del gruppo, comprese quelle consistenti nella proprietà e nell'amministrazione di immobili e nella gestione di servizi anche informatici* ✂ **società controllante, controllata, quotata** *'società quotata': società emittente strumenti finanziari negoziati sui mercati regolamentati italiani*

(N) **società o ente, società ed enti** ✂ **società capogruppo** ✂ **società di capitali** *si applicano le disposizioni del codice civile in materia di liquidazione delle società di capitali, relative alla cancellazione della società ed al deposito dei libri sociali* **società di persone, di revisione** ✂ **società del gruppo** ✂ **società per azioni** ✂ **amministratori, bilancio, controllo, costutuzione, liquidazione, scioglimento di una società** ✂ **partecipazioni in società** *le società fiduciarie che abbiano intestato a proprio nome partecipazioni in società appartenenti a terzi comunicano alla Banca d'Italia, se questa lo richieda, le generalità dei fiducianti*

(V) **società + controllare** *i commi 1, primo periodo (4), e 2 si applicano anche ai soggetti che esercitano i compiti ivi previsti presso le società che controllano le banche o che sono da queste controllate ai sensi dell'articolo 23*

(P) **presso una società** ✂ **in forma di società** *per il contatto con il pubblico, gli agenti in attività finanziaria che siano persone fisiche o costituiti in forma di società di persone si avvalgono di dipendenti o collaboratori iscritti nell'elenco di cui all'articolo 128-quater, comma 2* **per il tramite di società** *le disposizioni delle lettere b) e c) del comma 2 si applicano anche alle azioni o quote detenute, acquistate o alienate per il tramite di società fiduciaria o per interposta persona*

✎ *(SYNTACTIC NOMINAL)* **società in accomandita per azioni, società avente sede legale (in), società emittente titoli, società finanziaria capogruppo di un gruppo bancario iscritto nell'albo previsto dall'art. 1, società di gestione accentrata** *le iscrizioni contabili (presso la società di gestione accentrata) continuano a godere dello stesso trattamento fiscale, comprese le agevolazioni e le* *esenzioni, che la vigente normativa riconosce ai titoli di Stato* **società di gestione di mercati regolamentati, società incaricata della revisione contabile, società di partecipazione finanziaria mista capogruppo, società a responsabilità limitata** ✂ **società appartenenti ad un gruppo bancario / finanziario, società finanziarie ammesse al mutuo riconoscimento, società italiane con azioni quotate in mercati regolamentati, società italiane emittenti strumenti finanziari diffusi tra il pubblico in misura rilevante** *con proprio regolamento la CONSOB detta criteri in base ai quali è consentito alle società italiane di cui all'articolo 119 e alle società italiane emittenti strumenti finanziari diffusi tra il pubblico in misura rilevante ai sensi dell'articolo 116 di controllare imprese aventi sede in uno degli Stati di cui al comma 5*

✎ **società bancarie, finanziarie e strumentali** ✂ **la società cessionaria o la società emittente titoli** *la società cessionaria, o la società emittente titoli se diversa dalla società cessionaria, hanno per oggetto esclusivo la realizzazione di una o più operazioni di cartolarizzazione dei crediti* ✂ **bilancio della società estera controllata, dipendenti della società di revisione, organi di controllo delle società, valutazioni del rischio di credito rilasciate da società o enti esterni** ✂ **situazione economica, patrimoniale o finanziaria della società** ✂ **Commissione nazionale per le società e la borsa (CONSOB)** ✂ **costituito in forma di società** ✂ **per il tramite di società fiduciaria o per interposta persona** ✂ **deliberare la liquidazione della società** *in caso di mancato accoglimento delle istanze di cui al comma 4, lettere b), c) ed e), i soggetti ivi indicati deliberano la liquidazione della società ovvero modificano il proprio oggetto sociale, eliminando il riferimento ad attività riservate ai sensi di legge* ✂ **diritti di voto e gli altri diritti + consentire di influire sulla società** *non possono essere esercitati i diritti di voto e gli altri diritti che consentono di influire sulla società inerenti alle partecipazioni per le quali le autorizzazioni previste dall'articolo 19 non siano state ottenute ovvero siano state sospese o revocate* **forma di società per azioni + essere adottata, società + svolgere attività**

📖 Possible equivalents: firma, przedsiębiorstwo, SPÓŁKA (pl), company, corporation, firm, SOCIETY, UNDERTAKING (en)

SPESA (it)

Usually plural

(Adj) **spese applicabili** ✂ **eventuali spese** *le disposizioni del presente articolo non producono effetti sul pagamento di eventuali spese concordate tra prestatori di servizi*

di pagamento o soggetti di cui essi si avvalgono ✂ **spese imposte, sostenute** *il CICR individua i casi in cui la banca o l'intermediario finanziario possono chiedere al cliente un rimborso delle spese sostenute in relazione a servizi aggiuntivi da questo richiesti in occasione del recesso*

(V) **addebitare spese (a)** *le banche e gli intermediari finanziari non possono addebitare al cliente spese, comunque denominate, inerenti alle informazioni e alle comunicazioni previste ai sensi di legge trasmesse con strumenti di comunicazione telematica*

(P) **spese per** ✂ **senza spese** *la modifica si intende approvata ove il cliente non receda, senza spese, dal contratto entro la data prevista per la sua applicazione* ✂ **a cura e spese** *il provvedimento di applicazione delle sanzioni previste dall'articolo 144, commi 3, 3-bis e 4, è pubblicato, per estratto, entro il termine di trenta giorni dalla data di notificazione, a cura e spese della banca, della società o dell'ente al quale appartengono i responsabili delle violazioni, su almeno due quotidiani a diffusione nazionale, di cui uno economico* ✂ **senza penalità e senza spese** *l'utilizzatore di servizi di pagamento ha sempre la facoltà di recedere dal contratto quadro senza penalità e senza spese di chiusura*

📖 Possible equivalents: KOSZT, wydatek, OPŁATA (pl), charge, cost, expenditure, expense, FEE (en)

STATO (it)

(Adj) **stato comunitario, diverso, extracomunitario** *l'emissione di moneta elettronica da parte di un istituto di moneta elettronica con sede legale in uno Stato extracomunitario è subordinata all'apertura di una succursale in Italia autorizzata dalla Banca d'Italia ai sensi del presente articolo in presenza di condizioni corrispondenti a quelle del comma 1, lettere c), d), e) ed f)* ✂ **stato ospitante, partecipante** *con l'articolo 6 si autorizza il tesoro a ridenominare anche i propri prestiti emessi sui mercati esteri e denominati nella valuta di uno Stato partecipante, a condizione che lo Stato medesimo abbia provveduto a ridenominare il proprio debito pubblico, espresso nella propria moneta e disciplinato secondo il proprio diritto nazionale*

(N) **stato di appartenenza, di origine** ✂ **stato membro** ✂ **amministrazione, autorità, bilancio, debito, legge, valuta di uno stato** ✂ **sigillo dello Stato** *il*

presente decreto, munito del sigillo dello Stato, sarà inserito nella Raccolta ufficiale degli atti normativi della Repubblica italiana ✂ **titoli di stato** *'titoli di Stato': tutti i titoli, a breve e medio-lungo termine, emessi dal tesoro, nonché i prestiti emessi dalle Ferrovie dello Stato e riconosciuti come debiti dello Stato ai sensi dell'articolo 2, comma 12, della legge 23 dicembre 1996, n. 662*

✏ **stato dell'Unione europea** ✂ **autorità competente di uno stato di appartenenza** *gli istituti di moneta elettronica con sede legale in un altro Stato comunitario, che intendono operare in Italia, possono operare nel territorio della Repubblica anche senza stabilirvi succursali dopo che la Banca d'Italia sia stata informata dall'autorità competente dello Stato di appartenenza* **autorità di vigilanza di uno stato, decreto legislativo del capo provvisorio dello stato, decreto munito del sigillo dello stato, società aventi sede legale in uno stato** ✂ **denominato nella valuta di uno stato** *ridenominazione dei prestiti internazionali denominati nella valuta di uno Stato partecipante* **riconosciuto come debito dello stato** *il comma 4 specifica che il taglio minimo indicato dal prospetto di emissione è quello da prendere a riferimento per i titoli emessi dalle Ferrovie dello Stato e riconosciuti come debito dello Stato dalla legge n. 662 del 1996* ✂ **richiedere alle autorità competenti di uno stato di effettuare accertamenti** *la Banca d'Italia può richiedere alle autorità competenti di uno Stato comunitario di effettuare accertamenti presso i soggetti indicati nel comma 1, stabiliti nel territorio di detto Stato, ovvero concordare altre modalità delle verifiche* ✂ **essere disciplinati dalla legge di uno stato**

📖 Possible equivalents: kraj, PAŃSTWO (pl), COUNTRY, state (en)

STRUMENTO (it)

(Adj) **strumenti finanziari, giuridici, privati** *potranno essere ridenominati in euro anche gli strumenti finanziari privati, con le caratteristiche di cui sopra, denominati nelle valute di altri Stati aderenti all'Unione Europea che abbiano già proceduto alla ridenominazione* ✂ **strumenti emessi (da)**

(N) **strumento di debito** *nella Sezione II, composta dagli articoli 9 e 10, si delinea la disciplina per la ridenominazione degli strumenti di debito emessi da altri soggetti pubblici* **strumento di pagamento** ✂ **strumenti di comunicazione** ✂ **ridenominazione di strumenti** *la ridenominazione degli strumenti di cui*

all'articolo 11 è effettuata secondo i tempi e i modi indicati nell'apposito regolamento da emanarsi da parte della Consob, sentita la Banca d'Italia

✎ **strumenti finanziari computabili nel patrimonio a fini di vigilanza** *i provvedimenti particolari adottati ai sensi del comma 1 possono riguardare anche (...) il divieto di effettuare determinate operazioni e di distribuire utili o altri elementi del patrimonio, nonché, con riferimento a strumenti finanziari computabili nel patrimonio a fini di vigilanza, il divieto di pagare interessi* **strumenti finanziari diversi (da) / emessi (da**) *la Banca d'Italia, in conformità delle deliberazioni del CICR, disciplina l'emissione da parte delle banche delle obbligazioni non convertibili o convertibili in titoli di altre società nonché degli strumenti finanziari diversi dalle partecipazioni* **strumenti finanziari privati** ✂ **clienti aventi diritto alla restituzione di strumenti finanziari, ridenominazione in euro degli strumenti di debito, società italiane emittenti strumenti finanziari diffusi fra il pubblico in misura rilevante** *con regolamento della CONSOB sono stabiliti limiti al cumulo degli incarichi di amministrazione e controllo che i componenti degli organi di controllo delle società di cui al presente capo, nonché delle società emittenti strumenti finanziari diffusi fra il pubblico in misura rilevante ai sensi dell'articolo 116, possono assumere presso tutte le società di cui al libro V, titolo V, capi V, VI e VII, del codice civile* **utilizzo di un determinato strumento di pagamento** ✂ **emettere strumenti di pagamento**

📖 Possible equivalents: dokument, instrument, narzędzie, ŚRODEK (pl), DOCUMENT, INSTRUMENT, means, measure (en)

SUCCURSALE (it)

(N) **succursale di una banca, di un istituto** *'succursale di un istituto di pagamento': una sede che costituisce parte, sprovvista di personalità giuridica, di un istituto di pagamento e che effettua direttamente, in tutto o in parte, l'attività dell'istituto di pagamento*

(V) **stabilire succursali** *le banche italiane possono esercitare le attività ammesse al mutuo riconoscimento in uno Stato comunitario senza stabilirvi succursali, nel rispetto delle procedure fissate dalla Banca d'Italia*

(P) **succursale in Italia** *la Banca d'Italia iscrive in un apposito albo gli istituti di moneta elettronica autorizzati in Italia e le relative succursali nonché le succursali*

in Italia degli istituti di moneta elettronica con sede legale in uno Stato comunitario o extracomunitario

✎ **succursale di una banca comunitaria / extracomunitaria** *la Banca d'Italia informa dell'apertura della procedura di amministrazione straordinaria le autorità di vigilanza degli Stati comunitari che ospitano succursali della banca extracomunitaria* **succursale di un istituto di pagamento ✂ stabilire succursali nel territorio della Repubblica ✂ istituti di pagamento + stabilire succursali** *gli istituti di pagamento italiani possono stabilire succursali nel territorio della Repubblica e degli altri Stati comunitari nel rispetto delle procedure fissate dalla Banca d'Italia*

📖 Possible equivalents: filia, ODDZIAŁ (pl), branch (en)

T

TASSO (it)

(Adj) **tasso fisso, medio** *gli atti di cui all'art. 5 possono consentire che i proventi e gli oneri delle imprese suddette siano convertiti a tassi di cambio medi* **tasso nominale, variabile**

(N) **tasso di cambio, tasso di conversione, tasso d'interesse** *i contratti indicano il tasso d'interesse e ogni altro prezzo e condizione praticati, inclusi, per i contratti di credito, gli eventuali\ maggiori oneri in caso di mora* ✂ **tasso debitore** *le variazioni dei tassi di interesse adottate in previsione o in conseguenza di decisioni di politica monetaria riguardano contestualmente sia i tassi debitori che quelli creditori*

(V) **adottare, applicare il tasso** *il pagatore non può far valere ragioni legate al cambio, se è stato applicato il tasso di cambio di riferimento concordato con il prestatore di servizi di pagamento*

tasso di cambio corrente, tasso di cambio di riferimento, tasso di conversione irrevocabilmente fissato *si stabilisce che le suddette operazioni siano tradotte nella moneta di conto applicando i rispettivi tassi di cambio con l'euro irrevocabilmente fissati* **tasso effettivo globale medio** *per le operazioni di finanziamento, comunque denominate, è pubblicizzato il tasso effettivo globale medio previsto dall'articolo 2, commi 1 e 2, della legge 7 marzo 1996, n. 108* **tasso nominale minimo** *nei casi di assenza o di nullità delle relative clausole contrattuali il TAEG equivale al tasso nominale minimo dei buoni del Tesoro annuali o di altri titoli similari eventualmente indicati dal Ministro dell'economia e delle finanze, emessi nei dodici mesi precedenti la conclusione del contratto* **tasso ufficiale di sconto** ✂ **andamento dei tassi di cambio delle valute, modifica / variazione dei tassi d'interesse**

📖 Possible equivalents: kurs, stawka, STOPA (pl), rate (en)

TERMINE (it)

(Adj) **termine indicato (a)** *qualora la banca non provveda entro il termine indicato al comma 6-bis, il richiedente può presentare ricorso al presidente del tribunale nella cui circoscrizione è situato l'immobile* **termine stabilito (da), previsto (da)** ✂ **decorso il termine** *decorso il termine indicato senza che siano state proposte contestazioni ovvero definite queste ultime con sentenza passata in giudicato, i commissari liquidatori provvedono al riparto o alla restituzione finale in conformità di quanto previsto dall'articolo 91*

(N) **modalità e termini** *la Banca d'Italia stabilisce modalità e termini per l'invio delle comunicazioni di cui al comma 1-bis* ✂ **termine di 10 giorni / 2 mesi** ✂ **scadenza di un termine**

(P) **termine per** *qualora il termine per l'espressione del parere decorra inutilmente, i decreti legislativi possono essere comunque adottati* ✂ **termine di cui al comma 1** ✂**entro, oltre un termine** *la cancellazione dei dati del protesto è disposta dal responsabile dirigente dell'ufficio protesti competente per territorio non oltre il termine di venti giorni dalla data di presentazione della relativa istanza, corredata del provvedimento di riabilitazione* ✂ **nel termine** ✂ **secondo un termine** *alla riscossione delle sanzioni previste dal presente titolo si provvede mediante ruolo secondo i termini e le modalità previsti dal decreto del Presidente della Repubblica 23 settembre 1973, n. 602, come modificato dal decreto legislativo 26 febbraio 1999, n. 46.*

✎ **termine previsto dal comma 1** ✂ **termini di conclusione dei procedimenti amministrativi, stabiliti da norme di legge o di regolamento** ✂ **2 mesi prima della scadenza del termine indicato al comma 1** ✂ **entro il termine di 10 giorni dalla data (di)** ✂ **chiedere la comunicazione di dati e notizie e la trasmissione di atti e documenti, fissando i relativi termini** *per lo svolgimento dei propri compiti, l'Organismo può chiedere agli iscritti la comunicazione di dati e notizie e la trasmissione di atti e documenti, fissando i relativi termini, e può effettuare ispezioni* **trasmettere i bilanci con le modalità e nei termini stabiliti dalla Banca d'Italia** ✂ **inviare alla Banca d'Italia, con le modalità e nei termini da essa stabiliti, le segnalazioni periodiche nonché ogni altro dato e documento richiesto**

📖 Possible equivalents: OKRES, TERMIN (pl), DATE, deadline, duration, period, term (en)

TERRITORIO (it)

Usually singular

(N) **territorio della Repubblica** ✂ **Agenzia del territorio** *il creditore rilascia al debitore quietanza attestante la data di estinzione dell'obbligazione e trasmette al conservatore la relativa comunicazione entro trenta giorni dalla stessa data, senza alcun onere per il debitore e secondo le modalità determinate dall'Agenzia del territorio* **succursali nel territorio** *le banche italiane possono stabilire succursali nel territorio della Repubblica e degli altri Stati comunitari*

✏ **stabile organizzazione nel territorio della Repubblica** *l'iscrizione nell'elenco di cui all'articolo 128-sexies, comma 2, è subordinata al ricorrere dei seguenti requisiti: a) forma di società per azioni, di società in accomandita per azioni, di società a responsabilità limitata o di società cooperativa b) sede legale e amministrativa o, per i soggetti comunitari, stabile organizzazione nel territorio della Repubblica* ✂ **operare nel territorio della Repubblica, stabilire succursali nel territorio della Repubblica** ✂ **la sede legale e la direzione generale + essere situati nel territorio della Repubblica** *la Banca d'Italia autorizza gli intermediari finanziari ad esercitare la propria attività al ricorrere delle seguenti condizioni: a) sia adottata la forma di società per azioni, in accomandita per azioni, a responsabilità limitata e cooperativa b) la sede legale e la direzione generale siano situate nel territorio della Repubblica*

📖 Possible equivalents: obszar, teren, TERYTORIUM (pl), area, territory (en)

TESTO UNICO (it)

Usually singular

(Adj) **testo unico bancario** *nella presente legge si intende per 'testo unico bancario' il decreto legislativo 1 settembre 1993, n. 385, e successive modificazioni, recante il testo unico delle leggi in materia bancaria e creditizia*

(N) **titolo I del testo unico** *non rientra nell'ambito del presente decreto la regolamentazione in materia di vigilanza sulle banche, ivi compresa la disciplina*

delle crisi di cui al titolo IV del testo unico delle disposizioni in materia bancaria e creditizia, di cui al decreto legislativo 1° settembre 1993, n. 385

✎ **testo unico di cui al decreto legislativo 1 gennaio 2000 n. 1, testo unico delle disposizioni in materia di intermediazione finanziaria, testo unico delle leggi in materia bancaria e creditizia ✂ article 1, comma 1 del testo unico ✂ gruppo bancario iscritto nell'albo previsto dall'articolo 1 del testo unico** *le disposizioni del comma 2 si applicano in ogni caso alle società e agli enti finanziari che rientrano nei gruppi bancari iscritti nell' albo previsto dall'art. 64 del testo unico delle leggi in materia bancaria e creditizia* **sanzioni amministrative pecuniarie previste dal testo unico** *le sanzioni amministrative pecuniarie previste dal testo unico di cui al decreto legislativo 1° settembre 1993, n. 385, dal testo unico di cui al decreto legislativo 24 febbraio 1998, n. 58, dalla legge 12 agosto 1982, n. 576, che non sono state modificate dalla presente legge, sono quintuplicate* **sanzioni penali previste dal testo unico ✂ ai sensi dell'articolo 31 del testo unico di cui al decreto legislativo 1 gennaio 2000 n. 1** *la pena è raddoppiata se si tratta di società con titoli quotati in mercati regolamentati italiani o di altri Stati dell'Unione europea o diffusi tra il pubblico in misura rilevante ai sensi dell'articolo 116 del testo unico di cui al decreto legislativo 24 febbraio 1998, n. 58*

🕮 Possible equivalents: tekst jednolity (pl), consolidating act, consolidation act (en)

TITOLARE (it)

(N) **titolare dell'archivio** *il Ministero dell'economia e delle finanze è titolare dell'archivio e può avvalersi, per la gestione dell'archivio, di Consap S.p.A., di seguito denominato ente gestore* **titolare del conto** *il titolare del conto corrente ha la disponibilità economica delle somme relative agli assegni circolari o bancari versati sul suo conto (…) entro i quattro giorni lavorativi successivi al versamento* **titolare del diritto, delle partecipazioni** *la Banca d'Italia individua i soggetti tenuti a richiedere l'autorizzazione quando i diritti derivanti dalle partecipazioni indicate ai commi 1 e 2 spettano o sono attribuiti ad un soggetto diverso dal titolare delle partecipazioni stesse*

✎ **titolari di partecipazioni di cui all'articolo 1, titolari dei diritti indicati nel comma 1 ✂ i creditori e i titolari dei diritto** *entro quindici giorni dal ricevimento della raccomandata, i creditori e i titolari dei diritti indicati nel comma 2 possono* *presentare o inviare, mediante raccomandata con avviso di ricevimento, i loro reclami ai commissari, allegando i documenti giustificativi*

📖 Possible equivalents: WŁAŚCICIEL, POSIADACZ (pl), bearer, HOLDER, owner, possessor, proprietor (en)

TITOLO 1 (it)

Usually singular

(N) **disposizioni, norme del titolo I** *agli agenti in attività finanziaria, agli agenti previsti dall'articolo 128-quater, comma 7, e ai mediatori creditizi si applicano, in quanto compatibili, le norme del Titolo VI*

✎ **parte I, titolo I, capo I** ✂ **libro I, titolo I, capo I del codice penale** ✂ **titolo del presente decreto, titolo del testo unico bancario** ✂ **art. 1, comma 1, L. 1 gennaio 2000, n. 1, citato in nota al presente Titolo** *l'importo della sanzione è stato così aumentato ai sensi dell'art. 39, comma 3, L. 28 dicembre 2005, n. 262, citato in nota al presente Titolo, che ha disposto la quintuplicazione delle sanzioni amministrative pecuniarie previste dal testo unico* ✂ **disposizioni / sanzioni previste dal presente titolo, entrata in vigore delle disposizioni di attuazione del presente Titolo, norme del presente titolo** ✂ **attuazione della riforma del titolo 1, come sostituito dal d.lgs. 1 gennaio 2000 n. 1 e successive modificazioni** *norme applicabili ai soggetti operanti nel settore finanziario fino all'attuazione della riforma del titolo V, come sostituito dal d.lgs. 13 agosto 2010, n. 141, e successive modificazioni*

📖 Possible equivalents: dział, tytuł (pl), title (en)

TITOLO 2 (it)

Usually plural

(Adj) **titoli nominativi, obbligazioniari** *durante il periodo transitorio, le regioni che abbiano effettuato emissioni di titoli obbligazionari ai sensi degli articoli 35 e 37 della legge 23 dicembre 1994, n. 724 hanno facoltà di ridenominare in euro i relativi prestiti nei termini e con le modalità prescritti per gli strumenti finanziari privati, previsti negli articoli 12 e 13 del presente decreto* **titoli similari** *la presente legge si applica altresì alle operazioni di cartolarizzazione realizzate mediante la sottoscrizione o l'acquisto di obbligazioni e titoli similari ovvero cambiali finanziarie, esclusi comunque titoli rappresentativi del capitale sociale, titoli ibridi e convertibili,*

da parte della società emittente i titoli ✂ **titoli emessi (da), quotati (in)** *restano salve le disposizioni riguardanti gli enti e le società che abbiano emesso titoli quotati in borsa* **titoli ridenominati (in)**

(N) **crediti e titoli, obbligzioni e / o titoli** ✂ **titoli di credito, di debito, di Stato** *'titoli di Stato': tutti i titoli, a breve e medio-lungo termine, emessi dal tesoro, nonché i prestiti emessi dalle Ferrovie dello Stato e riconosciuti come debiti dello Stato ai sensi dell'articolo 2, comma 12, della legge 23 dicembre 1996, n. 662* ✂ **emissione di titoli** ✂ **portatori di titoli** *su ciascun patrimonio non sono ammesse azioni da parte di creditori diversi dai portatori dei titoli emessi per finanziare l'acquisto dei crediti stessi*

(V) **emettere titoli** *le banche possono emettere titoli di deposito nominativi o al portatore*

✎ **titoli quotati in borsa / mercati** *la pena è raddoppiata se si tratta di società con titoli quotati in mercati regolamentati italiani o di altri Stati dell'Unione europea o diffusi tra il pubblico in misura rilevante ai sensi dell'articolo 116 del testo unico di cui al decreto legislativo 24 febbraio 1998, n. 58* ✂ **società emittente titoli** ✂ **emettere titoli quotati in borsa**

📖 Possible equivalents: SECURITY (en), PAPIER WARTOŚCIOWY, TYTUŁ (pl)

V

VALORE (it)

(Adj) **valore monetario** *'moneta elettronica': il valore monetario memorizzato elettronicamente, ivi inclusa la memorizzazione magnetica, rappresentato da un credito nei confronti dell'emittente che sia emesso per effettuare operazioni di pagamento come definite all'articolo 1, comma 1, lettera c)* **valore nominale** ✂ **valore inferiore** *le immobilizzazioni materiali che, alla data di chiusura dell'esercizio, risultino durevolmente di valore inferiore al costo o al valore determinato a norma del comma 1 sono iscritte a tale minor valore* **valore superiore** ✂ **valori mobiliari** *il divieto previsto dal comma 2 non si applica agli organismi di investimento collettivo in valori mobiliari, per i quali valgono i limiti previsti dalla disciplina propria di ciascuno di essi*

valore nominale di un'azione *il valore nominale delle azioni non può essere inferiore a due euro* **valore nominale unitario** *i prestiti ridenominati sono costituiti da strumenti finanziari di taglio e valore nominale unitario pari ad un centesimo di euro* ✂ **accertamento dell'imposta sul valore aggiunto e delle imposte sui redditi** *la Banca d'Italia può effettuare ispezioni presso gli agenti insediati in Italia per conto di istituti di moneta elettronica o istituto di pagamento comunitari nonché presso il punto di contatto anche avvalendosi della Guardia di Finanza che agisce con i poteri ad essa attribuiti per l'accertamento dell'imposta sul valore aggiunto e delle imposte sui redditi, utilizzando strutture e personale esistenti in modo da non determinare oneri aggiuntivi*

Possible equivalents: cena, PAPIER WARTOŚCIOWY, WARTOŚĆ (pl), SECURITY, valore (en)

VALUTA (it)

(Adj) **valute aderenti, estere** ✂ **denominato in una valuta** *le differenze derivanti dalla conversione del patrimonio netto, denominato in valute aderenti, delle imprese controllate incluse nel consolidamento sono ricomprese nel patrimonio netto alla voce 'Riserva di conversione'*

(N) **valuta di uno stato** *il presente decreto si applica ai servizi di pagamento prestati in euro o nella valuta ufficiale di uno Stato membro non appartenente all'area dell'euro o di uno Stato appartenente allo Spazio economico europeo*

✎ **valute aderenti all'euro** *alla disciplina delle operazioni in corso soggette al rischio di cambio relativo ad una delle valute aderenti all'euro sono dedicati appositi articoli* **valuta di uno Stato partecipante** ✂ **andamento dei tassi di cambio delle valute aderenti** *s'impone l'adozione dei rispettivi tassi di conversione per la traduzione in moneta di conto degli elementi monetari il cui valore sia variabile in funzione dell'andamento dei tassi di cambio delle valute aderenti*

📖 Possible equivalents: WALUTA (pl), CURRENCY (en)

VIGILANZA (it)

Always singular

(Adj) **vigilanza informativa, ispettiva, regolamentare** *la CONSOB esercita sui soggetti abilitati e sulle imprese di assicurazione i poteri di vigilanza regolamentare, informativa e ispettiva di cui all'articolo 6, comma 2* ✂ **vigilanza consolidata** ✂ **sottoposto a vigilanza** *la Banca d'Italia pubblica un Bollettino (6) contenente i provvedimenti di carattere generale emanati dalle autorità creditizie nonché altri provvedimenti rilevanti relativi ai soggetti sottoposti a vigilanza*

(N) **esercizio della vigilanza** *le società indicate nell'articolo 65 forniscono alla capogruppo ovvero alla singola banca le situazioni, i dati e le informazioni richiesti per consentire l'esercizio della vigilanza consolidata*

(V) **esercitare la vigilanza** *al fine di esercitare la vigilanza su base consolidata, la Banca d'Italia richiede ai soggetti indicati nelle lettere da a) a c) del comma 1 dell'articolo 65 la trasmissione, anche periodica, di situazioni e dati, nonché ogni altra informazione utile*

(P) **vigilanza su** *le disposizioni del presente titolo non si applicano ai soggetti, individuati con decreto del Ministro dell'economia e delle finanze sentita la Banca d'Italia, già sottoposti, in base alla legge, a forme di vigilanza sull'attività finanziaria svolta*

✎ **autorità di vigilanza degli Stati membri, Istituto per la vigilanza sulle assicurazioni private e di interesse collettivo (ISVAP), soggetti inclusi nell'ambito della vigilanza consolidata** *la Banca d'Italia può scambiare informazioni con autorità amministrative o giudiziarie nell'ambito di procedimenti di liquidazione o di fallimento, in Italia o all'estero, relativi a banche, succursali di banche italiane all'estero o di banche comunitarie o extracomunitarie in Italia, nonché relativi a soggetti inclusi nell'ambito della vigilanza consolidata* **strumenti finanziari computabili nel patrimonio a fini di vigilanza ✂ consentire l'esercizio della vigilanza consolidata, esercitare i poteri di vigilanza, esercitare la vigilanza su base consolidata, ostacolare l'effettivo esercizio delle funzioni di vigilanza**

📖 Possible equivalents: KONTROLA, NADZÓR (pl), charge, control, supervision, surveillance (en)

VIGORE (it)

Always singular

(N) **entrata in vigore** *le disposizioni riguardanti le imprese di assicurazione si applicano decorsi dodici mesi dalla data di entrata in vigore del decreto di cui al comma 1*

(V) **entrare in vigore** *il presente decreto legislativo entra in vigore il 1° gennaio 1994*

✎ **entrata in vigore delle disposizioni attuative ✂ data di entrata in vigore della presente disposizione ✂ 10 giorni successivi alla data di entrata in vigore del presente decreto ✂ a decorrere dalla data di entrata in vigore dei corrispondenti articoli del decreto legislativo** *le disposizioni modificate, introdotte o sostituite dal presente decreto si applicano a decorrere dalla data di entrata in vigore dei corrispondenti articoli del decreto legislativo 13 agosto 2010, n. 141* **entro due mesi dalla data di entrata in vigore della presente legge, fino alla data di entrata in vigore delle disposizioni di attuazione**

📖 Possible equivalents: moc, życie (pl), effect, force (en)

6. Conclusions

The present work aimed at the creation of model of a multilingual dictionary of LSP collocations intended as an aid to those who aspire to compile dictionaries of the above-mentioned type. The model was presented in Chapter 5, which was devoted to the structure and content as well as the creation process of an example dictionary under discussion, i. e. collocational dictionary of English, Italian and Polish banking law. The above-mentioned dictionary, comprised in the work, constitutes an example result of the application of the model proposed.

The language of Polish, English and Italian banking law proved to possess numerous features typical of the language of law in general. They will be described in section 6.1 below. As far as section 6.2 is concerned, it comprises observations relating to the compilation of a dictionary according to procedures proposed in Chapter 5. Particular attention is devoted to problems and dilemmas encountered in the course of compiling the dictionary. Hopefully, the observations comprised in the section will prove helpful to individuals who will decide to create a dictionary based on the proposed model.

6.1. The language of Polish, English and Italian banking law

Before the discussion of characteristics of the language of banking law, it should be reminded that in this work it is understood as a polytechnolect, i.e. the logical sum of languages of members of a given group (or groups) of legislators who formulate normative acts pertaining to banking (cf. section 2.3). It should also be reminded that banking law as a domain of law has no clear-cut boundaries. The legislative acts which were included in the corpus were decided to be sufficiently related to banking law to be taken into account, i.e. they were qualified as devoted only or in majority to banking law.

Based on the experience gained in the process of compilation of the dictionary presented in this work, it can be observed that the language of banking law demonstrates features which are typical of the language of law in general. Let us turn firstly to its terminological and lexical features. At the outset, it should be stated that the language of banking law contains:

1) terms and other lexical items typical of the language of law
2) terms and other lexical items typical of the language of banking
3) vocabulary which is present in LGP

Furthermore, the language of banking law is characterised by the frequent use of nominalisations, absolute expressions and word combinations used to keep the broad broad or, conversely, restricted restricted (cf. section 2.4). They can be easily found in usage examples provided in the dictionary presented in this dissertation:

> *any reference in paragraph (4) above to a summary of the provisions of a scheme is a reference to a summary of those provisions which includes (but is not limited to) details of the level and scope of the protection afforded by the Scheme*

> *a reference in an enactment or other document to anything done under a provision applied by this Part of this Act includes a reference to the provision as applied*

> *a 'qualifying arrangement' means a voluntary arrangement which (b) includes a realisation of some or all of the assets of the credit institution, with a view to terminating the whole or any part of the business of that credit institution*

> *le somme di denaro detenute nei conti di pagamento costituiscono, per ciascun cliente, patrimonio distinto a tutti gli effetti da quello dell'istituto di pagamento e degli altri clienti dello stesso*

> *fino al completo soddisfacimento dei diritti dei soggetti a cui vantaggio la destinazione è effettuata, sul patrimonio destinato e sui frutti e proventi da esso derivanti sono ammesse azioni soltanto a tutela dei diritti dei predetti soggetti*

> *dyspozycja wierzyciela oznacza równocześnie jego zgodę na cofnięcie przez bank dłużnika obciążenia rachunku dłużnika i cofnięcie uznania rachunku wierzyciela w przypadku dokonanego przez dłużnika odwołania polecenia zapłaty, o którym mowa w ust. 6*

> *premia technologiczna przeznaczona na pokrycie wydatków, o których mowa w ust. 6, wraz z wszelką inną pomocą, w tym pomocą de minimis, udzielaną na pokrycie tych samych wydatków, nie może przekroczyć 50% wartości tych wydatków.*

However, it should be mentioned that the features under discussion are particularly easy to identify in the English part of the corpus. The reasons might lie in the differences between civil law tradition and common law tradition. As was stated in Chapter 2, common law texts tend to contain numerous details, whereas civil law texts are typically rather general (Gotti 2012: 58–59). Interestingly, the observations under discussion stand partially in contrast to some previous research, whose results suggested that nominalisations are more frequent in Italian legal texts than in English legal texts (Mattiello 2010, Garzone 2011: 223). Accordingly, they need to be confirmed by further, quantitative research on the subject.

So far, we have focussed, among others, on the absolute expressions, which are intended to ensure high precision and accuracy required from the texts of normative acts. Nevertheless, the texts included in the corpus proved to also contain vocabulary which can be perceived as ambiguous and flexible. Its examples are underlined below:

il finanziatore o l'intermediario del credito forniscono al consumatore chiarimenti adeguati, in modo che questi possa valutare se il contratto di credito proposto sia adatto alle sue esigenze e alla sua situazione finanziaria

la Banca d'Italia può stabilire ulteriori regole per garantire trasparenza e correttezza nei rapporti con la clientela

qualora risultino gravi irregolarità nell'amministrazione (...) la Banca d'Italia può disporre che uno o più commissari assumano i poteri di amministrazione dell'intermediario finanziario iscritto all'albo di cui all'articolo 106

la Banca d'Italia può richiedere alle autorità competenti di uno Stato comunitario di effettuare accertamenti presso i soggetti indicati nel comma 1, stabiliti nel territorio di detto Stato, ovvero concordare altre modalità delle verifiche

the duty to provide services and facilities in pursuance of the continuity obligation is subject to a right to receive reasonable consideration

any requirement in this Part to send a relevant notification to a creditor shall also be treated as satisfied if the conditions set out in paragraph (6) are satisfied

Komisja Nadzoru Finansowego może w szczególnie uzasadnionych przypadkach wyrazić zgodę na przekroczenie limitu, o którym mowa w ust. 2

właściwe władze nadzorcze mogą uzgodnić, że kryteriów, o których mowa w ust. 6 pkt 1–6, nie stosuje się, jeżeli są one niewłaściwe z uwagi na specyfikę banku, instytucji kredytowych lub względną istotność ich działalności w państwach członkowskich

The examples of ambiguous expressions seemed to be the most numerous in the Italian part of the corpus. Contrastingly, they were much more difficult to find in the English part of the corpus, which in a way completes the previous observations on the particularly frequent presence of absolute expressions in the texts under discussion. It should be reminded once again that in principle common law texts tend to be full of details, whereas civil law texts tend to be much more general (Gotti 2012: 58–59). The presence of absolute expressions and ambiguous expressions in the languages of law typical of common and civil law systems undoubtedly constitutes an especially interesting subject for more detailed research.

Furthermore, it should be mentioned that ambiguous expressions present in the corpus happen to be defined or accompanied by complex descriptions, as in the examples below:

In this section 'relevant person' means
(a) an institution authorised for the purpose of the Financial Services and Markets Act 2000(a) by the PRA or FCA,
(b) a parent of such an institution which
  (i) is a financial holding company or a mixed financial holding company; and
  (ii) is established in, or formed under the law of any part of, the United Kingdom,

or

(c) a subsidiary of such an institution or of such a parent which

(i) is a financial institution authorised by the PRA or FCA, and
(ii is established in, or formed under the law of any part of, the United Kingdom.

In this section '<u>small business</u>' means any person (other than an individual acting as a sole trader) carrying on a business which had a turnover in the relevant financial year of less than L1,000,000.

'costo <u>totale</u> del credito' indica gli interessi e tutti gli altri costi, incluse le commissioni, le imposte e le altre spese, a eccezione di quelle notarili, che il consumatore deve pagare in relazione al contratto di credito e di cui il finanziatore è a conoscenza

<u>działalność innowacyjna</u> – działalność polegającą na opracowaniu nowej technologii i uruchomieniu na jej podstawie wytwarzania nowych lub znacząco ulepszonych towarów, procesów lub usług

Besides, the definitions are frequently provided in the case of expressions whose meaning is specific to a given normative act or whose ambiguity is less obvious at the first glance, but which could be interpreted in various ways if they were not defined. Their examples are shown below:

<u>'electronic communication'</u> means an electronic communication within the meaning of the Electronic Communications Act 2000(a) the processing of which on receipt is intended to produce writing

in this regulation and regulation 4, <u>'relevant date'</u> means the 5th May 2004

<u>'Trattato':</u> il Trattato istitutivo della Comunità Europea, e successive modifiche e integrazioni

<u>'contratto di credito'</u> indica il contratto con cui un finanziatore concede o si impegna a concedere a un consumatore un credito sotto forma di dilazione di pagamento, di prestito o di altra facilitazione finanziaria

<u>badania</u> – badania naukowe w rozumieniu art. 2 pkt 3 ustawy z dnia 30 kwietnia 2010 r. o zasadach finansowania nauki (Dz. U. Nr 96, poz. 615);

<u>'budynek mieszkalny'</u> – budynek, w którym łączna powierzchnia wykorzystywanych zgodnie z przeznaczeniem lokali mieszkalnych wraz z powierzchnią pomieszczeń do nich przynależnych jest większa od łącznej powierzchni pozostałych lokali i pomieszczeń do nich przynależnych

The presence of significant numbers of definitions is another feature which is typical not only of the language of banking law, but also of the language of law in general, in particular as far as English and Polish legal systems are concerned (cf. subsection 2.4.4).

Let us now turn to collocational features of the corpus under discussion. The collocations that were identified in the corpus were sufficiently numerous to enable the creation of complex dictionary entries. They consisted of terms and common words (e.g. *to make a resolution instrument*) or of common words only (e.g. *to refrain from action*). Besides, some of the collocations constituted terms in themselves and were provided legislative definitions in the corpus (e.g. *a reverse property transfer instrument*).

Furthermore, the collocations identified in the corpus demonstrated various degrees of restrictedness and collocational strength (cf. Carter 1994, Hill 2000: 623–64 or section 1.3.). It should be noted that at the outset it was expected that the corpus would not contain semantically opaque collocations (cf. Chapter 1). Nevertheless, it proved to contain collocations which could be perceived as semantically opaque, i.e. multi-word terms (e.g. *papier wartościowy, testo unico*). Besides, initially it was assumed that the so-called free combinations (cf. Chapter 1) would not be granted the status of collocation in this work. Still, it should be mentioned that some of the word combinations identified and treated as collocations should be situated on the border between a collocation and a free combination. They will be devoted further attention in subsection 6.2.2 (cf. Chapter 5).

Furthermore, the collocations identified in the corpus were both simple (e.g. *to provide services)* and extremely complex (cf. Spohr 2012: 71–73). The corpus proved to encompass quite numerous binomials (e.g. *całość lub część, informazioni e/o comunicazioni, action or inaction, terms and conditions*), which are claimed to be particularly common in the language of law. Other collocations typical of the corpus were complex prepositions (e.g. *by virtue of, w drodze, nei confronti di*) as well as verb support construction, such as *to make a payment, dokonywać wypłat,* or *fare obbligo,* which are commonly indicated as a typical feature of legal texts (e.g. Jopek-Bosiacka 2010, Kłodawski 2012, Venturi 2013). Nevertheless, it is the presence of extraordinarily complex collocations that is the most conspicuous feature of the corpus under discussion. In some cases, the collocations identified were some complex that they constituted independent fixed sentences. The approach to especially complex collocations taken in the dictionary creation process is described in detail in subsection 6.2.2.

6.2. Dictionary compilation process

6.2.1. Rejected headwords

The dictionary compilation process involved the analysis of 346 potential headwords, out of which 53 were not included in the dictionary. According to the criteria described in Chapter 5, a potential headword was rejected if less than seven collocates were identified for it. The list of the headwords which were not included in the dictionary due to the insufficient number of collocations is demonstrated in *Figure 33:*

English Headwords	**Number of collocates**	**Italian Headwords**	**Number of collocates**	**Polish headwords**	**Number of collocates**
Amendment	6	Acquisto	3	Brzmienie	4
Annotation	1	Ambito	4	Finanse	5
Bail-in	6	Amministratore	5	Gospodarstwo	4
Connection	6	Azioni	6	Kancelaria	1
Draft	4	Base	4	Odnośnik	1
England	5	Beneficiario	5	Rozumienie	4
Extent	2	Capogruppo	5	Sejm	4
Failure	4	Cliente	3	Tekst	5
Force	6	Commissario	5	Zastrzeżenie	2
Help	2	Economia	2	Związek	5
Liquidation	4	Esecuzione	4	Życie	5
Account	3	Finanza	6		
Procedure	5	Finanziatore	2		
Reform	2	Oggetto	5		
Ring	10	Pagatore	2		
Scotland	3	Parola	6		
Stabilisation	6	Presidente	6		
Transfer	4	Prestatore	4		
Way	3	Somma	6		
Word	5	Tesoro	4		
		Utilizzatore	2		
Total: 20 out of 115 (**17 %**)		**Total:** 21 out of 127 (**16 %**)		**Total:** 11 out of 104 (**10 %**)	

Figure 33. The list of potential headwords that were rejected due to insufficient number of collocates.

In the case of the English headword *ring*, ten collocates were identified, but since the potential headword proved to constitute a part of compound words, it would need to be devoted two separate entries (i.e. *ring-fencing* and *ring-fenced body).* Therefore, the headword was finally rejected, since its acceptance would imply the inclusion of two entries containing five collocates.

Interestingly, as shown in *Figure 34*, it is around 17 % and 16 % of potential headwords that were rejected for English and Italian part of the dictionary respectively. When it comes to the Polish part, it is 10 % of the headwords:

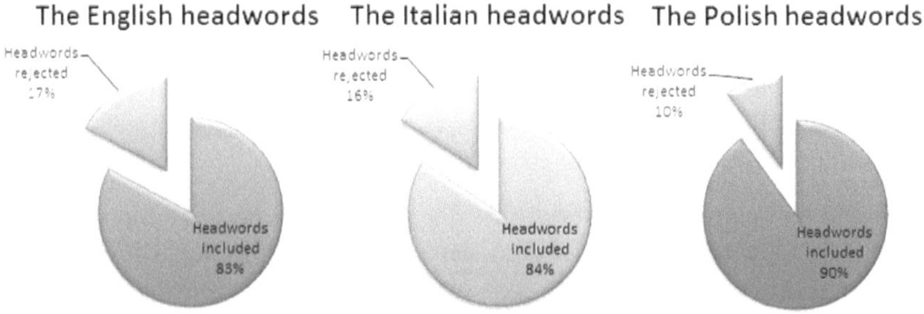

Figure 34. The percentage of potential headwords that were rejected due to the insufficient number of collocates.

The lower percentage of rejected headwords in the Polish part may be related to the fact that Polish is an inflected language, and its potential headwords were examined in their various inflectional forms (see Chapter 5). As the corpus was not tagged, the various inflectional forms were added manually already at the stage of searching for collocates. The procedure under discussion might result in an increased number of concordances for analysis, which in turn might lead to a larger number of identified collocates and consequently a lower number of rejected headwords.

Finally, it should be mentioned that some of the rejected headwords were added to the dictionary even though they did not meet the assumed frequency criteria, as they were considered crucial for the domain and are intuitively expected to be found in the dictionary under discussion. The terms under discussion are marked in *Figure 33* by bold font (cf. section 5.1.). The collocations presented in the corresponding entries were chosen at the discretion of the lexicographer, but still based on the corpus.

6.2.2. Problems related to statistical significance

Free combinations

One of the results of research conducted for the purposes this work was the formulation of a definition of collocation to be used by LSP lexicographers (cf. Chapter 1). It was decided that in the case of collocational LSP dictionaries, collocations should be understood most of all as word combinations which are semantically coherent, which occur in a given LSP habitually and which are statistically significant. Besides, it was proposed that in the context under discussion the notion of collocation should encompass:

1) grammatical and lexical collocations
2) collocations of two or more words
3) both simple and complex collocations as understood by Spohr (2012)
4) unique collocations, strong collocations and medium-strength collocations as understood by Hill (2000: 63–64)

It should be mentioned, however, that the above-mentioned assumptions may need to be adjusted by other LSP dictionary compilers, for instance due to specificity of a particular LSP. The definition presented herein was formulated bearing in mind the specificity of the corpus employed in this work.

Additionally, it should be highlighted that in the context of LSP lexicography, collocations should not be defined as any repeatedly occurring word combinations (cf. Chapter 1). Such definition, if accepted, would entail treating as collocations word pairs such as *of the*, which are frequent in most language corpora and which arguably should not be presented as one linguistic unit in any dictionary. Besides, it was decided that the expressions treated as collocations should not be required to be semantically unpredictable as understood by Herbst (1996, cf. subsection 1.1.1). The lack of semantic unpredictability does not seem to be a good reason to exclude any statistically significant and conventionally used collocation from a dictionary. Finally, the dictionary presented in this was supposed not to contain neither free combinations nor idioms, though it was stated that in the cases of some dictionaries their inclusion could be considered.

The assumptions under discussion were verified in practice in the course of the dictionary compilation and proved to be satisfactory. The only assumption which turned to be problematic was the one relating to the exclusion of free combinations. Initially, such word combinations were presumed to be redundant, since potential dictionary users were supposed to be advanced enough to form them with the aid of traditional dictionaries (cf. section 1.4.). Nevertheless, already in Chapter 5, which aimed at describing in detail the process of compilation of the dictionary presented in this work, it was noticed that the borderline between a collocation and a free combination is often vague and far from being obvious. Furthermore, it was stated that in the case of the vagueness under discussion, any word combination that seems to be potentially useful and results to be statistically significant should be treated as worth including in the dictionary.

At the stage of forming conclusions, it should be added that the dilemmas relating to the borderline between free combinations and collocations were especially acute in the case of particularly long word combinations. After careful consideration and based on the assumed criteria (cf. Chapter 1 and 5), the expressions under discussion were treated as collocations despite their length. Example collocations of this type are presented in the entry below:

LAW (it)

Uusally singular

(Adj) **foreign law** ✂ **law applicable (to)** *the effects of a relevant reorganisation or a relevant winding up on a netting agreement shall be determined in accordance with the law applicable to that agreement*

(N) **law of a country, a state** ✂ **insolvency law** ✂ **provision of the law, rule of law** *anything done by the bank in connection with the exercise of a stabilisation power under Part 1 of this Act is not a gratuitous alienation for the purpose of section 242 or any other rule of law*

(P) **under the law** *'appropriate authority' means the authority authorised, under the law of the EEA state mentioned in paragraph (d) of subsection (4), to enter into the joint determination mentioned in that paragraph,* **in accordance with the law**

general law of insolvency of the United Kingdom, law of an EEA State, law of the third country ✂ **application of insolvency law, partnership constituted under the law of Scotland** *this section does not apply in relation to partnerships constituted under the law of Scotland* ✂ **institution which is incorporated in or formed under the law of a country or territory outside the United Kingdom, institution which is incorporated in or formed under the law of any part of the United Kingdom** *'UK institution' means an institution which is incorporated in, or formed under the law of any part of, the United Kingdom* ✂ **to be determined in accordance with the law of a state**

It should be highlighted that all the relatively long word combinations which are treated as collocations in the dictionary presented in this work have met the assumed criterion of frequency (5 occurrences), and at least one of their collocates was identified based on MI test. It was decided that the word combinations under discussion should be included in the entries, since they simply seemed to be potentially very helpful to target users of the dictionary, which is production oriented and which is most of all intended to foster the efficient interlingual communication in the domain of law.

MI test and t-score test application

One of the initial assumptions regarding the process of compilation of the dictionary presented in this work was that the collocational research would be carried out with the aid of MI test, whose results were supposed to be compared with results of the T-score test. The proposed procedure was motivated by the fact that

MI test is assumed to give high scores to low-frequency collocations, whereas t-score tends to return high results for items occurring frequently (cf. section 3.6.2, Bartsch 2004: 103, McEnery, Xiao and Tono 2006: 57). Nevertheless, in the course of work it turned out that the number of collocations to be added to dictionary entries due to the application of the second statistical test is very limited (see *Figure 34*). By contrast, the number of collocations identified with the aid of the MI test was often very significant and allowed for the creation of long and complex dictionary entries. If, however, the number of collocates found with the aid of MI test was insufficient to include the entry in the dictionary, the application of the second test never helped. Therefore, as the profits proved not to be proportional to the input of efforts, the two tests were used only for the first 54 headwords analysed, whereas the remaining entries were created based on MI test only. The MI test seemed in a way preferable to t-score test, since the latter seemed to return larger numbers of insignificant results due to its focus on high-frequency items.

The headwords which were analysed with both MI and t-score test are presented in *Figure 35* together with the number of collocations that were added to the entries with the aid of t-score test:

Headword	**Number of collocations added with the aid of t-score test**	**Headword**	**Number of collocations added with the aid of t-score test**
Approval	0	conto	0
appointment	0	controllo	0
asset	0	conversione	0
authority	0	criterio	0
brzmienie	0	credito	0
bank (pl)	7	circumstances	1
banca	5	committee	0
bail	0	compensation	0
bank (en)	6	company	0
board	0	condition	0
body	0	copy	0
bridge bank	0	country	0
business	0	supervision	0
cel	2	creditor	0
cześć	1	dane	0
członek	0	decyzja	1
cambio	0	dzień	8
capitale	0	działalność	5

Figure 35. The number of collocations added with the aid of t-score test to headwords analysed with the aid of two statistical tests

Figure 35. Continued

Headword	Number of collocations added with the aid of t-score test	Headword	Number of collocations added with the aid of t-score test
capo	1	data	1
czynność	1	dati	0
caso	0	diritto	0
codice	0	disciplina	0
comma	8	document	0
comunicazione	0	decreto	2
consiglio	0	date	0
condizione	0	day	0
consumatore	0	decision	0
TOTAL: 49 collocates identified for 54 headwords analysed			

It should be mentioned that the t-score test usually permitted to add collocations to headwords whose entries proved to be particularly large anyway. Besides, is important to remind at this stage that as was mentioned in Chapter 5, the collocational analysis involved no more than 120 collocates for a single headword and the remaining collocates were simply omitted. The omitted collocates were those for which the test gave the lowest results. It seems highly probable that if all (or at least more than 120) of the collocates were analysed, the collocations identified with the aid of the t-score test would have been identified also with the aid of MI test. The characteristics of both tests relating to the dependency of their results on the item frequency in the corpus (cf. subsection 3.7.2) seems to make the assumption even more probable, since collocates with a relatively high t-score results tend to give relatively low MI test results.

Furthermore, it should be reminded that all the potential collocates that were analysed to be included in the dictionary got an MI score of at least 3 and a t-score of at least 2 (Hunston 2002: 72, McEnery, Xiao and Tono 2006: 56). Accordingly, though in this work the comparison of both tests was finally resigned from, it is strongly recommended in the case of collocational analysis that is limited to collocates with higher test results (e.g. MI test result > 7). Besides, the comparison of both tests is in general desirable in the case of research based on huge corpora, when the number of potential collocates is vast and needs to be severely restricted. Finally, it should be mentioned that in an ideal world with no time restrictions, the analysis with the aid of MI test should always be followed by an analysis based on t-score test. Even if no new collocations are identified with the aid of the latter, the analysis of t-score results gives opportunity of a second look on the potential collocates identified previously. At this time, some decisions may be changed, for instance some collocations may be added if they were previously omitted by accident or rejected for a controversial reason.

Meeting expectations of potential dictionary users

Should the choice of headwords be based solely on the frequency criterion, some terms that are intuitively expected to be found in a dictionary devoted to a given domain may not be included. Accordingly, the generated list of potential headwords should be verified by the lexicographer and, if necessary, completed at their discretion, possibly referring also to resources other than the corpus. The headwords that were added to the dictionary presented in this work regardless of the frequency criterion were indicated in section 5.1. It should be highlighted, however, that the number of the added headwords could have been much larger in order to further expand the dictionary and consequently to create an even more complete resource. For the purposes of this work, which aims at the creation a model and is supposed to provide an example of its practical application, but still remains to a large extent theoretical, it was considered sufficient to include the additional headwords listed in *Figure 32* in section 5.1. Still, undoubtedly, further expansion of the dictionary would positively influence its quality, especially if it contributed to a larger number of equivalent headwords present in all the three parts devoted to different languages. Taking the perspective of potential dictionary users, the more equivalent headwords included in the dictionary parts corresponding to various languages, the better the overall perception of the resource. Nevertheless, it is the frequency-based, automatic generation of headwords that ensures the best information on items which are actually often used in the language of banking law in a given area. The abovementioned information is also extremely significant to dictionary users, which is an important argument against the inclusion of additional headwords.

6.2.3. Fighting for consistency

While preparing for the process of compilation of the dictionary under discussion, the author tried to take all the possible decisions regarding its structure and content before the compilation had actually started. Nevertheless, it turned out that a myriad of less obvious issues had not been concerned at the planning stage and had to be approached already in the course of the dictionary compilation process. The situations involve the risk of consistency problems. It should be highlighted that consistency constitutes an enormous challenge for lexicographers, as virtually every entry is to some extent exceptional and entails dilemmas that may not be repeated in any other entry, but may also reappear after a couple of months of work. Thus, the lexicographer takes hundreds of minor decisions, each of which should be remembered till the end of the project. Preserving consistency is a demanding task, which nevertheless probably becomes easier with increasing experience.

Prepositional collocations

Particular consistency problems were encountered at the stage of creating subentries devoted to prepositions. Numerous collocations were obvious to be put into the prepositional subentries (e.g. *in reliance on a section* in the entry for *section*, or *with the approval / consent of the Treasury* in the entry for *Treasury*). Others, however, were placed in other subentries despite the presence of prepositions, as the choice seemed more intuitive. For the sake of example, the entry for *reference* contains numerous collocations which could have been placed in the prepositional subentry, but actually have been placed in the nominal subentry:

REFERENCE (en)

(Adj) **defined by reference (to)** *before making regulations under this section relating to a description of charges defined by reference to their being granted in favour of the Bank of England, or in connection with settlement arrangements provided by the Bank, the Secretary of State and the Treasury shall consult the Bank*
(N) **reference in an enactment** *a reference in an enactment or other document to anything done under a provision applied by this Part of this Act includes a reference to the provision as applied* **reference in Part 1, in section 1, in subsection (1)** ✂ **reference to an administrator, to a bank, to a committee, to a compay, to a deposit, to insolvency, to an institution, to liquidation, to a liquidator** *the modifications are that (a) a reference to the liquidator is a reference to the bank liquidator, (b) a reference to winding up is a reference to bank insolvency* **reference to an office, to a provision**

When we compare the content of the nominal subentry above with the prepositional subentry for the headword *decyzja* below, we will notice that the expressions with similar structures (i.e. headword + preposition + noun) are placed in different subentries. In the case of the entry for *reference*, it is probably the very high number of possible nominal collocations (*reference to an administrator, to a bank, to a committee, to a company, to a deposit, etc.)* that made the author feel that the data should be placed in the nominal subentry. In the case of the entry for *decyzja*, the expression *decyzja w sprawie* intuitively seemed an obvious candidate for the prepositional subentry and the expressions *decyzja o ustanowieniu* and *decyzja w przedmiocie* were treated analogically due to their internal structure.

DECYZJA (pl)

(Adj) **decyzja wydana** ✂ **określony w decyzji** *zarządca komisaryczny wykonuje również zadania określone w decyzji Komisji Nadzoru Finansowego o ustanowieniu zarządcy komisarycznego.*

(N) **doręczenie, podejmowanie, podjęcie, wydanie, wykonanie decyzji**

(V) **podejmować, podjąć, wydać decyzję (o)** ✂ **decyzja + dotyczyć, wygasać**

(P) **decyzja o** *w przypadku gdy decyzja o likwidacji kasy została podjęta przez jej członków, likwidacja prowadzona jest zgodnie z zasadami obowiązującymi przy likwidacji spółdzielni* ✂ **decyzja o ustanowieniu, decyzja w przedmiocie** *Komisja Nadzoru Finansowego wydaje decyzję w przedmiocie zezwolenia na utworzenie kasy w terminie 3 miesięcy od daty otrzymania wniosku lub jego uzupełnienia* **decyzja w sprawie** ✂ **w drodze decyzji** *Komisja Nadzoru Finansowego, w drodze decyzji, na wniosek kasy, w uzasadnionych przypadkach może zwolnić ją z obowiązków określonych w ust. 1 lub ograniczyć ich zakres*

Furthermore, as the entry above demonstrates, in some cases prepositions were put in parentheses, whereas in others not. The decisions to use or not to use parentheses were taken based on various criteria, which were frequently specific for a given entry. In general, however, if a preposition constitutes the only collocate that is presented (*decyzja o*) or placed in the middle of a collocation (*decyzja w sprawie*) it would be in a way unnatural to put it in parentheses. In some other cases, the parentheses were resigned from since the omission of the preposition would affect the grammatical case of a noun (e.g. collocations *w sprawie ogłoszenia, wniosku, zastosowania* in the entry for *sprawa)*. Contrastingly, as for the entry demonstrated above, in the expressions *podejmować, podjąć, wydać decyzję (o),* the parentheses suggest that the prepositional phrase is frequently omitted in the corpus. Finally, when it comes to the entry for *reference,* the parentheses in the collocation *defined by reference (to)* seem to focus attention on the essence of the collocation, which is related to the link between the participle *defined* and the noun *reference*.

The examples above demonstrate that the fight for consistency may be especially important within an entry as opposed to in between entries. Seemingly similar cases in various entries may encourage the compiler to make intuitive choices which negatively impact consistency as far as the entire dictionary is concerned. Nevertheless, the author of this dissertation would venture to state that in lexicography the intuitiveness of description is superior to strict rules in controversial and ambiguous cases, since dictionaries most of all constitute devices used by human beings in order to search for specific information. It is highly probable that the average user will enjoy consulting a dictionary in which the entries are structured in an intuitive way, as opposed to one with awkward entries, but always sticking to predetermined rules. Nevertheless, it is next to no doubt that dictionary compilers should not cease to fight for consistency. The only point is that it should not be done at the expense of intuitiveness of description or the general user friendliness of a given resource.

Verbal collocates

Numerous consistency problems were also related to verbal collocates. To give an example, in general, it was assumed that the collocates under discussion should be presented in their infinitive forms. Nevertheless, in numerous cases the above-mentioned rule was consciously broken to make the entry content more understandable and to show the actual form in which a given verb appears. The presentation of verbs in the inflected forms is in some cases felt to be more natural and user-friendly, as was previously suggested by Przybylska (2007). The entry fragment below contains collocations (here underlined) in which verbs were presented in their inflected forms:

USTAWA (pl)

(VERBAL) **przepisy ustawy + mieć zastosowanie** *odsetki skapitalizowane w okresie do dnia 31 grudnia 1999 r., przypadające od kredytów mieszkaniowych, do których mają zastosowanie przepisy ustawy, banki zaliczają do wyniku finansowego tego okresu, za który odsetki przypadają* **ustawa + określać zasady, tracić moc** *traci moc ustawa z dnia 28 października 1950 r. o zmianie systemu pieniężnego* **ustawa + wchodzić w życie po upływie 10 dni od dnia ogłoszenia / z dniem 1 stycznia 2000 r.** ✂ **ilekroć w ustawie jest mowa (o)** ✂ **stosuje**

się przepisy ustawy *kasa jest spółdzielnią, do której w zakresie nieuregulowanym ustawą stosuje się przepisy ustawy z dnia 16 września 1982 r. – Prawo spółdzielcze* ✂ **użyte w ustawie określenia oznaczają** ✂ **zmiany (tekstu jednolitego) wymienionej ustawy zostały ogłoszone w Dz. U. z 2000 r. Nr 1, poz. 1**

Another consistency dilemma concerned the perfective and imperfective aspect of verbs. On the one hand, some verbs occurred in the corpus only in one of their aspects and inclusion of the verb in the other aspect would signify going beyond the corpus data. On the other hand, the presence of only one of the verbal aspects in the entry may give the impression of some lack, inconsistency, or oversight. After careful consideration, it was decided that verbal collocates will occur in the entries only in the aspect in which they actually appear in the corpus. In most cases it was felt that the verb in the missing aspect did not seem to form a natural, typical, and actually employed collocation with the given headword, at least not in the corpus used in this work. The entry fragment below shows an example case in which the verbal collocate is presented only in one of the two aspects:

USTAWA (pl)

(Adj) **niniejsza ustawa** ✂ **ustawa budżetowa** *łączną kwotę, do wysokości której mogą być udzielane przez Skarb Państwa poręczenia i gwarancje, określa ustawa budżetowa, z zastrzeżeniem ust. 2* ✂ **wymieniona ustawa** *zmiany tekstu jednolitego wymienionej ustawy zostały ogłoszone w Dz. U. z 2012 r. poz. 1385 i 1529* ✂ **ustawa wymieniona w** ✂ **określony w ustawie** *wszelkie wartości pieniężne określone w ustawach oraz uchwałach Sejmu Rzeczypospolitej Polskiej przyjętych do dnia 31 grudnia 1994 r., a ogłoszonych po tym dniu, podlegają z dniem ogłoszenia przeliczeniu z mocy prawa w stosunku, o którym mowa w art. 2 ust. 2*

(N) **rozdział, tekst, zmiana ustawy** *zmiany ustawy zostały ogłoszone w Dz. U. z 1998 r. Nr 160, poz. 1063, z 2000* ✂ **przepisy ustawy**
(V) **ustawa + określać** *ustawa określa zasady grupowania i łączenia się niektórych banków w formie spółki akcyjnej*

Other consistency-related problems

The fight for maximum consistency within dictionary entries required taking numerous other decisions, some of which are summarised below:

1. How to present numerals in collocations?

The corpus happened to contain numbers expressed in different ways despite the similarity of context (e.g. *Part 2* and *Part II).* In this work it is Arabic numerals that were employed in such cases. Besides, it was decided that the number of numerals should be limited in the entries in which it would be particularly large, especially if the entries under discussion were of considerable size anyway (e.g. *article*, *section*, etc.).

2. How to approach articles in collocations?

It was decided that articles should be omitted wherever possible. If the article was felt to be needed, the indefinite article was preferred, unless the definite article seemed more logical. The entry fragment below shows example collocates with the article omitted as well as with the indefinite and definite article used. It should be mentioned that the headword *regulator* was typically accompanied in the corpus by the definite article, which is reflected in the entry.

REGULATOR (en)

Usually singular

(Adj) **appropriate regulator** ✂ **issuing regulator** *before issuing a statement of policy under section 63ZD, a regulator ('the issuing regulator') must (a) consult the other regulator, and (b) publish a draft of the proposed statement in the way appearing to the issuing regulator to be best calculated to bring it to the attention of the public*

(N) **regulator's functions, reasons** *the draft must be accompanied by (c) an explanation of the Payment Systems Regulator's reasons for believing that imposing the requirement is compatible with its duties under section 49* ✂ **reference to the regulator** *subsections (5) and (10) of that section have effect as if any reference to the PRA were a reference to the appropriate regulator*

✎ **EEA regulator, home state regulator** *'home state regulator', in relation to an EEA credit institution, means the relevant EEA regulator in the EEA State where its head office is located* ✂ **officer or member of staff of the regulator** *the function of issuing general guidance may not be discharged by an officer or member of staff of the Regulator or of the FCA* ✂ **appropriate regulator + to make rules, regulator + to charge a reasonable fee for providing a person with a copy (of)** *a regulator may charge a reasonable fee for providing a person with a copy of the statement published under this section* **regulator + to issue a statement** *if a statement issued under this section is altered or replaced by a regulator, the regulator must issue the* *altered or replacement statement* **regulator + to require the authorised person (to)** *the appropriate regulator may require the authorised person (a) to provide information which the person is required to give under this section in such form as the appropriate regulator may direct* **regulator + to take action**

3. In which cases the collocates should be presented in a row without repeating the headword?

Headwords were frequently repeated within the entries, since in many cases their repetition improved the general entry clarity, especially if the collocates consisted of more than two or three words. Besides, there were no prerequisites limiting the space of the dictionary, so the luxury of headword repetition could be afforded. Nevertheless, headwords were not repeated in the case of groups of structurally similar collocates. In fact, if the headword was repeated every time, including, for instance, very long rows of adjectival collocates, its repetition would not affect positively the clarity of the entry. Contrastingly, it would probably act as a distracting factor and would make the entry clumsy, so in such cases the repetition was avoided.

Furthermore, in some cases there was a need to shorten graphically particular groups of collocations and to separate their components using something else than a comma. It was decided to apply slashes (/) to this end. The entry below contains an example of their application in the section marked with the symbol of pen. Besides, the adjectival section below provides an example of situation in which the headword is not repeated in a row of structurally similar collocates:

PERIODO 1 (it)

Usually singular

(Adj) **periodo non inferiore (a), non superiore (a), transitorio** *ai documenti contabili obbligatori a rilevanza esterna redatti in euro nel periodo transitorio si applicano le disposizioni del comma 8*

(N) **periodo di tempo ✂ inizio di un periodo** *durante lo stesso periodo non possono essere iscritte ipoteche sugli immobili o acquistati altri diritti di prelazione sui mobili della banca se non in forza di provvedimenti giudiziali esecutivi anteriori all'inizio del periodo di sospensione*

(P) **durante, per un periodo** *il termine può essere prorogato dalla Banca d'Italia, in circostanze del tutto eccezionali per un periodo complessivo non superiore a 10 giorni lavorativi (3)* ✂ **nel periodo**

✎ per un periodo non inferiore / superiore a due anni

📖 Possible equivalents: OKRES (pl), period (it)

* * *

The present subsection has demonstrated the complex net of decisions that is involved in the dictionary compilation process. All in all, it should be highlighted that on the one hand, it is recommended to plan the dictionary structure as accurately as possible before the dictionary compilation is actually started. On the other hand, the compilation process is sufficiently complex to assume that it will probably always require taking some decisions already when it is in progress. The occurrence of such situation does not necessarily imply that the planning was not careful enough. Finally, every dictionary compiler should be aware that regardless of how much time they devote to the planning stage, in some cases they will be forced to make exceptions.

References

Aarts, J. (2002) Does corpus linguistics exist? Some old and new issues. In: Breivik, L. E., and Hasselgren, A. (eds.) *From the COLT's mouth… and others': Language corpora studies in honour of Anna-Brita*. Stenström, Editions Rodopi B.V. 1–19.

Adams, M. (ed., 2010) *'Cunning passages, contrived corridors' Unexpected Essays in the History of Lexicography*. Monza: Polimetrica.

Adolphs, S. and Knight, D. (2010) Building a spoken corpus: What are the basics? In: O'Keeffe, A., McCarthy, M. (eds.) *The Routledge Handbook of Corpus Linguistics*. London and New York: Routledge. 38–52.

Akasu, K. (2011) The first dictionary of English collocations in Japan. In: Szerszunowicz, J. et al., *Research on Phraseology in Europe and Asia: focal issues of phraseological studies. Vol 1*. Białystok: Univerity of Białystok Publishing House. 45–56.

Amussen, J. (2006) Towards a methodology for corpus-based studies of linguistic change. In: Wilson, A., Archer, D., Rayson, P. (eds.), *Corpus linguistics around the world*. Amsterdam: Editions Rodopi B. V. 33–48.

Antelmi, D. (2008) Vaghezza, definizioni e ideologia nel linguaggio giuridico. In: Garzione, G., Santulli, F. (eds.) *Il linguaggio giuridico: prospettive interdiscipliari*. Milano: Giuffrè Editore. 89–122.

Aodha, M. M. (ed., 2014) *Legal lexicography: A comparative perspective*. Farnham: Ashgate Publishing Limited.

Aprile, M. (2005) *Dalle parole ai dizionari*. Bologna: Il Mulino.

Atkins, B. T. and Rundell, M. (2008) *The Oxford Guide to Practical Lexicography*. New York: Oxford Universty Press.

Baker, P. (2006) *Using corpora in discourse analysis*. London, New York: Continuum.

Baker, P. (2010) Corpus Methods in Linguistics. In: Litosseliti, L. *Research Methods in Linguistics*. London: Continuum. 93–113.

Bambi, F. (2013) Introduzione. La lingua del diritto tra passato, presente e futuro. In: Marini, A. M., Bambin F. (eds.) *Lingua e diritto: Scritto e parlato nelle professioni legali*. Pisa: Pisa Univeristy Press. 11–14.

Barnbrook, G. (1996) *Language and computers: A practical introduction to the computer analysis of language*. Edinburgh: Edinburgh University Press.

Barnbrook, G., Mason, O., Krishnamurthy, R. (2013) *Collocation: Applications and Implications*. Basingstoke, New York: Palgrave Macmillan.

Bartoszewicz, E. (2011) Kilka uwag lingwistycznych na temat tekstów z zakresu prawa. In: *Lingwistyka Stosowana* 4. 221–228.

Bartsch, S. (2004) *Structural and functional properties of collocations in English.* Tűbengen: Gunterr Nar.

Bàzlik, M., Ambrus, P., Bęcławski, M. (2010) *The grammatical structure of legal English.* Warszawa: Translegis.

Benitez, P. F. (2009) The cognitive shift in terminology and specialized translaton. In: *MonTI: Monografías de Traducción e Interpretación* 1. 107–134.

Benson, M. (1989) The Collocational Dictionary and the Advanced Learner. In: Tickoo, M. L. (ed.) *Learners' Dictionaries: State of the Art. Anthology Series 23.* Singapore: Regional Language Centre SAMEO. 84–93.

Bergenholtz, H., Kaufmann, U. (1997) Terminography and lexicography. A critical survey of dictionaries from a single specialised field. In: *Hermes* 18. 91–125.

Berns, M. (2010) *A Concise Encyclopaedia of Applied Linguistics.* Oxford: Elsevier Ltd.

Białek, E. (2009) *Kolokacja w przekładzie. Studium rosyjsko-polskie.* Lublin: Wydawnictwo UMCS.

Biber, D. (1993a) Representativeness in Corpus Design. In: *Literary and Linguistic Computing* 8 (4). 243–257.

Biber, D. (1993b) Co-occurrence patterns among collocations: a tool for corpus-based lexical knowledge acquisition. In: *Computational linguistics* 19 (3). 549–556.

Biber, D. et al. (1998) *Longman Grammar of Spoken and Written English.* Harlow: Longman.

Biber, D., Conrad, S., Reppen, R. (1998) *Corpus Linguistics: Investigating Languages Structure and Use.* Cambridge: Cambridge University Press.

Biber, D., Jones, J. K. (2009) Quantitative methods in corpus linguistics. In: Lüdeling, A., Kytö, M. (eds.) *Corpus linguistics: an international handbook.* Berlin: Mouton de Gruyter. 1287–1304.

Biel, Ł. (2010) Corpus-Based Studies of Legal Language for Translation Purposes: Methodological and Practical Potential. In: Heine, C., Engberg, J. (eds.) *Reconceptualizing LSP. Online proceedings of the XVII European LSP Symposium 2009.* available at: http://www.asb.dk/fileadmin/www.asb.dk/isek/biel.pdf, access on 13 March 2012.

Biel, Ł. (2012) Areas of similarity and difference in legal phraseology: collocations of key terms in UK and Polish company law. In: Pamies, A., Manuel Pazos Bretaña, J., Luque Nadal, L. (eds.) *Phraseology and Discourse: Cross-Linguistic and Corpus-based Approaches.* Baltmannsweiler: Schneider Verlag, 225–233.

Bini, M., Pernas, A. and Pernas, P. (2007) Apprendimento / insegnamento delle collocazioni dell'italiano. Con I NUNC è più facile. In: Barbera, M., Corino, E. and Onesti, C. (eds.) *Corpora e linguistica in rete*. Perugia: Guerra Edizioni. 323–333.

Boguslavsky, I., Cardeňosa, J., Gallardo, C. (2008) A Novel Approach to Creating Disambiguated Multilingual Dictionaries. In: *Applied Linguistics* 30 (1). 70–92.

Boleszczuk, E., Szeczepański, P. (2011) Analiza porównawcza struktury dokumentów i języka prawniczego na przykładzie *Specyfikacji istotnych warunków zamówienia* i *Request for proposal*. In: Łukasik, M. (ed.) *Język bez granic*. Warszawa: Uniwersytet Warszawski. 13–23.

Bontempi, P. (2009) *Diritto bancario e finanziario*. Milano: Giuffrè Editore.

Borkowski, T. (2008) *Polsko-angielski tezaurus terminologii prawnej a harmonizacja prawa*. Unpublished doctoral work. University of Warsaw.

Borkowski, T. (2011) Terminologia prawna w ujęciu terminograficznym. In: *Komunikacja specjalistyczna* 4. 225–238.

Bowker, L. (2001) Towards a Methodology for a Corpus-Based Approach to Translation Evaluation. In: *Meta* 46 (2). 345–364.

Bowker, L. (2003) Specialized lexicography and specialized dictionaries. In: van Sterkenburg, P. (ed.) *A practical Guide to Lexicography*. Amsterdam, Philadelpphia: John Benjamins B. V. 154–164.

Bowker, L., Pearson, J. (2002) *Working with specialized language: a practical guide to using corpora*. London and New York: Routledge.

Brown, P. R. (1994) Lexical Collocations: a Strategy for Advanced Learners. In: *Modern English Teacher* 2 (3). 24–27.

Buczyński, A. (2006) Wybrane zastosowania programu 'Kolokacje' do badań lingwistycznych. In: Duszak, A., Gajek, E., Okulska, U. (eds.) *Korpusy w angielsko-polskim językoznawstwie kontrastywnym. Teoria i praktyka*. Kraków: TAiWPN Universitas. 427–447.

Burkhanov, I. (2003) Pragmatic specifications: Usage indications, labels, examples; dictionaries of style, dictionaries of collocations In: van Sterkenburg, P. (ed.) *A practical Guide to Lexicography*. Amsterdam, Philadelpphia: John Benjamins B. V. 102–113.

Bursill-Hall, G. L. (1966) Notes on the semantics of linguistic description. In: Bazell, C. E. et al. (eds.) *In memory of J. R. Firth*. London: Longmans. 40–49.

Cabré, M. T. (1996) Terminology today. In: Somers, H. (ed.) *Terminology, LSP and translation: studies in language engineering in honour of Juan C. Sager*. Amsterdam, Philadelphia: John Benjamins B. V. 15–33.

Cabré, M. T. (1999) *Terminology: theory, methods and applications*. Philadelphia: John Benjamins B. V.

Caldas-Coulthard, C. R. and Moon, R. (2010) 'Curvy, hunky, kinky': Using corpora as a tool for critical analysis. In: *Discourse & Society* 21 (2). 99–133.

Cane, P. (2011) *Administrative Law*. Oxford: Oxford University.

Cao, D. (2007) *Translating Law*. Clevendon: Multilingual Matters Ltd.

Caterina, R., Rossi, P. (2008) L'italiano giuridico. In: Pozzo, B., Timoteo, E. (eds.) *Europa e linguaggi giuridici*. Milano: Giuffrè Editore. 185–208.

Cavagnoli, S. (2007) *La comunicazione specialistica*. Roma: Carocci Editore.

Cavagnoli, S. (2013) *Linguaggio giuridico e lingua di genere: una simbiosi possibile*. Alessandria: Edizioni dell'Orso.

Carter, R. (1994) *Vocabulary: Applied Linguistics Perspective*. London and New York: Routledge.

Čermák, F. (2003) Source materials for dictionaries. In: van Sterkenburg, P. (ed.) *A practical guide to Lexicography*. Amsterdam, Philadelpphia: John Benjamins B. V. 18–25.

Church, K. W., and Hanks, P. (1990). Word association norms, mutual information, and lexicography. In: *Computational Linguistics* 16 (1). 22–29.

Chmielewska-Gorczyca, E. (1999) *Prawo Cywilne. Mikrotezaurus*. Warszawa: Wydawnictwo Sejmowe.

Choduń, A. (2007) *Słownictwo teksów aktów prawnych w zasobie leksykalnym współczesnej polszczyzny*. Warszawa: Wydawnictwo Trio.

Choduń, A. (2009) Uwagi o komunikatywności tekstów aktów prawnych. In: Niewiadomski, A., Mróz, A. Pawelec, M. (eds.) *Prawo i język*. Warszawa: Lingua Iuris. 127–132.

Chromá, M. (2004) *Legal translation and the dictionary*. Tübingen: Max Niemeyer.

Chromá, M. (2006) Synonymy and Polysemy in a Bilingual Law Dictionary. In: Corino, E., Marello, C., Onesti, C. (eds.) *Proceedings of XII EURALEX International Congress*. Turin: Edizioni dell'Orso. 735–741.

Clancy, B. (2010) Building a corpus to represent a variety of language. In: O'Keeffe, A., McCarthy, M. (eds.) *The Routledge Handbook of Corpus Linguistics*. London and New York: Routledge. 80–92.

Clear, J. (1993) From Firth Principles – Computational Tools for the Study of Collocation. In: Baker, M., Francis, G., Tognini-Bonelli, E. (eds.) *Text and Technology: In honour of John Sinclair*. Philadelpia, Amsterdam: John Benjamins B. V. 271–292.

Coffey, S. (2011) A new pedagogical dictionary of English collocations. In: *International Journal of Lexicography* 24 (3). 328–341.

Cowie, A. P. (ed., 2009) *The Oxford History of English Lexicography*. Oxford: Clarendon Press.

Cresti, E., Panunzi, A. (2013) *Introduzione ai corpora dell'italiano*. Bologna: Il Mulino.

Cruse, D. A. (1986) *Lexical Semantics*. Cambridge: Cambridge University Press.

Culver, K. (1999, ed.) *Readings in the philospohy of law*. Peterborough: Broadview Press Ltd.

Dash, N. (2005) *Corpus linguistics and language technology: with reference to Indian languages*. New Delhi: Mittal Publications.

Dechamps, C. (2004) Enseignement/apprentissage des collocations d'une langue de spécialité à un public allophone: l'exemple de la langue juridique. In: *Étude de Linguistique Appliquée* 135. 361–370.

Denisov, P. N. (2003) The typology of pedagogical dictionaries. In: Hartmann, R. R. K. (ed.) *Lexicogrpahy: Critical Concepts*. London, New York: Routledge. Vol 3. 70–89.

Dunning, T. (1993) Accurate Methods for the Statistics of Surprise and Coincidence. In: *Computational Linguistics* 19 (1). 61–74.

Dura, E. (2008) Synergies in term extraction from different corpora. In: Lewandowska-Tomaszczyk, B. (ed.) *Corpus Linguistics, Computer Tools and Applications: State of the Art*. Frankfurt: Peter Lang. 151–162.

Duva, G., Laursen, A.-L. (1995) User survey. In: Bergenholtz, H., Tarp, S. (eds.) *Manual of Specialized Lexicography: The preparation of specialised dictionaries*. Amsterdam/Philadelphia: Benjamins. 77–83.

Edwards, J. A. (1992) Design principles in the transcription of spoken discourse. In: Svartvik, J. (ed.) *Directions in Corpus Linguistics: proceedings of Nobel symposium 82, Stockholm 4–8 August 1991*. Berlin and New York: Mouton de Gruyter. 129–148.

Elementi di diritto e legislazione bancaria (2007). Napoli: Gruppo Editoriale Esselibri - Simone.

Ellis, N. C. (1997) Vocabulary acquisition: word structure, collocation, word-class, and meaning. In: Schmitt, N. and McCarthy, M. (eds.) *Vocabulary: Description, Acqusition and Pedagogy*. Cambridge: Cambridge University Press. 122–139.

Ellinger, E. P., Lomnicka, E., Hare, C. V. M. (2011) *Ellinger's Modern Banking Law*. Oxford: Oxford University Press.

Evison, J. (2010) What are the basics of analysing a corpus? In: O'Keeffe, A., McCarthy, M. (eds.) *The Routledge Handbook of Corpus Linguistics*. London and New York: Routledge. 122–135.

Firth, J. R. (1957) *Papers in linguistics 1934–1957*. London: Oxford University Press.

Flowerdew, L. (2004) The argument for using English specialized corpora to understand academic and professional language. In: Connor, U., Upton, T. A. (eds.) *Discourse in the Professions: Perspectives from Corpus Linguistics*. Amsterdam: John Benjamins B. V. 11–33.

Flowerdew, L. (2008) *Corpus-based analyses of the problem-solution pattern: a phraseological approach*. Amstedam, Philadelpia: John Benjamins B. V.

Flowerdew, J. (2009) Use of signaling nouns in a learner corpus. In: Flowerdew, J., Mahlberg, M. (eds.), *Lexical cohesion and corpus linguistics*. Amstedam, Philadelphia: John Benjamis B. V. 85–102.

Fontenelle, T. (1994) What on Earth are Collocations? In: *English Today* 40 / 10 (4). 42–48.

Fox, G. (1987) The case for examples. In: Sinclair, J. (ed.) *Looking up*. London and Glasgow: Collins ELT. 137–139.

Francis, N. (1992) Language corpora BC. In: Svartvik, J. (ed.) *Directions in Corpus Linguistics: proceedings of Nobel symposium 82, Stockholm 4–8 August 1991*. Berlin and New York: Mouton de Gruyter. 17–34.

Fuertes-Olivera, P. A. (2009) Systematic introductions in specialized dictionaries. Some proposals in relation to accounting dictionaries. In: Nielsen, S., Tarp, S. (eds.) *Lexicography in the 21st century*. Amsterdam, Philadelphia: John Benjamins B. V. 161–178.

Fuertes-Olivera, P. A., Arribas-Baño, A. (2008) *Pedagogical Specialized Lexicography: the representation of meaning in English and Spanish business dictionaries*. Amsterdam, Philadelphia: John Benjamins B. V.

Gabryś-Barker, D. (2005) *Aspects of Multilingual Storage, Processing and Retrieval*. Katowice: Wydawnictwo Uniwersytetu Śląskiego.

Gajda, S. (1990) *Wprowadzenie do teorii terminu*. Opole: Wyższa Szkoła Pedgogiczna im. Powstańców Śląskich.

Gajek, E. (2006) Zasoby i narzędzia internetowe w językoznawstwie korpusowym. In: Duszak, A., Gajek, E., Okulska, U. (eds.) *Korpusy w angielsko-polskim językoznawstwie kontrastywnym. Teoria i praktyka*. Kraków: TAiWPN Universitas. 311–328.

Gambaro, A. (2012) La prospettiva del privatista. In: Pozzo, B., Bambi, F. (eds.) *L'italiano giuridico che cambia*. Firenze: Accademia della Crusca. 33–47.

Gao, L. (2010) Historical Background of the Translatological Dictionaries. In: *Journal of Language Teaching and Research* 1 (3). 285–294.

Garner, B. A. (2014) Legal Lexicography: A View from the Front Lines. In: Aodha, M. M. (ed.) *Legal lexicography: A comparative perspective*. Farnham: Ashgate Publishing Limited. 45–58.

Garzone, G. (2011) Osservazioni sulla didattica della traduzione giuridica. In: Mazzotta, P., Salmon, L. (eds.) *Tradurre le microlingue scientifico-professionali. Riflessioni teoretiche e proposte didattiche.* Torino: UTET Università. 194–238.

Gledhill, C. (2000) *Collocations in Science Writing.* Tűbingen: Gunter Narr.

Gołąb, A. (2012) Lexical and syntactic description of the language of law. In: Niewiadomski, A., Sztymelska, E. (eds.) *Język współczesnego prawa.* Warszawa: Lingua Iuris. 97–121.

Gotti, M. (2012) Text and genre. In: Tiersma, P. M., Solan, L. M. (eds.) *The Oxford handbook of language nad law.* Oxford: Oxford University Press. 52–66.

Gotti, M. (2016) The translation of legal texts: interlinguistic and intralinguistic perspectives. In: *ESP Today* 4 (1). 5–21.

Gouadec, D. (1990) *Terminologie. Constitution des données.* Paris: Afnor.

Gouws, R. H. (1996) Bilingual Dictionaries and Communicative Equivalence for a Multilingual Society. In: *Lexikos* 6. 16–41.

Gouws, R. (2003) Types of articles, their structure and different types of lemmata. In: van Sterkenburg, P., (ed.) *A practical Guide to Lexicography.* Amsterdam, Philadelpphia: John Benjamins B. V. 34–43.

Gouws, R. H. (2004) State-of-the-art paper. Lexicology and lexicography: Milestones in metalexicography. In: van Sterkenburg, P. *Linguistics Today: Facing a Greater Challenge.* Amsterdam, Philadephia: John Benjamins B. V. 187–206.

Gouws, R. H. (2007) Sublemmata or main lemmata: a critical look at the presentation of some macrostructural elements. In: Gottlieb, H., Mogensen, E. J. (eds.) *Dictionary visions, research and practice.* Amsterdam, Philadelphia: John Benjamins B. V.

Gouws, R. H. (2009) Sinuous lemma files in printed dictionaries: Access and lexicographic functions. In: Nielsen, S., Tarp, S. (eds.) *Lexicography in the 21st Century: In Honour of Henning Bergenholtz.* Amsterdam: John Benjamins B. V. 3–21.

Goźdź-Roszkowski, S. (2005) Korpusy a języki specjalistyczne. In: Lewandowska-Tomaszczuk, B. (ed) *Podstawy Językoznawstwa Korpusowego.* Łódź: Wydawnictwo Uniwersytetu Łódzkiego. 174–200.

Górnicz, M. (2005) Terminologizacja. In: Lukszyn, J. (ed.) *Języki specjalistyczne. Słownik terminologii przedmiotowej.* Warszawa: KJS. 140.

Gramley, S., Pȁtzold, K. M. (2004) *A Survey of Modern English.* New York: Routledge.

Granger, S. (2002) A Bird's eye view of learner corpus research. In: Granger, S., Petch-Tyson, S. Hung, J. (eds.) *Computer learner corpora, second language acquisition and foreign language teaching.* Amsterdam, Philadelphia: John Benjamins B.V. 3–33.

Greaves, C., Warren, M. (2010) What can a corpus tell us about multi-word units? In: O'Keeffe, A., McCarthy, M. (eds.) *The Routledge Handbook of Corpus Linguistics*. London and New York: Routledge. 212–226.

Green, J. (1996) *Chasing the Sun: Dictionary Makers and the Dictionaries They Made*. New York: Henry Holt.

Greenbaum, S. (1970) *Verb-intensifier collocations in English. An experimental approach*. The Hague: Mouton & Co. N. V.

Greenberg, D. (2014) The challenges of compiling a legal dictionary. In: Aodha, M. M. (ed.) *Legal lexicography: A comparative perspective*. Farnham: Ashgate Publishing Limited. 59–74.

Gries, S. (2009a) *Quantitative corpus linguistics with R: a practical introduction*. New York: Routledge.

Gries S. (2009b) What is corpus linguistics? In: *Language and Linguistics Compass* 3. 1–17.

Gries, S. (2010) Useful statistics for corpus linguistics. In: Sànchez, A., Almela, M. (eds.) *A Mosaic of Corpus Linguisitcs: Selected Approaches*. Frankfurt am Main: Peter Lang. 269–291.

Groffier, E., Reed, D. (1990) *La lexicographie juridique. Principes et méthodes*. Cowanswille: Yvon Blais.

Grucza, F. (1983) *Zagadnienia metalingwistyki. Lingwistyka – jej przedmiot, lingwistyka stosowana*. Warszawa: Państwowe Wydawnictwo Naukowe.

Grucza, F. (1991) Terminologia – jej przedmiot, status i znaczenie. In: Grucza, F. (ed.), *Teoretyczne podstawy terminologii*. Wrocław: Ossolineum. 11–44.

Grucza, F. (1993a) Zagadnienia ontologii lingwistycznej: o językach ludzkich i ich (rzeczywistym) istnieniu. In: Bartmiński, J. et al. (ed.) *Opuscula Logopaedica. In honorem Leonis Kaczmarek*. Lublin: Wydawnictwo Uniwersytetu Marii Curie-Skłodowskiej. 25–47.

Grucza, F. (1993b) *Język, ludzie właściwości językowe, językowa zdolność ludzi*. In: Jędrzejczak, A. (ed.) *Człowiek w perspektywie ujęć biokulturowych*. Poznań: Wydawnictwo naukowe UAM. 151–174.

Grucza, F. (2008) Języki specjalistyczne – indykatory i/lub determinany rozwoju cywilizacyjnego. In: Lukszyn, J. (ed.) *Podstawy technolingwistyki I*. Warszawa: Euro-Edukacja. 5–23.

Grucza, F. (2010) O tekstach nazywanych 'ustawami', językowych brakach ustawy 'Prawo o szkolnictwie wyższym' oraz lingwistyce legislatywnej. In: *Lingwistyka Stosowana* 2. 7–39.

Grucza, S. (2007) O konieczności tworzenia korpusów tekstów specjalistycznych. In: Grucza, S., Kornacka, M., Marchwiński, A. (eds.) *W kręgu teorii i praktyki lingwistycznej*. Warszawa: Wydawnictwa Uniwersytetu Warszawskiego. 103–122.

Grucza, S. (2008) O konieczności tworzenia korpusów tekstów specjalistycznych. In: Lukszyn, J. (ed.) *Podstawy technolingwistyki* I. Warszawa: Euro-Edukacja. 197–224.

Grucza, S. (2009) Kategoryzacja języków (specjalistycznych) w świetle antropocentrycznej teorii języków ludzkich. In: *Komunikacja specjalistyczna* 2. 15–30.

Grucza, S. (2010) Główne cechy antropocentrycznej teorii języków. In: *Lingwistyka Stosowana* 2. 41–68.

Grucza, S. (2013) *Lingwistyka języków specjalistycznych*. Warszawa: Wydawnictwo Naukowe Instytutu Kultuturologii i Lingwistyki Antropocentrycznej Uniwersytetu Warszawskiego.

Gualdo, R., Telve, S. (2011) *Linguaggi specialistici dell'italiano*. Roma: Carocci.

Gustaffson, M. (1975) *Some Syntactic Properties of English Law Language*. Turku: University of Turku.

Grzelak, J. (2010) *Polski język prawa – w perspektywie glottodydaktycznej*. Unpublished doctoral work. Adam Mickiewicz University in Poznań.

Haas, M. R. (1978) *Language, Culture and History*. Stanford: Stanford University Press.

Hall, C. J., Smith, P. H., Wicaksono, R. (2011) *Mapping applied linguistics: a guide for students and practitioners*. London: Routledge.

Halliday, M. A. K. (1966) Lexis as a linguistic level. In: Bazell, C. E. et al. (eds.) *In memory of J. R. Firth*. London: Longmans. 148–162.

Handl, S. (2008) Essential collocations for learniners of English. The role of collocational direction and weight. In: Meunier, F., Granger, S. (eds.) *Phraseology in Foreign Language Learning and Teaching*. Amsterdam, Philadelphia: John Benjamins B. V. 44–66.

Hanks, P. (1990) Evidence and intuition in lexicography. In: Tomaszczyk, J., Lewandowska-Tomaszczyk, B., (eds.) *Meaning and Lexicography*. Amsterdam, Philadelphia: John Benjamins B. V.

Hannay, M. (2003) Types of bilingual dictionaries. In: van Sterkenburg, P., (ed.) *A practical Guide to Lexicography*. Amsterdam, Philadelphia: John Benjamins B. V. 145–153.

Hartmann, R. (1986) *The History of Lexicography*. Amsterdam, Philadelphia: John Benjamins B.V.

Hartmann, R. (2001) *Teaching and Researching Lexicography*. Essex: Pearson Education.

Hatch, E., Brown, Ch. (1995) *Vocabulary, Semantics and Language Education.* Cambridge and New York: Cambridge University Press.

Hausmann, F. J., Blumenthal, P. (2006) Présentation: collocations, corpus, dictionnaires. In: *Langue française* 2 (150). 3–13.

Hausmann, F. J., Wiegand, H. E. (2003) Component parts and structures of general monolingual dictionaries: a survey. In: Hartmann, R. R. K. (ed.) *Lexicography: Critical Concepts.* Vol 3. London, New York: Routledge. 207–254.

Herbst, T. (1996) What are collocations: sandy beaches or false teeth? In: *English Studies* 77 (4). 379–393.

Hill, J. (2000) Revising priorities: from grammatical failure to collocational success. In: Lewis, M. (ed.) *Teaching Collocation: Furher Developments in the Lexical Approach.* Hove: LTP Teacher Training. 47–69.

Hiltunen, R. (2012) The grammar and structure of legal texts. In: Tiersma, P. M., Solan, L. M. (eds.) *The Oxford handbook of language nad law.* Oxford: Oxford University Press. 39–51.

Hoffamnn, S., Lehmann, H. M. (2000) Collocational Evidence from the British National Corpus. In: Kirk, J. (ed). *Corpora galore: Analysis and Techniques in Describing English.* Amsterdam: Rodopi. 17–32.

Howarth, P. A. (1996) *Phraseology in English academic writing: some implications for language learning and dictionary making.* Tübingen: Niemeyer.

Hunston, S. (2002) *Corpora in applied linguistics.* Cambridge: Cambridge University Press.

Jackson, H. (2002) *Lexicography: An introduction.* London, New York: Routledge.

Jadacka, H. (2007) Przyczyny i skutki niejasnoci tekstów prawnych. In: A. Niewiadomski, A., Mróz, A., Pawelec, M. (eds.) *Współczesny język prawny i prawniczy.* Warszawa: Wydział Prawa i Administracji. Uniwersytet Warszawski. 33–37.

Jamrozik, E. (2014) Il lessico e le collocazioni nell'insegnamento delle lingue speciali. In: *Kwartalnik Neofilologiczny* LXI, 1/14. 163–176.

Johansson, S. (2007a) Seeing through multilingual corpora. In: Facchinetti, R. (ed.) *Corpus linguistics 25 years on.* Amsterdam, New York: Editions Rodopi B. V. 51–72.

Johansson, S. (2007b) *Seeing through multilingual corpora: on the use of corpora in contrastive studies.* Amsterdam, Philadelphia: John Benjamins B. V.

Johnson, K. (2008) *Quantitative Methods in Linguistics.* Oxford: Blackwell Publishing.

Jopek-Bosiacka, A. (2008) *Przekład prawny i sądowy*. Warszawa: Wydawnictwo Naukowe PWN.

Jopek-Bosiacka, A. (2010) *Legal communication – a cross-cultural perspective*. Warszawa: Warsaw University Press.

Jurkowski, M. (1991) Metajęzyk terminologii. In: Grucza, F. (ed.) *Teoretyczne podstawy terminologii*. Wrocław: Ossolineum. 45–60.

Kageura, K. (2002) *The Dynamics of Terminology. A descriptive theory of term formation and terminological growth*. Amsterdam, Philadelphia: John Bejnamins B.V.

Karpiński, Ł. (2008) Zarys leksykografii terminologicznej. Warszawa: KJS.

Kaszubski, R., Tupaj-Cholewa, A. (2010) *Prawo bankowe*. Warszawa: Wolters Kluwer Polska.

Kenning, M. M. (2010) What are parallel and comparable corpora and how we can use them? In: O'Keeffe, A., McCarthy, M. (eds.) *The Routledge Handbook of Corpus Linguistics*. London and New York: Routledge. 487–500.

Kielar, B. Z. (1977) *Language of the law in the aspect of translation*. Warszawa: Wydawnictwa Uniwersytetu Warszawskiego.

Kielar, B. Z. (2003) TS w układzie międzynarodowej komunikacji zawodowej (na przykładzie tłumaczenia tekstów prawnych). In: Kielar, B. Z., Grucza, S. (eds.) *Języki specjalistyczne 3. Lingwistyczna identyfikacja tekstów specjalistycznych*. Katedra Języków Specjalistycznych Uniwersytetu Warszawskiego. Warszawa.

Kielar, B. Z. (2007) Językowe i prawne aspekty tłumaczenia tekstu *Traktatu ustanawiającego Konstytucję dla Europy* podpisanego w 2004 roku. In: Grucza, S. Kornacka, M., Marchwiński, A. (eds.) *W kręgu teorii i praktyki lingwistycznej*. Warszawa: Wydawnictwa Uniwersytetu Warszawskiego. 147–156.

Kielar, B. Z. (2009) O prawie i jego językach. In: *Kounikacja specjalistyczna* 2. 43–52.

Kielar, B. Z. (2011) On Language(s) of the Law and a Guiding Principle in Translating Statutory Texts. In: *Lingwistyka Stosowana* 4. 75–86.

Kierzkowska, D. (2008) *Tłumaczenia prawnicze*. Warszawa: Translegis.

Kilgarriff, A., Kosem, I. (2012) Corpus tools for lexicographers. In: Granger, S., Paquot, M. (eds.) *Electronic lexicography*. Oxford: Oxford Uiversity Press. 31–56.

Kjær, A. L. (2000) On the structure of legal knowledge: The importance of knowing legal rules for understanding legal texts. In: Lundquist, L., Jarvella, R.J. (eds.) *Language, Text, and Knowledge. Mental Models of Expert Communication*. Berlin/New York: Mouton de Gruyter. 127–161.

Kjær, A. L. (2007) Phrasemes in legal texts. In: Burger, H., Dobrovol'skij D., Kühn, P., Norrick, N. R. (eds.) *Phraseologie / Phraseology: Ein internationales Handbuch zeitgenössischer Forschung / An International Handbook of Contemporary Research*. Vol. 1. Berlin: Walter de Gruyter. 506–516.

Kjellmer G. (1987) Aspects of English collocations. In Meijs, W. (ed) *Corpus Linguistics and Beyond. Proceedings of the seventh international conference on English language research on computerised corpora*. Amsterdam: Rodopi. 133–140.

Kjellmer, G. (1990) Patterns of collocability. In: Aarts, J., Meijs, W. (eds.) *Theory and Practice in Corpus Linguistics*. Amsterdam: Rodopi. 163–178.

Klejnowska-Borowska, M. (2014) Analiza wielojęzycznych słowników specjalistycznych z językiem polskim i rosyjskim wydanych w latach 1990–2012. In: Łukasik, M., Mikołajewska, B. (eds.) *Języki specjalistyczne wczoraj, dziś i jutro*. Warszawa: IKLA. 127–139.

Kłodawski, M. (2012) Pleonazmy i analityzmy – wyrażenia redundante pragmatycznie w języku prawnym. In: Niewiadomski, A., Sztymelska, E. (eds.) *Język współczesnego prawa*. Warszawa: Lingua Iuris. 121–132.

Koester, A. (2010) Building small specialized corpora. In: O'Keeffe, A., McCarthy, M. (eds.) *The Routledge Handbook of Corpus Linguistics*. London and New York: Routledge. 66–79.

Kohnen, T. (2009) Religious language in early English newspapers? In: Jucker, A. H. (ed.) *Early Modern English New Discourse*. Amsterdam, Philadelphia: John Benjamins B. V. 73–89.

Kornacka, M. (2005a) Termin. In: Lukszyn, J. (ed.) *Języki specjalistyczne. Słownik terminologii przedmiotowej*. Warszawa: KJS. 131.

Kornacka, M. (2005b) Typy terminów. In: Lukszyn, J. (ed.) *Języki specjalistyczne. Słownik terminologii przedmiotowej*. Warszawa: KJS. 151.

Kűbler, N., Aston, G. (2010) Using corpora in translation. In: O'Keeffe, A., McCarthy, M. (eds.) *The Routledge Handbook of Corpus Linguistics*. London and New York: Routledge. 501–515.

Kuratczyk, M. (2005a) Leksykografia terminologiczna. In: Lukszyn, J. (ed.) *Języki specjalistyczne. Słownik terminologii przedmiotowej*. Warszawa: KJS. 62.

Kuratczyk, M. (2005b) Quasi-termin. In: Lukszyn, J. (ed.) *Języki specjalistyczne. Słownik terminologii przedmiotowej*. Warszawa: KJS. 95.

Kuratczyk, M. (2005c) Hipotermin. In: Lukszyn, J. (ed.) *Języki specjalistyczne. Słownik terminologii przedmiotowej*. Warszawa: KJS. 35.

Kuratczyk (2005d) Słownik terminologiczny. In: Lukszyn, J. (ed.) *Języki specjalistyczne. Słownik terminologii przedmiotowej*. Warszawa: KJS. 105.

Kurartczyk, M. (2007) Nowe narzędzia w leksykografii dwujęzycznej (rosyjsko-polskiej i polsko-rosyjskiej). In: Grucza, S. Kornacka, M., Marchwiński, A., *W kręgu teorii i praktyki lingwistycznej*. Warszawa: Wydawnictwa Uniwersytetu Warszawskiego. 197–211.

Kurzon, D. (1997) 'Legal language': varieties, genres, registers, discourses. In: *International Journal of Applied Linguistics* 7 (2). 119–139.

van Laer, C. J. P. (2014) Bilingual Legal Dictionaries: Comparison without Precision? In: Aodha, M. M. (ed.) *Legal lexicography: A comparative perspective*. Farnham: Ashgate Publishing Limited. 75–87.

Landau, S. I. (2001) *Dictionaries: the art and craft of lexicography*. Cambridge: Cambridge University Press.

Langton, N. (2006) Cleaning up the Act: Using Plain English in Legislation. In: Wagner, A., Cacciaguidi-Fahy, S. (eds.) *Legal language and the search for clarity: practice and tools*. Bern: Peter Lang. 361–386.

Laufer, B. (2008) Corpus-based versus Lexicographer Examples in Comprehension and Production of New Words. In: Fontenelle, T. (ed.) *Practical Lexicography: a Reader*. Oxford: OUP. 213–218.

Laviosa, S. (2002) *Corpus-based Translation Studies*. Amsterdam, New York: Rodopi B. V.

Lawson, A. (2001) Collecting, aligning and analyzing parallel corpora. In: Ghadessy, M., Henry, A., Roseberry, R. (eds.) *Small corpus studies and ELT*. Amsterdam and Philadelphia: John Benjamins B. V. 279–310.

Lee, D. Y. W. (2010) What corpora are available? In: O'Keeffe, A., McCarthy, M. (eds.) *The Routledge Handbook of Corpus Linguistics*. London and New York: Routledge. 107–515.

Leech, G. (1992) Corpora and theories of linguistic performance. In: Svartvik, J. (ed.) *Directions in Corpus Linguistics: proceedings of Nobel symposium 82, Stockholm 4–8 August 1991*. Berlin and New York: Mouton de Gruyter. 105–122.

Leech, G. (2004) Corpora. In: Malmkjćr, K. (ed.) *The Linguistic Encyclopedia*, 2nd edition, London and New York: Routledge. 84–93.

Lenci, A., Montemagni, S., Pirelli, V. (2005) *Testo e computer: elementi di linguistica computazionale*. Roma: Carocci.

Leńko-Szymańska (2006) Problemy metodologiczne Kontrastywnej Analizy Interjęzyka. In: Duszak, A., Gajek, E., Okulska, U. (eds.) *Korpusy w angielsko-polskim językoznawstwie kontrastywnym. Teoria i praktyka*. Kraków: TAiWPN Universitas. 115–142.

Leśniewska, J. (2002) Multi-word items in vocabulary acquisition. In: Arabski, J. (ed.) *Time for Words: Studies in Foreign Language Vocabulary Acquisition.* Frankfurt: Peter Lang. 139–144.

Léon, J. (2007) Meaning by Collocation: The Firthian Filiation of Corpus Linguistics. In: Kibbee, D. (ed.) *History of Linguistics 2005: Selected Papers from the Tenth International Conference on the History of the Language Sciences.* Amterdam, Philadelphia: John Benjamins B. V. 404–415.

Lerat, P. (2014) Pour des dictionnaires juridiques multilingues du citoyen de l'Union européenne. In: Aodha, M. M. (ed.) *Legal lexicography: A comparative perspective.* Farnham: Ashgate Publishing Limited. In: 89–101.

Lewandowska-Tomaszczyk, B. (2005) Powstanie i rozwój językoznawstwa korpusowego. In: Lewandowska-Tomaszczyk, B. (ed.) *Podstawy Językoznawstwa Korpusowego.* Łódź: Wydawnictwo Uniwersytetu Łódzkiego. 9–26.

Lewandowska-Tomaszczyk, B. (2008) Translation studies: cognitive linguistics and corpora. In: Lewandowska-Tomaszczyk, B., Thelen, M. (eds.) *Meaning in Translation.* Frankfurt am Main: Peter Lang. 17–30.

Lewandowski, J. (2008) Paratypologie i quasi-klasyfikacje polskich języków profesjonalnych. In: Lukszyn, J. (ed.) *Podstawy technolingwistyki I.* Warszawa: KJS 87–100.

Lewis, M. (2000) Language in the lexical approach. In: Lewis, M. (ed.) *Teaching Collocation: Furher Developments in the Lexical Approach.* Hove: LTP Teacher Training. 126–154.

Liebetrau, A. (1983) *Measures of association.* Newbury Park, CA: SAGE.

Lindquist, H. (2009) *Corpus Linguistics and the Description of English.* Edinburgh: Edinburgh University Press.

Louw, P. A. (1999) Access Structures in a Standard Translation Dictionary. In: *Lexikos 9.* 108–118.

Lukszyn, J. (2008) Leksykon specjalistyczny – słownik terminologiczny – seria terminograficzna. In: Lukszyn, J. (ed.) *Podstawy technolingwistyki I.* Warszawa: KJS. 257–267.

Lukszyn, J. Zmarzer, W. (2001) *Teoretyczne podstawy terminologii.* Warszawa: KJS UW.

Luna, P. (2004) Not just a pretty face: The contribution of typography to lexicography. In: Williams, G. Vessier, S. (eds.). *Proceedings of the Eleventh Euralex International Congress.* Vol. II. Lorient: UBS UniversitÈ de Bretagne Sud. 847–858.

Lyons, J. (1966) Firth's theory of 'meaning'. In: Bazell, C. E. et al. (eds.), *In memory of J. R. Firth.* London: Longmans. 288–302.

Łukasik, M. (2007) *Angielsko-polskie i polsko-angielskie słowniki specjalistyczne (1990–2006). Analiza terminograficzna.* Warszawa: KJS.

Macko, D. (2011) Typical collocations in the judgements on appeal of the European Court of Justice. In: *Filologija, Edukologija* 19 (1). 67–80.

Maia, B., Barreiro, A., Fròis, C. (2008) N-grams in search of theories. In: Lewandowska-Tomaszczyk, B. (ed.) *Corpus Linguistics, Computer Tools and Applications: State of the Art*. Frankfurt: Peter Lang. 71–84.

Mahlberg, M. (2005). *English General. Nouns: A Corpus Theoretical Approach.* Amsterdam/Philadelphia. John Benjamins.

Malec, W. (2010) On the Asymmetry of Verb-Noun Collocations. In: Arabski, J., Wojtaszek, A. (eds.) *Neurolinguistic and Psycholinguistic Perspectives on SLA.* Bristol: Multilingual Matters. 126–144.

Malinowska, E. (2012) *Konstytucja jako gatunek tekstu prawngo.* Opole: Wydawnictwo Uniwersytetu Opolskiego.

Malinowski, A. (2006) *Polski język prawny. Wybrane zagadnienia.* Warszawa: LexisNexis.

Malinowski, A. (2012) *Polski tekst prawny. Opracowanie treściowe i redakcyjne.* Warszawa: LexisNexis.

Malkiel, Y. (1968) *Essays on Linguistic Themes.* Berkeley and Los Angeles: University of California Press.

Malkiel, Y. (2003) A typological classificication of dictionaries on the basis of dictinctive features. In: Hartmann, R. R. K. (ed.) *Lexicogrpahy. Critical Concepts.* London, New York: Routledge. Vol 3. 51–69.

Maniez, F. (2001) Extraction d'une phraséologie bilingue en langue de spécialité: corpus parallèles et corpus comparables. In: *Meta 46 (3).* 563.

Marazzini, C. (2009) *L'ordine delle parole. Storia di vocabolari italiani.* Bologna: Società editrice il Mulino.

Marzec-Stawiarska, M., Loranc-Paszylk, B. (2011) (Nie)modyfikowanie tekstów autentycznych a niezwykłe potrzeby uczących się języka prawnego i prawniczego. In: Piotrowski, S. (ed.) *O naczaniu i uczeniu się języka obcego dla potrzeb zawodowych.* Lublin: Werset. 32–43.

Mattiello, E. (2010) Nominalization in English and Italian normative legal texts. In: *ESP across cultures* 7. 129–146.

Mattila, H. E. S. (2012) Legal vocabulary. In: Tiersma, P. M., Solan, L. M. (eds.) *The Oxford handbook of language nad law.* Oxford: Oxford University Press. 25–38.

Mattila, H. E. S. (2013) *Comparative legal linguistics: Language of law, latin and modern lingua francas.* Farnham: Ashgate Publishing Limited.

McCarthy, M. (1994) *Vocabulary*. Oxford: Oxford University Press.

McEnery, T., Gabrielatos, C. (2006) English Corpus Linguistics. In: Aarts, B., McMahon, A. (eds.) *The handbook of English Linguistics*.Wiley-Blackwell. 33–71.

McEnery, T., Hardie, A. (2012) *Corpus Linguistics: Method, Theory and Practice*. New York: Cambridge University Press.

McEnery, T., Wilson, A. (2004) *Corpus Linguistics: an introduction*. Edinburgh: Edinburgh University Press.

McEnery, T., Xiao, R., Tono, Y. (2006) *Corpus-Based Language Studies. An Advanced resource book*. New York: Routledge.

McKeown, K. R., Radev, D. R. (2000) Collocations. In: Dale, R., Moisl, H., Somers, H. (eds.) *Handbook of natural language processing*. Basel, New York: Marcel Dekker. 507–523.

Meer, van der, G. (1998) Collocations as one particular type of conventional word combinations. Their definition and character. In: Fontenelle, T et al. (eds.), *Actes Euralex '98*. Liège: Université de Liège. 313–322.

Mellinkoff, D. (2004) *The language of the law*. Eugene: Wipf and Stock Publishers.

Metin, S. K., Karaoğlan, B. (2010) Collocation extraction in Turkish texts using statistical methods. In: Loftsson, H., Rőgnvaldsson, E. (eds.) *Advances in Natural Language Processing*. Berlin: Springer. 238–249.

Meyer, C. F. (2002) *English corpus linguistics: an introduction*. Cambridge: Cambridge University Press.

Michałowski, P. (2011) Rodzaj wiedzy a słownik terminologiczny. In: *Komunikacja specjalistyczna* 4. 148–167.

Mikos-Sitek, A., Zapadka, P. (2011) *Polskie prawo bankowe. Wybrane zagadnienia*. Warszawa: Wolters Kluwer Polska.

Moon, R. (1997) Vocabulary connections: multi-word items in English. In: Schmitt, N. and McCarthy, M. (eds.) *Vocabulary: Description, Acquisition and Pedagogy*. Cambridge: Cambridge University Press. 40–63.

Moon, R. (1998), On Using Spoken Data in Corpus Lexicography. In: Fontenelle, T. et al. (eds.) *ACTES EURALEX'98 Proceedings*. Vol II. Liège: University of Liège. 347–355.

Nasiadka, M. (2011) Jak nie należy tworzyć dzieła leksykograficznego (słownika terminologicznego). *Komunikacja specjalistyczna* 4. 53–61.

Nation, I. S. P. (2001) *Learning Vocabulary in Another Language*. Cambridge: Cambridge University Press.

Nepelski, P. (2012) Słowo w s(prawie) języka prawnika. In: Niewiadomski, A., Sztymelska, E. (eds.) *Język współczesnego prawa*. Warszawa: Lingua Iuris. 193–200.

Nelson, M. (2010) Building a written corpus: what are the basics?. In: O'Keeffe, A., McCarthy, M. (eds.) *The Routledge Handbook of Corpus Linguistics*. London and New York: Routledge. 53–65.

Nerima, L., Seretan, V., Wehrli, E. (2003) Creating a multilingual collocation dictionary from large text corpora. In: *Companion Volume to the Proceedings of the 10th Conference of the European Chapter of the Association for Computational Linguistics (EACL'03)*. Budapest. 131–134.

Nesselhauf, N. (2005) *Collocations in a learner corpus*. Amsterdam, Philadelphia: John Benjamins B. V.

Nielsen, S. (1995) Access structure. In: Bergenholtz, H., Tarp, S. (1995) *Manual of Specialized Lexicography. The preparation of specialised dictionaries*. Amsterdam/Philadelphia: Benjamins B. V. 219–223.

Nielsen, S. (2003) Mediostructure in bilingual LSP dictionaries. In: Hartmann, R. R. K. (ed.) *Lexicogrpahy. Critical Concepts*. Vol 3. London, New York: Routledge. 270–294.

Niewiadomski, A. (2007) Definicje legalne w wietle prawidłowego redagowania tekstów prawnych. In: Niewiadomski, A., Mróz, A., Pawelec, M. (eds.) *Współczesny język prawny i prawniczy*. Warszawa: Wydział Prawa i Administracji. Uniwersytet Warszawski. 49–54.

Niewiadomski, A. (2009) Europeizacja języka polskiego prawa na przykładzie regulacji praworolnych. In: Niewiadomski, A., Mróz, A., Pawelec, M. (eds.) *Prawo i język*. Warszawa: Lingua Iuris. 79–84.

Noël, J. (1992) Collocation and bilingual text. In: Leitner, G. (ed.) *New directions in English language corpora. Methodology, results, software developments*. Berlin: Mouton de Gruyter. 345–357.

Nuccorini, S. (2003) Towards an 'ideal' Dictionary of English Collocations. In: van Sterkenburg, P, (ed.) *A practical Guide to Lexicography*. Amsterdam, Philadelpphia: John Benjamins B. V. 366–388.

O'Keeffe, A., McCarthy, M., Carter, R., (2007) *From Corpus to Classroom: language use and language teaching*. Cambridge: Cambridge University Press.

Oakes, M. P. (1998) *Statistics for Corpus Linguistics*. Edinburgh: Edinburgh University Press.

Oakes, M. P., Krakowian, P., Uzar, R. (2005) Testy statystyczne w językoznawstwie korpusowym. In: Lewandowska-Tomaszczuk, B. (ed.) *Podstawy Językoznawstwa Korpusowego*. Łódź: Wydawnictwo Uniwersytetu Łódzkiego. 116–132.

Ofiarski, Z. (2011) *Prawo bankowe*. Warszawa: Wolters Kluwer Polska.

Okulska, U. (2006) Metody statystyczne w językoznawstwie. In: Duszak, A., Gajek, E., Okulska, U. (eds.) *Korpusy w angielsko-polskim językoznawstwie kontrastywnym. Teoria i praktyka*. Kraków: TAiWPN Universitas. 360–398.

Olpińska, M. (2009) Polski i niemiecki język specjalistyczny prawa – możliwości I ograniczenia dydaktyki tłumacznenia tekstów specjalistycznych. In: *Komunikacja specjalistyczna* 2. 79–92.

Osuchowska, D. (2002) Compiling a dictionary of collocation: problems and solutions. In: *Studia Anglica Resoviensia* 1. 79–85.

Osuchowska, D. (2007) *In search of the collocation value of EFL dictionaries.* Rzeszów: Wydawnictwo Uniwersytetu Rzeszowskiego.

Palmer, F. R. (1976) *Semantics. A new outline.* Cambridge: Cambridge University Press.

Paltridge, A. (2006) *Discourse Analysis.* London, New York: Continuum.

Parowenko, R. (2007) *Kluczowe terminy spcjokulturowe jako jednostki opisu leksykograficznego.* Unpublished doctoral work. University of Warsaw

Pawelec, M. (2007) Zrozumieć prawnika… Słownictwo fachowe z dziedziny prawa w dziełach leksykograficznych. In: Niewiadomski, A., Mróz, A., Pawelec, A. (eds.) *Współczesny język prawny i prawniczy.* Warszawa: Wydział Prawa i Administracji. Uniwersytet Warszawski. 23–32.

Pawłowski, A. (2003) Lingwistyka korpusowa – perspektywy i zagrożenia. In: *Polonica* XXII–XXIII. 19–31.

Pearson, J. (1998) *Terms in context.* John Benjamins B.V.

Peters, C., Picchi, E., Biagini, L. (2000) Parallel and cormparable bilingual corpora in language teaching and learning. In: Botley, S. C., McEnery, T., Wilson, A. (eds.) *Multilingual Corpora in Teaching and Research.* Amsterdam: Rodopi. 73–85.

Petzel, J. (2006) Język prawny w świetle lingwistycznej teorii rejestru językowego. In: *Studia Iuridica* XLV. 153–163.

Pieńkoś, J. (1999) *Podstawy juryslingwistyki.* Warszawa: Muza SA.

Pieńkoś, J. (2003) *Podstawy przekładoznawstwa.* Kraków: Zakamycze.

Piotrowski, T. (1993) *Z Zagadnień leksykografii.* Wrocław.

Piotrowski, T. (2001) *Zrozumieć leksykografię.* Warszawa: Wydawnictwo Naukowe PWN.

Pozzi, M. (1996) Quality assurance of terminology. In: Somers, H. (ed.) *Terminology, LSP and translation: studies in language engineering in honour of Juan C. Sager.* Amsterdam, Phladelphia: John Benjamins B. V. 67–82.

Pozzo, B. (2012) Le ragioni del convegno. L'italiano e la sfida del multilingualismo europeo. In: Pozzo, B., Bambi, F. (eds.) *L'italiano giuridico che cambia.* Firenze: Accademia della Crusca. 7–14.

Preite, C. (2012). Exemples de lexicographie juridique à orientation pédagogique en France: le Vocabulaire du juriste débutant et le Guide du langage juridique.

In: *Proceedings of the 15th EURALEX International Congress*, available at: http://www.euralex.org/elx_proceedings/Euralex2012/pp570-577%20Preite.pdf, access on 9 August 2015. 570–577.

Prонińska, A. (2005) Alcuni problem di comprensione del linguaggio giuridic-amministrativo italiano. In: Bogacki, K., Dutka-Mańkowska, A. (eds.) *Les relations sémantiques dans le lexique et dans le discours*. Warszawa: Uniwersytet Warszawski. 267–275.

Proost, K. (2007) *Conceptual structure in lexical items*. Amsterdam, Philadelphia: John Benjamis B. V.

Przepiórkowski, A. (2004) *Korpus IPI PAN. Wersja wstępna*. Warszawa: Instytut Podstaw Informatyki PAN.

Przybylska, R. (2007) Z problemów słownikowego opisu łączliwości rzeczownika. In: Żmigrodzki, P., Przybylska, R. (eds.) *Nowe studia leksykograficzne*. Kraków: Lexis. 69–77.

Reppen, R. (2010) Building a corpus: what are the key considerations? In: O'Keeffe, A., McCarthy, M. (eds.) *The Rroutledge Handbook of Corpus Linguistics*. London and New York: Routledge. 31–37.

Robinson, W. (2014) Translating legislation. The European Union Experience. In: *The theory and practice of legislation* 2 (2). 185–210.

Rokicka, T. (2007) Status kolokacji w Wielkim słowniku języka polskiego. In: Żmigrodzki, P., Przybylska, R. (eds.) *Nowe studia leksykograficzne*. Kraków: LEXIS. 79–87.

Roos, E. (1976) Contrastive collocational analysis. In: *Papers and Studies in Contrastive Linguistic* 5. 65–75.

Rosner, A. (2007) Zmagania z językiem prawa. Przykład polskiego przekładu Kodeksu Napoleona w Księstwie Warszawskim. In: Niewiadomski, A., Mróz, A., Pawelec, M., (eds.) *Współczesny język prawny i prawniczy*. Warszawa: Wydział Prawa i Administracji. Uniwersytet Warszawski. 9–22.

Royle, P. et al. (2009) Is Bigger Better? Corpus and Dictionary Use in the Search for Compounds, Collocations, Derived Forms and Fixed Expressions. In: *Meta* 54 (3). Montréal. 520–532.

Rudnicka, E. (2010) Leksykograficzne egzemplum. Sposoby wykorzystania cytatów i kolokacji w polskich słownikach ogólnych. In: Burkacka, I., Pawelec, R., Zdunkiewicz-Jedynak., D. *Słowa – kładki, na których spotykają się ludzie różnych światów*. Warszawa: wydział Polonistyki Uniwersytetu Warszawskiego. 111 - 126.

Rundell, M. (2012) The road to automated lexicography. In: Granger, S., Paquot, M. (eds.) *Electronic lexicography: an editor's viewpoint*. Oxford: Oxford Uiversity Press. 15–30.

Sag, I., Baldwin, T., Bond, F., Copestake, A., and Flickinger, D. (2002) Multiword expressions: a pain in the neck for NLP. In: Ivan, A., (ed.) *Proceedings of the Third International Conference on Computational Linguistics and Intelligent Text Processing*. London: Springer. 1–15.

Sandrini, P. (2014) Multilingual Legal Terminology in a Paper Dictionary? In: Aodha, M. M. (ed.) *Legal lexicography: A comparative perspective*. Farnham: Ashgate Publishing Limited. 141–151.

Šarčević, S. (1988) The Challenge of Legal Lexicography: Implications for Bilingual and Multilingual Dictionaries. In: SnellHornby, M. (ed.) *ZüriLEX '86 Proceedings*. Tubingen: Francke. 307–314.

Šarčević, S. (1990) Terminological incongruency in legal dictionaries for translation. In: en Magay, T., Zigány, J. (eds.), *BudaLEX '88 Proceedings*. Budapest: Akadémiai Kiadò. 439–446.

Šarčević, S. (2000) *New approach to legal translation*. The Hague: Kluwer Law International.

Schmitz, K. D. (2007) Indeterminacy of terms and icons in software localization. In: Antia, B. E. (ed.) *Indeterminacy in terminology and LSP*. Amsterdam, Philadelpphia: John Benjamins B. V. 49–60.

Scott, M. (2013) *WordSmith Tools Help. Liverpool: Lexical Analysis Software*. available at: http://www.lexically.net/downloads/version6/HTML/proc_tag_handling.html, access on 18.10.2013.

Seretan, V. (2011) *Syntax-based collocation extraction*. Geneva: Springer.

Seretny, A. (2011) Nauczanie języka specjalistycznego – kolejne wyzwanie glottodydaktyki polonistycznej. In: Piotrowski, S. (ed.) *O naczaniu i uczeniu się języka obcego dla potrzeb zawodowych*. Lublin: Werset. 106–121.

Scinetti, L. (2014) L'uso delle collocazioni: due gruppi di apprendenti a confronto. In: *Italiano LinguaDue* 5 (2). 109–131.

Siepmann, D. (2011) Sinclair revisited: beyond idiom and open choice. In: Herbst, T, Faulhaber, S., Uhrlg, P. (eds.) *Phraseological View of Language: A Tribute to John Sinclair*. Munchen: Walter de Gruyter. 59–86.

Sinclair, J. McH. (1966) Beginning the study of lexis. In: Bazell, C. E. et al. (eds.), *In memory of J. R. Firth*. London: Longmans. 410–430.

Sinclair, J. (1991) *Corpus, concordance, collocation*. Oxford: Oxford University Press.

Sinclair, J. (2003a) Corpora for lexicography. In: van Sterkenburg, P, (ed.) *A practical Guide to Lexicography*. Amsterdam, Philadelpphia: John Benjamins B. V. 167–177.

Sinclair, J. (2003b) Corpus processing. In: van Sterkenburg, P, (ed.) *A practical Guide to Lexicography*. Amsterdam, Philadelpphia: John Benjamins B. V. 179–192.

Sinclair, J., Jones, S., Daley, R. (2005) *English Collocation Studies: The OSTI Report*. London: Continuum.

Solan, L. M., Tiersma, P. M. (2012) Introduction. In: Tiersma, P. M., Solan, L. M. (eds.) *The Oxford handbook of language nad law*. Oxford: Oxford University Press. 1–9.

Spohr, D. (2005) *A description logic approach to modelling collocation*. Diploma work available at: http://courses.cs.tau.ac.il/0368-4341/shared/Papers/Collocations/diplomawork_spohr.pdf, access on 17.05.2015. Institut für Maschinelle Sprachveraibeitung. Universität Stuttgart.

Spohr, D. (2012) *Towards a multifunctional lexical resource: design and implementation of a graph-based lexicon model*. New York: Walter de Gruyter.

Sripicham, P. (2010) How we can prepare learners for using language corpora? In: O'Keeffe, A., McCarthy, M. (eds.) *The Routledge Handbook of Corpus Linguistics*. London and New York: Routledge. 371–384.

Stark, M. (2011) *Bilingual thematic dictionaries*. Berlin, Boston: Walter De Gruyter.

van Sterkenburg, P. (2003) 'The' dictionary: Definition and history. In: van Sterkenburg, P. (ed.) *A practical Guide to Lexicography*. Amsterdam, Philadelphia: John Benjamins B. V. 3–17.

Steyn, M. (2004) The access structure in Learner's Dictionaries. In: *Lexicos* 14. 275–298.

Stubbs, M. (2002) *Words and phrases: corpus studies of lexical semantics*. Oxford: Blackwell Publishing.

Sułkowska, M. (2013) *De la phraséologie à la phraséodidactique. Études théoretiques et pratiques*. Katowice: Wydawnictwo Uniwersytetu Śląskiego.

Swan, M. (1997) The influence of the mother tongue on second language vocabulary acquisition and use. In: Schmitt, N., McCarthy, M. (eds.) *Vocabulary: Description, Acquisition and Pedagogy*. Cambridge: Cambridge University Press. 156–180.

Swanepoel, P. (2003) Dictionary typologies. A pragmatic approach. In: van Sterkenburg, P. (ed.) *A practical Guide to Lexicography*. Amsterdam, Philadelpphia: John Benjamins B. V. 44–69.

Szemińska, W. (2011) Translating law into a dictionary. In: *Research in language* 9 (1). 177–186.

Szemińska, W. (2013) *Sposoby reprezentacji wiedzy specjalistycznej w slowniku dla tłumacza*. Unpublished doctoral work. University of Warsaw.

Śliwiński, W. (2008) Kolokacje rzeczownikowo-przymiotnikowe w dwudziestowiecznych tekstach konstytucji państwa polskiego. In: Karamańska, M., Młynarczyk, E., Stachurski, E. (eds.) *Annales Academiae Paedagogicae Cracoviensis 62. Stidia Linguistica IV*. Kraków: Wydawnictwo Naukowe Akademiii Pedagigicznej. 314–327.

Tarp, S. (1995a) Dictribution structure. In: Bergenholtz, H., Tarp, S. *Manual of specialized lexicography: the preparation of specialized dictionaries*. Amsterdam, Phladelphia: John Benjamins B. V. 188–190.

Tarp, S. (1995b) Special problems in central types of specialized dictionaries. In: Bergenholtz, H.,Tarp, S. *Manual of specialized lexicography: the preparation of specialized dictionaries*. Amsterdam, Phladelphia: John Benjamins B. V. 48–76.

Tarp, S. (1995c) Specialized dictionary functions. In: Bergenholtz, H., Tarp, S. *Manual of specialized lexicography: the preparation of specialized dictionaries*. Amsterdam, Philadelphia: John Benjamins B. V. 20–28.

Tarp, S. (2008) *Lexicography in the Borderland between Knowledge and Non-Knowledge. General Lexicograhical Theory with Particular Focus on Learner's Lexicography*. Max Niemeyer Verlag: Tűbingen.

Tarp, S. (2009) Beyond Lexicography: New visions and challenges in the information age. In: Bergenholtz, H., Nielsen, S., Tarp, S. (eds.) *Lexicography at a Crossroads. Dictionaries and Encyclopedias today, Lexicographical Tools tomorrow*. Bern: Peter Lang. 17–32.

Taylor, C. (2008) What is corpus linguistics? What the data says. In: *ICAME Journal* 32. 179–200.

Temmerman, R. (2000) *Towards new ways of terminology description: the sociocognitive approach*. Amsterdam, Philadelphia: John Benjamins B. V.

Teubert, W. (2001) Corpus Linguistics and Lexicography. In: *International Journal of Corpus Linguistics* 6. 125–153.

Teubert, W (2004) Units of Meaning, Parallel Corpora and their Implications for Language Teaching. In: Connor, U., Upton, T. A. (eds.) *Applied Corpus Linguistics: a Multidimensional Perspective*. Rodopi. 171–190.

Tiersma, P. M. (2000) *Legal language*. Chicago: The University of Chicago Press.

Thompson, P. (2010) Building a specialized audio-visual corpus. In: O'Keeffe, A., McCarthy, M. (eds.) *The Routledge Handbook of Corpus Linguistics*. London and New York: Routledge. 93–103.

Tognini-Bonelli, E. (2001) *Corpus linguistics at work*. Amsterdam: John Benjamins B. V.

Tognini-Bonelli, E. (2010) Building a corpus: What are the key considerations? In: O'Keeffe, A., McCarthy, M. (eds.) *The Routledge Handbook of Corpus Linguistics.* London and New York: Routledge.

Treffers-Daller, J. (2011) Grammatical collocations and verb-particles constructions in Brussels French: a corpus-linguistics approach to transfer. In: *International Journal of Bilingualism* 16 (1). 53–82.

Tribble, C. (2010) What are concordances and how are they used? In: O'Keeffe, A., McCarthy, M. (eds.) *The Routledge Handbook of Corpus Linguistics.* London and New York: Routledge. 167–183.

Tryuk, M. (1991) Stan organizacyjny działalności terminologicznej. In: Grucza, F. (ed.) *Teoretyczne podstawy terminologii.* Wrocław: Ossolineum. 95–116.

Tutin, A. (2005) Le dictionnaire de collocations est-il indispensable? In: *Revue française de linguistique appliquée* 10 (2). 31–48.

Tutin, A. (2010) Le traitement des collocations dans les dictionnaires monolingues de collocations du français et de l'anglais. In: Neveu F., Muni Toke V., Durand J., Klingler T., Mondada L., Prévost S. (eds.) *2e Congrès Mondial de Linguistique Française (CMLF).* New Orleans. 1075–1090.

Utri, R. (2013) A few remarks on Austrian languages for special purposes. In: *Lingwistyka Stosowana 7* 163–177.

Vetulani, G. (2000) Zasady budowy hasła słownikowego dla kolokacji werbo-nominalnych. In: *Scripta Neophilologica Posnaniensia II.* 173–190.

Vetulani, G. (2005) Répercussions des activités humaines dans les collocations verbo-nominales. In: *Neophilologica* 17. 153–161.

Vetulani, G. (2012) *Kolokacje werbo-nominalne jako samodzielne jednostki języka. Syntaktyczny słownik kolokacji werbo-nominalnych języka polskiego na potrzeby zastosowań informatycznych.* Część 1. Poznań: Wydawnictwo Naukowe UAM.

Vetulani, G. Vetulani, Z., Obrębski, T. (2008) Verb-Noun Collocation Syntex Dictionary – Corpus-Based Approach. In: Calzorali, N. et al. (eds.) *Proceedings of the 6th International Conference on Language Resources and Evaluation (LREC'08), Marrakech, Morocco.*: Paris: ELRA. 1561–1564.

Venturi, G. (2010) Legal language and legal knowledge management applications. In: Francesconi, E., Montemagni, S., Peters, W., Tiscornia, D. (eds.), *Semantic processing of legal texts* Berlin Heidelberg: Springer-Verlag. 3–26.

Venturi, G. (2013) Semantic annotation of Italian legal texts: a FrameNet-based approach. In: Fried, M., Nikiforidou, K. (eds.) *Advances in Frame Semantics.* Amsterdam, Philadelphia: John Benjamins B. V. 51–84.

Visconti, J. (2012) Prestiti e calchi: dove va la lingua giuridica italiana. In: Pozzo, B., Bambi, F. (eds.) *L'italiano giuridico che cambia*. Firenze: Accademia della Crusca. 185–193.

Waliński, J. (2005) Typologia korpusów oraz warsztat informatyczny lingwistyki korpusowej. In: Lewandowska-Tomaszczuk, B. (ed.) *Podstawy Językoznawstwa Korpusowego*. Łódź: Wydawnictwo Uniwersytetu Łódzkiego. 27–41.

Walker Read, A. (1986) The History of Lexicography. In: Ilson, R. (ed.) *Lexicography: An emerging international profession*. Manchester, Dover: Manchester University Press. 28–50.

Walsh, S. (2010) What features of spoken and written corpora can be exploited in creating language teaching materials and syllabuses? In: O'Keeffe, A., McCarthy, M. (eds.) *The Routledge Handbook of Corpus Linguistics*. London and New York: Routledge. 333–344.

Walter, E. (2010) Using corpora to write dictionaries. In: O'Keeffe, A., McCarthy, M. (eds.) *The Routledge Handbook of Corpus Linguistics*. London and New York: Routledge. 428–443.

Wanner, L. et al. (2005) The first steps towards the automatic compilation of specialized collocation dictionaries. In: *Terminology* 11 (1). 143–180.

Warburton, K. (2015) Managing terminology in commercial environments. In: Kockaert, H. J., Steurs, F. (eds.) *Handbook of terminology*. Vol. 1. Amsterdam, Philadelphia: John Benjamins B. V. 360–392.

Wehrli, E. (2007) Fips, a 'deep' linguistic multilingual parser. In: *Proceedings of ACL 2007 Workshop on Deep Linguistic Processing*, available at: http://dl.acm.org/citation.cfm?id=1608912&picked=prox, access on 15 May 2015. 120–127.

Wiechmann, D. (2008) On the computation of collostruction strenght. Testing measures of association as expressions of lexical bias. In: *Corpus Linguistics and Linguistic Theory* 4 (2). 253–290.

Wierzbicka, A. (2009) Exloring English Phraseology with two tools: NSM semantic methodology and Google. In: *Journal of English Linguistics* 37 (2). 101–129.

Wilcock, G. (2009) *Introduction to linguistic annotation and text analytics. Synwork Lectures on Human Language Technologies*. Morgan and Claypool Publishers.

Williams, G. (2006) La linguistique de corpus: une affaire prépositionelle. In: Rastier, F., Ballabriga, M. *Corpus en Lettres et Sciences Sociales: Des Documents Numériques à l'interprétation*. Paris: Texto. 151–158.

Wiltos, A. (2014) Znaczenie wykładni prawa w procesie tłumaczenia tekstów prawnych na przykładzie analizy użycia polskich pojęć narodowość i obywatelstwo oraz hiszpańskich nacionalidad i ciudadania. In: In: Łukasik, M., Mikołajewska, B. (eds.) *Języki specjalistyczne wczoraj, dziś i jutro*. Warszawa: IKLA. 424–439.

Wojtak, M. (2001) Styl urzędowy. In: Bartmiński, J. (ed.) *Współczesny język polski*. Lublin: Wydawnictwo Uniwersytetu Marii Curie-Skłodowskiej. 155–170.

Woźniak, J. (2014) Konwencjonalizacja w tekstach prawnych na przykładzie polskiej I niemieckiej wersji Traktatu Lizbońskiego. In: Łukasik, M., Mikołajewska, B. (eds.) *Języki specjalistyczne wczoraj, dziś i jutro*. Warszawa: IKLA. 440–453.

Woźnicka, A. (2004) Wiedza specjalistyczna a słownik terminologiczny. In: Lewandowski, J. (ed.) *Leksykografia terminologiczna – teoria i praktyka*. Warszawa: KJS. 73–84.

Wróblewski, B. (1948) *Język prawny i prawniczy*. Kraków: Polska Akademia Umiejętności.

Xiao, R. (2009) Well-known and influential corpora. In: Lüdeling, A., Kytö, M. (eds.) *Corpus linguistics: an international handbook*. Berlin: Mouton de Gruyter. 383–457.

Yong, H. and Peng, J. (2007) *Bilingual Lexicography from a Communicative Perspective*. Amsterdam, Philadelphia: John Benjamins B. V.

Zgusta, L. (1971) *Manual of Lexicography*. The Hague, Paris: Mouton.

Zmarzer, W. (2008) W kwestii typologii słowników terminologicznych. In: Lukszyn, J. (ed.) *Podstawy technolingwistyki I*. Warszawa: KJS. 248–256.

Zybert, J. (1999) *Errors in foreign language learning. The case of Polish learners of English*. Warszawa: Matrix.

Żmigrodzki, P. (2003) *Wprowadzenie do leksykografii polskiej*. Katowice: Wydawnictwa Uniwersytetu Śląskiego.

Żmigrodzki, P. (2008) *Słowo – słownik – rzeczywistość*. Kraków: Lexis.

Dictionaries:

Anioł-Kwiatkowska, J. (2003) *Wielojęzyczny słownik florystyczny*. Wrocław: Wydawnictwo Uniwersytetu Wrocławskiego.

Bar, L. (ed.) (1986) *Słownik prawniczy polsko-angielski. Polish-English dictionary of legal terms*. Wrocław: Ossolineum.

Białek, E. (2011) *Kolokacja w przekładzie. Słownik rosyjsko-polski*. Lublin: Wydawnictwo UMCS.

Broszkiewicz, H. et al. (1991) *Wielojęzyczny słownik terminów z zakresu własności przemysłowej*. Warszawa: Wydawnictwa Urzędu Patentowego RP.

Crowther, J. et al., (eds., 2002) *Oxford Collocations Dictionary for Students of English.* Oxford: Oxford University Press.

Dąbkowski, G. (2004) *Siedmiojęzyczny słownik terminów muzycznych: włosko-francusko-angielsko-niemiecko-rosyjsko-czesko-polski.* Warszawa: TAKT.

Douglas Kozłowska, Ch. (2004) *English Adverbial Collocations.* Warszawa: PWN.

Douglas Kozłowska, Ch., Dzierżanowska, H. (1993) *Selected English Collocations.* Warszawa: PWN.

Eksteen, L. C. et al. (eds., 1997) *Groot Woordeboek/Major Dictionary.* Cape Town: Pharos.

Garner, B. A. (ed., 2004) *Black's Law Dictionary.* Eighth edition. Saint Paul: Thomson West.

Geller, E., Dąbrówka, A. (2007) *Słownik stylistyczny języka polskiego.* Warszawa: Świat Książki.

Grelewicz-La Mela, M., Nuzzo, B. (2003) *Słownik prawniczy włosko-polski.* Warszawa: Dom Wydawniczy ABC.

Jędrzejko, E. (ed., 1998) *Słownik polskich zwrotów werbo-nominalnych.* Warszawa: Energeia.

Hartmann, R., James, G. (1998) *Dictionary of Lexicography.* London: Routledge.

Kwiatkowska, H. (2011) *Słownik terminologii prawniczej włosko-polski, polsko włoski.* Warszawa: C. H. Beck.

Lo Cascio, V. (ed., 2012) *Dizionario Combinatorio Compatto Italiano.* Amsterdam, Philadelphia: John Benjamins B. V.

Okoń, W., Dembska, J., Niemierko, B. (1990) *Pięciojęzyczny słownik terminów pedagogicznych.* Wrocław: Ossolineum.

Ożga, E (2006) *The great dictionary of Law and Economics. English-Polish.* Warszawa: C.H. Beck.

Ożga, E (2009) *The great dictionary of Law and Economics. Polish-English.* Warszawa: C.H. Beck.

Osuchowska, D. (2001) *English at Work. An English-Polish Dictionary of Selected Collocations.* Warszawa: Wydawnictwo Naukowe PWN.

De Palma, S. (2012) *Dizionario di inglese legale applicato inglese-italiano ~ italiano-inglese.* Bologna: Filodiritto.

Palmer, H. E. (1947) *A grammar of English words.* London, New York, Toronto: Longmans.

Picchi, F. (2011) *Economics & business. Dizionario enciclopedico economico e commerciale inglese-italiano con glossario italiano-inglese.* Bologna: Zanichelli.

Pieńkoś, J. (2004) *Polsko-angielsko-francusko-niemiecki glosariusz terminologii stosunków międzynarodowych i prawa międzynarodowego.* Kraków: Zakamycze.

Rundell, M. (ed., 2010) *Macmillan Collocations Dictionary for Learners of English.* Oxford: Macmillan Publishers Ltd.

Sinclair, J. et al (eds., 1987) *Collins Cobuild English Language Dictionary.* London: Collins.

Tiberii, S. (2012) *Dizionario delle collocazioni.* Bologna: Zanichelli.

Wrzosek, P. (1995) *Podręczny 4-języczny słownik samochodowy polsko-angielsko-francusko-polski.* Warszawa: KRAM.

Language corpora and databases:

The Bononia Legal Corpus (BoLC), available at: http://dslo.unibo.it/BOLCCorpQuery.html, access on 18 February 2012.

British National Corpus (BNC) Baby, available at: http://www.natcorp.ox.ac.uk/corpus/babyinfo.html, access on 13 March 2012.

Corpus of Contemporary American English (COCA), available at: http://corpus.byu.edu/coca/, access on 2 August 2014.

IATE terminology database, https://iate.europa.eu, access in February 2022

Michigan Corpus of Academic spoken English (MICASE), available at: http://quod.lib.umich.edu/m/micase/, access on 2 August 2014.

NewsgroupsUseNet Corpora (NUNC), available at: http://www.bmanuel.org/projects/ng-HOME.html, access on January 31 2012.

ParaConc, available at: http://www.athel.com/para.html, access on 29 February 2012.

Professional English Research Consortium (PERC) Corpus, available at: http://scn.jkn21.com/~percinfo/, access on 1 February 2012.

Legislation:

Bank of England act 1998 c. 11, available at: http://www.legislation.gov.uk/ukpga/1998/11/contents, access on 5 September 2015.

Banking Act 2009 c. 1, available at: http://www.legislation.gov.uk/ukpga/2009/1/contents, access on 5 September 2015.

Decreto legislativo 27 gennaio 1992, n. 87, Attuazione della direttiva 86/635/CEE, relativa ai conti annuali ed ai conti consolidati delle banche e degli altri istituti finanziari, e della direttiva 89/117/CEE, relativa agli obblighi in materia di pubblicità dei documenti contabili delle succursali, stabilite in uno Stato membro, di enti creditizi ed istituti finanziari con sede sociale fuori di tale Stato membro, available at: http://www.normattiva.it/atto/caricaDettaglioAtto?atto.dataPubblicazioneGazzetta=1992-02-14&atto.codiceRedazionale=092G0133&currentPage=1, access on 7 February 2015.

Decreto legislativo 1 settembre 1993, n. 385, Testo unico delle leggi in materia bancaria e creditizia, available at: http://www.normattiva.it/atto/caricaDettaglioAtto?atto.dataPubblicazioneGazzetta=1993-09-30&atto.codiceRedazionale=093G0428&currentPage=1, access on 27 January 2015.

Decreto legge 4 gennaio 1994, n. 1, Misure a garanzia del credito agrario, available at: http://www.normattiva.it/atto/caricaDettaglioAtto?atto.dataPubblicazioneGazzetta=1994-01-07&atto.codiceRedazionale=094G0007&currentPage=1, access on 9 September 2015.

Decreto legislativo 10 marzo 1998, n. 43, Adeguamento dell'ordinamento nazionale alle disposizioni del trattato istitutivo della Comunita' europea in materia di politica monetaria e di Sistema europeo delle banche centrali, available at: http://www.normattiva.it/atto/caricaDettaglioAtto?atto.dataPubblicazioneGazzetta=1998-03-14&atto.codiceRedazionale=098G0096&currentPage=1, access on 8 September 2015.

Decreto legislativo 24 giugno 1998, n. 213, Disposizioni per l'introduzione dell'EURO nell'ordinamento nazionale, a norma dell'articolo 1, comma 1, della legge 17 dicembre 1997, n. 433, available at: http://www.normattiva.it/atto/vediMenuExport?atto.dataPubblicazioneGazzetta=1998-07-08&atto.codiceRedazionale=098G0261, access on 8 September 2015.

Decreto legislativo 18 aprile 2006, n. 171, Ricognizione dei principi fondamentali in materia di casse di risparmio, casse rurali, aziende di credito a carattere regionale, enti di credito fondiario e agrario a carattere regionale, available at: http://www.normattiva.it/atto/caricaDettaglioAtto?atto.dataPubblicazioneGazzetta=2006-05-12&atto.codiceRedazionale=006G0196&currentPage=1, access on 9 September 2015.

Decreto legislativo 13 agosto 2010, n. 141, Attuazione della direttiva 2008/48/CE relativa ai contratti di credito ai consumatori, nonche' modifiche del titolo VI del testo unico bancario (decreto legislativo n. 385 del 1993) in merito alla disciplina dei soggetti operanti nel settore finanaziario, degli agenti in attività finanziaria e dei mediatori creditizi (10G0170), available at: http://www.normattiva.it/atto/caricaDettaglioAtto?atto.dataPubblicazioneGazzetta=2010-09-04&atto.codiceRedazionale=010G0170&currentPage=1, access on 9 September 2015.

Decreto legislativo 27 gennaio 2010, n. 11, Attuazione della direttiva 2007/64/CE, relativa ai servizi di pagamento nel mercato interno, recante modifica delle direttive 97/7/CE, 2002/65/CE, 2005/60/CE, 2006/48/CE, e che abroga la direttiva 97/5/CE, available at: http://www.normattiva.it/atto/caricaDettaglioAtto?atto.dataPubblicazioneGazzetta=2010-02-13&atto.codiceRedazionale=010G0027&currentPage=1, access on 10 October 2015.

Decreto legislativo 16 aprile 2012, n. 45, Attuazione della direttiva 2009/110/CE, concernente l'avvio, l'esercizio e la vigilanza prudenziale dell'attività degli istituti di moneta elettronica, che modifica le direttive 2005/60/CE e 2006/48/CE e che abroga la direttiva 2000/46/CE, available at: http://www.normattiva.it/atto/caricaDettaglioAtto?atto.dataPubblicazioneGazzetta=2012-04-28&atto.codiceRedazionale=012G0065&currentPage=1, access on 10 September 2015.

Financial services (banking reform) Act 2013 c. 33, available at: http://www.legislation.gov.uk/ukpga/2013/33/contents, access on 5 September 2015.

Legge 7 marzo 1996, n. 108, Disposizioni in materia di usura, available at: http://www.normattiva.it/uri-res/N2Ls?urn:nir:stato:legge:1996-03-07;108, access on 7 February 2015.

Legge 30 aprile 1999, n. 130, Disposizioni sulla cartolarizzazione dei crediti, available at: http://www.normattiva.it/atto/caricaDettaglioAtto?atto.dataPubblicazioneGazzetta=1999-05-14&atto.codiceRedazionale=099G0212&currentPage=1, access on 7 February 2015.

Legge 28 dicembre 2005, n. 262, Disposizioni per la tutela del risparmio e la disciplina dei mercati finanziari, available at: http://www.normattiva.it/atto/vediMenuExport?atto.dataPubblicazioneGazzetta=2005-12-28&atto.codiceRedazionale=005G0295, access on 9 September 2015.

The Bank Recovery and Resolution Order 2014 no. 3329, available at: http://www.legislation.gov.uk/uksi/2014/3329/contents/made, access on 28 September 2015.

The Credit Institutions (Protection of Depositors) Regulations 1995 no. 1442, available at: http://www.legislation.gov.uk/uksi/1995/1442/contents/made, access on 28 September 2015.

The Credit Institutions (Reorganisation and Winding up) Regulations 2004 no 1045, available at: http://www.legislation.gov.uk/uksi/2004/1045/contents/made, access on 28 September 2015.

Ustawa z dnia 28 grudnia 1989 r. o uporządkowaniu stosunków kredytowych, available at: http://isap.sejm.gov.pl/DetailsServlet?id=WDU19890740440, access on 25 January 2015.

Ustawa z dnia 3 lutego 1993 r. o restrukturyzacji finansowej przedsiębiorstw i banków oraz o zmianie niektórych ustaw, available at: http://isap.sejm.gov.pl/DetailsServlet?id=WDU19930180082, access on 25 January 2015, Dz.U. 1993 nr 18 poz. 82.

Ustawa z dnia 7 lipca 1994 r. o denominacji złotego, available at: http://isap.sejm.gov.pl/DetailsServlet?id=WDU19940840386, access on 27 January 2015, Dz.U. 1994 nr 84 poz. 386.

Ustawa z dnia 14 grudnia 1994 r. o Bankowym Funduszu Gwarancyjnym, available at: http://isap.sejm.gov.pl/DetailsServlet?id=WDU19950040018, access on 26 January 2015.

Ustawa z dnia 5 stycznia 1995 r. o dopłatach do oprocentowania niektórych kredytów bankowych, available at: http://isap.sejm.gov.pl/DetailsServlet?id=WDU19950130060, access on 26 January 2015.

Ustawa z dnia 26 października 1995 r. o niektórych formach popierania budownictwa mieszkaniowego oraz o zmianie niektórych ustaw, available at: http://isap.sejm.gov.pl/DetailsServlet?id=WDU19951330654, access on 25 January 2015.

Ustawa z dnia 30 listopada 1995 r. o pomocy państwa w spłacie niektórych kredytów mieszkaniowych, refundacji bankom wypłaconych premii gwarancyjnych oraz zmianie niektórych ustaw, available at: http://isap.sejm.gov.pl/DetailsServlet?id=WDU19960050032, access on 26 January 2015.

Ustawa z dnia 14 czerwca 1996 r. o łączeniu i grupowaniu niektórych banków w formie spółki akcyjnej, available at, http://isap.sejm.gov.pl/DetailsServlet?id=WDU19960900406, access on 25 January 2015.

Ustawa z dnia 8 maja 1997 r. o poręczeniach i gwarancjach udzielanych przez Skarb Państwa oraz niektóre osoby prawne, available at: http://isap.sejm.gov.pl/DetailsServlet?id=WDU19970790484, access on 26 January 2015.

Ustawa z dnia 29 sierpnia 1997 Prawo bankowe, available at: http://isap.sejm.gov.pl/DetailsServlet?id=WDU19971400939, access on 20 January 2014.

Ustawa z dnia 29 sierpnia 1997 r. o Narodowym Banku Polskim, available at: http://isap.sejm.gov.pl/DetailsServlet?id=WDU19971400938, access on 20 January 2015.

Ustawa z dnia 29 sierpnia 1997 o listach zastawnych i bankach hipotecznych, available at: http://isap.sejm.gov.pl/DetailsServlet?id=WDU20030990919, access on 20 January 2015.

Ustawa z dnia 17 lipca 1998 r. o pożyczkach i kredytach studenckich, available at: http://isap.sejm.gov.pl/DetailsServlet?id=WDU19981080685, access on 25 January 2015.

Ustawa z dnia 8 lipca 1999 r. o dopłatach do oprocentowania kredytów bankowych udzielonych na usuwanie skutków powodzi, available at: http://isap.sejm.gov.pl/DetailsServlet?id=WDU19990620690, access on 26 January 2015.

Ustawa z dnia 29 listopada 2000 r. o objęciu poręczeniami Skarbu Państwa spłaty kredytów mieszkaniowych, available at: http://isap.sejm.gov.pl/DetailsServlet?id=WDU20001221310, access on 26 January 2015.

Ustawa z dnia 7 grudnia 2000 r. o funkcjonowaniu banków spółdzielczych, ich zrzeszaniu się i bankach zrzeszających, available at: http://isap.sejm.gov.pl/DetailsServlet?id=WDU20001191252, access on 20 January 2015.

Ustawa z dnia 25 maja 2001 r. o skutkach wprowadzania w niektórych państwach członkowskich Unii Europejskiej wspólnej waluty euro, available at: http://isap.sejm.gov.pl/DetailsServlet?id=WDU20010630640, access on 27 January 2015.

Ustawa z dnia 8 czerwca 2001 r. o dopłatach do oprocentowania kredytów eksportowych o stałych stopach procentowych, available at: http://isap.sejm.gov.pl/DetailsServlet?id=WDU20010730762, access on 26 January 2015.

Ustawa z dnia 24 sierpnia 2001 r. o ostateczności rozrachunku w systemach płatności i systemach rozrachunku papierów wartościowych oraz zasadach nadzoru nad tymi systemami, available at: http://isap.sejm.gov.pl/DetailsServlet?id=WDU20011231351, access on 27 January 2015.

Ustawa z dnia 27 lipca 2002 r. Prawo dewizowe, available at: http://isap.sejm.gov.pl/DetailsServlet?id=WDU20021411178, access on 8 October 2015.

Ustawa z dnia 12 września 2002 r. o elektronicznych instrumentach płatniczych, available at: http://isap.sejm.gov.pl/DetailsServlet?id=WDU20021691385, access on 27 January 2015.

Ustawa z dnia 5 grudnia 2002 r. o dopłatach do oprocentowania kredytów mieszkaniowych o stałej stopie procentowej, available at: http://isap.sejm.gov.pl/DetailsServlet?id=WDU20022301922, access on 26 January 2015.

Ustawa z dnia 14 marca 2003 r. o Banku Gospodarstwa Krajowego, available at: http://isap.sejm.gov.pl/DetailsServlet?id=WDU20030650594, access on 25 January 2015.

Ustawa z dnia 8 września 2006 r. o finansowym wsparciu rodzin w nabywaniu własnego mieszkania, available at: http://isap.sejm.gov.pl/DetailsServlet?id=WDU20061831354, access on 26 January 2015.

Ustawa z dnia 30 maja 2008 r. o niektórych formach wspierania działalności innowacyjnej, available at: http://isap.sejm.gov.pl/DetailsServlet?id=WDU20081160730, access on 25 January 2015.

Ustawa z dnia 7 listopada 2008 r. o Komitecie Stabilności Finansowej, available at: http://isap.sejm.gov.pl/DetailsServlet?id=WDU20082091317, access on 25 January 2015.

Ustawa z dnia 12 lutego 2009 r. o udzielaniu przez Skarb Państwa wsparcia instytucjom finansowym, available at: http://isap.sejm.gov.pl/DetailsServlet?id=WDU20090390308, access on 25 January 2015.

Ustawa z dnia 5 listopada 2009 r. o spółdzielczych kasach oszczędnościowo-kredytowych, available at: http://isap.sejm.gov.pl/DetailsServlet?id=WDU20120000855, access on 25 January 2015.

Ustawa z dnia 19 czerwca 2009 r. o pomocy państwa w spłacie niektórych kredytów mieszkaniowych udzielonych osobom, które utraciły pracę, available at: http://isap.sejm.gov.pl/DetailsServlet?id=WDU20091150964, access on 25 January 2015.

Ustawa z dnia 12 maja 2011 r. o kredycie konsumenckim, available at: http://isap.sejm.gov.pl/DetailsServlet?id=WDU20111260715, access on 25 January 2015.

Software:

AntConc 3.4.3, available at: http://www.antlab.sci.waseda.ac.jp/antconc_index.html, access on 28 February 2012.

Annotate, available at: http://www.coli.uni-saarland.de/projects/sfb378/negra-corpus/annotate.html, access on 15 February 2014.

Bilingual Sentence Aligner, available at: http://research.microsoft.com/en-us/downloads/aafd5dcf-4dcc-49b2-8a22-f7055113e656/, access on 27 July 2014.

CLOC Collocation Package, available at: http://www.textworld.com/scp, access on 29 February 2012.

Coral, available at: http://takelab.fer.hr/coral/, access on 26 July 2014.

Kolokacje, available at: http://www.mimuw.edu.pl/polszczyzna/, access on 18 January 2012.

Multiconcord, available at: http://artsweb.bham.ac.uk/pking/multiconc/l_text.htm, access on 26 July 2014.

Simple Concordance Programme, available at: http://www.textworld.com/scp, access on 29 February 2012.

Sketch Engine, available at: http://www.sketchengine.co.uk/?page=Website/Prices, access on 28 July 2014.

WordSmith Tools, available at http://lexically.net/wordsmith/purchase/, accesss on 19 May 2017.

Index of Names

Studies in Linguistics, Anglophone Literatures and Cultures

Edited by Robert Kiełtyka and Agnieszka Uberman

Vol. 1 Marcin Kudła: A Study of *Attributive Ethnonyms* in the History of English with Special Reference to *Foodsemy*. 2016.

Vol. 2 Agnieszka Grząśko: On Invectives in Natural Language: A Panchronic Study of English Synonyms of 'Skinny'/'Fatty'. 2016.

Vol. 3 Małgorzata Martynuska / Elżbieta Rokosz-Piejko (eds.): Revolution, Evolution and Endurance in Anglophone Literature and Culture. 2017.

Vol. 4 Robert Kiełtyka / Agnieszka Uberman (eds.): Evolving Nature of the English Language. Studies in Theoretical and Applied Linguistics. 2017.

Vol. 5 Ewa Konieczna / Robert Kiełtyka (eds.): English versus Slavic. Lexicon in a Morphological and Semantic Perspective. 2017.

Vol. 6 Małgorzata Martynuska / Elżbieta Rokosz-Piejko (eds.): New Developments in Postcolonial Studies. 2017.

Vol. 7 Beata Kiersnowska: Ideologies and Forms of Leisure and Recreation in Victorian Manchester. 2017.

Vol. 8 Magdalena Grabowska / Grzegorz Grzegorczyk / Piotr Kallas: Narrativity in Action: Language, Culture and Text. 2017.

Vol. 9 Magdalena Trinder: The Influence of Level of Extroversion, Locus of Control and Gender on Listening and Reading Proficiency in Second Language Acquisition. 2017.

Vol. 10 Jarosław Wiliński / Joanna Stolarek (eds.): Norm and Anomaly in Language, Literature, and Culture. 2017.

Vol. 11 Agnieszka Uberman / Marta Dick-Bursztyn (eds.): Language in the New Millennium. Applied-linguistic and Cognitive-linguistic Considerations. 2018.

Vol. 12 Lucyna Harmon / Dorota Osuchowska (eds.): Translation Studies across the Boundaries. 2018.

Vol. 13 Mária Matiová / Martin Navrátil (eds.): A Reflection of Man and Culture in Language and Literature. 2019.

Vol. 14 Bożena Duda / Robert Kiełtyka / Ewa Konieczna (eds.): Culture, Cognition, Discourse and Grammar. Cognitive Considerations on Formulaic Language. 2019.

Vol. 15 Patrycja Austin / Elżbieta Rokosz-Piejko (eds.): Re-Imagining the Limits of the Human. 2019.

Vol. 16 Michał Organ (ed.): Translation Today: Literary Translation in Focus. 2019.

Vol. 17 Michał Organ (ed.): Translation Today: Audiovisual Translation in Focus. 2019.

Vol. 18 Michał Organ (ed.): Translation Today: Applied Translation Studies in Focus. 2019.

Vol. 19 Marcin Grygiel / Robert Kiełtyka (eds.): Cognitive Linguistics in the Year 2017. 2019.

Vol. 20 Andrej Zahorák: Intercultural Aspect in Translation and Reception of Precedent Phenomena. 2019.

Vol. 21 Dorota Osuchowska / Lucyna Harmon (eds.): Contents, Use, Usability. Dictionaries from the Perspective of a Translator and a Language Teacher. 2019.

Vol. 22 Lucyna Harmon / Dorota Osuchowska (eds.): Nationality in Translation. 2019.

Vol. 23 Ewa Kusz: Musical Intelligence and Its Impact on English Pronunciation Skills in the Process of Second Language Acquisition. 2019.

Vol. 24 Michał Organ (ed.): Translation Today: National Identity in Focus. 2019.

Vol. 25 Łukasz Barciński (ed.): National Identity in Literary Translation. 2019.

Vol. 26 Judyta Pawliszko: Sociolinguistic analysis of Mexican-American bilingualism: Spanglish as a sociocultural phenomenon. 2020.

Vol. 27 Lucyna Harmon / Dorota Osuchowska (eds.): Translation and Power. 2020.

Vol. 28 Robert Oliwa: Design and Management of the Virtual Learning Environment for Foreign Language Instruction in Adult Learner Groups. 2020.

Vol. 29 Dorota Osuchowska: Occupational Inequality and Sex-Role Stereotyping in Dictionaries of English: A Causal Link? 2021.

Vol. 30 Arkadiusz Pietluch: Energising Directed Motivational Currents Through Learners' Agency. 2021.

Vol. 31 Bożena Kochman-Haładyj: Anglo-American and Polish Proverbs. A Contrastive Perspective of Linguistic Representation of Traditional Values. 2021.

Vol. 32 Robert Kiełtyka (ed.): Studies in the Evolution of the English Language. 2021.

Vol. 33 Tomasz Paciorkowski: Native Speakerism. Discriminatory Employment Practices in Polish Language Schools. 2022.

Vol. 34 Katarzyna Góra: Predicates of Gratification in English and Polish. A Semantic-Syntactic Perspective. 2022.

Vol. 35 Anna Zagórska: Dictionaries of LSP Collocations. The Process of Compilation Based on Polish, English and Italian Banking Law. 2022.

www.peterlang.com

www.ingramcontent.com/pod-product-compliance
Ingram Content Group UK Ltd.
Pitfield, Milton Keynes, MK11 3LW, UK
UKHW041824100926
8556IPUK00002B/7

9 783631 871522